Foundations of Art

Foundations of Art Therapy

Theory and Applications

Edited by

Meera Rastogi

Rachel Paige Feldwisch

Michelle Pate

Joseph Scarce

Academic Press is an imprint of Elsevier
125 London Wall, London EC2Y 5AS, United Kingdom
525 B Street, Suite 1650, San Diego, CA 92101, United States
50 Hampshire Street, 5th Floor, Cambridge, MA 02139, United States
The Boulevard, Langford Lane, Kidlington, Oxford OX5 1GB, United Kingdom

ISBN 978-0-12-824308-4

For information on all Academic Press publications
visit our website at https://www.elsevier.com/books-and-journals

Publisher: Nikki P. Levy
Acquisitions Editor: Joslyn Chaiprasert-Paguio
Editorial Project Manager: Samantha Allard
Production Project Manager: Omer Mukthar
Cover Designer: Christian J. Bilbow

Typeset by STRAIVE, India

Dedication

We dedicate this book to our art therapy founders who created such a rich field, to our students who teach us something new every day, to our clients whose resilience inspires the work we do, and to our families for their continued support on this journey.

Contents

4. Intersections of neuroscience and art therapy

Meera Rastogi, PhD, ATR-BC, Christianne Strang, PhD, ATR-BC, Ilya Vilinsky, PhD, and Kristopher Holland, PhD

5. Approaches to research in art therapy

Girija Kaimal, EdD, ATR-BC, Asli Arslanbek, MA, ATR, and Bani Malhotra, MA, ATR-BC

7. Psychoanalytic and Jungian approaches to art therapy

Leah Friedman, MA, ATR-BC and
Jessica Whitesel, MA, LPC, ATR-BC

8. Humanistic approaches to art therapy: Existentialism, person-centered, and gestalt

Elizabeth Hadara Hlavek, DAT, LCPAT, ATR-BC and
Rachel Paige Feldwisch, PhD, MAAT, LMHC, ATR-BC

Part III
Art therapy with specific populations: Painting the picture

10. Child development and artistic development in art therapy

Michelle Itczak, MA, ATR-BC, ATCS, LMHC

11. Art therapy for psychological disorders and mental health

Meera Rastogi, PhD, ATR-BC and Janet K. Kempf, MA, ATR-BC, LPC, NCC

12. Art therapy and older adults

Erin Elizabeth Partridge, PhD, ATR-BC

The URL for this book's companion website is https://www.elsevier.com/books-and-journals/book-companion/9780128243084

Contributors

Numbers in parentheses indicate the pages on which the authors' contributions begin.

Asli Arslanbek, MA, ATR (159), Creative Arts Therapies Program, College of Nursing and Health Sciences, Drexel University, Philadelphia, PA, United States

Vittoria Daiello, PhD (493), Art Education, College of Design, Architecture, Art, and Planning, University of Cincinnati, Cincinnati, OH, United States

Heather J. Denning, MA, ATR-BC, ATCS, LSW (451), Art Department, Mercyhurst University, Erie, PA, United States

Dana Elmendorf, MA, ATR-BC, LPC (543), Art Therapy Program, Seton Hill University, Greensburg, PA, United States; Accreditation Council for Art Therapy Education, Alexandria, VA, United States

Rachel Paige Feldwisch, PhD, MAAT, LMHC, ATR-BC (3, 235), Department of Counseling, University of Indianapolis, Indianapolis, IN, United States

Leah Friedman, MA, ATR-BC (211), Transpersonal Art Therapy, Naropa University, Boulder, CO, United States

Elizabeth Hadara Hlavek, DAT, LCPAT, ATR-BC (235), Hlavek Art Therapy, LLC, Annapolis, MD, United States

Kristopher Holland, PhD (123), Art Education, School of Art, University of Cincinnati, Cincinnati, OH, United States

Michelle Itczak, MA, ATR-BC, ATCS, LMHC (291), Department of Counseling, University of Indianapolis, Indianapolis, IN, United States

Girija Kaimal, EdD, ATR-BC (159), Creative Arts Therapies Program, College of Nursing and Health Sciences, Drexel University, Philadelphia, PA, United States

Janet K. Kempf, MA, ATR-BC, LPC, NCC (335), Psychology and Pre-Art Therapy Programs, University of Cincinnati, Clermont College, Batavia; Good Samaritan Hospital, Cincinnati, OH, United States

Bani Malhotra, MA, ATR-BC (159), Creative Arts Therapies Program, College of Nursing and Health Sciences, Drexel University, Philadelphia, PA, United States

Eileen Misluk-Gervase, MPS, LPC, ATR-BC, LMHC, CEDCAT (197), Graduate Art Therapy Department, Herron School of Art and Design, IUPUI, Indianapolis, IN, United States

Molly O'Neill Haaga, PhD, ATR-BC, LPC (31), Art Therapy Department, Ursuline College, Cleveland, OH, United States

Erin Elizabeth Partridge, PhD, ATR-BC (379), Art Therapy, Dominican University of California, San Rafael; Experiential Researcher-In-Residence, Elder Care Alliance, Alameda, CA, United States

Michelle Pate, DAT, LCMHC, ATR-BC (493), Psychology and Applied Therapies, Lesley University, Cambridge, MA, United States

Meera Rastogi, PhD, ATR-BC (123, 335, 493), Department of Social Sciences; Psychology and Pre-Art Therapy Programs, University of Cincinnati, Clermont College, Batavia, OH, United States

Marcia L. Rosal, PhD, ATR-BC, HLM (259), Florida State University, Tallahassee, FL, United States

Joseph Scarce, PhD, ATR-BC (413), University of Tampa, Tampa, FL, United States

Jennifer B. Schwartz, MAAT, ATR-BC, ATCS (31), Art Therapy Department, Ursuline College, Cleveland, OH, United States

Stella A. Stepney, MS, ATR-BC, LCAT (81), Herron School of Art and Design, Indiana University Purdue University, Indianapolis, IN, United States

Christianne Strang, PhD, ATR-BC (123), Department of Psychology, University of Alabama at Birmingham, Birmingham, AL, United States

Ilya Vilinsky, PhD (123), Neuroscience, Department of Biological Sciences, University of Cincinnati, Cincinnati, OH, United States

Jessica Whitesel, MA, LPC, ATR-BC (211), Transpersonal Art Therapy, Naropa University, Boulder, CO, United States

Cynthia Wilson, PhD, ATR-BC (413), UniQue ImAging Art Therapy and Photo Therapy Techniques, Boise, ID; UniQue ImAging Art Therapy and Photo Therapy Techniques, Modesto, CA, United States

About the Editors

Meera Rastogi, PhD, MAAT, ATR-BC, CGP, is a licensed psychologist, board-certified art therapist, certified group psychotherapist, and professor at the University of Cincinnati, Clermont College. She teaches psychology and art therapy courses and directs the University's Pre-Art Therapy Certificate Program. Dr. Rastogi offers weekly art therapy groups for people with chronic illness and for those focused on mental health recovery. Her research interests include the intersections between psychology, neuroscience, and art therapy; art therapy and mental health conditions; and higher education.

Rachel Paige Feldwisch, PhD, MAAT, LMHC, ATR-BC, is a board-certified art therapist, licensed mental health counselor, and licensed school counselor. She worked as an art therapist and counselor for about a decade before returning to graduate school for a PhD in counseling psychology. She is currently the Director of Counseling Programs at the University of Indianapolis, where she oversees the graduate and undergraduate art therapy programs; provides art therapy training; and conducts research in art therapy, counseling, and trauma-informed practice.

Michelle Pate, DAT, LCMHC, ATR-BC, holds a doctorate in art therapy from Mount Mary University. She is a board-certified art therapist and licensed clinical mental health counselor. She teaches undergraduate art therapy at Lesley University and currently chairs the AATA Education Committee and cochairs the AATA Undergraduate Education Subcommittee. Her current research focuses on the inclusion of diversity in the undergraduate education curriculum.

Joseph Scarce, PhD, ATR-BC, provides art therapy to medical hospitals and substance abuse facilities. He edited the first book on art therapy in disaster response: *Art Therapy in Response to Natural Disasters, Mass Violence, and Crises*. Dr. Scarce is an assistant professor at the University of Tampa and coordinates the BA in Art Therapy program. He partners with the Tampa Museum of Art, working with undergraduate students of the University of Tampa to provide art therapy to underserved populations through the Art Space Program.

Part I

Fundamentals of art therapy: Prepping the canvas

Chapter 1

History, profession, and ethics of art therapy

Rachel Paige Feldwisch, PhD, MAAT, LMHC, ATR-BC
Department of Counseling, University of Indianapolis, Indianapolis, IN, United States

Voices from the field

To know the history of art therapy is to find your ancestors who light the path for you. The history of art therapy is context for all the work you do as an art therapist. To know the history of art therapy is to understand where you came from, who you are now and where you might go.

Maxine Borowsky Junge, PhD, LCSW, ATR
(personal communication, July 10, 2020)

Learning outcomes

After reading this chapter, you will be able to

1. Provide a definition of art therapy.
2. Discuss historical events and movements that influenced the development of art therapy as a profession.
3. Name key figures and explain their contributions to the history of art therapy.
4. Identify professional organizations that are associated with the field of art therapy.
5. Explain the role of credentialing boards, including the Art Therapy Credentials Board in the United States.
6. Define the term "ethical code" and discuss the contents of the Ethical Principles of the American Art Therapy Association.

Chapter overview

This chapter provides definitions of art therapy and describes the profession of the art therapist. Movements in psychology, education, and visual art are discussed as influential to the early beginnings of the profession. Readers will be introduced to important figures and events that are relevant to the history of art therapy. Established professional organizations are reviewed, followed by discussion and application of Ethical Principles for Art Therapists.

Foundations of Art Therapy. https://doi.org/10.1016/B978-0-12-824308-4.00007-7

What is art therapy?

Likely, you have started reading this text and potentially enrolled in a course because you have some interest in the intersection of fine arts and psychology. However, providing a straightforward definition of art therapy is somewhat complicated because the terms art and therapy are abstract and may be described differently depending upon the context.

When you hear the word art, what comes to mind? Take a moment to reflect on this concept and write down a few thoughts. The word art may conjure a mental image of a visual creation, a product that resulted from someone's urge to use their creative drive to make a two-dimensional or three-dimensional piece. Your personal definition of the word art may also be influenced by your culture of origin and past experiences with making or viewing art. As you progress through this chapter and the subsequent chapters of this text, you will discover that many art therapists emphasize the artistic process over the resulting artistic product.

Therapy is also an abstract concept that may conjure up traditional images of psychotherapy or physical therapy, occupational therapy, or other medical interventions. Your views regarding what constitutes therapy may also be influenced by your culture; for example, people from Asian and Native American or Indigenous cultures may imagine religious or traditional healing practices that occur within their communities (Moodley et al., 2013; Wendt & Gone, 2016). Take a moment to write or sketch what the word therapy means to you.

How do art therapists define art therapy? Well, that depends! The way that art therapists describe their professional work may be influenced by the places where they were trained, the clinical work that they do, the settings where they practice, the countries where they reside, and their theoretical or philosophical beliefs about art and healing. Susan Hogan, an art therapist and academic at the University of Derby, wrote that in Australia and most of Europe the term art therapy is used to describe the work of the art therapist without much disagreement or debate (Hogan, 2001). In contrast, American Art Therapist Judith Rubin explained that art therapists in her country call their work "art as therapy...art psychotherapy…expressive analysis, clinical art therapy, psycho-aesthetics, or expressive therapy" (Rubin, 2010, p. 25). With so many different descriptive terms for the work that they do, it is not surprising that art therapists also have differing opinions regarding the definition of art therapy.

Even when we collectively agree upon the term art therapy, the way that we define art therapy may be quite different depending upon our beliefs regarding practice. For example, Rubin (2010) dedicated an entire chapter of her book *Introduction to Art Therapy: Sources and Resources* to exploring the definition by sharing perspectives from art therapy pathfinders (such as Margaret Naumburg and Elinor Ulman) and comparing and contrasting art therapy to other professional disciplines (such as art education). Rubin landed on the assumption that "most practitioners would agree with Elinor Ulman that whatever is called 'art therapy' needs to be true to both art and therapy" (2010, p. 47).

Other art therapists have emphasized relational and social factors when defining art therapy. During their study of art therapists in the Eastern world, Coss and Wong (2015) found that art therapists in Asia emphasized collectivist values that are more focused on family and community than the Western concept of the self. Bruce Moon, an art therapist in the United States, explored the definition of art therapy and the work of art therapists as connected to love. Moon (2016) suggested that making art is an act of love for art therapists, and therapy is an act of attending to others. Moon explained, "For art therapists, then, the question is how to best attend to and care for clients through art processes" (2016, p. 10). Cliff Joseph, an art therapist, also focused on relationships, but at both the interpersonal level and the systemic level. Joseph was "chiefly interested in the use of art as an agent for community development, self-determination, and social change" (Joseph, 1973, p. 1). Joseph's work paved the way for a new definition of art therapy that is rooted in social justice.

Professional associations, such as the American Art Therapy Association (AATA), bring groups of professionals together and may release definitions, ethical standards, and values statements associated with a profession. The AATA released its first official definition of art therapy in 1977 (Junge, 2010). The following definition from the AATA (2017a, 2017b) evolved over time with input from practitioners and scholars in the field:

> ***Art therapy*** *is an integrative mental health and human services profession that enriches the lives of individuals, families, and communities through active art-making, creative process, applied psychological theory, and human experience within a psychotherapeutic relationship. Art therapy, facilitated by a professional art therapist, effectively supports personal and relational treatment goals as well as community concerns. Art therapy is used to improve cognitive and sensorimotor functions, foster self-esteem and self-awareness, cultivate emotional resilience, promote insight, enhance social skills, reduce and resolve conflicts and distress, and advance societal and ecological change.*
>
> (AATA, 2017a, 2017b, para. 1)

What are the authors of this definition trying to communicate by providing this description? First, art therapy is a helping profession that focuses on improving the mental health and well-being of individuals and groups of people. While art is central to this process, art therapists also understand psychological theory and the development of therapeutic relationships. Second, art therapy is not something that simply happens when someone opens a coloring book; art therapy is a relational process that occurs between the client, the art, *and* the art therapist. A **client** is the recipient of art therapy services and the focus of the art therapy intervention. Alternatively, when working in a hospital or other medical setting, the art therapist may refer to the person who receives art therapy services as a **patient**. Other entities, such as community practice settings, may refer to the person engaged in art therapy as a **consumer**.

As American Art Therapist Elinor Ulman (2001) explained, "the definition of art therapy is intimately intertwined with the definition of art therapists. Who are they? How did they get to be what they are?" (p. 16). According to the American Art Therapy Association (2017a, 2017b), an **art therapist** is a professional with a master's degree that includes specific coursework and supervised clinical experience in the practice of art therapy. In other countries, art therapists may have different levels of experience and types of training, or may still be in the process of establishing their work as a professional discipline (Gussak & Rosal, 2015).

As explained by Junge at the start of this chapter, learning the history of art therapy will help you not only to understand how the profession developed but also will provide a context for the profession of art therapy as it exists today.

A history of art therapy

In searching for a definition of art therapy, you might wonder where the profession began and how it developed. Perhaps, through exploring the origins of art therapy, we can paint a better picture of what art therapy has become. Dissanayake (2000) made a compelling case for the connections between the arts and all essential elements of human existence. The use of art in healing rituals occurred long before there was ever a profession called art therapy (Junge, 2010). Nonetheless, we must respectfully consider how language, religious and spiritual belief systems, and historical and cultural contexts influenced what *might or might not* have been called art therapy by people from cultures that may be different from our own. For example, the languages of Indigenous or Native American cultures of the United States do not have a direct translation of the word art, and historically have not had a practice named art therapy (Napoli, 2019). The practices of shamans, traditional healers in Eastern and Indigenous cultures, were often passed through oral history or were documented by social scientists who were nonnative to their cultures and, therefore, susceptible to misrepresenting the cultural differences associated with making art as part of their practice. To claim knowledge of a direct connection between the rituals of healers from Indigenous cultures and the formation of a profession that is rooted in theories that primarily originated in Europe and the United States could be short sighted (Napoli, 2019), yet to ignore the history of art-making as fundamental to our development and well-being as humans would also be problematic. Before continuing this reading, take a moment to reflect upon how art has contributed to your own personal history, the histories of people in your family, and your culture(s) of origin. What does your history tell you about the meaning and purpose of making art?

When studying any written history, it is important to consider the origins of that history and who is telling the story. The history of art therapy that has been documented in the Western part of our world is one version of a story with voices that are predominantly White, cisgender females (**cisgender** describes people whose gender identity aligns with their assigned sex at birth) (American Psychological Association, 2015). According to this historical account, art therapy was first recognized as a distinct profession in the United States in the 1940s (Junge, 2010). Around this time, Margaret Naumburg brought together the synchronized movements that had been taking place in the fields of psychology, art, and education to name what she called "dynamically oriented art therapy" (Naumburg, n.d., as cited by Junge, 2010).

The segments that follow will introduce you to the historical movements and events that have been documented as precursors to the profession of art therapy in the Western world. In addition, the emerging history of art therapy in other parts of the world will be covered briefly and with the hope that subsequent editions of this textbook will see more information emerge regarding the international origins of art therapy.

Developments in psychology

Advancements in psychology around the turn of the 20th century paved the way for the field of art therapy to emerge as a distinct discipline during the decades that followed. In the early 1900s, the work of Sigmund Freud and the Vienna Psychoanalytic Society became popular throughout the Western world (Junge, 2010; Malchiodi, 2003). Fascination with the **unconscious**, the part of the mind that is outside of the conscious awareness of a person, prompted by Freud's psychoanalytic theory, led to experimentation with different techniques that could be used to tap into this mysterious function of the mind (Rubin, 2010). For example, Freud observed patients' desire to draw dreams, which were considered to be an expression of the unconscious, even though they were unable to describe them. According to psychoanalytic personality theory, the ability to depict mental processes that cannot be captured in words confirms the idea that drawings can provide a pathway to the unconscious (Malchiodi, 2003).

Jung, a psychoanalyst and former colleague of Freud, had a personal interest in art and recognized the ways in which the arts were able to provide access to feelings and promote self-understanding (Jung, 1964). Jung regularly encouraged his patients to draw visual representations of their thoughts and dreams and encouraged discussion of artistic images during therapy sessions. The writings of Jung and Freud promoted the idea that images are symbolic forms of expression that increase our understanding of the inner mind in ways that words often cannot. Some art therapists would argue that if not for the development of the idea of the unconscious by Freud and others during the early 20th century, we most likely would never have uncovered the variety of ways in which art can be used for, in, and as therapy (Malchiodi, 2003; Rubin, 2010). For more information regarding psychoanalytic theory, see Chapter 7, Psychoanalytic and Jungian approaches to art therapy.

Freud and Jung were not the only innovators in the field of psychology who were interested in the concept of art as a reflection of the unconscious. Many professionals began examining the artwork of people who were mentally ill simply out of curiosity, whereas others began to see the relationship between internal conflicts and artistic expression (Rubin, 2010). In 1876, French Psychiatrist Paul-Max Simon became one of the first to publish comprehensive studies of the drawings of individuals who had mental illnesses. Simon believed that the content of the artwork could be related to symptoms, an idea that influenced the later use of drawing as a diagnostic tool. In 1922, an art historian turned psychiatrist named Hans Prinzhorn published a series of 5000 pieces from 500 patients in his publication *Artistry of the Mentally Ill*, the most extensive study ever of its kind. Prinzhorn was most interested in the creative drive to make art that he believed to be inherent in all people and in ways that art contributes to wellness and psychological well-being (Vick, 2003). Prinzhorn's goal was to discover commonalities in all art without specific regard to the mental condition of the creator. Unlike Simon, he was not interested in how art might aid in diagnosis, nor did he consider the therapeutic advantages of art (Junge, 2010).

Several drawing tests were also invented during the time of Freud. Fritz Mohr, a German psychologist, was the first to develop drawing tests to be used for psychological purposes in 1906 (Rubin, 1986). In 1926, Florence Goodenough designed the "Draw-a-man" assessment for children that was intended to measure intelligence but was a better estimate of personality. During this assessment, the patient was told to draw a person and then the therapist analyzed the drawing. Psychoanalysts believed that the drawing could be representative of the patient's self-image, and therefore, used drawings as indicators of psychological problems. This test, now called the Human Figure Drawing Test, and other art-related methods of testing are still used today (Rubin, 2010).

Even though art therapy had not yet been named as a professional discipline, the presence of art in psychoanalysis, the treatment of individuals with mental illnesses, and psychological testing laid the foundation for the development of art therapy.

A new focus in fine art

In addition to innovations in the field of psychology that led to greater exploration of the arts in relation to self, the climate was also right in the world of fine art in that a propensity toward knowing, exploring, and representing inner thoughts and feelings through creative work was becoming more widely accepted. Postimpressionism, symbolism, and art nouveau stretched the boundaries and limitations of art-making in the late 1800s. Around the time when psychoanalysts were examining the mysteries of dreams and free association in the early 1900s, American and European artists were moving their attention away from the re-creation of the outer world and began to focus on self-expression (Junge, 2010). Movements such as Expressionism and Surrealism stemmed from the new importance of depicting inner thoughts and feelings through artwork, as can be seen in Edvard Munch's "The Scream," in which emotional turmoil is depicted through color and line (Prideaux, 2005). Likewise, Salvador Dali's surreal landscapes stemmed from dreams, a primary mechanism of the unconscious (Rubin, 2010). Many artists from this time period were interested in depicting internal thoughts and emotions through their work, which increased public acceptance of the power of art as a form of self-expression.

Movements in education

Likewise, movements in education at the turn of the twentieth century had an impact on the emergence of art therapy as a discipline. Theorists such as John Dewey, Jean Piaget, and Maria Montessori stressed the need for attention to individual needs within school systems. As a result, the Progressive Education Movement developed, which emphasized educating the whole child (Junge, 2010). The concept of educating the whole child included the creative and artistic abilities of the developing person, as well as other areas of development that were not typically emphasized in educational settings. Consequently, the regular inclusion of art in the school curriculum began, which was a precursor of art therapy with children (Junge, 2010).

Franz Cizek and Viktor Lowenfeld were two of the pathfinders of the modern art education movement. Cizek was Lowenfeld's mentor and a firm believer in the importance of allowing free expression of creativity and imagination in artwork (Junge, 2010). Lowenfeld, who studied psychoanalysis in Vienna before coming to the United States, proposed a stage theory of development that is evidenced by a child's artwork. Lowenfeld's (1947) book *Creative and Mental Growth* expanded on the connection between creative development and intellectual growth proposed by other educational theorists. Lowenfeld also used artwork to facilitate identity development with children who had developmental disabilities (Junge, 2010). For more information regarding Lowenfeld's stages, see Chapter 10, Child development and artistic development in art therapy.

The new emphasis on the need for a well-rounded curriculum led to the use of art in education, then in special education. The advancements in education led Margaret Naumburg, an educator with knowledge of psychoanalytic theory and direct contact with emerging expressive artists, to question how the advancements in these three fields could be brought together.

The emergence of art therapy in the United States

Margaret Naumburg

In the 1930s, Margaret Naumburg synthesized the corresponding developments that had been taking place in the fields of psychology, art, and education into a practice that she called "art therapy" (Naumburg, 1958, p. 511). Naumburg earned the title of "Mother of Art Therapy" both through her work and through her eloquent writing, which defined the new profession (Vick, 2003, p. 9). Naumburg studied with John Dewey and Maria Montessori and was known to socialize with Georgia O'Keefe, Charlie Chaplin, Alfred Stieglitz, and other popular artists of the early twentieth century (Junge, 2010). Thus she was familiar with the greater emphasis on the whole child in education and the greater emphasis on self-expression in art that were taking place in the early twentieth century. In addition, Naumburg had experience and understanding of psychoanalytic theory, Jungian psychotherapy, child development, and art education (Rubin, 2010). Naumburg's eclectic knowledge base and interests influenced the newly emerging field of art therapy (Fig. 1.1).

An outcome of Naumburg's psychoanalytic orientation was her belief that art was a form of symbolic speech that, like dreams, stemmed from the unconscious and could best be understood through the artist's own free association. She believed that the artist's interpretations should be respected during the analysis of this unconscious symbolic content and that this process required verbalized insight from the client in addition to artistic expression (Naumburg, 1987). Despite Naumburg's forward thinking, she faced an obstacle because most young people and adults at the time still held the belief that creating art involved a series of copying or tracing, an idea that was promoted by traditional education (Naumburg, 1947). Interestingly, contemporary art therapists must often encourage clients to set aside what is considered to be good art by traditional standards in order to make art that is therapeutic and personally meaningful (Rubin, 2010).

As a result of her desire to create an institution dedicated to spontaneous creative expression and self-motivated learning, Naumburg founded the Walden School in New York City in 1914. Her philosophical perspective of education was based on her belief in the importance of the emotional development of children and a rejection of the traditional, standardized, intellectual model (Naumburg, 2001; Rubin, 2010). She acted as the director of the school but often taught art

FIG. 1.1 *Margaret Naumburg.*
(Photograph courtesy of Judith Rubin.)

classes as well with her sister, Florence Cane, the art teacher at the Walden School (Junge, 2010). It was in the art classroom at the Walden School that Margaret Naumburg first conceptualized art therapy and concluded that, in addition to art's importance in education, spontaneous art-making could be an essential component of psychological assessment and psychotherapy (Naumburg, 1947).

Following her work at the Walden School, Margaret Naumburg went on to research spontaneous art in therapy with Nolan C. Lewis at the New York State Psychiatric Unit. The results of Naumburg's research were published in *Studies of the "Free" Art Expression of Behavior Problem Children and Adolescents as a Means of Diagnosis and Therapy* (Naumburg, 1947). Graduate courses in the methods and principles of art therapy based on Naumburg's work began at New York University in 1958. Naumburg continued to write throughout her career, and she traveled throughout the United States conducting seminars and giving lectures (Levick, 1983). The work of Margaret Naumburg at the Walden School inspired other educators and mental health professionals to explore the use of art in therapy.

Florence Cane

Alongside her sister, Cane developed unique methods such as the use of sound and movement as part of the art-making process that she believed helped to stimulate creativity (Junge, 2010). Cane (1951, 1983) developed and described the scribble technique as involving the use of a scribble followed by development of unconscious imagery that emerges from the scribble. In addition to teaching at the Walden School, Cane served as the Director of Art at the Counseling Center for Gifted Children of the School of Education at New York University in Manhattan (Junge, 2010). Cane's book *The Artist in Each of Us* (Cane, 1951, 1983) described her innovative techniques and widely influenced the fields of art therapy and art education.

Cane explained the steps of the scribble drawing as follows: "The making of this rhythmic pattern is the first step of the scribble...The scribble reflects the state and nature of the person drawing it much as handwriting does...Having made the scribble, the student now should be asked to sit down quietly at a distance and contemplate it...After he has discovered a definite pattern in the scribble, the pupil should emphasize the lines that will bring out what he has seen" (Cane, 1983, p. 56).

Edith Kramer

Art therapist and author Edith Kramer developed her ideas about the use of art as therapy a short time after Naumburg and Cane. Kramer was born in Vienna, Austria, and fled Europe in 1938 to avoid the Nazis (Junge, 2010). Prior to immigrating to the United States, Kramer taught art classes with children who were refugees of Nazi Germany. While her early work as an art facilitator and teacher could have been classified as art therapy, Kramer was first called an art therapist by an American psychologist who served on the school board for Wiltwyck

FIG. 1.2 *Edith Kramer.*
(Photograph courtesy of Judith Rubin.)

School for Boys (Junge & Wadeson, 2006). From 1950 to 1957, Kramer worked with children at Wiltwyck who had emotional and behavioral disturbances. Throughout her career, Kramer strongly promoted the significance of the creative process itself in art therapy, stressing "art as therapy" over the art psychotherapy approach advocated for by Naumburg (Junge, 2010, p. 43). Kramer called the people whom she worked with students instead of clients and did not classify herself as a psychotherapist. Her book *Art as Therapy with Children* (1971) included examples of art therapy with children who were blind, undergoing psychiatric hospitalization, and receiving treatment in a residential facility (Fig. 1.2).

Mary Huntoon and Don Jones

In 1946, Art Therapist Mary Huntoon organized one of the first art therapy studios in the United States at the Menninger Clinic in Topeka, Kansas (Junge, 2010). At that time, the Menninger Clinic served veterans and was one of the largest psychiatric research and training centers in the United States. Huntoon's approach to art therapy aligns with the community arts approach that is still popular among art therapists today. Huntoon's colleague at the Menninger Clinic, Don Jones, later moved to Ohio where he created a similar program at Harding Hospital. Don Jones was influential in forming one of the first state associations of art therapists, the Buckeye Art Therapy Association (BATA) in Ohio, with fellow Art Therapist Bernard Stone. However, Elinor Ulman later insisted that the Wisconsin Art Therapy Association was the first statewide art therapy association (Ulman, 1969, as cited by Potash & Ramirez, 2013). The debate has continued in more recent art therapy literature (e.g., Junge, 2010; Potash & Ramirez, 2013; Potash et al., 2016).

Elinor Ulman

Elinor Ulman was an artist with training in landscape architecture who taught art and worked as a cartographer, draftsperson, and technical illustrator before she became an art therapist (Junge, 2010). As she transitioned into the profession of art therapy, Ulman worked with children who had developmental disabilities and with adults who had substance-use concerns. In the 1950s, Ulman organized Margaret Naumburg's lecture series, established an art therapy program at Washington DC General Hospital, and developed the Ulman Assessment Procedure. Ulman was the first person to publish a scholarly journal that was devoted to the profession of art therapy, *Bulletin of Art Therapy*, in 1961. Ulman later cofounded the George Washington University art therapy program in 1971 with Art Therapist Bernard Levy.

Hanna Yaxa Kwiatkowska

Naumburg's first documented art therapy trainee was a Polish immigrant named Hanna Yaxa Kwiatkowska (Junge, 2010). Beginning in 1955, Kwiatkowska worked as an art therapist at St. Elizabeth's Hospital in Washington DC, where she developed a program that served adult patients with schizophrenia. Kwiatkowska designed and implemented research and later continued her studies at the National Institute of Mental Health, where she worked from 1958 to 1972. She was one of the first art therapists to conduct published quantitative research. Kwiatkowska is widely known for inventing family art therapy, a technique that she described in her book *Family Therapy and Education Through Art* (1978). Kwiatkowska found that treatment outcomes for individuals who have schizophrenia and other serious mental health conditions improved significantly when their families were involved in art therapy.

Myra Levick

Myra Levick began her work as an art therapist at the Albert Einstein Medical Center in Philadelphia in 1963. She created the first graduate-level training program in art therapy at Hahnemann Hospital and Medical College in 1967 and later became the first president of the American Art Therapy Association. Levick wrote over 40 published journal articles on the topic of art therapy and created the Levick Emotional and Cognitive Art Therapy Assessment (LECATA), a measure that is based upon developmental norms.

Georgette Powell

Georgette Powell was the only art therapist of color profiled in the initial publication of *A History of Art Therapy in the United States* (Junge & Asawa, 1994). The extent of Powell's contributions are well documented in a recent article by Stepney (2019). Powell led several arts-based initiatives in New York beginning in the 1930s with funding from the Federal Arts Program of the Works Project Administration. She advocated for her artwork to be included on the walls of Harlem Hospital, a mural titled *Recreation in Harlem* that depicted Black children of the surrounding neighborhood. Powell began identifying as an art therapist in the late 1950s and learned from Edith Kramer at the Turtle Bay Music

School. In the early 1960s, Powell relocated to Washington DC, where she established several community-based art therapy programs for children (Junge, 2010) and worked at Washington DC General Hospital with Elinor Ulman. Powell also worked as an art therapist at St. Elizabeth's Hospital and was a supervisor and mentor to students from George Washington University (Boston & Short, 2006). She was a founding member of the National Alliance of Third World Creative Therapists in the 1970s alongside Lucille Venture, Cliff Joseph, Charles Anderson, and other art therapists of color (Stepney, 2019). The ad hoc committee later formed the Mosaic Committee and subsequently was renamed the Multicultural Committee of the AATA.

Cliff Joseph

Cliff Joseph, an Afro-Caribbean art therapist, was the first person who identified as Black to become a Registered Art Therapist (AATA, 2017a, 2017b). Joseph (2006) noted that he entered the field of art therapy in 1963 when he transitioned from being a commercial artist to being an artist who promotes individual and systemic change. During his early years as an art therapist, he worked as the Director of Art Therapy at Albert Einstein College of Medicine Hospital in New York City. Like Powell, Joseph had connections to Edith Kramer, who invited him to attend an initial meeting of the AATA in the late 1960s. Joseph described being the only person of color at the initial meetings of the AATA and subsequently organized meetings and panels that focused on the needs of clients and art therapists of color (Joseph, 1973). Joseph later became a faculty member at the Pratt Institute in Brooklyn, where he taught for 11 years and served as a thesis advisor and mentor (Junge, 2010). Throughout his life, Joseph continued to be involved in advocacy efforts that highlighted the mental health needs of urban communities of color and the impact of institutional racism (Stepney, 2019) (Fig. 1.3).

FIG. 1.3 *Cliff Joseph.*
(Photograph courtesy of Judith Rubin.)

Lucille Venture

Lucille Venture was a high school art teacher in Baltimore, MD, for over 25 years (Stepney, 2019). During a leave of absence from her teaching position, Venture began practicing art therapy at a psychiatric hospital where she developed a Crisis Art Therapy program that focused on crisis intervention. She later developed an art therapy program with targeted prevention efforts at the Lafayette Multipurpose Center called the Kid's Room. Venture became a Registered Art Therapist in 1973 and was the first art therapist in the United States to publish a doctoral dissertation that was specific to art therapy, titled *The Black Beat in Art Therapy Experiences* (Venture, 1977). Although Venture earned a doctoral degree, she voiced support for allowing art therapy to be practiced with less than a master's degree and presented an alternative pathway for art therapy education that she viewed as being more inclusive. Throughout her professional life, Venture was an advocate for students, art therapists, and clients of color who left a lasting impression upon the field of art therapy (Potash, 2005).

Charles Anderson

Charles Anderson was the first chairperson of the Mosaic Committee of the AATA and a leader of efforts to bring multicultural awareness and diversity to the field of art therapy (Stepney, 2019). Anderson began working with Don Jones at the Menninger Clinic in 1962 and was employed there until 2003. He also served in the military during the 1960s and worked as a recreation specialist with Vietnam veterans. Anderson's influence on the field of art therapy may be lesser known because he did not publish written work to the same extent as other art therapists of this time period, but his contributions in terms of leadership and advocacy through his spoken word and artwork were important to the development of the profession (J.A. Rubin, personal communication, February 1, 2021). Anderson also had an impact upon future generations of art therapists whom he trained and mentored through several universities (Emporia State, Avila, and Washburn) and supervised at the Menninger Clinic (Stepney, 2019).

Christine Wang

Recently identified as one of the first advocates for research in the profession of art therapy, Christine Wang was an art therapist and researcher who entered the profession in the early 1960s (Potash, 2021). Early in her career, Wang conducted research using the Draw-A-Person test with John Money at Johns Hopkins Hospital. In the late 1960s, she led art therapy groups with young women who were pregnant and contributed to the literature in this area. Wang interacted with many of the US art therapy pathfinders who were previously mentioned in this chapter, was a founding member of the AATA, and was the first Chinese American to become a registered art therapist. Despite her active roles in research, practice, and training, little was widely known about Wang until a recent article by Potash (2021) that highlighted her numerous and important contributions to the profession.

Wayne Ramirez

Wayne Ramirez first learned about art therapy from his mother in Puerto Rico, who stated that art therapy would be "a wonderful thing to do as a career" (Potash & Ramirez, 2013, p. 169). Later, while completing his Master of Fine Arts at the University of Pennsylvania, Ramirez shared his passion for art with young people at the Southern Home for Children in South Philadelphia. Here began the transition from practicing studio artist to practicing art therapist, an experience that would lead to Ramirez being offered the position of art therapist at Devereaux School in 1963 and subsequently accepting a position at the Milwaukee Psychiatric Hospital in Wisconsin as director of the Art Therapy Department in 1964 (Potash & Ramirez, 2013). While in Wisconsin, Ramirez was integral in forming the Wisconsin Art Therapy Association and served as the first president of the state association. Ramirez was identified as an "active leader" in the early days of the AATA (Potash & Ramirez, 2013, p. 171) and established a successful undergraduate art therapy program that still exists today at Mount Mary University (Fig. 1.4).

FIG. 1.4 *Wayne Ramirez.*
(Photograph courtesy of Wayne Ramirez.)

The emergence of art therapy in the United Kingdom

Art Therapist Susan Hogan (2001) documented the emergence of art therapy in the United Kingdom. According to Hogan (2001), the work of Margaret Naumburg and other American art therapists was not well known in Europe until the mid-1950s. However, a British art therapist named Adrian Hill simultaneously developed his rendition of art therapy around the same time as Naumburg, Cane, and Kramer.

Adrian Hill

Hill reported that he first used the term art therapy in 1942 to describe his work at King Edward VII Sanatorium at Midhurst, where he provided services to injured soldiers (Hill, 1951). A **sanatorium** was a medical facility that was designed to help patients recuperate from long-term illnesses during this time period (Kanabus, 2020). Hill witnessed the power of art to help patients develop a more positive outlook as a strategy for coping with physical illness (Hogan, 2001). Hill (1945) was a survivor of tuberculosis and was instrumental in helping other survivors cope with the debilitating illness as documented in his first book on the subject of art therapy, *Art Versus Illness*. Hill emphasized the importance of direct interaction between art therapist and patient as "essential to the success of the work" (Hogan, 2001, p. 145). Hill's work could be viewed as a predecessor to **medical art therapy,** which was later defined as "the use of art expression and imagery with individuals who are physically ill, experiencing trauma to the body, or who are undergoing aggressive medical treatment" (Malchiodi, 2003, p. 2).

In addition to his work in medical settings, Hill also advocated for art therapy and the arts in health care. He formed a relationship with the British Red Cross and subsequently helped develop a traveling exhibit of patient artwork that was displayed in hospitals. Hill lectured and led discussions regarding patient artwork in hospitals throughout Great Britain, helping to generate interest and enthusiasm regarding art therapy in medical settings (Hogan, 2001). As the chairperson of the Art Therapy Committee of the South West Metropolitan Hospital Board (SWMHB), Hill helped to develop and disseminate a survey of hospital-based art therapy programs in 1949 (Hill, 1951). Survey results indicated an overall positive view of art therapy in British hospitals, documenting the recreational aspects, diagnostic significance, therapeutic benefits, and aesthetic value of art-making in hospital settings.

Other UK art therapists in medical settings

The SWMHB survey provided evidence that art therapy was being practiced in this region of Great Britain in several hospital facilities by the late 1940s (Hill, 1951). Several of the hospital-based art therapists in the area were trained by Hill, including Frank Brakewell, who was an artist and had been Hill's patient. Edward Adamson, an art therapist who worked at Netherne Hospital in Surrey, worked with Hill in a sanatorium that served patients with tuberculosis (Hogan, 2001).

North of this area in Birmingham, Art Therapist Elsie Davies worked at the City Sanitarium, but her work differed from Hill and his predecessors in that her approach was methodical and highly structured (Hogan, 2001). She referred to her method as the Arthur Segal Method because it was based upon the work of the hospital-based artist who worked with patients in psychiatric wards (Davies, 1936, as cited by Hogan, 2001).

Joyce Laing was the first art therapist to initiate an art therapy department at a hospital in Scotland in the 1950s. Laing worked primarily with military veterans and described feeling deeply connected to this work. According to Hogan (2001), Laing did not publish writing about her work but communicated deep connections to her patients, the setting, and the profession of art therapy during a personal interview with Hogan in 1995.

Growth of community-based art therapy in the United Kingdom

While much of the growth of art therapy in Europe occurred in hospitals, British Art Therapist Rita Simon established an art therapy group in 1946 within what was then called a social club, a place where people with mental health issues would gather for treatment and socialization (Hogan, 2001). The art group emphasized self-expression and each session would end with a group painting. The approach that Simon described in her writing involved encouraging participants to form connections, strengthen relationships, and find a sense of belonging within a community of artists (Simon, 1964, as cited by Hogan, 2001). As Hogan (2001) explained, "Simon's approach to art therapy was essentially radical, as she perceived mental illness as something generated in the interaction between people and society" (p. 207).

Also in the 1940s, Irene and Gilbert Chapernowe formed Withymead, a therapeutic community in Great Britain that was dedicated to art therapy. The Chapernowes initially created Withymead as a home and refuge for people who were impacted by World War II (Hogan, 2001). The 14-room house afforded places for people to live and make art, and subsequently became a place where people would come for long-term art therapy treatment. Led by Psychoanalyst Irene Chapernowe, European art therapists including Jo Guy, Norah Godfrey, Peter Lyle, Elizabeth Wills, Richard Fritzsche, and others all worked at Withymead. Hogan (2001) explained that Withymead was a predecessor of the therapeutic community movement, which took place in both Europe and the United States. For more information regarding community art therapy, see Chapter 15, Community-based art therapy and community arts.

The emergence of art therapy in Canada

At the time of this writing, a complete history of art therapy in Canada has yet to be published. However, two authors have recently published brief writings on the topic, including Lois Woolf (2003) and Janis Timm-Bottos (2015).

Woolf (2003) explained that art therapy emerged in Canada in the late 1940s. The first Canadian art therapy innovator was identified by Woolf as Psychiatrist Martin Fischer. Fischer utilized art at Lakeshore Psychiatric Hospital in Toronto with psychiatric patients. Later, Fischer introduced the concept of child art therapy to the Ontario Children's Aid Society. Around this same time period, Selwyn and Irene Dewdney introduced art therapy to London Psychiatric Hospital and the Westminster Veteran's hospital in London, Ontario. The fourth Canadian art therapist of this time period was Marie Revai, an art teacher and artist who worked with children and psychiatric patients.

In her coverage of the history of art therapy in Canada, Timm-Bottos (2015) asserted, "While it was men who were first acknowledged for developing and disseminating art therapy in Canada, it was a larger-by-far group of women who stayed close to the work, often without the recognition they deserved" (Timm-Bottos, 2015, p. 691). Readers who are interested in learning more about the history of art therapy in Canada are encouraged to refer to Timm-Bottos' (2015) brief but interesting account, which also documented the sociopolitical factors influencing the development of art therapy in Canada.

The emergence of art therapy in Australia

A history of art therapy in Australia was published recently by Gilroy et al. (2019). The book highlighted the origins of art therapy in Australia as being similar to its origins in the United Kingdom but occurring a little bit later. Gilroy et al. (2019) documented the contributions of Guy Grey-Smith in Perth, Western Australia, where he worked with tuberculosis survivors and psychiatric patients in hospital settings in the late 1950s. Unlike Canada and the United States where professional organizations emerged in the 1970s, professional organizations were not initiated in Australia until the late 1980s. Readers who are interested in learning more about the history of art therapy in Australia are encouraged to refer to *Art Therapy in Australia* (Gilroy et al., 2019).

The emergence of art therapy in Israel

Regev and Lev-Wiesel (2015) wrote that art therapy was first introduced in Israel in the 1960s when immigrants from Europe and the United States began practicing art therapy in educational and medical settings. The Israeli Association of Creative and Expressive Therapies (IACET) was formed in 1971, and the first art therapy educational program at the University of Haifa opened in 1981. Art therapy has been recognized as a paramedical profession and overseen by the Ministry of Health since 1988. According to Regev and Lev-Wiesal (2015), art therapy is currently "an integral part of the human services provided in Israel's medical and educational domains" (p. 728).

The emergence of art therapy throughout Asia

The use of arts in healing in parts of Asia was documented centuries ago and continues as part of modern practice. An important source of information in English regarding the development of art therapy is the book *Art Therapy in Asia: To the Bone or Wrapped in Silk* (Kalmanowitz et al., 2012). Kalmanowitz et al. (2012) explained, "The development of art therapy in Asia is as diverse as the countries themselves" (p. 29). The contributors to *Art Therapy in Asia* do not focus on art therapy pathfinders; instead, a series of authors describe current work of art therapists who practice within their cultural contexts, including historical traditions. Similarly, Coss and Wong (2015) focused more on current developments in Asian countries and less on the historical development of art therapy in China, Taiwan, Korea, Japan, Hong Kong, India, Pakistan, and Sri Lanka. An art therapy program in Hong Kong is mentioned as originating in the 1980s. Art therapy training was cited as having been established in the 1990s, including at Daegu University Graduate School in Korea and at Soochow University in China. A more detailed account of the history of art therapy in the countries mentioned here was not found in the current literature.

Instead of viewing the history of art therapy in Asia and other parts of the world as something in need of being uncovered or discovered (as may be typical of a Western cultural stance), readers are encouraged to maintain a genuine curiosity and cultural humility regarding what we could learn from the practices of art therapists who reside in other cultural contexts. The international and cross-cultural use of art therapy and sharing of insights gained from research and practice in other countries are areas of growing interest in the field.

Art therapy today: A brief overview of recent trends

In addition to interest in sharing ideas across countries and cultures, several trends have emerged in the literature, including a focus on social justice and an emerging specialization in virtual art therapy. Reviewing current journal articles such as those published in *Art Therapy: The Journal of the American Art Therapy Association* or *The Arts in Psychotherapy* is one way of learning more about current topics. For example, the January 2021 issue of *Art Therapy* featured a qualitative research study on the experiences of art therapy graduate students of color and provided suggestions for improving educational experiences for art therapy trainees (Johnson et al., 2021). Another method for learning about contemporary issues in art therapy is visiting the websites of our professional organizations. For example, current foci of materials found at www.arttherapy.org, the website of the American Art Therapy Association (AATA), include a progress report on diversity, equity, and inclusion within the AATA and a report on the findings of the Coronavirus Impact Survey. Beginning in the year 2020, the COVID-19 pandemic had a significant impact on the profession of art therapy and the world, including an influence on the expansion of telehealth and virtual art therapy (AATA, 2020). The AATA has also recently released statements related to Black Lives Matter and US law enforcement responses to mental health crises (AATA, 2020). The next section of this chapter explains the role of professional associations and names several national organizations that support art therapy and art therapists.

Professional associations

Professional associations are organizations that bring together groups of people who work in the same or similar fields and help to define, promote, and set standards for a profession (University of Sydney Career Centre, 2020). Professional associations also offer opportunities for professionals to network, share ideas, and collectively advocate for the profession. According to Bordonaro (2015), more than two dozen countries have organized art therapy associations. While several of the larger art therapy professional associations will be discussed, readers are also encouraged to learn more by visiting the Global Art Therapy Alliance webpage at http://www.arttherapyalliance.org/GlobalArtTherapyResources.html.

The American Art Therapy Association (AATA)

The American Art Therapy Association (AATA) began as a series of meetings in the late 1960s where US art therapists met to discuss the possibility of forming a new professional association (Junge, 2010). Prior to these meetings, the organization where many art therapists connected and exchanged ideas was the International Society for Psychopathology of Expression (IPSE), a professional group that primarily consisted of psychiatrists who were mainly focused on visual markers of psychopathology in artwork. Art therapists decided to organize a new association that focused on the clinical work of art therapists and the profession of art therapy (Junge, 2010). The initial meeting's attendees were pathfinders in the field, including Naumburg, Ulman, Kwiatkowska, Levick, Joseph, and Jones. The first official AATA meeting occurred in 1968 and Myra Levick, a key organizer of the new professional association, was elected as president (Junge, 2010). Subsequently, the association formed an ad hoc committee to locate all art therapists across the United States and Canada and invite them to join. An executive board was elected and the decision made that only those who identified as art therapists could be voting members and hold office in the AATA, a tradition that is maintained in the organization to this day (Junge, 2010).

In the beginning, the AATA had approximately 50 members. Currently, over 5000 art therapists from the United States, Canada, and other countries are members of the AATA (C. Woodruff, personal communication, September 9, 2020). Memberships are also available for students, international members, affiliates, and associates (see www.arttherapy.org for additional information).

The British Association of Art Therapists (BAAT)

The British Association of Art Therapists (BAAT) was also founded in the 1960s by a group of art therapists in the United Kingdom, including Adamson, Hill, and others. Waller (2013) documented the formation of BAAT in her book *Becoming a Profession.* In the United Kingdom, art therapists are regulated by the Health and Care Professions Council (HCPC), and professionals must be deemed qualified by the HCPC before they can join BAAT as professional members (BAAT, 2020). However, as with the AATA, associate and trainee memberships are available for individuals who are not qualified art therapists. For more information, visit www.baat.org.

The Canadian Art Therapy Association (CATA-ACAT)

The Canadian Art Therapy Association, also known as l'Association Canadienne d'Art Thérapie (CATA-ACAT), was founded by Martin Fischer in 1977 (CATA-ACAT, 2020). The association offers professional level memberships to individuals with graduate-level education in art therapy and also offers associate and student memberships. For more information, visit www. https://www.canadianarttherapy.org.

The Australian, New Zealand, and Asian Creative Arts Therapies Association (ANZACATA)

While art therapists in Australia may belong to associations in other countries, most belong to the Australian, New Zealand, and Asian Creative Arts Therapies Association (ANZACATA, 2020). The organization began in 1987 as the Australian National Art Therapy Association Inc. and later incorporated other associations and countries to form ANZACATA (for a detailed timeline, visit https://www.anzacata.org/About-ANZACATA). In addition to offering professional memberships to art therapists from the corresponding region, ANZACATA offers professional categories that are open to graduates from approved programs in the United States, United Kingdom, and Canada in addition to provisional, student, and affiliate memberships. For more information, visit www.anzacata.org.

International Expressive Arts Therapy Association (IEATA)

Many art therapists from the United States, the United Kingdom, Canada, and Australia may also be members of the International Expressive Arts Therapy Association (IEATA). The IEATA defines **expressive arts therapies** as practices "that combine the visual arts, movement, drama, music, writing, and other creative processes to foster deep personal growth and community development" (IEATA, 2020, para 3). Founded in 1994 and based in San Francisco, California (USA), the IEATA provides opportunities for art therapists and other creative art therapists to network and learn from one another (IEATA, 2020). The IEATA also credentials Registered Expressive Arts Therapists (REAT). A variety of membership types are available. For more information, visit https://www.ieata.org/.

Ethical standards

An important function of most professional associations is the establishment of ethical codes and principles. **Ethical codes** are standards of professional conduct that should be followed by members of a group in order to protect the general public and preserve the integrity of the profession. Each of the previously mentioned professional groups has a code of ethics as named in Table 1.1. At the time of this writing, the ethical codes for each association could be found on their websites.

In the United States, art therapists must follow two sets of ethical codes, those of the AATA and those determined by the **Art Therapy Credentials Board** (ATCB, 2020). The ATCB issues and oversees credentials for art therapists in the United States including the **Registered Art Therapist (ATR)** credential. **Credentialing** involves reviewing and approving the educational and clinical experience of an applicant in order to attest to their qualifications to practice in a particular profession. All art therapists who hold a credential that is issued by the ATCB must comply with their Ethics and Standards of Conduct or they could face disciplinary action (ATCB, 2020).

The Ethical Principles of the American Art Therapy Association will be reviewed in detail as *one example* of standards of conduct that may guide a practicing art therapist. Readers who are situated outside of the United States are strongly encouraged to review the standards in their home country.

TABLE 1.1 Professional associations and corresponding ethical codes.

	Country or region	Name of document
AATA	United States	Ethical Principles
ATCB	United States	Code of Ethics, Conduct, and Disciplinary Procedures
BAAT	United Kingdom	Code of Ethics and Principles of Professional Practice
CATA-ACAT	Canada	Standards of Practice
ANZACATA	Australia, New Zealand, and Asia	Standards of Professional Practice and Code of Ethics
IEATA/REAT	International	Code of Ethics

Ethical principles for art therapists (AATA)

The Ethical Principles for Art Therapists published by AATA (2013) can be found at www.arttherapy.org/ethics/. Additionally, best practice papers, guides to ethical decision-making, and AATA Values Statements are found on this website. The purpose of the Ethical Principles is to provide guidance to art therapists with the intention of safeguarding clients. The principles address many situations that an art therapist could encounter through their professional practice of art therapy and also provide direction regarding education and supervision of art therapy trainees. The Ethical Principles may also be used as an educational tool for students, professionals, and the public (AATA, 2013). The Ethical Principles connect to the six core values listed as follows, which are intended to be aspirational in nature and "affirm basic human rights" (AATA, 2013, p. 1):

Autonomy: Art therapists respect clients' right to make their own choices regarding life direction, treatment goals, and options. Art therapists assist clients by helping them to make informed choices, which further their life goals and affirm others rights to autonomy as well.

Nonmaleficence: Art therapists strive to conduct themselves and their practice in such a way as to cause no harm to individuals, families, groups, and communities.

Beneficence: Art therapists promote well-being by helping individuals, families, groups, and communities to improve their circumstances. Art therapists enhance welfare by identifying practices that actively benefit others.

Fidelity: Art therapists accept their role and responsibility to act with integrity toward clients, colleagues, and members of their community. Art therapists maintain honesty in their dealings, accuracy in their relationships, faithfulness to their promises, and truthfulness in their work.

Justice: Art therapists commit to treating all persons with fairness. Art therapists ensure that clients have equal access to services.

Creativity: Art therapists cultivate imagination for furthering understanding of self, others, and the world. Art therapists support creative processes for decision-making and problem-solving, as well as meaning-making and healing.

The first five values (autonomy, nonmaleficence, beneficence, fidelity, and justice) are similar to values expressed by other helping professions [see, for example, the General Principles of the American Psychological Association Code of Ethics (https://www.apa.org/ethics/code) or the American Counseling Association Code of Ethics Preamble (https://www.counseling.org/resources/aca-code-of-ethics.pdf)].

The sixth value is unique to art therapy and reflects the importance of creative expression to the work of art therapists. While the distinctiveness of art-making as a therapeutic process has long been known and described by art therapists, recent research literature has reported psychological, interpersonal, and physical benefits of art-making (De Witte et al., 2021). For more information regarding art therapy research, see Chapter 5, Approaches to research in art therapy. Since art therapists value art-making as a mechanism of change and the art product as an important artifact of the therapy session, special consideration must be given regarding what happens with the art after the session concludes. Art therapists must consider the implications of artwork being displayed, as well as the need for client consent and protection of client welfare associated with the exhibition of artwork (Rubin, 2010).

The subsequent principles address the following categories: (1) responsibility to clients; (2) confidentiality; (3) assessment methods; (4) client artwork; (5) exhibition of client artwork; (6) professional competence and integrity; (7) multicultural and diversity competence; (8) responsibility to art therapy students and supervisees; (9) responsibility to research participants; (10) responsibility to the profession; (11) financial arrangements; (12) advertising; (13) independent practitioner; (14) initial and ending phases in art therapy; (15) professional use of the internet, social networking sites, and other electronic or digital technology; (16) conducting art therapy by electronic means; (17) abiding by the Ethical Principles for Art Therapists; and (18) inquiries and complaints (AATA, 2013). Art therapists use ethical decision-making models to review and apply the ethical codes. The following case study provides an example of an art therapist's decision-making process in action, referencing the AATA Ethical Principles for Art Therapists.

Case study: The art therapist and the board member

An art therapist works in a public children's hospital in an inner city. Many of the families she works with receive public assistance, including Medicaid. An influential member of the hospital board is quite excited about art therapy and wants to support the hospital's art therapy program. She contacts the art therapist directly and shares her intention to raise money to expand the art therapy program to provide outpatient services to underserved groups in the surrounding community. She asks to attend an inpatient pediatric art therapy group to learn more about the work of the art therapist. In addition, the board member suggests that she is willing to purchase children's artwork produced during art therapy sessions for the purpose of displaying the artwork in her own home, and also would like to help the art therapist transform client artwork into greeting cards that can be sold in the hospital gift shop as a fund raiser for the art therapy program. How should the art therapist proceed?

First, the art therapist should consider the potential harm (nonmaleficence) and potential benefits (beneficence) to her clients. What is the potential for harm to current pediatric clients if the board member attends their group, purchases/exhibits their artwork, and facilitates the sale of reproductions of the client artwork? How might clients benefit from the funding of an outpatient art therapy program in the future? According to the first set of ethical principles, the art therapist has a responsibility first and foremost to her clients. Principle 1.2 tells the art therapist that she must seek informed consent from the parent or guardian. **Informed consent** involves providing information to the client (or in this case, the legal guardian) at the onset of services so that they can make decisions regarding treatment. The informed consent process includes explaining what will happen during treatment, providing information regarding risks and benefits, discussing alternative options, and ultimately respecting the client's or guardian's decision regarding treatment (Center for Ethical Practice [CEP], 2020). The legal guardians of the children would need to provide consent for the board member to attend the group because they were not informed of a board member's potential attendance when they consented to services. In addition, it would be prudent for the art therapist to talk with group members to gauge their comfort level with having a visitor, as the visitor's presence may impact the art therapy group.

The art therapist would also need to consider confidentiality. **Confidentiality** involves protecting the client's right to privacy concerning their protected health information (CEP, 2020). Allowing an outside person (the hospital board member) to attend an art therapy group would provide access to confidential information discussed within the group. Principle 2.6 tells the art therapist that consent must be obtained from the parent or legal guardian prior to release of confidential information.

The art therapist must also consider standards related to client artwork. Art therapists consider client artwork created during sessions to be protected health information; therefore, the art therapist cannot release images of the client artwork (Principle 4.3) and cannot exhibit or sell client artwork (Principles 5.6 and 5.7) without signed consent from the parent or legal guardian. The art therapist should also be advised to discuss the potential exhibition, sale, and distribution of artwork with the client(s) because the Ethical Principles (AATA, 2013) indicate that the artwork belongs to the client, not the art therapist.

The profession of art therapy

In this chapter, you have examined definitions of art therapy and art therapists, explored the roots of the profession, been introduced to the pathfinders, become acquainted with the major professional organizations, and reviewed a set of ethical standards. The information presented here is intended to provide a context for the work of art therapists, which is covered in the next several chapters. As you continue reading, you will encounter answers to the questions, "What informs the work of art therapists?" and more specifically, "What do art therapists do?" In Chapter 16 of this book, you will revisit some of the information provided in this chapter as you learn more about pathways to becoming a professional art therapist.

Art experientials and reflection questions

1. Create a "scribble drawing" as discussed in the work of art therapy pioneer Florence Cane.

2. Make your own pictorial timeline of important events in the history of art therapy.
3. Locate, read, and summarize an article describing the history or practice of art therapy in a country outside of the country where you reside.
4. Given what you know about the cultures of "Eastern" and "Western" countries where art therapists live and work, why do you think that art therapists in the United States may be more interested in documenting art therapy pathfinders (or key figures)? For example, how might the cultural values of art therapists in China influence what they prioritize and document in relation to their work?
5. Visit the website of a professional association mentioned in this chapter and provide a summary of the resources available on the website.
6. Should the art therapist described in the case example, "The Art Therapist and the Board Member" allow the board member to attend her group with the permission of the parents/guardians? Should she allow clients' artwork to be sold? Why or why not?

Additional resources

Videos and Films:

Art Therapy: The Movie: https://www.imdb.com/title/tt3898052/
Art Therapy has Many Faces: https://www.psychotherapy.net/video/art-therapy
Wheels of Diversity: Pioneers of Color in Art Therapy: https://vimeo.com/search?q=Wheels%20of%20Diversity%3A%20Pioneers%20of%20Color%20in%20Art%20Therapy

Websites:

American Art Therapy Association: www.arttherapy.org
Art Therapy Credentials Board: https://www.atcb.org/
Australian, New Zealand, and Asian Creative Arts Therapies Association: https://www.anzacata.org
British Art Therapy Association: www.baat.org
Canadian Art Therapy Association: l'Association Canadienne d'Art Thérapie: https://www.canadianarttherapy.org
Ethical Principles for Art Therapists: https://arttherapy.org/wp-content/uploads/2017/06/Ethical-Principles-for-Art-Therapists.pdf
International Expressive Arts Therapy Association: https://www.ieata.org/

Chapter terms

American Art Therapy Association
Art Therapy
Art Therapist
Art Therapy Credentials Board

Australian, New Zealand, and Asian Creative Arts Therapies Association
Autonomy
Beneficence
British Art Therapy Association
Canadian Art Therapy Association
Client
Confidentiality
Creativity (as described in AATA's Ethical Principles)
Credentialing
Ethical Code
Expressive Art Therapies
Fidelity
Informed Consent
International Expressive Arts Therapy Association
Justice
Medical Art Therapy
Nonmaleficence
Professional associations
Registered Art Therapist
Sanatorium
Shaman
Unconscious

References

American Art Therapy Association. (2020). *COVID resources for art therapists, December 5.* https://arttherapy.org/covid-19-resources/.

American Art Therapy Association. (2013). *Ethical standards for art therapists.* https://arttherapy.org/wp-content/uploads/2017/06/Ethical-Principles-for-Art-Therapists.pdf.

American Art Therapy Association. (2017a). *About art therapy.* https://arttherapy.org/about-art-therapy/.

American Art Therapy Association. (2017b). *Multicultural subcommittee.* https://arttherapy.org/multicultural-sub-committee/.

American Psychological Association. (2015). Guidelines for psychological practice with transgender and gender nonconforming people. *The American Psychologist, 70*(9), 832–864. https://doi.org/10.1037/a0039906.

Art Therapy Credentials Board. (2020). *Code of ethics, conduct, and disciplinary procedures.* https://www.atcb.org/Ethics/ATCBCode.

Australian, New Zealand, and Asian Creative Arts Therapies Association. (2020). *About ANZACATA, December 5.* https://www.anzacata.org/About-ANZACATA.

Bordonaro, G. P. W. (2015). International art therapy. In D. Gussak, & M. L. Rosal (Eds.), *The Wiley handbook of art therapy* (pp. 675–682). John Wiley & Sons.

Boston, C., & Short, G. (2006). Georgette Seabrook Powell. *Art Therapy: Journal of the American Art Therapy Association, 23*(2), 89–90. https://doi.org/10.1080/07421656.2006.10129649.

British Association of Art Therapists. (2020). *Benefits of joining the BAAT and how to join, December 5.* https://www.baat.org/About-BAAT/Membership.

Canadian Art Therapy Association. (2020). *CATA-ACAT fact sheet.* https://static1.squarespace.com/static/5e84c59adbbf2d44e7d72295/t/5e94eb91badd4454b3a670a4/1586817943147/CATA-fact-sheet-April-2018.pdf.

Cane, F. (1951). *The artist in each of us.* Pantheon.

Cane, F. (1983). *The artist in each of us* (Revised ed.). Art Therapy Productions.

Center for Ethical Practice. (2020). *Practice resources.* https://centerforethicalpractice.org/ethical-legal-resources/practice-resources/.

Coss, E., & Wong, J. (2015). Cultural context and the practice of art therapy in Asia. In D. Gussak, & M. L. Rosal (Eds.), *The Wiley handbook of art therapy* (pp. 718–726). John Wiley & Sons.

De Witte, M., Orkibi, H., Zarate, R., Karkou, V., Sajnani, N., Malhotra, B., & Koch, S. C. (2021). From therapeutic factors to mechanisms of change in the creative arts therapies: A scoping review. *Frontiers in Psychology*, *2525*.

Dissanayake, E. (2000). Finding and making meaning. In *Art and intimacy: How the arts began* (pp. 72–98). University of Washington Press.

Gilroy, A. J., Linnell, S., McKenna, T., & Westwood, J. (Eds.). (2019). *Art therapy in Australia*. Brill. https://doi.org/10.1163/9789004368262.

Gussak, D. E., & Rosal, M. L. (Eds.). (2015). *The Wiley handbook of art therapy*. John Wiley & Sons.

Hill, A. K. G. (1945). *Art versus illness: A story of art therapy*. G. Allen and Unwin.

Hill, A. (1951). *Painting out illness*. William and Norgate Ltd.

Hogan, S. (2001). *Healing arts: The history of art therapy*. Jessica Kingsley Publishers.

International Expressive Arts Therapy Association. (2020). *About us*. https://www.ieata.org/.

Johnson, T., Deaver, S. P., & Doby-Copeland, C. (2021). Art therapy students of color: The experience of seven graduate students. *Art Therapy: Journal of the American Art Therapy Association*, *38*(1), 50–56. https://doi.org/10.1080/07421656.2020.1862603.

Joseph, C. (Ed.). (1973). *Art therapy and the third world: A panel discussion* (publisher not identified).

Joseph, C. (2006). Creative alliance: The healing power of art therapy. *Art Therapy: Journal of the American Art Therapy Association*, *23*(1), 30–33. https://doi.org/10.1080/07421656.2006.10129531.

Jung, C. G. (1964). *Man and his symbols*. Dell Publishing Company.

Junge, M. B. (2010). *The modern history of art therapy in the United States*. Charles C. Thomas.

Junge, M. B., & Asawa, P. P. (1994). *A history of art therapy in the United States*. American Art Therapy Association.

Junge, M. B., & Wadeson, H. (Eds.). (2006). *Architects of art therapy: Memoirs and life stories*. Charles C. Thomas.

Kalmanowitz, D., Potash, J., & Chan, S. M. (2012). *Art therapy in Asia: To the bone or wrapped in silk*. Jessica Kingsley Publishers.

Kanabus, A. (2020). *Sanatorium: From the first to the last*. https://tbfacts.org/about-us/.

Levick, M. F. (1983). *They could not talk and so they drew: Children's styles of coping and thinking*. Charles C. Thomas.

Lowenfeld, V. (1947). *Creative and mental growth: A textbook on art education*. Macmillan.

Malchiodi, C. A. (2003). *Handbook of art therapy*. Guilford.

Moodley, R., Gielen, U. P., & Wu, R. (Eds.). (2013). *Handbook of counseling and psychotherapy in an international context*. Routledge.

Moon, B. L. (2016). *Introduction to art therapy: Faith in the product*. Charles C. Thomas.

Napoli, M. (2019). Ethical contemporary art therapy: Honoring an American Indian perspective. *Art Therapy: Journal of the American Art Therapy Association*, *36*, 175–182. https://doi.org/10.1080/07421656.2019.1648916.

Naumburg, M. (1947). Studies of the "free" art expression of behavior problem children and adolescents as a means of diagnosis and therapy. *Nervous & Mental Disorders Monograph Series*. Grune & Stratton.

Naumburg, M. (1958). Art therapy: Its scope and function. In E. F. Hammer (Ed.), *The clinical application of projective drawings* (pp. 511–517). Charles C. Thomas.

Naumburg, M. (1987). *Dynamically oriented art therapy: Its principles and practices, illustrated with three case studies*. Magnolia Street Pub.

Naumburg, M. (2001). Spontaneous art in education and psychotherapy. *American Journal of Art Therapy*, *40*(1), 46. https://search.proquest.com/docview/199310225/fulltextPDF/F3FE92E3D46545AEPQ/1?accountid=28917.

Potash, J. S. (2005). Rekindling the multicultural history of the American Art Therapy Association, Inc. *Art Therapy: Journal of the American Art Therapy Association*, *22*(4), 184–188.

Potash, J. S. (2021). Christine Wang: Pioneering Chinese-American art therapist. *Art Therapy: Journal of the American Art Therapy Association*. https://doi.org/10.1080/07421656.2020.1859916.

Potash, J., Burnie, M., Pearson, R., & Ramirez, W. (2016). Restoring Wisconsin Art Therapy Association in art therapy history: Implications for professional definition and inclusivity. *Art Therapy*, *33*(2), 99–102.

Potash, J. S., & Ramirez, W. A. (2013). Broadening history, expanding possibilities: Contributions of Wayne Ramirez to art therapy. *Art Therapy: Journal of the American Art Therapy Association*, *30*(4), 169–176.

Rubin, J. A. (1986). From psychopathology to psychotherapy through art expression: A focus on Hans Prinzhorn and others. *Art Therapy: Journal of the American Art Therapy Association*, *3*(1), 27–33. https://doi.org/10.1080/07421656.1986.10758816.

Regev, D., & Lev-Wiesel, R. (2015). Art therapy in Israel: Current status and future directions of the profession. In D. Gussak, & M. L. Rosal (Eds.), *The Wiley handbook of art therapy* (pp. 727–734). John Wiley & Sons.

Prideaux, S. (2005). *Edvard Munch: Behind the scream*. Yale University Press.

Rubin, J. (2010). *Introduction to art therapy: Sources & resources*. Routledge.

Stepney, S. A. (2019). Visionary architects of color in art therapy: Georgette Powell, Cliff Joseph, Lucille Venture, and Charles Anderson. *Art Therapy: Journal of the American Art Therapy Association*, *36*(3), 115–121.

Timm-Bottos, J. (2015). Art therapy in Canada: A place-based métissage. In D. Gussak, & M. L. Rosal (Eds.), *The Wiley handbook of art therapy* (pp. 691–700). John Wiley & Sons.

Ulman, E. (2001). Art therapy: Problems of definition. *American Journal of Art Therapy*, *40*(1), 16.

University of Sydney Career Centre. (2020). *Professional associations*. https://www.sydney.edu.au/careers/students/career-advice-and-development/professional-associations.html.

Venture, L. D. (1977). *The black beat in art therapy experiences (Doctoral dissertation)*. Union for Experimenting Colleges and Universities.

Vick, R. M. (2003). A brief history of art therapy. In C. Malchiodi (Ed.), *Handbook of art therapy* (pp. 5–15). Guilford.

Waller, D. (2013). *Becoming a profession: The history of art therapy in Britain 1940-82*. Routledge.

Wendt, D. C., & Gone, J. P. (2016). Integrating professional and Indigenous therapies: An urban American Indian narrative clinical case study. *The Counseling Psychologist*, *44*(5), 695–729.

Woolf, L. (2003). Art therapy in Canada: Origins and explorations. *Canadian Art Therapy Association Journal*, *16*(2), 2–9. https://doi.org/10.1080/08322473.2003.11434764.

Chapter 2

Understanding media: Laying the groundwork for art-making

Molly O'Neill Haaga, PhD, ATR-BC, LPC and Jennifer B. Schwartz, MAAT, ATR-BC, ATCS

Art Therapy Department, Ursuline College, Cleveland, OH, United States

Voices from the field

When individuals engage in art making, the inherent properties of the materials and physical action of the process put the control back into their hands. Mixing, cutting, brushing, shaping, drawing, tearing, centering each require specific actions. This action-based, nonverbal process creatively engages our psychic properties in unique ways that move us even when we are depressed, blocked, or physically limited. The result is a dynamic collaboration that allows the creator to use art media and techniques to discover or recover parts of the self that are new or have been lost.

Mary (Mickie) K. McGraw, BFA, MA, ATR-BC
(personal communication, March 31, 2021)

Art therapy is not magic. It is an evidence-based profession founded on the knowledge of basic art skills and experience with various materials and techniques. Without this artists' 'tool box' we can not effectively integrate art into our therapeutic work with others. Each art experience leads to the next, as the patient builds self-confidence with the materials, and begins to understand the art therapy process.

Martha C. Stitt, ATR-BC, LPCC-S, LICDC-CS
(personal communication, March 31, 2021)

Learning outcomes

After reading this chapter, you will be able to

1. Describe a broad range of visual art media and their unique characteristics.
2. Explain how art materials and processes can carry personal, social, and cultural meanings.
3. Identify the expressive potential of a variety of art media.
4. Discern the media variables that affect interactions with art materials.

Foundations of Art Therapy. https://doi.org/10.1016/B978-0-12-824308-4.00013-2

5. Identify the theoretical background and components of the Expressive Therapies Continuum and provide examples that show how visual art processes can engage these components.
6. Develop strategies to safely implement and adapt art materials to promote success with all participant populations.
7. Summarize research that supports the application of art media for health and wellness.

Chapter overview

This chapter addresses the characteristics of a range of art materials used within health, wellness, and educational settings. The first part explores the foundations of art media, including media understanding and rationale for media selection, as described through the lenses of historical backgrounds, theoretical viewpoints, and culturally relevant practices. Contributing factors in successful media facilitation are discussed in terms of quality and variety of materials, accessibility, adaptations, and safety. The second part of the chapter provides a breakdown of a range of art materials, identifying key properties such as fluidity and structure, sensory impact, symbolic potential, practical considerations, and literature supporting the use of a broad scope of materials in art facilitation and art therapy practice. Art experientials and reflection questions will help the reader explore media components and develop firsthand knowledge and skills using a variety of materials.

Art media foundations

Ancient media, ancient practice

The roots of each art material discussed in this chapter trace back to prerecorded history. Handprints, paintings, and drawings have left evidence of human creativity on cave walls in ancient places across the globe. Early humans sourced local **pigments** from minerals and plants, using them to draw or paint scenes that appear to tell stories of animal and human interaction, dating back to at least 25,000 BCE (Stokstad & Cothren, 2011). Beads formed of shell and bone, and cloth made of native plants and animal sources, were fashioned to create clothing and adornments, with craftsmanship that went beyond the purely functional. Pictorial symbols carved onto tablets by the Sumerians around 3300 BCE, as well as paintings, drawings, and inscriptions made upon papyrus scrolls dating back to at least 2400 BCE, were meant to communicate ideas and connect with others (Diringer, 2011; Stokstad & Cothren, 2011). Figurines carved from marble around 3000 BCE provide more evidence of human imagination and ingenuity in utilizing raw materials to express concepts in three dimensions (such as the ancient Near East marble sculpture seen here https://www.clevelandart.org/art/1993.165). From our earliest experiences with painting on rocks, to creating digital art installations that make use of 21st-century technologies, we find ways to use art media to satisfy our creative urges. Researchers from a variety of disciplines conclude that this artistic behavior of transforming, with care and craftsmanship, the raw materials we have at hand into extraordinary, nonutilitarian objects, is a survival skill that has enabled our species to thrive for many hundreds of generations (Puccio, 2017).

Scientists, historians, anthropologists, philosophers, and artists alike have questioned what purpose these drawings served for their makers. For art therapists and many artists, understanding this behavior from an evolutionary perspective, as a survival skill that has been naturally selected as an adaptive function, makes a lot of sense. Dissanayake (2003) describes artistic survival skills as creative behaviors that "make special" normal objects, giving them aesthetic adjustments. Over time, these "making special" behaviors evolved as people utilized materials at hand to sketch, draw, plan, imagine, recount stories, and eventually write out their histories, myths, and insights. With the support of art facilitators and art therapists, people will continue to find value in art-making for many generations to come.

Media understanding

In art-making, **media** (or **mediums**) are the materials and tools used to create artistic expression. In the field of art therapy, the media we use are the conduits that enable creativity, problem-solving, play, experimentation, and exploration. The art media we use can be both familiar and unknown, traditional and nontraditional. While media possibilities are endless, bound only by one's imagination, they might include drawing materials (pastel, charcoal, crayon, ink, etc.); painting materials (watercolors, acrylics, tempera, spray paint, etc.); sculptural and three-dimensional materials (clay, metal, wood, found objects); fiber and textiles (yarn, muslin, reeds, etc.); digital materials (photography, art apps, tablets, etc.); natural materials (leaves, stones, branches, etc.); surfaces (canvas, cardboard, paper, etc.); and tools (paintbrushes, adhesives, erasers, etc.). In working with such a diverse array of media, the art therapist must begin with acceptance of material's power and significance. When incorporated into art-making, these materials will transform in matter and meaning—taking on symbolic energy, capable of eliciting change (Seiden, 2001). For example, in Fig. 2.1, the artist included everyday objects to represent personal metaphors.

Art therapy practitioners underscore the importance of developing personal knowledge, experience, and skills with media (Moon, 2010; Rubin, 2011). Gaining an understanding of the continuum of media through firsthand experience and exploration is an essential component of art therapy training and education. It is through such experience with a range of creative art media and processes that we become intimately familiar with the processes and pitfalls that our participants face. This is truly one of the cardinal rules of art therapy practice: Do it yourself first! However, the importance of media understanding is not limited to art therapy alone. Whether facilitating a community arts project, leading an after-school art club, teaching a painting class, or just creating on your

FIG. 2.1 *Ladder of Growth.*
Found object sculpture (6″ × 23″) by Charisse Green.

own, being mindful of the media you choose is an important step to ensuring a successful and meaningful art-making experience.

Elements and principles of art

The practice of art therapy requires knowledge of the creative process, as well as the visual arts. Fundamental to the art therapy student's art education is an understanding of these formal elements and principles of art. The elements of line quality, shape, form, space, texture, color, and value (see Fig. 2.2) are tools for designing a visual **composition**, while the principles of balance, pattern, movement, contrast, emphasis, unity, and proportion (see Fig. 2.3) provide a framework for how these elements can be deployed to affect the composition, and ultimately the viewer's perceptions (Field, 2018). Like art educators, art therapists and facilita-

ART
Elements

Line creates boundaries, delineates form, and leads the eye by connecting points. Variation in line (e.g., direction, width, visibility) can communicate meaning.

Shape is created by combining lines to form 2-D figures with height and width. Shapes can carry physical associations and evoke feeling in response to their character (e.g., simple/complex, smooth/jagged).

Form is shape that takes on depth to become 3-D. Form can be actual (e.g., clay sculpture) or implied through the use of elements like value (e.g., charcoal drawing).

Space is the area around, between, within, or occupied by objects. Space can enhance visual engagement by creating a focal point (e.g., negative space) or the illusion of depth (e.g., overlapping space).

Texture refers to the surface quality of the artwork. It can be real or visually implied. Texture can add visual interest and stimulate tactile memories and associations.

Color often holds symbolic meaning. Color combinations and arrangements (e.g., monochromatic, warm, cool, primary) can add visual complexity, alter visual perceptions, and impact mood and emotion.

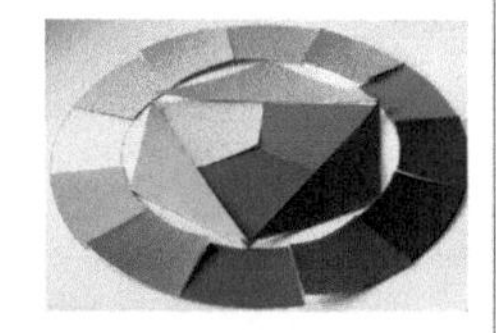

Value is the degree of lightness or darkness of color. Value creates dimension and evokes feeling based on the arrangement of varying tones.

FIG. 2.2 *Art Elements.*
Infographic created on CANVA.com with information adapted from Field, J. (2018). *An illustrated field guide to the elements and principles of art and design*. Hot Iron Press.
(No permission required.)

ART
Principles

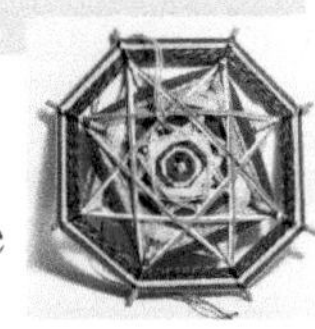

Balance is the even distribution of design elements, achieved when an image has equal visual "weight." This conveys a sense of wholeness and stability.

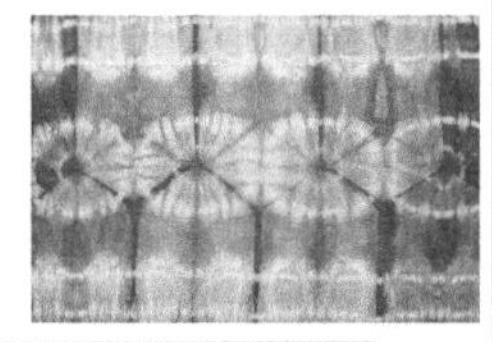

Pattern provides a structural framework for the repetition of elements. It emphasizes regularity in design and can help to establish the rhythm of the composition.

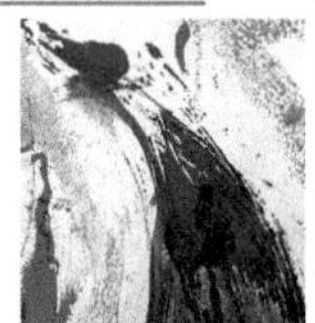

Movement shows action and gives the impression of motion. Movement also creates the visual narratives of the composition and directs the viewer's eye through the artwork.

Contrast refers to opposing or dramatic differences between elements (e.g., value, texture, size, proportion) that capture the viewer's attention. Contrast is most commonly associated with a change from light to dark values.

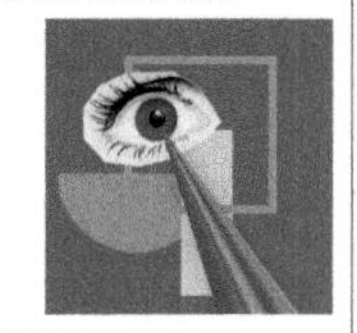

Emphasis is perceived prominence of one element over another. The emphasized element draws the viewer's attention and provides the image with a focal point. Emphasis helps define the artist's message.

Unity is achieved by positioning similar elements together to create a cohesive composition. Unity can impart feelings of completeness and harmony, while lack of unity can be used to cause tension.

Proportion refers to perceived size relationships between elements. Proportion can be used to create balance and familiarity or dominance and emphasis.

FIG. 2.3 *Art Principles.*
Infographic created on CANVA.com with information adapted from Field, J. (2018). *An illustrated field guide to the elements and principles of art and design*. Hot Iron Press.
(No permission required.)

tors may help participants understand these fundamentals of art, as they support them in their efforts to express themselves more clearly through their artwork. In this respect, a "successful" composition is not measured by the aesthetics achieved but rather by the message and the mood evoked. The communicative potential of the elements of art is vast, which demonstrates why they play a role in guiding the art-making process, as well as evaluation of the art product. Art therapy research shows that combinations of certain formal elements within artwork can be indicative of aspects of mental health and functioning (Gantt & Anderson, 2009; Haeyen & Hinz, 2020; Pénzes et al., 2018, 2020). When combined with the client's verbal processing of their artwork, looking at the art product in these terms can enhance understanding for both client and therapist.

Sociocultural context

Archeologists, sociologists, art historians, and artists alike note that the raw materials used to create art have intrinsic **symbolic value** (Bar-Yosef Maeyer & Bosch, 2019). Throughout this chapter, readers will notice examples of artists using each media to symbolically represent abstract ideas and real-life experiences that can be difficult and sometimes impossible to articulate with words. In supporting the artist's ability to tell their story through the use of artistic media, we must also consider the inherent messages conveyed by individual art materials. Facilitating therapeutic encounters with art-making requires consultation with the artist to select media that are **ego-syntonic**—aligned with the individual's sense of self. In this act, the facilitator should recognize and honor that the meanings and associations an individual attaches to certain art media are born from their personal and cultural history. For example, socioeconomic status can directly affect access to what have traditionally been considered "fine art" materials. Social norms, practiced by cultural and community groups, can determine how art materials are valued. Cultural and ethnic identity is tied in with how art materials have been used to depict the life experiences of different populations. Environmental considerations may affect how and where art materials should be sourced. Regional economies and infrastructures dictate what materials are sustainable. By their own nature, art materials cannot be adequately understood without consideration of the sociocultural context from which they were born and have been applied (Joseph, 2006; Moon, 2010; Orr, 2010; Park et al., 2020; Potash et al., 2017). Application of culturally meaningful art media can enhance the therapeutic process by promoting greater emotional engagement and personal expression (Hinz, 2020; Moon, 2010). In working toward building multicultural competence in this area, readers are encouraged to question the dominant narratives that shape their own, as well as their participants' understandings, beliefs, values, and choices related to art materials.

Media selection and interaction

Seminal authors from the fields of art education, art therapy, and psychology have emphasized the importance of understanding the influence of art materials on the creative process (Arnheim, 1989; Hinz, 2020; Junge, 2016; Kramer, 1971; Lowenfeld, 1952; Lusebrink, 1990; McNiff, 1998; Moon, 2010; Naumburg, 1958, 1966; Rubin, 2011; Wadeson, 1987). Art therapy is rooted in the interactive process between the client and the art materials. To best facilitate this **media interaction**, art therapists use their extensive media training to select art materials based on several factors including client needs, preferences, and abilities, as well as the art therapist's therapeutic approach (Pénzes et al., 2014, 2015). While conceptualization and characterization of media use in art therapy have been rooted in the psychoanalytic perspective of the first noted practitioners, contemporary art therapy practices emphasize more eclectic, interdisciplinary, and diverse approaches to understanding media selection and interaction.

Art therapy founder Margaret Naumburg emphasized the value of using easily accessible art materials that were fluid in nature, such as paint or clay, to promote spontaneous expression and draw out unconscious psychic content (Junge, 2010; Naumburg, 1958). The durability of the art products created with such materials was also cited as an effective way to preserve authorship, meaning, and memory (Naumburg, 1958). Art Therapist Edith Kramer expanded the definition of art therapy practice to include an emphasis on material selection and uses (Junge & Asawa, 1994). Kramer (1971) argued that requiring basic art materials, such as tempera paint, pastels, charcoal, clay, and a kiln, in the art therapy studio allowed for greater versatility. For Kramer, media manipulation was seen as giving structure and form to art materials, as well as to emotions, and her assessment practices focused on evaluation of not only the end product, but also the ways in which the individual interacted with and responded to the art materials (Kramer, 1971; Kramer & Gerity, 2001). Art therapist and visionary Cliff Joseph identified group mural making as an effective intervention for building connection and community in his work with psychiatric patients, as well as within community activism and protest art (Harris & Joseph, 1973; Joseph, 2006; Stepney, 2019). Lucile Venture (1977) also focused on art therapy within her community, placing primary importance on preventative practices. By introducing play media in the form of multicultural dolls into art therapy work with Black children, Venture sought to address the importance of early perceptions of race and skin color and encourage children to embody the positive imagery of the multicultural dolls to discover a more positive self-image (Stepney, 2019; Venture, 1977). Similarly, Art Therapist Sarah McGee (1979) applied play media in her work with migrant mothers, using puppetry to facilitate communication of trauma and act out traditional and indigenous healing practices. She also utilized familiar, everyday art materials as personally relevant vehicles for expressive art (Doby-Copeland, 2019). Harriet Wadeson (1987) identified four influential media characteristics: ***control*** (different media allow for more or less control); ***commitment*** (certain media are permanent while others are transformative, providing opportunities for change); ***color intensity*** (media can span from pale to vivid or include a range of intensity); and ***drawing*** or coloring (media like pencils and pens are usually more appropriate for drawing while paints are the preferred option for coloring). Visual perception Psychologist Rudolph Arnheim (1989) wrote extensively about the psychology of art and contended that art materials have character. Arnheim argued that the individual attributes of a material that attract one person may repel another or result in feelings of indifference, showing that the physical properties of art materials are inseparably tied to psychological connotations. According to Art Therapist and Psychologist Judith Rubin (2011) simple, unstructured media should be prioritized in art therapy and argued that materials like clay, pastels, and paint hold infinite potential for unique visual creations, thus encouraging projection of personal meaning. Additionally, unstructured media can be easier to use within limited timeframes and is applicable to all ages and skill sets, with less need for instruction. Finally, emphasizing the sensory benefits of media, Art Therapist Michael Franklin (2017) noted that using art materials helps ground us in the present moment, and that natural materials can help some artists feel physically and emotionally interconnected with all life.

Conceptual models

Media dimension variables

To describe the potential for creative expression that art media and interaction with art media are capable of eliciting, Art Therapists Sandra Kagin and Vija Lusebrink (1978) identified three structural elements of art intervention with the **media dimension variables** (MDV) model. These include the physical properties of the art media, the complexity of the tasks associated with using the given media, and the structure of the media experience. The variables act as a continuum along which art materials may be arranged (Kagin & Lusebrink, 1978; Lusebrink, 1990). **Media properties** are classified as **Fluid/Resistive**. **Fluid media** are those whose properties are soft, malleable, liquid, and easy to manipulate, such as watercolors, pastels, fingerpaints, etc. Across the spectrum are **resistive media** whose properties are defined as hard, nonmalleable, brittle, and difficult to manipulate, such as pencil, metal, wood, hard clay, etc. (Graves-Alcorn & Green, 2013; Lusebrink, 1990). The **low complexity/high complexity** classification refers to the number of steps required to work with the media. **Simple media tasks** (e.g., rubber stamping) will not require as much complex information processing as more complicated **multistep media tasks** (e.g., quilting), which necessitate cognitive planning and problem-solving. The **unstructured/structured** classification distinguishes between nondirected and directed media experiences. **Unstructured media experiences** (e.g., scribbling) are not associated with a specific outcome and allow for less preparation and instruction. **Structured media experiences** (e.g., printmaking) are designed to achieve a specific outcome and often involve additional tools and techniques, along with several stages of creating to achieve success (Hinz, 2020; Lusebrink, 1990).

Expressive therapies continuum

The **Expressive Therapies Continuum** (ETC) is a systems-based theoretical model that incorporates and expands upon historical perspectives of media interaction in art therapy (Hinz, 2020; Lusebrink & Hinz, 2020). Originally conceived by Kagin and Lusebrink (1978), the ETC bridges theoretical orientations and approaches to "...describe how qualities of the media or the experiences chosen, interact with each persons' preferred style of information processing and image formation to convey content or meaning" (Hinz, 2020, p. 25). For the trained art therapist, the ETC can serve as a practical and theoretical guide in conducting art therapy evaluations, tracking client progress, understanding neurological implications of art-making, and determining appropriate use of media and techniques (Graves-Alcorn & Kagin, 2017; Hinz, 2020).

The ETC is organized as a bottom-up developmental hierarchy (see Fig. 2.4) that explains how individuals perceive and process information as they move from simple to increasingly complex interactions with art media to create mental and artistic imagery (Hinz, 2020; Kagin & Lusebrink, 1978). The first three levels of the ETC each have two poles with one component on either end of a continuum of information processing. When both components are activated in an art-making experience, they work together to facilitate **optimal creative**

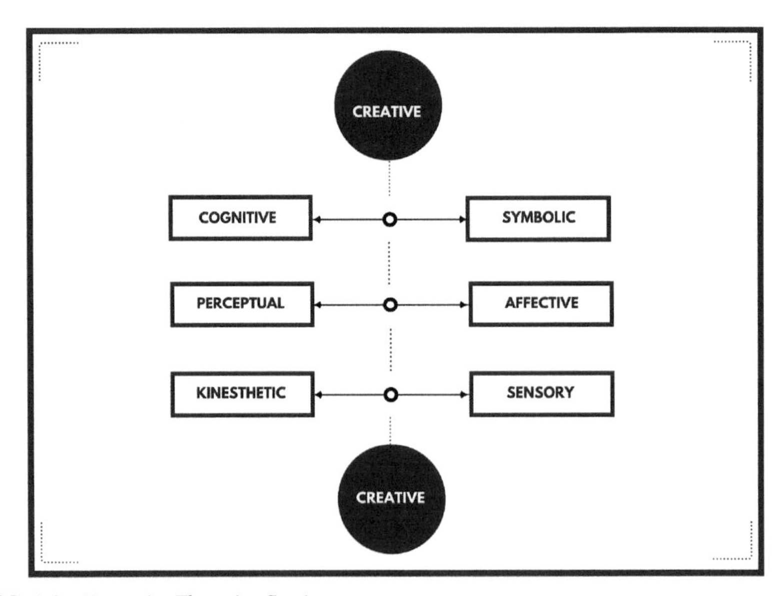

FIG. 2.4 *Expressive Therapies Continuum.*
Adapted from Haeyen, S., & Hinz, L. (2020). The first 15 min in art therapy: Painting a picture from the past. *The Arts in Psychotherapy, 71*(20). https://doi.org/10.1016/j.aip.2020.101718.
(No permission required.)

functioning. When information processing with one component is dominant, the opposing component recedes and is eventually deactivated. Lusebrink describes this type of relationship as **bipolar** (Hinz, 2020; Lusebrink, 1990).

The **Kinesthetic/Sensory** (K/S) level is an exploratory level where basic, preverbal information processing begins using tactile, rhythmic, and sensory experiences. The **kinesthetic** component refers to sensations and awareness of bodily movements, actions, and rhythm. Media experiences at this end of the K/S level focus on releasing energy through bodily movement. Art materials that tend to promote physical action and release include resistive materials such as hard clay or wood (Hinz, 2020; Kagin & Lusebrink, 1978). At the opposite end is the **sensory** component, which involves both internal and external sensations in response to media interaction and derives information from the five senses (sight, sound, smell, taste, and touch).

The **Perceptual/Affective** (P/A) level requires a more sophisticated degree of information processing to translate internal experiences into external visual images. The **perceptual** component focuses on representation of mental imagery with emphasis on the formal elements (as illustrated in Fig. 2.2) and structural qualities of the art materials. Media experiences on the perceptual end of the P/A level provide symbolic boundaries and limits to help contain the emotional release that often accompanies expression of personal perceptions (Hinz, 2020; Lusebrink, 1990). For example, providing smaller paper and limiting drawing materials may provide a sense of organization and containment. In contrast, the **affective** component, which refers to feeling, emotion, or mood, encourages affective release through interaction with art media. Art-making at this end often uses materials that are fluid, colorful, and quick to fill the page, such as chalk pastels or tempera paint, to enhance emotional expression without regard to structure and form (Hinz, 2020).

The **Cognitive/Symbolic** (C/Sy) level is where advanced information processing happens. The **cognitive** component involves complex thought processes. With an emphasis on facts and logical thinking, this component is reliant upon abstract thinking, planning, sequencing, and problem-solving. Media experiences at the cognitive end of the C/Sy level use structured materials, such as digital drawing tools and multistep activities like **collage**, to promote cognitive functioning and skill building. At the opposing end is the **symbolic** component, which involves intuitive thinking and symbolic expression of personal and universal meanings with potential to build self-knowledge. Media experiences might include themes such as self-discovery, duality, or acceptance. Symbols often include kinesthetic, sensory, and affective dimensions, which can aid in determining the media qualities that are best suited for supporting their creation and expression (Hinz, 2020; Kagin & Lusebrink, 1978; Lusebrink, 1990).

The **Creative** (CR) level, represented by the vertical axis running through the three horizontal levels, is indicative of creative functioning, which can occur at any level or be an integration of characteristics across the entire continuum. **Creativity** in this context is understood as "...an affective experience of closure and a sense of unity between the medium and the message" (Lusebrink, 1990, p. 95). The creative state is one of discovery, synthesis, wholeness, satisfaction, and ultimately self-actualization and growth (Hinz, 2020; Kagin & Lusebrink, 1978; Lusebrink, 1990).

Application of ETC-MDV

Applying an ETC-MDV perspective to understanding media selection and interaction means that we aim to identify and understand the ways in which media properties and processes shape individual experiences. Kagin and Lusebrink (1978) posited that fluid media, which flow quickly and easily, making them more difficult to control, promote spontaneous exploration and tend to produce an affective response. In contrast, resistive media, which may be easier to control and promote a more intentional approach, tend to produce a more cognitive response (Hinz, 2020). Media experiences that offer low complexity and low structure, allowing for free expression, are associated with affective or symbolic functioning while those that offer high complexity and structure evoke cognitive functioning (Hinz, 2020).

When applied within multiculturally competent practice, the ETC theory assumes individual responses to media interaction mimic preferred ways of processing information across environments, both in and outside of the therapy session (Haeyen & Hinz, 2020; Hinz, 2020). Application of the ETC and its MDV assists the therapist in designing media experiences that not only help to identify issues with patterns of information processing but also intentionally stimulate and direct the client's focus of attention, rerouting the flow of energy and information toward kinesthetic, emotional, and intellectual resources that can aid in improving mental states and overall resilience (Graves-Alcorn & Kagin, 2017).

Quality of materials

The word "material" literally means the substance of which something is made. It can also mean "significant," as in "you have made material contributions to this group project." Likewise, the materials we choose to use play a significant role in the success of a project. Commercial art materials are manufactured in a range from student- to professional-grade. Student-grade materials are made from less expensive components and have a lower concentration of pigments, while **professional-grade media** typically include higher quality vehicles and concentrated pigment levels. In general, facilitators should offer participants the highest quality of materials that budgets allow, while at the same time steering clear of materials that may seem too precious to use freely. For example, although paper is generally plentiful in industrialized cultures, we should keep in mind that paper may be a luxury to some people and should be respected as a valuable commodity. Ultimately, we want our participants to enjoy the process and succeed in forming the materials to their satisfaction, and it's sometimes challenging to accomplish this with low quality supplies. Art Therapist Shaun McNiff (1998) suggested avoiding low-quality supplies, as participants may wrongly attribute a displeasing result with their own perceived shortcomings rather than their use of low-quality materials, which can make good results difficult to achieve for anyone. Conversely, Art Psychotherapist Michelle Dean (2016) noted that using materials with more substance or a professional feel can produce pressure to create a piece that adheres to a perceived standard worthy of the materials (p. 57). Ultimately, the crux of this decision rests upon the specific needs of the participant population, the type of setting, and the goals of the program.

Supply packaging is also relevant, as art therapists are constantly considering ways to make art experiences inviting and inclusive. We should always be aware of commercial art materials that create initial impressions through their packaging, which can impact the participant's willingness to engage with them. For example, a paint tube labeled "flesh" colored will rarely match a participant's skin tone, as there is no one color of human skin. An identity affirming, empowering approach would be to show participants how to mix the skin tone they desire. Likewise, some art supply vendors may espouse corporate values that conflict with participants' views regarding environmental, economic, or social justice issues. Attention to details such as these can go a long way to help participants who identify as part of marginalized groups feel safe, accepted, and affirmed.

Variety of materials

Art materials inspire. Trying something new or reconnecting with something familiar are often motivating factors in media choice. Having a wide variety of culturally relevant materials on hand is another way to individualize the art-making process and promote self-expression and control. It is the task of the art therapist to provide a diverse array of materials, with a range of qualities, while also remaining mindful to not overwhelm the participant with too many choices at once.

Additional rationale for introducing a variety of materials includes the need to balance skill and familiarity with novelty and challenge. For example, when engaged in creative activity, there is the potential to hit a state of **flow**, a psychological state of optimal and effortless concentration and engagement in which time seems to float away (Csikszentmihalyi, 2013). Conditions that promote flow include clear goals, a balance between skill and challenge, and immediate feedback (Csikszentmihalyi, 2014). Therefore, when using art media to promote creativity and flow, the art therapist who is able to provide a variety of materials is better prepared to attend to the client's interests and ensure they are fully engaged in the creative process. It is especially important here to avoid materials that are too difficult for the client to master and may exacerbate anxiety and frustration, or too familiar and lack challenge, resulting in boredom—scenarios that impede therapeutic gain and prevent flow (Hinz, 2020; Snir & Regev, 2013). See Box 2.1 for more on the effects of flow.

Box 2.1 Did you know?

As Frances Kaplan (2000) described, "when art making partakes of the characteristics of 'flow,' it provides the kind of optimal experience that produces feelings of psychological growth and makes life in general more worth living" (p. 76). Recent findings from neuroscience research support this claim, showing changes in brain activity (Katahira et al., 2018) and increases in dopamine (Gold & Ciorciari, 2020) while in a state of flow.

Accessibility of materials

Art can happen anywhere: in bathtubs, kitchens, hallways, offices, classrooms, studios, and on city streets. Art therapy sessions have been held in prison blocks, chemotherapy stations, public parks, and have been supported in remote places using technology interfaces. However, some projects and processes require special equipment and space to be effective. As part of the project design process, facilitators must consider every aspect of the media process in terms of what space and equipment are needed in a particular session. In a restrictive setting, the absence of space and equipment will render some processes impractical and impossible. Ingenuity is needed to develop adaptations and substitutions, and creativity is needed to identify alternative processes that can achieve the same objectives. For example, while quarantining during the COVID-19 pandemic, the authors were tasked with helping students in their art therapy courses to navigate art-making experientials from home, using whatever materials they had on hand. An example of this included salt dough sculptures, made from ingredients found in our kitchens, to represent the quarantine experience. Making use of supplies that are readily available in one's home is another way of increasing accessibility and ownership of the entire process.

Media adapting

Adapting art materials to help individuals use them successfully is a skill that art therapists and facilitators cultivate throughout their training and professional life. Our goal is to always promote the maximum level of independence for each participant, which manifests differently for everyone. While some may need verbal cueing to guide them through an unfamiliar process, others may need an adaptive device such as a thick foam handle or strap to enable them to grip a paintbrush. Artists with impaired vision may need to have the edges of their paper taped or marked so they have a clear, tactile sense of where boundaries lie. And for participants who are uncomfortable with the sensation of messy printing inks, paints, or clay on their hands, facilitators can offer non-latex gloves (being careful to avoid latex allergies) to improve their experience. Art therapists also adapt the workspace to promote freedom of expression. Preparing the area with a tablecloth is another way to help participants feel free to experiment without the worry of messes. Organizing supplies and arranging them in easy to reach spots in the creative space makes them more accessible. Storing them in clear plastic bins with large print labels will make them easy to find in a pinch. Arranging them in a "chroma-logical" order can also help novice artists feel more grounded when opening a box of pastels. Using familiar materials is another way to keep them accessible and meaningful.

Media safety

A core value in art therapy practice is **nonmaleficence**, meaning "do no harm." Thus safety is always a central concern. Safety involves managing a physically safe studio environment, using physically safe art supplies and processes, and also tending to an emotionally safe creative space where participants can feel accepted and free to be themselves. To assess art media's chemical components, art therapists and facilitators pay attention to **toxicity** labels on supplies and generally work with materials carrying a nontoxic designation. Any supplies without the nontoxic label are kept in a locked cabinet with current **Materials Safety Data Sheets** (MSDS) and poison control information on hand. MSDS can be obtained from supply manufacturers, distributors, and online databases. Emergency contact information is kept readily available. In medical settings and under certain infection control conditions, such as those we endured under the COVID-19 pandemic, we follow Centers for Disease Control standard disinfecting procedures for art supplies. In some cases where disinfecting supplies is not enough, we can offer disposable supplies that the participant may keep or discard. In settings where patients may be at risk for accidentally or purposefully self-harming, art therapists are vigilant about the use of sharps (e.g., scissors, pens, needles, etc.) and potential inhalants, using safer alternatives or doing without.

Art materials breakdown

Drawing

History and definition

Drawing is the act of creating lines or textures across a surface. A drawing is a visual expression of boundaries and divided space. To draw is to symbolize, represent, or reconstruct one's environment, bringing intrinsic imaginings into extrinsic form (Dean, 2016). Drawing is a human activity so essential that we could fill volumes with examples, across cultures and throughout time. Among the earliest known human artworks, Paleolithic drawings and paintings have been preserved in caves around the globe. The earliest known drawing on archeological record, made around 73,000 years ago, was recently found in a South African cave. Distinguishing this ancient artifact from earlier Paleolithic markings is the fact that it is indeed a drawing—a cross-hatched design created with an ochre pigment crayon, and thus clearly intentional (Henshilwood et al., 2018). Drawing materials have remained fairly simple since the beginning. While drawing with a stick of charcoal, lead, and eventually graphite was eventually upgraded with a wooden casing to create the modern pencil, we use drawing implements in much the same way. Because of the simplicity of drawing, as well as its capacity to incorporate many details, drawing has been widely used as a way of understanding our inner experiences, most notably how we think. In Western medicine, drawings have been, and remain, a focus of study across mental health disciplines for their diagnostic and therapeutic potential.

Some of our first creative acts are drawn markings signifying, "I am here." These marks serve as affirmations that we have power and can be effective in life. The spontaneous drawing of childhood elicits pride, enhances communication with our caregivers, and promotes the development of problem-solving skills and spatial abilities. However, in Western societies, many of us stop drawing after adolescence, when it is presented as an option rather than a requirement in school (Lowenfeld & Brittain, 1987). In contrast, the power to choose is a luxury not afforded to many children across the world, who do not have access to even the most basic of drawing materials. Consequently, adult drawings often resemble the developmental stage at which the individual stopped actively drawing and often have a childlike quality (Lowenfeld & Brittain, 1987; Seiden, 2001). However, in the context of art therapy, drawings take on meaning far beyond aesthetics. Art Therapist Pat Allen (1995) defines drawing as "energy made visible" and asks the artist to shift their focus from knowing "how to draw" to "drawing-as-energy" (pp. 21–23). For example, drawing an object is an exercise in getting to know the essence of that object, rather than rendering a realistic portrayal. In adopting this new perspective, the concept of drawing expands and takes on new forms, including drawing as play, experimentation, connection, relationship, meditation, and a way to reflect and change energy states (Allen, 1995).

Drawing media

As the foundation and scaffolding by which many artistic endeavors are built and supported, drawing can take many forms. From pencil, to paint pens, to digital drawing, there are a multitude of drawing media and techniques to choose from. The following provides a brief overview of some of the most common drawing media used in the field of art therapy.

Oil pastels

Oil pastels consist of pigments bound together with oil and wax. They come in different quantities, qualities, and thicknesses. Many find that oil pastels offer a rather controlled way of drawing, allowing for maintaining boundaries and preventing messiness. However, drawing techniques such as smearing and smudging can enhance fluidity and bring out the sensual qualities of the medium, stimulating a sense of play and enabling emotional expression, release, and creativity (Snir & Regev, 2013).

Charcoal and chalk pastel

Charcoal and **chalk pastels** are both powdered pigments mixed with binding agents. They are available in a range of hard to soft, with soft having less binder and more pigment. Hard charcoal and chalk pastel can create fine details when used on the point, while softer forms are easier to blend and smudge. Both forms can be used to layer colors and when used on the side are handy for filling in or covering large areas. These properties make charcoal and chalk pastel materials some of the least resistive drawing materials. However, with their fluidity comes a lack of control, specifically in their tendency to break, crumble, and emit dust.

Markers

Markers are another familiar medium for children and adults alike. Relatively easy to control, markers can be especially useful for precision work or filling in drawings with color. Water-soluble markers are appropriate for use across a variety of settings, as they offer a multitude of bold colors and can be easily washed from the skin. Permanent markers are good for creating bold outlines and graphics. Calligraphy markers are great for hand lettering. Oil-based and acrylic paint markers work on a variety of surfaces like canvas, glass, or ceramics. Ranging from fine point to thick point, markers can be versatile in their application. However, their resistance to mixing, blending, or erasing pigment can also inhibit creativity and self-expression, resulting in feelings of frustration (Horovitz, 2018; Snir & Regev, 2013).

Pencil

The pencil often elicits memories of school, note taking, doodling, testing, and drafting. When using pencils for art-making, one should take care to avoid the typical "school pencil," when possible, and use artist pencils instead. Artist pencils are available on a spectrum from hard to soft. Harder pencils make a lighter, gray mark and may tug and scratch the paper while softer pencils produce darker, gray/black lines and release more graphite for blending and shading, as demonstrated in Fig. 2.5. Colored pencils provide the artist with an added element of expression. They come in a wide spectrum of hues and can also be layered. Pencils are commonly perceived as rigid, offering much control, but may limit affectual expression (Horovitz, 2018; Snir & Regev, 2013).

Grounds

Drawing in an arts setting is usually done on a **ground**—a support or surface, typically a piece of paper (Ocvirk et al., 2012). Just like the drawing materials themselves, grounds also influence **material interaction**. The size of the drawing surface can be used to increase or diminish structure, and therefore control.

FIG. 2.5 *Target.*
Graphite and charcoal drawing (9″ × 12″) by Chantaisa White.

For example, drawing within a circle to create a mandala on a typical 9″ × 12″ piece of paper may encourage a tighter, more controlled drawing response as compared to the same activity on a piece of posterboard. Similarly, it is important to note that not all drawing materials are appropriate for all grounds. For example, photocopier paper can easily rip if it gets too saturated by marker or is submitted to repeated pencil marks, whereas pastel paper will have some "tooth," or texture, to allow for layering, rubbing, and blending in pigment without tearing (Dean, 2016). In addition to testing out materials before application with participants, it is also important to check drawing papers and other surfaces you intend to use for adherence, saturation, breakdown, and archival qualities.

Practical considerations

Drawing is often associated with childhood and can therefore elicit a sense of familiarity or nostalgia. The ubiquitous nature of drawing materials makes them easier to access and apply across a diverse array of settings (Moon, 2010). When compared with other materials, such as clay or photography, drawing media do not typically require additional materials or tools, and are usually nontoxic, easy to store, transport, and clean up. Most drawing media are resistive, as the act of making marks is generally more intentional and contained, allowing the artist structure and control (Kagin & Lusebrink, 1978). Drawing materials can provide comfort in their predictability, as well as flexibility, allowing for layering, blending, scratching, reworking, and erasing. As such, drawing media can be particularly useful in limiting opportunities for regression and promoting successful outcomes in the context of art therapy.

Despite the advantages outlined above, there are also several influential factors that determine an individual's response to drawing media. For example, drawing calls for focus and cognitive problem-solving to overcome the challenge of translating cognitive and emotional content into visual imagery (Kozbelt, 2001). This may prove difficult with populations that are dealing with cognitive issues such as learning disorders or dementia. The physical act of drawing involves fine motor control, which can be difficult for individuals with physical limitations. For some, sensory issues may dictate material choice and for many, concerns about artistic ability will be reflected in their response. For example, individuals who approach a drawing task with associations to fine art may feel pressure to depict their subject matter in a realistic way. This in turn can influence the content of the drawing as focus shifts toward anxiety over having their artwork interpreted inaccurately (Rafaelli & Hartzell, 2016). This may be especially true when creating art in a group, where self-consciousness and comparison are heightened. See Chapter 10: Child Development and Artistic Development in Art Therapy on ways to adapt materials for children and adolescents, and Chapter 12: Art Therapy and Older Adults, for additional information on media considerations with older adults.

Recognizing the influential factors in material choice and then working to promote success by ensuring accessibility and adaptation can help individuals overcome many of the characteristic challenges of drawing. For example, beginning with a doodling icebreaker or visual prompt can provide a starting point and decrease performance anxiety. For children, offering thicker drawing materials that will not break as easily when grasped with the fist can help prevent anxiety about "ruining" the materials and affords more control. Another consideration is color variety. Because the mixing of pigments is not always possible with many drawing materials, color choices can be limited, prohibiting realistic portrayal of important elements like tone, hue, or dimension. Creating a comprehensive array of color choices can limit frustration and help the individual to feel seen.

Painting

History and definition

Paint is formed from pigments mixed with a binder such as linseed oil. The first paint pigments used by ancient humans were created from naturally occurring yellow, brown, and red iron oxides called ochre. Rocks served as grinding tools to turn the ochre into a powder. The powder was then mixed with binding agents, often in the form of animal fat or marrow. Animal bones served as the first mixing and painting tools, and natural vessels, such as shells, provided storage (Graf, 2018). While the purpose for which ancient humans created paint remains speculative, archeologists have found evidence of ochre used as body paint for sun protection, rituals, and decorative purposes; as a colorant for vessels and ornaments; in burial practices; and of course, to adorn the walls of ancient caves dating back to before 40,000 BCE (Graf, 2018; Hodgskiss & Wadley, 2017; Morriss-Kay, 2010; Stokstad & Cothren, 2011). Looking at the Egyptian, Chinese, Roman, and Mayan civilizations that followed, the pursuit to bring color into the world continued. Developing natural dyes, creating synthetic pigments, and finding the most effective binders to preserve the unique colors they created, these ancient paint-making processes serve as early examples of chemistry (Graf, 2018).

Painting is about perception. Painting can serve as a way to document or reproduce reality. With the use of perspective, depth, and other elements of design, the painter observes and reports back what is objectively true (Dean, 2016). Painting can also be a communicative act, conveying the artist's personal experience of the world. Painters observe their environment, embody an idea or concept, and transform their perceptions into symbolic creations (Gardner, 1994). Each painting we encounter, whether as artist or viewer, offers a chance for connection, reflection, and a change of perspective. Painted murals offer a great example of the multifaceted meanings that a painted surface can hold. The word *mural* derives from the Latin *muralis* meaning *wall* (Moss, 2010). The common, shared wall has been the grounds for mural making since prehistoric cave paintings and continues to serve our human need for community connection through documentation of important events, expression of social and political views, portrayal of cultural customs, paying tribute to important figures, and providing a space for mourning and remembrance. In current times, community murals have become an art form that intersects public art and street art, bringing together neighbors, community members, graffiti artists, and an idea with which to begin a visual dialogue (Moss, 2010).

As philosopher and Psychologist John Dewey (2005) explained, just as the physical materials that are used to create a painting change throughout the art-making process, so too do the artist's "…'inner' materials, images, observations, memories and emotions" (p. 77). Painting can be both a mindful and meditative practice of filling in color and building depth, and a sensory-stimulating exercise in blending, layering, texturizing, working, and reworking. The action of painting is one of rhythm and repetition. As McNiff (2014) explained, tapping into the movement of painting can release new understandings. From the first brushstroke, the marks we create hold meaning. Repeating the rhythm of these marks, not only through the stroke of the brush but also through full-body movement at the same time, quiets the mind and allows for personal transformation (McNiff, 1998).

Painting media

Most art and art therapy programs incorporate water-based paints such as acrylic, watercolor, or tempera. These provide a plethora of safe, nontoxic options that are easy to work with and clean up. Manufacturers regularly develop innovations in paints, making them available in different forms with unique applications.

Acrylics

Acrylic paint comes in tubes, jars, and sprays and can be found in many viscosities. Acrylics can also be mixed with water or acrylic mediums to thin or thicken to the desired consistency. This provides the versatility to create a range of painting effects, from watercolor-like transparency to textured, dimensional opaqueness, as seen in Fig. 2.6. Acrylic paint dries quickly to a water-resistant finish and can be easily painted over. Applying a finishing coat of varnish or gloss will seal the work while also creating the luster or sheen of an oil painting.

FIG. 2.6 *Tribal Dance.*
Acrylic and mixed media painting (32″ × 40″) by Scott Mars. Photo courtesy of Art Therapy Studio.

Tempera

Tempera paint, also known as gouache, is available in tubes, blocks, sticks, bottles, and powders. Tempera can provide opaque coverage but is usually thinner than acrylics and dries faster. Tempera paintings will dry to a matte, powdery finish, and colors will become more muted once dry. Tempera is a popular painting material in school settings, as well as art therapy workshops, because of its low cost, easy application, and quick-drying quality.

Watercolors

Watercolor paint comes in tubes, dry pans, bottles, and sprays. Watercolor pans make this type of paint compact and easier to work with. Known for their translucent and transparent effects, watercolors are also capable of opaque coverage, depending on quality and layering techniques. While this type of paint can produce unique and dynamic effects, frustration can stem from its fluidity and need to fully dry before layering. Reworking an image can easily turn into a muddy mess. Thus, this medium requires patience and is best approached with beginners as an experimental and spontaneous creative activity (Horovitz, 2018; Snir & Regev, 2013).

Painting grounds and tools

In terms of paint surfaces, almost any porous or nonporous surface can be painted. Canvas and papers are the obvious choices, but any kind of object or surface, such as cardboard, wood, books, rocks, clothing, or shoes, can be painted if the correct **primer** is applied to prepare the surface and the correct paint is used. Effective primers include acrylic paint or gesso. In contrast to acrylic or tempera, watercolor does not adhere as easily to surfaces and requires a porous surface, capable of holding water, such as paper with a textured quality, or "tooth." Paint can be applied using traditional tools like brushes, palette knives, or fingers and hands, but is also easily loaded onto a toothbrush, sponge, roller, or kitchen utensil to produce an array of interesting textures.

Regardless of the kind of paint or tools used, paint media have powerful transformative characteristics. For example, tempera paints introduce the power of color, which can greatly enhance expressive potential and emotional, or affective release (Hinz, 2020; Snir & Regev, 2013). Finger painting with materials like tempera can be a sensory stimulating and kinesthetic creative exercise and has been shown to elicit playful responses regarding physical contact with the material, decreased ability for precision, and the possibility of getting dirty or lacking control (Snir & Regev, 2013). However, paint can also trigger emotional regression, especially for those who typically exercise cognitive control to suppress affect (Hinz, 2020; Kramer, 2001). In these instances, the use of a brush or other painting tool can help mediate direct contact with the paint and create boundaries by decreasing paper size. Distance from the material may result in more reflective cognitive thought about the art-making process, while a smaller painting surface can provide a sense of safety through containment of emotional expression (Hinz, 2020).

Practical considerations

Painting can be messy. Its fluid and free nature may make it difficult to control. Paint colors bleed, run, and mix. Without knowledge of color theory, painters may be surprised when colors become muddy or do not match their desired hue. Additionally, the painted picture reveals how the material was applied. Lack of familiarity with brushes or other painting implements may hinder the creative process when the painter's tools produce unwanted textures or effects. Success is very much dependent on the facilitator's experience with paint products and processes and ability to recognize when painting may and may not be beneficial.

Painting can be a simple, unstructured activity when presented in a spontaneous or exploratory manner. However, mixing colors, creating texture, and establishing form add complexity. Using limited palettes, painting in layers, arranging simple compositions, and teaching technique, can all provide control and lead to increased confidence with the media.

Most commercial artist paints are available in nontoxic forms. When clients are interested in particular materials that don't always adhere to this standard, such as spray paints and sealers which can be dangerous to inhale, care is taken to provide protective equipment.

Clay

History and definition

Clay has provided the foundation for some of humankind's most ancient handicrafts. A naturally occurring material born from the Earth's crust, clay has been used for functional, aesthetic, and creative endeavors since prehistoric times. Clay consists of fine particles of decomposed rock and other organic minerals, primarily aluminum silicate. When hydrated, clay becomes a plastic modeling compound, meaning it can hold its shape when manipulated (Henley, 2002; Staubach, 2005). Clay's plasticity, combined with its abundance and durability, has made it a valuable material across time, culture, and civilization (Seiden, 2001; Staubach, 2005). Used to make vessels for cooking and storing food; to build dwellings and other structures; to create objects for ritual, celebration, and play; and applied within modern industries including computer and space sciences, biotechnology, and publishing; clay is rooted in our history, mythology, and connection to Earth's origins (Seiden, 2001; Staubach, 2005). In its versatility, clay provides almost endless opportunities for the creation of both form and meaning.

Working with clay has been described as an alchemy-like process, whereby manipulation of the clay body results in a transformation of the soul as well as the material. In contrast to other art media, the physical properties of clay change throughout the art-making process, moving from different states of plasticity and taking on new textures and forms through stages of construction, deconstruction, and reconstruction. These stages mirror the phases and cycles of life, while the clay creations that emerge serve as residual meaning and metaphor (Nan, 2021; Sholt & Gavron, 2006). As the clay moves from wet to dry, formless to distinct form, it gains strength along the way and is endowed with the chance to begin anew. Its final challenge is trial by fire, to test its strength in preserving its form through the transformation of clay to ceramic. This alchemy of matter runs parallel with the alchemy of the artist's soul as it confronts adversity, learns from pain and failures along the way, and becomes stronger and more resilient (Nan, 2021).

Clay media

Although clay is often associated with mud, dirt, and other natural wet materials, it exists in an array of physical states. Clay particles are suspended in water or oil, with very different results. Natural clays are composed of minerals, water, and other raw materials. The most common types are earthenware, stoneware, and porcelain. They come in a variety of colors including white, gray, brown, beige, and red. Natural clays can be watered down to a paste, dried out to a frail and chalky solid, or fired in a **kiln** to create a solid and permanent material (Seiden, 2001).

Synthetic clays are not made of clay materials but mimic its fluid and malleable qualities. Water-based, air-dry clay can be similar in consistency to mineral clay but is composed of plant-based materials and cannot be fired. It will harden upon losing moisture and can then be painted. Air-dry clay can be homemade, in the form of salt dough, or purchased from art supply vendors. Oil-based clays are natural clays that have been infused with oil and wax. They do not harden and remain in a plastic state. Plasticine is one of the most commonly used oil-based clays and comes in a number of bright and bold colors, as well as different levels of firmness. Polymer clay is an oven-bake clay with a plastic base that allows for soft and malleable modeling but can be hardened to a variety of finishes. Polymer clays come in flat, metallic, and pearlescent colors and can mimic glass, wood, stone, and ceramics. In addition to polymer clay, there are many types of soft modeling clays or doughs, offering a great deal of versatility for anyone who might not have the hand strength to manipulate firmer clay materials.

In plastic form, clay can be thrown, wedged, smoothed, pounded, paddled, divided, built up, added onto, joined, cut, carved into, stamped, scratched, rolled, torn, or hollowed out. Hand building techniques include pinching, creating slabs, casting, and sculpting (as seen in Fig. 2.7). Working with a potter's wheel can be used to create symmetrical works (Nan, 2021). Useful tools for working with and shaping clay include wire tools, scraper tools, pin tools, loop tools, popsicle sticks, paddles, sponges, canvas boards, sandpaper, and glazing brushes. Of equal importance to the creation of form is the process of decorating. Clay pieces that have been air-dried or bisque-fired, meaning fired once and now solid ceramic, can be painted or glazed. Acrylic paints provide a straightforward approach for air-dry clay creations that cannot be fired. **Glazes** are ceramic paints that when fired to the appropriate temperature will melt and fuse to the clay piece. Composed of milled silica, alumina, oxides, and various colorants and additives, glazes come in transparent or opaque colors and produce flat or glass finishes.

Clay can be used in a myriad of ways and evoke a wide range of responses. The unstructured, malleable, and three-dimensional qualities of clay present an opportunity for cognitive and symbolic thinking, as the artist is asked to create something out of nothing. Focusing on the form and structure of a clay piece requires perceptual awareness, which may effectively divert attention away from emotional distress and evoke a sense of calm (Henley, 1991; Hinz, 2020). When used for unstructured play and tactile exploration, clay can encourage a kinesthetic

FIG. 2.7 *Precious Madness Series.*
Earthenware sculptures (6″ × 19″ and 6″ × 12″) by Charisse Green.

release of energy and stimulate a somatosensory response (Czamanski-Cohen & Weihs, 2016; Elbrecht & Antcliff, 2014; Nan & Ho, 2017). This sensory component of clay work can enhance body awareness, promote mindfulness, and provide a positive affective experience (Nan, 2021). In contrast, the individual who struggles to wedge a cold, unyielding hunk of clay or create structural form from an overworked stick of plasticine that has become too soft may feel frustration, disgust, and even anger. Resistance or lack of boundaries may cause confusion and anxiety (Rubin, 2011; Seiden, 2001). Overall, the particular qualities of clay can stimulate both pleasurable/unpleasant and positive/negative responses. Therefore, the propensity of clay to promote regressive behaviors is a primary consideration in material choice and interaction across all participant populations. As the research clearly indicates (more on this in Box 2.2), clay work can offer abundant clinical benefits when implemented carefully.

Box 2.2 Did you know?

A comprehensive review of 35 clinical studies involving the use of clay work in the therapeutic process found six common therapeutic factors: facilitation of emotional expression, catharsis, rich and deep expression, and verbal communication; expression of unconscious materials; and concretization and symbolization (Sholt & Gavron, 2006). Using clay in art therapy has also been shown to help with emotional regulation, relieve depressive symptoms, improve daily functioning, improve general mental health (Nan & Ho, 2017), enhance overall well-being (Nan & Ho, 2017; Puig et al., 2006), and reduce negative mood states (Kimport & Robbins, 2012).

Practical considerations

Clay, in its many forms, can range from soft and fluid to work with, or stiff and restrictive. Methods can range from simply forming a shape out of a chunk of air-dry clay to more structured and complex handbuilding or wheelwork. The ideal conditions for working with most types of clay are small, short-term projects in which the facilitator can store each participant's work in an airtight wrapping in between work sessions to control moisture levels. Water-based clay can dry out and crack as the artist is working so it is important to keep the clay moist. However, adding too much water can weigh down the material and result in sagging. Plasticine clay leaves an oily residue behind and can easily melt in sun or high temperatures, both considerations for work and display surfaces.

Safety concerns are also part of clay work. For example, when working with natural clays, it is important to minimize clay dust, which can be harmful to the lungs over time. Surfaces should be cleaned with a wet sponge or mop, as dusting or sweeping can kick up clay dust. Facilitators must also be careful to check the labels of all clay products for the presence of toxic materials. Polymer clay can sometimes contain phthalate plasticizers, which have been shown to pose possible health risks (Roy, 2012). Finally, the types of clay tools used will vary according to the participant population and should involve consideration of individual needs, abilities, and safety.

Printmaking

History and definition

Among the earliest known human artworks are handprints found on Paleolithic cave walls and rock faces across the globe. Stamp seals, made from carved stone incised with designs, were used to impress signatures and marks of ownership. These first stamping tools have been discovered in ancient Near-Eastern excavations sites dating back to the end of the 4th millennium BCE (Glenn, 2021). Woodblock printing of text and images began in China around 600 CE before spreading to Korea and Japan to inspire other printmaking traditions that supported the growth of religion, literacy, and commerce (https://education.asianart.org/resources/the-invention-of-woodblock-printing-in-the-tang-and-song-dynasties/). Mechanizing this process in 1450, the Gutenberg press revolutionized intellectual progress in Germany and throughout Europe as it provided an efficient way to disseminate religious, political, economic, and scientific information. Still known in modern times as the peoples' medium, printmaking enables the proliferation of the printed image and word to the masses (https://www.highpointprintmaking.org/about/about-printmaking). And just as in ancient times, printmaking is still used to express universal human experiences, indicate ownership, and convey cultural symbols, such as the West-African adinkras (White, 2002).

Printmaking is an art form that involves printing an image, usually multiple times, from a prepared block or plate. White (2002) wrote about the essential components of printmaking harnessed by art therapists. These include the engaging element of surprise and the reworking of images that don't come out as originally intended. The repetitive physical production of multiple images, the multisensory stimulation, the delayed gratification, the multistep process, the control and containment, and the intrinsic messiness all provide therapeutic entry points to facilitate growth and healing. Additionally, when designing artwork with the intention of making multiples (prints), the inherent idea is that one's message is worth spreading and that one's voice will connect with many others (Dean, 2016). With so many steps involved, the process can be a focal point in which we learn that experimentation helps us grow and that we can rework images that don't come out as initially intended. The process involves "making an impression," which we aspire to do upon ourselves and others. Other symbolic themes that can be explored in printmaking include reversed images, positive and negative space, the multistep ritualistic process, attending to mysteries, and surrendering control (Dean, 2016).

Printmaking media

Printmaking is a multistep process which can include preparing the plate, inking the surface, pressing the paper upon the inked plate, and then lifting off to reveal the image that has been transferred onto the paper. The resulting prints can appear in a range of effects including detailed line drawings (such as those seen in Fig. 2.8), juicy paintings, and bold graphics. Methods for creating images upon these blocks involve various carving, incising, gluing, painting/inking, rubbing, and stenciling processes. Each of these methods incorporates the perception of negative and positive space, which is usually a novel concept for participants.

Printmaking requires studio space, allowing for the use of special tools and equipment, a messy process, a water source, and storage space for multiple prints to dry. While these needs can be minimized with adaptations, some table space and cleaning cloths are always a minimum requirement. The preparation of blocks or plates can involve special carving or cutting tools and glues. Nontoxic, water-based inks are essential for safety and easy clean up. Some relief printing can involve the use of everyday items, such as fruits; vegetables; leaves; and the artist's fingers, hands, and feet. Once the block is prepared, ink is spread onto a flat palette and rolled onto the block. For an extensive list of media and process ideas, refer to White's (2002) book *Printmaking as Therapy: Frameworks for Freedom.*

Printmaking engages the artist through the sounds of ink being worked on the palette and the tactile satisfaction derived from rubbing or transferring prints by hand. Whether making a simple, stamped print from a carving or working with the mechanics of a printing press, the printmaking process involves kinesthetic movement throughout as the artist prepares the materials, blends and spreads the ink, moves the paper, pulls a print, and then starts all over again. A different sense of stimulation is derived from the perceptual and cognitive challenge of creating and carving images in the reverse into what are often hard, resistive materials.

FIG. 2.8 *Grief.*
Intaglio series (11″ × 14″) by Mariah Yoder.

Practical considerations

Printmaking processes range from highly fluid to firmly restrictive, so art therapists choose elements that best meet the needs of their participants. Physical properties can be loose, as when smearing thick paint onto a monoprint palette, or tight, as when we refine a linoleum block with a carving tool to achieve precise image edges. Printmaking processes are generally complex, executed in multiple steps that can require planning and yield a significant distance between idea and product. Art therapists capitalize on this reflective distance as a way to help clients work through difficult personal matters they are addressing in their work. Visual perception can be challenged in this process, as printmaking always results in a reversed image. Without the support of an experienced printmaker, this can present frustrations for the novice.

Due to the kinesthetically engaging elements of the process, some participants may need physical assistance to accomplish their visions. The main safety concern in printmaking involves the use of sharp carving tools and scissors. Commercially available soft linoleum is recommended, as it requires minimal applied pressure to cut, which relieves some safety concerns. Nontoxic water-based inks are alternatives to oil-based ink. Common household items can be incorporated into printmaking processes, rendering them within reach both physically and economically. For example, colographs use basic white glue, corrugated cardboard, masking tape, and other textured items. The process itself generates innovation in the way we use materials, think and produce prints, challenging the participant to develop novel ways of approaching their problems. This "peoples' art form" is an effective way to liberate the imagination, harness emotions, and invigorate creative thinking.

Fiber

History and definition

Fibers have long been used in rituals and rites to infuse ceremonies with special meaning, celebrate cultural traditions, record history, tell stories, and inspire social and political change (Schoeser, 2003). The earliest known needles, dating from 26,000 to 20,000 BCE, enabled early humans to join animal skins to create clothing and to embellish them with pebbles, shells, seeds, and teeth (Schoeser, 2003). In southwestern Native American tribal creation stories, Spider Woman weaves the universe into existence (Leeming, 1992). In the Christian Bible, a woman named Dorcas is an apostle who spent her life using her sewing skills to help indigent women and children (King James Bible, 2021) (Acts 9: 36–42). In the southern United States, quilts were used to guide escaping slaves to freedom along the Underground Railroad (Tobin & Dobard, 1999). In Chile, throughout the brutal dictatorship of the 1970s and 1980s, women used cloth patchwork pictures called Arpilleras to smuggle news out of the country, eventually leading to the downfall of the Pinochet regime (Agosin, 2008). Started in San Francisco in the late 1980s, the *Names Project* collects handmade quilt panels, made by loved ones of those lost to the AIDS virus. Each panel is added onto what is known as the *AIDS Quilt*, bringing awareness to the need for medical research, impacting government policy, and providing an outlet for expression of grief and loss (Kausch & Amer, 2007). In contemporary Western cultures and art schools, fiber arts have generally been relegated to the status of craft, a result of longstanding social biases (Leone, 2021). Yet there is so much power in fiber that these traditional crafts can rightfully be incorporated into a variety of programs. An example of research findings on the benefits of fiber art can be found in Box 2.3.

Box 2.3 Did you know?

Fiber handcrafts have been studied for their wellness benefits. One international study of 831 nonprofessional fiber crafters found that the primary reasons for engaging in these crafts were to cope with stress, to create something beautiful, to express themselves, and to ground the crafter in manual, rhythmic sensory engagement with the materials (Collier, 2011). An example of the rewarding process of fiber art can be seen here, in a crochet piece that took 50 hours to complete (Fig. 2.9).

FIG. 2.9 *Blanket Mandala: Self-Expression Woven Through the Fibers.* Worsted weight acrylic yarn crochet blanket (4 ft. diameter) by Megan Fortney.

When fiber art is made of old clothing it can be ideal for processing issues of identity, development, or grief. Functional objects such as blankets and scarves that physically warm and comfort the user carry metamessages. In dye work, being immersed in something or steeped in hot water can hold meaning as we look at how challenging experiences can transform us. Art Therapist Savneet Talwar notes that in embroidery (and quilting), the process of forming the image or message involves "stabbing the fabric" multiple times with a sharp implement, which can be satisfying when working through frustrations or anger (personal communication, February 24, 2017). For example, Fig. 2.10 shows the subversive power of needlework to express vulnerability and empowerment simultaneously in addressing matters of social justice. Collier (2011) describes many process metaphors involved in fiber work, such as the challenge of piecing one's life back together, just as we experience the challenges of piecing together a quilt, being tied up in knots, as in macramé or crochet, or "weaving a yarn," as in telling a story.

FIG. 2.10 *Break the Silence Stop the Violence.*
Embroidered mini-quilt (6″ × 7″) by Catherine Casey.

Fiber art includes works made of natural and synthetic fibers, often stitched, knit, woven, or knotted. Fiber is a ubiquitous part of human life, from the moment we are born and wrapped in a blanket, until the time of death, when we might be buried in clothing or wrapped in cloth. For this reason, most everyone can relate to fiber and use fiber to tell stories about their lives. Almost every culture on Earth has some kind of fiber-art tradition, using fibers native to its place of origin. Fiber-art products can be useful as well as aesthetically compelling. Quilts can tell stories and hold memories of loved ones and ancestors through symbolic image narratives or through incorporation of personal and familial fabrics. Soft fiber sculptures can take the form of vessels, convey imagery, or be functional, such as toys or dolls, which can personify any character, idea, or archetype. Wearable fiber art can be traditional or ceremonial, as a full garment or small piece of jewelry, mask, hat, or other adornments. Fiber art can even take the form of a larger installation or environmental piece.

Fiber media

Common fiber arts include dye work, sewing, quilting, embroidery, soft sculpture, weaving, felting, knitting, and crochet. Fibers come in a huge variety of materials and textures, such as plush velvet, cozy fleece, soft flannel, sturdy denim, sleek satin, delicate lace, rough burlap, etc.—the list goes on! Fiber stimulates the senses through the color and patterns we see, the textures we touch, the scents it might hold, and even the sound it creates when handled. This sensory stimulation can then evoke memory, emotion, and meaning, paving the way for a rich creative experience. Fibers can be drawn upon, painted, and embellished with beads and other meaningful objects of all kinds. They can be glued, stitched, melded together, ripped, cut, or singed. The physical activity involved in fiber arts can range from large gross motor gestures, such as ripping fabric or working a large wooden loom, to smaller arm movements like ironing fabric, to fine motor movements involved in crochet or knitting.

Practical considerations

Except for surface treatments like paints and dyes, fiber work is generally a resistive media. Fiber-art processes range in complexity from a simple immersion tie dye to a layered quilt that can take years to complete. While most processes require many steps, they can be broken down and simplified. Dye work, machine sewing, and large-weaving-loom work require equipment and studio space, but most other processes, such as embroidery and crochet, can be done almost anywhere there is good light. Work with fabric can require extra storage space, as fabrics can be bulky.

For some fiber-art processes, such as sewing, embroidery, and weaving, the use of a blunt needle is a safety adaptation. Some people are allergic to animal-based fibers, such as wool, or are vegan and do not use animal products altogether. Therefore, appropriate substitutions must be available. Used or upcycled fabrics can contain dust, mold, or animal hair and should be washed to remove them before use. Many fiber-art processes can be time intensive and thus must be extended over multiple sessions.

Mixed-media sculpture

History and definition

Sculpture involves working raw or found materials into three-dimensional art. Reviewing sculptural art of the past is a study in the history of human ingenuity. The oldest known representational sculptures were carved out of mammoth ivory and volcanic rock. Early humans of the upper Paleolithic period carved stone into recognizable images (Morriss-Kay, 2010). Many of the earliest known sculptures were female figurines and **petroglyphs**, relief sculptures with flat images carved into the sides of cave walls. Embellished sculptural objects are believed to have served utilitarian religious and aesthetic purposes (Puccio, 2017). Archeologists date beads, sculpted for human ornamentation, to the middle-Paleolithic era, roughly 82,000 years ago (Bar-Yosef Maeyer & Bosch, 2019). Examples have been found across the globe. The earliest surviving beads were made of natural objects such as shells, stones, eggshells, and bones. They adorned clothing, ceremonial objects, and tools, and were valued commodities in trade. Such adornments represented individual and group identities, showed social status, and told stories conveying cultural values. As technologies advanced, artisans incorporated new materials such as metals, paper, and glass into sculpture, which continue to be widely used. Sculpture continues to play an integral part in spiritual and religious expression across cultures (e.g., prayer beads, gravestones, statues, altars, etc.), helping elevate the mundane into the sacred, and enabling worshipers to participate actively in prayer and ceremony.

Sculpture has a physical presence that other art forms do not. It exists in space, just as we do, and can be worked and interacted with from multiple sides. As in clay work, negative space in sculpture enables the formation of vessels, boxes, and other containers. **Kinetic sculpture**, or sculpture that moves on its own, can be suspended in the air as a mobile or mounted on a base.

The symbolic potential of sculpture is as varied as the materials themselves. Locally sourced materials can represent home and environment. Wood, and other organic materials that were once alive, can have symbolic associations with elements of the natural world. Metal shines and is reflective, holding the potential to represent these qualities. Metal can also be associated with weapons, money, religious objects, or even factory work. Glass is transparent, fragile, and carries light; it can be reflective and hold an ethereal quality. Found objects tell the story of searching and discovering along one's path (Wong, 2021). Using recycled materials in sculpture holds value as an environmentally conscious decision. **Upcycling** often begins with materials chosen specifically because of associations with their former uses or owners. In essence, both recycling and upcycling transform the original meaning of an object and give it an entirely new purpose.

Sculpture media

Considering the nature of sculpture, materials that can be incorporated into the work seem limitless. Wood, metal, glass, wax, plaster, paper, plastics, fabric, yarn, and all sorts of natural and fabricated found objects can be formed into meaningful sculpture (see Fig. 2.11). Objects such as plastic packaging that once served a commercial function can be subversively transformed to serve the creative needs of the artist. Upcycling involves transforming an object, often old and outdated, into something new and useful. Materials can be shaped and combined through modeling, carving, burning, bending, welding, nailing, tying, cutting, stitching, gluing, and other methods. Upcycled items may need some deconstruction initially, which can involve an emotional catharsis and release that can be a meaningful first step before a new image is formed.

Practical considerations

Sculptural work is resistive, with clearly delineated boundaries that hold their shape. For example, vessels, containers, and boxes can clearly represent figures and forms in relationship to each other. Since the materials are resistive by nature, they predictably go where they are put, sometimes requiring special tools and adhesives. Working with these materials is usually a structured experience,

FIG. 2.11 *Blood Roses: The Eternal Internal.*
Mixed media sculpture (approximately 10×12×8 in.) by Mo Mzik.

involving planning and problem-solving to assess the complexity of the project and what special tools, adhesives, and steps are needed.

Depending on the materials, creating sculptural artwork might involve using dangerous machinery and tools (e.g., chisels, saws, soldering tools, heat guns, toxic adhesives, etc.). However, there are safer methods and alternatives (Stallings & Clark, 2021). Using recycled and upcycled materials is resourceful and the raw materials cost nothing. Gathering them together takes time and can be a way of engaging participants outside the session.

Many household materials can be used to make sculpture accessible. Aluminum foil, duct tape, paper mâché made of newspaper strips, coat hangers, nylon stockings and socks, old clothing, paper towel tubes, straws, and food items can be formed into imagery. Even a simple sheet of paper can be cut, folded, and glued to represent a house, a person, an animal.

Paper craft and collage

History and definition

The first paper was papyrus, made from the flattened reeds of the plant of that name in ancient Egypt around 2900 BCE (Capua, 2015). Paper in the form widely used today, created from plant pulp which is reconstituted on a screen and then pressed flat, was invented in China in 105 CE (Bloom, 2017). As papermaking spread slowly across Asia and Europe, paper replaced silk, papyrus, and parchment (Bloom, 2017) and became the primary material used to record information in words and images. Cultural groups around the world developed unique paper crafts using methods of cutting, coiling, folding, forming, and gluing with locally sourced materials. Scrapbooks trace back to the Renaissance when people collected personally meaningful quotes and memorabilia and chronicled their life stories in "commonplace" books (Helfand, 2008). Collage, a method of adhering paper and/or other media onto a surface to create an assemblage, was made popular by European artists Charles Braque and Pablo Picasso in 1912, who used the term to describe their playful incorporation of wallpaper, newspaper, and other found papers in their paintings and drawings, challenging the viewer to discern the real from the rendered (Gardner et al., 1991). The longstanding accessibility, cultural relevance, and expressive potential of working with paper media are supported by a growing body of research, like the studies described in Box 2.4.

Box 2.4 Did you know?

Studies have shown scrapbook programs to be beneficial in processing and healing grief among children and adults (Kohut, 2011; Williams & Lent, 2008), treating trauma among children and adolescents (Karns, 2002; Lowenstein, 1995), improving coping among hospitalized school-aged children (Romero, 1986), and enhancing coping for groups of parents of pediatric oncology patients (McCarthy & Sebaugh, 2011).

Thin and delicate, easy to crumple and tear, paper can represent impermanence. Paper can be translucent like a veil, allowing yet obscuring the view of what's behind it. The materials from which paper is made, as well as the colors or patterns it holds, carry symbolic elements. Working with paper often involves both destructive and constructive processes, as it is cut or ripped from its original form and then manipulated, rearranged, and applied into a new design. Metaphor can be found in the breaking down of original form and then putting the pieces back together in a way that makes sense, incorporating new meaning that the artist controls. Collaging sometimes involves resurrecting or redefining paper and other materials once discarded or forgotten, which may resonate personally and can parallel healing processes (Moon, 2010). Layering, overlapping, and experimenting with placements before securing items with glue can be similarly meaningful. As in life, it's wise to explore one's options before committing to a decision.

Paper media

Paper craft

A diverse array of paper arts and crafts have been developed throughout history and across cultures. Paper-surface-design methods are plentiful, including aspects of painting, printmaking, marbling, and collage. Paper-folding, such as origami, can create sculptural art without the need for scissors or glue. Paper puppets can be constructed with moving parts. Paper-cutting traditions range from the simple fold-and-cut paper snowflake to Mexican folk art (papel picado), Polish paper cutting (Wycinanki), or German **paper cutting** (Scherenschnitte), which each involve intricate designs cut into paper with scissors or a blade. Paper pulp can be sculpted with molds or combined with glue to form paper mâché. Paper **quilling**, also called filigree, is a process of coiling and shaping thin strips of colored papers and adhering them to a flat surface, forming a three-dimensional design. Book media can offer a range of simple to complex processes that may incorporate booklet construction methods, folding, stitching together bundles of pages, printmaking, scrapbooking, collage, and journaling. Books can be made in a variety of sizes, shapes, and formats. Altered books involve upcycling old books that have existing text and imagery, providing a potentially meaningful starting point and interesting design elements to explore.

Certain paper crafts are most successful when specialty and craft papers are used. For example, cardstock ensures that paper-cutting artwork will withstand lots of physical handling and will not tear along the way. The thinner quality of origami and quilling papers makes them better able to be creased and coiled. When designing three-dimensional sculptures or forms, the paper used will depend on its strength and flexibility.

Collage

Paper collage takes many forms, each of which involves the basic steps of selecting interesting materials, cutting or tearing shapes, assembling them on a surface to form an image, and gluing them in place. **Decoupage** involves decorating an object (e.g., table, frame, box, jar, etc.) by gluing down and then covering flat, thin papers with a protective sealant to preserve the collage underneath. **Photomontages**, or collages incorporating meaningful photographs, can provide a powerful way of incorporating visual memories into artwork. In **mixed-media collage**, any kind of paper or meaningful object can be collected and arranged on a flat surface. In paper collage painting, colored paper is glued down to form original imagery. Paper mosaics can be created with different paper shapes, fitted together to form a pattern.

There are a plethora of interesting papers to be collaged, and not just those available from art and craft stores. These include magazine images and words, newsprint, old calendar images, tissue paper, personal photographs, maps, stamps, pages from old books, junk mail, written quotes or poems, wrapping paper, stickers, memorabilia (e.g., concert tickets, birthday cards, business cards, etc.), even old or abandoned art pieces. **Mixed-media found objects** are often natural embellishments for paper collages and include anything that can be glued down (e.g., fabric, yarn, beads, coins, buttons, pressed flowers, leaves, feathers, jewelry, etc.), as seen in Fig. 2.12. The sensory and expressive potential of this versatile medium makes it a common process in many programs.

FIG. 2.12 *Unknown Rune: African Ancestry.*
Mixed media collage (18″ × 24″) by Angela Hulett.

Each of these materials, along with the different processes used in working with them, holds potential for rich creative experiences and layers of meaning. Paper can be assembled into a wide variety of forms that carry on traditional cultural themes and artistic practices, serves as visual storytelling, preserve memories and mementos, and provide an outlet for symbolic expression. Collage art is rich with the metaphor of materials used, as well as the processes involved. Hunting, gathering, assessing, deciding, and then placing are all cognitive exercises in creativity of expression. Books can provide comfort, as they hold many secrets inside. The three basic sections of a book—the covers, the contents, and the connecting spine—offer a structured "container" that can help organize complex ideas and feelings that might have been previously inaccessible.

Practical considerations

There are many ways to adhere items in paper craft and collage work, well beyond the use of glue. Anything with a binder in it, including acrylic paint and some homemade mixtures of common kitchen ingredients, can function as glue. Liquid glues, solid pastes, and glue sticks each offer different benefits for adhering special items. Tapes can be transparent, reflective, textured, patterned, or otherwise decorative. Metal items such as brads, grommets, fasteners, clips, wire, and staples can offer their unique symbolic potential as attachment hardware. Decorative effects can be achieved by stitching papers together with yarn, string, or threads.

Paper-surface-design techniques such as marbling and various dye methods can have fluid qualities. Paper craft and books are resistive processes and present a good deal of structure and complex steps. Testing out media and methods and designing prototypes are key practices in working with this type of media, as there is much room for mistakes. Care should be taken to simplify steps as needed. Paper collage is an accessible starting place for people with limited art-making experience (Dean, 2016; Henley, 1992; Landgarten, 1993; Levy et al., 1974). The structure and control of the media makes for an activity many individuals will be able to do with minimal assistance.

Paper cutting and assembling methods often involve precision scissors, craft knives, awls, and needles. This can be problematic for individuals who may have difficulty with coordination and control or lack a tight **pincer grasp** to pick up and hold the papers or tools. Adaptive scissors in various designs are available to enable many participants who have difficulty cutting, while hand-over-hand assistance can help mitigate the risk of using sharps. In work with individuals who may have a history of self-harm or harm to others, tearing is a safer alternative to cutting. While most adhesives used in art therapy settings are nontoxic, hot glue guns, spray adhesives, and commercial cements/glues require careful oversight, as they can harm skin and/or be dangerous to inhale.

Although paper is generally plentiful in industrialized cultures, we should keep in mind that paper may be a luxury to some people and should be respected as a valuable commodity. Public libraries frequently sell in bulk or give away large quantities of picture books, magazines, and books with interesting texts. Old books can be used as grounds for collages and altered books. To ensure longevity, permanent, archival-quality glues and papers are ideal. Art therapists often present precut images to participants for collage work in order to promote focus, ease of access, and reduce distractions. Try organizing them by color or theme in an accordion file, and soon you will have many options at your fingertips.

Technology-based media: Photography and digital art

History and definitions

Since its invention in the 1830s, photography has shaped the way we receive and perceive history. Once confined to the realm of professional work, requiring specialized equipment, photography is now accessible to anyone with a cell phone. Photography has played an important role in documenting reality and sharing information; promoting social change; and preserving communal, familial, and individual experiences, while paving the way for other expressive art forms like film and digital art.

The word **photography** means "drawing with light," derived from the Greek photo, meaning light, and graph, meaning to draw (Gardner et al., 1991). In photography, an optical image is recorded on a light-sensitive surface or digital interface. Photography methods and techniques rely primarily on the subject matter, composition, and tone to create and convey the photographer's overall message. Photographs can be carefully composed, just as a painter composes an artwork, and can range from simple snapshots of what immediately appeals to the senses, to framing a shot that captures a feeling or moment in time. In the therapeutic context, photographic media permit examination of the experiences we have preserved as 'fact,' highlighting the range of realities we may project onto photographs (Weiser, 2015).

Digital innovations affect countless aspects of our lives, including the way we create and experience the arts. **Digital arts** involve any creative product that is generated using a computer-based device and software program. The first digital images were created by computer engineers and mathematicians in the 1960s (Victoria and Albert Museum, 2016). Emerging digital technologies were expensive and not widely embraced by art therapists of the time, who were still striving to articulate the role of traditional drawing, painting, and sculpture media in their practices (Orr, 2016). By the 1970s, photography and video were used in some art therapy programs, and by the mid-1980s, as digital cameras and home computers became more widely available, art therapists began documenting their clinical application of digital tools and media (Malchiodi, 2000; Orr,

2016). Distinct practices of phototherapy and therapeutic photography emerged as specialized disciplines. Throughout the late 20th and early 21st centuries, practitioners in multiple human services professions sought to develop methods for using assistive technology, including those that create digital imagery, to improve communication and creative engagement for people with physical and cognitive challenges. At the same time, multimedia artists incorporated available technology, including video and audio, to understand contemporary problems and seek innovative solutions.

The use of digital media in art therapy greatly expanded in 2020, as many practitioners were forced to practice telehealth during the COVID-19 pandemic. Art therapists capitalized on free software applications that clients could access via their smartphones, tablets, or computers. While telehealth technologies improved creative engagement for many isolated participants, too often low-income people lacked accessibility as libraries and other public resources providing the essential elements of electricity, internet connections, and hardware, closed their doors. The pandemic made the digital divide more apparent and spurred new efforts to eradicate barriers to using these powerful tools for artistic expression, communication, and therapeutic intervention.

Technology-based media

Photography media include personal photographs, family photographs, self-portraits, and photographic material in the form of images taken from magazines, newspapers, internet sources, postcards, calendars, and more. Using photographs in the art-making process can evoke a sense of familiarity with the glossy shine and sturdy paper at our fingertips, or we may find comfort in the controlled environment of digital editing. Shooting photographs engages not only our visual perception, but can engage the whole body kinesthetically, as we move through landscapes, set up shots, or model. As the individual exercises their cognitive problem-solving skills to turn complex materials into artistic expression, the art materials are transformed into symbolic representations of memories and meaning. Art Therapist and Psychologist Weiser (2015) cites several important functions of photographic media, including connecting with the moment; sensory stimulation; considering alternative realities; bridging unconscious content; bypassing filters and defenses typically used in verbal expression; and assisting in the therapeutic tasks of remembering, exploring, confronting, and imagining.

In digital art, we also find meaning inherent in whichever other art media is represented, such as painting, found-object sculpture, or collage. However, the interface of artist and material is unique in digital artwork, as a growing variety of electronic tools are used to interact with and manipulate the bytes that are the building blocks of digital art (Orr, 2010). These **digital mediators** include keypads, hand controllers, voice recognition apps, eye-tracking devices, headsets, head-mounted displays, cameras capturing stills and video, screen displays, and more. Other hardware, such as scanners and printers, are useful in manipulating images both on and off the screen. Software suites and apps provide the palette with which to work, as well as a myriad of inspiring and innovative capabilities.

The sensory impact of digital art is unique, providing a clean and sometimes portable interface. While our tactile senses feel tools that are made of plastic, metal, and glass, our visual and auditory senses are fully engaged in limitless possibilities that mimic the widest range of visual and audio effects. Nowadays, art therapists can use immersive environments, artistic animations, and even virtual reality to fully immerse and engage participants in kinesthetic, gestural art, sometimes enhanced with olfactory sensations and visual effects that appear to defy the laws of gravity (Carlton, 2017; Hacmun et al., 2018; Kaimal et al., 2020). While digital effects allow for a dynamic sensory experience, the power in this media also lies in its workability. The undo and redo buttons enable experimentation, while the boundary of the screen serves to contain emotions. Images can be built with the instantaneous click of a mouse, using templates, effects, and layers, or printed and enhanced using traditional art media.

Practical considerations

In general, the mechanical properties of cameras and computers, and fixed image of a photograph or digital design make these materials more resistive than fluid in nature. While many digital interfaces are user-friendly, photographic and digital media can also offer complex experiences. Processes can range from highly structured multistep techniques involving special equipment to less structured: point, shoot, print, and title.

A central consideration for working with digital media and photographs is preservation. Taking care to electronically save, print, and pass on digital artwork to its creator honors the art-making process and makes it possible to revisit images in future work. Storing, scanning, and photocopying are especially important first steps when using original photographs. These preservation processes honor their importance as historical records and allow the artist to focus on artistically altering the image as a process of transformation of meaning, rather than a destruction of memory.

While sharing photographic images is a common, and therefore relatively comfortable, activity in modern society, there remains a certain unease in being photographed. Art-making activities involving photography must respect personal boundaries and obtain consent from all involved in the process. Additional ethical concerns to consider with photographic and digital media include issues of confidentiality, secure storage, permanence, technology failures, equal accessibility, fluidity of meaning, rapid evolution of new technologies, lack of practitioner training, and depersonalization (Orr, 2016). These concerns are addressed in the Art Therapy Credentials Board code of ethics (https://www.atcb.org/ethics/). However, as described in Box 2.5, a growing amount of research shows that when these problems are overcome, many participants can benefit from this exciting contemporary medium.

Box 2.5 Did you know?

In settings that can afford some basic tools and successfully navigate the inherent ethical challenges, digital art plays a unique role in improving accessibility to art expression for several populations. For individuals with limited motor abilities, digital art can be a game changer in increasing accessibility and general ease of use (Carlton, 2017; Weinberg, 1985). For patients in healthcare settings where infection control is paramount, tablets and similar devices provide portable, sterilizable, and mess-free expressive tools. The smooth tactile interface with technology devices provides an accessible option for individuals such as some on the autism spectrum who have adverse reactions to messier tactile media like chalk, paint, and clay (Darewych et al., 2015). Artificial intelligence technology and digital art tools can also enhance creative engagement for people with dementia (Mihailidis et al., 2010). Digital art is essential in art therapy work with young people and for all forthcoming generations of "digital natives" (Carlton, 2014; Zeevil, 2021).

Conclusions

Art therapists and art facilitators are adept at harnessing the inherent, essential, beneficial elements of art media and art-making processes. Art therapists' training deepens their understanding of the use of art media to address psychosocial issues, beyond that of art facilitators who focus primarily on art educative processes. However, both art therapists and art facilitators utilize the same essential elements of materials, setting, process, culture, and storytelling to design and implement beneficial art experiences. Each of these elements should be attended to within every studio session to promote the participants' success. Just as artists are constantly changing and expanding the definition of what constitutes "art," new and emerging materials shape our understanding of media. This requires us to stay informed and to remain committed to the idea that the right art materials for the right art-making situation form the foundation of a successful process and product. These decisions facilitate a return to our ancient drive to create art in a way that gives voice to our human experiences.

Art experientials and reflection questions

1. Art media journal: provide a visual record of your experiments with art media. Include written reflections describing the media properties

(fluid/resistive), the art-making process, and its impact on you in terms of physical movements, sensory engagement, holistic perception, emotional reaction, thoughts and memories, and associations to meaning. Chart your experiences using Media Exploration Chart (please see Appendix).

2. Study the expressive qualities of some formal art elements with this classroom group exercise designed by art therapy educator Kay Stovall (June 25, 1992). Each person will need a set of oil pastels and four pieces of small paper (5"×7" to 9"×12"), and a quick demonstration from the instructor about how to blend and layer the pastels. Using shapes, lines, and colors, use the oil pastels to represent: (1) love, (2) anger, (3) fear, and (4) another feeling of your choice. Each of these should be made on a separate piece of paper. When they are done, post them together in four groups (one group of love, etc.). As a class, discuss the common elements of each group and notice any differences. Discuss what these commonalities and differences can tell us about the nature of these feelings, the potential of art to communicate such abstract concepts, and potential pitfalls of making assumptions about imagery in art.
3. Create a mixed media piece, incorporating elements from three different media included in this chapter. Consider creating art on themes such as elements of self, personal cultural identity, the role of art in society, or a theme decided by your class.
4. For those who have barriers to making art, such as someone in a community art group whose arthritis causes difficulty with fine motor skills, what adaptations might be needed to help this person use art materials more effectively?
5. For any of the earlier mentioned media, identify ways of changing the media dimension variables within a project to make it more successful for a variety of participant abilities.
6. What are ethical concerns facing art therapists who use with digital art? Develop an argument for or against the use of digital art media. Do the benefits outweigh the concerns? Debate with your classmates, providing specific examples and situations where the benefits outweigh the risks. Articulate strategies you could use to mitigate the risks.

Additional resources

Art Material Safety Guide: https://www.cpsc.gov/s3fs-public/pdfs/blk_media_5015.pdf
Art Material Safety for Kids: https://kinderart.com/blog/art-supply-safety-kids/
Material Safety Data Sheet Database: https://msds.com/
National Poison Control: https://www.poison.org/

Appendix

MEDIA EXPLORATION							
MEDIA	CLAY	MAGAZINE COLLAGE	CHALK PASTELS	TEMPERA PAINT	MELTED CRAYON	WATERCOLOR PENCIL	SANDTRAY
Personal Experience							
NEW							
TRIED ONCE OR TWICE							
EXPERIENCED/FAMILIAR							
Comfort Level							
COMFORTABLE							
UNCOMFORTABLE							
Control & Quality							
HARD TO CONTROL (FLUID)							
EASY TO CONTROL (RESISTIVE)							
IN BETWEEN (MANAGABLE)							
NEEDED ARM/GROSS MOTOR							
NEEDED HAND/FINE MOTOR							
Emotional Response							
HAPPY							
SAD							
QUIET							
PLAYFUL							
EXCITED							
FRUSTRATED							
BORED/UNINSPIRED							
OTHER (BE SPECIFIC)							
Thoughts/Associations							
REMINDED ME OF...							
MAKES ME THINK OF...							
SYMBOLS THAT EMERGED...							
WOULD LIKE TO GO FURTHER							
WOULD LIKE TO SIMPLIFY							

Media exploration chart.

Chapter terms

Affective
Balance
Bipolar
Chalk pastels
Charcoal
Cognitive
Cognitive/Symbolic Collage
Color Color intensity
Commitment Composition
Contrast
Control
Creative
Creativity
Decoupage
Digital arts
Digital mediators
Drawing
Ego-syntonic
Emphasis
Expressive Therapies Continuum
Fiber art
Flow
Fluid media
Fluid/Resistive
Form
Glazes
Ground
Kiln
Kinesthetic
Kinesthetic/Sensory
Kinetic sculpture
Line
Low Complexity/High Complexity
Material interaction
Materials Safety Data Sheets
Oil pastels
Media Dimension Variables
Media interaction
Media properties
Media/mediums
Mixed-media collage
Mixed-media found objects
Movement
Multistep media tasks
Nonmaleficence
Optimal creative functioning
Paper cutting
Pattern
Perceptual
Perceptual/Affective
Petroglyphs
Photography
Photomontages
Pigments
Pincer grasp
Primer
Printmaking
Professional-grade media
Proportion
Quilling
Resistive media
Sculpture
Sensory
Shape
Simple media tasks
Space
Structured media experiences
Symbolic
Symbolic value
Texture
Toxicity
Unity
Unstructured media experiences
Unstructured/Structured
Upcycling
Value

References

Agosin, M. (2008). *Tapestries of hope, threads of love: The arpillera movement in Chile*. Rowan & Littlefield Publishers.
Allen, P. (1995). *Art as a way of knowing*. Shambhala.

Arnheim, R. (1989). *Thoughts on art education*. The Getty Center for Education in the Arts.

Bar-Yosef Maeyer, D. E., & Bosch, M. D. (2019). Humans' earliest personal ornaments: An introduction. *PaleoAnthropology*, *2019*, 19–23. https://doi.org/10.4207/PA.2019.ART121.

Bloom, J. (2017). Papermaking: The historical diffusion of an ancient technique. In H. Jöns, P. Meusburger, & M. Heffernan (Eds.), *Mobilities of knowledge* (pp. 51–66). Springer. https://doi.org/10.1007/978-3-319-44654-7_3.

Capua, R. (2015). *Papyrus-making in Egypt*. Metropolitan Museum of Art. https://www.metmuseum.org/toah/hd/pyma/hd_pyma.htm.

Carlton, N. R. (2014). Digital culture and art therapy. *The Arts in Psychotherapy*, *41*(1), 41–45. https://doi.org/10.1016/j.aip.2013.11.006.

Carlton, N. R. (2017). Grid + pattern: The sensory qualities of digital media. In R. L. Gardner (Ed.), *Digital art therapy: Materials, methods, and applications* (pp. 22–39). Jessica Kingsley.

Collier, A. F. (2011). The well-being of women who create with textiles: Implications for art therapy. *Art Therapy: Journal of the American Art Therapy Association*, *28*(3), 104–112. https://doi.org/10.1080/07421656.2011.597025.

Csikszentmihalyi, M. (2013). *Creativity: The psychology of discovery and invention*. Harper Collins.

Csikszentmihalyi, M. (2014). *Flow and the foundations of positive psychology*. Springer.

Czamanski-Cohen, J., & Weihs, K. L. (2016). The bodymind model: A platform for studying the mechanisms of change induced by art therapy. *The Arts in Psychotherapy*, *51*, 63–71.

Darewych, O. H., Carlton, N. R., & Farrugie, K. W. (2015). Digital technology use in art therapy with adults with developmental disabilities. *Journal on Developmental Disabilities*, *21*(2), 95–102.

Dean, M. (2016). *Using art media in psychotherapy: Bringing the power of creativity to practice*. Routledge.

Dewey, J. D. (2005). *Art as experience*. Penguin (Original work published 1934).

Diringer, D. (2011). *The book before printing: Ancient, medieval, and oriental*. Dover Publications.

Dissanayake, E. (2003). The core of art: Making special. *Journal of the Canadian Association of Curriculum Studies*, *1*(2), 16–38.

Doby-Copeland, C. (2019). Intersections of traditional healing and art therapy: Legacy of Sarah E. McGee. *Art Therapy: Journal of the American Art Therapy Association*, *36*(3), 157–161. https://doi.org/10.1080/07421656.2019.1649548.

Elbrecht, C., & Antcliff, L. R. (2014). Being touched through touch. Trauma treatment through haptic perception at the clay field: A sensorimotor art therapy. *International Journal of Art Therapy: Inscape*, *19*(1), 19–30. https://doi.org/10.1080/17454832.2014.880932.

Field, J. (2018). *An illustrated field guide to the elements and principles of art and design*. Hot Iron Press.

Franklin, M. A. (2017). *Art as contemplative practice: Expressive pathways to the self*. State University of New York Press.

Gantt, L., & Anderson, F. W. (2009). The Formal Elements Art Therapy Scale: A measurement system for global variables in art. *Art Therapy: Journal of the American Art Therapy Association*, *26*, 124–129.

Gardner, H. (1994). *The arts and human development*. Basic Books.

Gardner, H., De la Croix, H., Tansey, R. G., & Kirkpatrick, D. (1991). *Gardner's art through the ages* (9th ed.). Harcourt Brace Jovanovich.

Glenn, A. (2021). *Ancient cylinder seals*. Johns Hopkins Archaeological Museum. https://archaeologicalmuseum.jhu.edu/staff-projects/ancient-cylinder-seals/.

Gold, J., & Ciorciari, J. (2020). A review on the role of the neuroscience of flow states in the modern world. *Behavioral Sciences (Basel, Switzerland)*, *19*(9), 137. https://doi.org/10.3390/bs10090137.

Graf, C. (2018). Coloring the world of the ancients. *Faces*, *34*(9), 12.

Graves-Alcorn, S., & Green, E. (2013). The expressive arts therapy continuum: History and theory. In E. Green, & A. Drewes (Eds.), *Integrating expressive arts and play therapy with children and adolescents* (pp. 1–15). Wiley.
Graves-Alcorn, S., & Kagin, C. (2017). *Implementing the expressive therapies continuum: A guide for clinical practice*. Routledge.
Hacmun, I., Regev, D., & Salomon, R. (2018). The principles of art therapy in virtual reality. *Frontiers of Psychology, 9*. https://doi.org/10.3389/fpsyg.2018.02082.
Haeyen, S., & Hinz, L. (2020). The first 15 min in art therapy: Painting a picture from the past. *The Arts in Psychotherapy, 71*(20). https://doi.org/10.1016/j.aip.2020.101718.
Harris, J., & Joseph, C. (1973). *Murals of the mind: Image of a psychiatric community*. International Universities Press.
Helfand, J. (2008). *Scrapbooks: An American history*. Yale University Press.
Henley, D. R. (1991). Facilitating the development of object relations through the use of clay in art therapy. *American Journal of Art Therapy, 29*(3), 69–76.
Henley, D. R. (1992). *Exceptional children exceptional art: Teaching art to special needs*. Davis.
Henley, D. R. (2002). *Clayworks in art therapy: Playing the sacred circle*. Jessica Kingsley.
Henshilwood, C. S., d'Errico, F., van Niekerk, K. L., Dayet, L., Queffelec, A., & Pollarolo, L. (2018). An abstract drawing from the 73,000-year-old levels at Blombos Cave, South Africa. *Nature, 562*(7725), 115–118. https://doi.org/10.1038/s41586-018-0514-3.
Hinz, L. D. (2020). *Expressive therapies continuum: A framework for using art in therapy* (2nd ed.). Routledge.
Hodgskiss, T., & Wadley, L. (2017). How people used ochre at Rose Cottage Cave, South Africa: Sixty thousand years of evidence from the Middle Stone Age. *PLoS ONE, 12*(4). https://doi.org/10.1371/journal.pone.0176317.
Horovitz, E. (2018). *A guide to art therapy materials, methods, and applications: A practical step-by-step approach*. Routledge.
Joseph, C. (2006). Creative alliance: The healing power of art therapy. *Art Therapy: Journal of the American Art Therapy Association, 23*(1), 30–33. https://doi.org/10.1080/07421656.2006.10129531.
Junge, M. M. (2010). *The modern history of art therapy in the United States*. Charles C. Thomas.
Junge, M. M. (2016). History of art therapy. In D. E. Gussack & M. L. Rosal (Eds.), *The Wiley handbook of art therapy* (pp. 7–16). John Wiley & Sons.
Junge, M. M., & Asawa, P. P. (1994). *A history of art therapy in the United States*. American Art Therapy Association.
Kagin, S. L., & Lusebrink, V. B. (1978). The expressive therapies continuum. *The Arts in Psychotherapy, 5*, 171–180. https://doi.org/10.1016/0090-9092(78)90031-5.
Kaimal, G., Carroll-Haskins, K., Berberian, M., Dougherty, A., Carlton, N., & Ramakrishnan, A. (2020). Virtual reality in art therapy: A pilot qualitative study of the novel medium and implications for practice. *Art Therapy: Journal of the American Art Therapy Association, 37*(1), 16–24. https://doi.org/10.1080/07421656.2019.1659662.
Kaplan, F. (2000). *Art, science, and art therapy: Repainting the picture*. Jessica Kingsley.
Karns, J. T. (2002). Scrapbooking during traumatic and transitional events. *Journal of Clinical Activities, Assignments & Handouts in Psychotherapy Practice, 2*(3), 39–47. https://doi.org/10.1300/J182v02n03_05.
Katahira, K., Yamazaki, Y., Yamaoka, C., Ozaki, H., Nakagawa, S., & Nagata, N. (2018). EEG correlates of the flow state: A combination of increased frontal theta and moderate frontocentral alpha rhythm in the mental arithmetic task. *Frontiers of Psychology, 9*. https://doi.org/10.3389/fpsyg.2018.00300.

Kausch, K. D., & Amer, K. (2007). Self-transcendence and depression among AIDS memorial quilt panel makers. *Journal of Psychosocial Nursing and Mental Health Services*, *45*(6), 44–53. https://doi.org/10.3928/02793695-20070601-10.

Kimport, E. R., & Robbins, S. J. (2012). Efficacy of creative clay work for reducing negative mood: A randomized controlled trial. *Art Therapy: Journal of the American Art Therapy Association*, *29*(2), 74–79. https://doi.org/10.1080/07421656.2012.680048.

King James Bible. (2021). *King James bible online*. https://www.kingjamesbibleonline.org/Acts-Chapter-9/.

Kohut, M. (2011). Making art from memories: Honoring deceased loved ones through a scrapbooking bereavement group. *Art Therapy: Journal of the American Art Therapy Association*, *28*(3), 123–131. https://doi.org/10.1080/07421656.2011.599731.

Kozbelt, A. (2001). Artists as experts in visual cognition. *Visual Cognition*, *8*(6), 705–723. https://doi.org/10.1080/13506280042000090.

Kramer, E. (1971). *Art as therapy with children*. Schocken Press.

Kramer, E. (2001). Art and emptiness: New problems in art education and art therapy. *American Journal of Art Therapy*, *40*(1), 6–15.

Kramer, E., & Gerity, L. (2001). *Art as therapy: Collected papers*. Jessica Kingsley.

Landgarten, H. (1993). *Magazine photo collage: A multicultural assessment and treatment technique*. Brunner/Mazel.

Leeming, D. (1992). *The world of myth: An anthology*. Oxford University Press.

Leone, L. (2021). *Craft in art therapy: Diverse approaches to the transformative power of craft materials and methods*. Routledge.

Levy, B. I., Kramer, E, Kwiatkowska, H. Y., Lachman, M., Rhyne, J., & Ulman, E. (1974). Symposium: Integration of divergent points of view in art therapy. *American Journal of Art Therapy*, *14*(1), 13–17.

Lowenfeld, V. (1952). *Creative and mental growth* (2nd ed.). Macmillian.

Lowenfeld, V., & Brittain, W. L. (1987). *Creative and mental growth* (8th ed.). Macmillian.

Lowenstein, L. B. (1995). The resolution scrapbook as an aid in the treatment of traumatized children. *Child Welfare*, *74*(4), 889–904.

Lusebrink, V. B., & Hinz, L. (2020). Cognitive and symbolic aspects of art therapy and similarities with large scale brain networks. *Art Therapy: Journal of the American Art Therapy Association*, *37*(3), 113–122. https://doi.org/10.1080/07421656.2019.1691869.

Lusebrink, V. B. (1990). *Imagery and visual expression in therapy*. Plenum Press.

Malchiodi, C. (2000). *Art therapy and computer technology: A virtual studio of possibilities*. Jessica Kingsley.

McCarthy, P. G., & Sebaugh, J. G. (2011). Therapeutic scrapbooking: A technique to promote positive coping and emotional strength in parents of pediatric oncology patients. *Journal of Psychosocial Oncology*, *29*(2), 215–230. https://doi.org/10.1080/07347332.2010.548443.

McGee, S. E. (1979). Art therapy as a means of fostering parental closeness in a migrant preschool. In L. Gantt (Ed.), *Focus on the future: The next ten years. Proceedings of the 10th Annual Conference of the American Art Therapy Association* (pp. 32–35). American Art Therapy Association.

McNiff, S. (1998). *Trust the process: An artist's guide to letting go*. Shambhala.

McNiff, S. (2014). The role of witnessing and immersion in the moment of arts therapy experience. In L. Rappaport (Ed.), *Mindfulness and the arts therapies: Theory and practice* (pp. 38–50). Jessica Kingsley.

Mihailidis, A., Blunsden, S., Boger, J., Richards, B., Zutis, K., Young, L., et al. (2010). Towards the development of a technology for art therapy and dementia: Definition of needs and design constraints. *The Arts in Psychotherapy*, *37*(4), 293–300. https://doi.org/10.1016/j.aip.2010.05.004.

Moon, C. H. (2010). *Materials & media in art therapy: Critical understandings of diverse artistic vocabularies*. Routledge.

Morriss-Kay, G. M. (2010). The evolution of human artistic creativity. *Journal of Anatomy*, *216*(2), 158–176. https://doi.org/10.1111/j.1469-7580.2009.01160.x.

Moss, K. L. (2010). Cultural representation in Philadelphia murals: Images of resistance and sites of identity negotiation. *Western Journal of Communication*, *74*(4), 372–395. https://doi.org/10.1080/10570314.2010.492819.

Nan, J. K. M. (2021). From clay to ceramic: An alchemical process of self-transformation. In L. Leone (Ed.), *Craft in art therapy: Diverse approaches to the transformative power of craft materials and methods* (pp. 55–71). Routledge.

Nan, J. K. M., & Ho, R. T. H. (2017). Effects of clay art therapy on adults outpatients with major depressive disorder: A randomized controlled trial. *Journal of Affective Disorders*, *217*, 237–245. https://doi.org/10.1016/j.jad.2017.04.013.

Naumburg, M. (1958). Art therapy: Its scope and function. In E. F. Hammer (Ed.), *The clinical application of projective drawings* (pp. 511–517). Charles C. Thomas.

Naumburg, M. (1966). *Dynamically oriented art therapy*. Grune & Stratton.

Ocvirk, O., Stinson, R., Wigg, P., Bone, R., & Cayton, D. (2012). *Art fundamentals: Theory and practice* (12th ed.). McGraw-Hill.

Orr, P. (2010). Social remixing: Art therapy media in the digital age. In C. H. Moon (Ed.), *Materials and media in art therapy: Critical understandings of diverse artistic vocabularies* (pp. 89–100). Routledge.

Orr, P. (2016). Art therapy and digital media. In D. E. Gussak, & M. L. Rosal (Eds.), *The Wiley handbook of art therapy* (pp. 188–197). John Wiley & Sons.

Park, S., Lee, H., Kim, S., & Kim, Y. (2020). Traditional Korean art materials as therapeutic media: Multicultural expansion through materials in art therapy. *Art Therapy: Journal of the American Art Therapy Association*, *38*(2), 60–68. https://doi.org/10.1080/07421656.2020.1729077.

Pénzes, I., van Hooren, S., Dokter, D., & Hutschemaekers, G. (2018). How art therapists observe mental health using formal elements in art products: Structure and variation as indicators for balance and adaptability. *Frontiers in Psychology*, *9*, 1611. https://doi.org/10.3389/fpsyg.2018.01611.

Pénzes, I., van Hooren, S., Dokter, D., & Hutschemaekers, G. (2020). Formal elements of art indicate aspects of mental health. *Frontiers in Psychology*, *11*, 2507. https://doi.org/10.3389/fpsyg.2020.572700.

Pénzes, I., van Hooren, S., Dokter, D., Smeijsters, H., & Hutschemaekers, G. (2014). Material interaction in art therapy assessment. *The Arts in Psychotherapy*, *41*(5), 484–492. https://doi.org/10.1016/j.aip.2014.08.003.

Pénzes, I., van Hooren, S., Dokter, D., Smeijsters, H., & Hutschemaekers, G. (2015). Material interaction and art product in art therapy assessment in adult mental health. *Arts & Health*, *8*(3), 213–228. https://doi.org/10.1080/17533015.2015.1088557.

Potash, J. S., Bardot, H., Moon, C. H., Napoli, M., Lyonsmith, A., & Hamilton, M. (2017). Ethical implications of cross-cultural international art therapy. *The Arts in Psychotherapy*, *56*, 74–82. https://doi.org/10.1016/j.aip.2017.08.005.

Puccio, G. J. (2017). From the Dawn of humanity to the 21st century: Creativity as an enduring survival skill. *Journal of Creative Behavior*, *51*(4), 330–334. https://doi.org/10.1002/jocb.203.

Puig, A., Lee, S. M., Goodwin, L., & Sherrard, P. A. D. (2006). The efficacy of creative arts therapies to enhance emotional expression, spirituality, and psychological well-being of newly diagnosed stage I and stage II breast cancer patients: A preliminary study. *The Arts in Psychotherapy*, *33*(3), 218–228. https://doi.org/10.1016/j.aip.2006.02.004.

Rafaelli, T., & Hartzell, E. (2016). A comparison of adults' responses to collage versus drawing in an initial art-making session. *Art Therapy: Journal of the American Art Therapy Association, 33*(1), 21–26.

Romero, R. (1986). Autobiographical scrapbooks: A coping tool for hospitalized school children. *Issues in Comprehensive Pediatric Nursing, 9*(4), 247–258. https://doi.org/10.3109/01460868609009779.

Roy, K. (2012). Modeling safety in clay use. *Science and Children, 50*(4), 84–85.

Rubin, J. A. (2011). *The art of art therapy: What every art therapist needs to know*. Routledge.

Schoeser, M. (2003). *World textiles: A concise history*. Thames & Hudson.

Seiden, D. (2001). *Mind over matter: The use of materials in art, education and therapy*. Magnolia Street Publishers.

Sholt, M., & Gavron, T. (2006). Therapeutic qualities of clay-work in art therapy and psychotherapy: A review. *Art Therapy: Journal of the American Art Therapy Association, 23*(2), 66–72. https://doi.org/10.1080/07421656.2006.10129647.

Snir, S., & Regev, D. (2013). A dialog with five art materials: Creators share their art making experiences. *The Arts in Psychotherapy, 40*(1), 94–100. https://doi.org/10.1016/j.aip.2012.11.004.

Stallings, J., & Clark, S. (2021). Healing with fire: The use of hot glass in art therapy. In L. Leone (Ed.), *Craft in art therapy: Diverse approaches to the transformative power of craft materials and methods* (pp. 40–54). Routledge.

Staubach, S. (2005). *Clay: The history and evolution of humankind's relationship with the earth's most primal element*. University Press of New England.

Stepney, S. A. (2019). Visionary architects of color in art therapy: Georgette Powell, Cliff Joseph, Lucille Venture, and Charles Anderson. *Art Therapy: Journal of the American Art Therapy Association, 36*(3), 115–121. https://doi.org/10.1080/07421656.2019.1649545.

Stokstad, M., & Cothren, M. W. (2011). *Art history*. Prentice Hall.

Tobin, J. L., & Dobard, R. G. (1999). *Hidden in plain view: A secret story of quilts and the underground railroad*. Anchor Books.

Venture, L. (1977). *The Black beat in art therapy experiences*. Union for Experimenting Colleges and Universities. Publication No. 7720887, Doctoral dissertation, Proquest Dissertations and Theses Database.

Victoria and Albert Museum. (2016). *A history of computer art*. http://www.vam.ac.uk/content/articles/a/computer-art-history/.

Wadeson, H. (1987). *The dynamics of art psychotherapy*. John Wiley & Sons.

Weinberg, D. J. (1985). The potential of rehabilitative computer art therapy for the quadriplegic, cerebral vascular accident and brain trauma patient. *Art Therapy: Journal of the American Art Therapy Association, 2*(2), 66–72. https://doi.org/10.1080/07421656.1985.10758788.

Weiser, J. (2015). Establishing the framework for using photos in art therapy (and other therapies) practices. In *Arteterapia. Papeles de Arteterapia y Educación Artística Para La Inclusión Social*. https://doi.org/10.5209/rev_ARTE.2014.v9.47490.

White, L. M. (2002). *Printmaking as therapy: Frameworks for freedom*. Jessica Kingsley.

Williams, K., & Lent, J. (2008). Scrapbooking as an intervention for grief recovery with children. *Journal of Creativity in Mental Health, 3*(4), 455–467. https://doi.org/10.1080/15401380802547553.

Wong, D. (2021). Materials: Potential and found objects. In D. Wong, & R. P. Lay (Eds.), *Found objects in art therapy: Materials and processes* (pp. 25–38). Jessica Kingsley.

Zeevil, L. S. (2021). Making art therapy virtual: Integrating virtual reality into art therapy with adolescents. *Frontiers in Psychology, 12*, 1–10. https://doi.org/10.3389/fpsyg.2021.584943.

Chapter 3

Multicultural and diversity perspectives in art therapy: Transforming image into substance

Stella A. Stepney, MS, ATR-BC, LCAT
Herron School of Art and Design, Indiana University Purdue University, Indianapolis, IN, United States

Voices from the field
Let the students know that we are all here on Earth together as members of the human family, allied in the task of bringing health to the world.
And please share with them my love.

Cliff Joseph, Art Therapy Pathfinder

Learning outcomes

After reading this chapter, you will be able to

1. Identify basic terminology associated with multicultural and diversity perspectives.
2. Describe contemporary demographic pragmatics that impact the art therapy profession.
3. Summarize the historical context of multiculturalism in the United States.
4. Identify the types of multicultural awareness, knowledge, and skills that reflect multicultural and diversity competence in art therapy.
5. Compare the concepts of cultural competence and cultural humility in the delivery of art therapy services.
6. Discuss the impact of intersectionality on contemporary art therapy practice.
7. Identify models of racial, ethnic, and cultural identity development.
8. Implement the concepts presented in the chapter through experiential learning opportunities.

Foundations of Art Therapy. https://doi.org/10.1016/B978-0-12-824308-4.00010-7

Chapter overview

Culture is the belief systems and value orientations that influence customs, norms, practices, and social institutions, including psychological processes and organizations. Culture is characterized as the embodiment of a worldview through learned and transmitted beliefs, values, and practices, including religious and spiritual practices. In essence, culture encompasses a way of living informed by the historical, economic, ecological, and political forces on racial, ethnic, and cultural groups.

The purpose of this chapter is to examine multicultural and diversity competence as it relates to culturally responsive art therapy practice. Art therapists are expected to demonstrate expertise and competence in the services they offer. Therefore, they must be able to work effectively with a broad variety of clients, each of whom has been shaped by a different mix of cultural and social influences.

The Ethical Principles for Art Therapists (2013) provides aspirational values and principles that cover many situations encountered by art therapists. The goal of this document is to safeguard the welfare of the individuals and groups with whom art therapists work. Ethical Principle 7.0 addresses MULTICULTURAL AND DIVERSITY COMPETENCE:

Multicultural and diversity competence in art therapy refers to the capacity of art therapists to continually acquire cultural and diversity awareness of and knowledge about cultural diversity with regard to self and others, and to successfully apply these skills in practice with clients. Art therapists maintain multicultural and diversity competence to provide treatment interventions and strategies that include awareness of and responsiveness to cultural issues (American Art Therapy Association, 2013).

Multicultural and diversity competence is essential to ethical practice, and this competence must become the cornerstone for effective art therapy practice. By gaining the requisite awareness, knowledge, and skills necessary to be culturally competent, art therapists can actualize their professional commitment to nondiscrimination and equal access for all clients.

Introduction

The Statue of Liberty is a neoclassical sculpture on Liberty Island in New York Harbor within New York City in the United States. The statue, which was a gift from the people of France to the people of the United States, was dedicated on October 28, 1866. The statue is a figure of the robed Roman liberty goddess Libertas. She holds a torch above her head with her right hand, and in her left hand carries a tablet with dovetail handles inscribed July 4, 1776, in Roman numerals, the date of the U.S. Declaration of Independence. A broken shackle and chain lie at her feet as she walks forward, commemorating the 1865 ratification of the 13th Amendment to the U.S. Constitution in the aftermath of the Civil War, which abolished slavery in the United States. Following its dedication, the statue became an icon of freedom and of the United States, seen as a symbol of welcome to immigrants arriving by sea ("Statue of Liberty," 2021) (Fig. 3.1).

The United States of America (U.S.) is a federal republic of 50 states. Besides the 48 states which have a common boundary, the United States includes the state of Alaska and the island state of Hawaii. It is the fourth largest country in the world in area. The major characteristic of the United States is its great variety. The country embraces some of the world's largest urban concentrations and some of the most extensive areas that are devoid of habitation (Editors of Encyclopaedia Britannica, 2021).

The United States has a highly diverse population. Unlike a country that largely incorporates indigenous peoples, the United States has a diversity that has come from immense and sustained global immigration. No other country has a wider range of racial, ethnic, and cultural groups. In addition to the presence of surviving Native Americans, including American Indians, Aleuts, and Eskimos, and the descendants of Africans taken as enslaved persons to the New World, the national character of the United States has been enriched, tested, and constantly redefined by millions of immigrants who have come to America hoping for greater social, political, and economic opportunities (Editors of Encyclopaedia Britannica, 2021).

From the 1830s onward, a steady stream of immigrants formed a pool of foreign-born persons unmatched by any other nation. Many immigrants were driven to the New World seeking escape from political or economic hardship, while others were drawn by opportunities. Americans migrated internally, exhibiting a restlessness that thrived in the open land and on the frontier. The Land of Opportunity was realized dramatically in the 20th century with the emergence of the United States as a world power. However, at the dawn of

FIG. 3.1 *Statue of Liberty (Liberty Enlightening the World).*

the 21st century, tensions stemming from social and economic inequalities began to threaten the fabric of the country. Many Americans perceived the tensions as the product of the nation's failure to extend the dream of **equality of opportunity,** which is the idea that all people should be able to compete on equal terms (Editors of Encyclopaedia Britannica, 2021).

A society in which people are chosen and moved into positions of success, power, and influence on the basis of their demonstrated abilities and merit, or conduct deserving reward, honor, or esteem is referred to as **meritocracy** (Merriam-Webster, n.d.-c). As a widely held but false belief, meritocracy is a myth. In the United States, this myth has perpetuated and unified Americans throughout the country's history. The **myth of meritocracy** claims that social, political, economic, and religious freedom would assure the like treatment of everyone, so that all could achieve goals in accord with their individual talents, *if only they worked hard enough* (Editors of Encyclopaedia Britannica, 2021).

The systems of knowledge, concepts, rules, and practices that are learned and transmitted across generations are referred to as **culture** (American Psychiatric Association, 2013). Within the United States, individuals and groups are exposed to multiple cultures, which may be used to develop cultural identities and make sense of experiences. The discipline of **cultural anthropology** focuses on how people develop and use culture as a tool. Basically, it is the study of the learned behavior of groups of people in specific environments. How people have been accepted and treated within the context of society or culture has a direct impact on how they perform in that society or culture. Human cultural behavior is learned. Within this context, culture is the conceptual system developed by a society to structure the way people view the world. Cultural anthropologists have concluded that the current racial and ethnic inequalities in the United States are by-products of historical and contemporary social, economic, educational, and political circumstances (American Anthropological Association, 2021).

United States demographics: The changing face of America

The statistical study of human populations with reference to size and density, distribution, and vital statistics is referred to as **demography** (Merriam-Webster, n.d.-a). The U.S. Census Bureau is the federal government's largest statistical agency dedicated to providing current facts and figures about America's people, places, and economy. The Decennial Census is the once-a-decade population and housing count of all 50 states, the District of Columbia, Puerto Rico, and the Island Areas as required by the U.S. Constitution (U.S. Census Bureau, 2019). In addition, the Census Bureau estimates the population and characteristics. Population projections are based on future demographic trends (U.S. Census Bureau, 2019) (Fig. 3.2).

FIG. 3.2 *Diversity in the U.S. population.*

Understanding culture, race, and ethnicity in the United States

Culture is the conceptual system developed by a society to structure **worldviews**, which are composed of people's attitudes, values, and beliefs that affect how people think, define events, make decisions, and behave (Sue & Sue, 2016). Culture is not a definable entity to which people belong or do not belong. However, culture is a primary force in the creation of a person's identity. Within a nation, race, or community, people belong to multiple cultural groups and negotiate multiple cultural expectations. These expectations, or **cultural norms**, are spoken and unspoken rules or standards for a given group that indicate whether a social event or behavior is appropriate or inappropriate.

The term culture can be applied to not only racial and ethnic group populations but also to other groups on the basis of age, socioeconomic status, disability, and sexual orientation. Therefore individuals embrace their culture(s) in a unique way and there is considerable diversity within and across races, ethnicities, and cultural heritage (Substance Abuse and Mental Health Services Administration [SAMHSA], 2014). The diverse racial, ethnic, and cultural groups in the United States can have very different life experiences, values, and traditions. Therefore understanding the diversity within a specific culture, race, or ethnicity is essential.

The culturally constructed category of identity that divides humanity into groups based on a variety of superficial physical traits attributed to some hypothetical intrinsic characteristics is referred to as **race** (American Psychiatric Association, 2013). Although the construct of race has no consistent biological definition, the concept of race is important in discussing multicultural and diversity competence. The perception that people who share physical characteristics also share beliefs, values, attitudes, and ways of being can have a profound impact on people's lives whether they identify with the race to which they are ascribed by themselves or others (SAMHSA, 2014).

The culturally constructed group identity used to define peoples and communities is referred to as **ethnicity** (American Psychiatric Association, 2013). Although the term ethnicity is sometimes used interchangeably with the term race, there is a distinction between the two. Ethnicity is a social identity and mutual sense of belonging that defines groups of people through common historical or family origin, beliefs, and other standards of behavior (i.e., culture). Ethnicity can also refer to identification with a clan or group whose identity can be based on race as well as culture (SAMHSA, 2014). Notably, ethnicity may be self-assigned or attributed by others. New mixed, multiple, or hybrid ethnic identities may be defined by increased mobility, interracial marriage, and intermixing of cultures.

The Census Bureau collects race data according to the U.S. Office of Management and Budget (OMB) guidelines, and this data is based on self-identification. The racial categories included in the census questionnaire reflect a social definition of race recognized in the United States and not an attempt to define race biologically, anthropologically, or genetically. It is recognized that the categories of race include racial, national origin, or sociocultural groups. People may choose to report more than one race. The racial categories include White, Black or African American, American Indian or Alaska Native, Asian, and Native Hawaiian or Other Pacific Islander.

White: A person having origins in any of the original peoples of Europe, the Middle East, or North Africa.

Black or African American: A person having origins in any of the Black racial groups of Africa.

American Indian or Alaska Native: A person having origins in any of the original peoples of North and South America (including Central America) and who maintains tribal affiliation or community attachment.

Asian: A person having origins in any of the original peoples of the Far East, Southeast Asia, or the Indian subcontinent including, for example, Cambodia, China, India, Japan, Korea, Malaysia, Pakistan, the Philippine Islands, Thailand, and Vietnam.

Native Hawaiian or Other Pacific Islander: A person having origins in any of the original peoples of Hawaii, Guam, Samoa, or other Pacific Islands (U.S. Census Bureau, 2020a).

Hispanic Origin can be viewed as the heritage, nationality, lineage, or country of birth of the person or the person's parents or ancestors before arriving in the United States. The OMB requires federal agencies to use a minimum of two ethnicities in collecting and reporting data. A person of Cuban, Mexican, Puerto Rican, South or Central American, or other Spanish culture or origin, regardless of race, is defined by OMB as **Hispanic or Latino** (U.S. Census Bureau, 2020b).

Demographic trends and population projections in the United States

Population projections for the years 2020–2060 indicate that the year 2030 will mark a major demographic point for the United States. Three demographic milestones are expected to make the 2030s a transformative decade for the U.S. population. First, beginning in 2030, all **baby boomers**, individuals born between 1946 and 1964, will be older than 65 and by 2034 it is projected that older adults will outnumber children for the first time in U.S. history. Second, immigration is projected to overtake natural increase, or the excess of births over deaths, as the primary driver of population growth. Third, net international migration is expected to overtake natural increase, even as levels of migration are projected to remain flat (Vespa et al., 2020).

By 2028 the foreign-born share of the U.S. population is projected to be higher than at any time since 1850. Beginning in 2045, the non-Hispanic White population is no longer projected to make up the majority of the U.S. population. The fastest-growing population in the United States is people who are of two or more races. Foreign-born people living in the United States are not a single population, they are made up of people from different countries and backgrounds. By 2058 the U.S. population is expected to cross the 400-million threshold with a projected population of 401.3 million people. By 2060 the number of immigrants living in the United States is projected to total more than 69 million people or about one in six people living in the United States (Vespa et al., 2020).

The transformative trends indicate that the United States is becoming a more racially and ethically pluralistic society. Art therapy theory and practice are impacted by the ever-increasing diversity of client populations, which reflects the changing demographics and social dynamics of the 21st century. To adequately serve art therapy clients from diverse cultures, a new vision of service delivery must be established based on **cultural competence**, which is the ability to provide effective helping services cross-culturally. Diller (2015) highlights that developing cultural competence also provides "enormous personal growth in the form of increased self-awareness, cultural sensitivity, nonjudgmental thinking, and broadened consciousness" (p. 33).

Demographic trends in other multicultural populations in the United States

Sexual orientation and gender identity

A part of an individual's identity that includes a person's sexual and emotional attraction to another person and the behavior and/or social affiliation that may result from this situation is referred to as **sexual orientation** (American Psychological Association, 2020). Sexual orientation can be conceptualized by the degree to which a person feels sexual and emotional attraction and as having a gendered directionality of attraction. The acronym LGBTQIQ is used in reference to multiple groups of people. The ALGBTIC LGBQQIA Competencies Taskforce (2013) defines the specific terms for LGBTQIQ orientations:

> **Lesbian**: A woman who is emotionally, physically, mentally, and/or spiritually oriented to bond and share affection with other women.
> **Gay:** A man who is emotionally, physically, mentally, and/or spiritually oriented to bond and share affection with other men.
> **Bisexual:** A man or woman who is emotionally, physically, mentally, and/or spiritually oriented to bond and share affection with men and women.
> **Transgender (or trans)**: An umbrella term used to describe people who challenge social gender norms, including gender-queer people, and gender-nonconforming people.
> **Queer:** Individuals who identify outside of the heteronormative imperative and/or gender binary (e.g., those from the LGBTQIQ community).
> **Intersex**: An individual who was born with male and female characteristics in the internal/external sex organs, hormones, chromosomes, and/or secondary sex characteristics.
> **Questioning**: Individuals who are unsure if they are emotionally, physically, mentally, and/or spiritually attracted to women, men, or both (pp. 40–45).

In the United States, there has been a notable rising trend in the percentage of American adults identifying as Lesbian, Gay, Bisexual, Transgender, and Queer (LGBTQ) individuals. This population has risen to 4.5%, up from 4.1% in 2017 and 3.5% in 2012. Extrapolation to the latest U.S. Census estimate of adults 18 and older suggests that more than 11 million adults identify as LGBTQ. According to Newport (2018), the expansion in the number of Americans who identify as LGBTQ is driven by the cohort of **millennials**, individuals born between 1980 and 1999. The U.S. Census does not include questions relating to sexual and gender orientation in its population updates. Therefore the upward trajectory of the estimates between 2012 and 2017 of the LGBTQ adult population provides an important social indicator relating to this key aspect of contemporary American society (Newport, 2018).

In the United States, LGBTQIQ individuals live in a heterosexual society expecting "normative" gender behavior and sexuality where they face the challenge of developing a healthy self-identity in the midst of societal norms. Although there is increased societal acceptance of the LGBTQIQ community within the United States, intense stressors which can range from microaggressions up to and including the threat or actuality of physical violence and even death are prevalent. Therefore social justice must play an important role in addressing systemic issues that are responsible for stressors in the lives of LGBTQIQ individuals, groups, and communities.

Income inequality and poverty

Socioeconomic status (SES) encompasses quality of life attributes and opportunities afforded to people within society and is a consistent predictor of an array of psychological outcomes. The SES includes income, educational attainment, occupational prestige, and subjective perception of social status and social class (American Psychological Association, 2020). A state or condition in which a person or community lacks the financial resources and essentials for a minimum standard of living is referred to as **poverty** (Chen, 2020). The Census Bureau uses a set of money income thresholds that vary by family size and composition to determine who is in poverty. In 2020 the poverty threshold for a family of four, two adults and two children, was $26,246 (U.S. Census Bureau, n.d.).

Census Bureau statistics on income shed light on income inequality in the United States. **Income inequality** refers to how unevenly income is distributed throughout the population. The less equal the distribution, the higher income inequality is. Income inequality is accompanied by **wealth inequality**, which is the uneven distribution of wealth. An **income gap** refers to the difference in income earned between demographic segments. Income distributions by demographic segmentation form the basis for examining income inequality and income disparity (Kopp, 2020). A stark gap exists in the wealth of Americans across race and ethnicity. The difference in assets owned by different racial or ethnic groups is referred to as the **racial wealth gap**. The current gap is viewed as a result of historical and continuing patterns of wealth inequality. Over time, income inequality, governmental housing policies, representation and political disenfranchisement, limited educational opportunities, and a lack of social support have contributed to the racial wealth gap (Mollenkamp, 2021).

In an industrialized society like the United States, particular demographic groups are vulnerable to long-term poverty, referred to as **concentrated collective poverty** (Editors of Encyclopaedia Britannica, 2020). Victims of concentrated collective poverty are found in parts of the city in which members of a minority group live, especially as a result of social, legal, or economic pressure. Victims are also found in regions bypassed or abandoned by industry, and in areas where agriculture or industry is inefficient and cannot compete profitably. The chief economic traits for victims of concentrated collective poverty are unemployment and underemployment, unskilled occupations, and job instability (Editors of Encyclopaedia Britannica, 2020).

Although poverty does not constitute a true cultural designation, the challenges of life in poverty diverge enough from mainstream life to warrant consideration. Access to good schools, healthcare, financial resources, and essentials for a minimum standard of living remains elusive for many individuals living in poverty. For those who are able to move out of poverty, progress is often temporary. The damage that poverty exacts upon people's physical and emotional well-being calls for advocating for the eradication of poverty.

Responding to poverty is becoming integral to the practice of art therapy. Feen-Calligan (2013) advocates, "Strengthening capabilities such as imagination, thought, personal awareness, expression of emotions, motivation, and agency can be accomplished regardless of financial, economic, or other external resources. Moreover, these capabilities can be fostered through art therapy"

(p. 398). Emotional stability, motivation, energy levels, and general life satisfaction are referred to as **well-being**. Critical inquiry into how a person's social environment supports or detracts from well-being, coupled with helping people to be advocates for themselves and for social change, can and should be among the functions of art therapists working with people living in poverty and/or experiencing homelessness (Feen-Calligan, 2013).

Health disparities

Within the United States, the policies, economic systems, and other institutions have produced **health disparities**, which are differences in access, utilization, and quality of care. These disparities have been linked to **structural racism**, defined as laws, rules, or official policies in a society that result in and support a continued unfair advantage to some people and unfair or harmful treatment of others based on race (Cambridge Dictionary, 2021). Structural racism is a threat to the physical, emotional, and social well-being of every person in a society that allocates privilege on the basis of race.

Karcher (2017) asserts that art therapists cannot ignore the social and political sources of oppression and the trauma experienced by those who live with marginalized identities. If art therapists are not aware of their power and privilege, they will be ineffective at treating the unique experiences of trauma that are exacerbated by oppression. Art therapists hold power within the therapeutic relationship due to their position as the "helper" and they may hold privilege due to access to higher education, financial status, race, sexual orientation or gender, citizenship, or religion. Karcher (2017) posits, "When one belongs to, or is assumed to belong to, a group seen as the 'norm' (e.g., white people, men, middle or upper class, straight people, Christians, etc.), the person holds privilege" (p. 125). Therefore it is important for art therapists to question the ways they participate or remain complicit in the oppression of other people.

Art therapists have the opportunity to use art interventions with clients to facilitate critical consciousness, which entails decoding broader social contexts and developing mastery to take action to transform their world. When bringing these elements to life, art therapists operationalize social justice frameworks and recognize the important position of artistic creation. Art therapists hold a unique position of masterfully facilitating the healing process through creative expression coupled with the use of art for social change (Karcher, 2017).

Marginalization

The process in which individuals or entire cultural groups are systematically blocked from or denied full access to various rights, opportunities, and resources that are normally available to members of the dominant cultural group is referred to as **marginalization** (Lee & Ali, 2019). Gladding and Newsome (2018) cautioned that when people live in a social environment characterized by oppression, harassment, discrimination, prejudice, and microaggressions, they may "exhibit behaviors and attitudes that appear dysfunctional but are, in fact, healthy coping mechanisms for living in that environment" (p. 67). Any emotional, physical, social, economic, or other factors that disrupt the normal physiological, cognitive, emotional, or behavioral balance of an individual is referred to as a **stressor** (American Psychiatric Association, 2013). Oppression, harassment, discrimination, prejudice, and microaggressions are stressors for marginalized individuals, groups, and communities. Through advocacy efforts for equality and equity, injustices impacting marginalized groups can be rectified and health disparities decreased. These changes can improve not only the structure of people's lives but also their mental health and wellness (Caraballo, 2019).

Sociopolitical barriers to equality and equity

The existence of the same treatment for every person in a community or society, irrespective of social group membership, is referred to as **equality**. The requirement that all individuals have fair access to society's resources and the opportunity to use their access in order to be successful is referred to as **equity**. Equity goes beyond equal treatment and addresses the marginalized positions of individuals and groups compared to members of the dominant group (Grothaus et al., 2013). The lens of social equality and equity is one that art therapists can intentionally employ to sharpen their focus on the ways in which access and opportunity are denied and advocate for dismantling systemic barriers to success that are present within American society.

Oppression

The condition of being subject to another group's power is **oppression**. The intentional disadvantaging of groups of people based on their identity while advantaging members of the dominant group is referred to as **systemic oppression** (National Equity Project, n.d.). Oppression exists across cultural identities and it can be actively or subtly expressed in various forms. An oppressive and especially discriminatory attitude or belief is referred to as an **ism** (Merriam-Webster, n.d.-b). Within the United States, the isms (e.g., racism) are viewed as contemporary forms of oppression (Grothaus et al., 2013; Capodilupo, 2019).

Microaggressions

The everyday slights, put-downs, invalidations, and insults directed at socially devalued group members by people who may be unaware that they have engaged in biased and harmful behaviors are referred to as **microaggressions** (Sue & Sue, 2016). Microaggressions manifest in American society as microassaults, microinsults, and microinvalidations. Each manifestation reflects that the dominant group's values permeate the culture so that the nondominant groups' values are seen as nonexistent or wrong (Grothaus et al., 2013; Capodilupo, 2019).

A **microassault** is a blatant verbal, nonverbal, or environmental attack intended to convey discriminatory and biased sentiments. For example, assuming an Asian American is foreign born and asking, "Where are you from?" or "Where were you born?" The subtle message is "You are not American."
A **microinsult** is an unintentional behavior or verbal comment that conveys rudeness or insensitivity or demeans a person's race, ethnicity, sexual orientation, gender, ability, or religion. For example, pathologizing cultural communication styles by asking, "Why do Blacks have to be so loud?" The subtle message is "They should assimilate to the dominant culture's communication style."
A **microinvalidation** is a verbal comment or behavior that excludes, negates, or dismisses the psychological thoughts, feelings, or experiential reality of a target group. For example, when a White person denies individual racism by saying, "I am not racist; I have several (Black/African American or Native American or Asian, or Native Hawaiian) friends." The subtle message is "I am immune to racism because I have friends who are People of Color."

Colorblind ideology

Colorblind ideology is a form of racism and the statement, "When I look at you, I don't see color" is offensive because it ignores the ways in which race profoundly affects the lives of people of color. Within America, colorblindness creates a society that denies the negative racial, ethnic, or cultural experiences of people of color, rejects their cultural heritage, and invalidates their unique perspectives (Williams, 2011; Grothaus et al., 2013).

Acton (2001) addresses colorblindness in the art therapy profession and cautions that problems occur when art therapists enter a therapeutic relationship with the perspective that all people should be treated equally without the acknowledgment of race, ethnicity, or culture. Acton (2001) maintains that in ignoring important information, the "color blind" art therapist is not able to have a true understanding of their clients. "Instead of closing our eyes to the ethnic and cultural diversity of our clients, we can look to those differences to inform and guide the creation of effective treatment models" (Acton, 2001, p. 112).

Privilege

The unearned special rights, immunities, and societal advantages that are granted on the basis of membership in a dominant social identity group are referred to as **privilege** (American Psychological Association, 2017). Privilege is often invisible to those who possess it and generally goes unexamined. In a sense, privilege is the opposite of oppression. While dominant group members who are enjoying the benefits of a privileged status may not recognize the advantages, members of nondominant groups are acutely aware of their nonprivileged condition (Grothaus et al., 2013).

Advocacy for social equality and equity in America

Advocacy is a process that focuses on injustices and environmental conditions that warrant change for the welfare of clients and communities. Advocacy plays a vital role in the well-being of clients and communities because it includes outreach, empowerment, social justice, and social action. Initiating behaviors toward people in need for the purpose of making a helpful difference is referred to as **outreach**. Efforts that identify barriers while simultaneously developing advocacy skills and resources to help overcome these barriers are referred to as **empowerment**. Active engagement and action in working toward equal access and opportunity for all people and fighting injustice in all its forms is referred to as **social justice.** Behaviors designed to promote social justice are referred to as **social action** (Gladding & Newsome, 2018; Sue & Sue, 2016).

The civil rights era of the 1960s and 1970s in America was a struggle for social justice, which placed a focus on issues of oppression, privilege, and social inequalities. This era ushered in a period of activism for equality and equal rights. The legacies of the Civil Rights Movement, Women's Rights Movement, and the Gay Rights Movement all point to the importance of understanding the lived experiences of marginalized groups, who have been relegated to unimportant and powerless positions within American society. These three movements stirred up passions and pointed out particular needs within U.S. society that warranted advocacy.

The Civil Rights Movement

The **Civil Rights Movement** was a struggle for social justice that took place during the 1950s and 1960s for African Americans to gain equal rights under the law in the United States (History.Com Editors, 2020a, 2020d). Following the Civil War, African American citizens continued to endure the devastating effects of racism, especially in the South under **Jim Crow Laws,** which were a collection of state and local statutes that legalized racial segregation. These laws, which remained on the books in the South until 1968, were formulated to marginalize African Americans by denying them the right to vote, hold jobs, and get an education (History.Com Editors, 2020c). The Civil Rights Movement advocated social action. It was a time of great personal courage and forward movement, which included Sit-in movements in 1960, Freedom Rides in 1961, Integration of Ole Miss in 1962, "I Have a Dream" speech in 1963, Civil Rights Act of 1964, Freedom Summer in 1964, and the Selma to Montgomery March in 1965.

Junge (2010) maintains that the Civil Rights Movement was an important influence on the development of art therapy as a separate profession. Junge (2010) asserts:

The brave struggles and lessons of the Civil Rights Movement are many. Its meaning to the development of art therapy is that it may well have been used as a model for change and growth. The clear message of the Civil Rights Movement was that those who were concerned needed to become activists…It began to be widely recognized that if art therapy was to become a separate and respected mental health profession, it needed to be accomplished by art therapists themselves (p. 101).

Art therapy pathfinder Clifford "Cliff" Joseph (1927–2020) was standing at the foot of the Lincoln Memorial when Dr. Martin Luther King, Jr. delivered his "I Have a Dream" speech on August 28, 1963. "I was so moved…I decided I would get out of commercial art. If I hadn't had the inspiration that I got through the civil rights movement, I might have remained there, but this awakened me" (O'Donnell, 2020). As an activist, Joseph worked primarily in communities of racial and economic oppression and on behalf of individuals whose voices were marginalized.

The Women's Rights Movement

The **Women's Rights Movement** marks July 13, 1848 as its beginning. There were two waves of the Women's Rights Movement in America. The first wave of activism in the 19th and early 20th centuries focused on women's legal rights, especially women's suffrage, or the right to vote. The second wave of activism during the 1960s and 1970s was a diverse social movement that sought equal rights and opportunities and greater personal freedom for women. Feminism grew out of the second wave (Eisenberg & Ruthsdotter, 1998).

Friedan (1963) published a landmark book *The Feminine Mystique* which inspired women to look for fulfillment beyond the role of homemaker. In 1966 the National Organization for Women (NOW) was organized to address the needs of specific groups of women. As issues emerged, groups of women within communities worked on grassroots projects such as battered women's shelters, rape crisis hotlines for victims of sexual abuse and domestic violence, child care centers so women could work outside their homes for pay, and women's clinics to provide birth control and family planning counseling (Eisenberg & Ruthsdotter, 1998).

Junge highlights that the Women's Movement was another important influence on the development of art therapy as a separate profession. The American Art Therapy Association (AATA), which is the governing body for the profession in the United States, was formed on June 27, 1969 in Louisville, Kentucky. Art therapy pathfinder Myra Levick (1924–2020), who has been described as "a feminist before there was feminism," became the driving force and energy that helped create the American Art Therapy Association and was elected the first President. Junge (2010) contends:

Through forming the American Art Therapy Association (AATA), the field of art therapy would begin to proclaim itself a special and significant field with well-trained practitioners whose skills and expertise are distinctive from other mental health disciplines and which could add immeasurable to them (p. 101).

The Gay Rights Movement

The term **homosexual** has been used historically to describe an individual who is emotionally, physically, mentally, and/or spiritually oriented to bond and share affection with those of the "same" sex (ALGBTIC LGBQQIA Competencies Taskforce et al., 2013). In 1966 three men who were dedicated to fighting for gay rights set out to disrupt the political and social climate of New York City by demonstrating that bars in the city discriminated against homosexuals.

The practice of refusing service to homosexuals in bars was common at the time. Intimate encounters between two men were deemed disorderly, so gay men were often refused service at bars. Bars that served homosexuals ran the risk of having their liquor license revoked and were often the targets of police raids. Using the model of the "Sit-ins" of the Civil Rights Movement, the men staged a "Sip-in." As a result, gay patrons were allowed freedom that they had not experienced before, which was empowering for the gay community. The landmark 1969 Stonewall Riots may not have happened if the gay community had not reaped the benefits of the "Sip-in" (Morgan, 2019).

The Stonewall Riots began on June 28, 1969, when New York City police raided the Stonewall Inn, a gay club located in Greenwich Village. The raid sparked a riot among bar patrons and neighborhood residents which led to 6 days of protests and violent clashes with law enforcement outside of the bar. Although the Stonewall Riots did not start the gay rights movement, it served as a catalyst and became a galvanizing force for LGBTQ political activism, leading to gay rights organizations such as the Gay Liberation Front, Human Rights Campaign, GLAAD, and PFLAG. The gay rights movement in the United States has seen tremendous progress. However, it continues to be a long road for gay rights proponents, who advocate for employment, housing, and transgender rights (History.Com Editors, 2020b, 2021a, 2021b).

Cultural pluralism in America

A state of society in which members of diverse ethnic, racial, religious, or social groups maintain and develop their traditional culture or special interest within the confines of a common civilization is referred to as **pluralism** (Merriam-Webster, n.d.-e). The theory and mechanics of pluralism are applied not only in government but also in the areas of culture and religion. In government, pluralism anticipates that people with different interests, beliefs, and lifestyles will coexist peacefully and be allowed to participate in the governing process.

Cultural **pluralism** describes a condition in which minority groups participate fully in all areas of the dominant society, while maintaining their unique cultural identities (Longley, 2019).

Art therapists' knowledge of and sensitivity to cultural pluralism are important characteristics of professional behavior and practice. By contrast, art therapists who define reality according to one set of cultural assumptions show insensitivity to cultural variations among individuals, and are trapped in one way of thinking that resists adaptation and rejects alternatives exhibit **cultural encapsulation** (Corey et al., 2015).

Diversity is a fundamental quality of humanness. It is associated with concepts of difference, tolerance, and multicultural engagement. Moon (2015) asserts that art therapists and their clients bring beliefs, attitudes, biases, mores, experiences, and values to the therapeutic situation. Multiple views and voices exist, and cultural differences are real and influence all human interactions. Diversity and complexity are the new realities in America. Addressing these new realities requires seeking new and diverse sources of information. Understanding the cultural context is essential for effective practice.

Culturally responsive art therapy practice in America

A "lens" is a metaphor that communicates the idea of looking at an event, experience, and data through a particular perspective. The extension of this metaphor is that art therapists can look at what is occurring and construct an interpretation and a subsequent action based on the "lens" being employed at any given time. Cultural identity, cultural identity development, and intersectionality are sources of information for understanding the cultural context. Each represents a "lens" that art therapists can intentionally employ to sharpen their focus on the ways in which individuals see themselves in their world and how they understand and experience their world.

Cultural identity in the United States

The individual differences in characteristic patterns of thinking, feeling, and behaving are referred to as **personality** (American Psychological Association, 2021). It is important to understand that human personality is a manifestation of one's identity and that identity develops within a cultural context. An individual's sense of belonging to a specific group and the part of one's personality that is attributable to membership in that group are referred to as **cultural identity**. As a construct, cultural identity forms the core personality dimensions that characterize distinct cultural realities and worldviews for an individual (Lee & Ali, 2019).

Cultural identity is not only due to cultural differences but also a result of how differences are perceived in American society (Sue et al., 2019). Throughout American history, cultural identity differences have sparked tensions. Cultural identity clashes have and continue to occur over race, ethnicity, gender, age, SES status/class, religion, sexual orientation, language, and mental/physical ability. By not accepting cultural identities, individuals create limited worldviews and perceptions of others (Serai, 2018).

Cultural identity acts as a lens and a frame of reference for making the meaning of the world and current events (Serai, 2018). Art therapists can utilize critical thinking in working toward understanding cultural identity. This involves thinking about sources of information and asking questions. Critical thinking also expands art therapists' perceptions, beliefs, and attitudes.

Cultural identity development in the United States

Individuals' understanding of themselves as racial beings and how it impacts their perception of the world in relationships with others are referred to as a **racial awakening** (Sue & Sue, 2016). A racial awakening has strong implications for cultural identity development. Cultural identity development models are utilized to describe how people come to understand their cultural identities. The models highlight the importance of cultural identity in understanding clients' lived experiences and suggest that individuals at different stages of development may exhibit very different needs and values and may feel differently about what is therapeutic in a helping situation (Diller, 2015). Three foundational models provide insight into cultural identity development: Racial/Cultural Identity in People of Color, White Racial Identity, and Sexual Identity.

Racial, ethnic, cultural identity development in people of color

People of color have been socially marginalized into an "otherness" status based upon race, including societal pressure to fit into specific racial categories. The Racial/Cultural Identity Development (R/CID) model describes five levels of development: conformity, dissonance, resistance and immersion, introspection, and integrative awareness. Sue et al. (2019) provide an overview of the characteristics of individuals in the development of racial, ethnic, cultural (REC) identity:

1. **Conformity status**: People of color have an unequivocal preference for dominant-held cultural values.
2. **Dissonance status**: People of color become more aware of inconsistencies between dominant-held views and those of their own group, resulting in a sense of dissonance. This occurs when individuals encounter information or experiences that are inconsistent with their culturally held beliefs, attitudes, and values. An encounter leads to questioning and challenging previous attitudes and beliefs and causes individuals to begin to reinterpret their world, resulting in a shift in worldviews.
3. **Resistance and immersion status**: People of color endorse minority-held views completely and completely reject the dominant-held values of society. Anger is directed outwardly toward oppression and racism.

4. **Introspection status**: For people of color, two factors work in unison: self-reflection and rethinking of rigidly held racial beliefs and their relationship to whiteness. There is a need for a positive self-definition and many group views may now be seen as conflicting with individual views.
5. **Integrative awareness status**: People of color develop an inner sense of racial security and can own and appreciate unique aspects of their culture as well as those of U.S. culture. With an integrative awareness status, the person has a strong commitment and desire to eliminate all forms of oppression (pp. 239–249).

Even after a person of color has completed all five stages in the R/CID model, life circumstances, such as new encounters with racism, may cause the individual to recycle through the stages. For art therapists who work with culturally diverse populations, the R/CID framework is a useful exploratory tool. It can alert art therapists working with clients of color to certain likely challenges associated with each status of Racial, Ethnic, Cultural (REC) consciousness and may provide suggestions of what may be the most culturally responsive therapeutic interventions.

White racial identity development

In American society, White people have been viewed as **monolithic**, or consisting of a massive undifferentiated and often rigid group; as having been in America for a long time; as the dominant group in America; and as privileged (Richmond & Guidon, 2013). However, Europeans who immigrated to the United States were not a homogeneous group. They came to America from different countries at different times and for different reasons. Therefore art therapists who work with White clients must understand not only their clients' unique cultural worldviews but also how they develop a White racial identity. In other words, "What does it mean to be White in America?"

According to Sue et al. (2019), one of the greatest barriers to racial understanding for White Americans is the invisibility of their Whiteness and/or its impact on their lives. "Many Whites appear oblivious to the meaning of their *Whiteness*, how it intrudes and disadvantages people of color, and how it affects the way they perceive the world" (Sue et al., 2019, p. 257). Sue et al. (2019) contend that **Whiteness** is associated with privilege. However, privilege is not equally distributed among all White Americans. With respect to identity, privilege is contextual, which means that a privileged identity in one cultural context may not be privileged in another.

The Process of White Racial Identity Development: A Descriptive Model identifies a seven-phase process of development: naiveté, conformity, dissonance, resistance and immersion, introspective, integrative awareness, and commitment to antiracist action. Sue et al. (2019) provide an overview of the characteristics of individuals in the development of White racial identity:

1. **Naiveté phase:** White people are relatively neutral with respect to racial/cultural differences.
2. **Conformity phase**: White peoples' attitudes and beliefs are very ethnocentric. The White culture is viewed as highly developed, and all others are primitive or inferior.
3. **Dissonance phase**: Movement into this phase occurs when the White person is forced to deal with inconsistencies that have been compartmentalized or encounters information/experiences at odds with denial. Individuals are forced to acknowledge *Whiteness* at some level and examine their own cultural values.
4. **Resistance and immersion phase:** White people begin to question and challenge their own racism and that of others in society. Racism is seen everywhere (e.g., advertising, television, educational materials, interpersonal interactions).
5. **Introspective phase:** This phase is a state of relative quiescence, introspection, and reformulation of what it means to be White. The process may involve addressing the questions: "What does it mean to be White?" "Who am I in relation to my whiteness?" "Who am I as a racial/cultural being?"
6. **Integrative awareness phase:** This phase is characterized by an understanding of self as a racial/cultural being. It involves being aware of sociopolitical influences regarding racism, appreciating racial/cultural diversity, and becoming more committed toward eradicating oppression.
7. **Commitment to antiracist action phase:** This phase is characterized by social action. Objecting to racist jokes; trying to educate family, friends, and coworkers about racial issues; and taking action to eradicate racism in school and the workplace and in social policy are examples of actions taken by individuals (pp. 254–267).

An identity in which White people recognize their own racial biases and make an internal commitment to eradicate racism is referred to as a **nonracist White identity.** White supremacy must be seen through a larger lens of individual, institutional, and societal racism. Tatum (2007; as cited in Sue et al., 2019) uses the term *White ally* to describe a White person who understands that it is possible to use one's privilege to create more equitable systems.

Kaiser (2017) asserts that whiteness in art therapy has led to deeply embedded systems of structural racism and oppression that perpetuate the silencing of marginalized voices. White art therapists comprise the majority of the American Art Therapy Association (AATA) membership and white art therapists dominate the scholarly texts on art therapy history and theory used in higher education curricula. According to Carr (2016; as cited in Kaiser, 2017), this is problematic:

Since Whiteness is extensive, often elusive, well protected, nebulous, and extremely difficult to unravel and identify, it is essential that discussions, deliberations, and action plans be conceptualized and implemented to address, at myriad levels, White power, and privilege in and through education (p. 154).

Toxic whiteness refers to the confluence of harmful psychological effects of living and being socialized in a white supremacist society. Hamrick and Byma (2017) maintain that one way that toxic whiteness can manifest itself is through **white fragility**, defined as a psychological intolerance and lack of emotional stamina for critical conversations about race. Hamrick and Byma (2017) expound:

This intolerance is due to the fact that white supremacist culture shields white people from race-based stress. Shame, blame, anger, fear, and guilt are emotions that often emerge for people from dominant cultures when confronted with discussions about their privilege and complicity in oppressive systems. These emotions can lead to stress responses including resistance, defensiveness, and aggression, any one of which can result in markedly antisocial behavior (p. 107).

Hamrick and Byma (2017) argue that dominant whiteness in art therapy negatively affects white art therapists by "limiting their social skills, self-awareness, and ability to engage in productive dialogue about race and other structures of oppression with clients and peers" (p. 107). Hamrick and Byma (2017) provide recommendations for white art therapists to critically engage and collectively participate in dismantling white supremacy in the field of art therapy:

Listen closely to the testimony of people of color describing their experiences of racism and racial violence… Notice with honesty… emotional responses to discussions about whiteness, race, and privilege…Become acquainted with the truth that [art therapists] have perpetuated violence in their lifetimes…Violence occurs in many forms, including psychological (e.g., microaggressions) (p. 108).

Sexual identity development

Sexual identity is conceptualized as how individuals consider themselves in terms of their sexual orientation, which is the degree to which a person feels sexual and emotional attraction, and as having a gendered directionality of attraction. An individual who is emotionally, physically, mentally, and/or spiritually oriented to bond and share affection with those of the "opposite" sex is referred to as **heterosexual.** By contrast, the term homosexual was historically used to describe an individual who is emotionally, physically, mentally, and/or spirituality oriented to bond and share affection with those of the "same" sex (ALGBTIC LGBQQIA Competencies Taskforce et al., 2013).

In 1979 Cass published, *Homosexual Identity Formation: A Theoretical Model*, which presents a six-stage model based upon individuals' perceptions of their own behavior and actions within the viewpoint of American society. Cass (1979) maintains that the model of homosexual identity formation describes the process by which a person comes "first to consider and later to acquire the identity of 'homosexual' as a relevant aspect of self" (p. 219). According to Cass (1979), identity is attained through a developmental process and interactions that occur between individuals and the environment.

A prestate is included within this model, which is characterized by an assumption of one's sexual orientation as part of the heterosexual group. In this prestate, heterosexuality is viewed as a norm or dominant status and homosexuality is viewed as a nondominant status (Kenneady & Oswalt, 2014). The six stages of Cass's homosexual identity formation model include identity confusion, identity comparison, identity tolerance, identity acceptance, identity pride, and identity synthesis. Kenneady and Oswalt (2014) provide an overview of the characteristics of individuals in the Cass (1979) model:

1. **Stage 1: Identity confusion**: Individuals recognize a difference in their own behavior from the dominant heterosexual norm and question that behavior as being that of a lesbian or gay male. There is a disconnect between previously considering oneself as a heterosexual and the current perception of oneself.
2. **Stage 2**: **Identity comparison**: There is vacillation between acceptance of a possible homosexual identity ("I may be a gay male or lesbian") and complete denial, often concluding with acknowledging that one's identity as a gay male or lesbian is probably true to self. One is faced with feelings of alienation as distinctions between self and heterosexuals become more clear.
3. **Stage 3: Identity tolerance:** There is a movement toward the acknowledgment of a gay male or lesbian identity with the sexual identity not being fully accepted. The individual can fall into three groups of people: those who find this desirable; those who consider it undesirable; and those who feel partly positive about themselves by accepting the "probably" statement. As individuals begin to make more friends or contact with other gay males or lesbians, they increase self-esteem and reduce alienation.
4. **Stage 4: Identity acceptance:** Identity is clearer, and the individual has a more positive self-image as a gay male or lesbian and develops greater security in a gay male or lesbian role. Involvement in the gay male or lesbian subculture and the network of gay male and lesbian friends increases and becomes more frequent.
5. **Stage 5: Identity pride**: Individuals exhibit feelings of pride toward their gay male or lesbian identity and are loyal toward gay male and lesbian groups, creating a sense of belonging. Individuals become consumed with gay male and lesbian culture and literature. To promote the validity and equality of gay males and lesbians, anger about society's stigmatization of gay males and lesbians leads to disclosure and purposeful confrontations with heterosexuals.
6. **Stage 6**: **Identity synthesis**: Personal and public sexual identities are synthesized into one image, and a sense of oneself as a gay male or lesbian fully develops. Anger, alienation, frustration, and pride are more controlled. The development process is complete with one now being able to combine a gay male or lesbian identity with all aspects of self. Self-disclosure has become automatic and a nonissue (pp. 231–232).

Intersectionality in the United States

The way in which individuals are shaped by and identify with a vast array of cultural, structural, sociobiological, economic, and social contexts is referred to as **intersectionality** (American Psychological Association, 2020). Intersectionality addresses the multiple dimensions of identity and social systems as they intersect with one another. From an intersectional perspective, the cultural identity dimensions of race, ethnicity, gender, age, SES status or class, religion, sexual orientation, language, and mental or physical ability are linked and an understanding of the multidimensionality of cultural identity offers a fuller understanding of personality. All of the dimensions affect an individual in both a unique and interactive fashion (Lee & Ali, 2019).

Diversity occurs not only across racially, ethically, and culturally diverse groups but also within each racial, ethnic, and cultural group. According to SAMHSA (2014), there are cross-cutting factors across and within race, ethnicity, and culture. These factors include language and communication; geographical location; worldviews, values, and traditions; family and kinship; gender roles; socioeconomic status and education; immigration and migration; acculturation and cultural identification; heritage and history; sexuality; perspectives on health, illness, and healing; and religion and spirituality.

The concept of intersectionality can provide a framework for assessing the multiple dimensions of client identity and how they interact. Within this context, Lee and Ali (2019) highlight three implications of intersectionality for culturally competent practice:

First, it is important that [practitioners] assume that clients' realities are composed of multiple identities…Second, it is essential to consider how the client makes meaning from each of the recognized identities…Third, it is important to understand the degree to which the client's multiple identities overlap and subsequently interact (p. 27).

Intersectionality is understood as the convergence and interactions of the multiple dimensions that have an effect on an individual's personality and worldview. Without this perspective, there is the risk of minimizing a client's cultural worldview by ignoring multiple aspects of identity that may be essential in understanding the individual's overall reality. Sue et al. (2019) highlight five principles to enhance the ability to work cross-culturally:

Learn from the groups you hope to understand.
Learn from healthy and strong people of the culture.
Learn from experimental reality.
Learn from constant vigilance of fears and biases.
Learn from being committed to anti-bias action (p. 274).

Cultural dimensions in clinical assessment

The integration of traditional assessment methods within a cultural competency framework is referred to as **culturally competent assessment** (Sue & Sue, 2016). Infusing cultural relevance into clinical assessments entails (a) incorporating the clients' understanding of the presenting problem or disorder; (b) exploration of trauma history (e.g., racial, ethnic, cultural, or historical); (c) the identification of strengths; and (d) an exploration of clients' multiple identities within the environmental context (Sue et al., 2019).

From a contextual viewpoint, both therapist and client are embedded within cultural systems, which means that assessment is best conceptualized as being influenced by both client and therapist variables. Therefore, in conducting culturally responsive assessments, art therapists must be alert for diagnostic errors in clinical judgment. Sue et al. (2019) highlight these common diagnostic errors during the assessment:

Confirmatory strategy. Searching for evidence or information that supports one's hypothesis and ignoring data that is inconsistent with this perspective.
Attribution error. Holding a different perspective on the problem than that of the client and using it to define problems and to propose solutions.
Judgmental heuristics. Commonly used quick-decision rules, which short-circuit the ability to engage in self-correction.
Diagnostic overshadowing. Misdiagnosing a problem by focusing on a salient characteristic that has nothing to do with the presenting problem.

Art therapists must be aware of their beliefs and values when working with clients and their specific presenting problems. Art therapists who remember that errors in judgment are possible can reduce their effect by utilizing self-corrective strategies.

ADDRESSING cultural influences

The **ADDRESSING Framework**, developed by Hays (2016), is a guide to assessment and personal data collection, which evaluates various aspects of cultural identity. As an assessment method within a culturally responsive framework, ADDRESSING is a tool for developing hypotheses and questions closer to clients' realities. By looking within and across various cultural influences, hypotheses are likely to emerge about the meaning of cultural influences as well as possible client problems and concerns (Diller, 2015).

The ADDRESSING framework encompasses nine key cultural influences that shape clients' beliefs and behaviors. The first letter of each cultural influence is used to create the ADDRESSING acronym:

Age and generational influences.
Development or other **D**isability.
Religion and spirituality.
Ethnic and racial identity.
Socioeconomic status.
Sexual orientation.
Indigenous heritage.
National origin.
Gender.

By calling attention to multiple identities and context, the ADDRESSING framework can help art therapists avoid inaccurate generalizations on the basis of characteristics such as a client's physical appearance, name, or language. Hays (2016) asserts that the more therapists recognize the complexity of human experience and identity, the more they are able to understand and build a positive therapeutic alliance.

Sexual orientation: Coming out

The term **coming out** refers to two processes: (a) a personal (coming out to oneself) process of understanding, accepting, and valuing one's affectional orientation and gender identity; and (b) an interpersonal (coming out to others) process of sharing that information with others (ALGBTIC LGBQQIA Competencies Taskforce et al., 2013). Notably, many of the emotional and physical risk factors for LGBTQ individuals are most prominent during the process of coming out. Increased risk is attributed to stress stemming from social stigma, discrimination, and the coming out process. LGBTQ youth face additional pressures in school as a result of their membership in a stigmatized minority.

Pelton-Sweet and Sherry (2008) advocate that the use of art therapy during the coming out process increases well-being in the LGBTQ population. Clients in the midst of clarifying their sexual orientation may be able to protect their physical and emotional health while learning more about, and ultimately becoming, their authentic selves through art therapy. Pelton-Sweet and Sherry (2008) highlight an art therapy assessment/intervention ideally suited for clients struggling with identity. "Inside Me, Outside Me" involves the creation of two self-portraits: one of the publicly presented self, the other of the private, internal self. For LGBTQ clients in the early phases of coming out, there may be two very different portraits. Pelton-Sweet and Sherry (2008) point out that the idea of creating self-portraits is a means for externalizing feelings and qualities of the self that are too delicate to expose verbally. The self-portraits can be utilized as a springboard for discussion and reflection.

Pelton-Sweet and Sherry (2008) highlight core competences that are required for effective care for LGBTQ populations: "knowledge of the social, cultural, and health issues facing this population, a non-judgmental attitude, and skill in counseling [LGBTQ] clients" (p. 173). Art therapists should have an understanding of sexual identity development coupled with an awareness of social stigma, discrimination, homophobia, and transphobia, and the ways in which these factors threaten the emotional and physical health of LGBTQ populations (Pelton-Sweet & Sherry, 2008).

Gender identity and sexuality

In the United States, the cultural bias that everyone follows or should follow traditional norms of heterosexuality is referred to as **heteronormative**. This bias also includes **cisgender** in which gender identity aligns with the sex and gender individuals were assigned at birth. Heteronormative bias includes the idea that both individuals have cisgender identity, where males identify with and express masculinity and females identify with and express femininity (ALGBTIC LGBQQIA Competencies Taskforce et al., 2013).

As a category of social identity, **gender identity** refers to an individual's identification as male, female, or "occasionally, some category other than male or female" (American Psychiatric Association, 2013, p. 822). The way individuals experience and express themselves sexually is referred to as **sexuality.** Millen (2019) posits that although gender identity and sexuality exist on separate continuums, there can be multiple points of intersection because, "inevitably, the two are intertwined because sexual orientation is largely defined by attraction to the same or different gender identity" (p. 201). Within a cultural approach, Millen (2019) maintains that the more gender identity and sexuality are deconstructed, "the greater the flexibility in meeting individuals where they are, and allowing freedom of expression" (p. 205).

Millen (2019) developed a self-study art therapy protocol for an LGBTQ population utilizing portraiture and mixed media. Through engagement in a series of artworks, individuals can explore their sense of self through concepts of identity, external perceptions, attraction and comfort, aesthetic preferences, and gender roles. According to Millen (2019), participants of the protocol are challenged to:

- develop a greater understanding of how they feel internally about themselves.
- consider how the perceptions of others impact the sense of self.
- explore feelings and attitudes of connection, comfort, and attraction to multiple/one/no genders.
- reflect on how experiences in culture, family of origin, and social systems.
- influence the expression of self both aesthetically and behaviorally (p. 207).

Within the self-study protocol, each session begins with a series of questions. The progression of sessions begins with concrete and historical knowledge and becomes increasingly abstract:

1. How was I perceived, and how do I remember myself as a child?
2. Development of sexual identity.
3. Development of gender identity.
4. Influential experiences.
5. Perceptions of others, social/cultural messages, and heteronormism.
6. How am I?
7. Where am I?
8. Who am I? What makes me, me?

Millen (2019) recommends that prior to utilizing the art therapy protocol with LGBTQ populations, art therapists should first complete the protocol, as a way to identify heteronormative bias. Working cross-culturally, a practitioners' own gender identity and sexuality can influence their views of self and others.

"By breaking down the barriers between masculine and feminine, social and behavioral, gender and sexuality, we can attempt to build new definitions and ideas with each individual patient" (Millen, 2019, p. 214).

Cultural dimensions in clinical practice

In 2017 the American Art Therapy Association adopted a Vision Statement that conceptualized, "The services of licensed culturally proficient art therapists are available to all individuals, families, and communities" (American Art Therapy Association, 2017a, 2017b). The practice of art therapy within a pluralistic society involves self-awareness, knowledge of culturally diverse groups, specific clinical skills, and the ability to intervene at the individual, group, institutional, and societal levels.

The ability to provide services cross-culturally in an effective manner is referred to as **cultural competence**. Art therapists commit to and demonstrate cultural competence by attaining and utilizing the following qualities: (a) **cultural sensitivity**, an awareness and appreciation of human cultural diversity; (b) **cultural knowledge**, the factual understanding of basic anthropological knowledge about cultural variation; (c) **cultural empathy**, the ability to connect emotionally with the client's cultural perspective; and (d) **cultural guidance**, the ability to assess whether and how a client's problems are related to cultural factors and experiences and suggesting therapeutic interventions that are based on cultural insight (Vasquez, 2010).

Diversity, equity, and inclusion (DE&I)

The array of differences that exists among groups of people with definable and unique cultural backgrounds is referred to as **cultural diversity** (Diller, 2015). Equity acknowledges that individuals should have fair access to society's resources and the opportunity to use their access in order to be successful. Inclusion is diversity in practice. It is the act of welcoming, supporting, respecting, and valuing diverse individuals and groups. Diversity, Equity, and Inclusion (DE&I) encompass the symbiotic relationship, philosophy, and culture of acknowledging, embracing, supporting, and accepting all racial, ethnic, and cultural groups (Dunn, 2020).

Diversity, equity, and inclusion are core values in advancing the vision of the American Art Therapy Association. In 2019 the Association adopted the following DE&I Mission Statement and Vision Statement:

- The DE&I Mission Statement affirms, "The AATA critically examines our structures, values, and actions to ensure the continuous integration of diversity, equity, and inclusion within the organization and the art therapy community" (AATA, 2019).
- The DE&I Vision Statement asserts, "The AATA demonstrates equity and belonging in all aspects of the association and in the profession of art therapy" (AATA, 2019).

Equity is viewed as the goal of diversity and inclusion. Within a disproportionate society, equity attempts to correct its imbalance by creating opportunities for marginalized individuals and groups who have historically had less access. Belonging infers that an equitable organization is in place and functioning to make all people, regardless of their differences, feel welcome. In essence, DE&I initiatives work to *transform society into a more just place* (Dunn, 2020).

Multicultural and diversity competence

Multicultural and diversity competence is conceptualized as a three-stage developmental sequence from awareness to knowledge and comprehension to skills and application. It implies a specific and measurable set of deliberate actions and results that increase the ability to communicate, interact, negotiate, and intervene on behalf of clients from diverse backgrounds and advocate for the development of policies and practices that are more responsive to all groups.

The Art Therapy Multicultural and Diversity Competencies (2015) are based on attitudes, knowledge, and skills within three domains: (a) awareness of personal values, biases, and assumptions; (b) knowledge of clients' worldviews; and (c) skills in developing and/or implementing appropriate interventions, strategies, and techniques. Within the three domains are three competency areas: (a) attitudes and beliefs, (b) knowledge, and (c) skills. The competency areas speak to a wide range of multicultural and diversity issues and contain comprehensive statements. These statements describe the behaviors and practices that support and reflect multicultural and diversity competence in art therapy.

Therapeutic alliance

The ethical practice of art therapy involves the development of a strong **therapeutic alliance**, which refers to the importance of interpersonal bonds such as collaboration, empathy, warmth, and genuineness, which are all factors known to be critical for effective cross-cultural therapy (Sue & Sue, 2016). The strength of the working relationship between the client and the therapist is referred to as the **therapeutic bond** (Sue & Sue, 2016).

The quality of the therapeutic alliance is related to treatment outcomes in which clients feel understood, safe, and encouraged to disclose information. A strong therapeutic relationship is comprised of three elements: (a) an emotional or interpersonal bond between the therapist and the client; (b) mutual agreement on appropriate goals, with an emphasis on changes valued by the client; and (c) intervention strategies or tasks that are viewed as important and relevant by both the client and the therapist (Sue et al., 2019, pp. 196–197).

Culturally responsive intervention strategies which are presented in an atmosphere of respect can strengthen the therapeutic alliance and enable clients to explore their issues within the context of a familiar cultural experience.

Ethics

Ethics focus on principles and standards that govern relationships between individuals, such as the therapeutic alliance between art therapists and clients. Art therapists are guided by core values that affirm basic **human rights**, which are universal legal rights that protect individuals and groups from behaviors that interfere with freedom and human dignity (American Psychological Association, 2017). Moon (2015) developed *Five Tenets of Ethical Multicultural Competence in Art Therapy*:

1. In order to appreciate and honor differences in clients' cultures, art therapists must be aware of and value their own cultural backgrounds.
2. Art therapists need to be aware of how their cultural and aesthetic biases influence their assumptions and values about clients' artwork and behavior.
3. Art therapists need to be sensitive to their clients' cultural backgrounds, and cognizant of culture-specific meanings associated with artistic expression, colors, forms, and symbols.
4. Art therapists must be aware that an individual client's dysfunction develops in a sociocultural context. The cultural context influences the particular nature and form of the dysfunction, as well as what constitutes normal behavior.
5. Art therapists must develop treatment plans and interventions appropriate to working with people from different cultural backgrounds (p. 230).

Cultural humility

A complementary component to cultural competence associated with an open attitudinal stance or a multiculturally open orientation to work with diverse clients is referred to as **cultural humility** (Sue & Sue, 2016). Cultural competence is characterized by a "way of doing." Cultural humility is characterized by a "way of being." The lens of cultural humility is a lens that art therapists can intentionally employ to sharpen their focus on the importance of continually engaging in self-reflection and self-critique as lifelong learners and reflective practitioners (Tervalon & Murray-Garcia, 1998).

Jackson (2020) advocates that the principles set forth in cultural humility offer art therapists a way of developing worldviews with integrity and respect for oneself and their clients. "It can bring dignity to those who have felt stripped of their sense of self as well as lending empowerment to those whose voices have been denied witnessing" (Jackson, 2020, p. 19). The ability to self-reflect is a key component of cultural humility. Art that is made by art therapists to contain, explore, and express clinical work is referred to as **response art** (Fish, 2019). Jackson (2020) points out that response art can also be used by art therapists to recognize sources of discomfort with cultural differences that may exist between themselves and clients with respect to race, ethnicity, and culture.

Responsive art making offers art therapists opportunities to apply the principles of cultural humility in work with culturally diverse clients. Transference and countertransference are terms that refer to personal reactions of clients and therapists to one another. In cross-cultural therapy, the terms take on a different meaning. Diller (2015) maintains that cultural **transference** and **countertransference** refers to "cross-cultural relationships, conflicts, and power imbalances in the real world that get stimulated between therapist and client with regard to each other" (p. 44). Therefore art therapists' awareness of their own cultural identities is viewed as essential in dealing with complex interactions related to issues of transference and countertransference across cultural identities (Fig. 3.3).

Therapeutic intervention

Culturally competent art therapists are able to design and offer art therapy interventions and experiences that take into consideration their clients' diverse art traditions, preferences for art materials, and beliefs and practices related to the creation of imagery (American Art Therapy Association, 2015). Art therapy is founded upon the therapeutic use of art media and art materials. Through integrative methods, art therapy engages the mind, body, and spirit. Kinesthetic, sensory, perceptual, affective, cognitive, and symbolic opportunities invite alternative modes of receptive and expressive communication, which can circumvent the limitations of language (American Art Therapy Association, 2017a, 2017b).

An **art therapy technique** is a "concrete implementation of theory introduced by the art therapist at the appropriate time to facilitate creative and therapeutic change" (Robbins, 1994, p. 168). Robbins (1994) points out that techniques have a *function* and a *focus*. Function addresses the question, toward what goal does the therapist aim to use the energy released through the activity? Focus indicates the specific area of development the technique

FIG. 3.3 *Cultural humility.*

intends to facilitate (Robbins, 1994). Rubin (2010) expounds, "The source of artistic technique…is for… art therapists to have digested and assimilated a theory so well that [they are] then able to respond with disciplined spontaneity" (p. 165).

As a foundational theory in art therapy, the **Expressive Therapies Continuum (ETC)** is a theoretical and practical guide that describes and represents the ways in which people interact with various art materials or experiential activities to process information and form images. Notably, the ETC advocates the use of culturally sensitive art materials. Hinz (2020) points out that maintaining multicultural competence is an ethical obligation that involves, in part, "acquiring education about art media and experiences that might be particularly therapeutic for the diverse groups with whom art therapists work" (p. 33).

Cultural differences can influence a client's comfort level with various art media and art therapists are encouraged to provide clients with culturally sensitive and meaningful materials (Hinz, 2020). The use of materials that are culturally meaningful can allow for greater emotional investment in the artistic process and more personal expression in the art product. Hinz (2020) advises that when working with diverse clients, art therapists should research which materials and processes would offer the most cultural relevance. Hinz (2020) asserts that the Expressive Therapies Continuum (ETC) model offers a theory to "recognize that numerous features of the media properties, art experience, and finished product can aid healing" (p. 37).

Global literacy

The knowledge base that every culturally competent individual should possess in today's interconnected world is referred to as **global literacy** (Lee, 2019). It is the breadth of information that extends over the major domains of human diversity. Global literacy warrants getting out of one's cultural comfort zone and experiencing cultural diversity firsthand in all aspects of life.

Kapitan (2014) regards global literacy as a necessary condition for responsible and ethical art therapy practice. Globally literate art therapists do not hesitate to explore diverse cultural perspectives before framing problems or proposing solutions to clients' concerns. They are critically aware of the cultural, historical, and theoretical assumptions from which they conduct research or practice. Kapitan (2014) affirms that most importantly, global literacy means that "we recognize how the lives and fates of people in other parts of the world—or in the next neighborhood—affect and are affected by our own" (p. 101).

Social action

Active engagement and action in working toward equal access and opportunity for all people and fighting injustice in all its forms are referred to as social justice (Sue & Sue, 2016). Lee (2013) views social justice as "promoting access and equity to ensure full participation in the life of a society" (p. 16). Equal access and opportunity, fair distribution of power and resources, and empowering individuals and groups with a right to determine their own lives are warranted to ensure the welfare of an American democratic society (Sue et al., 2019).

Behaviors designed to promote social justice are referred to as social action. Social action strives to make collective change. Individuals do not exist within a social vacuum. They cannot be separated from the cultural settings in which they live and by which they have been influenced. Kaplan (2007) believes that art therapists must take into account the culture or variety of cultures that clients come from and to which they will return. Art therapists must also "honor [clients'] backgrounds and yet assist them in dealing with aspects of society that have contributed to their suffering" (Kaplan, 2007, p. 14).

A social action model of art therapy locates the concept of advocacy at the center of practice. Advocacy is a process that focuses on injustices and environmental conditions that warrant change for the welfare of clients and communities. Advocacy enhances a client's sense of personal power and/or fosters change in the broader sociopolitical environment. An art therapist's role as advocate can range from developing and implementing interventions that empower individual clients to taking actions that influence public policy and systemic change.

Empowering individuals and diminishing societal forces that cause powerlessness among marginalized groups are viewed as ways to promote psychological health and well-being (Gladding & Newsome, 2018).

Transforming image into substance

A figure of speech in which a word or phrase literally denoting one kind of object or idea is used in place of another to suggest a likeness or analogy between them is referred to as a **metaphor** (Merriam-Webster, n.d.-d). In essence, something is like something else. Metaphors juxtapose one thing with another, exchange meaning, and open up new possibilities and understanding. They provide a powerful means for expressing ideas and feelings that might otherwise remain unspoken, unwritten, or understood.

Moon (2003) conceptualizes an **image** as the inner visualized form that emerges within an individual's imagination and, as such, the image should be regarded as a living entity. Whatever form emerges, the image should be viewed as having life. Images are not concrete; they will always be ambiguous, communicative, and subject to change. Moon (2003) uses the image of the "canvas mirror" as a metaphor for the introspective processes that are the foundation for art making. Moon (2003) refers to art therapists as "metaphoreticians," who look at, listen to, and share stories through metaphoric action. "In art therapy, metaphors can be found in both actions and objects in which (the client) is described in terms of the other (the image or artistic process)" (Moon, 2003, p. 137).

As "metaphoreticians," art therapists make a leap beyond comparison to an identification or fusion of action and object, resulting in a new entity that has characteristics of both. In essence, the image is transformed into **substance**, an ultimate reality that underlies all outward manifestations and change (Merriam-Webster, n.d.-f). In art therapy, visual metaphors hold in tension the potential for multiple interpretations, their purpose being to illuminate truths about clients' feelings, thoughts, and experiences (Moon, 2003).

Conclusions

The mirror, as a reflective surface, reveals a clear image, which affirms that self-reflection and self-transparency are cornerstones of the work of art therapists. Empathy is one way to locate and explore what is emotionally alive in visual imagery. Such attuned understanding gathers information about another's internal life; empathic responses are the successful communication of this information reflected back to self. Neuroscientist Vittorio Gallese (as cited in Jaffe, 2019) states, "It seems we're wired to see other people as similar to us, rather than different. At the root, as humans, we identify with the person we're facing as someone like ourselves" (para. 1).

The term "**mirror neuron**" was coined to describe a class of neurons that modulate their activity when an individual executes a specific motor act and when they observe the same or similar act performed by another individual (Kilner & Lemon 2013). It is not necessary to physically replicate what is observed to have this effect; the motor system engages *as if* the action has been replicated (Franklin, 2010). The concept of embodied simulation has had a profound effect on the field of social cognition.

The ability to empathize with others is reflected when individuals observe the emotional experiences of someone else and then connect with that emotion within themselves. Empathic awareness results from conscious and preconscious material filtered through an art therapist's personal inventory of the client's many cues. The progression of empathic insight and reason begins with a contemplative mindful lens, in which the art therapist's intention should be to slow down and remain present without judgment.

The effectiveness of art therapy depends on the ability of the art therapist and the client to understand and relate to each other. The process that bridges the cultural gap between the art therapist and the client is referred to as **culturally sensitive empathy**. It is viewed as the ability to "perceive the cultural frame of reference from which the client operates, and which guides the clients' perceptions" (Gladding & Newsome, 2018, p. 108).

Cultural competence is recognized as a *way of doing*. Cultural humility is comprehended as a *way of being*. Culturally sensitive empathy is distinguished as a *way of seeing*. Doing, being, and seeing encompass the symbiotic relationship that fosters diversity, equity, and inclusion (DE&I) in art therapy to ensure that all clients, no matter their differences, feel welcomed, supported, respected, and valued.

Art experientials and reflection questions

An approach that enables individuals to become aware of both internal and external experiences is referred to as **experiential learning**. Experiential learning encourages individuals to consider the contexts that influence behaviors, attitudes, and beliefs. The capacity to gain a deep intuitive understanding of concepts is referred to as **insight**. Utilizing the concept of reflective learning, the experiential activities are designed to explore the chapter content in multidimensional ways and relate them to the emergence of insight into multicultural and diversity perspectives in art therapy.

1: Self-assessment of identity privilege

Utilizing the acronym ADDRESSING, Hays (2016) identified nine categories of cultural areas for both dominant and nondominant group members in the United States. Within each ADDRESSING category, a dominant cultural identity is described. Within each category, Hays (2016) identified an area of privilege in the United States. The Self-Assessment of Identity Privilege can be utilized by art therapists to not only recognize identity privilege but also recognize the ways in which identity can affect their lives and work with diverse clients.

Instructions: Answer the question for each **ADDRESSING** category and follow the directions for the placement of a star (*).

Age and generational influences [A]: If you are between 30 and 60 years old (i.e., a young to middle-aged adult), place a star (*) on the letter A.

Developmental or other **D**isability [DD]: If you do not have a disability (i.e., if you are a member of the nondisabled majority), place a star (*) on the letters DD.

Religion and spiritual orientation [R]: If you grew up in a secular or Christian home, place a star (*) on the letter R.

Ethnic and racial identity [E]: If you are of European American heritage, place a star (*) on the letter E.

Socioeconomic status [S]: If you were brought up in a middle- or upper-class family or are currently of middle- or upper-class status, place a star (*) on the letter S.

Sexual orientation [S]: If you are heterosexual, place a star (*) on the letter S.

Indigenous heritage [I]: If you have no Indigenous heritage, place a star (*) on the letter I.

National origin [N]: If you live in the country in which you were born and grew up, place a star (*) on the letter N.

Gender identity [G]: If you are a cisgender male, place a star (*) on the letter G.

Look at the ADDRESSING self-description with attention to the stars. The starred (*) letter denotes an area of privilege for individuals in the United States. Answer the following queries:

1. In which identity categories do you hold privilege?
2. In which identity categories do you experience marginalization?
3. What did you learn from this activity?
4. How will you use what you have learned from this activity?

2: Art experiential: Exploring gender identity and sexuality through portraiture and mixed media

Utilizing the concept of responsive art making, Millen (2019) developed a self-study protocol to explore gender identity and sexuality with an LGBTQ population. A **self-portrait** is a pictorial representation of oneself created by oneself. Self-portraits can be utilized for externalizing feelings and qualities of self that may be too delicate to expose verbally.

Response art is art that is made by art therapists to contain, explore, and express clinical work. Millen (2019) recommends that art therapists seeking to repeat the protocol in their clinical work would be well served by first completing the self-study. Millen (2019) cautions that in order to do meaningful work with LGBTQ clients, it is necessary to understand how personal identity may impact the dialogue.

Materials

1. Assorted surfaces for drawing, painting, collage.
2. Assorted drawing media.
3. Assorted painting media.
4. Assorted magazine images.
5. Assorted collage material.
6. Adhesives.
7. Mediators/tools.
8. Supplies for clean-up.

Instructions: At any age, an individual's sense of gender identity and sexuality may be clearly understood or may have layers of ambiguity. Read and reflect on the series of questions that begins each session. Create a self-portrait in response to the questions. The pictorial representation of the self can be a drawing, painting, collage, or mixed media with the content portrayed as either representational or nonrepresentational/abstract.

Session 1: How was I perceived, and how do I remember myself as a child?

Consider how you may have been perceived and influenced as a child. What were the behavioral expectations? How did you prefer to express yourself in outward appearance and behaviors? Were these expressions impacted by the prescribed gender role, and how? Who did you seek out for friendship and closeness?

Session 2: Development of sexual identity

At what point did you become aware of yourself as a sexual being, or become aware of attraction to others as shown through affection and desired closeness? How has this changed over time?

Session 3: Development of gender identity

How do you identify yourself now? How have you identified in the past? How has this changed or not changed over time? What does "female-ness" or "male-ness" mean to you?

Session 4: Influential experiences

Are there any experiences that affected your sexual or gender identity/affiliation, or relationship to your body? How much do you think your environment has impacted your expression of self? If relevant, this may also include exploration of trauma.

Session 5: Perceptions of others, social/cultural messages and heteronormism

How did the perceptions of others influence, shape, alter, or confirm your inward sense of who you are, and who you are attracted to?

Session 6: How am I?

How do you act? What are the behaviors and outward expressions of who you are? If salient, you may also include how you appear/look/dress.

Session 7: Where am I?

How do you see yourself in the greater landscape of gender, sexuality, and affiliation?

Session 8: Who am I? What makes me, me?

Having explored the previous seven sets of concepts, attempt to represent or symbolize your sense of who you are from any/some/all/none of the previous dimensions. What is most important to know about you? What has changed? (Millen, 2019, pp. 208–213).

3: Assessment of multicultural and diversity competence in art therapy

Multicultural and diversity competence implies a specific and measurable set of deliberate actions and results that increase the ability to communicate, interact, negotiate, and intervene on behalf of clients from diverse backgrounds and advocate for the development of policies and practices that are more responsive to all groups.

Instructions: Within the three art therapy competency domains, check the statements that describe the behaviors and practices that support and reflect multicultural and diversity competence.

Domain: Awareness of personal values, biases, and assumptions

Art therapists believe that cultural self-awareness and sensitivity to one's own cultural heritage are essential.

Art therapists have specific knowledge about their own race, ethnicity, culture, nationality, age, acculturation, gender, gender identity/expression, religion, socioeconomic status, political views, sexual orientation, geographic region, physical capacity, physical, mental or developmental disability, and historical experiences with the dominant culture.

Art therapists are constantly seeking to understand themselves and actively seek a nonracist and nondiscriminatory identity.

Domain: Knowledge of clients' worldviews

Art therapists are aware of their negative and positive emotional reactions toward racial, ethnic, and cultural groups that may prove detrimental to the therapeutic relationship. They are willing to differentiate their own beliefs and attitudes with diverse groups of clients in a nonjudgmental fashion.

Art therapists possess specific knowledge and information about the racial, ethnic, and cultural groups with whom they are working. They are aware of the life experiences, cultural heritage, cultural identity, artistic traditions, cultural identity, artistic traditions, and historical background of their clients.

Art therapists familiarize themselves with relevant research and the latest findings regarding mental health and mental disorders that affect racial, ethnic, cultural, and other diverse groups.

Domain: Skills in developing and/or implementing appropriate interventions, strategies, and techniques

Art therapists demonstrate respect for the clients' religious and/or spiritual beliefs and values, including attributions, taboos, symbolic traditions, and preferred methods of treatment, because they affect worldview, psychological functioning, and expression of distress.

Art therapists have knowledge of culturally specific resources (i.e., interpreters/translators) and are aware of barriers (i.e., transportation) that prevent clients from various groups in accessing and utilizing mental health services.

Art therapists are able to design and offer art therapy interventions and experiences that take into consideration their clients' diverse art traditions, preferences for art materials, and beliefs and practices related to the creation of imagery.

Additional resources

Crawford, J., & Clifton, D. (Directors). (2017). *America: Promised land,* Part 1 & Part 2. [Films]. A&E Television Networks.

Peck, R. (Director). (2016). *I am not your Negro: James Baldwin and race in America* [Film]. Kino Lorber Essential Collection.

Young, J., Morris, S., Jhally, S., & Wise, T. (Filmmakers). (2013). *White like me: Race, racism & white privilege in America* [Film]. Media Education Foundation.

Yu, L. (Filmmaker). (2018). *American experience: The Chinese Exclusion Act*. Public Broadcasting System (PBS).
Skurnik, J., & Vasquez, R. (Filmmakers). (2012). *The thick dark fog: Reclaiming Native American identity* [Film]. New Day Films.
Chamberlain, M. (Filmmaker). (2017). *We breathe again: The stories of four Alaska Native Peoples* [Film]. Vision Maker Media.
Mancha, L. (Filmmaker). (2014). *Inner borderlines: Visions of America through the eyes of Alejandro Morales*. Pragda.
Prodo, A. (Filmmaker). (2008). *Children in no man's land* [Film]. Impacto Films.

Chapter terms

ADDRESSING framework
Advocacy
American Indian or Alaska Native
Art therapy technique
Asian
Baby boomers
Bisexual
Black or African American
Cigender
Civil Rights Movement
Color blind ideology
Coming out
Concentrated collective poverty
Countertransference
Cultural anthropology
Cultural competence
Cultural diversity
Cultural empathy
Cultural encapsulation
Cultural guidance
Cultural humility
Cultural identity
Cultural knowledge
Cultural norms
Cultural pluralism
Cultural sensitivity
Culturally competent assessment
Culturally sensitive empathy
Culture
Demography
Empowerment
Equality
Equality of opportunity
Equity
Ethnicity
Experiential learning
Expressive Therapies Continuum
Gay
Gay Rights Movement
Gender identity
Global literacy
Health disparities
Heteronormative
Heterosexual
Hispanic or Latino
Hispanic origin
Homosexual
Human rights
Image
Income gap
Income inequality
Insight
Intersectionality
Intersex
Ism
Jim Crow Laws
Lesbian
Marginalization
Meritocracy
Metaphor
Microaggressions
Microassault

Microinsult
Microinvalidation
Millennials
Mirror neuron
Monolithic
Myth of meritocracy
Native Hawaiian or Other Pacific Islander
Nonracist White identity
Oppression
Outreach
Personality
Pluralism
Poverty
Privilege
Queer
Race
Racial awakening
Racial wealth gap
Response art
Self-portrait
Sexual orientation
Sexuality
Social action
Social justice
Socioeconomic status (SES)
Stressor
Structural racism
Substance
Systemic oppression
Therapeutic alliance
Therapeutic bond
Toxic whiteness
Transference
Transgender
Wealth inequality
Well-being
White
White fragility
Whiteness
Women's Rights Movement
Worldviews

References

Acton, D. (2001). The "color blind" therapist. *Art Therapy: Journal of the American Art Therapy Association*, *18*(2), 109–112. https://doi.org/10.1080/07421656.2001.10129749.

ALGBTIC LGBQQIA Competencies Taskforce, Harper, A., Finerty, P., Martinez, M., Brace, A., Crethar, H. C., et al. (2013). Association for lesbian, gay, bisexual, and transgender issues in counseling competencies for counseling with lesbian, gay, bisexual, queer, questioning, intersex, and ally individuals. *Journal of LGBT Issues in Counseling*, *7*(1), 2–43. https://doi.org/10.1080/15538605.2013.755444.

American Anthropological Association. (2021). *AAA statement on race*. http://www.americananthro.org/ConnectWithAAA/Content.aspx?ItemNumber=2583.

American Art Therapy Association. (2013). *Ethical principles for art therapists*. https://arttherapy.org/wp-content/uploads/2017/06/Ethical-Principles-for-Art-Therapists.pdf.

American Art Therapy Association. (2015). *Art therapy multicultural and diversity competencies*. https://www.arttherapy.org/upload/Multicultural/Multicultural.Diversity%20Competencies.%20Revisions%202015.pdf.

American Art Therapy Association. (2017a). *About art therapy*. http://arttherapy.org/aata-aboutus/.

American Art Therapy Association. (2017b). *Our mission*. http://arttherapy.org/aata-aboutus/.

American Art Therapy Association. (2019, September 5). *AATA board of directors approves diversity, equity, and inclusion (DE&I) mission and vision statements*. https://arttherapy.org/news-dei-mission-and-vision-statements/.

American Psychiatric Association. (2013). *Diagnostic and statistical manual of mental disorders* (5th ed.).

American Psychological Association. (2017). *Multicultural guidelines: An ecological approach to context, identity, and intersectionality*. http://www.apa.org/about/policy/multicultural-guidelines.pdf.

American Psychological Association. (2020). *Publication manual of the American Psychological Association* (7th ed.).

American Psychological Association. (2021). *Personality*. https://www.apa.org/topics/personality/.

Cambridge Dictionary. (2021). Structural racism. In *Dictionary* Cambridge.org. https://dictionary.cambridge.org/dictionary/english/structural-racism.

Capodilupo, C. M. (2019). Microaggressions in counseling and psychotherapy. In D. W. Sue, D. Sue, H. A. Neville, & L. Smith (Eds.), *Counseling the culturally diverse: Theory and practice* (8th ed., pp. 119–141). John Wiley & Sons, Inc.

Caraballo, J. E. (2019, December 26). *Understanding the minority stress model*. Talkspace. https://www.talkspace.com/blog/minority-stress-model/.

Cass, V. V. (1979). Homosexual identity formation: A theoretical model. *Journal of Homosexuality*, *4*(3), 219–235.

Chen, J. (2020, September 4). *Poverty*. Investopedia. https://www.investopedia.com/terms/p/poverty.asp#:~:tex.

Corey, G., Corey, M. S., Corey, C., & Callanan, P. (2015). *Issues and ethics in the helping profession* (9th ed.). Cengage Learning.

Diller, J. V. (2015). *Cultural diversity: A primer for the human services* (5th ed.). Cengage Learning.

Dunn, L. (2020, November 6). *What is diversity, equity & inclusion (DEI)?* InclusionHub. https://www.inclusionhub.com/articles/what-is-dei.

Editors of Encyclopedia Britannica. (2020, December 31). Poverty. In *Encyclopedia Britannica*. https://www.britannica.com/topic/poverty.

Editors of Encyclopedia Britannica. (2021, March 21). United States. In *Encyclopedia Britannica*. https://www.britannica.com/place/United-States.

Eisenberg, B., & Ruthsdotter, M. (1998). *History of the women's rights movement*. National Women's History Alliance. https://nationalwomenshistoryalliance.org/history-of-the-womens-rights-movement/.

Feen-Calligan, H. (2013). Art therapy, homelessness, and poverty. In D. E. Gussak, & M. L. Rosal (Eds.), *The Wiley handbook of art therapy* (pp. 397–407). John Wiley & Sons.

Fish, B. J. (2019). Response art in art therapy: Historical and contemporary overview. *Art Therapy: Journal of the American Art Therapy Association*, *36*(3), 122–132. https://doi.org/10.1080/07421656.2019.1648915.

Franklin, M. (2010). Affect regulation, mirror neurons, and the third hand: Formulating mindful empathic art interventions. *Art Therapy: Journal of the American Art Therapy Association*, *27*(4), 160–167. https://doi.org/10.1080/074216556.2010.10129385.

Friedan, B. (1963). *The feminine mystique*. W.W. Norton.

Gladding, S. T., & Newsome, D. W. (2018). *Clinical mental health counseling in community and agency settings* (5th ed.). Pearson Education, Inc.

Grothaus, T., McAuliffe, G., Danner, M., & Doyle, L. (2013). Equity, advocacy, and social justice. In G. McAuliffe, & Associates (Eds.), *Culturally alert counseling: A comprehensive introduction* (2nd ed., pp. 45–73). SAGE Publications, Inc.

Hamrick, C., & Byma, C. (2017). Know history, know self: Art therapists' responsibility to dismantle white supremacy. *Art Therapy: Journal of the American Art Therapy Association*, *34*(3), 106–111. https://doi.org/10.1080/0721656.2017.1353332.

Hays, P. A. (2016). *Addressing cultural complexities in practice: Assessment, diagnosis, and therapy* (3rd ed.). American Psychological Association.

Hinz, L. D. (2020). *Expressive therapies continuum: A framework for using art in therapy* (2nd ed.). Routledge.

History.Com Editors. (2020, June 23). *Civil rights movement.* https://www.history.com/topics/black-history/civil-rights-movement.

History.Com Editors. (2020, June 26). *Stonewall riots.* https://www.history.com/topics/gay-rights/the-stonewall-riots.

History.Com Editors. (2020, August 19). *Jim Crow laws.* https://www.history.com/topics/early-20th-century-us/jim-crow-laws.

History.Com Editors. (2020, February 10). *Civil Rights Act of 1964.* https://www.history.com/topics/black-history/civil-rights-act.

History.Com Editors. (2021, February 24). *Civil rights movement timeline.* https://.history.com/topics/civil-right-movement/civil-reghts-movement-timeline.

History.Com Editors. (2021, January 25). *Gay rights movement.* https://www.history.com/topics/gay-rights/history-of-gay-rights.

Jackson, L. C. (2020). *Cultural humility in art therapy: Applications for practice, research, social justice, self-care, and pedagogy.* Jessica Kingsley Publishers.

Jaffe, A. (2019, July 17). *A look in the mirror neuron: Empathy and addiction.* Psychology Today. https://www.psychologytoday.com/us/blog/all-about-addiction/201907/look-in-the-mirror-neuron-empathy-and-addiction.

Junge, M. B. (2010). *The modern history of art therapy in the United States.* Charles C Thomas Publisher, Ltd.

Kaiser, D. H. (2017). What do structural racism and oppression have to do with scholarship, research, and practice in art therapy? *Art Therapy: Journal of the American Art Therapy Association, 34*(4), 154–156. https://doi.org/10.1080/07421656.2017.1420124.

Kapitan, L. (2014). The world we share: Four challenges worthy of art therapists' attention. *Art Therapy: Journal of the American Art Therapy Association, 31*(3), 100–101. https://doi.org/10.1080/07421656.2014.937270.

Kaplan, F. F. (2007). Introduction. In F. F. Kaplan (Ed.), *Art therapy and social action* (pp. 11–17). Jessica Kingsley Publisher.

Karcher, O. P. (2017). Sociopolitical oppression, trauma, and healing: Moving toward a social justice art therapy framework. *Art Therapy: Journal of the American Art Therapy Association, 34*(3), 123–128. https://doi.org/10.1080/07421656.2017.1358024.

Kenneady, D. A., & Oswalt, S. B. (2014). Is Cass's model of homosexual identity formation relevant to today's society? *American Journal of Sexuality Education, 9*(2), 229–246. https://doi.org/10.1080/15546128.2014.900465.

Kilner, J. M., & Lemon, R. N. (2013). What we know currently about mirror neurons. *Current Biology, 23*(23), PR1057–R1062. https://www.cell.com/action/showPdf?pii=S0960-9822%2813%2901326-2.

Kopp, C. M. (2020, June 17). *Income inequality.* Investopedia. https://www.investopedia.com/terms/i/income-inequality.asp.

Lee, C. C. (2013). The cross-cultural encounter: Meeting the challenge of culturally competent counseling. In C. C. Lee (Ed.), *Multicultural issues in counseling: New approaches to diversity* (4th ed., pp. 13–19). American Counseling Association.

Lee, C. C. (2019). Multicultural competency: A conceptual framework for counseling across cultures. In C. C. Lee (Ed.), *Multicultural issues in counseling: New approaches to diversity* (5th ed., pp. 3–13). American Counseling Association.

Lee, C. C., & Ali, S. (2019). Intersectionality: Understanding the complexity of identity in counseling across cultures. In C. C. Lee (Ed.), *Multicultural issues in counseling: New approaches to diversity* (5th ed., pp. 23–30). American Counseling Association.

Longley, R. (2019, July 31). *What is pluralism? Definition and examples*. https://www.thoughtco.com/pluralism-definition-4692539.

Merriam-Webster. (n.d.-a). Demography. In *Merriam-Webster.com dictionary*. https://www.merriam-webster.com/dictionary/demography.

Merriam-Webster. (n.d.-b). Ism. In *Merriam-Webster.com dictionary*. https://www.merriam-webster.com/dictionary/ism.

Merriam-Webster. (n.d.-c). Meritocracy. In *Merriam-Webster.com dictionary*. https://www.merriam-webster.com/dictionary/meritocracy.

Merriam-Webster. (n.d.-d). Metaphor. In *Merriam-Webster.com dictionary*. https://www.merriam-webster.com/dictionary/metaphor.

Merriam-Webster. (n.d.-e). Pluralism. In *Merriam-Webster.com dictionary*. https://www.merriam-webster.com/dictionary/pluralism.

Merriam-Webster. (n.d.-f). Substance. In *Merriam-Webster.com dictionary*. https://www.merriam-webster.com/dictionary/substance.

Millen, M. (2019). Exploring gender identity and sexuality through portraiture and mixed media. In B. MacWilliam, B. T. Harris, D. G. Trottier, & K. Long (Eds.), *Creative arts therapies and the LGBTQ community: Theory and practice* (pp. 201–215). Jessica Kingsley Publishers.

Mollenkamp, D. T. (2021, February 24). *Race and income inequality*. Investopedia. https://www.investopedia.com/the-racial-wealth-gap-5105010.

Moon, B. L. (2003). *Essentials of art therapy education and practice* (2nd ed.). Charles C Thomas Publisher, Ltd.

Moon, B. L. (2015). *Ethical issues in art therapy* (3rd ed.). Charles C Thomas Publisher, Ltd.

Morgan, T. (2019, June 12). *The gay 'sip-in' that drew from the civil rights movement to fight discrimination*. History.com. https://www.history.com/gay-rights-sip-in-juslius-bar.

National Equity Project. (n.d.). *Lens of systemic oppression*. https://www.nationalequityproject.org/frameworks/lens-of-systemic-oppression.

Newport, F. (2018, May 22). *U.S., estimate of LGBT population rises to 4.5%*. Gallup. https://news.gallup.com/poll/234863/estimate-lgbt-population-rises.aspx.

O'Donnell, M. (2020, December 11). *Cliff Joseph, Chicago artist, art therapist who corresponded with MLK, dead at 98*. Chicago Sun-Times. https://chicago.suntimes.com/2020/12/11/22168899/cliff-joseph-artist-mlk-martin-luther-king-nelson-mandela-obituary.

Pelton-Sweet, L. M., & Sherry, A. (2008). Coming out through art: A review of art therapy with LGBT clients. *Art Therapy: Journal of the American Art Therapy Association*, *25*(4), 170–176. https://doi.org/10.1080/07421656.2008.10129546.

Richmond, L. J., & Guidon, M. H. (2013). Culturally alert counseling with European Americans. In G. McAuliffe, & Associates (Eds.), *Culturally alert counseling: A comprehensive introduction* (2nd ed., pp. 231–262).

Robbins, A. (1994). *A multi-modal approach to creative art therapy*. Jessica Kingsley Publisher.

Rubin, J. A. (2010). *Introduction to art therapy: Sources & resources*. Routledge.

Serai, Y. (2018). *What is cultural identity?* https://classroom.synonym.com//what-is-culture-identity-12082328.html.

Statue of Liberty. (2021, February 26). *Wikipedia*. https://en.wikipedia.org/wiki/Statue_of_Liberty.

Substance Abuse and Mental Health Services Administration. (2014). Improving cultural competence. *Treatment Improvement Protocol (TIP) Series No. 59*. Health and Human Services (HHS). https://store.samhsa.gov/sites/default/files/d7/priv/sma14-4849.pdf.

Sue, D. W., & Sue, D. (2016). *Counseling the culturally diverse: Theory and practice* (7th ed.). John Wiley & Sons, Inc.

Sue, D. W., Sue, D., Neville, H. A., & Smith, L. (2019). *Counseling the culturally diverse: Theory and practice* (8th ed.). John Wiley & Sons, Inc.

Tervalon, M., & Murray-Garcia, J. (1998). Cultural humility versus cultural competence: A critical distinction in defining physician training outcomes in multicultural education. *Journal of Health Care for the Poor and Underserved*, *9*(2), 117–125.

U.S. Census Bureau. (2019, October 25). *About*. https://www.census.gov/about/what/census-at-a-glance.html.

U.S. Census Bureau. (2020, October 16). *About race*. https://www.census.gov/topics/population/race/about.html.

U.S. Census Bureau. (2020, October 16). *About Hispanic origin*. https://www.census.gov/topics/population/hispanic-origin/about.html.

U.S. Census Bureau. (n.d.). *Income and poverty*. https://www.census.gov/topics/income-poverty.html.

Vasquez, M. J. (2010). Ethics in multicultural counseling practice. In J. Ponterotto, J. Casas, L. Suzuki, & C. Alexander (Eds.), *Handbook of multicultural counseling* (3rd ed., pp. 127–145). SAGE Publication, Inc.

Vespa, J., Medina, L., & Armstrong, D. M. (2020, February). *Demographic turning points for The United States: Population Projections for 2020 to 2060*. U.S. Census Bureau. https://www.census.gov/content/dam/Census/library/publications/2020/demo/p25-1144.pdf.

Williams, M. T. (2011, December 27). *Colorblind ideology is a form of racism*. Psychology Today. https://www.psychologytoday.com/us/blog/culturally-speaking/201112/colorblind-ideology-is-form-racism#:#:~:text=Colorblindness%20is%20the%20racial%20ideology%20that%20posits%.

Chapter 4

Intersections of neuroscience and art therapy

Meera Rastogi, PhD, ATR-BC[a], Christianne Strang, PhD, ATR-BC[b], Ilya Vilinsky, PhD[c], and Kristopher Holland, PhD[d]

[a]*Department of Social Sciences, University of Cincinnati, Clermont College, Batavia, OH, United States,* [b]*Department of Psychology, University of Alabama at Birmingham, Birmingham, AL, United States,* [c]*Neuroscience, Department of Biological Sciences, University of Cincinnati, Cincinnati, OH, United States,* [d]*Art Education, School of Art, University of Cincinnati, Cincinnati, OH, United States*

Voices from the field

Bridging the gap between art therapy and neuroscience potentially can resolve questions regarding the appropriate role of scientific evidence in art practice as well as engagement in art practice for scientific research. Ultimately, such positive changes can potentially propel art therapy from the outskirts of the mental health field to the front line of care, where it rightfully belongs...

Guseva (2019, p. 48)

Learning outcomes

After reading this chapter, you will be able to

1. Describe the evolution of how humans came to make art.
2. Define and describe the basic physiology of the nervous system and its major divisions.
3. Define and describe how neurons communicate with one another.
4. Identify how neural plasticity is connected to the practice of Art Therapy Relational Neuroscience.
5. Identify key brain networks that may be at work when engaging in creative acts.
6. Describe and illustrate how our brain processes visual information.
7. Explain studies that examine the effects of art-making on sight and the brain.
8. Identify key parts of the eye.
9. Develop an understanding of empirical research that connects the neurobiological basis of perception and behavior to the theory and practice of art therapy.

Chapter overview

This chapter identifies specific ways that the field of art therapy can benefit from neuroscience. We begin by learning how and why humans began making art.

Foundations of Art Therapy. https://doi.org/10.1016/B978-0-12-824308-4.00014-4

To enhance the connections between these two fields, we learn about the basics of the nervous system, the neuron, and the brain. Next, we explore the process in which visual information is received by our eye, interpreted by the brain, and integrated with other sensory, emotional, and memory systems to form the basis of our behaviors and actions. Our approach demonstrates the power of transdisciplinary knowledge and provides a multilayered approach that explores why humans make art and why art-making is central in art therapy.

How did humans start to make art?

Art-making predates farming, writing, and many other technologies, and therefore making art is a vital part of the human story (Rutherford, 2019). Let's begin with our ancestors (called **hominins**) who developed behaviors for tool and art-making through simple interaction with the world around them. Hominins refers to the group of animals that includes modern humans, extinct human-like species (like **Neanderthals**), and any immediate ancestors to us (Rutherford, 2019). What is important to understand is that all of these nonhomosapien animals developed multiple ways to change the surroundings to make the environment work better for them (called **niche construction;** Fuentes, 2017).

One of the ways hominins crafted their environment was through the use of stone tools. They improved the quality of these stone tools through a technique called knapping. **Knapping** is a process where one stone serves as a hammer instrument to shape the other stone (Mateos et al., 2019). While "Most archeologists would agree that the first intentionally modified stone tools appear in the archeological record of Africa at least 2.6 million years ago, before any fossil evidence of significant hominin brain expansion... [the] Stone tools have given hominins a window into a whole new set of skills and ways of thinking that allow for great variation and flexibility" (Malafouris, 2013, p. 169).

We also know **Neanderthals** developed stone and other forms of tool making, musical instruments, cave drawings, and paintings before our species appeared in the archeological record (Rutherford, 2019). Neanderthals, now extinct, are part of the hominin lineage on the tree of life, like we are (Sykes, 2020). Increasingly more and more evidence is being found as to these hominims' amazing role in the birth of art-making, as Sykes (2020) stated: "The weight of evidence from more and more cases or pigment use and mark making is increasingly leading even skeptics to accept that Neanderthals had an aesthetic, symbolic element to their lives" (p. 255). Sykes suggested the first great art projects were an installation in a cave at Bruniquel France 174,000 years ago which she described as "monumental in scale and vision" (Sykes, 2020, p. 264).

Stone tool usage expanded in material and among different groups. Groups began to utilize wood, animal parts, mud, and other materials to further transform the places they inhabited. The influence of hominin interactions with each other appears to have had an impact on each other's evolution in material and psychological ways. Each species learned from seeing others make and do things, and borrowing imaginative uses for the material world from many other species of hominins.

Homo sapiens, our species, built on our ancestor's tool- and art-making innovations to construct new environments that played to our strengths of cooperation and social organization to survive. We not only took things and moved them into better places, but we also took things from the environment and reshaped them, smashed them, cooked them, marked them, shattered them, flaked them, and connected them. In doing this, we also changed our brains.

This is the story of smashing rocks, yes, but not just that. It is also the story of how we imagined rocks as something else. How we use our imaginations, which in turn shaped our brain's physicality, to be able to shape the material world into evermore combinations and aesthetic choices to make our lives different. We cannot know exactly how our hominin ancestors thought of those rocks three million years ago, but we can thank them for beginning the processes that led us to the use of art-making as a form of survival, way of life, and a catalyst for how our brain has evolved over time.

Introduction to neuroscience

Neuroscience is the study of the brain and the nervous system at the physiological (biochemical, cellular, network) level to understand the foundations of behavior and cognition/thinking (Purves et al., 2018). What on earth does neuroscience have to do with art therapy? What does the brain have to do with making art? Can art-making change our brain? How can this information be useful for art therapists?

You might be surprised to find out that neuroscience has been integrated into the field of art therapy since as early as 2008 (Hass-Cohen & Carr, 2008). There are several reasons why art therapists believe that understanding the brain can improve the knowledge and practice of art therapy. First, art therapists value the connection between BOTH the mind and the body versus traditional treatments that only target the mind OR the body (Kaplan, 2008). Second, basic knowledge in neuroscience can help art therapists to "recognize neurotypical functioning and better understand clients' psychological symptoms" (Hinz, 2019, p. 225). Third, neuroscience research can help art therapists understand how art-making and creativity affect, and change, the brain (Hass-Cohen, 2008a; Hinz, 2019) and explain how art therapy works (Lusebrink & Hinz, 2020). Therefore "Creative Arts Therapists and neuroscientists need to evolve [an] existing common language that will allow for communication and connection across disciplines and cultural barriers…to provide insight into the links between cognitive, affective, and symbolic expression and brain function" (King, 2018, p. 2). This chapter seeks to do just that: to provide you with basic language and information about the brain, nervous system, and eye in order to facilitate stronger conversations between the fields of art therapy and neuroscience. It is our hope that this information will inspire some of you to become the future generation of art therapy neuroscientists that can provide explanations of how art therapy works.

The nervous system

How do animals make their way in the world? Animals actively move through the environment, reacting to stimuli positively or negatively by moving toward desired goals and away from threats. An animal must constantly take a survey of the environment and act accordingly. Animals use a specialized organ system, the **nervous system**, whose sole purpose is to take in information, process and store it, and issue commands to muscles and other organs. The nervous system receives external sensory information (sights, sounds, textures, smells, and tastes), transforms that information into electrical and chemical impulses that can be analyzed and interpreted in the brain, and this information can result in learning and behaviors that promote survival. The brain processes and interprets information in a parallel way, where thousands of operations occur simultaneously, each one influencing many others as it proceeds (Pinker, 2009). The result is that the animal can move through, manipulate, and ultimately change its environment based on the information received and interpreted by our nervous system.

The nervous system has two main divisions: the central and the peripheral nervous systems (Hass-Cohen, 2008a). The **central nervous system** (CNS) is made up of the brain and spinal cord. The **peripheral nervous system** (PNS) consists of the cranial and spinal nerves as well as ganglia (clusters of nerves and neurons) located outside the brain and spinal cord. The PNS receives and sends messages from, and to, the CNS where the CNS interprets the messages on a deeper level. The PNS has two divisions: the somatic and autonomic nervous systems. The **somatic nervous system** (SoNS) sends sensory information to the CNS and receives direction from the CNS on how to change behavior through bodily movement. The **autonomic nervous system** (ANS) is divided into two systems: sympathetic and parasympathetic nervous systems. The **sympathetic nervous system** (SNS) is what is activated in emergencies and what causes a number of bodily reactions to stressful situations (usually referred to as the flight or fight response; when your body gets ready to escape a situation or confront a situation). The **parasympathetic nervous system** (PSNS) helps our system return to normal and leads to relaxation. Please see Fig. 4.1 for a summary of the structure of the nervous system.

According to Hass-Cohen (2008b), art therapists work with these activating (SNS) and relaxing nervous (PSNS) systems through the selection and engagement with the art materials. For example, an art therapist might help the client select materials that the client finds soothing (e.g., clay; and this may lead to parasympathetic nervous system activation). The art therapist can then assist the client in interacting with the materials in a way that activates (e.g., pounding the clay; activating the sympathetic nervous system) or relaxes the nervous

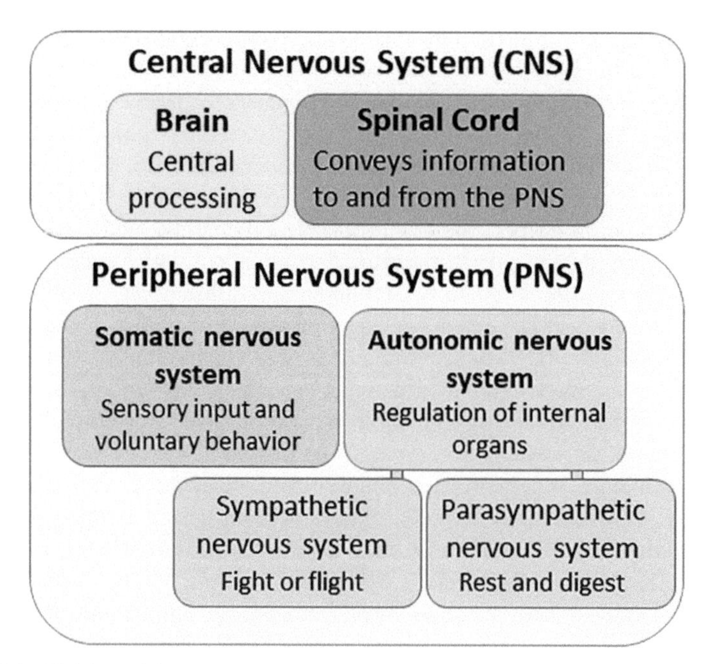

FIG. 4.1 *Divisions of the nervous system.*

system (e.g., smoothing out the clay with water; activating the parasympathetic nervous system).

How do the nervous system and brain work?

To comprehend how we perceive, understand, and then act on our environment, we start with the basic elements that comprise the nervous system. We begin our understanding in the mid-1800s through the artwork of Scientist Santiago Ramon Y Cajal. Santiago Ramon Y Cajal (1852–1934; Newman et al., 2017) won the Nobel Prize in 1906 for his theories on brain organization, specifically the identity of neurons as discrete, individual cells that connect to one another. From an early age, Cajal expressed great interest in drawing and photography and wanted to be an artist. Cajal's father, who ultimately wanted Cajal to pursue medicine, lured him toward medicine by asking Cajal to teach anatomy to medical students and use his drawings to create an anatomical atlas. After learning about another scientist's, Camillo Golgi's, staining method to study brain cells, Cajal combined his skills in medicine and drawing. His cell stains led to approximately 3000 drawings "that reveal the microscopic anatomy of the brain…as we now understand it" (p. 22). These microscopic and artistic studies yielded two major findings: The Neuron Doctrine and the Theory of Dynamic Polarization. The **Neuron Doctrine** states that the nervous system is made up of neurons that interact with one another through their interconnections (this will be explained next). **The Theory of Dynamic Polarization** describes the flow of information within a cell (see action potentials later). To view some of Cajal's beautiful drawings, please check out *A Deep Dive Into the Brain, Hand-Drawn by the Father of Neuroscience: The breakthrough drawings of Santiago Ramón y Cajal are undeniable as art and First Drawings of Neurons.* So what are neurons?

Neurons are the cells in the brain that take in, generate, and process information. Neurons enable a person or animal to adapt to circumstances and make their way through life. While a typical human brain has about 86 billion neurons, there are also approximately as many **glial cells**, the other major cell type in the nervous system. Both are critical for nervous system function (Purves et al., 2018). Glia work together with neurons to shape and control information flow. The coordinated activity of specific populations of neurons and glia underlies the network activity of the nervous system.

As shown in Fig. 4.2, neurons exhibit branched projections, called **dendrites**, which take information into the cell. Sensory neurons have dendritic specializations that allow the conversion of stimuli from the world into electrical signals. For example, when we touch paint we feel cool, wetness. Mechanoreceptor and temperature receptor neurons sense the paint texture and temperature and this information is processed in the brain where we realize the coolness and dampness of the paint. These electrical messages are passed throughout the neuron, which

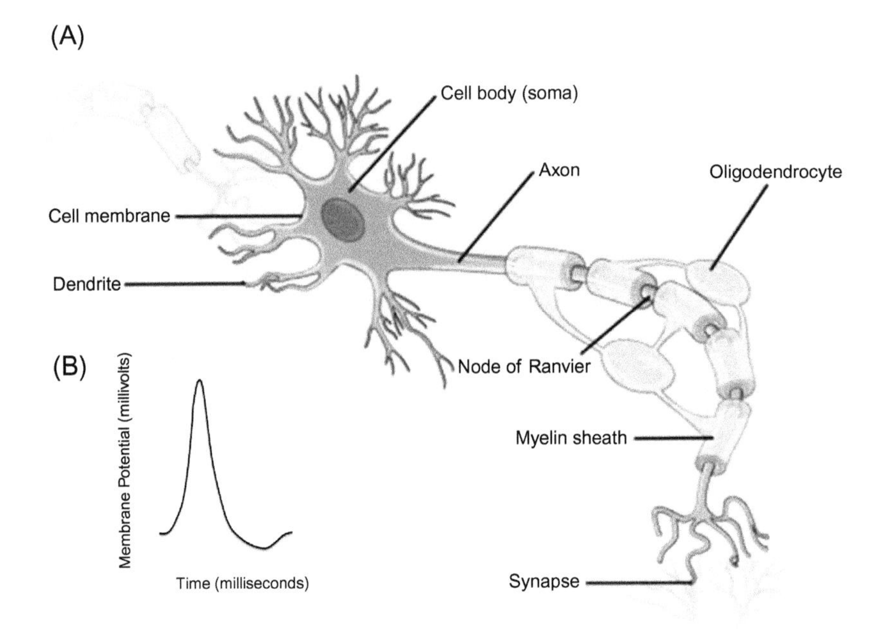

FIG. 4.2 *Parts of the neuron. (A) The main parts of the neuron include: (1) dendrites, (2) axon, (3) myelin sheath, and (4) synapse. (B) An illustration of an action potential.*
(Elsevier.)

contains a long **axon** which is a membranous structure extending from the cell body (this was described as dynamic polarization in Cajal's drawings). The axon makes contact with other neurons through chemical messengers known as neurotransmitters. Information flow within neurons is electrical, while signals between neurons are chemical.

How do neurons communicate?

Communication with other neurons occurs between the **axon terminal** and dendrite (Purves et al., 2018). The **synapse** is the patch of cell membrane of the neuron where this contact occurs. **Neurotransmitter** molecules are specific chemical compounds used for communication between cells and come from the **presynaptic** "sending" neuron. Neurotransmitters float across the gap between cells, called the **synaptic cleft**, and bind and activate receptor proteins in the cell membrane of the **postsynaptic** "receiving" neuron or muscle cell. The way in which a cell reacts to the neurotransmitters depends on the type of receptor in the postsynaptic cell. Some receptors are specific proteins called **ion channels** that can open and allow charged molecules, ions, to flow across the cell membrane. Moving ions make electric currents that cause voltage changes. The amount and direction of change is determined by positive or negative ions flowing through the receptor channel. Generally, the flow of positive ions results in excitatory, positive voltage changes, while the flow of negative ions results in inhibitory, negative voltage changes. Positive membrane voltages push the neuron toward firing *more* action potentials, while negative membrane voltages *inhibit* action potentials. When enough excitatory voltages sum together, specific ion channels open, allowing more charged ions to flow across the cell membrane, causing further voltage change, resulting in a large, self-perpetuating voltage spike called the **action potential** (Kandel et al., 2013) shown in Fig. 4.2B. The excitatory and inhibitory inputs into a neuron sum together to determine the rate at which action potentials are "fired" by that neuron. This "rate code" reflects the level of neuronal activity which informs a person about the strength and importance of the message and determines the amount of overall neurotransmitter released by active neurons to send this message.

Action potentials travel down the axon. Some axons are wrapped by a **myelin sheath** made of specialized glia, oligodendrocytes and Schwann cells, to insulate and speed action potential transmission along their length (similar to the rubber coating around an electrical cord). When an action potential reaches the axon terminal, the positive voltage changes trigger the release of neurotransmitter molecules onto the dendrites of the next neuron in the circuit.

You may be wondering what neurons, dendrites, axons, and action potentials have to do with art therapy? We chose two examples of connections between neuron communication and art therapy to review in this section based on our experience and knowledge. First, you will learn about the disturbance in neural communication that is the cause of multiple sclerosis (MS) and how art therapy can help people cope with the symptoms of MS. Next, you will learn about neuroplasticity and how art therapy might help strengthen positive neural communication. Both of these examples are based on theory and have not yet been empirically studied. We hope these connections can be empirically studied in the future to provide evidence for the connections between changes in neuronal functioning and the complex behaviors involved in the art therapy process.

Neural communication and implications for art therapy: Case of multiple sclerosis

When communication among neurons is disrupted and nerve signals are reduced or blocked, this can lead to sensory and motor control problems. **Multiple sclerosis** (MS) is an example of what can happen when communication among neurons is disrupted. MS is an autoimmune disease where the body attacks its glia cells and thus damages the myelin sheath (the insulating coating on the axon) and disrupts neuron communication (Brugge, 2018). This damage causes scars on the neurons called **sclerotic plaques** in the central nervous system; the location of the plaques determines the type of symptoms the patient experiences.

When the first author started coleading a group for patients with multiple sclerosis more than 2 years ago, she was surprised to learn about the range of symptoms caused by MS. You may be familiar with the more well-known physical symptoms of MS which include muscle weakness and stiffness, impaired coordination, and sometimes pain (Brugge, 2018), but did you know that MS also has numerous psychological symptoms? As stated before, MS affects communication among neurons and thus the damage causes a wide range of both motor and psychological symptoms. The psychological symptoms include cognitive impairment (slower information processing, impaired memory, and concentration), fatigue (Brugge, 2018), and higher rates of depression than found in the general population (Arnett et al., 2019). The first author was additionally surprised to learn that vision problems are one of the first symptoms that lead people to an MS diagnosis. Vision problems can result from "inflammation and demyelination at the level of the optic nerve" (Brugge, 2018, p. 69).

Having knowledge and understanding of how MS affects the central nervous system can inform art therapy practice. For example, by understanding the neurobiological links of MS which cause cognitive impairments, higher risk for depression, and vision problems, the art therapist can adapt the art therapy sessions. To adapt to cognitive impairments, the art therapist can provide art prompts in multiple ways (such as verbal, written, and individual assistance). The art therapist may want to provide one task at a time and/or repeat the directions for those with slower information processing and/or memory problems. Additionally, the art therapist can find ways to explore feelings of depression through art prompts and discussions with the client or group with the understanding that there may be a strong chemical cause of the depression versus environmental causes.

In an interesting study, Shella (2020) found statistically significant differences in the artwork of patients with different types of MS (progressive MS and relapsing-remitting MS). Shella scored the drawings of patients using the Formal Elements of Art Therapy Scale (FEATS; Gantt & Tabone, 2012)) and found that those with the progressive type of MS "were less likely to add details to their drawings, or use much space on the page, perhaps due to lack of interest in completing the drawing, loss of energy, and psychomotor agitation or retardation" (p. 151). Shella also noted that those with progressive type of MS used more graphic indicators of depression in their drawings as compared to those with the relapsing-remitting type of MS.

Finally, to adapt art therapy to those patients with vision impairments, the art therapist might use tape on the edges of paper so the client can feel the edge of the paper. Having knowledge of the broad-reaching symptoms caused by MS (cognitive, psychological, visual, and motor) prepares the art therapist to better adapt the art therapy sessions to the patient group. Next, we will explore neural communication and neuroplasticity.

Neural communication and implications for art therapy: Neuroplasticity

After early childhood, the human nervous system mostly stops making new neurons, except in a few restricted brain regions. Unlike the liver or the skin, the nervous system has to work with a pretty well-set number of neurons throughout our lifespan; in fact, neurons die off naturally as we age, and every person experiences some degree of age-related neural degeneration. How can we reconcile this observation with what we know to be the purpose of our brain, which is to continually adapt and learn? How can we explain someone who recovers from brain injury, heals from trauma, and changes unhealthy and destructive patterns of behavior?

You might be surprised to learn that the brain can reorganize connections in response to learning, experience, or even damage; this is called neuroplasticity. **Neuroplasticity** is used to refer to changes in the brain and brain networks. Neuroplasticity, or the change in connections between neurons and brain networks, arises because the synaptic connections between neurons change in response to activity and experience. According to Doidge's *The Brain that Changes Itself* (Doidge, 2007), synapses typically get stronger if they are more active and weaken if they are used less frequently. Moreover, synapses from different presynaptic neurons, that merge signals on a single, common postsynaptic neuron, can strengthen when they fire together. In this way, different neurons reinforce each other's synaptic strengths when they coordinate their action potential streams if they have the same target cell. "Cells that fire together, wire together" is commonly used to describe this process by neuroscientists and mental health professionals. Ebbs and flows of coordinated action potential firing therefore reinforce or scale back activity in specific networks, depending on how these networks are used. This process of synaptic strength change is called **synaptic plasticity.** In general, the term neuroplasticity is used to refer to changes in the brain and brain networks, while the term synaptic plasticity is used to refer to changes in the strength of the synapses themselves.

Synaptic plasticity is what is happening in your brain and is the physical source of memories, associations, recognition, and learning. When a synapse strengthens, it is physically changed. More vesicles full of neurotransmitters may be shuttled to the terminal of the presynaptic sending neuron. More receptors may be packed in the membrane of the postsynaptic receiving cell, and the entire synaptic connection grows larger. The opposite processes happen when synapses weaken as they are less frequently used. When we learn new facts or associations or establish new habits, the physiology of our brain changes in a very real way. Right now, as you read, your synapses are moving and changing, hopefully establishing strong connections corresponding to the material that you are experiencing. Far from being "hard-wired," your brain is better represented as a dense network of flexible filaments with active, mobile ends that constantly project and retract connections with their neighbors. This is the physiological basis of learning.

We have come to understand that the connections between cells in the brain are not static; in fact, these cells are *not designed* to be static. New connections can take on tasks that were formerly damaged circuits. Old associations can be weakened and be forgotten or reassociated with other stimuli and memories. Plasticity is thus a process fundamental to how brains work. It is key to normal neural function and critical in the process of therapy. We may be able to recognize the effects of neuroplasticity on a large scale when learning new behaviors or changing old behaviors. When we first try a new behavior, it may be difficult to remember and enact all of the steps, but with repetition, the behavior becomes easier or more automatic. For example, when a client first comes into an art therapy studio, they may be hesitant and uncertain about their artistic skills. They may ask about how to mix paint or apply it to canvas. As they explore and become familiar with the materials, they may mix and apply colors with more confidence. Have you noticed this about your own interactions with art-making? Has your confidence and skill level increased the more you work with a specific art material? Remember: "Cells that fire together, wire together!"

Synaptic plasticity and art therapy

Hass-Cohen developed a framework for art therapy interventions based on the principle of synaptic plasticity. **Art Therapy Relational Neuroscience** (ATR-N) integrates relational and interpersonal neuroscience with the practice of art therapy (Hass-Cohen & Findlay, 2015) and focuses on creating new healthy attachments by facilitating interactions that allow "cells that fire together" to form new connections that "wire together." ATR-N identifies six key components in art therapy practice that focus on replacing negative interpersonal associations with new positive interpersonal associations. For example, if a client has grown up in an emotionally invalidating environment they may have developed negative associations when interacting with others. The art therapist can use the ATR-N approach to create new, positive, and adaptive associations by employing six components. The six ATR-N components are *C*reative Embodiment, *R*elational Resonating, *E*xpressive Communicating, *A*daptive Responding, *T*ransformative Integrating, and *E*mpathizing and Compassion (CREATE; Hass-Cohen, 2008a).

The ATR-N framework articulates the way the art therapist can facilitate neurobiological and relational changes in clients and the framework also helps "art therapists understand the neurological underpinnings of psychopathology and allows for the fine-tuning of art therapy interventions and theories of change" (Hass-Cohen, 2008a, p. 283). A description of the six components follows.

Creative Embodiment refers to the bodily movements experienced in art-making (e.g., the client moving a paintbrush on a piece of paper or pounding clay). During this first stage in art therapy, the client is taking risks to engage in art-making and silencing their inner critic while the art therapist utilizes nonverbal signs of attention and acceptance of the client (Hass-Cohen & Findlay, 2015). The physical movement of the client simultaneously stimulates additional parts of the nervous system which helps to integrate the client's "actions, emotions, and thoughts" (p. 10) as the client moves, feels, and thinks about the next step in the art-making process. **Relational Resonating** is created from the connection and stable relationship between the art therapist and client and has "the potential to activate and mend attachment wounds, alter attachment states, stabilize affect regulation, and update autobiographical memories" (p. 10). **Expressive Communicating** is the client's emotional expression via artwork and the meaning making of the art piece within a safe therapeutic environment. **Adaptive Responding** is the art therapy intervention that helps to "balance and support" (p. 11) the client. **Transformative Integrating** develops over time with repeated experiences from the principles mentioned before. Through repeated sharing of art images and processing in a safe, therapeutic environment, the client can develop a different understanding of self or experiences with others. Over time, **Empathizing and Compassion** develops in the client for themselves, and others, and thus shows signs of increased emotion regulation and new interpersonal neurological connections.

The previous sections examined the intersections between neuroscience and art therapy. Both examples highlight how neuroscience can inform art therapy practice in two ways: (1) helping the art therapist understand the way certain diseases affect the brain and in turn affect art therapy sessions and (2) how art therapy might help clients form adaptive connections in the brain. Next we will learn about different brain regions.

The brain regions

To continue building our basic knowledge of neuroscience and its implications for art therapy, we will now explore different regions of the brain. Populations of different classes of neurons comprise different brain regions, each of which performs specific computational tasks that ultimately give rise to perceptions, behaviors, and sense of self. The brain is divided into three main regions, the forebrain, the midbrain, and the hindbrain, based on developmental origins. The **forebrain** includes the cortex, the outermost layer of the brain, and subcortical structures involved in learning, memory, and emotion. The **midbrain** is part of the brainstem and is involved with sensory reflexes and alertness. The **hindbrain** includes the medulla, pons, and cerebellum which are structures associated with the regulation of breathing, heart rate, and the coordination of sensory and motor reflexes (Kandel, 2012). Overall, the brain is divided into two **hemispheres** that are anatomically connected by the **corpus callosum**. The corpus callosum is made of axons that transfer information between the two hemispheres.

We will begin exploring the higher brain, or the neocortex, which oversees our most advanced functioning and is divided into four **cortical lobes** (see Fig. 4.3). These lobes include the machinery for conscious sensory perception, cognition, and motor behavior. The **occipital lobe** contains the visual cortex. It receives and processes visual information. The **temporal lobe** receives and processes auditory information and contributes to visual processing, while the **parietal lobe** receives and processes tactile and somatosensory information. The parietal lobe also contains regions that are specialized for the integration of

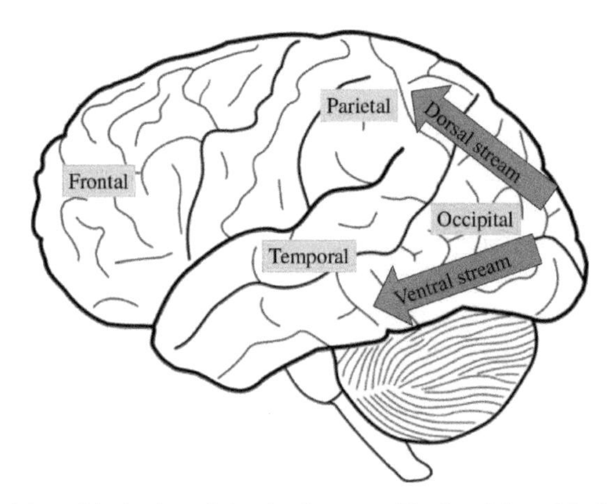

FIG. 4.3 *The lobes of the brain and the visual streams. The four lobes of the brain include the (1) frontal lobe, (2) temporal lobe, (3) parietal lobe, and (4) occipital lobe. This image also features the dorsal and ventral visual streams (labeled red arrows) that arise from primary visual cortex (V1) in the posterior occipital lobe.*
(Elsevier.)

touch, vision, and auditory information. Information from the occipital, temporal, and parietal lobe feed to the **frontal lobe.** The frontal lobe contains the **prefrontal cortex** which performs executive and cognitive functions and the **motor cortex** which is responsible for voluntary motor outputs (Kandel et al., 2013). **Executive functions** include the behaviors of planning, prediction, attentional focus, and coordinating complex behaviors. **Cognitive functions** include functions that deal with memory, learning, and thinking. The cortex also receives and integrates information from subcortical and brainstem structures that are organized in **nuclei**, groups of neurons that perform specific tasks.

Like the regions of the cortex, each subcortical region is represented in both hemispheres and is responsible for functions such as sensory integration (thalamus), motor control (basal ganglia and cerebellum), and homeostatic functions (hypothalamus). Subcortical forebrain structures include the **limbic system** (limbic means borders). "The limbic system structures include the basal ganglia, caudate nucleus, amygdala, thalamus, hippocampus, and hypothalamus" (Hass-Cohen & Findlay, 2015, p. 35). Spatial and explicit memory is integrated by the hippocampus, a bilateral structure deep within the temporal lobe, while emotions and emotional memories are processed by the amygdala.

The brainstem is responsible for autonomic and motor outputs that regulate such functions as heart rate, breathing, sleeping, and digestion. All sensory inputs from the periphery and all motor output to the periphery pass through the **brainstem** and **spinal cord** (Kandel et al., 2013). Together, the electrical signals within neurons and chemical signals between populations of neurons underlie the flow and integration of information through the nervous system. So how are these brain regions connected to art therapy?

Brain regions and the expressive therapies continuum

The **Expressive Therapies Continuum** is a conceptual framework for art therapy that has been linked to a human neurobiological framework of information processing (ETC; Kagin & Lusebrink, 1978 as cited by Hinz, 2019; Lusebrink, 2010). This model consists of three levels that are arranged hierarchically (from basic, simple interactions to more advanced levels) for how clients interact with art materials to create artwork. The three levels parallel both cognitive and artistic stages of development (Hinz, 2019) and thus coincide with typical psychological and biological stages of development. The ETC also provides art therapists with a framework for assisting clients in selecting art media based on their needs and preferences and can be used by art therapists for the assessment of creative, affective, and cognitive functioning. The ETC states that people who are psychological healthy can engage with materials on all levels while those who exhibit psychological issues will likely express difficulty with some of the components (Hinz, 2019). Each of the levels has been mapped to specific brain structures (Lusebrink, 2010).

The most basic level, **kinesthetic-sensory,** is preverbal and does not require the ability to produce words. Kinesthetic and sensory interactions are the way we gather information as infants (Hinz, 2020) and thus engagement with art materials on this level requires minimal cognitive involvement. This level has been mapped to basic sensory processing in the visual and somatosensory cortices and kinesthetic feedback from subcortical motor control regions (see the brain regions section above).

The second, more advanced level on the hierarchy is the **perceptual-affective** level. The perceptual level focuses on the creation of line and shape in artwork while the affective component emphasizes the expression of emotion. This second level can be mapped to the perception of sensory information located in the higher-level cortical processing areas. The affective level is mapped to direct connections between the limbic system and cortex (see the brain regions section above). These interactions can result in dynamic changes that reflect new relationships between the art process, experiences, emotions, and memory (Lusebrink & Hinz, 2020).

The third, advanced level is the **cognitive-symbolic** where the client must plan and think about the art therapy prompt in order to create artwork. Processes at this level are mediated by regions of the prefrontal cortex. The activity in the prefrontal cortex integrates the lower levels of the hierarchy and underlies the ability to make deliberate and conscious expressive choices for communication and problem solving (see the brain regions section above). Creativity can occur at all levels of the hierarchy. (More information about the ETC can be found in the Art Materials chapter.)

Understanding the brain regions that are likely to be activated during art-making is the first stage in understanding the connections between neuroscience and art therapy. However, as the tools that we use to measure brain activity and function become more sophisticated, we are learning that complex cognition and behaviors, including creativity, require interactions and connections between many brain regions. Accordingly, art therapy neuroscience research has recently shifted from attributing art-making actions to specific brain structures (as described before) to attributing actions to complex brain networks. Cognitive processing, behavioral flexibility, and creativity reflect the activation and connectivity with large-scale networks among different brain regions (Bressler & Menon, 2010; Lusebrink & Hinz, 2020). We explore these networks next.

Shift from brain regions to networks

More recent research from electrophysiological and functional neuroimaging studies demonstrates that complex processing (such as thoughts that involve memory, learning, planning, and creativity) is due to connections and dynamic interactions within **large-scale brain networks** (LSBN) of different brain regions (Bressler & Menon, 2010). Thus, complex thinking like creativity and mental flexibility utilizes large-scale interacting brain networks on both sides of the brain. These networks use multiple regions involved in sensation, perception, emotion, cognition, and movement (Khalil et al., 2019). Beaty et al. (2015) argued that three networks, the default mode network (DMN), the central executive network (CEN; also identified as the executive control network, below), and the salience network (SN), work together when engaging in creative thinking. Interactions and disconnections in these three networks are also implicated in psychological disorders (Menon, 2011); this overlap has the potential to explain the association of why creativity can help with healing. We next explore these three large-scale brain networks and discuss their role in the creative process.

The **default mode network** (DMN) "comprises midline and posterior inferior parietal regions that show increased metabolic activity in the absence of most externally presented cognitive tasks" (Beaty et al., 2015, p. 88). The DMN is active when there is no stimulus and our mind wanders "because this is what the brain defaults to when individuals are not actively engaged in an externally directed task" (Hinz, 2019, p. 231). This network focuses on our *internal* experiences that result in daydreaming, reminiscing, and future planning. Activation of the DMN helps us generate and expand our thinking (Abraham, 2019). This network is thought to underlie the ability to notice and observe one's inner self and explore how one might react in different situations (Koban et al., 2021). Beaty et al. (2015) states that "activation of default mode regions during improvisation indicates internally-driven, self-referential mechanisms, which allow the improviser to suspend conscious monitoring and enter a 'flow-like' state" (p. 111). See Box 4.1 to learn more about flow.

Bolwerk et al. (2014) measured the default mode network activity and psychological resilience by comparing two groups: (1) an art-making group versus (2) an art discussion group. Twenty-eight retired adults (average age was

Box 4.1 Flow

A flow state is defined as "a subjective state that people report when they are completely involved in something to the point of forgetting time, fatigue, and everything else but the activity itself" (Csikszentmihalyi, 2014, p. 230). Flow results when a task requires maximum engagement combined with maximum enjoyment (Snyder et al., 2011). Chilton (2013) examined the implications of flow on art therapy practice. She argued that the creative process in art therapy can facilitate a flow state that lowers the client's anxiety while increasing their interactions in the art-making process. To increase a state of flow, she suggested that art therapists might provide a short meditation to help clients become present and provide clear directions and support so that the client can immerse themselves into the experience. To help clients shift out of the flow state, Chilton suggested environmental cues (e.g., turning off or changing the background music). Scarce (2019) noted that art therapists can develop the skills to assess and monitor their own flow and to use the clinician's flow state to facilitate a shared art-making experience with their clients.

63.5 years) were recruited for the 10-week study. One half of participants were in a group that made art 2 hours per week and the other half were in the art discussion group for 2 hours per week (this served as the control group). **Functional magnetic resonance imaging** (fMRI) is a method that can display activity levels of different brain regions using measurements of oxygenated blood flow which is used to indicate brain activity. Participants received a pre- and post-fMRI scan and completed a self-report survey on resilience. The results indicated that the art-making group demonstrated greater connections in the DMN as compared to the art discussion group. The researchers also found stronger connections between resilience and brain connectivity in the art-making group, which "was interpreted to mean that through their use of art making, the study subjects experienced or learned greater cognitive control over emotions" (Hinz, 2019, p. 231).

An alternative state occurs when the **cognitive or executive control network** (ECN) is active. This network activity is associated with our sense of self, cognition, metacognition, symbolism, and decision making (Koban et al., 2021). These functions involve interactions between several brain regions in both hemispheres. The ECN is activated when we need to have focused attention, use our working memory, switch tasks, and/or evaluate the ideas generated by the default network. This network helps us evaluate creative ideas and is responsible for problem solving and reasoning (Abraham, 2019). When pianists are asked to generate a specific pitch versus music that expresses emotions, those focused on the pitch had ECN activation and connections to cognition and motor areas (Pinho et al., 2016). Those focused on expressing emotion revealed increased connections in the control network and the default network (King & Parada, 2021).

The **salience network** (SN) mediates between the DMN and ECN. The salience network helps in directing our focus externally and internally as needed (Abraham, 2019) and aids in communication between brain areas and helps us switch networks as needed (Hinz, 2019). Cognitive and emotional problems can result when there are problems with the SN (Lusebrink & Hinz, 2020). To strengthen the SN, an art therapist might ask clients about what they see, then the therapist can ask how they feel about the images, and finally, what does the client see as the most important element in the art image. This shift from visual perception to emotional awareness to discernment is a way that might engage the SN since the brain is activating multiple areas to engage with the therapist's questions (Hinz, 2019).

How do these networks work together when we are making art? Mather (2021) and Hinz (2019) believed these large-scale brain networks work in complementary ways while people engage in art-making. Mather (2021) described an fMRI study (Ellamil et al., 2012) that found that while participants were sketching ideas for a book cover their DMN was more active which may indicate a state of flow or openness to generating ideas. When the participants were trying to decide on the best sketch, the ECN was at work which may indicate evaluation of the sketches to determine the best one. In his summary of the study, Mather (2021) argued that "art really does give all of our cognitive functions a full work-out" (p. 21).

The shift from specific structures to looking at large-scale brain networks in the process of creativity offers new ways to categorize and research on how art-making affects the brain (Beaty et al., 2015; Hinz, 2019). The shift toward large-scale brain networks moves art therapy research toward new avenues of exploration since there is still so much we do not know about how making art affects the brain. Additional research comparing different forms of creativity and their effects on the brain is needed (McPherson & Limb, 2018).

Vision

Another area of neuroscience that has connections to the field of art therapy is the area of vision. Why should we know about vision? How can knowledge of our visual systems enhance our understanding of art-making and art therapy? Despite the heavy emphasis on vision in art therapy, connections between the field of art therapy to our brain's visual system have been widely understudied by art therapists. Neuroscientists, vision researchers, and psychology researchers have been studying vision, visual perception of art, and art-making. Kandel (2016) argued that "To appreciate what brain science can tell us about…how we respond to a work of art—we need to first understand how our visual experiences are generated by the brain" (p. 24). This section of the chapter provides basic information about how the eye works and aids in processing visual information. We will also explore how the visual system underlies our ability to make and view art. Understanding the pathways and connections is crucial to understanding how visual perception is inextricably linked to cognition, emotion, and memory. We begin this section by examining why our sense of vision is so well developed in our brain.

Vision is a central sense for humans

The ability to perceive visual images is the single most important sensation that humans possess (Gregory, 2015). Seeing is the sense that allows people to position themselves in the world, to orient in space, and to perceive the form and the relationships among objects around them. Vision is also the primary mode for imagination and dreams. The richness, variation, distance, and speed of this process set vision apart from other senses such as hearing, smell, taste, and touch. Some estimate that about 80% of a person's sensory input consists of vision (Livingstone, 2014) and our brain has dedicated more areas to our visual senses as compared to the others (Freberg, 2016; Mather, 2014). The sense of sight has been studied so much that it is one of the best-understood sensory systems in humans.

Why are humans so visually focused? The answer likely lies in the evolutionary history of the human species. Humans evolved in a complex environment where long-range detection of landscape, food sources, animals, and other humans was critically important. Additionally, humans used fine-tuned manipulation of objects that needed precise control of tools as ways to alter one's environment (called **niche construction** as discussed at the beginning of the chapter). The ability to manipulate objects using skills developed to control tools required detailed, high-resolution sensory feedback, something that vision excels at. As we will see, the human eye is specifically adapted for sharp resolution and color discrimination in the short to medium distance range. This range was perfect for finding a comfortable cave shelter, identifying a useful plant, and targeting prey animals, or enemies, with a stone or spear that helped us survive. Vision also helps with creating art work (Kass, 2013).

Art-making, the eye, and the brain

Psychology professor Pascal Mamassian argued that "Master painters are also keen observers of human vision and perception...they use that knowledge to create pictures that don't just lie flat" (Dingfelder, 2010, p. 34). So, how do artists make images that do not just lie flat? Does making art eventually change our brain? Or fine-tune our vision? Abraham (2019) reported that artists reveal different visual and thinking patterns from nonartists. Artists display higher levels of **divergent thinking**, or ability to generate new ideas, advanced ability to visualize figure movement, superior performance on perception and drawing tasks, visual restructuring speed, and better memory for recalling visual features of pictures than nonartists (Abraham, 2019). Making and responding to art relies extensively on visual information. But do artists just see and think about things differently? Can making art change the way nonartists see and think?

To answer this question, Schlegel et al. (2015) examined the brain structure changes after a 3-month drawing or painting course. Thirty-five undergraduate students participated in the study, 17 completed a 3-month-long drawing or painting course (the experimental group) while 18 students did not study art (these students served as the control group). All participants completed the Torrance Tests of Creative Thinking Figural Form A (TTCT; Torrance, 1974; this test provides a composite creativity index) and all participants had a magnetic resonance imaging (MRI) scan while observing a visual drawing and making a 30-second gesture drawing. These assessments were completed before and after 3 months.

Results revealed significant differences after 3 months between the students in the art class (the experimental group) versus students who did not take the art class (the control group) on the TTCT. The authors concluded that the students in the art class scored higher on creative thinking, divergent thinking, modeling of systems and processes, and imagery. The MRI scans indicated prefrontal white matter decreases in the art class students which the authors argued indicates an increased "ability to model systems and processes creatively" (p. 449). The authors believed that the art training may lead to more efficient, creative processing which accounts for the decrease in white matter because the students' brains were being more efficient. Similar to the MRI scan findings, the art class students improved scores on creative cognitive ability and technical skills on the gesture drawing assessment. While the participants were drawing, functional MRI scans displayed the largest activity in parts of the cerebellum and motor cortex; these are areas associated with fine motor control, understanding where one is in space, hand-eye coordination movements. The authors argue that these changes may only be revealed when vision and action/motor movement are paired together "such as the skilled strokes of a paintbrush" (p. 449). This study provides an argument that making art can change the way we see, take in visual information, and shape our brain. How does an external image enter the eye? And how do we make sense of the information our eye receives?

The eye

What we actually see is light, which is electromagnetic energy (Mather, 2014) produced from the sun, from glowing heat and fire, or emitted from artificial illumination. This energy consists of photons traveling as waves of different wavelengths. Photons bounce off or are absorbed by the surface of opaque objects, or change direction when passing through transparent objects (Freberg, 2016). Eyes are fundamentally organs for absorbing photons and determining their wavelength, amount, and location of origin. These qualities are perceived as color, intensity, and location by the eye. In this way, we can determine the shape, color, size, and distance of objects in our surroundings by the patterns of reflection, absorption, or refraction of photons.

Neurobiologists often describe the eye in the same terms that we would use to describe a camera. The eyes of all vertebrates, including humans, follow a basic pattern known as the camera-type eye. However, even though human eyes have structural similarities to the camera, the camera structure does not reveal how the eye is built, how it functions, and how it allows us to see and perceive.

The eye is roughly spherical, about 25 mm (not quite an inch) across in humans and is composed of a tough scleral sheet that contains a transparent, gelatinous **vitreous humor**. At the front of the eye is a transparent covering, the **cornea**, which begins the bending of light before entering the pupil. The **pupil** itself is a round hole that is surrounded by a colorful tissue, the iris. The **iris** is composed of pigment cells and muscles that dilate or constrict in response to external light levels. "Pupil diameter is also affected by your emotional states through the activity of the autonomic nervous system" (Freberg, 2016, p. 181). When we are in a heightened state our pupils dilate. The resulting increase or decrease in pupil size allows more or less light into the eye, serving as a first response to regulate light levels. Controlling the amount of light entering the eye is critical for vision, as the difference in light levels between a sunny day outside and even a well-lit interior room can be a factor of one thousand or more. To be

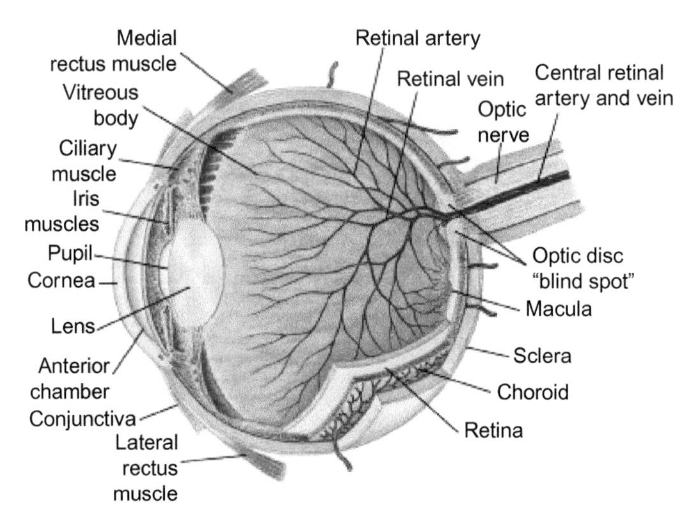

FIG. 4.4 *Diagram of the eye. This diagram of the eye includes the (1) cornea, (2) iris, (3) lens, (4) ciliary muscle, (5) vitreous fluid, (6) retina, and (7) optic nerve.*

able to see both in full daylight on a plain day as well as in moonlight in a thick forest, we need to be able to adjust our vision (Livingstone, 2014). See Fig. 4.4 for a diagram of the eye.

Behind the pupil is a clear refracting **lens** that further bends light rays, so that the image of an object falls on the retina at the back of the eyeball. The place where the image falls on the retina is determined by the distance of the object, its location in space, and the exact shape of the lens. The lens is held by connective fibers attached to the ciliary muscle. Contraction of the ciliary muscles shapes the lens and brings closer objects into focus. As we get older, our lens tends to harden and lose elasticity, reducing its ability to accommodate to near distances. For this reason, almost everyone requires corrective lenses, or reading glasses, to accommodate for near distances as they get older. Art therapists working with older adults, or those with vision impairments, may observe patients squinting or moving a visual image closer or farther to focus. These behaviors might indicate vision issues; art therapists will need to adapt images and art materials to accommodate vision issues.

At the back of the eye lies the **retina** which contains cells to process information about the image. Cells in the retina respond to different types of stimuli (Kandel et al., 2013). The **rods** are cylinder-shaped photoreceptors that respond with vision at night. **Cones** are triangular shaped and respond in brighter light and are responsible for daylight vision and send us information about color. The messages from rods and cones are sent to the retinal bipolar cells and then to the retinal ganglion cells. **Retinal ganglion cells** integrate the signals and fire action potentials along their axons. The axons form a bundle and exit the eyeball, forming the **optic nerve**.

From the optic nerve, the view on the left side of the visual field, from both eyes, projects to the right hemisphere of the brain, while the view from the right projects to the left hemisphere (Fig. 4.5). To accomplish this, axons from the retinal ganglion cells from both eyes that view the left visual field connect to the right thalamus and are relayed to the right visual cortex. Axons from the retinal ganglion cells from both eyes that view the right visual field connect to the left thalamus and are relayed to the left visual cortex. The point at which the axons cross is called the **optic chiasm.**

Because humans have eyes placed at the front, there is a large binocular overlap in the view of the left and right visual fields that results in parallel, overlapping copies of a majority of the total visual field (Kandel et al., 2013).

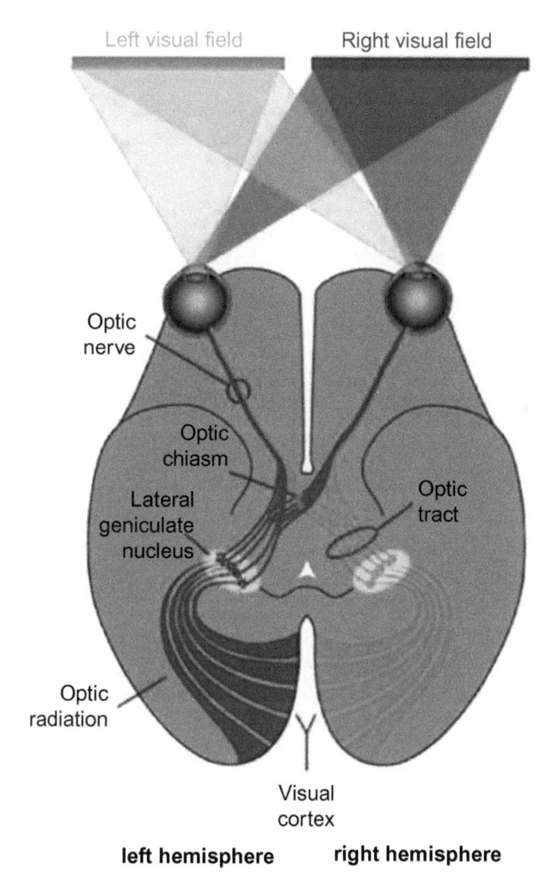

FIG. 4.5 *Visual pathways of both eyes. The image on the left side of the visual field, from both eyes, projects to the right hemisphere of the brain, while the view from the right projects to the left hemisphere. Portions of the optic nerves cross over at the* ***optic chiasm****. The information then goes to the thalamus and is relayed to visual cortex.*
(Elsevier.)

Using two eyes is like having two cameras trained on the world, each one with a slightly different perspective. Seeing a scene from two different angles is a phenomenon known as **parallax**. It not only expands the field of view but also allows the brain to compare the two overlapping images, noting similarities and discrepancies. These different views allow you to determine the distance, relative size, and relative position of objects. All this computation is done in the visual cortex where the information from the optic nerves are first integrated and then the information from each eye is compared and combined. The *Parallax Effect* exhibition showcased the work of several artists who used the concept of parallax to create movement and dimension in their graphic designs. The artists play with the visual images from two different angles in one art piece so the images feel like they are moving; Adam Sorensen's Fogo (2014) is the best example of this effect in the exhibit (Fig. 4.6).

The **thalamus** is a subcortical region of the forebrain and one of its main functions is to act as a preprocessing and relay center for sensory information (Hwang et al., 2017). The thalamus sorts and evaluates information before it is

FIG. 4.6 *Fogo. As you can see in this image, the objects feel like they are moving despite this image being stationary.*
(Adam Sorensen.)

passed on for a higher-level processing in the cortex. Only the sense of smell is sent to the cortex without first going through the thalamus. Within the thalamus, a region called the **lateral geniculate nucleus** receives information from the optic nerve. After preprocessing, the information is sent to the **visual cortex** which is located in the occipital lobe at the back of the head, under the part of the skull directly above the neck (Kandel, 2016). What happens in the visual cortex?

The visual cortex and the processing streams

At the back of the occipital lobe is the **primary visual cortex** (called area V1) (Kandel et al., 2013). This area sends visual information in two different processing streams: the dorsal (directed toward the top of the cortex) or ventral (directed toward the bottom of the cortex) (Milner & Goodale, 2008) (Fig. 4.3). The **dorsal stream** informs the viewer "where" an object is or "how" an object is moving by sending information from the visual cortex to the parietal lobe (Kravitz et al., 2013). The information then helps us determine motion, location, and relationship of objects. This pathway operates quickly but is weakly linked to conscious awareness and contributes relatively little to long-term memory (Kandel, 2012).

To process information about "what" are the objects and faces we are seeing, the **ventral visual stream** takes information from the visual cortex to the inferior temporal lobes, located on the sides of the cerebral cortex, right above the ears relative to the head (Kandel, 2016, Kravitz et al., 2013). This visual stream identifies objects, forms, and faces, and defines items in context. The ventral stream operates more slowly than the dorsal and has a greater ability to discriminate detail in a scene, information is more available to conscious awareness, and it contributes to long-term memory formation (Kandel, 2012).

Both visual streams send signals to the prefrontal cerebral cortex. The **prefrontal cortex** is a major integration center that is involved in executive functions. Remember, **executive functions** include planning, prediction, attentional focus, coordinating complex behaviors, personality, and conscious perception of the self.

There is now extensive evidence of crosstalk between the dorsal and ventral streams so that neither one can be said to function independently of the other. In addition, both streams are also influenced by the prefrontal cortex and visual information is integrated with information from other senses, cognition, memories, and emotions (Kandel et al., 2013). Neural processing is said to occur in circuits where data is sent back and forth between sensory regions to planning and emotional control regions (and this is true for our other senses). Thus complex experiences and behaviors arise from the activity of large-scale overlapping neural networks. Vision is not the only sense where computation and perception are performed by many parallel circuits, each working on a different aspect or quality of the sensation. So, it is impossible to say where exactly a specific object is seen, heard, or felt in the brain; the answer is that perception is widely distributed and experienced as a coherent activation of different circuits (Zeki & Bartels, 1999). How can art therapists use this knowledge of vision and the brain to improve their work?

Vision and implications for art-making and art therapy

As described earlier in the chapter, different diseases (such as multiple sclerosis) or brain damage can cause problems with vision. As we have discussed, a large portion of the brain is dedicated to visual processing, so brain damage and disease can easily have an impact on vision (Mather, 2014) and therefore can affect the ability to view and make art.

Mather (2014) described several artists who experienced brain damage and how the brain damage affected their artwork. For example, an artist who experienced **visual agnosia** after a stroke (inability to recognize objects) created art images that lacked structure. Mather also describes another artist who had a stroke that affected his right parietal cortex and subsequently the artist tended to draw images on the right side of the canvas and was unable to develop full details on the left side of the canvas. If you want to learn more about these types of cases, you might check out the Neurologist Oliver Sacks', book about several of his unusual cases [*The Man Who Mistook His Wife for a Hat* (Sacks, 1985)].

If brain damage can affect art-making, can art therapy enhance vision? Recent research has explored whether engaging in art therapy might improve the visual-cognitive functions and eye movements in patients with Parkinson's disease (Cucca et al., 2021). Most people know that Parkinson's disease causes problematic motor/body movements in patients, but most Parkinson's patients will also have problems with mood, cognitive impairments (such as problems with information processing, memory, attention, and planning), psychosis, and sensory impairments that may cause perceptual problems (Brugge, 2018). Visual problems due to Parkinson's can include problems with contrast, adapting to light, differentiating among colors, impaired motor perception, visual recognition, and space.

Cucca et al. (2021) created a study to explore if art therapy can improve the vision of patients with Parkinson's. Participants engaged in 90-min group art therapy sessions, twice a week, for 10 weeks. The art interventions included work with clay, painting, collage, drawings, and murals. Participants completed a number of assessments that included several visuospatial assessments and an fMRI scan. Results revealed that the Parkinson's patients had decreased involuntary eye movements and improved scores on the visuospatial tests. The fMRI scans displayed significant changes in visual connectivity networks (Fig. 4.3) and increased functional connectivity. The researchers concluded that "Overall, our findings suggest that art therapy may enhance visuoperceptual skills in patients with PD" (p. 151).

Neuroaesthetics

An area of neuroscience that offers promising connections to the field of art therapy is neuroaesthetics. **Neuroaesthetics** is a subfield of cognitive neuroscience and is traditionally defined as the scientific study of the biological mechanisms involved in our experiences with beauty (Chatterjee & Vartanian, 2014; Pearce et al., 2016). Utilizing advanced technology and a variety of brain imaging instrumentation, researchers in neuroaesthetics examine how the brain responds to experiencing and creating beauty (i.e., aesthetic experiences) (Diessner, 2019). Neuroaesthetics utilizes a framework called the aesthetic triad (Chatterjee & Vartanian, 2014). The **aesthetic triad** is made up of three neural systems that create our experiences with beauty, and includes the (1) sensory-motor system, (2) emotion-valuation system, and (3) meaning-knowledge system. Our sensory-motor systems are activated when viewing something beautiful and/or seeing an image with movement in it (Diessner, 2019). Our emotion-valuation system determines whether we find the aesthetic experience pleasing while our meaning-knowledge system connects our present experience to our prior knowledge and experience. King and Parada (2021) and King (2018) are working toward a systematic integration of the science of neuroaesthetics with theory, practice, and research in art therapy. King argued that neuroaesthetics research might help in understanding the reward systems that operate when we make and view art, exploring how neuroplasticity and art therapy might aid people with neurodegenerative disease and injury, and help clarify scientifically sound art therapy intervention strategies.

Connecting our understanding of vision to learning how to draw

How do artists use information about how we see to enhance their art-making? Betty Edwards begins her famous book *Drawing on the Right Side of the Brain* (Edwards, 1989) stating that "Drawing is a curious process, so intertwined with seeing that the two can hardly be separated. Ability to draw depends on ability to see the way an artist sees, and this kind of seeing can marvelously enrich your life" (p. 2). Edwards (1989) used information about the eye and brain to create exercises that "shut off" advanced visual processing so the student-artists focus on drawing exactly *what* they see (lines and shapes), not what they *think* they see (a person). For example, she asked readers to draw images upside down to help the viewer focus on line, angles, and shape. This exercise "disorients" the meaning-making processing stream and thus the student-artist must focus on what they see (abstract lines, shapes, shadows). In another exercise, she had student-artists create a "pure contour drawing" (p. 86) of the outer edge or contour of the hand without looking. This exercise allows the student-artist to focus on learning how to use the edge, or contour, versus relying on engrained higher-level brain processing memories of how we typically draw a hand. These skills also parallel findings by researchers who have found that artists tend to focus on details of objects (such as line, edge, contours) versus the overall conceptual of the object (e.g., drawing an apple) (Drake et al., 2010; Pring et al., 1995).

Margaret Livingstone's *Vision and Art: The Biology of Seeing* (2014) similarly highlighted how artists use the knowledge of our visual system to enhance the viewer's experience in particular ways. Livingstone studied the paintings of the Impressionist Monet (Dingfelder, 2010). The impressionist painters lacked definition and were criticized for presenting "unfinished" works to viewers at the time. Livingstone believed that Monet minimized the colors in his artwork "to achieve visual effects that were more alive, and lively, than more realistic paintings preceding them" (Livingstone, 2014, p. 161). She explained that the lack of color contrast in Monet's work stimulates our *where* system of visual processing over the *what* system "because the Where system has higher contrast sensitivity to the What system" (p. 167) and this stimulation makes the piece more vibrant to the viewer.

These are just two examples about how knowledge of our visual process affects the art we make. Although art therapy is not focused on the accuracy of art work, understanding how drawing and vision are connected can be helpful when working with clients and for developing our own art work. For additional ways art therapists might adapt the art therapy session for those with vision impairments, please see Box 4.2.

Box 4.2 Art therapy adaptations for persons with vision impairments.

When clients are squinting, moving images back and forth to focus, or coloring off the page, art therapists might suspect the client may be having issues with their vision. As we have discussed earlier, art therapists can adapt the art-making and viewing process to make things easier for clients. Art therapists will want to make sure the room is well lit to ensure optimal vision; however, lighting can also cause a glare which can hamper vision (Wagenfeld, 2015). Placing the art tools within sight of the client (some clients may have a difficult time with peripheral view) is important or moving the client's hands so they feel the tools and the location can be helpful. Additionally, consistently placing the tools in the same place and orally stating their location can help clients orient themselves to subsequent sessions more easily. Creating labels with large and bold font, puff paint, or tactile markers (such as rubber bands or paper clips) will help clients to work independently (Wagenfeld, 2015). As mentioned earlier, using painter's tape to identify the edges of the paper adds a tactile indication for the client-artist of where to draw.

Teepa Snow, a well-known occupational therapist and advocate for people with neurocognitive disorders (NCD), trains caregivers to be sensitive to NCD-related vision impairment by describing how vision changes from wearing goggles (having social vision) to wearing binoculars (only having task vision) and eventually covering one eye (causing impairments in depth perception). We encourage you to try the exercises described in this Teepa Snow video so that you can see how impairments in vision might affect art therapy sessions: https://www.youtube.com/watch?v=t--mkzfHuIE. Please see the chapter on Older Adults for more information about art therapy for older adults.

Additional art therapy research and connections to neuroscience

For our final section we will explore art therapy neuroscience research. We will begin looking at several studies that examine the brain, art-making, and art therapy. There are a number of methods to measure the functioning of the brain in response to art-making and to art therapy. These methods include electroencephalography (EEG), measurement of cortisol levels, and brain scans (fMRI, MRI, etc.). We begin with early studies that measured brain waves using EEG recordings and end with new technologies for measuring the effects of art therapy on the brain.

EEG, art materials, and the brain

How does the use of different art materials affect the brain? An **electroencephalogram** or EEG records the combined electrical activity from the region of the brain underneath scalp electrodes. Immediate changes in activity in response to interventions, like art-making, can be measured using the EEG.

In 2014, Belkofer et al. (2014) found that after participants made art using oil pastels, brain regions associated with visual, somatosensory, and association processes showed an increase in alpha activity. **Alpha waves** are an indicator of a relaxed yet awake state and thus the researchers suggest that creating art with oil pastels may be associated with an awake and relaxed state. Kruk et al. (2014) found that when participants worked with clay and when drawing there were increases in executive control and sensory association areas. Both clay and drawing increased gamma activity; however, those who only worked with clay revealed a shift from gamma to theta activity. **Gamma** activity happens when we are actively attending to information or when our brain is engaged in synaptic plasticity, memory and motor control. **Theta** waves usually occur at the beginning of NREM sleep or indicate "imaginative states or internal focus, such as meditation" (p. 53). The shift from gamma to theta activity can indicate sensory and memory processes such as working memory (Jones et al., 2020; Lisman & Jensen, 2013). See Table 4.1 for a summary of these brain wave patterns. These EEG studies indicate that art-making results in changes in visual, somatosensory, association, and executive areas and the specific changes depend on the art material.

Cortisol and art therapy

Can art-making also affect our stress hormones? The stress hormone, **cortisol**, is in our blood and saliva and is regulated by the brain. Cortisol levels provide an objective measure of stress level changes (Kaimal et al., 2016). In 2016, Kaimal et al. had participants work with three types of art media: collage,

TABLE 4.1 Brain wave patterns.

Brain waves	Description of state
Gamma	Actively attending to information
Beta	Awake and alert
Alpha	Awake and relaxed
Theta	Meditative state

modeling clay, or markers. Participants provided salivary cortisol samples pre- and post-art-making so that researchers could assess the effects of making art on individual stress levels. After 45 min of art-making, participants showed a statistically significant decrease in salivary cortisol levels. **Significance testing** is a statistical method that quantifies whether or not the results are likely to be due to chance or to real changes in the variable of interest. Thus the statistical significance of changes in cortisol levels indicated that the differences were likely to be related to art-making and not by chance. Open-ended responses from participants indicated that they found the art-making to be enjoyable and relaxing. Together, these results indicated that art-making can decrease both objective (cortisol levels) and subjective (open-ended responses) measures of stress.

Beerse et al. (2020) also used salivary cortisol to compare participants who were randomly assigned to an online-delivered mindfulness-based art therapy (MBAT) intervention or a neutral clay task (NCT) for 5 weeks. Saliva samples were taken before and after the study and participants also completed instruments to measure generalized anxiety and perceived stress. Seventy-seven participants completed the study and while participants in both groups had statistically significant decreases in salivary cortisol over time, only the participants in the MBAT had significant reductions in generalized anxiety and perceived stress, suggesting that art therapy intervention can enhance positive outcomes as compared to art-making by itself.

Brain scans and art therapy

Functional near-infrared spectroscopy (fNIRS) is wearable and portable brain-monitoring technology that uses near-infrared light sources and detectors on the scalp to monitor cortical blood flow that can be used to study the effects of art-making. The fNIRS measurements are similar to the **blood oxygenation level-dependent** signal measured in fMRI studies. Both brain technologies (fNIRS and fMRIs) measure the ratio of oxygenated to deoxygenated blood as an indirect measure of neuronal activity because regions receiving an increased ratio of oxygenated blood can be presumed to be activated.

Kaimal et al. (2017) used fNIRS to examine responses in the medial prefrontal cortex as a measure of the level of reward associated with specific drawing activities (coloring, doodling, and free drawing). Participants completed a five-question pre- and postsurvey about self-perception of creativity, drawing experience, and feedback on the study. Eleven men and 15 women (eight identified as artists) participated in all three art tasks (coloring, doodling, and free drawing). All three tasks increased blood flow in the reward pathway (medial prefrontal cortex). Interestingly, those that identified as artists had the highest amount of activity when doodling as compared to coloring and free drawing, supporting connections between artistic training and the brain.

In 2018, Walker, Stamper, Nathan, and Riedy (2018) analyzed the resting state connectivity of the Default Mode Network (DMN) and brain region connectivity in active-duty military service members diagnosed with **traumatic brain injury** (TBI) and **posttraumatic stress disorder** (PTSD). The researchers found that the individuals who made masks with themes of injury and trauma had higher PTSD scores, high symptomatology scores, and an average of 14 brain scars. fMRI scans revealed a pattern of low default mode network activity and low thalamic connectivity. As mentioned earlier in the chapter, default mode network activity is associated with internal experiences such as daydreaming, future planning, and the ability to notice and observe one's inner self, while thalamic connectivity is associated with attentional (Antonucci et al., 2019) and cognitive processes (Kang et al., 2018) and the engagement of sensory pathways (Walker et al., 2018). Individuals who made masks with patriotic themes had low PTSD scores, low symptomatology scores, and an average of one brain scar on the anatomical MRIs. Functional MRI scans showed a pattern of high thalamic connectivity and high default mode network activity. Fewer scars on the anatomical scans may indicate less severe injury, while the differences in brain connectivity and activation may have indicated reengagement of sensory pathways disturbed by traumatic events and the ability to cope with or compensate for traumatic events.

New Technology for Measuring the effects of art therapy

Mobile, wearable fNIRS equipment and mobile brain/body imaging (MoBI) have the potential to expand the measurement of brain function and associated changes affect and stress *during* art-making and art therapy, not just before and after (King & Parada, 2021). MoBI is more portable, less cumbersome, and can be used in various settings (from hospital to lab settings). King et al. (2019) encouraged more art therapists to utilize evidence-based information produced by mobile scans about the interaction between art-making, emotional expression, and physiological and neurological changes in art therapy practice. These studies can also provide clear, accurate information to clients about the effects of art therapy and can aid the art therapist in selecting the best therapeutic interventions (King et al., 2019).

Summary

This chapter made connections between neuroscience and art therapy. We first learned how our present brain was shaped by our interactions with tools, art-making, and the environment. We also explored how the brain receives information from our environment and translates this information through multiple complex and intricate processes. Synaptic plasticity helps us to understand how the work in art therapy can lead to psychological changes as described by Art Therapy Relational Neuroscience. While the Expressive Therapies Continuum has implications for activation in specific brain regions, newer research is exploring how brain networks may help explain the shifts experienced when making and evaluating art. Our sense of sight plays a major role in art-making and art therapy and therefore we learned about how the structure of the eye takes in light waves that subsequently send images to be interpreted by other parts of the brain. The chapter concludes with the beginnings of evidence that art-making can alter activity in brain regions and that art made in therapy may produce specific activation patterns in the brain. We hope this chapter provides you with the basic language of neuroscience. We look forward to future evidence of the connections between neuroscience and art therapy.

Experientials

1. Numerous online tutorials can help you create a three-dimensional model of the neuron. Identify the main parts of the neuron: (1) dendrites, (2) axon, (3) terminal button, (4) neurotransmitters, and (5) glial cells/myelin sheath. Following are several sites that offer different ways to build a neuron: https://faculty.washington.edu/chudler/chmodel.html; https://i.pinimg.com/originals/d3/cf/f6/d3cff6fed71488b8e5d019c82cbbe952.jpg; https://www.simplyneuroscience.org/ggsxsn-lesson-plans.
2. After exploring the drawings of Cajal, answer the following questions: (1) In what ways do you think Cajal's interests in drawing and photography aided his understanding of brain cells? (2) In what ways can you relate to Cajal's struggle with wanting to be an artist and the pressure he felt to go into medicine? (3) Are you able to identify the key structure of a neuron in Cajal's drawings?

   Check out: A Deep Dive Into the Brain, Hand-Drawn by the Father of Neuroscience: The breakthrough drawings of Santiago Ramón y Cajal are undeniable as art. https://www.nytimes.com/2018/01/18/arts/design/brain-neuroscience-santiago-ramon-y-cajal-grey-gallery.html.

   Check out: First Drawings of Neurons: https://boingboing.net/2015/10/26/the-first-drawings-of-neurons.html.
3. Find an online tutorial to help you create a drawing of the eye. Identify the key structure of the eye: (1) pupil, (2) cornea, (3) vitreous humor, (4) retina, and (5) optic nerve. Here is an online tutorial that describes an easy way to draw the eye: https://www.youtube.com/watch?v=pohaP-TA-pY.

4. Find an online tutorial to draw the brain. Identify the visual cortexes described in the text. This is an online tutorial to help you draw the brain: https://www.youtube.com/watch?v=g8K5rWGZxjU.

Resources for further exploration

1. Explore the 2012 exhibit entitled Brains: The Mind as Matter. https://we-make-money-not-art.com/brains_the_mind_as_matter/. This Brains Exhibit contained real brains and parts of brains as well as other methods we have used over time to understand how the brain functions.
2. Explore 3D images of the human brain. https://www.livescience.com/42227-3d-images-human-brain.html. This website hosts brain-anatomy images collected by Dr. Albert Rhoton of the University of Florida.
3. Learn about artists who are teaching doctors about illness through art. UCLA Medical School's "Guest Artist" Is Helping To Teach Doctors About Disease. https://www.huffpost.com/entry/ted-meyer-geffen-medical-school_n_7325072.
4. Listen to Radio Lab's Unraveling Bolero to learn about how frontotemporal dementia affects art and music making. https://www.wnycstudios.org/podcasts/radiolab/articles/unraveling-bolero.
5. Watch Flow, the secret to happiness Mihaly Csikszentmihalyi to learn more about Flow. https://www.ted.com/talks/mihaly_csikszentmihalyi_flow_the_secret_to_happiness/up-next?language=en.
6. Explore Dawn Hunter's artwork based on the work of Cajal. She utilizes pen and ink to recreate drawings similar to Cajal. See her portfolio here: https://www.dawnhunterart.com/.

Chapter terms

Action potential
Adaptive responding
Alpha waves
Art therapy relational neuroscience
Autonomic nervous system
Axon
Brain stem
Central nervous system
Cognitive functions
Cognitive/symbolic
Cones
Control network
Cornea
Corpus callosum
Cortical lobes
Creative embodiment
Default mode network
Dendrites
Divergent thinking
Dorsal stream
Empathizing and compassion
Executive control network
Executive functions
Expressive communicating
Expressive Therapies Continuum
Flow state
Forebrain
Frontal lobe
Functional magnetic resonance imaging

Functional near-infrared spectroscopy
Gamma waves
Glial cells
Hemispheres
Hindbrain
Hominins
Ion channel
Iris
Kinesthetic/sensory
Knapping
Large-scale networks
Lateral geniculate nucleus
Lens
Limbic system
Midbrain
Multiple sclerosis
Myelin sheath
Neanderthals
Nervous system
Neuroaesthetics
Neuron
Neuron doctrine
Neuroplasticity
Neuroscience
Neurotransmitter
Niche construction
Nuclei
Occipital lobe
Optic chiasm
Optic nerve
Parallax
Parasympathetic nervous system
Parietal lobe
Perceptual/affective
Peripheral nervous system
Postsynaptic
Prefrontal cortex
Presynaptic
Primary visual cortex
Pupil
Relational resonating
Retina
Retinal ganglion cells
Rods
Salience network
Sclerotic plaques
Somatic nervous system
Spinal cord
Sympathetic nervous system
Synapse
Synaptic cleft
Synaptic plasticity
Thalamus
Theory of dynamic polarization
Theta waves
Transformative integrating
Ventral stream
Visual agnosia
Visual cortex
Vitreous humor

References

Abraham, A. (2019). *Neuroscience of creativity*. Cambridge University Press.

Antonucci, L. A., Di Carlo, P., Passiatore, R., Papalino, M., Monda, A., Amoroso, N., et al. (2019). Thalamic connectivity measured with fMRI is associated with a polygenic index predicting thalamo-prefrontal gene co-expression. *Brain Structure & Function*, *224*(3), 1331–1344. https://doi.org/10.1007/s00429-019-01843-7.

Arnett, P. A., Barwick, F. H., & Beeney, J. E. (2019). *Cognitive and affective neuroscience theories of cognition and depression in multiple sclerosis and Guillain–Barré syndrome* (pp. 443–461). Springer International Publishing. https://doi.org/10.1007/978-3-030-14895-9_20.

Beaty, R. E., Benedek, M., Silvia, P. J., & Schacter, D. L. (2015). Creative cognition and brain network dynamics. *Trends in Cognitive Sciences*, *20*(2), 87–95. https://doi.org/10.1016/j.tics.2015.10.004.

Beerse, M. E., Van Lith, T., & Stanwood, G. (2020). Therapeutic psychological and biological responses to mindfulness-based art therapy. *Stress and Health*, *36*(4), 419–432. https://doi.org/10.1002/smi.2937.

Belkofer, C. M., Van Hecke, A. V., & Konopka, L. M. (2014). Effects of drawing on alpha activity: A quantitative EEG study with implications for art therapy. *Art Therapy: Journal of the American Art Therapy Association*, *31*(2), 61–68. https://doi.org/10.1080/07421656.2014.903821.

Bolwerk, A., Mack-Andrick, J., Lang, F. R., Dorfler, A., & Maihofner, C. (2014). How art changes your brain: Differential effects of visual art production and cognitive art evaluation on functional brain connectivity. *PLoS ONE*, *9*(7). https://doi.org/10.1371/journal.pone.0101035, e101035.

Bressler, S. L., & Menon, V. (2010). Large-scale brain networks in cognition: Emerging methods and principles. *Trends in Cognitive Sciences*, *14*(6), 277–290. https://doi.org/10.1016/j.tics.2010.04.004.

Brugge, F. V. D. (2018). *Neurorehabilitation for central nervous system disorders*. Springer. https://doi.org/10.1007/978-3-319-58738-7.

Chatterjee, A., & Vartanian, O. (2014). Neuroaesthetics. *Trends in Cognitive Sciences*, *18*(7), 370–375. https://doi.org/10.1016/j.tics.2014.03.003.

Chilton, G. (2013). Art therapy and flow: A review of the literature and applications. *Art Therapy: Journal of the American Art Therapy Association*, *30*(2), 64–70. https://doi.org/10.1080/07421656.2013.787211.

Csikszentmihalyi, M. (2014). *Flow and the foundations of positive psychology: The collected works of mihaly csikszentmihalyi* (2014th ed.). Springer. https://doi.org/10.1007/978-94-017-9088-8.

Cucca, A., Di Rocco, A., Acosta, I., Beheshti, M., Berberian, M., Bertisch, H. C., et al. (2021). Art therapy for Parkinson's disease. *Parkinsonism & Related Disorders*, *84*, 148–154. https://doi.org/10.1016/j.parkreldis.2021.01.013.

Diessner, R. (2019). *Understanding the beauty appreciation trait: Empirical research on seeking beauty in all things*. Palgrave Macmillan. https://doi.org/10.1007/978-3-030-32333-2.

Dingfelder, S. F. (2010). The scientist at the easel. *Monitor on Psychology*, *41*(2), 34–38.

Doidge, N. (2007). *The brain that changes itself*. Penguin.

Drake, J. E., Redash, A., Coleman, K., Haimson, J., & Winner, E. (2010). 'Autistic' local processing bias also found in children gifted in realistic drawing. *Journal of Autism and Developmental Disorders*, *40*(6), 762–773. https://doi.org/10.1007/s10803-009-0923-0.

Edwards, B. (1989). *Drawing on the right side of the brain*. Jeremy P. Tarcher, Inc.

Ellamil, M., Dobson, C., Beeman, M., & Christoff, K. (2012). Evaluative and generative modes of thought during the creative process. *NeuroImage*, *59*(2), 1783–1794. https://doi.org/10.1016/j.neuroimage.2011.08.008.

Freberg, L. A. (2016). *Discovering behavioral neuroscience: An introduction to biological psychology*. Cengage Learning.

Fuentes, A. (2017). *The creative spark: How imagination made humans exceptional*. Dutton.

Gantt, L., & Tabone, C. (2012). *The formal elements art therapy scale: The rating manual*. Gargoyle Press.

Gregory, R. L. (2015). *Eye and brain: The psychology of seeing*. Princeton Science Library.

Guseva, E. (2019). Art therapy in dementia care: Toward neurologically informed, evidence-based practice. *Art Therapy*, *36*(1), 46–49. https://doi.org/10.1080/07421656.2019.1564613.

Hass-Cohen, N. (2008a). CREATE: Art therapy relational neuroscience principles (ATR-N). In N. Hass-Cohen, & R. Carr (Eds.), *Art therapy and clinical neuroscience* (pp. 283–309). Jessica Kingsley.

Hass-Cohen, N. (2008b). Partnering of art therapy and clinical neuroscience. In N. Hass-Cohen, & R. Carr (Eds.), *Art therapy and clinical neuroscience* (pp. 21–42). Jessica Kingsley Publishers.

Hass-Cohen, N., & Carr, R. (2008). *Art therapy and clinical neuroscience*. Jessica Kingsley Publishers.

Hass-Cohen, N., & Findlay, L. J. (2015). *Art therapy & the neuroscience of relationships, creativity & resiliency: Skills an practices*. WW Norton & Company.

Hinz, L. D. (2019). *Expressive therapies continuum: A framework for using art in therapy*. Taylor & Francis Group.

Hwang, K., Bertolero, M. A., Liu, W. B., & D'Esposito, M. (2017). The human thalamus is an integrative hub for functional brain networks. *Journal of Neuroscience*, *37*(23), 5594–5607. https://doi.org/10.1523/JNEUROSCI.0067-17.2017.

Jones, K. T., Johnson, E. L., & Berryhill, M. E. (2020). Frontoparietal theta-gamma interactions track working memory enhancement with training and tDCS. *NeuroImage (Orlando, Fla.)*, *211*, 116615. https://doi.org/10.1016/j.neuroimage.2020.116615.

Kaimal, G., Ayaz, H., Herres, J., Dieterich-Hartwell, R., Makwana, B., Kaiser, D. H., et al. (2017). Functional near-infrared spectroscopy assessment of reward perception based on visual self-expression: Coloring, doodling, and free drawing. *The Arts in Psychotherapy*, *55*, 85–92. https://doi.org/10.1016/j.aip.2017.05.004.

Kaimal, G., Ray, K., & Muniz, J. (2016). Reduction of cortisol levels and participants' responses following art making. *Art Therapy: Journal of the American Art Therapy Association*, *33*(2), 74–80. https://doi.org/10.1080/07421656.2016.1166832.

Kandel, E. R. (2012). *The age of insight: The quest to understand the unconscious in art, mind, and brain, from Vienna 1900 to the present*. Random House.

Kandel, E. R. (2016). *Reductionism in art and brain science: Bridging the two cultures*. Columbia University Press.

Kandel, E. R., Schwartz, J. H., Jessell, T. M., Siegelbaum, S. A., Hudspeth, A. J., & Mack, S. (2013). *Principles of neural science* (5th ed.). McGraw-Hill Education LLC.

Kang, L., Zhang, A., Sun, N., Liu, P., Yang, C., Li, G., et al. (2018). Functional connectivity between the thalamus and the primary somatosensory cortex in major depressive disorder: A resting-state fMRI study. *BMC Psychiatry*, *18*(1), 339. https://doi.org/10.1186/s12888-018-1913-6.

Kaplan, F. (2008). Foreword. In N. Hass-Cohen, & R. Carr (Eds.), *Art therapy and clinical neuroscience* (pp. 13–14). Jessica Kingsley Publishers.

Kass, J. (2013). Perspectives from clinical neuroscience: Mindfulness and the therapeutic use of the arts. In F. Chang, E. Mullin, J. Surrey, & S. Trantham (Eds.), *Mindfulness and the arts therapies: Theory and practice*. Jessica Kingsley Publishers.

Khalil, R., Godde, B., & Karim, A. A. (2019). The link between creativity, cognition, and creative drives and underlying neural mechanisms. *Frontiers in Neural Circuits*, *13*, 18. https://doi.org/10.3389/fncir.2019.00018.

King, J. L. (2018). Summary of twenty-first century great conversations in art, neuroscience and related therapeutics. *Frontiers in Psychology*, *9*, 1428. https://doi.org/10.3389/fpsyg.2018.01428.

King, J. L., Kaimal, G., Konopka, L., Belkofer, C., & Strang, C. E. (2019). Practical applications of neuroscience-informed art therapy. *Art Therapy: Journal of the American Art Therapy Association*, *36*(3), 149–156. https://doi.org/10.1080/07421656.2019.1649549.

King, J. L., & Parada, F. J. (2021). Using mobile brain/body imaging to advance research in arts, health, and related therapeutics. *The European Journal of Neuroscience*. https://doi.org/10.1111/ejn.15313.

Koban, L., Gianaros, P. J., Kober, H., et al. (2021). The self in context: Brain systems linking mental and physical health. *Nature Reviews. Neuroscience*, *22*, 309–322. https://doi.org/10.1038/s41583-021-00446-8.

Kravitz, D. J., Saleem, K. S., Baker, C. I., Ungerleider, L. G., & Mishkin, M. (2013). The ventral visual pathway: An expanded neural framework for the processing of object quality. *Trends in Cognitive Sciences*, *17*(1), 26–49. https://doi.org/10.1016/j.tics.2012.10.011.

Kruk, K. A., Aravich, P. F., Deaver, S. P., & deBeus, R. (2014). Comparison of brain activity during drawing and clay sculpting: A preliminary qEEG study. *Art Therapy: Journal of the American Art Therapy Association*, *31*(2), 52–60. https://doi.org/10.1080/07421656.2014.903826.

Lisman, J., & Jensen, O. (2013). The theta-gamma neural code. *Neuron (Cambridge, Mass.)*, *77*(6), 1002–1016. https://doi.org/10.1016/j.neuron.2013.03.007.

Livingstone, M. (2014). *Vision and art: The biology of seeing (revised edition)*. Abrams.

Lusebrink, V. (2010). Assessment and therapeutic application of the expressive therapies continuum: Implications for brain structures and functions. *Art Therapy: Journal of the American Art Therapy Association*, *27*(4), 168–177.

Lusebrink, V. B., & Hinz, L. D. (2020). Cognitive and symbolic aspects of art therapy and similarities with large scale brain networks. *Art Therapy: Journal of the American Art Therapy Association*, *37*(3), 113–122. https://doi.org/10.1080/07421656.2019.1691869.

Malafouris, L. (2013). *How things shape the mind: A theory of material engagement*. The MIT Press.

Mateos, A., Terradillos-Bernal, M., & Rodríguez, J. (2019). Energy cost of stone knapping. *Journal of Archaeological Method and Theory*, *26*(2), 561–580. https://doi.org/10.1007/s10816-018-9382-2.

Mather, G. (2014). *The psychology of visual art: Eye, brain and art*. Cambridge University Press.

Mather, G. (2021). *The psychology of art*. Taylor & Francis Group.

McPherson, M. J., & Limb, C. J. (2018). Artistic and aesthetic production: Progress and limitations. In R. E. Jung, & O. Vartanian's (Eds.), *The Cambridge handbook of the neuroscience of creativity* (pp. 517–527). Cambridge University Press. https://doi.org/10.1017/9781316556238.030.

Menon, V. (2011). Large-scale brain networks and psychopathology: A unifying triple network model. *Trends in Cognitive Sciences*, *15*(10), 483–506. https://doi.org/10.1016/j.tics.2011.08.003.

Milner, A. D., & Goodale, M. A. (2008). Two visual systems re-reviewed. *Neuropsychologia*, *46*(3), 774–785.

Newman, E. A., Araque, A., Dubinsky, J. M., Swanson, L. W., King, L. S., & Himmel, E. (2017). *The beautiful brain: The drawings of santiago Ramón y cajal*. Abrams.

Pearce, M. T., Zaidel, D. W., Vartanian, O., Skov, M., Leder, H., Chatterjee, A., et al. (2016). Neuroaesthetics: The cognitive neuroscience of aesthetic experience. *Perspectives on Psychological Science*, *11*(2), 265–279. https://doi.org/10.1177/1745691615621274.

Pinho, A. L., Ullén, F., Castelo-Branco, M., Fransson, P., & De Manzano, Ö. (2016). Addressing a paradox: Dual strategies for creative performance in introspective and extrospective networks. *Cerebral Cortex*, *26*(7), 3052–3063. https://doi.org/10.1093/cercor/bhv130.

Pinker, S. (2009). *How the mind works*. W. W. Norton and Company.

Pring, L., Hermelin, B., & Heavey, L. (1995). Savants, segments, art and autism. *Journal of Child Psychology and Psychiatry, and Allied Disciplines*, *36*(6), 1065–1076. Retrieved from http://search.ebscohost.com/login.aspx?direct=true&db=mnh&AN=7593399&site=ehost-live.

Purves, D., et al. (2018). *Neuroscience* (6th ed.). Sinauer Associates.

Rutherford, A. (2019). *Humanimal: How Homo sapiens became nature's most paradoxical creature: A new evolutionary history*. The Experiment New York.

Sacks, O. (1985). *The man who mistook his wife for a hat and other clinical tales*. Summit Books.

Scarce, J. (2019). *The art therapists experience of making art with clients: A generic qualitative study* (publication no. 2305194622) [Doctoral dissertation, Capella University]. ProQuest Dissertation Publishing.

Schlegel, A., Alexander, P., Fogelson, S. V., Li, X., Lu, Z., Kohler, P. J., et al. (2015). The artist emerges: Visual art learning alters neural structure and function. *NeuroImage*, *105*, 440–451. https://doi.org/10.1016/j.neuroimage.2014.11.014.

Shella, T. (2020). FEATS score differences and comorbid depression within in persons diagnosed with multiple sclerosis. *Art Therapy: Journal of the American Art Therapy Association*, *37*(3), 147–154. https://doi.org/10.1080/07421656.2020.1738314.

Snyder, C. R., Pedrotti, J. T., & Lopez, S. J. (2011). *Positive psychology: The scientific and practical explorations of human strengths*. Sage Publications.

Sykes, R. W. (2020). *Kindred: Neanderthal life, love, death and art*. Bloomsbury Sigma.

Torrance, E. P. (1974). *The Torrance tests of creative thinking: Technical-norms manual*. Scholastic Testing Services.

Wagenfeld, A. (2015). *Foundations of theory and practice for the occupational therapy assistant*. Wolters Kluwer Health.

Walker, M., Stamper, A., Nathan, D., & Riedy, G. (2018). Art therapy and underlying fMRI brain patterns in military TBI: A case series. *International Journal of Art Therapy*, *23*(4), 180–187. https://doi.org/10.1080/17454832.2018.1473453.

Zeki, S., & Bartels, A. (1999). Toward a theory of visual consciousness. *Consciousness and Cognition*, *8*(2), 225–259.

Chapter 5

Approaches to research in art therapy

Girija Kaimal, EdD, ATR-BC, Asli Arslanbek, MA, ATR, and Bani Malhotra, MA, ATR-BC
Creative Arts Therapies Program, College of Nursing and Health Sciences, Drexel University, Philadelphia, PA, United States

Voices from the field

"We are convinced that it is imperative that art therapists broaden their range of inquiry past the more traditional philosophies and methods and that they have the confidence and commitment to discover their own identity as researchers. Continuing investigations into new developments and paradigms in human sciences research will help to achieve that. Their natural tendencies as clinicians—to work intuitively and metaphorically—do not have to be sacrificed in the interests of rigor. And training programs need no longer support the anomalous contradiction between excellence in clinical training (emphasizing creativity, relationship, and subjectivity) and traditional research methods (emphasizing analysis, measurement, and objectivity). Rather, as we develop research more integral to and synchronous with our own proclivities, we may contribute important research about the human condition in our own voices and from our own ways of being and knowing" (Junge & Linesch, 1993, p. 66). Junge and Linesch (1993) emphasized the need in art therapy to find research approaches that capture the unique qualities of artistic inquiry and expression. This call to action is mirrored in the diversity of research approaches that contribute to the evidence base for art therapy.

Learning outcomes

After reading this chapter, you will be able to

1. Identify the key steps of developing a research study.
2. Recall the meaning and purpose of key sections in a research study paper.
3. Identify central terms and definitions relevant to research.
4. Describe the history of art therapy research.
5. Identify the differences among research paradigms in social sciences that are relevant to art therapy.

Foundations of Art Therapy. https://doi.org/10.1016/B978-0-12-824308-4.00001-6

6. Compare and contrast the types of research methods used in art therapy, including quantitative, qualitative, mixed methods, participatory, arts-based approaches, and program evaluation.
7. Articulate the importance of the role of ethics review and Institutional Review Boards (IRBs).
8. Describe the components of program evaluation and explain how program evaluation is a doorway to research.
9. Identify innovations and new media in art therapy as implications and future directions for research in art therapy.

Chapter overview

In this chapter, we provided an overview of approaches to research in art therapy in the past, present, and future. Over the past decades since the discipline was established, the conceptualization of art therapy research has expanded from descriptive case studies to empirical studies, arts-based knowledge, and community-based research (Kaimal, 2017). In this chapter, we included an overview of current research in art therapy while addressing challenges of conducting research in the discipline, including limited funding and research capacity, small sample sizes, and inclusion of artwork as data. Topics we covered in this chapter include most commonly used and accepted research designs (quantitative, qualitative, mixed methods, arts-based approaches, and program evaluation), how research can be used to improve clinical practice, tools to evaluate research quality, the importance of participatory and community-based research, and ethical issues when conducting art therapy research. We also included a section on implications and future directions, as well as art experientials and reflective questions to review and further consider the materials.

Introduction

This chapter presents a range of approaches and methods that have been used in art therapy research and proposes ideas for future inquiry from our perspective. As authors, we bring to this chapter our experiences as art therapists with personal histories in India, Turkey, and the United States. Our unique developmental experiences in different parts of the world, and with differing ethnic identities as well as our experiences as artists, art therapists, and scholars inform our approach to this chapter and the work we do in the discipline. We assert that in the 21st century, art therapy needs research led by scholars and practitioners from within the field. We need to conduct, claim, and share art therapy research done by art therapists and not be dependent on narratives and approaches defined by other professionals. Through an interdisciplinary approach, we believe art therapist researchers can build on research from other disciplines while accessing the unique ways of knowing through art-making as well as art therapy.

But, where do we start? Research starts with curiosity! Think about a topic in art therapy that intrigues you and makes you curious. This topic could be a phenomenon itself, or could be related to a specific population or a setting. For example, individuals with specific mental health or medical diagnosis, or settings such as art therapy in schools, forensic settings, or medical settings. Next, reflect upon what about the population, setting, or topic that interests you and then make a list of things you know or are familiar about this topic without performing a search at this point. For example:

> *I'm curious to know how art can be used to facilitate empathy in individuals with autism [this statement includes both the topic, empathy, and population, those on the autism spectrum]. I am interested in this topic because I have worked with individuals on the autism spectrum and noted that maybe art can help understand other's emotions [this statement explains my motivation for the topic and prior experience with the population]. Empathy is understood to be largely absent/deficit in autistic individuals. I want to understand whether art therapy can help cultivate empathy, if so how? [Here, we understand what I think I know about the topic and what I want to find out]. I know about the Theory of Mind (ToM) that explains perspective taking as part of cognitive development and that there may be a difference in the ToM in children with autism. [This initial process became the basis for Bani's master's capstone project at the George Washington University; read Malhotra (2019) to learn more].*

After this initial reflective work on a possible area, make a list of possible questions you would like to answer as part of your research. These will help in formulating a research question. Once you identify your research interests, the different ways in which the particular research question will be answered will depend on your worldview and methodology. Let's learn more about these!

Developing a research study

As we mentioned before, research starts with curiosity. Do you have a burning question about a certain phenomenon related to art therapy? Good! Now, we will discuss the basic steps of developing a research study. Before deciding whether the question you pose is worth examining, it is important to know if somebody else asked the same question before you. To learn this, you can do a detailed search about your phenomenon of interest. Let's say you are interested in a research area, such as art therapy with refugees. How will you access relevant literature on this topic? One of the databases you may use is your university's library. You may also use your university access to other databases and search engines such as PubMed, JSTOR, Google Scholar, or Elsevier Science Direct.

After you have found several articles through a database search, how will you know which article is a reliable source of information? The first thing you should look at is if the article has been published in a peer-reviewed journal. Publishing in a **peer-reviewed journal** requires a rigorous review process where more than one reviewer reads and evaluates the manuscript. **Reviewers** assist the editor of the journal to decide whether to accept, reject, or ask for further revisions to the manuscript. Another question you may want to ask is whether the researchers address study limitations. Does the researcher share how they addressed these limitations and discrepancies that may have influenced their findings? Sharing study limitations shows how open the researchers are to sharing their weaknesses and how they were willing to tackle them to make their research credible. Does the researcher clearly and openly share every step of the research procedure such as data collection and analysis? If you are left with questions about methodology, methods, findings, or limitations of a study, then it is likely that the authors did not cover every aspect of writing a research paper. In her book *Introduction to Art Therapy Research*, Kapitan (2010) recommended a checklist of what to look for in a research paper. According to this checklist, readers should look for whether the sections of the research paper address their purpose appropriately. We will explain these sections and their purpose now.

In a research article, these key sections are typically included: abstract, introduction (literature review), methodology, data analysis, findings, discussion, and conclusion. The **abstract** section is where the researcher explains their research topic, purpose (why it is important), how and with whom the study was conducted, and what they have found through their research. In the **introduction** section, the reader is familiarized with the topic. The authors provide detailed background information about previous research efforts on the area and explain why and where there is a gap in the field. The **methodology** section explains the method the authors chose to investigate the phenomenon. The methodology, as we mentioned earlier, is often chosen based on the research question, which usually emerges through the researchers' worldview. In this section, you will usually find details about the study such as the participant demographics, procedures, and data collection methods. The **data analysis** section describes what approaches researchers engaged in analyzing the data. Some data may require statistical analysis, thus researchers may use a statistical analysis program to examine the data. Other data such as interview transcripts may require qualitative analysis, where researchers will engage in a detailed coding process to identify and categorize the data to find connections. There are various data analysis approaches based on the methodology. In the **findings** (or **results**) section, researchers map out what they have found. This section is where authors report their research findings without interpretation. The **discussion** is where the researchers interpret their findings. In this section, the researchers explain what the findings may mean, and why the findings are important. In this section, some authors discuss implications and limitations of the research too, while other research articles may have a separate section for implications and limitations. If the academic journal does not have a distinct guideline about how to structure these sections, researchers may decide whether they would like to discuss implications and limitations in a separate section or under the discussion section. In addition to the key sections mentioned before, there are other sections that can be added based on whether the author needs further clarifications in these areas. These sections are recommendations, implications, ethical considerations, and limitations. **Recommendations** provide insights and advice to service providers and researchers based on their research findings. The **implications** explain the usefulness of the study. This is also the area where authors discuss the implications of their findings on other research areas and pose new research gaps (if applicable). You may find research articles that explain the implications in the discussion section as well. **Ethical considerations** are the precautions the researchers took to minimize risks to the participants. In this section, authors explain how they ensured confidentiality and minimized emotional or physical risks of harm. The **limitations** are the weaknesses in the study such as problems in the study design, any unexpected events that may have happened during data collection, or other considerations that may have influenced their findings. Pointing out the limitations of the study means the researchers are aware of the weaknesses of their study.

You will likely find several research articles that connect to your research interests. But do these sources answer the same question you are asking? If they do, is there a gap in the methods or unexplained research procedures in the research you have found? You can still ask the same questions, as long as your method aims to address the areas previous research failed to do. Once you are confident that you know the research literature on your topic, start thinking about formulating your research question. What is the nature of your question? Are you interested in understanding participant experiences in art therapy, or effectiveness of an intervention, or exploring an uncharted phenomenon? The type of questions you ask will determine what kind of methodology and research methods you choose to investigate your research question. For instance, if you are interested in *examining* the impact of art therapy on anxiety, using an experimental approach, your methodology is likely to be quantitative. You may choose to use standardized instruments (e.g., an anxiety assessment), or biological indicators that are related to anxiety (such as heart rate or blood pressure). Your methodology will also determine your sample size. For example, if you are looking to make generalizable statements on the effectiveness of art therapy on anxiety of a population, you will need a large and diverse sample that is representative of the population.

After determining the research studies or literature that relates to your research area, formulating your research question, explaining the importance of your research question, and identifying your method, you may now write a research proposal. A research proposal typically includes a literature review (summary of research in the area), research question in relation to the gap in the field, an explanation about why this question is significant and worth exploring, and methods to conduct this research. Once your proposal is approved by your instructor, advisor, or supervisor, you may start contacting potential sites, plan your intervention, and prepare to collect your data. However, if your research project involves human subjects, then you will also be required to submit specific paperwork to the Institutional Review Board, a process that is explained later in this chapter.

So far, you have read about how and why we do research. If you are interested in learning more and engaging in hands-on research activities, you can start investigating which professors in your university conduct research. If professors or research labs employ or accept undergraduate students as interns, you may want to contact them and ask if they have any availability. Moreover, you can ask researchers in your institution to mentor you with your own thesis study. Working on a research project will teach you how to take responsibility as a team member, expand your knowledge about research in art therapy, and observe how researchers conduct research. In the next sections, we will look at the brief history of art therapy research, and start learning about paradigms, methodologies, and common research methods used in art therapy.

Historical overview of art therapy research

Art therapy as a profession has gained national momentum with increased licensure and credentialing structures in place to guide clinical work (American Art Therapy Association, n.d.). Research in art therapy continues to evolve as new understandings emerge to contribute to the knowledge of how and why art therapy is beneficial. Continued research responds to the ongoing need of improving art therapy services we provide to different populations in varied settings. Art therapy research has evolved over the years and has growing recognition within the field.

The main framework and core principles of art therapy as a mental health intervention have traditionally been psychoanalytic. In psychoanalytic art therapy, artworks are used as tools to bring unconscious conflicts to the surface and to act as a reflection of the inner self. Early art therapy research predominantly focused on psychoanalytic inferences on the material and content of art products through qualitative case studies, assessment, and theoretical concept building (Betts & Deaver, 2019; Eaton et al., 2007; Reynolds et al., 2000). Betts and Deaver (2019) described how art therapy research began in the 1970s with three emergent topics: assessment and diagnosis, effectiveness, and art therapy in professional settings. Research that involved art assessments used individuals' art to differentiate diagnoses or conditions. Levy and Ulman (1967) used paintings of psychiatry patients for their diagnostic purposes. Silver and Lavin (1977) used diagnostic art-making tasks to determine intervention effectiveness. Research efforts included inquiry into the professional settings such as art therapy educational programs and workplaces. Anderson and Landgarten (1974) designed a large-scale survey to assess the knowledge and interest in art therapy in hospital settings. Landgarten (1978) published another research paper on the status of art therapy in the Los Angeles area. Langarten (1978) looked at the perceptions of art therapy within the mental health field. In the 1980s, the scope of research expanded due to the emphasis on formal research courses in graduate art therapy programs. Scholarly contributions grew and the American Art Therapy Association (AATA) published *A Guide to Conducting Art Therapy Research* in 1992 to support greater diversity in research endeavors (Kapitan, 2017).

Art therapy research has conventionally been rooted in the clinical practice paradigm of case studies, theoretical perspectives, and descriptive and observational studies (Robb, 2015). An evolving conceptualization of art therapy research has led to a shift from exploratory work mainly including descriptive case studies to evidence-based practices, arts-based knowledge, and community-based research (Junge & Linesch, 1993; Kaimal, 2017; Kaiser, 2015; Talwar, 2016). Increased focus on empirical research allowed art therapy as a discipline to make evidence-based and generalizable claims. **Empirical research** broadly refers to studies where a hypothesis is tested and outcomes can be measured. **Generalizability** refers to how research findings can be applicable to a wider population. For instance, findings of a research study on the effectiveness of art therapy with adult cancer patients could yield to similar results if the study was to be reproduced with a new group or sample (Mertens, 2015).

Although illustrative of the individual human experience, several limitations of case studies have been noted (Reynolds et al., 2000). While **case studies** provide a detailed, in-depth understanding of the phenomena under examination, they are limited in their generalizability to larger groups beyond the individual (or small sample) on the value of art therapy with respect to behavioral outcomes (Reynolds et al., 2000). Art therapy as a profession has been around for more than a century; however, empirical art therapy research is fairly new (Reynolds et al., 2000). In recent years there have been more empirically tested studies measuring outcomes in art therapy.

Art therapists have identified the need for **outcome studies**, which is an umbrella term to describe studies that aim to investigate the treatment outcomes of health interventions. Art therapy outcome studies may include studies that investigate treatment outcomes of art therapy with patients undergoing chemotherapy treatments, or effects of art therapy on depression of women living with HIV (Kaiser & Deaver, 2013). Kaiser and Deaver (2013) underscored the need for more valid and reliable studies of art therapy assessments. **Validity** refers to the extent that a method measures what is intended to be measured. **Reliability** refers to the consistency that a method will yield similar results at different time points.

Art therapy research today

In the past decade, art therapy research has expanded due to increased understanding of a range of methodologies and approaches, interest in diverse populations, applications in various settings, and increased support from funding sources. AATA established a research task force in the 2000s in order to extend support through research awards and seed grants (https://arttherapy.org/research/). AATA's research committee is dedicated to encouraging and promoting art therapy research grounded in diverse methodologies and honors professional and student research activity by maintaining a registry of *Art Therapy Outcomes Bibliography*, *Art Therapy Assessment Bibliography*, and the *National Art Therapy Thesis and Dissertation Abstract Compilation*. The committee has also provided recommendations for possible research focus based on a Delphi study with art therapy researchers (Kaiser & Deaver, 2013). A **Delphi study** is an approach that involves gathering perspectives from experts through multiple discussions and then distilling findings to generate conclusions. To expand art therapy practices around the globe, researchers are focusing also on how art therapy works in cross-cultural settings (Kaimal, 2017).

Art therapy research ensures the quality and validity of art therapy interventions, as well as generates an evidence base to advance the field. Thus scholars and clinicians continue to emphasize the importance of art therapy research today (Betts & Deaver, 2019; Deaver, 2002; Gantt, 1998; Kaimal, 2017; Kapitan, 2017; Kaplan, 2001). However, the perceived ability of art therapists to conduct research continues to be a challenge (Linesch, 1995). Obstacles facing art therapy researchers include limited educational support and opportunities for research (Kaiser & Deaver, 2013), and relatively low levels of interest in research compared with clinical practice (Robb, 2015). Apprehensions have been noted about multiple issues that include lack of time to conduct research, statistical skills, funding and training in conducting research (Betts & Laloge, 2000), unacknowledged fears, anxieties, and a culture of resistance to conducting research (Huet et al., 2014).

Art therapists can address research questions through different paradigms, depending on the nature of their question and their philosophical stance as a researcher. In this part of the chapter, we will describe different paradigms for approaching research and different research methodologies that have been and can be useful in answering different types of research questions. The limitations facing the field of art therapy can be mitigated through increased attention to art therapy research in master's level and undergraduate level art therapy training.

Research paradigms (worldview) relevant for art therapy

As humans, we are shaped by our knowledge, beliefs, and perceptions of the world around us. The things we value; the aims we hope to achieve; and how we perceive, think, and know the truth forge our paradigmatic lens. To give an example of how paradigmatic stance can change the way a phenomenon is understood, let's look at how people perceive undocumented immigration. For some, migration is a human right, and every person is entitled to seek a better life. For others, undocumented immigration is unlawful and it is a criminal act. It is difficult to say which of these stances is correct because both views are informed by different sets of assumptions. Understanding the paradigmatic lens is not only essential in defining a research methodology, but it is also important to position ourselves in the world. Paradigms represent our assumptions; paradigms are the lens through which we perceive the world. They guide us about how we will construct the meaning in the research that we conduct.

Paradigm, or in other words worldview, provides a philosophical perspective to position the reasons to choose among research approaches. **Paradigms** are defined as "a coherent, systematic view of what is believed to be true, real and of value" (Paul, 2005, p. vi). Paradigms are the researcher's set of assumptions that drive their research interests, the type of questions they ask, and which research approach they will choose to investigate a phenomenon. Research approaches come out of philosophical assumptions about human motivations and functioning. In this section, we will provide an overview of how our worldview and approach to knowledge relates to the kinds of methods we might choose to use.

Positivism and postpositivism. As Guba and Lincoln (1994) described, a **positivistic** approach to research assumes one reality exists and can be found through experimental and manipulative methodologies. In contrast, a postpositivist researcher believes reality exists but cannot be comprehended completely since the human mind and perception are flawed (Mertens, 2015) and therefore reality can only be grasped "imperfectly and probabilistically" (Guba & Lincoln, 1994, p. 110). **Postpositivists** believe that not all data can be observable through experiments (like positivists believe), and unobservable realities also exist. Postpositivists use self-report data such as those extracted from interviews and questionnaires as ways to gather evidence (Clark, 1998). Positivists and postpositivists tend to be dedicated to ensuring standardized implementation of the intervention and rigor of the method. The postpositivist investigator has the role of the expert, who seeks generalizable cause and effect relationships in research to make "efficient predictions and control" (Guba & Lincoln, 1994, p. 113). For a postpositivist researcher, "developing numeric measures of observations and studying the behavior of individuals becomes paramount" (Creswell, 2014, p. 51), leading postpositivist researchers to gravitate toward quantitative methods. Indeed, quantitative methods are predominantly used in postpositivist paradigm, although the paradigm is also open to qualitative methods as unobservable scientific evidence can be accumulated through qualitative inquiries (Mertens, 2015). In both positivist and postpositivist paradigms, research is aimed to be **value free**, meaning researcher's values and stance are (assumed to be) left out (Guba & Lincoln, 1994) as one's values may pose a threat to objectivity. Postpositivist researchers acknowledge that a researcher may have their own biases, assumptions, and background knowledge about a phenomenon; however, they adhere to the objectivity by remaining "neutral to prevent values or biases from influencing the work by following prescribed procedures rigorously" (Mertens, 2015, p. 63).

Pragmatism. Pragmatist researchers are led by the desire to solve problems and to ensure that research addresses social challenges. Pragmatists accept that there are multiple realities and focus on solving "practical problems in the real world" (Feilzer, 2010, p. 8). Pragmatists use a range of methods and are led by research creative approaches and methods that are best suited for a specific context in order to comprehensively answer research questions. Examples of pragmatic research are studies that want to establish causality between treatment and outcome while also paying attention to the impact on society or community of the intervention. Pragmatists emphasize the "effect and consequences" of a research study when evaluating the study's value (Noddings, 2005, p. 57). This paradigm prioritizes an increase in understanding what the researcher was researching about (Feilzer, 2010). Pragmatic approaches value the ethic of care and are responsive to social needs and issues. Researchers with this philosophical stance are sensitive to the social context and impact of their work beyond the commitment of methodological rigor alone.

Constructivism. Constructivist researchers are of the belief that there are multiple realities in the world. They propose that all research studies conducted by human beings with other human beings are essentially coconstructed in the interactions with each other. Unlike postpositivists, constructivists believe that all knowledge is subjective and a representation of our unique experiences in the world. The realities explored through research are constructions "situated in historical time and social history, language and culture" (Kapitan, 2010, p. xxii). Examples of constructivist research are studies that want to understand the lived experiences of participants in relation to the phenomenon under study. Constructivists believe that knowledge is a construction of the person who collects the data, the type of data that is collected, and the individuals analyzing and presenting it. In art therapy research, this manifests often in case studies and qualitative research designs.

Critical and poststructuralist theories. Critical theorists and poststructural researchers work to uncover disparities, injustices, and hierarchies in society to examine prevailing assumptions that might need to be changed. They seek to illuminate unexamined biases underlying social constructs and what we know to be knowledge. An example of critical and poststructuralist research in art therapy can be research that emphasizes the voices of minority and marginalized groups or communities. Critical and poststructural approaches often challenge and offer alternative ways of knowing compared with commonly accepted research methods. Poststructuralist researchers in particular work to unpack and question that which we hold to be true. For example, critical theorists and poststructuralists tend to be the scholars who bring attention to systemic forms of discrimination and the challenges faced by subjugated and marginalized groups.

When you think about researching a topic in art therapy, what approach might you take? Would you want to understand the lived experiences of research participants as a constructivist researcher would, or would you be more interested in determining cause and effect relationships through a postpositivist lens?

Types of research methods used in art therapy

In this section, we will share examples of research studies in art therapy, including qualitative, quantitative, arts-based, participatory, mixed methods, and program evaluation research. Table 5.1 highlights the many ways in which

TABLE 5.1 Types of research methods in art therapy: Terms and definitions.

Terms	Definitions
Qualitative research	Method that involves collection and analysis of nonnumerical data such as notes, interviews, memos, or audio or video recordings
Quantitative research	Method that involves collection and analysis of quantifiable data through statistical, computational, or mathematical tools
Mixed methods research	Method that involves both qualitative and quantitative research methods in the data collection and analysis process
Program evaluation research	Method that involves collection and analysis of data often in order to understand the effectiveness of programs and projects
Participatory action research	Research that emphasizes a collective process where participants are actively involved in theory building, data collection and analysis, and dissemination of collected information
Case study	The detailed study of a particular group, individual, event, or phenomenon
Theoretical perspective	A preconceived set of assumptions that informs the kind of questions the researcher asks
Exploratory research	Research that involves investigation of a research question or phenomenon that has not been sufficiently addressed in the literature before
Evidence-based research	The gathering of information that is collected through a transparent, evidence-based process
Arts-based research	Research that involves the use of art as a primary tool during data collection, analysis, and dissemination of information
Community-based research	Research that takes place in a community setting and focuses on the collaboration between the community members to encourage social action and draw attention to social justice
Outcome studies	Outcome studies measure the effects of art therapy on a targeted outcome (such as improved physical or psychological well-being)

research can be conducted in art therapy. In our view as authors, no one method is superior, rather each approach is suited to the type of questions being investigated. The main purpose in research, we believe, should be to first identify the question of interest and then use the appropriate method to gather data to answer that question. Research methods can be visualized as a painting palette with each color having its unique strengths that allow for specific aspects of the human experience to be understood. Research in art therapy can take many forms.

Each type of research methodology has its own set of assumptions around what constitutes knowledge, values, and guidelines around how we create that knowledge. **Methodology** is the systematic way to address a research question. **Methodological framework** informs the research methods a researcher will use. Methods are informed by methodologies, and they refer to the strategies and techniques researchers use to generate and analyze data. Examples of research methods include experiments, interviews, surveys, or observations. The way researchers construct, collect, analyze, interpret, and disseminate data is based on the methodology they use. For example, an art therapist working with adults with posttraumatic stress disorder (PTSD) might want to know several ways in which art therapy might influence the client's quality of life, relationships, or symptomology. The art therapist might want to know if their use of an intervention helps reduce a mental health symptom. With a different focus, the therapist might want to see if art therapy influences the relational dynamics within the client's family, or the therapist might want to learn more about the lived experience of the client with trauma in art therapy. These different research interests will require different ways to investigate the phenomenon. Art therapy research, in particular, offers the potential to connect and combine many different approaches. Depending on the question that inspires the study, research approaches can be seen as a palette of possibilities (Fig. 5.1).

FIG. 5.1 *Art therapy research palette. This palette highlights the many ways in which research can be conducted in art therapy.*

Qualitative approaches in art therapy research

Qualitative research involves the collection and analysis of nonnumerical data such as notes, interviews, memos, or audio or video recordings and focuses on understanding the phenomena through the meanings the participant of the study assigns to them. Qualitative research data collection methods include semistructured and unstructured interviews, focus groups, documents, archival material, observation notes, and recordings. Various methods can be used during data analysis to generate meaning from the data such as content analysis or thematic analysis (Braun & Clarke, 2006). **Content analysis** allows the researcher to identify and organize certain words, phrases, concepts, or themes used in qualitative data such as texts. Content analysis helps researchers quantify qualitative data. **Thematic analysis** is a qualitative research tool that helps researchers look for patterns across data and identify overarching categories and themes. Qualitative inquiry, especially case studies, has been widely available in the art therapy literature (Reynolds et al., 2000). There are several different methods/approaches to qualitative research that are chosen based on the researcher's goals. Some of these approaches are phenomenology, grounded theory, narrative studies, qualitative synthesis, case studies, heuristic research, and ethnography.

Phenomenology research involves understanding the lived experiences of the research participant. In phenomenological research, the researcher wants to explore an individual experience and understand the phenomenon under study. An example of phenomenological research is Van Lith and colleague's (2011) study on the lived experiences in art-making of participants who took part in arts-based psychosocial rehabilitation services. In this phenomenological research, the authors aimed at identifying the views of participants regarding the role of art-making in supporting their mental health recovery. Data collection included qualitative in-depth interviews and authors employed interpretative phenomenological analysis in their interviews. A total of 11 major themes emerged which were organized into three main areas. These main areas were "qualities conducive to the art making process, how the art making process benefits mental health recovery, and how the image or art product benefits mental health recovery" (p. 652). Participants found that art-making allowed them to feel stronger and more confident, and they felt that they were more capable of being in control of their journey toward recovery.

Grounded theory is an exploratory method that collects, codes, and analyzes data to discover emerging concepts (Glaser et al., 1968). Grounded theory is used as a method when there is limited documentation on the topic. A researcher engaged in grounded theory compares all data to find patterns, categories, and ideas. Hypotheses arise during the time of analysis, which are then tested against the data to find core categories and theories that shed light on the phenomena. Linesch et al. (2012) used grounded theory to understand the immigration and cultural transition experiences of Latino families. The researchers used art interviews, focus groups, and questionnaires to collect information.

During the first phase of the data analysis process, researchers used open and axial coding to determine preliminary themes. **Open coding** is when the researcher breaks the textual data into separate codes. **Axial coding** refers to making connections between, and organizing those separate codes. Once the emergent themes were identified, in the second phase of data analysis, the researchers used selective coding to regroup themes, identify core categories, and systematically cluster categories as they relate to one another (**selective coding** is when the researcher connects the categories under an umbrella category). Results of this study proposed that fathers struggled with stress and anxiety, and mothers dealt with the fear of losing the cultural traditions, while their children showed resiliency as bilingual agents between the family and the new culture.

Collie et al. (2006) used a narrative research approach to gain a deeper understanding of how women with breast cancer in the United States and Canada used art therapy and art-making for the psychosocial need of meaning making. The authors addressed how art therapy and art-making were valuable in identifying therapeutic mechanisms of art. In this research, **narrative research methods** served the purpose of investigating the stories around identity transition from being a patient to a survivor. The interviews yielded four storylines about the experiences of participants in art therapy. These storylines showed that art therapy helps cancer patients feel "affirmed, confirmed and proclaimed" (p. 761). Narrative interviews are common means of data collection in qualitative methods and aim to generate a story through the interview. In contrast to a question and answer format in a standard interview, in a narrative interview, the interviewer asks open-ended questions that invite interviewees to narrate their stories (Kartch, 2017). For instance, the interviewer might ask an open-ended question such as, "Can you tell me about your experiences in art therapy?"

Qualitative synthesis research involves incorporation of multiple research studies to answer the research question and employs a narrative format to report the research findings. An example for narrative synthesis in art therapy was on effectiveness of artistic activities in emotion regulation (**emotion regulation** refers to a person's ability to manage their emotional states) (Gruber & Oepen, 2018). The authors' review confirmed that art-making stood as an efficient emotion regulation strategy (Gruber & Oepen, 2018).

One of the most common approaches in qualitative art therapy research, **case studies** focus on a case or cases to make an in-depth exploration of the phenomenon. Walker et al.'s (2016) study of an active duty military service member can be an example of case studies. The authors used a variety of data to gain an in-depth understanding of the case, including medical records, therapist's notes, patient's reflections, patient's artworks, and patient narratives.

In **heuristic research**, the researcher engages in self-inquiry, a systematic self-dialogue, and exploration to find answers about a certain phenomenon about the human experience. A heuristic research question can be about the researcher's challenges or curiosities about themselves and their life. Even though the research process is autobiographic, heuristic research questions have a social significance (Moustakas, 1994). A researcher's senses, thoughts, and feelings are at the center to illuminate the research question. Data sources of such inquiry include transcripts, notes, and other personal written, audio, or visual documents such as poems, diaries, and artworks. Heuristic research does not mean that the only participant of the study is the researcher. Instead, the researcher may include participants as coresearchers to their inquiry. However, even when coresearchers are involved, the researcher will remain dedicated to their interpretations to illuminate coresearchers' experiences. There is not a strict recipe for heuristic methodology. Instead, the creative process is at the heart of this research approach, which allows the researcher to stay flexible and explorative (Moustakas, 1994). An example of heuristic research in art therapy is Arslanbek's (2021) research on exploring the adolescent self through visual and written diaries. In this research, the author engaged in exploring her adolescent diaries, artworks, and poems to understand whether this exploration will enhance her current self-understanding. Arslanbek (2021) concluded that through exploring her adolescent diaries and artworks, she found important correlations between her past experiences and her current self, which enhanced her self-understanding.

Ethnographic research focuses on a culture-sharing group. Individuals who identify with a certain ethnicity or religion, women with similar displacement experiences (such as refugees), or people who share the same profession (like social workers or art therapists) can all be considered a culture-sharing group. Researchers who engage in ethnography look for patterns of the group and trust on participant self-reports, field notes, and participant observations (Creswell & Poth, 2018). In order to collect data, an ethnographer spends an extensive amount of time in the daily life of their participants. The researcher observes, takes notes, and interviews the participants to understand their behaviors, values, language, as well as the relationship between the group members. It is imperative for the ethnography researcher to have an understanding of cultural anthropology and sociocultural systems in order to recognize how ethnicity, religion, economy, and politics influence cultures (Creswell & Poth, 2018). There is a risk of *going native* when doing ethnography, when the researcher is so immersed in the world of their participants that they lose their objectivity which may result in ending the research project without completion. In an earlier research study, Spaniol (1998) attempted to understand the role of art, and perceptions of art therapy with individuals living with psychiatric disabilities. The author described how art therapists can approach their participants as a member of a culture just as an ethnographer would. For example, the author poses that approaching a patient group as a microculture will position the patient as an expert, who can teach art therapy researchers about their condition.

As identified in the prior examples, there are a range of qualitative methods that can be used in art therapy research. Data sources can include interviews, artwork, and documents related to sessions. Qualitative approaches to research provide comprehensive and detailed information. Unless the study has a large sample size, in general, qualitative research studies are not expected to lead to generalizable results.

Quantitative approaches in art therapy research

Quantitative research is the most commonly used approach in social and behavioral sciences. This approach emphasizes the use of statistical or numerical techniques and experimental methods to evaluate causal and correlational associations between natural and social phenomena. The aim of quantitative methods is often to produce findings that can be generalized. While sample sizes in quantitative research can be large or small, quantitative research with large sample sizes often provides better generalizable results. While providing generalizable outcomes, quantitative research comes with several limitations. These include limited flexibility in designing the study, limited capacity to capture emotions, behavioral observations and other qualitative information, and a smaller focus on capturing the phenomenon within the context it occurs (Queirós et al., 2017). Some examples of quantitative research methods include randomized controlled trials and quasi-experimental designs. Researchers use research instruments such as survey questionnaires, biological indicators, and statistical measures to collect and analyze numerical data (Babbie, 2020; Steckler et al., 1992).

In the social sciences, quantitative research often involves the use of standardized and validated psychological instruments. **Standardization** refers to uniform administration of the measurement, scoring, and interpretation of the test results. These standardized instruments are tested to be usable for specific mental health conditions or over time. In addition to these validated psychological instruments, survey questions and self-report data are also used to collect quantitative data which may or may not have been standardized.

Experimental methods are methods that look at the effect of one variable on the other. Experimental methods in art therapy may use standardized instruments and biomarkers. They measure whether the intervention results in desired outcomes under ideal circumstances. Experimental methods are often designed as controlled trials where participants are randomly assigned to either a treatment or control group.

Randomized controlled trials (RCTs) are considered the ideal experimental research methodology for studies that measure the effect of an intervention or program (Hariton & Locascio, 2018). In RCTs, participants are assigned randomly into **experiment groups** (those who receive the intervention) and **control groups** (those who do not receive the intervention). Random assignment of treatment and control group is used to reduce the risk of bias and to ensure that the outcomes emerge from the intervention, and not other confounding factors. **Random assignment** refers to assigning participants to a treatment or control group using a chance process. **Confounding factors** are variables that affect both the dependent and the independent variable. After the data is collected, researchers measure the differences in outcomes between control group and experiment group. Sandmire et al., (2012) studied psychological outcomes of art-making with undergraduate students. They randomly assigned participants to art-making or control groups and used surveys before and after the intervention to determine causal relationships between art-making and anxiety scores (see Fig. 5.2 for study set up). The control group did not engage in art-making but sat in a comfortable chair in a separate room. The researchers concluded that art-making had an anxiety-reducing effect on undergraduate students (Sandmire et al., 2012).

Quasi-experimental designs are a way to assess change in participants when it is not viable, or if it is difficult to recruit a control group. In this design, change is assessed before and after an intervention with the same group of participants; that is, the quasi-experimental designs do not have a control group or randomization (Kapitan, 2010). Chandraiah et al. (2012) evaluated the potential benefits of weekly group art therapy sessions with psychiatric outpatient participants during 8-week long session, groups consisted of six to eight patients. By using pretest and posttest, the authors found that the mean group scores of the standardized Center for Epidemiological Studies Depression Scale (CES-D; Radloff, 1977) significantly declined after art therapy treatment, suggesting that outpatient group art therapy may help reduce depressive symptoms in people with psychiatric diagnosis (see Fig. 5.3 for study setup).

Neurobiological mechanisms refer to what happens in the human brain and body when we create art, and how and why art therapy changes our functioning. A recent development in art therapy research is the use of **biological indicators** (such as heart rate or blood pressure) or **biomarkers** (such as saliva cortisol). Biomarkers are inspired by findings in neuroscience. Most biological indicators and biomarkers tend to be used more in quantitative designs. These can include brain imaging technologies (such as EEG, qEEG, fMRI, or fNIRS) or stress hormones and inflammatory markers which are used in identifying changes in depressive feelings, anxiety, or stress.

Belkofer and Konopka (2008) used electroencephalograph (EEG) data to measure the neural patterns of participants when they engaged in an hour of painting and drawing. In another study, Belkofer et al. (2014) used pre-/post-treatments within groups by analyzing the quantitative electroencephalogram

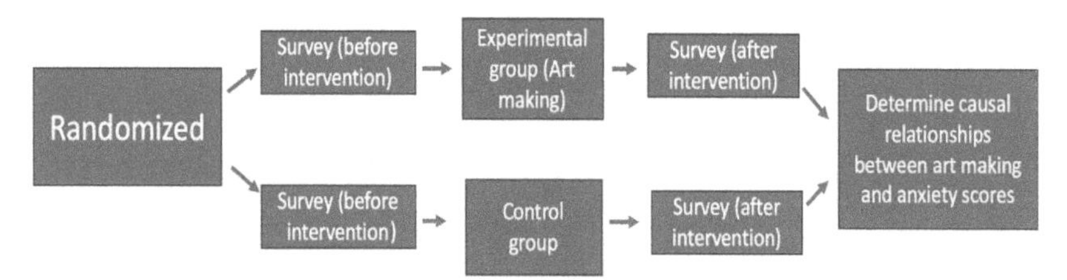

FIG. 5.2 *Sandmire et al. (2012) study setup.*

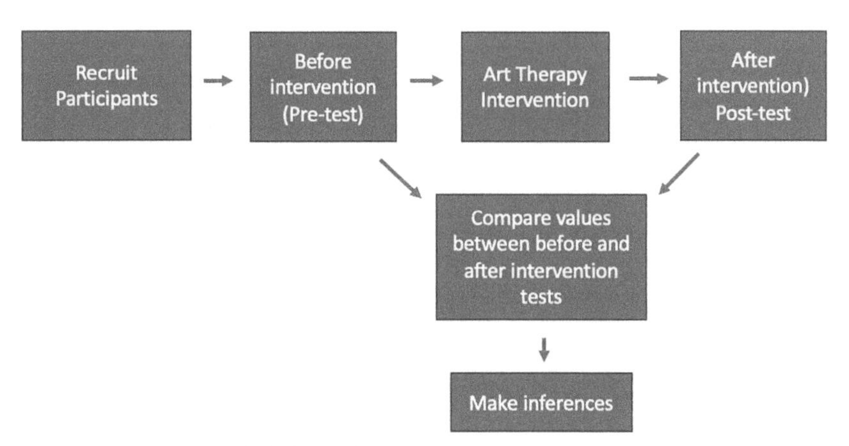

FIG. 5.3 *Chandraiah et al. (2012) study setup.*

(qEEG) to measure the residual impacts of materials used in art therapy in the brain following 20 min of drawing. The authors recorded qEEG values before and after 10 participants created drawings using oil pastels. Their results showed significant differences in qEEG levels between pre- and postdrawing. The authors also found that different areas of the brain were activated in artists compared to nonartists. In another study, Kaimal et al. (2017) investigated brain activation while coloring, doodling, and free drawing through using the functional near-infrared spectroscopy (fNIRS) technology. Authors concluded that art-making activated the medial prefrontal cortex, which may suggest that art-making evoked reward pathways in the brain. Walker et al. (2018) investigated brain activation while creating art with military service members who had chronic traumatic brain injury (TBI). Authors used functional magnetic resonance imaging (fMRI) technology to see whether art products created by military members and their fMRI results had connections. Walker et al. (2018) found that those who created artwork with themes of pride and patriotism had fMRI results closer to noninjured control group, whereas those who had artwork content suggesting injury and trauma had abnormal fMRI results. In a study where Kaimal et al. (2016) investigated the effect of art therapy on stress levels, they collected saliva samples before and after a 45-min art-making session from healthy adults. Their results showed statistically significant reduction of saliva cortisol levels after art-making. Haiblum-Itskovitch et al. (2018) measured heart rate variability (HRV) between using different art materials in order to understand the emotion eliciting qualities of materials. Authors used an electrocardiogram to measure HRV when creating art with pencil, crayons, or gouache paint.

Table 5.2 summarizes some of the commonly used quantitative research methods in art therapy.

TABLE 5.2 Commonly used quantitative research methods.

Experimental research methods	Nonexperimental research methods
Randomized controlled trial (RCT)	*Observational research design*
RCT is a clinical trial that aims to reduce selection bias by randomly assigning participants to experimental and control group. This design is done to ensure that any findings can be attributed to the study intervention alone	In observational research design, data is collected without manipulation of any variable. Rather they are observed and described as they naturally occur in the place of study. Some observational designs include longitudinal and cross-sectional research, case–control studies, cohort studies, and retrospective-prospective research
Quasi-experimental designs	*Survey design*
Like RCTs, quasi-experimental designs aim to investigate causal relationships. However, unlike RCTs, quasi-experiments may not use random assignment of participants. They may involve participant groups that are of different characteristics. Potential sample bias must be carefully examined in findings. Studies might also use pre–post designs without a control group	Survey design is a popular descriptive data collection method. A survey includes a group of questions that can both be conducted in written, oral, or electronic format. This method is useful to understand the practices, values, and ideas of a specific group
Single subject design	*Systematic reviews and meta analyses*
In single subject design, the study participant functions as their own control. Measurements are taken at multiple time points before, during, and after an intervention to assess changes in the same participant	Different from the traditional review approach, systematic reviews entail a rigorous search, review, and summarizing process of existing literature on the topic. They describe selection criteria and explain the methods that are used to evaluate the information that is included. Studies where results are combined using statistical analysis to develop an overall effect estimate are called meta-analyses

Mixed methods approach in art therapy research

Even though qualitative and quantitative research serve different purposes, in mixed methods research, they are used in combination when one method alone does not suffice to answer the research question. **Mixed methods research** designs typically include a quantitative and qualitative approach used in combination. Mixed methods research designs were developed to address the limitations of using a single approach (qualitative or quantitative). Some of the criticisms of quantitative approaches are that they do not capture the uniqueness and individuality of human experiences. Similarly, qualitative approaches have been critiqued for small sample sizes and the challenges in drawing conclusions to a larger population. Mixed methods designs help address these challenges to an extent by offering more comprehensive data and information about the topic being researched. For example, a study might include surveys and then incorporate a smaller set of case studies to better describe the findings. Alternatively, a study might include interviews first, which then help to develop a survey to be disseminated to a larger population. There are many ways to do mixed methods research and the ways vary depending on how the researchers want to combine the methods. Creswell and Clark (2017) offer terminology for commonly used mixed methods research designs. The most commonly used approaches are parallel or convergent, explanatory, and sequential designs (see Table 5.3).

Parallel or convergent mixed methods refer to studies when qualitative and quantitative research are conducted as part of a research study at the same time independently and the findings are brought together and integrated in the end. In this design, both qualitative and quantitative elements are given equal weight. An example of this would be a study where participants offer narrative responses and also fill out a survey.

In an **explanatory sequential study** the researcher will first use quantitative methods to collect data. Then in the second phase of research, they will collect qualitative data. Finally, they will bring qualitative and quantitative findings together to integrate and explain the phenomenon. An explanatory study might use quantitative methods as the main approach and might add qualitative component to better understand the results. For example, a study might initially use surveys (a quantitative tool) to understand the phenomenon, but also include interviews (a qualitative tool) to better understand the survey results.

An **exploratory sequential study** uses qualitative methods initially to understand the phenomenon. Then in the second phase, the researcher will collect quantitative data. Finally, in the third phase, both findings will be brought together. For instance, a study might use unstructured interviews to understand the lived experiences of a group. The qualitative data will then be used to develop a new quantitative measure (Creswell & Clark, 2017).

TABLE 5.3 Mixed method designs.

Parallel/convergent mixed method design	Qualitative and quantitative research is conducted at the same time independently and integrated at the end of the study
Explanatory sequential design	Quantitative method is used to explain the qualitative method
Exploratory sequential design	Qualitative method is used to explain the quantitative method

Examples of recent mixed method research in the field of art therapy include Walker et al. (2018) and Kaimal et al. (2018) studies with military service members, Kaimal, Carroll-Haskins, et al. (2019) study with caregivers of cancer patients study, and Kaimal and Ray (2017) study on the effects of individual studio-based free visual art making on affect and self-efficacy.

Participatory research approaches

In **participatory approaches**, research is planned and conducted *with* the participants (Bergold & Thomas, 2012). The research is participative and collaborative in nature and participants are often referred to as coresearchers or coinquirers. The focus of this research is to aid in the transformation of the participants as well as the environment. Action research is also called participatory action research (PAR), community-based action research, emancipatory research, or collaborative inquiry. In participatory research, the distinction between the researcher and the researched is challenged as participants are given the opportunity to take an active role in addressing the issues that affect them, their families, or communities (Brydon-Miller, 1997).

Participatory action research (PAR) is focused on social change with an underlying agenda of empowering the participants (Creswell & Poth, 2018). PAR is context specific and promotes social change by challenging inequality and creating a political debate and discussion for change to occur. Participatory research involves researchers and participants working together to understand and/or bring about a desired change. Researchers adopting these approaches utilize a range of methods including both quantitative and qualitative that are relevant to the context of the study, e.g., participant observation, interviews, focus groups, storytelling, drama, photography, and art. Participatory approaches integrate community members as partners in the research, especially when doing research with minority groups including indigenous communities (Pain, 2004).

Participatory and community-based art therapy approaches are emerging in the field to promote practice-based research in alternate environments (Kapitan, 2009). Spaniol (2005) documented participatory action research through a two-day conference which incorporated art therapy to foster dialogue and collaboration between art therapists and consumers of art therapy. The arts-based approach to PAR enabled participants to articulate commonalities and differences and to envision new practices and perspectives in their professional practice.

Indigenous and traditional voices incorporated in art therapy research

Indigenous voices are increasingly being recognized as long-standing forms of knowledge in contrast to the more recent western research methodologies. **Indigenous research frameworks** value traditional ways of knowing that are borne of years of observations, stored in memories and expressed in oral and physical forms including storytelling, fables, songs, dances, language, and rituals (Chilisa, 2012). Chilisa's (2012) book *Indigenous Research Methodologies* advocated for critiquing and resisting the widely accepted Euro-western research methodological practices regarded as scientific and objective. She emphasized alternative ways to generate knowledge and practice. Chilisa (2012) stressed the perspectives and concerns of the marginalized, and urged indigenous researchers to pay utmost attention to developing tests and measures that were culturally and contextually aligned with the community.

Since the emergence of art therapy as a mental health field in 1960s, the western psychological frameworks have influenced the art therapy practices including the understanding of symptoms, material use, interventions, and approaches. There is a growing interest in critically examining art therapy that is based on a westernized framework. This is especially important when practicing art therapy in other nonwestern communities in order to engage in cross-cultural collaboration and cultural competency. Art therapists have made attempts to incorporate indigenous and traditional art-making practices into art therapy clinical practice. Kaimal and Arslanbek (2020) have reviewed these attempts and highlighted some of the important issues of cultural considerations and competency as well as risks of misappropriation. Campanelli (1996) underlined that integration of indigenous symbols into art-making allows participants to take cultural pride and increases belonging within the group. When incorporating arts-based practices of other cultures, it is important to consider culturally respectful practices. Art therapists have been cautioned against the risk of misinterpretation and misappropriation of traditional and indigenous healing practices (Napoli, 2019). Researchers adopt qualitative, participatory, mixed methods, and ethnographic methodologies while examining indigenous and traditional art practices in relation to art therapy (Campanelli, 1996; Huss & Cwikel, 2005; Lu & Yuen, 2012; Warson et al., 2013).

Arts-based research approach

When doing art therapy research, it is common to use art works for various purposes including data analysis. However, there is one research method that uses artistic practice and art-making as an integral part of the process of learning and generating knowledge. **Arts-based research** (ABR) asserts the fundamental belief that artistic practice and art-making are an integral part of the process of learning and generating knowledge. Active art-making to gather information, make sense of it and disseminate it, makes art the unique foundation of systematic investigation in ABR (Barone & Eisner, 2012; McNiff, 2011). The goal of the ABR research is to highlight and express meaning, emotions, and thoughts which would otherwise be inexpressible (Barone & Eisner, 2012). Historically, arts-based research is intended to include all art disciplines such as dance, drama, music, visual arts, and poetry, with roots in arts education, anthropology, and archeology (Chilton & Leavy, 2014). The researcher is also involved in some form of direct art-making as part of the systematic inquiry (McNiff, 2011). Through engaging in the artistic process themselves, researchers strive for understanding of the phenomenon, predictable outcomes, and systematic steps that can be repeated through an artistic experience (McNiff, 2011).

In contrast to traditional research methods where emphasis may be on "exact replication of results in experiments using the same conditions, the arts encourage variation and even uniqueness in both methods and outcomes" (McNiff, 2011, p. 387). In order to assess the quality of ABR, the focus is on its aesthetic quality such as artistic elements and practices engaged in the inquiry, its ability to get to the heart of the issue, the capacity of the research to engage the audience and encourage reflection and dialogue, and its expressive power in terms of feelings evoked in the audience by the research (Barone & Eisner, 2012). ABR is noted to be especially significant to the field of art therapy with creative expression as a primary "way of knowing" (McNiff, 2011, p. 387), and generating meaning, insight, awareness, and behavioral change (Potash, 2019). Thus there is a perceived natural fit between arts therapies and ABR, both of which espouse art as the primary action in research and therapy (Kapitan, 2010).

ABR has been used as a systematic method for self-inquiry such as inquiring about one's beliefs, thoughts, and feelings. Potash (2019) highlighted the use of arts-based processes as an opportunity for researchers to use their own artistic experiences to contribute to new knowledge and insights that enhance understanding of one's self, relationships, and the community. As an example, Franklin (2012) wrote about art as an awakening of the self through arts-based contemplative methods in art therapy to demonstrate the fragility and resilience in times of personal crisis. Franklin (2012) explored the media of clay and charcoal, and combined practices of art and meditation in order to transform a difficult experience into a meaningful one. By engaging in intentional artistic processes such as digging, squeezing, or pulling the clay, the author simultaneously reflected on the qualities of transformation of the art material. The mindful presence with the creative process allowed new meaningful symbols and artworks to emerge through this arts-based exploration.

In a doctoral study, Scotti and Gerber (2017) used arts-based research to explore the experience of first-time mothers in the process of transitioning to motherhood. The arts-based method and *beyond_words* phenomena were used to capture the multidimensional and embodied nature of the experience, otherwise inexpressible in words. The researchers worked with five women and created a special method for data generation and analysis through montage portraiture, which included visual/textual interview in which the participants were asked to create a self-portrait by tracing photographs of themselves and their child. This technique was specifically designed by the first author for the purpose of the study. During this process, the researchers generated arts-based memos and arts-based analysis. Scotti used her personal artistic practice to create montage portraits of the participants based on content analysis of the text and visual data to capture and represent the participants experiences as authentically as possible. The final synthesis of this study comprised of a group portrait and a cross case analysis in the form of a dramatic play which was exhibited and performed on the premises of Drexel University in Philadelphia, PA.

More recently, arts-based research is being aligned with social activism to challenge the sociopolitical landscape (Gerber et al., 2020) with its underlying assertions of aesthetic power, emotional insight, social accessibility, and radical discourse (Barone & Eisner, 2012). In sum, ABR expands knowledge into the unknown, emphasizes creative inquiry, and opens new platforms for sharing knowledge with a worldview that understands art as the source of knowledge and adopts art making as the method to access knowledge.

The research approaches we mentioned earlier incorporate research questions that arise out of a combination of the researchers clinical interests and worldview. Such research provides the field of art therapy with answers to knowledge gaps, improves the quality of service delivery, and offers preliminary data for future research explorations. Next, we will explore another research approach that targets questions specifically about the service delivery, effectiveness, and quality of art therapy programs.

Program evaluation as an approach to bridge art therapy practice and research

Have you ever wondered if the clinic where you see your therapist evaluated their interventions for effectiveness in achieving the targeted health outcomes?

Program evaluation is a systematic way to analyze and evaluate the efficacy of programs and projects. Program evaluations can be conducted in most settings and are often referred to as quality improvement or quality assurance. This indicates that program evaluations are considered a way to gather data that can help improve clinical services.

Program evaluation connects clinical practice to research. In their paper, Kaimal and Blank (2015) explain how program evaluation can be a doorway to research in art therapy. Although not considered research in the traditional sense, program evaluation can help provide information that can lead to the development of larger scale studies. Program evaluation as a method developed in the 1960s and 1970s was a way to track outcomes of large federal investment in education and social services. Program evaluation can measure if the implemented program or intervention is applied as intended, if it is achieving the targeted outcomes, and if the program is cost-efficient. Program evaluations and studies in community settings often adopt a pragmatist approach. The program evaluation design will depend on what research questions are asked and what the worldview of the evaluator is. Commonly used tools for program evaluation in art therapy include surveys, interviews, focus groups, memos, and field notes.

There have been several program evaluation studies in art therapy. Klorer and Robb (2012) examined outcomes of an art therapy intervention with children in a Head Start program using program evaluation. In this study, the authors gathered feedback over 5 years as part of an art enrichment program that was run by art therapy graduate students at Head Start centers. At the end of the program year, facilitators gave evaluation surveys to the teaching and coordinating staff of the center. These surveys aimed to gather feedback about the students' experience and the overall rating of the program. Both quantitative survey responses and qualitative written comments and recommendations were analyzed. Results showed that teachers and coordinators considered the art enrichment program to be enjoyable and exciting for students, and professional and helpful for teachers and coordinators. The qualitative coding of written responses showed that the program helped students with increased communication skills, impulse control, self-esteem, and attention span.

Feldman et al. (2014) used program evaluation to assess the impact of art therapy interventions for patients undergoing HIV/AIDS treatment. The authors used process evaluation and outcome data indicators from the last 5 years that included a total of 255 clients who attended either group or individual art therapy at a community-based organization in New York. **Process evaluation** examines if the interventions are implemented as they are intended to be. **Outcome indicators** assess if the program achieved target outcomes. To assess outcome measures, the researchers used standardized questionnaires that measured depression severity and quality of life related to mental health. Findings suggested that art therapy decreased the severity of depression symptoms and improved mental health-related quality of life among individuals living with HIV/AIDS.

Evaluations have also been used in military art therapy settings. Kaimal et al. (2018) analyzed feedback from service members (SMs) with posttraumatic stress and traumatic brain injury who had received art therapy over a 2-year period. The SMs had been given a series of surveys to gather their feedback at 3 weeks, 6 weeks, and at the end of treatment (1–2 years). The feedback was used by the treatment team to improve art therapy clinical care on site as well as track changes over time in the SMs' perceptions of the value and contributions of art therapy in their treatment. The survey responses indicated that SMs found art therapy was initially useful in addressing issues around identity struggles. However, later in treatment, art therapy helped surface issues around grief and loss that were the underling challenges of posttraumatic stress and traumatic brain injury (TBI). The survey feedback helped illuminate the SMs' experiences and provided valuable insights into how art therapy can help service members in the short and long term.

The role of ethics review and institutional review boards

Doing research with human participants can pose ethical risks including risks to physical and emotional safety. **Research ethics** refers to the codes and principles researchers follow to ensure they conduct and publish research without bringing harm to the research participants or the society at large. To ensure this, any research with human participants is conducted after approval from an **Institutional Review Board (IRB)**. IRBs are offices within universities and research units that provide protections to participants and oversight of researchers to ensure ethical practices are followed in research studies. As with all research that involves human beings, legal and ethical protections have been developed to ensure the safety of participants in studies. Any human research study should have some type of IRB approval so that the researchers and the participants are ensured legal and ethical protections. The requirements are led by guidelines from the federal government to ensure that participants in research studies are not abused or mistreated in any way (About ORI, 2021). Many of the guidelines for human participants' protections were introduced after incidents of research misconduct were discovered in medical and psychological research in the 20th century. The examples highlighted the dangers of not having IRB oversight which in turn can result in harmful outcomes for participants. Some examples of misconduct have included withholding medical treatment of Black men with syphilis (while White male patients received treatment) to track the course of the illness, not disclosing full details of an experimental study of military service members on the impact of harmful certain chemical weapons, as well as allowing participants to engage in deceitful interpersonally destructive activities that resulted in mental health distress (Brawley, 1998; Rice, 2008).

IRB applications usually involve the inclusion of a study protocol, informed consent forms, and all data collection tools. A **study protocol** is a document where researchers describe the methodology in detail and share the outline of their planned intervention. **Informed consent** is a process of including participants in a study in a way that ensures that they are fully aware of the risks and benefits of participation. Researchers are all expected to be proficient and trained in the ethical conduct of research. CITI training (https://about.citiprogram.org/en/homepage/) is one such program that teaches prospective researchers the need for and guidelines for the ethical conduct of research. Once a study is approved, participants can be recruited and once they sign the informed consent form, they can be included as participants. Research participants have many protections including the freedom to leave a study at any time without any penalty. All these protections are included in the informed consent form.

The prioritization of research participants' physical and mental health is one of the main goals of IRBs. In all research, it is understood that there is some level of risk involved and the goal of the IRB is to determine the level of risk and ensure that the benefits of the research outweigh the risks. The process of review of research falls mainly into three categories: exempt, expedited, and full review. **Exempt research** is considered minimal risk and typically involves studies that are conducted with adults using social science research methods. **Expedited reviews** involve more than a minimal risk but potentially include sensitive topics or tools for data collection. **Full reviews** are needed for studies involving high-risk populations or for study procedures that are considered invasive. For example, some populations like pregnant women, children, prisoners, and those unable to consent (due to cognitive challenges) are considered vulnerable groups. Inclusion of individuals in these categories leads to a study being categorized as higher risk and requires that the researchers include processes to ensure the ethical protection of participants. What other steps do researchers need to take to ensure that participant rights are protected?

Research in art therapy typically involves collecting data about participants' experiences in clinical sessions and/or the artwork created as part of treatment. Research participants might belong to a range of clinically vulnerable populations. Inclusion of information for a study needs to ensure that participant voices and visual representation are valued and protected. Both the interpersonal aspects of art therapy practice as well as artwork involves risk in terms of loss of privacy as well as an incomplete or inaccurate representation of participant experiences. Artwork is also a potential source of vulnerability, patients and clients might not want their artwork shared in any public forum despite protections of personal identity. As stated under the Responsibility to Research Participants section in the *Art Therapy Credentials Board (ATCB) Code of Ethics, Conduct and Disciplinary Procedures* (ATCB, 2019), art therapy researchers "must treat information obtained about research participants during the course of the research protocol as confidential" (p. 5).

The way to address the concerns stated before is to affiliate with a research partner and work together to develop the appropriate protocol for the study and get it reviewed and approved by an IRB. The most robust studies in art therapy tend to involve clinician and researcher partnerships and help to capture the clinical relevance as well as ensure research protections and rigor. Given the recognized need for rigorous research in art therapy, there are many potential areas for further systematic inquiry.

Implications and future directions for research in art therapy

Art therapy is emerging as an influential discipline in contributing to the knowledge of health care and well-being. The different approaches to research in art therapy offer diverse pathways for systematic investigation through the integration of clinical knowledge and critical inquiry. Varying perspectives of knowledge and knowing call for a commitment to creating a valued space for researchers guided by different colors of the art therapy research palette. The different methodologies not only offer tools to integrate physiological and psychological outcomes where needed, but also challenge our understanding by questioning art therapy applicability, accessibility, and adaptations in a global setting. The different approaches can add critical value in advancing our understanding of art therapy with various populations in various settings and cultures. As evidence of the impact of art therapy grows so does the potential for interdisciplinary collaborations with disciplines like neuroscience, aesthetics, education, health care, technology, and museum studies among others.

Expanding research on mechanisms of change and the impact of art therapy in complementary and integrative care in diverse settings will also help position art therapy as a strong evidenced-based clinical practice. Widening the accepted research paradigms to nontraditional research practices such as indigenous, participatory, and arts-based methodologies will allow rigorous methodologies to foster a holistic view while maintaining a critical stance on the evolving culture of science. The expansion of multidisciplinary, multilevel studies with art therapists as primary investigators will furthermore impact nationwide licensure and advocacy efforts and may aid in enforcing appropriate title protection and educational standards.

Expanding research opportunities internationally, cross-culturally, and at various educational levels (undergraduate, graduate, doctoral, and postdoctoral) will help the discipline and the populations art therapists serve. Offering funding support to Black, indigenous, and other people of color is especially relevant to breaking the trend of White, middle-class art therapists in the United States that tend to be the majority. Studies might also use **longitudinal** data, namely, data that is collected sequentially from the same participants over a period of time to understand changes and trends over time. By implementing art therapy treatments over longer periods, researchers can observe the participants, and they can continuously collect quantitative or qualitative data based on surveys, standardized tests, or observations. Slayton et al. (2010) wrote about studies measuring the efficacy of art therapy based on interventions that lasted from 4 months to 3 years. They outlined several complications in art therapy outcome studies such as "lack of standardized reporting and utilization of control groups, and a tendency to use anecdotal case material to demonstrate treatment outcomes rather than measured results" (Slayton et al., 2010, p. 116). Further funding is also needed to demonstrate the feasibility and efficacy of art therapy, generalizability, and cost-effectiveness of art therapy.

Art therapy is continuing to build research capacity with over six doctoral programs preparing researchers in art therapy. Gerber et al. (2020) mapped the development of doctoral education in art therapy to emphasize the continual need for robust research as an emerging priority. Gerber et al. (2020) highlighted the current status of doctoral education as relatively new with exemplars of six U.S. programs and offered recommendations for future developments of programs to nurture research potential. An area of ongoing investigation is also the mechanisms of art therapy. At present, three theoretical models attempt to explain how art therapy works. These include the Expressive Therapies Continuum (ETC, Lusebrink et al., 2013), the Bodymind model (Czamanski-Cohen & Weihs, 2016), and the Adaptive Response Theory (ART, Kaimal, 2019). The **ETC** delineates three levels of engagement with art media—kinesthetic/sensory, perceptual/affective, and cognitive/symbolic—that are interconnected by the creative level. The **Bodymind model** outlines specific psychological and physiological mechanisms of change that are impacted as a result of engaging in art therapy. The **ART**, based on evolutionary biology and human development perspective, suggests that art therapy works through the dynamic interplay of the art therapist, the patient/client, the art-making process, and the art product to facilitate different adaptive responses.

In conclusion, as explored in this chapter, there are a variety of possibilities to select and combine research methodologies in the art therapy research palette. Researchers can choose from a range of perspectives, methods, and tools based on their research question and paradigm. Art therapy researchers have adapted research tools from social sciences to address the questions relevant to our discipline. The art therapy field can benefit from studies that aim to understand the adaptation of emergent methods and tools into art therapy research. Art therapy and arts-based interventions are widely and globally used. In line with the global expansion of art therapy, there is a greater need for more research on art therapy in culturally diverse international settings. Further research is also needed to better understand how art therapy practices might be implemented ethically with training and undergraduate level preparation including where there are no higher education programs available in art therapy. As the body of evidence continues to grow on mental health benefits of art and creativity, arts-based mental health services will inevitably continue to expand. It is important to continue thinking about art therapy's global applicability and adaptability. As art therapy continues to expand to a larger global context, there is a greater need for research on cultural and contextual adaptations and changes in art therapy delivery, while protecting the integrity of our profession.

Art experientials

1. Identify a topic of interest to you. Describe how this topic could be explored using any three different approaches discussed in this chapter. Take 20 min to draw a literal or abstract image of a research topic that interests you. Put the image at a distance and reflect on the composition for another 15–20 min. Jot down the setting of the image, the number of people in the drawing, your metaphoric or literal presence (or absence) in the artwork, and any other relevant components (colors, objects). Use this image to reflect on any approach among those discussed in this chapter that may resonate more with you and why.
2. Select a journal in creative arts therapies such as the *Arts in Psychotherapy* and find three studies that used different research methodologies. For example, one study might be a phenomenological case study, another might be arts-based research with adolescent males, and another study may have conducted a randomized controlled trial. Step 1: After identifying these studies and methods, reflect on how these methods can be represented visually. Draw or paint literal or abstract representations of these three methodologies on three separate papers. You may use pencils, crayons, oil pastels, or acrylic. Choose an appropriate paper thickness according to your medium, but make

sure you are using the same paper size as each methodology is different but weighted equally. While visualizing the methodologies reflect on these questions: If this methodology had a weight, shape, and size, what would it look like? What ideologies does this methodology represent for me? Step 2: At this point, think of other research methodologies that you have learned and interests you. If they are different than the three methodologies you created an image for, make sure to create and include visual representations of other methodologies that interest you among these. Step 3: After drawing or painting all methodologies, lay them out and think of these methodologies as pieces of a map. There are many other research methodologies that will not be included in this visual map, but if you wish, you can visualize them too. After laying down the artworks think of their relationship to each other. What do they have in common? Which ones are far away and which are closer to each other? Finally, think of your own research interest and which methodologies you find yourself closer to. You may find an imagined location in between these methodologies for your own research interest.

Chapter reflection questions

1. Think of your own areas of interest in art therapy and write down research questions related to your interests. After reading the material in this chapter, which research approaches appeal most to you? What approach do you think might best answer your research question?
2. What have you learned about research through this chapter? Do you think there are any absolute truths and forms of knowledge? What is the nature of truth to you? Is it generated by scientific research or constructed by the researcher?
3. After seeing the research methods in art therapy in this chapter, what do you think are some of the gaps in art therapy research today? What is a dream study you might want to do?
4. What collaborative study would you want to be involved in? Identify a major/department in your university and a potential topic of interest that intersects with art therapy.

Chapter terms

Abstract
Adaptive response theory
Arts-based research (ABR)
Axial coding
Biological indicators
Biomarkers
Bodymind model
Case studies
Conclusion
Confounding factors
Constructivism
Content analysis
Control group
Critical and poststructuralist theories
Data analysis
Delphi study

Emotion regulation
Empirical research
Ethical considerations
Ethnography
Experimental group
Experimental methods
Explanatory study
Exploratory study
Expressive Therapies Continuum
Generalizability
Grounded theory
Heuristic research
Indigenous and traditional voices
Indigenous research frameworks
Informed consent
Institutional Review Board (IRB)
Introduction
Limitations
Longitudinal
Method
Methodology
Mixed methods research
Narrative research
Neurobiological mechanisms
Objectivist
Open coding
Outcome studies
Paradigm
Parallel or convergent mixed methods
Participatory action research (PAR)
Participatory approaches
Participatory research-program evaluation
Peer-reviewed journal
Phenomenological research
Positivistic
Postpositivism
Pragmatism
Program evaluation
Qualitative research
Qualitative research approaches
Qualitative synthesis
Quantitative research
Quantitative research approaches
Quasi-experimental designs
Random assignment
Randomized controlled trials
Recommendations
Reliability
Research ethics
Research paradigms
Research proposal
Results
Reviewer
Selective coding
Standardization
Study protocol
Thematic analysis
Validity
Value free

References

About ORI. (2021). Retrieved from https://ori.hhs.gov/about-ori.

American Art Therapy Association. (n.d.). *Credentials and licensure*. Retrieved from https://arttherapy.org/credentials-and-licensure/ (6 December 2021).

Anderson, F. E., & Landgarten, H. (1974). Art in mental health: Survey on the utilization of art therapy. *Studies in Art Education*, *15*(3), 44–48.

Arslanbek, A. (2021). Exploring the adolescent-self through written and visual diaries. *The Arts in Psychotherapy*, *75*, 101825. https://doi.org/10.1016/j.aip.2021.101825.

ATCB. (2019). *Code of ethics, conduct, and disciplinary procedures*. Retrieved January 12, 2021, from https://www.atcb.org/Ethics/ATCBCode.

Babbie, E. R. (2020). *The practice of social research* (15th ed.). Cengage.

Barone, T., & Eisner, E. (2012). *Arts based research*. Sage.

Belkofer, C. M., & Konopka, L. M. (2008). Conducting art therapy research using quantitative EEG measures. *Art Therapy: Journal of the American Art Therapy Association*, *25*(2), 56–63. https://doi.org/10.1080/07421656.2008.10129412.

Belkofer, C. M., Van Hecke, A. V., & Konopka, L. M. (2014). Effects of drawing on alpha activity: A quantitative EEG study with implications for art therapy. *Art Therapy: Journal of the American Art Therapy Association*, *31*(2), 61–68. https://doi.org/10.1080/07421656.2014.903821.

Bergold, J., & Thomas, S. (2012). Participatory research methods: A methodological approach in motion. *Historical Social Research—Historische Sozialforschung*, 191–222. https://doi.org/10.17169/fqs-13.1.1801.

Betts, D., & Deaver, S. (2019). *Art therapy research: A practical guide*. Routledge.

Betts, D., & Laloge, L. (2000). Art therapists and research: A survey conducted by the Potomac Art Therapy Association. *Art Therapy: Journal of the American Art Therapy Association*, *17*(4), 291–295. https://doi.org/10.1080/07421656.2000.10129765.

Braun, V., & Clarke, V. (2006). Using thematic analysis in psychology. *Qualitative Research in Psychology*, *3*, 77–101. https://doi.org/10.1191/1478088706qp063oa.

Brawley, O. W. (1998). The study of untreated syphilis in the Negro male. *International Journal of Radiation Oncology, Biology, Physics*, *40*(1), 5–8. https://doi.org/10.1016/S0360-3016(97)00835-3.

Brydon-Miller, M. (1997). Participatory action research: Psychology and social change. *Journal of Social Issues*, *53*(4), 657–666. https://doi.org/10.1111/0022-4537.00042.

Campanelli, M. (1996). Pioneering in Perth: Art therapy in Western Australia. *Art Therapy: Journal of the American Art Therapy Association*, *13*(2), 131–135. https://doi.org/10.1080/07421656.1996.10759209.

Chandraiah, S., Ainlay Anand, S., & Avent, L. C. (2012). Efficacy of group art therapy on depressive symptoms in adult heterogeneous psychiatric outpatients. *Art Therapy: Journal of the American Art Therapy Association*, *29*(2), 80–86. https://doi.org/10.1080/07421656.2012.683739.

Chilisa, B. (2012). *Indigenous research methodologies*. Sage Publications.

Chilton, G., & Leavy, P. (2014). Arts-based research practice: Merging social research and the creative arts. In P. Leavy (Ed.), *The Oxford handbook of qualitative research* (pp. 403–422). Oxford University Press.

Clark, A. M. (1998). The qualitative-quantitative debate: Moving from positivism and confrontation to post-positivism and reconciliation. *Journal of Advanced Nursing*, *27*(6), 1242–1249.

Collie, K., Bottorff, J. L., & Long, B. C. (2006). A narrative view of art therapy and art making by women with breast cancer. *Journal of Health Psychology*, *11*(5), 761–775. https://doi.org/10.1177/1359105306066632.

Creswell, J. W. (2014). *Research design: Qualitative, quantitative and mixed methods approaches*. Sage.

Creswell, J. W., & Clark, V. L. P. (2017). *Designing and conducting mixed methods research*. Sage Publications.

Creswell, J. W., & Poth, C. (2018). *Qualitative inquiry and research design*. Sage.

Czamanski-Cohen, J., & Weihs, K. L. (2016). The Bodymind model: A platform for studying the mechanisms of change induced by art therapy. *The Arts in Psychotherapy*, *51*, 63–71. https://doi.org/10.1016/j.aip.2016.08.006.

Deaver, S. (2002). What constitutes art therapy research? *Art Therapy: Journal of the American Art Therapy Association*, *19*(1), 23–27. https://doi.org/10.1080/07421656.2002.10129721.

Eaton, L. G., Doherty, K. L., & Widrick, R. M. (2007). A review of research and methods used to establish art therapy as an effective treatment method for traumatized children. *The Arts in Psychotherapy*, *34*(3), 256–262. https://doi.org/10.1016/j.aip.2007.03.001.

Feilzer, Y. M. (2010). Doing mixed methods research pragmatically: Implications for the rediscovery of pragmatism as a research paradigm. *Journal of Mixed Methods Research*, *4*(1), 6–16. https://doi.org/10.1177/1558689809349691.

Feldman, M. B., Betts, D. J., & Blausey, D. (2014). Process and outcome evaluation of an art therapy program for people living with HIV/AIDS. *Art Therapy: Journal of the American Art Therapy Association*, *31*(3), 102–109. https://doi.org/10.1080/07421656.2014.935593.

Franklin, M. (2012). Know thyself: Awakening self-referential awareness through art-based research. *Journal of Applied Arts & Health*, *3*, 87–96. https://doi.org/10.1386/jaah.3.1.87_1.

Gantt, L. (1998). A discussion of art therapy as a science. *Art Therapy: Journal of the American Art Therapy Association*, *15*(1), 3–12. https://doi.org/10.1080/07421656.1989.10759306.

Gerber, N., Kapitan, L., Forinash, M., Gussak, D., Civita, J. L., & Kaimal, G. (2020). Doctoral education in art therapy: Current trends and future directions. *Art Therapy: Journal of the American Art Therapy Association*, 1–8. https://doi.org/10.1080/07421656.2020.1761735.

Glaser, B. G., Strauss, A. L., & Strutzel, E. (1968). The discovery of grounded theory; strategies for qualitative research. *Nursing Research*, *17*(4), 364.

Gruber, H., & Oepen, R. (2018). Emotion regulation strategies and effects in art-making: A narrative synthesis. *The Arts in Psychotherapy*, *59*, 65–74. https://doi.org/10.1016/j.aip.2017.12.006.

Guba, E. G., & Lincoln, Y. S. (1994). Competing paradigms in qualitative research. In N. K. Denzin, & Y. S. Lincoln (Eds.), *Handbook of qualitative research* (pp. 105–117). Sage.

Haiblum-Itskovitch, S., Czamanski-Cohen, J., & Galili, G. (2018). Emotional response and changes in heart rate variability following art-making with three different art materials. *Frontiers in Psychology*, *9*, 968. https://doi.org/10.3389/fpsyg.2018.00968.

Hariton, E., & Locascio, J. J. (2018). Randomised controlled trials—The gold standard for effectiveness research. *BJOG: An International Journal of Obstetrics and Gynaecology*, *125*(13), 1716.

Huet, V., Springham, N., & Evans, C. (2014). The art therapy practice network: Hurdles, pitfalls and achievements. *Counseling and Psychotherapy Research: Linking Research With Practice*, *14*(3), 174–180. https://doi.org/10.1080/14733145.2014.929416.

Huss, E., & Cwikel, J. (2005). Researching creations: Applying arts-based research to Bedouin women's drawings. *International Journal of Qualitative Methods*, *4*(4), 44–62. https://doi.org/10.1177/160940690500400404.

Junge, M., & Linesch, D. (1993). Our own voices: New paradigms for art therapy research. *The Arts in Psychotherapy*, *20*(1), 61–67. https://doi.org/10.1016/0197-4556(93)90032-W.

Kaimal, G. (2017). The road ahead: Preparing for the future of art therapy research. In R. Carolan, & A. Backos (Eds.), *Emerging perspectives in art therapy* (pp. 58–73). Routledge.

Kaimal, G. (2019). Adaptive response theory (ART): A clinical research framework for art therapy. *Art Therapy: Journal of the American Art Therapy Association*, *36*(4). https://doi.org/10.1080/07421656.2019.1667670.

Kaimal, G., & Arslanbek, A. (2020). Indigenous and traditional visual artistic practices: Implications for art therapy clinical practice and research. *Frontiers in Psychology*, *11*, 1320. https://doi.org/10.3389/fpsyg.2020.01320.

Kaimal, G., Ayaz, H., Herres, J., Dieterich-Hartwell, R., Makwana, B., Kaiser, D. H., & Nasser, J. A. (2017). Functional near-infrared spectroscopy assessment of reward perception based on visual self-expression: Coloring, doodling, and free drawing. *The Arts in Psychotherapy*, *55*, 85–92.

Kaimal, G., & Blank, C. L. (2015). Program evaluation: A doorway to research in the creative arts therapies. *Art Therapy: Journal of the American Art Therapy Association*, *3*(2), 89–92. https://doi.org/10.1080/07421656.2015.1028310.

Kaimal, G., Carroll-Haskins, K., Mensinger, J. L., Dieterich-Hartwell, R. M., Manders, E., & Levin, W. P. (2019). Outcomes of art therapy and coloring for professional and informal caregivers of patients in a radiation oncology unit: A mixed methods pilot study. *European Journal of Oncology Nursing*, *42*, 153–161. https://doi.org/10.1016/j.ejon.2019.08.006.

Kaimal, G., Jones, J. P., Dieterich-Hartwell, R., Acharya, B., & Wang, X. (2018). Evaluation of art therapy programs for Active Duty Military service with TBI and post-traumatic stress. *The Arts in Psychotherapy*. https://doi.org/10.1016/j.aip.2018.10.003.

Kaimal, G., & Ray, K. (2017). Free art-making in an art therapy open studio: Changes in affect and self-efficacy. *Arts & Health*, *9*(2), 154–166. https://doi.org/10.1080/17533015.2016.1217248.

Kaimal, G., Ray, K., & Muniz, J. (2016). Reduction of cortisol levels and participants' responses following art making. *Art Therapy: Journal of the American Art Therapy Association*, *33*(2), 74–80. https://doi.org/10.1080/07421656.2016.1166832.

Kaiser, D. H. (2015). What should be published in art therapy? What should art therapists write about? *Art Therapy: Journal of the American Art Therapy Association*, *32*(4), 156–157. https://doi.org/10.1080/07421656.2015.1107376.

Kaiser, D., & Deaver, S. (2013). Establishing a research agenda for art therapy: A Delphi study. *Art Therapy: Journal of the American Art Therapy Association*, *30*(3), 114–121. https://doi.org/10.1080/07421656.2013.819281.

Kapitan, L. (2009). The art of liberation: Carrying forward an artistic legacy for art therapy. *Art Therapy: Journal of the American Art Therapy Association*, *26*(4), 150–151. https://doi.org/10.1080/07421656.2009.10129618.

Kapitan, L. (2010). *Introduction to art therapy research*. Routledge/Taylor & Francis.

Kapitan, L. (2017). *Introduction to art therapy research* (2nd ed.). Routledge.

Kaplan, F. F. (2001). Areas of inquiry for art therapy research. *Art Therapy: Journal of the American Art Therapy Association*, *18*(3), 142–147. https://doi.org/10.1080/07421656.2001.10129734.

Kartch, F. (2017). Narrative interviewing. In M. Allen (Ed.), *The SAGE encyclopedia of communication research methods*. Sage Publications. https://doi.org/10.4135/9781483381411.

Klorer, G., & Robb, M. (2012). Art enrichment: Evaluating a collaboration between head start and a graduate art therapy program. *Art Therapy: Journal of the American Art Therapy Association*, *29*(4), 180–187. https://doi.org/10.1080/07421656.2012.730920.

Landgarten, H. (1978). The state of art therapy in greater Los Angeles, 1974: Two-year follow-up study. *Art Psychotherapy*, *5*, 227–233. https://doi.org/10.1016/0090-9092(78)90038-8.

Levy, B., & Ulman, E. (1967). Judging psychopathology from paintings. *Journal of Abnormal Psychology*, *72*, 182–187. https://doi.org/10.1037/h0024440.

Linesch, D. (1995). Art therapy research: Learning from experience. *Art Therapy: Journal of the American Art Therapy Association*, *12*(4), 261–265. https://doi.org/10.1080/07421656.1995.10759176.

Linesch, D., Aceves, H. C., Quezada, P., Trochez, M., & Zuniga, E. (2012). An art therapy exploration of immigration with Latino families. *Art Therapy: Journal of the American Art Therapy Association*, *29*(3), 120–126. https://doi.org/10.1080/07421656.2012.701603.

Lu, L., & Yuen, F. (2012). Journey women: Art therapy in a decolonizing framework of practice. *The Arts in Psychotherapy*, *39*(3), 192–200. https://doi.org/10.1016/j.aip.2011.12.007.

Lusebrink, V. B., Mārtinsone, K., & Dzilna-Šilova, I. (2013). The expressive therapies continuum (ETC): Interdisciplinary bases of the ETC. *International Journal of Art Therapy*, *18*(2), 75–85. https://10.1080/17454832.2012.713370.

Malhotra, B. (2019). Art therapy with puppet making to promote emotional empathy for an adolescent with autism. *Art Therapy: Journal of the American Art Therapy Association*, *36*(4), 183–191. https://doi.org/10.1080/07421656.2019.1645500.

McNiff, S. (2011). Artistic expressions as primary modes of inquiry. *British Journal of Guidance and Counselling*, *39*(5), 385–396. https://doi.org/10.1080/03069885.2011.621526.

Mertens, D. M. (2015). *Research and evaluation in education and psychology: Integrating diversity with quantitative, qualitative, and mixed methods* (4th ed.). Sage Publications.

Moustakas, C. (1994). *Phenomenological research methods*. Sage Publications.

Napoli, M. (2019). Ethical contemporary art therapy: Honoring an American Indian perspective. *Art Therapy: Journal of the American Art Therapy Association*, *36*(4), 175–182. https://doi.org/10.1080/07421656.2019.1648916.

Noddings, N. (2005). Perspective 2: Pragmatism. In J. L. Paul (Ed.), *Introduction to the philosophies of research and criticism in education and the social sciences* (pp. 57–60). Pearson.

Pain, R. (2004). Social geography: Participatory research. *Progress in Human Geography*, *28*(5), 652–663. 10.1191%2F0309132504ph511pr.

Paul, J. L. (Ed.). (2005). *Introduction to the philosophies of research and criticism in education and the social sciences*. Prentice Hall.

Potash, J. S. (2019). Arts-based research in art therapy. In D. Betts, & S. Deaver (Eds.), *Art therapy research: A practical guide* (pp. 119–146). Routledge.

Queirós, A., Faria, D., & Almeida, F. (2017). Strengths and limitations of qualitative and quantitative research methods. *European Journal of Education Studies*. https://doi.org/10.5281/zenodo.887089.

Radloff, L. S. (1977). The CES-D scale: A self-report depression scale for research in the general population. *Applied Psychological Measurement*, *1*(3), 385–401.

Reynolds, M. W., Nabors, L., & Quinlan, A. (2000). The effectiveness of art therapy: Does it work? *Art Therapy: Journal of the American Art Therapy Association*, *17*(3), 207–213. https://doi.org/10.1080/07421656.2000.10129706.

Rice, T. W. (2008). The historical, ethical, and legal background of human-subjects research. *Respiratory Care*, *53*(10), 1325–1329.

Robb, M. (2015). An overview of historical and contemporary perspectives in art therapy research in America. In D. E. Gussak, & M. L. Rosal (Eds.), *The Wiley handbook of art therapy* (pp. 609–616). John Wiley & Sons.

Sandmire, D. A., Gorham, S. R., Rankin, N. E., & Grimm, D. R. (2012). The influence of art making on anxiety: A pilot study. *Art Therapy: Journal of the American Art Therapy Association*, *29*(2), 68–73. https://doi.org/10.1080/07421656.2012.683748.

Scotti, V., & Gerber, N. (2017). Rendering beyond_words in transitioning to motherhood through visual and dramatic arts. In *Voices* (3rd ed., Vol. 17). A World Forum for Music Therapy.

Silver, R., & Lavin, C. (1977). The role of art in developing and evaluating cognitive skills. *Journal of Learning Disabilities*, *10*(7), 27–35. https://doi.org/10.1177/002221947701000704.

Slayton, S. C., D'Archer, J., & Kaplan, F. (2010). Outcome studies on the efficacy of art therapy: A review of findings. *Art Therapy: Journal of the American Art Therapy Association*, *27*(3), 108–118. https://doi.org/10.1080/07421656.2010.10129660.

Spaniol, S. (1998). Towards an ethnographic approach to art therapy research: People with psychiatric disability as collaborators. *Art Therapy: Journal of the American Art Therapy Association*, *15*(1), 29–37.

Spaniol, S. (2005). "Learned hopefulness": An arts-based approach to participatory action research. *Art Therapy: Journal of American Art Therapy Association*, *22*(2), 86–91. https://doi.org/10.1080/07421656.2005.10129446.

Steckler, A., McLeroy, K. R., Goodman, R. M., Bird, S. T., & McCormick, L. (1992). Toward integrating qualitative and quantitative methods: An introduction. *Health Education Quarterly*, *19*(1), 1–8. https://doi.org/10.1177/109019819201900101.

Talwar, S. (2016). Is there a need to redefine art therapy? *Art Therapy: Journal of the American Art Therapy Association*, *33*(3), 116–118. https://doi.org/10.1080/07421656.2015.1068632.

Van Lith, T., Fenner, P., & Schofield, M. (2011). The lived experience of art making as a companion to the mental health recovery process. *Disability and Rehabilitation*, *33*(8), 652–660. https://doi.org/10.3109/09638288.2010.505998.

Walker, M. S., Kaimal, G., Koffman, R., & DeGraba, T. J. (2016). Art therapy for PTSD and TBI: A senior active duty military service member's therapeutic journey. *The Arts in Psychotherapy*, *49*, 10–18. https://doi.org/10.1016/j.aip.2016.05.015.

Walker, M. S., Stamper, A. M., Nathan, D. E., & Riedy, G. (2018). Art therapy and underlying fMRI brain patterns in military TBI: A case series. *International Journal of Art Therapy*, *23*(4), 180–187.

Warson, E., Taukchiray, W., & Barbour, S. (2013). Healing pathways: American Indian medicine and art therapy. *Canadian Art Therapy Association Journal*, *26*(2), 33–38. https://doi.org/10.1080/08322473.2013.11415584.

Part II

Theoretical orientations: Gathering the tools

Chapter 6

Overview of theoretical orientations

Eileen Misluk-Gervase, MPS, LPC, ATR-BC, LMHC, CEDCAT
Graduate Art Therapy Department, Herron School of Art and Design, IUPUI, Indianapolis, IN, United States

Voices from the field
The purpose of psychotherapy is to set people free.

Rollo May (1981, p. 19)

How does psychotherapy set people free? This chapter intends to help answer this question. The purpose is to provide students with an overview of psychological theories and a wide variety of theoretical approaches, how they are used, and the primary assumptions that define each movement. These assumptions include the therapist's role, the role of the client, and the etiology of the presenting issues. These assumptions are the foundation of theories, approaches, and interventions applied to answer the question mentioned previously.

Learning outcomes

After reading this chapter, you will be able to

1. Define the three primary theories that shaped the foundation of psychology and art therapy.
2. Define the primary assumptions of each movement including the role of the therapist, role of the client, and the etiology of presenting issues.
3. Explain art therapy theoretical approaches and the role of the art-making process and product.

Chapter overview

Psychology is the science of mental and behavioral patterns and theory is an "integrated set of statements that summarizes and explains" (Sdorow, 1998, p. G11). Psychological theory is a set of statements that summarizes and explains mental

Foundations of Art Therapy. https://doi.org/10.1016/B978-0-12-824308-4.00009-0

and behavioral patterns within the context of society and culture. During the first half of the 20th century, three theories emerged that shaped the foundation of psychology: psychoanalysis, behaviorism, and humanism (Brooks-Harris, 2008). Psychoanalysis and behaviorism viewed human behavior as determined but disagreed on the source. Psychoanalysis believed that internal drives (id, ego, superego) and the unconscious determined human behavior. Behaviorism considered that environment, reward, and punishment drove behaviors. Contradictory to both, humanism emphasized free will and choice. In practice, these theories are approaches to understanding pathology, behavior, and wellness.

Psychoanalysis dominated the first half of the 20th century with foundational ideas of the **unconscious**, **resistance**, **defenses**, and **transference** (Karon & Widener, 1995). The **unconscious** contains thoughts, feelings, and memories that influence us without awareness (Sdorow, 1998). The goal of psychoanalytic therapy is to bring unconscious content into consciousness. **Resistance** emerges because of the inability to bring unconscious content to consciousness by repressing thoughts, experiences, or feelings (Gehart, 2016). **Defenses** operate unconsciously and are a normal part of development and functioning (Tyson & Tyson, 1990). Examples of defenses are denial, avoidance, isolation, and displacement. **Transference** is the way that people reenact situations and emotions, often painful, and experience these repeatedly with other individuals (Tyson & Tyson, 1990). **Libidinal types**—erotic, obsessional, and narcissistic—are based on libido or sexual energy emerging from the id, ego, and superego in the psyche (American Psychological Association, 2020). **Countertransference** is the therapist's conscious and unconscious reactions to the client's transference based on the therapist's own psychological needs and conflicts (American Psychological Association, 2020). The traditional role of the psychoanalyst in therapy as passive and neutral supports unconscious content to transfer onto the therapist (Rubin, 2016). Analyzing these relationship patterns supported unconscious content to be brought to consciousness and then understood. Followers of psychoanalysis further developed psychodynamic theories. Alfred Adler emphasized social constructs, interpersonal interactions, cognitive organization, and mastery as behavioral drivers. Carl Jung combined soul, spirit, and idea to develop a theory of the psyche as well as the personal, transpersonal, and archetypal layers of the unconscious (Gehart, 2016). Critics of psychoanalytic approaches found the theory to be steeped in metaphor and lacking empirical evidence (Brooks-Harris, 2008).

How is **behaviorism** different than psychoanalysis? Behaviorism challenged psychoanalysis with its focus on observable actions rather than unconscious drives and metaphoric language. Researchers who opposed psychoanalysis such as Ivan Pavlov, B.F. Skinner, John Watson, and Joseph Wolpe used scientific rigor with a focus on **classic** and **operant conditioning** to address the behaviors and attitudes of human beings (Brooks-Harris, 2008). The result of this research became the foundation of behaviorism. **Classical conditioning** is the pairing of a neutral stimulus to a behavior and **operant conditioning** is the process of increasing or decreasing the probability of behaviors based on certain circumstances (Sdorow, 1998). Early behaviorists felt that this approach contrasted with psychoanalysis, mainly the principle of **reciprocal inhibition**. **Reciprocal inhibition** is the pairing of a contradictory action to an emotion to reduce the intensity and interrupt the conditioned response to the emotion (Heriot & Pritchard, 2004). For example, using relaxation techniques to reduce anxiety.

What makes humanism different than psychoanalysis and behaviorism? **Humanism** and existentialism emerged as contradictory to both psychoanalysis and behaviorism. These theories rejected the idea of the role of the therapist as the expert on the client. In humanism, the therapist's role is to assist the client by relying on their individual drive and autonomy. It emphasizes the present rather than the past, and the feelings that emerge from these experiences. The relationship between the client and therapist was an essential component of the therapeutic process and client growth. This approach, later named by the founder Carl Rogers as client-centered therapy, hypothesized that individuals have the capacity to constructively handle experiences that come into conscious awareness (Rogers, 1951). Fritz Perls developed Gestalt Therapy which focused on the here and now, promoting the creative power of clients, and using experiments to engage in authentic experiences (Brooks-Harris, 2008). Both approaches focused on the direct lived experiences of the client and the impact of an authentic therapeutic relationship.

How did these three theories evolve? In the second half of the 20th century, a second evolution of these three theories evolved into more complementary approaches rather than contradictory ones. The theories that emerged supported the practice of using one or multiple ideas or strategies from theories rather than a single approach (Brooks-Harris, 2008). Interpersonal theory from psychodynamic focuses on interpersonal relationships and the influence on internal experiences and behavioral implications. Cognitive theory from behaviorism relies on gaining an understanding of internal thought processes that influence behaviors. Experiential theory from humanism emphasized the emotions within the lived experiences to understand behaviors.

This second evolution of theory leads to further complexity as theories emerge, emphasizing family and cultural systems that influence human behavior. Family Therapist Virginia Satir found that families behave as a unit and when one member is in pain the entire family is affected (Haber, 2002). The family unit must be treated, rather than the individual. Systemic theory explores the impact of family, social, cultural, and other social systems on the thoughts, feelings, and behaviors of an individual. The feminist and the multicultural theory emerged because of previous approaches not meeting the needs of women and people of color. Feminist theory emphasizes the contradictory roles and messages that shape women's behaviors. Multicultural theory recognizes the social and cultural impacts that shape relationships, thoughts, feelings, and actions.

Additionally, a focus on the relationship between physical health and mental well-being influenced the emergence of the biopsychosocial and health psychology approach. This approach helped merge the gap between psychiatry and psychology as it integrates social, cultural, and psychological influences of health and illness (Brooks-Harris, 2008). Influenced by family, systemic and cognitive theory, constructivist theory maintains that individuals construct their reality through family, social, and cultural impacts. Individuals develop and revise personal hypothesis throughout life by focusing on lived experiences and personal meaning (D'Andrea, 2000).

The field of psychology is continuously evolving to address client's needs with the changing social and cultural landscape resulting in the emergence of new or adapted approaches. In the *Handbook of Innovative Therapy*, Corsini compiled a list of different theoretical approaches, leading to 250 entries which all emerged from the three foundational approaches—psychoanalysis, behaviorism, and humanism (Corsini, 2001).

Art therapy theory

What is the role of psychological theory in art therapy? Art therapy theory integrates psychological theory principles on pathology and the role of the client and therapist with an understanding of the kinesthetic, sensory, and organizing principles of art-making and materials. **Pathology** is the deviation in thoughts and/or behaviors from what is considered healthy or adaptive (American Psychological Association, 2020). Art therapists use this integration to conceptualize cases, develop treatment plans, and assess progress. These theories will be explored in greater depth in the following chapters.

"Art therapy is an active therapeutic process that integrates the mind and body, allowing an individual to uncover, explore, and process emotional content through art-making" (Misluk-Gervase, 2020, p. 89). Art therapy often pairs fear-arousing emotions with art-making to enhance coping and regulation (Hass-Cohen and Loya, 2008). Art therapists encourage spontaneity, support attention, and create a holding space for overwhelming emotional experiences (Shore, 2014).

Art therapy theory provides a framework for understanding the "roots" of thoughts, feelings, and actions of clients. With varying degrees, theories take into consideration the role of history in presenting issue(s) and their influence on treatment outcomes; and external and internal forces that drive thoughts, actions, and emotions. Theory guides the development of assessments, directives, interventions, and goals. Theories identify general outcomes that reflect the effectiveness of therapy and the attainment of goals. Some therapists work from a single theory, while others use an integrated approach. Art therapists who use multiple or integrated approaches base their decision on the needs of the client and their therapeutic goals.

Just as theories in the field of psychology developed, art therapists applied those foundational theories to the creative process resulting in the development of unique art therapy theories. Within all theoretical frameworks, art therapy provides an opportunity for clients to explore imagery, thoughts, feelings, and memories using art materials. The following section will provide an overview of three broad theoretical frameworks: psychoanalytic and Jungian, humanistic, and cognitive behavior therapy. It includes an understanding of the assumptions of the theory in the field of art therapy and the use of art-making and creative processes that support client needs. **Creative processes** are broad practices that encompass a wide range of art-making approaches, materials, and activities used within the therapeutic setting. For example, this includes traditional or fine art materials (e.g., drawing and painting), craft (e.g., sewing, weaving), visual journaling, and art-making from found objects.

Psychodynamic approaches in art therapy

Psychoanalytic and psychodynamic art therapy

Psychoanalytic approaches place a focus on uncovering, exploring, and understanding the meaning behind personal imagery, thoughts, and feelings hidden in the unconscious. Using the psychoanalytic intervention, free association, art therapists encourage clients to use the creative process to uncover and gain insight into the self (Rubin, 2016). Through the creative process of exploring images and objects, the relationship between the client and therapist will develop along with hidden conflicts and feelings that can be further explored (Edwards, 2004). Unlike classical psychoanalysts, psychoanalytic art therapists may not be able to remain neutral and passive. Although, maintaining a level of neutrality in session encourages transference from the client and enhances a deeper understanding of the client's functioning (Rubin, 2016). The act of remaining neutral inhibits a safe therapeutic space to explore unconscious content through the creative process. Art-making provides a concrete, tangible experience with a product that chronicles the therapeutic experience and provides documentation for unconscious content. The art product is analyzed to gain a deeper understanding of defense mechanisms, symbols, and metaphors.

The exploration of personal symbols is a "fundamental and intrinsic form of self-expression" (Hogan, 2016, p. 35). Symbols are present in all social and cultural groups across time. Exploration of personal symbols also includes an understanding of cultural symbols and archetypes. **Archetypes** are universal symbols that have been passed down from our ancestors and can be found in art, dreams, and religion (Sdorow, 1998). Art therapy supports the exploration of archetypes and personal symbols that emerge in the psychoanalytic process.

Jungian art therapy

The Jungian approach emphasizes the collective unconscious through dreams, life patterns, and themes that emerge to build a relationship between the ego and the self (Gehart, 2016). Jung's belief in the power of creative expression in expanding the relationship between the ego and unconscious is supported by his explorations in art-making (Swan-Foster, 2016). Jungian art therapists use the creative process to gain a deeper understanding of the collective unconscious where archetypes and universal symbols reside. Jung believed that symbols can be either healing or destructive, and that everyone has certain archetypes—self, anima/animus, and shadow—that exist while other archetypes express themselves at various times (Gehart, 2016). Furth elaborates on the function of symbols as they emerge in art therapy (Furth, 2002). Symbols are thought to have a compensatory or complementary function that seeks to balance a person's psyche (Furth, 2002). A **compensatory** image expresses a hidden or neglected area and brings this area into awareness so that it can be further understood (Hogan, 2016), while a **complementary** symbol emerges from the unconscious to reflect the current conscious state. In addition to archetypes, Jungian art therapists focus on exploring individual symbols that emerge and support the exploration from the unconscious to the conscious. **Complexes,** as Jung defined, are emotionally charged images and ideas in the psyche that remain dormant in the unconscious (Swan-Foster, 2016). For complexes to surface, there must be enough psychic energy. **Psychic energy** is innate, carrying thoughts, feelings, and instincts that are brought from the unconscious to the conscious by images, relationships, and dreams, and at times, back to the unconscious (Swan-Foster, 2016). Psychic energy is a foundational concept in Jungian theory, flowing from the complex into an archetype (Swan-Foster, 2016). Jungian art therapists focus on the archetypal imagery as a source for healing and transformation. The images that emerge as a result of the exploration of archetypes have the potential to organize, attract, and contain psychic energy, and move unconscious content into consciousness aiding in personal transformation and insight (Swan-Foster, 2016). Jungian art therapy embeds art-making in the exploration of archetypes and images and supports the process through the creation of visual representations. The role of the Jungian art therapist is to facilitate the process without interference, supporting the client's natural exploration rather than directing the session (Hogan, 2016). The resulting product is not analyzed as it would be in a psychoanalytic framework but rather is used to engage in dialogue that further supports the creative process (Hogan, 2016). A Jungian approach to art therapy requires an understanding that the uncovering, exploring, and healing process cannot be rushed or dictated.

Under the umbrella of psychoanalytic art therapy additional approaches exist including archetypal art therapy, object relations art therapy, and self-psychology art therapy. While each theory differs from one another, the core psychoanalytic principles of libidinal drive and determined behaviors remains foundational.

Behavioral approaches in art therapy

As stated before, behavioral approaches place an emphasis on environment, reward, and punishment. The focus is on pairing contradictory action to reduce the intensity of a feeling or emotion and in turn interrupting the conditioned response to develop new behavioral responses. Many approaches emerged from behaviorism including cognitive, behavioral, developmental, systems, cognitive behavioral, and dialectical behavior therapy.

Cognitive behavior art therapy

Cognitive behavior art therapy (CBAT) utilizes thinking, sensing, identifying, and understanding emotions through the creative process (Rubin, 2016). Art-making requires planning, problem-solving, and memory recall, which are foundational concepts in CBAT. To address fears, CBAT therapists will use exposure, either in vivo (live) or imaginal, in the therapeutic setting. This allows the client to directly practice reciprocal inhibition, the pairing of a contradictory action to an emotion. CBAT art therapy uses the creative process to employ "imaginal exposure" to thoughts, feelings, and/or situations that are feared (Hogan, 2016). The use of art materials allows clients' control over the rendering of the images and in turn provides a sense of control over the "imaginal exposure." Accompanying this approach is "imaginal rescripting" where clients are using mental images to explore new emotional and behavioral responses to situations (Hogan, 2016). CBAT supports this technique by providing materials that result in a concrete image to document the process. Art therapists are encouraged to use guiding questions as well as identify negative thinking and triggers (Hogan, 2016).

Incorporating art-making that uses self-soothing practices, connecting mind and body, supports the balancing of internal thoughts and external behaviors. These processes explore and reframe negative and potentially overwhelming experiences through the organizing principles of art-making. The resulting products of these explorations serve to track therapeutic processes; review goals and ideas; and externalize internal thoughts, feelings, and stimuli. Homework is a crucial component of CBAT to utilize therapeutic strategies in everyday life. Homework assignments may include symptom logs, journals, and structured activities like exposure and response to certain stimuli. Homework is organized into three categories: psychoeducational homework, self-assessment homework, and modality-specific homework (Tang & Kreindler, 2017). CBAT art therapy would use creative processes, such as reflective visual journaling to explore therapeutic topics outside of the session (Malchiodi & Rozum, 2002).

Other behavioral approaches

Art therapists also use other behavioral approaches such as developmental art therapy, systems art therapy, cognitive art therapy, behavioral art therapy, and dialectical behavioral art therapy. Developmental art therapy is used to explore sensory stimulation, develop skills, and adapt to changing situations (Malchiodi et al., 2002). This approach is primarily used with individuals with intellectual or developmental disabilities. Dialectical behavioral therapy (DBT) integrates concepts of mindfulness and acceptance to change behavioral patterns (Linehan, 1993). Dialectical behavioral art therapy uses creative mindfulness to increase insight into emotions, along with nonjudgmental reflections from the therapist to reframe negative thoughts (Clark, 2016). Art-making supports self-soothing, self-exploration, and identity formation while providing reflective distance from potentially overwhelming experiences.

Humanistic approaches in art therapy

Existential art therapy

Existential theory is concerned with existential questions about life, purpose, and existence in accordance with the individual subjective experience (Gehart, 2016). The theory values the "I–thou" relationship between therapist and client, the here and now experience, and promotes responsibility and independence (Gehart, 2016). Existential art therapy employs the creative process to explore the concepts mentioned earlier. Creativity offers opportunities for free choice, meaning-making, and mindfulness (Malchiodi, 2002). The existential art therapist aims to develop an authentic relationship with the client where mutual art-making supports the shared journey of the therapist and client (Moon, 2016). The creative process allows clients to make decisions, which promotes responsibility and independence. This leads clients to engage in the creative struggle as mirror for the concerns of human existence such as aloneness, suffering, meaning, and death (Moon, 2016). The art product is not meant to be interpreted by the therapist. Instead, the art therapist creates the holding environment for the client to explore their artwork, make meaning from the struggle, and support the healing that results from this process.

Person-centered art therapy

The humanistic orientation requires the art therapist to engage in three primary tasks: being present and open, honoring thoughts and feelings as they arise in the moment, and engaging in authentic art-making alongside clients (Moon, 2016) with the goal of creating a safe and supportive environment where growth can occur (Hogan, 2016). Person-centered art therapy actively engages the client in the creative process through client-generated ideas. There is a greater emphasis on the process of creating than on the product, although, the product serves as a place of exploration and discussion to gain personal insight (Rogers, 1951).

Gestalt art therapy

Gestalt therapy focuses on the here and now, reconciling unfinished business and understanding of the self in the world. Gestalt art therapy uses the creative process and art-making to explore experiences in the "here and now" and allows the product to be the focus of attention and a representation of the evoked feelings (Hogan, 2016). It requires the client to actively engage; connect with the "whole" self; and become acquainted with movement, internal sensation, and visual productions (Rhyne, 2016). The gestalt art therapist is authentic and empathetic and engages in honest and direct communication to establish a space where the enactment of personal experiences through the creative process is safely explored.

Transpersonal art therapy

Transpersonal art therapy will not be further explored in the upcoming chapters, although this brief explanation helps to frame this approach within the field. Transpersonal theory recognizes a spiritual dimension existing beyond the individual and culture (Brooks-Harris, 2008). Transpersonal art therapy uses art-making for grounding and a method of spiritual practice (Allen, 2016). The creative process supports the exploration of opposites, personal lessons, and exposes polarities (Allen, 2016). The transpersonal art therapist is not the expert; the therapist and client learn together to understand the self and one another.

In conclusion, regardless of the theoretical framework, all approaches require an understanding of the tenants of the theory, and role of the therapist and client. This understanding shapes the conceptualization of the clinical case and therapeutic goals (Fig. 6.1).

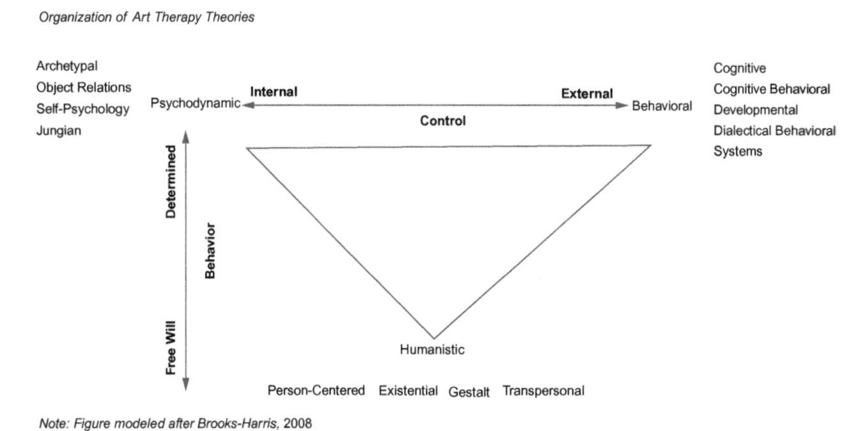

FIG. 6.1 *Organization of art therapy theories.*
(No permission required.)

Case conceptualization and treatment planning

Overview

How are theory and art-making applied to clinical cases? Therapists use case conceptualizations. A **case conceptualization** is the clinician's overall understanding of the client's presenting issue(s) viewed through a particular theory and this understanding is guided by the biological, psychological, symptomology, and social and cultural influences (John & Segal, 2015). A well-rounded case conceptualization uses a theoretical orientation to provide a framework for developing a clinical narrative that identifies presenting issue(s), internal and external supports, and barriers. A formal or informal intake process is used to gather biological, psychological, and social history (biopsychosocial history). This will include the client's understanding of their presenting concern, precipitating factors, triggers, and strengths through the lens of the identified theory. **Biological history** will include the physical development of the client, medications, and medical procedures that are important for the therapist to know. For example, if the client is a child, it would be important to know if they sat up, walked, and talked consistently with peers their age. **Psychological history** includes prior therapy, psychiatric treatment, psychiatric medications, and familial history of mental illness. A **social history** will include family patterns, social and/or cultural affiliations, spiritual or religious affiliations, and community relationships. The **presenting issue(s)** is the reason that the individual is seeking treatment. **Precipitating factors** are the experiences that preceded the presenting issue(s). **Triggers** are experiences that exacerbate the presenting concern or increase the severity. Identifying client strengths and existing support systems such as familial, financial, and community supports determine the need for additional providers or community resources. Case conceptualizations provide a detailed overview for treatment.

Treatment planning

Treatment planning involves the art therapist's use of case conceptualization to inform a plan for treatment. The structure used in the development of a treatment plan was originally influenced by the medical field to meet the needs of third-party payors also known as insurance companies (Gehart, 2016). Gehart found that this type of treatment plan focused solely on symptoms leading to a lack of theoretical focus (Gehart, 2016). To address this concern, theory-based models of treatment planning for counseling and psychotherapy were developed to align to the assumptions and goals of the identified theory (Berman, 1997; Gehart & Tuttle, 2003). The treatment plan includes the mode of treatment (e.g., individual, group, and/or family therapy) and an understanding of diversity issues that influence treatment approaches, interventions, and outcomes. Treatment plans include long-term goals and short-term objectives that guide the therapeutic process. Art therapists use formal and informal assessments to aid in treatment planning. Formal assessments such as the Person Picking an Apple from a Tree (PPAT), Diagnostic Drawing Series (DDS), and the Levick Emotional and Cognitive Art Therapy Assessment (LECATA) provide standardized administrative guidelines and rating instruments (Brooke, 2004). Informal assessments include guidelines for administration and rating but do not provide standardized tools. These assessments are used to develop treatment goals, assess progress, and support termination once goals are met.

Therapy in action

Therapeutic process includes building rapport and exploring the presenting issue(s) through the creative process. **Rapport** is the development of a trusting and honest relationship between the client and therapist. **Therapeutic progress** is the tracking of progress on short-term objectives and long-term goals. Lambert found that four common factors influence success in therapy: the client, relationship, theory, and a placebo (Lambert, 1992). Client factors include motivation, supports, and resources. The quality of the therapeutic relationship from the perspective of the client is extremely important in making therapeutic progress. The theory, approaches, and interventions utilized by the therapist influence the success of therapy. The last factor is the placebo effect or the level of hope that engaging in therapy will improve presenting issue(s). Lambert suggests that out of these four, the most important are the client factors and the relationship between the client and therapist (Lambert, 1992).

Dependent on the theoretical framework, the art therapist uses verbal and nonverbal therapeutic interventions which include structured and unstructured directives. The strategies used in verbal processing vary across theories. The role of verbal processing supports articulating thoughts, actions, and emotions in a supportive environment, which leads to deeper insights. In turn, this process aids in the development of skills to make sense of the current situation. Structured directives provide a theme or suggestion for the session, and unstructured directives allow the client to select the themes (McNeilly, 1983). Art materials may be offered by the therapist or selected by the client and used to explore concepts, feelings, memories, experiences, and any other content that may arise during therapy as they relate to the presenting issue(s) and theoretical focus.

Many therapists use an integrated approach, which means that they are selecting aspects of theories that will best support the varying needs of their clients. For example, art therapists may assign homework (behavioral approach) as part of their treatment plan while using a Jungian approach in session focusing on archetypes. The creative process serves to uncover, explore, take risks, externalize, and contain experiences and emotions. It provides a space to visually explore the "unseen" internal world. Art-making is diagnostic and interactional. The content explored in session supports the therapeutic goals, serves as a tool for communication, and the art product is evidence of therapeutic dynamics (Junge, 2010). The following chapters will provide an in-depth understanding of psychodynamic, cognitive behavior, and humanistic theory and approaches in art therapy. This will include detailed explanations and clinical case examples to further elucidate these theories in practice.

Art experientials and reflection questions

1. In what other ways can art therapists integrate theories?
2. Using symbols in art-making helps art therapists learn about clients, what symbols would best describe you?
3. Based on your understanding, what theory resonates with you and why?
4. Select an image for each theory and create a chart exploring the relationship between the three theories.
5. Create a visual diagram of the relationship between the therapist and client for each theory.
6. Select an image that represents the components of a case conceptualization and create a visual diagram.

Additional resources

Sommers-Flannigan, J. & Sommers-Flannigan, R. (Directors). (2014). Clinical interviewing: Intake, assessment and therapeutic alliance [Film]. Psychotherapy.net. https://www.psychotherapy.net/video/clinical-interview-intake-assessment-training.

Sommers-Flannigan, J. & Sommers-Flannigan, R. (Directors). (2014). Counseling and psychotherapy theories in context and practice: Skills, strategies, and techniques [film]. Psychotherapy.net. https://www.psychotherapy.net/video/counseling-psychotherapy-theories.

Menninger Foundation (Director). (1986). Art therapy: The healing vision [Film]. Expressive Media. https://www.expressivemedia.org/product/art-therapy-the-healing-vision/.

Smith, S. (Host). (2016–2019). The thoughtful counselor [Audio podcast]. Palo Alto University's division of Continuing & Professional Studies. https://thethoughtfulcounselor.com/.

Chapter terms

Archetypes
Behaviorism
Biological history
Case conceptualization
Classical conditioning
Compensatory
Complementary
Complexes
Countertransference
Creative process
Defenses
Humanism
Libidinal types
Operant conditioning

Pathology
Precipitating factors
Presenting issues
Psychic energy
Psychoanalysis
Psychological history
Rapport
Reciprocal inhibition
Resistance
Social history
Transference
Treatment planning
Treatment process
Treatment progress
Triggers
Unconscious

References

Allen, P. (2016). Art making as a spiritual path. In J. A. Rubin (Ed.), *Approaches in art therapy* (3rd ed., pp. 271–285). Routledge.

American Psychological Association. (2020). In *APA dictionary of psychology*. American Psychological Association. https://dictionary.apa.org/pathology.

Berman, P. S. (1997). *Case conceptualization and treatment planning: Exercises for integrating theory and clinical practice*. Sage.

Brooke, S. L. (2004). *Tools of the trade: A therapist's guide to art therapy assessments* (2nd ed.). Charles C. Thomas.

Brooks-Harris, J. E. (2008). *Integrative multitheoretical psychotherapy*. Lahaska Press.

Clark, S. M. (2016). *DBT-informed art therapy: Mindfulness, cognitive behavior therapy, and the creative process*. Jessica Kingsley.

Corsini, R. J. (2001). *Handbook of innovative therapy* (2nd ed.). John Wiley & Sons.

D'Andrea, M. (2000). Postmodernism, constructivism, and multiculturalism: Three forces reshaping and expanding our thoughts about counseling. *Journal of Mental Health Counseling*, *22*(1), 1–16.

Edwards, D. (2004). *Art therapy*. Sage.

Furth, G. (2002). *The secret world of drawings: A Jungian approach to healing through art* (2nd ed.). Inner City Books.

Gehart, D. (2016). *Theory and treatment planning in counseling and psychotherapy* (2nd ed.). Cenage Learning.

Gehart, D. R., & Tuttle, A. R. (2003). *Theory-based treatment planning for marriage and family therapists: Integrating theory and practice*. Brooks/Cole.

Haber, R. (2002). Virginia Satir: An integrated, humanistic approach. *Contemporary Family Therapy*, *24*(1), 23–34. https://doi.org/10.1023/A:1014317420921.

Hass-Cohen, N., & Loya, N. (2008). A visual system in action. In N. Hass-Cohen, & R. Carr (Eds.), *Art therapy and clinical neuroscience*. Jessica Kingsley.

Heriot, S. A., & Pritchard, M. (2004). "Reciprocal inhibition as the main basis of psychotherapeutic effects" by Joseph Wolpe (1954). *Clinical Child Psychology and Psychiatry*, *9*(2), 297–307. https://doi.org/10.1177/1359104504041928.

Hogan, S. (2016). *Art therapy theories: A critical introduction*. Routledge.

John, S., & Segal, D. L. (2015). Case conceptualization. In R. L. Cuatin, & S. O. Lilienfeld (Eds.), *The encyclopedia of clinical psychology*. John Wiley & Sons, https://doi.org/10.1002/9781118625392.wbecp106.

Junge, M. B. (2010). *The modern history of art therapy in the United States*. Charles C. Thomas.

Karon, B. P., & Widener, A. J. (1995). Psychodynamic therapies in historical perspective. In B. Bonger, & L. E. Beutler (Eds.), *Comprehensive textbook of psychotherapy: Theory and practice*. Oxford.

Lambert, M. J. (1992). Psychotherapy outcome research: Implications for integrative and eclectic counselors. In J. C. Norcross, & M. R. Goldfried (Eds.), *Handbook of psychotherapy integration* (pp. 94–129). Basic Books.

Linehan, M. M. (1993). *Skills training manual for treating borderline personality disorder*. Guilford.

Malchiodi, C. (2002). Humanistic approaches. In *Handbook of art therapy* (2nd ed., pp. 58–71). Guilford.

Malchiodi, C., Kim, D., & Choi, W. S. (2002). Developmental art therapy. In C. Malchiodi (Ed.), *Handbook of art therapy* (2nd ed., pp. 93–105). Guilford.

Malchiodi, C., & Rozum, A. L. (2002). Cognitive-behavioral and mind body approaches. In C. Malchiodi (Ed.), *Handbook of art therapy* (2nd ed., pp. 72–81). Guilford.

McNeilly, G. (1983). Directive and non-directive approaches in art therapy. *The Arts in Psychotherapy*, *10*(4), 211–219. https://doi.org/10.1016/0197-4556(83)90021-7.

Misluk-Gervase, E. (2020). Art therapy and the malnourished brain: The development of the nourishment framework. *Art Therapy: Journal of the American Art Therapy Association*, *38*(2), 87–97. https://doi.org/10.1080/07421656.2020.1739599.

Moon, B. (2016). Art therapy: Humanism in action. In J. A. Rubin (Ed.), *Approaches to art therapy* (3rd ed., pp. 203–211). Routledge.

Rhyne, J. (2016). Gestalt art therapy. In J. A. Rubin (Ed.), *Approaches to art therapy* (3rd ed., pp. 212–229). Routledge.

Rogers, C. R. (1951). *Client-centered therapy*. Houghton-Mifflin.

Rubin, J. A. (2016). *Approaches to art therapy: Theory and technique*. Routledge.

Sdorow, L. M. (1998). *Psychology* (4th ed.). McGraw Hill.

Shore, A. (2014). Art therapy, attachment, and the divided brain. *Art Therapy: Journal of the American Art Therapy Association*, *31*(2), 91–94. https://doi.org/10.1080/07421656.2014.903827.

Swan-Foster, N. (2016). Jungian art therapy. In *Approaches to art therapy: Theory and technique* (3rd ed., pp. 167–188). Taylor & Francis. https://doi.org/10.4324/9781315716015.

Tang, W., & Kreindler, D. (2017). Supporting homework compliance in cognitive behavioural therapy: Essential features of mobile apps. *JMIR Mental Health*. https://doi.org/10.2196/mental.5283, e20.

Tyson, P., & Tyson, R. L. (1990). *Psychanalytic theories of development: An integration*. Yale University Press.

Chapter 7

Psychoanalytic and Jungian approaches to art therapy

Leah Friedman, MA, ATR-BC and Jessica Whitesel, MA, LPC, ATR-BC
Transpersonal Art Therapy, Naropa University, Boulder, CO, United States

Voices from the field
Both Carl Jung and Sigmund Freud took as fact that unseen realms exist and that those realms are teeming with images. This alone secures their foundational value to art therapists. What is of the greatest importance, however, is to remember that each man's most critical theories emerged from the study of his own images, Freud through his dreams and Jung through active imagination, and in that way they serve as mentors to all of us who practice art therapy.

Pat B. Allen

Learning outcomes

After reading this chapter, you will be able to

1. Describe the chapter authors' queering approach and rationale as they explore the contributions of Freud and Jung to art therapy.
2. Describe Freud's model of the psyche and the role of the psyche in art and symbolism.
3. Articulate the ways art therapists expanded on Freud's approach to treatment.
4. Examine the purpose of defense mechanisms and describe examples of defense mechanisms.
5. Explain the role of the art object in therapy.
6. Describe the role of sublimation in art therapy.
7. Describe Jung's Red Book and how he used active imagination to explore his psyche.
8. Explain Jung's view of art and the art image in therapy.
9. Describe Jung's model of the psyche.
10. Identify the role of the shadow in one's process to become whole.
11. Describe some of the criticisms of Jung's beliefs.
12. Explain two examples of Jungian art therapy methods.

Foundations of Art Therapy. https://doi.org/10.1016/B978-0-12-824308-4.00004-1

Chapter overview

This chapter explores the foundational contributions of both Freud and Jung to the field of art therapy while at the same time critically examining psychoanalytic thought and Jungian or analytic theory. The chapter first describes the major contributions of Freud. Art therapy methods that are based on psychoanalytic thought are described and explored with a case example. This section concludes with the first author's cultural and historical connection to psychoanalysis. The second half of the chapter described the influence of Jung or analytic approach to art therapy. Jung's approach to the psyche is described. Several Jungian art therapy methods are described and explored with a case example. The chapter concludes with experiential activities and additional resources.

Authors' approach to this chapter

In this chapter, we as coauthors seek to acknowledge the foundational contributions of both Freud and Jung to the field of art therapy in its formative stages of development and to outline central concepts of both branches of psychoanalytic thinking, especially those which have influenced art therapy approaches. This chapter also thinks critically about the ways in which psychoanalytic thought and Jungian or analytic theory have historically caused harm; perpetuated theories that marginalized women, people of color, and the LGBTQIA+ community; and reinforced the biases of historical and current psychological paradigms. This task requires a recognition that social justice is not an addendum to the current theory but a necessary integration of critical consciousness to the theory itself.

In the field of art therapy, sometimes students will wonder aloud if art therapists have a "magic decoder ring" that offers the meaning of images and if this secret decoder will allow them unfettered access to the minds of their clients. Franklin and Politsky (1992) acknowledged this challenge and explained that there are many interpretive strategies and that the very nature of symbolism implies multiple meanings. By imagining that the therapist has magical all-knowing wisdom, the client/artist can also be swept up in this fantasy. For the therapist, there can be a powerful desire to be seen by the client as a special caregiver with the power to heal.

The idea that art can contain symbolism and meaning, which may be hidden even from the artist, is compelling. It creates a fantasy that a skillful art therapist need only examine an artwork to uncover a secret map that reveals one's psyche with all the needed insight for healing. Do you think art therapists can "read" art? Does art reveal something deeper?

Understanding where these ideas come from can give us insight into the ways we look at **interpretation** explaining the meaning of an image. There is a notion that suggests interpreting an image is necessary for validity, which ultimately privileges the perspective of the analyst over the maker of the image (Hogan, 2001). This puts the analyst in a position of authority and power that may or may not be problematic but certainly requires acknowledgment (Hoffman, 1998).

For art therapists, it is imperative to keep these dynamics in mind in order to avoid possible abuse of power and to centralize the client's voice and perspective. We must keep in mind that the interpretation occurs within a framework that also assumes certain things, such as analyzing the transference to the therapist as central to the "cure." This assumption alone does not acknowledge either the imbalance of power between art therapist and client, or the cultural context as relevant to both parties.

Art therapists and students must also ask themselves—what ideas define us? What parts of art therapy's history do we reject, redefine, or subvert? Questioning historical context adds valuable layers of insight without elevating our predecessors (Freud and Jung) to deity status. This chapter seeks to unpack Freud and Jung's valuable contributions while queering our perspective to, at last, include voices who have been marginalized and pathologized throughout previous texts. **Queering** our perspective, in this context, refers to questioning dominant or assumed paradigms, identifying underrepresented voices, and surfacing systemic inequity.

A queering perspective includes (1) deconstructing the notion that the therapist knows everything, while acknowledging the sociocultural context of both therapist and client; (2) centralizing the client/artist's role in their own meaning making; and (3) questioning cultural and historical context which leads to pathologizing facets of identity as "sick." Students and practitioners of helping professions must look at internalized forms of oppression as well as oppression on institutional, ideological, and interpersonal levels. In seeking to integrate this perspective, we must remain in the paradox of both recognizing and challenging the value of Freud and Jung's theories. By remaining in this tension, we envision a future cocreated space for art therapy education and practice.

Introduction

What are the first things that come to your mind when you hear the names Freud and Jung? Both names carry with them powerful connotations and relationships to the field of psychology. A judgment or belief about these men may come to mind as you begin this chapter. Perhaps as you read this now, you might pause and ask yourself if you have any thoughts, feelings, or images associated with these names? It is important to notice this internal response and acknowledge the way the topic is loaded; perhaps it is based on prior education, experience with the theory, or even pop culture references to the names. Reflecting on the history of art therapy requires acknowledgment of the field's relationship to Freud and Jung's theories. At the same time, art therapists and students must look critically at their theory and practice, approaching it with a contemporary lens (Talwar et al., 2019). To do so requires a deep dive into some basic assumptions about art therapy. In other words, art therapists and students must utilize the essence of important historical theory while also applying their current views.

Both Freud and Jung sought strategies to access the client's **unconscious** (defined as whatever one is not aware of in a given moment) in order to reveal the layers beneath the conscious mind. Freud (1961) believed that unconscious material left unexplored led to pathology, and that revealing and gaining insight into the unconscious created health and well-being. Jung and Freud disagreed on the nature of the unconscious; Freud saw unconscious processes as defensive and requiring intervention, while Jung saw the unconscious as a necessary and healing part of the overall self.

We can find meaningful theory and relevant applications by translating works through a critical lens, locating ourselves in relationship to the original words, and questioning existing assumptions. It is also important to note that a traditional analytic approach takes many years to complete, which is both impractical and inaccessible for most people who seek mental health care. It is common for managed care to dictate a number of allowed sessions (sometimes as few as three to six), so this multiyear analytic approach might be considered inaccessible for many people. However, as art therapists, we are inherently well equipped to adapt by applying a creative lens and the power of art-making as an always evolving practice. Utilizing art-based therapeutic techniques can invite an individual into a relationship with their own art that can endure long beyond therapy.

Freud's psychoanalytic theory

To fully unpack Freud's influence on art therapy, it is important to examine several of the key concepts he introduced in his work, such as art and symbolism, art and relationship, and sublimation. He observed that many patients described dreams, memories, and experiences primarily in images and the way images became useful in analysis points to some of his early use of art in a therapeutic context (Malchiodi, 2003). In its most basic form, the psychoanalytic process was meant to make the client's unconscious thoughts, feelings, desires, and fantasies accessible to the conscious mind (Freud, 1961). He believed humans employ defense mechanisms or strategies which allow the conscious mind to avoid stress and anxiety. Several of these defense mechanisms include: **projection** (attributing unwanted personal attributes onto another), **repression** (pushing away unwanted thoughts or memories), **sublimation, and displacement** (discussed later in this chapter), to name a few. Utilizing imagery described by clients, Freud took this observation further and postulated that to fully understand an art image it must be interpreted or analyzed for meaning.

Art and symbolism

Some of Freud's early theories on symbolism came from work with dreams and dream imagery. He wrote about how dreams are often the disguised, repressed, or hidden wishes and urges of the dreamer (Freud, 1961). Imagery that is unacceptable to a person by day emerges at night and reveals itself during sleep. This idea is key to Freud's belief that each individual is made up of drives and urges that are deemed acceptable or not, which leads to a person's desire to push away the urge (which is called **repression**) or be unaware of the urge (therefore the urge becomes part of the **unconscious**).

Freud's model of the psyche includes the **id** (our instincts), **ego** (the reality), and **superego** (our ideals). According to Freud, urges that may not be deemed appropriate or socially acceptable are **id impulses**, which are tempered by the governing function of the ego (Tobin, 2015). In this way, a symbol, a dream, or a fantasy might be an id impulse being expressed in a way that is easier for us to receive. For example, you might dream about running through open space as a symbol of feeling trapped or a desire to run away. Through the dream image, the id impulse is communicated through metaphor. Freud would then utilize this described imagery as a way to gain insight about the patient's unconscious. He suggested the drive to create was the attempt to bypass unproductive or destructive urges into a form that would be more socially acceptable.

Talwar et al. (2019) discussed how Freud influenced art therapy theories and techniques by suggesting that artwork is a way to make the human psyche readable. Talwar et al. (2019) expressed concern about how Freudian interpretive strategies may be applied to clients without regard to social and cultural influences. This helpful critique suggests that if standards of development and pathology have been based on psychoanalytic values without cultural context, such systems create othering. **Othering** is labeling anything that is different from the "norm," which can lead to marginalization. Othering may occur when patients are only seen within Freud's own context. While we can imagine how this impacts our understanding of Freud's theory, it simultaneously challenges the assumption that all art should be interpreted for meaning (Mann, 2006).

Margaret Naumburg is credited with expanding Freud's approach by moving from the use of verbal descriptors of images to directly asking patients to create images (1987). She believed this furthered Freud's concept of **free association** or speaking aloud without filter as a gateway to the unconscious, which allowed patients to create imagery spontaneously in order to bypass the ego's self-consciousness that comes with speech. Naumburg approached the imagery as communication that came in both pictures and words noting that often her patients could draw something they struggled to describe (Naumburg, 1987). She also described how the art object itself holds at least a portion of the transference or feelings that the patient may have about the therapist (Rubin, 2011). Naumburg is associated with the early defining of art therapy and she held a strong psychoanalytic lens. It is sometimes described that she preferred to focus less on the art-making and more on how the art product could be useful for diagnostic and analytic purposes (Cohen, 2017).

While Naumburg operated inside the systemic model of the time, she also helped to convince her psychiatric peers that children's art with unusual perspectives (e.g., two opposing views of the same situation) was a creative expression rather than an indication of pathology. Naumburg's approach was to separate the goal of interpretation and meaning making from art-making and this approach challenged the analytic approach (Franklin & Politsky, 1992; Hogan, 2001). Thus early art therapists were thinking about how to center the clients they worked with beyond the psychiatric curiosity about mental illness (MacGregor, 1992).

Art and relationship

The concept of object relations is central to the way in which psychodynamic art therapy thinks about the therapeutic process. **Object relations** come directly from Winnicott's (1969) theory that humans move from dependence on a caregiver to autonomy or independence through the use of a self/other development (Aron et al., 2018). We do not speak about relationships anymore as self/object so this language can be confusing. However, this basic idea outlines how humans learn to be in relationship with and are deeply impacted by early caregivers. Ainsworth and Bowlby (1991) described how individuals develop both internal relationships (**self-intrapersonal**) and relationships with others (**other-external object relations**), which become relationship styles and may emerge during therapy. This basic idea outlines how humans learn to be in relationship with, and are deeply impacted, by early caregivers. Modern-day attachment theory and relational psychoanalysis have both examined this work from many directions, thus attempting to take the theory beyond an overly simplified story of damaged early caregiver relationship as the root of all problems.

Art therapy uses the triadic relationship among the artist/ client, therapist, and the artwork as a rehearsal ground for improving relationships (Rubin, 2011). The art serves as a relationship to be cultivated and developed; the art materials possess personalities to be interacted with and committed to; and the art product serves as a transitional object. A **transitional object** is a soothing object (such as a blanket or a stuffed animal) that a child invests with meaning in the absence of a caregiver. Likewise, the art object can hold the meaning it is imbued with as well as a representation of the relationship to the artist and therapist (Rubin, 2011). This means the art acts as a transitional object and represents the significant relationship with therapist and client/artist or another primary relationship. For instance, a client who wishes to keep the art made during therapy sessions may be holding on to both the symbolic representation of the relationship with their therapist *and* the important work done in therapy. The role of the therapist is to remain in relationship with the client/artist and their many internal parts as well as the art process and product.

Sublimation

Edith Kramer (1993), one of the founding mothers of art therapy, developed the prevailing theory on artistic **sublimation** that examines how, through the art-making process, an unacceptable urge can be transformed into a symbolic equivalent. For example, rather than smashing an object out of anger, someone might intentionally and thoughtfully break an object to create specific sizes and shapes to craft a mosaic. The artwork then serves as a satisfactory representation of the original impulse (smashing due to anger) in a new creative form, allowing for what she described as inner harmony following the resolution of tension. Kramer explained that the art process strengthens the ego by delaying the impulse and channeling the unacceptable urge into something that is more socially acceptable, ultimately leading to a more mature and complete version of the original impulse. While smashing something out of anger might be relieving, it would create what Kramer called **displacement**, which moves the energy out, but does not transform it in any way. If we were to simply create art from the place of impulse (id), it would not fulfill what Kramer described as successful sublimation (Kramer, 1993).

This process of sublimation then becomes a tool for the art therapist who is engaging with both the client/artist's struggle and their process of inner revolution. Kramer (1993) described the art therapist's role as occasionally acting as the auxiliary ego. The **auxiliary ego** is a stand-in for the client/artist as they work to cultivate their own inner resources. This idea translates very clearly within the art experience as the art therapist knows the art process, the materials, and can even offer what Kramer (1993) called "**a third hand intervention**," where the therapist uses themselves as a bridge between the client/artist's unformed image and a satisfactory complete image. In Kramer's description of this process, we see that she was already advocating for a more relational style of therapy than traditional psychoanalytic theory proposed. This provided a meaningful step away from the singular authority of the therapist or analyst.

While there are certainly urges (representing one's id) or desires that create problems for an individual, we as art therapists now must question vigorously what may have been previously pathologized based on bias. Early Art Therapist Mala Betensky (1995) also spoke about this notion and suggested that creative drive is more than simply an effort to conceal shameful aspects of the self. Perhaps, she was suggesting artistic expression was valuable in giving voice to all facets of identity.

The art therapy process, as outlined by Kramer (1993) seemingly ends with the resolution of a troubling issue; however, this approach will not work with some problems. Therapists must work with clients to surface long-held shame connected to racial and sexual hierarchies that come from internalized ideologies (Belkin & White, 2020). For example, if one believes that their own sexual identity is unacceptable, attempting to sublimate that urge away can be damaging. If these internalized hierarchies are not made conscious, art therapists will continue to contribute to the development of practices that assist in assimilating those outside of the norm.

Freud (2012) believed that sexuality was often a primary drive and symbolic focus in dream imagery. His willingness to explore the meaning of the sexual lives of his patients opened up territory that we are still exploring today. In fact, his early model of human development framed childhood as a drive for pleasure based on erogenous zones of the body, oral (ages 0–1), anal (ages 1–3), and phallic (ages 3–5). Notably, he framed feminine development only in relation to lack of or wishing/envy of the phallus (Leiper & Maltby, 2004). However, Freud's frequent references to sexual imagery and symbolism have at this point become a punch line with little reference to his original thinking.

It becomes the work of modern-day therapists to expand his important ideas about human drive beyond a reductive **gender binary** (Belkin & White, 2020) where sexuality is bound by preconceived and defined gender roles. Current critical psychoanalytic theory is quick to problematize this history and to examine ways in which **intersectional identities** (defined as all facets of personal identity) can be surfaced and welcomed without pathology (Belkin & White, 2020). This timely reexamination of theory forces us to acknowledge how systemic scientific racism and homophobia crafted diagnostic criteria while only recognizing normalcy within the **cis-heteronormative** life trajectory that assumes that everyone is straight and identifies with their assigned biological sex. This trajectory excludes anyone whose culture, gender, sexuality, or ability is different from the socially defined dominant "norms."

It feels irresponsible not to note that perhaps Freud, Naumburg, Kramer, and others were developing strategies to face their own oppression or marginalization based on gender, race, religion, or sexuality. We must look at how the process of artistic sublimation can allow for integration and the coexistence of intersectionality without seeking a resolve that banishes an important facet of identity. Art-making uniquely offers us an opportunity for multiple images and perspectives to exist on a single page.

Methods in psychoanalytic art therapy: Scribble drawing

Edith Kramer (1993) expanded Florence Cane's work with scribbles, developing an art therapy method known as a **scribble drawing**. The purpose of the scribble is to access the unconscious without the conscious mind controlling the image. Using a large piece of drawing paper, the artist takes a moment to create a scribble on the page. Use of a nondominant hand or even closed eyes can help to avoid the ego's desire to control even the scribbled line. The therapist and client/artist then look at the scribble the way one might look at a cloud waiting for an image to emerge. The client/artist then uses the art materials to emphasize and draw out the image they see.

I often utilize this technique with art therapy students who are capable artists and sometimes find that allowing an image to emerge without control is quite challenging. The following is a student's description (Ramona) of her experience with the scribble drawing in class (Fig. 7.1).

I hold the pastel in my nondominant hand and survey the blank paper. I close my eyes, take a deep breath, and begin to scribble rather aggressively. I am rushing and lose contact with the paper, so the line skips down the page momentarily. I want the exercise to be over. I can only tolerate this unknown

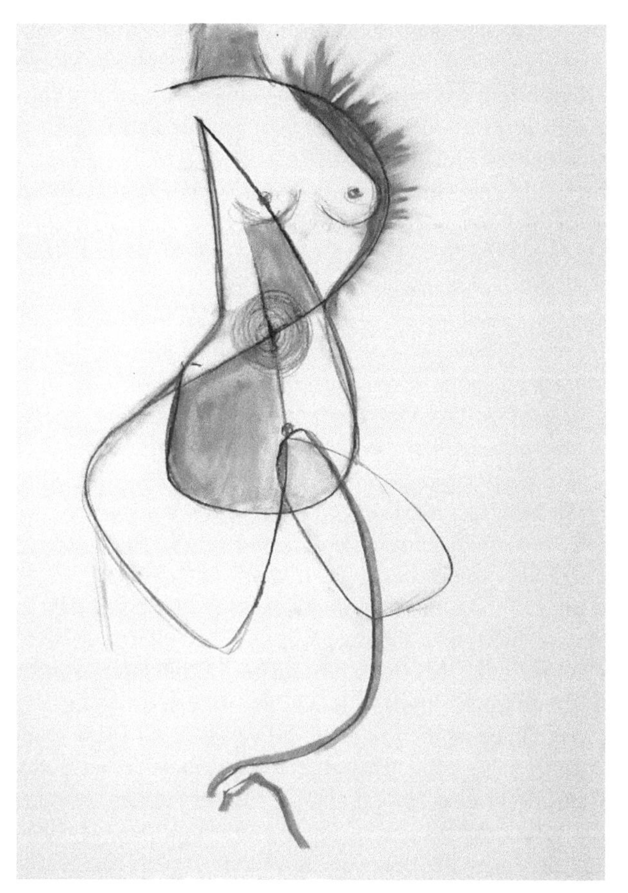

FIG. 7.1 *Beyond the cord.*
(No permission required.)

for so long. Finally, I open my eyes to face my scribble and immediately see a woman's figure. At first, I invert the scribble and try to make it the back of a woman, but the form is clearly facing forward. I wish it was her back and become self-conscious about the exposure. In this moment, the figure seems to be me. I begin to notice her curved back, big butt, and a round belly with an umbilical cord. Then the way the lines cross through the vortex over my solar plexus meeting in the middle and forming an "x." I have a profound desire to soften the lines around her and the spaces inside of her. A question echoes in my head—what is at the end of the cord?

Together, with the watchful eyes of the class at our backs, we look at the image Ramona has created. I check in with her to both validate the vulnerability of being seen by the entire class and to empower her to drive the experience. Quickly, Ramona begins to analyze and explain the image before us. I gently bring her attention back to the lines on the page as a way to stay with the formal elements before jumping to content (Franklin, 2017). Even with a scribbled line, a conscious mind might worry about being embarrassed or too vulnerable, and wants to step in and control the narrative. After the exercise, Ramona described our exchange in her own words:

I gave a brief analysis about what I thought the image represented, then my professor drew attention to the area over my solar plexus and I described it as a vortex. She said, "Is the vortex going in or out?" I knew viscerally that it was in fact going in and then immediately went back to focus on the parts that I had already considered on my own. I began to verbally analyze the way the lines crossed over the solar plexus and, as I relayed my analysis, my professor observed that the figure didn't have a head. At once, I dropped into my body and feelings. In that moment I was the figure without a head who finally had access to the feelings of sadness, fear, and shame that the vortex held. I began to cry and my professor, sensing that I had gone far enough, tenderly brought me back into the room. To be witnessed by my professor offered me an essential objectivity as well as a deeper subjectivity simultaneously, that facilitated a connection with the parts of the scribble, and my self, that I had avoided.

From the image on the page, Ramona's ego (conscious mind) immediately went to work explaining how the image fit with her internal self-structure. My observations helped guide her to go beyond her initial defense to recognize the pain she was attempting to bypass. It was my intention to support her in having her own experience of the image by reflecting what I saw and did not see (the figure's head) on the page. This observation follows what Betensky (1995) described in her **phenomenological** approach to art therapy, an approach which centralizes the direct experience of the client/artist. She suggested that staying focused on the form and structure of an image more accurately represents the inner reality of the client's emotional experience. This is an example of a Freudian relational approach that does not jump to an all-knowing interpretation, but rather is a more collaborative experience where the client/artist can discover and uncover meaning and emotion (Naumburg, 1987).

Cultural context and author's personal experience

Kuriloff (2014) stated that it is impossible not to acknowledge the deep impact of the Holocaust on Freud and other psychoanalytic thinkers and theory since one's emotional experience is deeply and directly affected by the culture of the time. There is likewise an interesting connection to art therapy history here, raising the question about how Jews were involved in the early formation of the field and how that influenced the development of therapeutic practices (Kuriloff, 2014). Kuriloff (2014) examines how dissociation as a survival tool became psychic ingenuity and was a necessary strategy to avoid the traumatic devastation that was caused by the Nazis. Survivors were forced to split off from the trauma experienced, dissociate, in order to move forward. Kuriloff (2014) also speculated that Freud and many of his contemporaries were forced to deny any Jewish identity as it was associated with negative traits and even failed masculinity. This forced denial may have contributed to the notion that the therapist must project neutrality and blankness in order to avoid any dependence on or attachment to the therapist, which was a common practice in psychoanalysis. It is mind blowing to think that **autonomy,** or self-reliance, as the ultimate sign of health may have come out of traumatic loss. It is important to think about the anti-Semitism Freud faced since he is a household name and this struggle is not often discussed.

During WWII, Friedl Dicker-Brandeis, Art Therapist Edith Kramer's painting instructor (Wix, 2011), was taken to the infamous concentration Camp Terezin where she lived for 17 months until she was killed. Her time in the camp is well documented as she created a secret school for the children and taught them painting. The artwork created was, by her design, intended to stimulate emotional and intellectual growth in spite of the horrific conditions (Ius & Sidenberg, 2017). Dicker-Brandeis believed that her role as a teacher was to have as little impact as possible on the work created, which mirrors the psychoanalytic value of projection and therapeutic neutrality. The artworks made by her students in the camps have been studied extensively in the context of trauma, development, and resilience.

While in Terezin, Dicker-Brandeis met a young woman named Erna Furman (aged 16) whom she had an enormous influence upon. Furman eventually was liberated from the camp in 1945 and went on to work with Sigmund's daughter, Anna Freud, who continued her father's work after he died in 1939. The two women developed theories on child development and psychoanalysis in England before Furman traveled to the United States where she developed a psychoanalytic program for children and became a widely published author.

Furman's work with Anna Freud was hugely influential on the development of child psychology and we would be remiss not to consider how the field of art therapy has been impacted by these women. For example, it was impossible for anyone who was working with children in the late 1940s to ignore the impact of loss or war trauma. Further, we might imagine how paramount the themes of war and looming death with central therapeutic values of autonomy and expression were to the evolution of psychoanalytic theory. All three of these women (Kramer, Anna Freud, and Furman) believed that children's creation of artwork was powerful communication beyond the limitation of verbal expression (Ius & Sidenberg, 2017).

Furman was still an active therapist at the time that my own personal story (Leah Friedman) overlaps. At age 2, I became a student in the psychoanalytic preschool and began my own analysis 5 days a week. I continued full analysis for the next 10 years ending at age 12. This is a complex section of my own history both as a therapist and as an individual. Often upon sharing this story, I am asked how this decade influenced me, which is by nature an impossible question to answer. As it was part of my everyday routine and life, it was not something I imagined as unique or outside of the realm of others' experience. My memories are highly subjective and influenced by time, my own family, and trauma.

As part of the first fully postwar generation, with Holocaust survivors on both sides of my family, the evidence and fallout from intergenerational trauma was present but subtle. My parents have shared with me their experience of the survivors from our family, but similar to the values expressed by Dicker-Brandeis (Wix, 2011) it was modeled that trauma should be dealt with best by moving forward and pursuing success. The abandonment and lives lost caused by the Holocaust for survivors meant that autonomy was prized over all other goals. To be in therapy provided a strategy for the pursuit of autonomy as a means of transcending trauma. For Jewish families, seeking insight through therapy was intended to support healing, yet it became linked to anti-Semitic tropes, which posit that intellectual pursuit masks hunger for power, money, and control. With a complex identity and religion, Jewish people are often othered, neither considered white (although some are white identifying) nor all people of color.

As a young child in analysis, I often felt that success meant being able to narrate my inner world, identify my drives and internal motivation, and reflect a profound self-reliance that has been pervasive in my development. It has taken me nearly 12 years of practice as a therapist myself to tease apart the ways these values were built into my character and to decide how they serve me or don't. In therapy, I was frequently paraphrased and reflected accurately; however, that is not the same as experiencing attunement or feeling cared for. As art therapists, our clients often wish to know they have value or hold a place in our mind beyond the hour of appointment. There is important dialogue to be had about how intersectionality and relational therapeutic practice can begin to address marginalized identities and voices (Belkin & White, 2020) and modern psychoanalysis and psychodynamic theory have attempted to dismantle some of the previously rigid values.

I find myself with reverence for the art therapists and theorists who came before me. I know there is a long history of art therapy not being seen as a legitimate form of treatment. It is perhaps this deep fear of fraudulence that has driven some of the practices that have created marginalization within the art therapy community. When I read some of the original texts from Freud or Jung, my eyes grow wide as I attempt to conjure the context in which they were working, dreaming, and living. I wonder how art therapists can deconstruct what has been deeply damaging while honoring some of the more valuable theoretical constructs. In this way, we can cultivate more intersectional identities as therapists while holding both complex history and personal vulnerabilities (Talwar et al., 2019) and take responsibility for our own process in looking at how meaning is made.

Jungian and analytic approaches

Although in this chapter we have separated Jung and Freud into distinct sections, the two men had significant influences on each other. Much has been written about their charged relationship, their differences, and their eventual split;

this split had profound impacts on each of their theories and the psychological community as a whole. While a comprehensive comparison of their psychologies and beliefs is beyond the scope of this chapter, we acknowledge that each brought powerful cultural influences to understanding and interpreting the nature of the psyche. Early art therapists were influenced by, and drew from both Freudian and Jungian thought (Swan-Foster, 2016); thus, the division between these two men's influences on art therapy is in some ways overemphasized—they are inextricably linked and deeply intertwined.

Jung and the Red Book

In 2009 Jung's (2009) *Red Book* was published, almost 50 years after his death, giving readers access to unseen images and writings that had been kept hidden throughout his lifetime and led to the development of his analytic theory. In many ways, Carl Jung took responsibility for his own meaning-making process by creating the images that appear in the *Red Book*. Art Therapist Shaun McNiff (2011) described the *Red Book* as the "most elegant object published in art therapy's history" (p. 145). The paintings in the *Red Book* reflect Jung's deep involvement with his creative process and his own method for creative self-inquiry. The book illustrates his approach to working with the unconscious through **active imagination**, an experiential method for engaging with the unconscious (Swan-Foster, 2018). Created during the years after his break with Freud, between 1913 and 1930, Jung used images to explore the language of his own **psyche** (defined as the totality of one's conscious and unconscious mind and described in more depth later). The *Red Book* shows the approaches that Jung would use with his patients throughout his life. Jungian Scholar Sonu Shamdasani described this approach as helping people develop their own cosmologies (Hillman & Shamdasani, 2013, p. 15) using images, dreams, and myth to cultivate his patients' own meaning and self-understanding.

Have you looked at the images in the *Red Book*? My own copy of the *Red Book* (Jessica Whitesel) sits on the floor of my office, leaning against the wall. It is a massive hardbound book, so it is difficult to know where to put it, since it is larger than any other book in my office, although similar in weight to the *Diagnostic and Statistical Manual of Mental Disorders (DSM)* (American Psychiatric Association, 2013). Like the *DSM*, it is not a casual read, but also like the *DSM*, it seems to signify some kind of authority that gives me pause. It is not a book anyone ever asks to borrow or flip through. When I do peruse it, which is not often, it feels as intimate as someone's private journal but also as confusing and inscrutable as a stranger's half-remembered dream. It is this combined sense of mystery and magic, of confusion and complexity that draws me into Jung's work, while also challenging my critical capacity. As a White, middle-class, college-educated, cisgender female, I realized Jung's work satisfies my desire to step outside systems of dominance within psychology while still existing within the privileged boundaries of academic thought. It seems many in traditional psychology have either summarily dismissed Jung's ideas, sending him to the margins of history, or embraced his theory wholeheartedly and with devotion, without critique or acknowledgment of bias. I imagine the value of Jungian thought for art therapists and students exists somewhere between these polarities, and perhaps through holding the tension of these opposites, we can find meaningful new ways to utilize his theory while making visible those concepts that have caused harm.

The nature of the psyche

Jung described the **psyche**, the totality of the conscious and unconscious mind, as "image," centralizing the notion of using images within a therapeutic frame (Swan-Foster, 2018). Jung encouraged his own patients to paint (Edwards, 1987) and saw his patient's pictures as a "concrete manifestation of the imaginal world" (Schaverien, 1992, p. 23). His move toward depathologizing symptoms, of seeing symptoms as one's attempt to self-correct or move toward wholeness, shifts illness from a focus on past causes to a more meaningful and purposeful process with the inherent possibility of change and healing.

Jung proposed a model of the psyche that included both a **personal unconscious,** containing individual psychic material unavailable to consciousness, as well as a **collective unconscious**, which contains universal material and imagery that spans across culture and time (Hauke, 2006). The concept of the collective unconscious emerged out of Jung's interest and study of mythology, positing that mythic or **archetypal images** which are universal or primordial patterns or forms that exist below the personal unconscious (Jung, 1953), connecting people to their ancestors and their history. Working with his own fantasies and inner images helped Jung identify what Shamdasani (2009) called the "myth-creating function of the mind" (p. 199) and the idea that mythic themes and primordial images exist in our collective unconscious. (See Red Book project section for example.)

According to Jung, the **shadow** lives within our personal and collective unconscious. The shadow contains personal, collective, and archetypal dimensions (Casement, 2006) and includes all the aspects of a person that are distasteful or unacceptable to us. Murray Stein (1996) stated: "The first duty of any ethically-minded person is, from Jung's psychological perspective, to become as conscious as possible of his or her own shadow. If they (shadow qualities) are repressed, they are unconscious and are projected into others. When this happens, there is usually strong moral indignation and the groundwork is laid for a moral crusade. Filled with righteous indignation, persons can attack others for perceiving in them what is unconscious shadow in themselves, and a holy war ensues (p. 17)." This way of framing shadow work as one's own ethical responsibility offers a frame of reference for how art therapists, or any practitioner, might consider what **self-reflexive** (considering one's self in relation to others) process is required for them to work effectively with others, both in one's personal and collective shadow. For example, the shadowy or disavowed aspects of myself are those qualities, attributes, or identities that I deny in myself. I am then more likely to project those qualities or attributes onto another, whether that be an individual, a group, a community, or a country. To become more aware of these aspects in yourself, some questions you might ask yourself include: What assumptions do I make about others? What am I not conscious of? What do I fear, and how do I project these fears onto others? Asking these questions of one's self builds a link between individual shadow work and critiquing or dismantling assumptions about others.

Jung's theory of complexes imagines a theory of the self in which we are multiple, made up of a variety of inner selves, or parts. A **complex**, according to Jung, is a "splinter psyche" or split-off part of the self, which has an emotional charge, and can function outside of one's conscious control (Brewster, 2020; Shalit, 2002). Complexes are made up of associations, ideas, memories, and emotions, and can be known or expressed through an image (Swan-Foster, 2018). Complex theory provides a strength-based view of our inner selves as being comprised of many parts (Noll, 1989; Wilkinson, 2005). Jung's complex model assumes multiplicity, which foreshadows and aligns with an intersectional lens of self-identity, and allows fluid concepts of self to exist at the same time, recognizing the many modes of knowing one's self and others that are possible (Harris, 2009).

Using complexes as a template of inner experience allows art therapists to move away from psychological categories that are **binary** (either/or) or hierarchical in nature, in favor of theories that promote complexity, subjectivity, and multiplicity. For example, a client experiencing anxious thoughts might state, "I'm anxious." Holding in mind a multiple model of the psyche acknowledges both the "anxious part" of the client and the possibility of other parts existing simultaneously. Giving form to both the "anxious part" and "another part" visually allows both parts to be seen at once, validating the complexity and multiplicity of one's inner experience, rather than defining the client as singularly "anxious." It lends itself to a both/and approach, rather than either/or, recognizing that no one is, as the Novelist Adichie (2009) explained, "a single story." By shifting from a patriarchal expectation that we are either this or that, Jung's model of the psyche potentially allows more complexity in how one languages and imagines one's own identity and clients' identities.

However, Jung's theory of **anima** (the inner image of a woman in a man) and **animus** (the inner image of man in a woman) (Swan-Foster, 2018) has been criticized as essentializing and reinforcing gender binaries. Post-Jungian James Hillman (1985) suggested that an archetype cannot be gender specific, and Samuels (1989) argued that masculine and feminine definitions of psychology are always culture bound and not innate. Some Jungians frame the anima/animus more generally as wisdom figures, or a "mysterious stranger" within the psyche who is experienced as a spiritual "other" (Kast, 2006).

Jung and racism

My experience in teaching the Jungian Approaches class at Naropa University was powerful and transformative, in part because the students in this course challenged some of the basic assumptions about Jung's work. Questioning Jung's description of the shadow and his essentialist ideas about gender (the notion that some traits are inherently masculine/male or others inherently feminine/female) forced me into a deeper level of self-reflection around my privileged location. As a group, we grappled with these ideas and explored places in Jung's work that seemed to highlight his biases or personal shadow material, our own shadow material or complexes as individuals, and the collective material that manifests in our larger community. Holding the tension collectively was a challenge, allowing or making space for conflicting beliefs or attitudes. Don Kalsched (2020) described this process as a way in which **democratic inner work**—building tolerance for the diverse inner parts of the self, holding conflict, and allowing marginalized parts to have their own voice—reflects and mirrors the work of an outer democracy.

In her book *The Racial Complex*, Fanny Brewster (2020) discussed how Jung explored issues of race long before others addressed this within the field of psychology. At the same time, however, the colonial and racist ideas that permeate Jung's work, especially regarding indigenous people and those of African and Indian descent, have led to both "inner and outer harm" in individuals and in communities (Open Letter, 2018). In his essay, "Notes on White Supremacy," Hillman (1986) boldly described modern psychology as white consciousness attempting to create a psychic geography that reflects only itself. The unconscious, according to Hillman, is an invention of white consciousness that is seeking to understand and "discover" otherness, but is ultimately serving itself, a kind of 'Manifest Destiny' of the psyche, justifying exploration and colonization for its own power and purpose.

In the foreword to *White Fragility*, Michael Eric Dyson described how whiteness "dresses in camouflage as humanity" and to deconstruct it, one must be "a magician of the political and the social, an alchemist of the spiritual and psychological, too" (Diangelo & Dyson, 2018, p. x). This means that we need to recognize and deconstruct the way oppressive concepts exist within our history, ourselves, and our current therapeutic models, which requires powerful inner resources. At its best, I believe that Jungian therapeutic approaches make space for incorporating the alchemical and spiritual, as well as the political and the social, and offer a framework for inner exploration that can bring such unconscious material to light, both within one's self and one's larger world. Perhaps a Jungian approach could offer meaningful perspectives or methods for dismantling the systems that colonize our thinking, raising the question of whether or not the master's tools could in fact dismantle the master's house (Lorde, 1984). In other words, Jungian concepts can help us engage in dialogue and stay in relationship with ideas that we might find abhorrent. Doing so creates the tension that allows something new to emerge without denying history or conforming to it (Brewster, 2021).

Methods in Jungian art therapy

Jung (1975) described **active imagination** as his basic analytical method of psychotherapy, which allows unconscious material to emerge in order to heal the self. The method involves allowing clients or patients to draw, paint, or sculpt the images that arise, after lowering one's consciousness or turning inward, and then bringing in conscious awareness (Shamdasani, 2009; Swan-Foster, 2018). The experiential exercise at the end of the chapter offers a way to begin to experiment with such an approach. Students often find themselves both struggling to lower their consciousness enough to allow images to emerge and expressing genuine surprise at the evocative psychic material that emerges.

Mandalas, from the Sanskrit word for "circle," are also used as an art therapy directive. Drawing within a circular form or mandala can provide a useful structure or container for a client to create an image, which symbolically evokes a sense of wholeness and contemplation (Swan-Foster, 2018). Jung (1968) considered mandalas to be an image of the self as well as an organizing principle of the self, describing them as a "kind of central point within the psyche, to which everything is related, by which everything is arranged, and which is itself a source of energy" (CW 9i, para. 634).

Student examples

Jung advocated for analysis, or therapy, for all clinicians. This is a requirement for many students in graduate art therapy training as well. This requirement allows space for powerful content that emerges in class to be attended to and worked with outside the academic setting. Exploring one's own imagery and engaging in a practice of inquiry, alone, in a group, or with a therapist allows students to begin to relate to their own identity in images, helping them grieve their own losses, recognize their reasons for entering the field (both public and private motivations) (Page, 1999), and develop an understanding of their own inner and outer work to be done. Students in the Jungian Approaches class work throughout the semester on creating their own personal Red Book, honoring Jung's own example of how to use images to work with the unconscious.

Red book project

I asked H, a White, queer, nonbinary art therapy graduate student, the following questions about her personal Red Book to evoke her thoughts about Jung and working with images in her unconscious. Her answers brought a critical lens to Jung's theory.

Questions:

1. How did you engage with your unconscious using the art process?

By taking Jung's perspective that image is psyche, engaging the art process is a fairly direct way to dialogue with unconscious material. For me, accessing the personal unconscious through art may take several different forms. Art is the language of metaphor and creates a conduit for my unconscious to speak. I often use watercolors to illustrate dreams because the blurred edges capture the surreal quality of details I cannot quite remember. The fluidity of the media also feels congruent with unconscious content relating to my gender and sexuality, which are fluid by nature.

2. What parts of your identity did you explore, and what surprised you? How does engaging with your shadow relate to social justice work?

Exploring my gender identity pulled me into some shadowy or unknown corners of my unconscious. I was assigned female at birth, was socialized as a woman, and have considered myself a woman up until quite recently. Engaging with shadow material on a personal level taps into the deeper collective oppression of the LGBTQIA+ community and the discrimination, demonization, and erasure it has endured. When Jung refers to the "collective," does he truly include all people, or only those whose traditions, mythology, and ways of being uphold a narrative of white goodness, superiority, and "normalcy"? Is the collective simply a euphemism for white, Western culture? Jung's relationship with his own shadow work certainly reveals racist and potentially homophobic tendencies. Collective shadow should not be confused with white shadow.

A Red Book illustration of a dream in which drag superstar Trixie Mattel appeared at a lake near my home. Watercolor pencil and graphite (Fig. 7.2).

One of the most valuable practices I learned in keeping an illustrated dream journal is that the associations of dream images (**latent content** is the underlying meaning) *can unlock just as much information as the dream images themselves* (**manifest content** are the actual images in the dream). *Early in the semester I dreamt that the drag queen appeared at a lake near my home, and we swam, played in the water with my two younger cousins, and floated down some rapids on an inner tube. Just as Trixie Mattel and I played in the lake in my dream, so too can I dip in and out of gendered expression, and allow myself to become immersed in the symbolic fluidity of gender expression and identity.*

In painting her dream and allowing the dream figures to speak, H was able to explore and play with an image of gender fluidity, giving form and expression to a previously unexplored part of her psyche. This important representation reflected in drag culture created the context for H to find and honor underrepresented and invalidated aspects of her own identity. If you never see heroes that look like you, how can you imagine that you are the hero of your own story? The lack of public images, stories, and faces from diverse communities narrows access and creates unique challenges to mythologize one's own story.

Conclusions

Freud and Jung both loom large in the history of 20th century psychology and each deeply influenced the field of art therapy, providing at various times a theoretical ground, societal legitimacy, and practical validation for emerging

FIG. 7.2 *Splashing with gender.*
(No permission required.)

art therapists of the time. Their eventual break continues to be debated widely in both Freudian and Jungian circles. Personal as well as theoretical differences led to their eventual split, but several formative voices in art therapy, including Margaret Naumburg, Florence Cane, and Irene Champernowne drew from both Freudian and Jungian thought (Swan-Foster, 2018).

The influence of Freudian and psychoanalytic approaches has been well documented throughout the history of art therapy, while Jungian influence has been more sparingly acknowledged. Swan-Foster (2018) suggested that this alliance with psychoanalytic thinking gave art therapy credence within the established medical community of the 20th century. This push to define art therapy psychoanalytically prioritized the influence of early art therapists like Naumburg, Kramer, and Ulman. While this effort to legitimize the field aligned art therapy with dominant therapeutic paradigms of the time, it consequently marginalized the voices of art therapists like Lucille Venture, who called out the lack of inclusivity in the emerging field of art therapy; Mary Huntoon, who focused on an artistic perspective; and Sarah McGee, who focused on communal and systemic approaches with migrant families (Gipson, 2019; Talwar et al., 2019).

As 21st century art therapists, the authors seek to both acknowledge and question these roots, thinking critically about the invisible assumptions built into Freudian and Jungian paradigms and finding ways to include voices that have been marginalized and pathologized in the past. Let's ask ourselves: what grips us as reflections of those parts of our personal, familial, cultural, national, and ethnic history that unconsciously define and guide us, for better or for worse? How can the most valuable parts of Freud's and Jung's theories evolve to also include a queered perspective? Where might you as a reader locate yourself in relationship to these historical figures?

Experiential activities

1. We invite you to try having a dialogue between two parts. For this activity, select an issue, situation, or conflict you have between two choices, two parts of yourself, or two people. Create an image for each part in this dynamic. Imagine the two parts speaking to each other. What would each part say to the other? Allow yourself to imagine this dialogue and continue the process as long as each part has more to say. Sometimes, at the end of such an exercise, a new "third" image or idea may emerge, a manifestation of what Jung called **the transcendent function** (Jung, 1960) in which the tension held between two polarities gives rise to a new possibility.
2. Create a dream journal for yourself. Keep it close to where you sleep, so you can document your dream upon waking, either through words or images.
3. Trace a circle on a page in a sketchbook. Start a daily practice of creating a **mandala** each day for yourself, noting repeating themes or changes. Jung engaged in this practice for a period of time, describing his process in *Memories, Dreams, and Reflections* (1961): "...sketching every morning in a notebook a small circular drawing, a mandala, which seemed to correspond to my inner situation at the time. With the help of these drawings I could observe my psychic transformations from day to day."
4. Create your own scribble drawing by holding a drawing material in your hand (or perhaps nondominant hand) and moving your arm freely on the page for around 15 s. Take several minutes to examine your scribble, step back, maybe squint your eyes and wait for an image to reveal itself. Once you've identified an image, use your materials to bring forth and embellish your image.

Additional resources

Books

Jung, C.G. (2009). *The Red Book: Liber Novus*, S. Shamdasani (Ed.) New York: W.W. Norton.

Swan Foster, N. (2017). *Jungian Art Therapy: Images, Dreams, and Analytical Psychology*. New York: Routledge.

Volvakova, H. (1994). *I Never Saw Another Butterfly: Children's Drawings and Poems from the Terezin Concentration Camp, 1942–1944*. Schocken; 2nd edition.

Films

Thomas, J. (Producer) & Cronenberg, D. (Director). (2011). *A Dangerous Method*.

Malmberg, J., Putnam, T., Radecki, M., Shellen, C., Walsh, K. (Producers) & Malmberg, J. (Director). (2010). *Marwencol*.

Chapter terms

Active imagination
Anima/animus
Archetypal images
Autonomy
Auxiliary ego
Cis-heteronormative
Collective unconscious
Complex
Democratic inner work
Displacement
Dissociation
Ego
Free association
Freud
Gender binary
Id
Interpretation
Intersectional identities
Jung
Latent/manifest content
Mandalas
Marginalization
Object relations
Oppression
Othering
Personal and collective unconscious
Phenomenological
Projection
Psyche
Queering
Racism
Repression
Scribble drawing
Self-reflexive
Shadow
Sublimation
Superego
Symbolism
Third hand intervention
Transcendent function
Transitional object

References

Adichie, C. N. (July 2009). *Chimamanda Ngozi Adichie: The danger of a single story [Video file]*. Retrieved from https://www.ted.com/talks/chimamanda_ngozi_adichie_the_danger_of_a_single_story.

Ainsworth, M. D. S., & Bowlby, J. (1991). An ethological approach to personality development. *American Psychologist*, *46*, 331–341.

American Psychiatric Association. (2013). *Diagnostic and statistical manual of mental disorders* (5th ed.). American Psychiatric Association.

Aron, L., Grand, S., & Slochower, J. (Eds.). (2018). *De-idealizing relational theory: A critique from within*. Routledge.

Belkin, M., & White, C. (Eds.). (2020). *Intersectionality and relational psychoanalysis: New perspectives on race, gender and sexuality*. Routledge.

Betensky, M. (1995). *What do you see? Phenomenology of therapeutic art expression*. Jessica Kingsley.

Brewster, F. (2020). *The racial complex: A Jungian perspective on culture and race*. Routledge.

Brewster, F. (February, 2021). *Our collective shadow: Racism, trauma, and privilege*. Talk presented via Zoom hosted by Pacifica Graduate Institute.

Casement, A. (2006). The shadow. In R. Papadopoulos (Ed.), *The handbook of Jungian psychology*. Routledge.

Cohen, R. (2017). *Outsider art and art therapy: Shared histories, current issues, and future identities*. Jessica Kingsley.

Diangelo, R., & Dyson, M. E. (2018). *White fragility: Why it's so hard for white people to talk about racism*. Beacon Press.

Edwards, M. (1987). Jungian analytic art therapy. In J. Rubin (Ed.), *Approaches to art therapy: Theory and technique* (1st ed., pp. 92–113). Brunner/Mazel.

Franklin, M. (2017). *Art as contemplative practice: Expressive pathways to the self*. SUNY Press.

Franklin, M., & Politsky, R. (1992). The problem of interpretation: Implications and strategies for the field of art therapy. *The Arts in Psychotherapy*, *19*(3), 163–175.

Freud, S. (1961). *The ego and the id*. W. W. Norton & Co.

Freud, S. (2012). *A general introduction to psychoanalysis*. Wordsworth Editions.

Gipson, L. (2019). Envisioning black women's consciousness in art therapy. In S. K. Talwar (Ed.), *Art therapy for social justice: Radical intersections* (pp. 96–120). Routledge.

Harris, A. (2009). *Gender as soft assembly*. Routledge.

Hauke, C. (2006). The unconscious: Personal and collective. In R. Papadopoulos (Ed.), *The handbook of Jungian psychology*. Routledge.

Hillman, J. (1985). *Anima: An anatomy of a personified notion*. Spring.

Hillman, J. (1986). Notes on white supremacy: Essaying an archetypal account of historical events. *Spring*, *46*, 29–58.

Hillman, J., & Shamdasani, S. (2013). *Lament of the dead: Psychology after Jung's red book*. W.W. Norton and Company.

Hoffman, I. (1998). *Ritual and spontaneity in the psychoanalytic process: A dialectical-deconstructionist view*. Routledge.

Hogan, S. (2001). *Healing arts: The history of art therapy*. Jessica Kingsley.

Ius, M., & Sidenberg, M. (2017). The all-powerful freedom: Creativity and resilience in the context of Friedl Dicker-Brandeis' art teaching experiment. *Proceedings*, *1*, 904. https://doi.org/10.3390/proceedings1090904.

Jung, C. G. (1953). *Psychology and alchemy. Collected works* (Vol. 12). Princeton University Press.

Jung, C. G. (1960). *The structure and dynamics of the psyche. Collected works* (Vol. 8). Princeton University Press.

Jung, C. G. (1968). *The archetypes and the collective unconscious. Collected works* (Vol. 9i). Princeton University Press.

Jung, C. G. (1975). In G. Adler (Ed.), *Letters Vol. 2: 1951–1961*. Princeton University Press. R. F. C. Hull, Trans.

Jung, C. G. (2009). In S. Shamdasani (Ed.) (Trans. M. Kyburz, J. Peck, & S. Shamdasani), *The red book*. W.W. Norton.

Kalsched, D. (2020). Wrestling with our angels: Inner and outer democracy in America under the shadow of Donald Trump. In T. Singer (Ed.), *Cultural complexes and the soul of America: Myth, psyche, and politics* (pp. 53–88). Routledge.

Kast, V. (2006). Anima/animus. In R. Papadopoulos (Ed.), *The handbook of Jungian psychology*. Routledge.

Kramer, E. (1993). *Art as therapy with children* (2nd ed.). Magnolia Street Publishers (Original work published 1971).

Kuriloff, E. (2014). *Contemporary psychoanalysis and the legacy of the Third Reich: History, memory, tradition*. Routledge.

Leiper, R., & Maltby, M. (2004). *The psychodynamic approach to therapeutic change*. Sage Publications.

Lorde, A. (1984). The master's tools will never dismantle the master's house. In *Sister outsider: Essays and speeches* (pp. 110–114). Crossing Press.

MacGregor, J. (1992). *The discovery of the art of the insane*. Princeton University Press.

Malchiodi, C. (Ed.). (2003). *Handbook of art therapy*. The Guilford Press.

Mann, D. (2006). Art therapy: Re-imagining a psychoanalytic perspective—A reply to David Maclagan. *International Journal of Art Therapy*, *11*(1), 33–40.

McNiff, S. (2011). The red book [liber novus]. *Art Therapy: Journal of the American Art Therapy Association*, *28*(3), 145–146.

Naumburg, M. (1987). *Dynamically oriented art therapy*. Magnolia Street Publishers (Original work published 1966).

Noll, R. (1989). Multiple personality, dissociation, and C. G. Jung's complex theory. *Journal of Analytical Psychology*, *34*, 353–370.

Open Letter. (2018). Open letter from a group of Jungians on the question of Jung's writings on and theories about 'Africans'. *British Journal of Psychotherapy*, *34*(4), 673–678.

Page, S. (1999). *The shadow and the counsellor*. Routledge.

Rubin, J. A. (2011). *The art of art therapy* (2nd ed.). Routledge (Original work published 1984).

Samuels, A. (1989). *The plural psyche*. Routledge.

Schaverien, J. (1992). *The revealing image: Analytical art psychotherapy in theory and practice*. Routledge.

Shalit, E. (2002). *The complex: Path of transformation from archetype to ego*. Inner City Books.

Shamdasani, S. (Ed.). (2009). Introduction. In M. Kyburtz, J. Peck, & S. Shamdasani (Trans.), *The red book: A reader's edition* (pp. 1–113). W.W. Norton.

Stein, M. (Ed.). (1996). *Jung on evil*. Princeton University Press.

Swan-Foster, N. (2016). Jungian art therapy. In J. Rubin (Ed.), *Approaches to art therapy: Theory and technique* (3rd ed., pp. 167–187). Routledge.

Swan-Foster, N. (2018). *Jungian art therapy: A guide to dreams, images, and analytical psychology*. Routledge.

Talwar, S. K., Clinton, R., Sit, T., & Ospina, L. (2019). Intersectional reflexivity: Considering identities and accountability for art therapists. In S. K. Talwar (Ed.), *Art therapy for social justice: Radical intersections* (pp. 66–95). Routledge.

Tobin, M. (2015). *A brief history of art therapy: From Freud to Naumburg and Kramer*. https://doi.org/10.13140/RG.2.1.4211.6003/1.

Wilkinson, M. (2005). Undoing dissociation. Affective neuroscience: A contemporary Jungian clinical perspective. *Journal of Analytical Psychology*, *50*, 483–501.

Winnicott, D. W. (1969). The use of an object. *The International Journal of Psycho-Analysis*, *50*, 711–716.

Wix, L. (2011). Aesthetic empathy in teaching art to children: The work of Friedl Dicker-Brandeis in Terezin. *Art Therapy: Journal of the American Art Therapy Association*, *26*(4), 152–158.

Chapter 8

Humanistic approaches to art therapy: Existentialism, person-centered, and gestalt

Elizabeth Hadara Hlavek, DAT, LCPAT, ATR-BC[a] and Rachel Paige Feldwisch, PhD, MAAT, LMHC, ATR-BC[b]
[a]*Hlavek Art Therapy, LLC, Annapolis, MD, United States,* [b]*Department of Counseling, University of Indianapolis, Indianapolis, IN, United States*

Voices from the field

I am drawn to the notion that each person is ultimately responsible for his or her own meaning. When push comes to shove, I would argue that all therapies are essentially different flavors of humanism and existentialism. Cognitive behaviorism, neuroscience, etc., are really just different lenses through which to understand the ultimate concerns of human beings.

Bruce Moon, PhD, ATR-BC, HLM

Learning outcomes

After reading this chapter, you will be able to

1. Demonstrate an understanding of the essential elements of humanistic theoretical orientation.
2. Identify Yalom's four existential concerns and articulate how these concerns informed Moon's tenets of existential art therapy.
3. Explain how Roger's core conditions of therapeutic change inform the work of person-centered art therapists.
4. Describe the theory underlying gestalt art therapy and corresponding techniques used by art therapists.
5. Distinguish the differences between humanistic theoretical approaches from other approaches.
6. Discuss the applicability of humanistic art therapy to cross-cultural contexts.

Chapter overview

Have you ever wondered what your purpose is in life? Have you experienced unconditional positive regard from someone? Have you ever considered your

Foundations of Art Therapy. https://doi.org/10.1016/B978-0-12-824308-4.00005-3

life experience in relation to others? These are questions that are addressed with a humanistic approach to psychotherapy. Humanistic psychology began as a philosophical movement to understand what it truly means to be human. Early humanistic scholars and philosophers rejected the popular branches of psychology like psychoanalysis and behaviorism, viewing them as **reductionistic** and therefore limiting (Moss, 2014). The term reductionist refers to the approach of simplifying human behavior to one contributing source, instead of viewing behaviors as a result of complex and varying causes. This approach can be limiting, as it neglects the impact of the multitude of influences on human behavior. Early humanistic therapists aimed to help their clients in a **holistic** manner, by looking at the whole of the individual (such as their passions, lived experiences, and relationships) beyond psychiatric conditions. A humanistic approach to psychotherapy is one that focuses on the whole of the individual. It is built on the notion that all humans possess the capacity to achieve their full potential in life (Joseph & Linley, 2004). The humanistic philosophies emphasize the individual as being capable of growth and change even with the presence of pathology.

Humanistic philosophies are also typically **nondirective**. This does not mean that there is no direction to therapy, but rather that the therapist creates an environment in which the client is empowered to take ownership of their therapy. In doing so, the client guides the direction of their therapy, while the therapist accompanies them on the journey. The humanistic therapist provides space for the client to express their concerns and feelings, then helps the client reflect and clarify on what they have shared.

Although there are various theories and modalities that fall under the umbrella of humanistic approaches, in this chapter we will focus on three of the most developed frameworks: **existential**, **person-centered**, and **gestalt**.

Existential psychotherapy

An existential approach to therapy considers the experience of existence as a human in the world. Existentialism is a **holistic** philosophy, taking an individual's cultural, political, and social background into account. Although the term existentialism can sound heavy, it is actually a philosophy that aims to understand a person's most basic condition: being human. An existentially oriented therapist views their client's distress as a response to the struggles of humanity. Those engaged in existential psychotherapy may ask broad, contemplative questions such as, "What is my purpose in life?", "What am I contributing to the world?", or "How can I qualify the value of my life?"

Historical background of existential philosophy

Existentialism in Western psychotherapy provided a paradigm that helped psychotherapists understand their clients as whole beings apart from their pathology. Influenced by the philosophies of Sartre, Soren Kierkegaard, and

Friederich Nietzsche, 20th century existential psychotherapists considered the chaotic, transient, and circumstantial nature of human existence, from which they challenged the postulations of conventional psychotherapy practice (May & Yalom, 2000). In addition to including a spiritual, distinctly human element in therapy, early existential therapists believed that a psychotherapy session was a place to explore and discuss the uncomfortable but relevant, ultimate concerns of existence. These therapists postulated that the *awareness of existence* is the root of anxiety. Existential psychotherapy guides the client to understand their concerns as embedded in an increased awareness and genuine fear surrounding their own existence. In this paradigm, psychiatric conditions are not idiosyncratic but rather are viewed as universal to the human condition.

One of the most notable figures in the existential psychology movement of the 20th century was Viktor Frankl, a psychiatrist who studied the value of suffering in his auto-ethnographic memoir of Auschwitz, finding that a sense of meaning and purpose was life enhancing (Frankl, 1973, 2006). Frankl began exploring existentialism in psychotherapy in the 1930s while working in psychiatric clinics in Austria. Frankl was concerned that psychiatry and psychology had become consumed by science and neglected an individual's spirituality. He conceived of **logotherapy** as "meaning-centered psychotherapy" (Frankl, 2006, p. 98), stemming from the Greek word *logos*, which implies reason or intent. In logotherapy, the client strives to develop a future-oriented meaning of self, thereby breaking away from maladaptive patterns and behaviors (e.g., substance abuse or self-injury) that negatively impact one's life (Frankl, 2006). Thus **meaning** in logotherapy is associated with a stable mood, positive outlook, reduction in stress, and stronger self-awareness (Schulenberg et al., 2008). Frankl, along with subsequent existentialists, was adamant that the spiritual, intellectual dimension of humans should be taken into account in psychotherapy. He additionally believed that finding meaning is life enhancing, and that psychotherapy should help the client in their search for meaning.

Contemporary existential theory

Existentially oriented therapists today veer away from the medical model of treatment (guided by DSM or ICD code) and instead consider the whole of an individual, not just their diagnosis. These therapists engage clients to achieve self-awareness, clarity, and a deepened sense of meaning and purpose. van Deurzen and Arnold-Baker (2018) categorized four dimensions of human existence as a framework for therapists to understand the whole of their clients. These four dimensions represent the different ways in which individuals relate to and experience their world: **physical**, **social**, **personal**, and **spiritual** (Fig. 8.1). Deurzen encourages therapists to consider each as a pane of a client's existence that are intertwined and at times paradoxical.

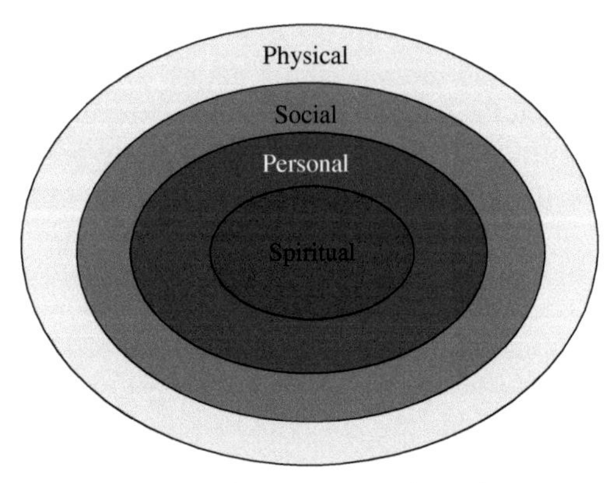

FIG. 8.1 *Deurzen's four dimensions of human existence dimensions.*

Finding meaning

A search for meaning is at the crux of existential philosophy. Hoffman (2009) emphasized the importance of finding meaning, arguing that it is a central aspect of human existence. Per existentialist thought, meaningfulness comes into fruition by an individual's actions in response to circumstance. For example, when a survivor of domestic violence finds meaning in their own horrific experiences through becoming an advocate for abuse victims. Robbins (1999) made the point that chaos cannot lead to meaning unless the individual experiencing it is "overwhelmed by the anxiety and the psychic forces" (p. 125) involved.

By engaging in art-making, one can move into a place of acute awareness and contemplation, and can therefore find meaning within the experience. May (1975) suggested that by creating, artists allow themselves to evolve by conjuring new ideas and perceptions. Uncertainty can be reframed and new understandings can emerge. Creativity requires a sense of free will and a confidence to make choices in the progression of the creative act, which can contribute to agency and self-confidence. Creativity ultimately leads to a sense of organization amid confusion and turmoil (Robbins, 1999). Robbins (1999) viewed creativity as a process of construction and deconstruction, and stated that art-making is an opportunity to reorganize fragments of chaos, which leads the individual to find meaning.

Yalom's four concerns

Although not originally an existentialist, Irving Yalom is a psychiatrist known for articulating a clear relationship between existential philosophy and psychotherapy practice, which was rooted in European and Western philosophy. Yalom's (1980) theory centers on four primary concerns pertaining to existence: death, freedom, isolation, and meaninglessness. These "givens," described in detail below, shape human experience and comprise the most basic levels of existence. In this framework, all psychological stressors and struggles can be distilled down to manifestations of these core existential concerns.

Death

The concern regarding death is foremost in Yalom's theory. He alleged that a persistent fear of death, manifested as a **death anxiety**, occurs throughout one's life (Yalom, 2008). Like his predecessors, Yalom believed that most anxieties stem from a fear of human mortality that causes individuals to ignore or deny the subject completely. He advised confronting rather than avoiding the subject of mortality, to make it less daunting and overwhelming: "We should contemplate our ultimate end, familiarize ourselves with it, dissect and analyze it, reason with it, and discard terrifying childhood death distortions" (1980, p. 276). Existentialism views the definiteness of life and death to be interchangeable, thereby making the subject of death a critical topic in psychotherapy. If an individual is able to accept their mortality, Yalom argued, then they can live a more authentic life, appreciating the simplicity of living.

Freedom

The concern of freedom relates to free will and responsibility. Yalom viewed freedom as a lack of structure and guidance. He believed that "one is also entirely responsible for one's life, not only for one's actions, but for one's failures to act" (Yalom, 1980, p. 220). This concept of freedom is built on Sartre's (1949) theory of tension between authentic choice and ersatz comfort. Sartre asserted that humans have the freedom to live authentically, governed by their own moral compass. Such freedom can cause anxiety when one senses "groundlessness" (Yalom, 1980) in the absence of firm external direction. The ability to act and to choose freely also involves a significant responsibility, which can contribute to anxiety or fear if experienced as overwhelming. An example of this **groundlessness** often occurs when students are preparing for college graduation. Throughout their life, they may have been guided by a clear pathway of grades K-12, followed by college. However, the period after graduation presents a less paved pathway. College seniors and recent graduates may feel overwhelmed and anxious by the options of directions (job searching, graduate school, volunteer work) they can take.

Isolation. Existential isolation is a broad concept, which Yalom referred to as a "gap" in the human experience. "Each of us enters existence alone and must depart from it alone. The existential conflict is thus, the tension between our awareness of our absolute isolation and our wish to be part of a larger whole" (Yalom, 1980, p. 9). The concern of existential isolation is experienced in individuals who are close to death, as they become acutely aware that they will leave their life alone, regardless of the close connections they may have made throughout life. The development of relationships throughout one's life may be a defense against existential isolation (May & Yalom, 2000) as individuals strive for a sense of connectedness.

Meaninglessness

The fourth existential concern, meaninglessness, relates to an individual's purpose, ideals, values, and ambitions. Meaninglessness is found in the absence of purpose, cohesion, and explanation (Wong, 2017), and can result in feelings of dysphoria, helplessness, and spiritual emptiness. Existentialists viewed emptiness as contrary to meaningfulness, as it lurks in the void of meaning. For example, Frankl believed that spiritual emptiness could lead to an individual ultimately capitulating to circumstance (Schulenberg et al., 2008). Without a perception of meaning, a person lacks substance and subsequently loses motivation and drive to live an authentic existence. Meaning distinguishes individuals as uniquely human.

The element of choice is critical to meaningfulness. By experiencing freedom of choice, humans are given regular opportunities to respond in ways that align with personal values, thereby achieving meaning (Schulenberg et al., 2008). However, when a person's responses conflict with their individual values, goals, and overall essence, the result is a sense of meaninglessness. Frankl (1973) identified two stages of existential meaninglessness as they appear in psychotherapy. An **existential vacuum** (Frankl, 1973; Yalom, 1980) is a state of apathy and hopelessness in which one experiences no sense of intent or purpose. In an attempt to fill the existential vacuum, an individual enters the **existential neurosis** that is characterized by depression, angst, and/or maladaptive behavior. In this construct, Frankl viewed psychiatric symptoms as a reaction to the experience of meaninglessness. Thus he emphasized that humans must find a meaning for existence and live accordingly.

With these four givens, Yalom provided a framework that makes existential theory more applicable to psychotherapy practice. Later practitioners built on Yalom's framework to further advance existential psychotherapy (see Schneider, 2015; Schneider & Krug, 2010; Hoffman, 2019). How then, do art therapists use existential theory in their work?

Existential art therapy

Moon (2009) is considered the first art therapist to formally integrate existential psychotherapy philosophies with art therapy, which he defined in theory as "a dynamic approach to the therapeutic use of arts processes and imagery that focuses attention on the ultimate concerns of human existence" (2009, p. 31). Confronted with the products of his own art practice, Moon searched for a sense of meaning in and reconciliation of painful personal experiences. He described working through issues, both petty and significant, through extended engagement in painting. Moon's artistic experience lent support to his belief that art-making results in a meaningful experience by providing the artist with an opportunity for contemplation and reflection. Applied to art therapy practice, Moon endorsed a relaxed, nondirective approach in which the client makes decisions about their artwork with guidance from the art therapist. Moon's approach encouraged the client to define and embrace their spiritual, uniquely human dimensions through art-making.

According to Moon, existential art therapy rests on three tenets. The first is **being with**, in which a shared artistic journey is encouraged. Moon wrote that he creates art alongside clients to model authentic engagement and his commitment to accompanying them through the therapeutic process. For example, Moon painted while his clients painted.

The second tenet, **being open to**, emphasizes the need for an authentic and respectful relationship between art therapist and client. Moon supported transparency in the therapeutic relationship in order for clients to see their therapist as a fellow person, rather than a transference figure or representation of an authoritarian healthcare system. He also stated that the therapist must be open to and accepting of all that the client brings to the session. Art Therapist Robbins (1999) also supported the notion of *being open to*. To acquire a sense of relatedness between art therapist and client, the art therapist must be accepting and tolerant of the transient nature of emotion and creation. To demonstrate this openness, the art therapist must serve as a witness to their client's art process and product, regardless of the nature of the work. The art therapist can remind their client that art-making may evoke strong responses, all of which will be respected within the session.

Moon's third tenet, **honoring pain**, is also influenced by the contributions of Nietzsche and Frankl. Moon proposed that the role of an art therapist using an existential approach is not to reduce pain but instead to acknowledge it. Clients bring their pain into sessions; it will not dissolve in the span of an hour. By honoring a client's pain, the art therapist normalizes pain as a matter of human experience, and encourages clients to fully experience its impact on their life concerns, instead of trying to deny it. Moon quoted Frankl (1959), "For what matters above all is the attitude we take toward suffering, the attitude in which we take our suffering upon ourselves" (p. 138). Art therapists can honor their client's pain by responding to the artwork with acknowledgment of what the client chose to share, and asking follow-up questions about the artwork and life experience that inspired it. Honoring pain requires that the art therapist be a witness not just to the artwork but to the client's life experience. The case example at the end of this first section highlights Moon's tenets.

The creative process has been associated with existential theory outside of art therapy literature. May (1975) theorized that there is a highly relevant relationship between creativity and existentialism. In his view the creative process is paramount in finding meaning. May asserted that life struggles may foster a sense of meaning that can be achieved through creativity. The capacity to recognize beauty is to recognize meaning, regardless of the despair that may have bred it. May described authentic creativity as "bringing something new into being" (1975, p. 38) and argued that creativity represents a high level of emotional health and self-actualization. May also pondered the place of death anxiety in creativity, asserting that the purpose of creativity is "the passion to live beyond one's death" (1975, p. 31). He believed that creative engagement offers a sense of wholeness. It evokes a sensation of ecstasy and joy (May, 1975) and results in a grounding, comprehensive understanding of the self.

Furthering the connection between creativity and existential theory, Schneider and Krug (2017) stated that individuals have the capacity to grow and make changes through the creative process, which, according to the authors, is the "basic assumption of existential therapy" (p. 29).

Case example

Contemporary art therapists practicing through an existential lens recognize that their clients are in the throes of distress. Although they may have previously experienced a traumatic event, they are contending with day-to-day struggles that impact their existence. To retain a sense of humanity and facilitate growth, we, the authors, believe it is imperative that the art therapist's approach is one that humanizes.

To further this point, we will share an example from an art therapy session. A 24-year-old self-identified queer Black female client who uses she/her pronouns came to her weekly appointment and immediately announced that her mother died the day before. Her mother had been hospitalized for liver failure and the client knew that she would not survive the illness, but neither she nor her art therapist expected that death was imminent. As the client spoke, the art therapist realized how fresh her pain was. In the past 24 hours, her entire world had changed. Together they drew with pastels while the client tearfully placed blame on the hospital, her father, and her siblings for her mother's death. From a technical standpoint, her drawing was impoverished. She used minimal space on the paper and positioned her drawing in an odd, unanchored spot (see Fig. 8.2). Although abstract, the shapes and colors looked hurried and incongruent. Despite this, the existential art therapist did not attribute these features to the client's chronic depression or social anxiety, the conditions that initially brought her into art therapy. Instead, the art therapist saw the artwork as an expression of the client's very recent loss. How could her drawing possibly be cohesive when her entire existence had just been shaken?

During the session, the art therapist was aware of Moon's (2009) tenets of *being with, being open to*, and *honoring pain*. The therapist was powerless to change her client's situation and nothing the therapist said or offered could bring the client's mother back or mitigate the suffering. The existential art therapist's role was not to do any of those things, but rather to be in the client's presence, draw with her, and witness her pain. The client's aching expressions were given witness to exist, and she was able to safely express herself, without fear of judgment or evaluation. She manifested her pain into her artwork and used the art process as an opportunity to experience and express her range of emotions.

FIG. 8.2 *Drawing in response to death drawing from art therapy session.*

Summary: Existential art therapy

Existential therapy considers the client's day-to-day struggles with the burdens of existence. According to existentialism, meaning is essential for persevering through hardship. The discovery of meaning from adversity or suffering is what an existentially oriented art therapist strives to help clients achieve. Even though it cannot change their past experiences or their current realities, art therapy can guide individuals to find meaning and purpose regardless of circumstance. Through art-making, individuals gain acute awareness and contemplation, and therefore can begin to identify meaning within a painful experience, which makes the reality of their existence more tolerable. Now that you have a better understanding of existential theory, let's move on to another humanistic approach: person-centered therapy.

Person-centered therapy

Have you ever considered that, despite your flaws and struggles, you have the capacity for positive growth and change? Like existentialism, person-centered therapy is a nondirective orientation in which the therapist's empathic approach empowers and motivates the client in the therapeutic process to reach their full potential. Psychologist Carl Rogers is widely known as the creator of person-centered therapy, which was also called client-centered therapy in his early work (Rogers, 1961). Rogers' theory consistently emphasized the importance of the therapist demonstrating three core conditions: empathy, genuineness, and unconditional positive regard. While other conceptualizations exist, Carl Rogers' definition of **empathy** involved the therapist accurately communicating their perceptions regarding the client's internal reality (Neukrug et al., 2013). Empathy involves the therapist imagining what it would be like to exist within the lived experience of the other person, then sensitively expressing emotional and cognitive reactions to the person's lived experience. During a video-recorded explanation of the core conditions, Rogers described how empathy involves understanding the "inner world" of a person and seeing the world "through her eyes" (Shostrom, 1965). Experiencing and expressing empathy helps the therapist and client to process not only the superficial meanings of the client's lived experiences but also the deeper meanings that shape a person's life.

Genuineness means being sincere and truthful when reacting to a client (Rogers, 1961). According to Rogers (1961), genuineness not only facilitated the development of therapeutic relationships, but also helped clients to identify and explore areas of themselves that lack genuineness or incongruence. In his writings, Rogers described the related concept of **congruence** both as a trait of the therapist and as a goal for the client. Rogers defined **congruence** as the match between communication, experience, and awareness (Rogers et al., 1967). For example, a therapist who feels anger when a client speaks of being mistreated by another person would express and communicate that anger, saying something like, "When I hear how you were treated by this other person, I feel angry." When a person is acting genuinely and congruently, their outward physical and verbal expressions match their internal thoughts and feelings. However, Rogers emphasized that therapist's expressions of thoughts and emotions must be carefully done so as not to impose the therapist's feelings onto the client (Shostrom, 1965).

Another key element of the person-centered therapeutic relationship is unconditional positive regard. Rogers defined **unconditional positive regard** as acceptance, caring, and genuine warmth expressed by the therapist (Rogers et al., 1967). During a recorded interview, he described this way of interacting with people as "acceptance" and "nonpossessive love" (Shostrom, 1965). Rogers further explained that expressions of positive regard must be genuine and affirmations must be truthfully expressed by the therapist. In other words, the therapist must truly feel unconditional positive regard toward their clients in order for it to be effective.

Rogers believed that the three core conditions (empathy, genuineness, and unconditional positive regard) set the stage for a client to experience growth in therapy. Researchers have found that expressions of empathy (Elliott et al., 2011), genuineness or congruence (Kolden et al., 2011), and unconditional positive regard (Farber & Doolin, 2011) positively impact the therapeutic relationship. Interestingly, researchers have discovered that genuine expressions of positive regard and affirmation are even more impactful when a therapist from a dominant or privileged culture works with a client from a nondominant or marginalized culture; for example, when a person of color engages in therapy with a White therapist (Farber et al., 2018).

Rogers' beliefs regarding the therapeutic relationship greatly differed from the teachings of Freud and Strachey (1964) and other psychoanalysts during the 20th century in several ways. In addition to differing views regarding the core conditions associated with the therapeutic relationship, Rogers (1961) also defined different goals for therapy. Rogers (1961) identified the facilitation of self-exploration, personal growth, and self-actualization as the objectives of person-centered therapy. He explained that therapeutic goals could be achieved through the relationship between client and therapist without the need for elaborate interpretation or analysis by the therapist. The client, not the therapist, was viewed as the expert regarding their experience. Rogers also explained that motivation to change is initiated by a person's tendency toward self-actualization; in other words, the client is intrinsically motivated toward change. Rogers emphasized that therapists could be most helpful by openly identifying and clarifying the emotions of the client (Rogers, 1961). While Freud may have been one of the first clinicians to advocate for a talking cure, Rogers' person-centered therapy also made a remarkable and enduring impact on the practice of psychotherapy.

Person-centered therapy in contemporary practice

In contemporary practice, person-centered therapy includes a series of brief statements and summarizations by the therapist that deepen and broaden the client's understanding of thoughts, feelings, and other aspects of the self (Neukrug et al., 2013). The stated reflections of modern-day person-centered therapists utilize the client's own words along with reflection of deeper feelings and observations regarding discrepancies or contradictions within the client's self-expression. Person-centered therapists may also utilize creative descriptions of visual images, analogies, and metaphors with the goal of deepening a client's self-awareness and understanding. For example, the second author worked with a teenage client who identified "feeling gray" and described experiences with peers that left her feeling sad and lonesome. I helped her to connect to the emotions associated with "feeling gray" and subsequently used the client's association with the color gray to help her to explore her experiences with depressed mood.

In addition, person-centered therapists utilize selectively targeted self-disclosure regarding here-and-now reactions to the client (Neukrug et al., 2013). **Self-disclosure** involves the therapist sharing their own thoughts, feelings, and experiences directly with a client. For example, a person-centered therapist might disclose their internal reactions or emotional responses that relate directly to what the client is expressing in the here-and-now experience of the therapy session. While modern-day person-centered therapists may be a bit more interactive or slightly more directive than Rogers, the emphasis on qualities that define the therapeutic relationship remains imperative in person-centered therapy. During the late 1900s, person-centered techniques became more popular in the field of art therapy (Rubin, 2016). Two Art Therapists Natalie Rogers and Liesl Silverstone contributed to the development of person-centered art therapy.

Person-centered art therapy

Art Therapist Judith Rubin published the first comprehensive book on application of psychological theory to art therapy in the United States in 1987, titled *Approaches to Art Therapy: Theory and Technique.* In her introduction to the humanistic theories, Rubin (1987) explained:

> *Although many art therapists, especially students in training, utilize a "nondirective" approach, none has specifically embraced Rogers' theory as a primary framework for his or her work. Perhaps that is in part because it emphasizes the necessary conditions for good therapeutic work (e.g., a psychologically safe environment, empathy, and positive regard on the part of the therapist) that alone—like art alone—are not always enough. (p. 136)*

Natalie Rogers. Art therapist and daughter of Carl Rogers, Natalie Rogers subsequently developed what she called Person-Centered Art Therapy (Rogers, 2016). In her contribution to Levine and Levine's *Foundations of Expressive Arts Therapy* (1999), Rogers expressed her belief that self-analysis and self-knowledge are the goals of expressive arts therapy. According to Rogers, self-discovery can develop from any form of art that relates to one's emotions. Her expansion of person-centered theory suggests that just as talking about feelings is helpful to people, expressing feelings through art is also helpful. Rogers also emphasized using the arts to release emotions and express oneself without judging the aesthetic beauty of the piece; in other words, a focus on the process rather than the product that clearly fits within the here-and-now approach of person-centered therapy.

Natalie Rogers developed a comprehensive person-centered expressive arts therapy program and described her work in her 1993 book *The Creative Connection: Expressive Arts as Healing.* In her book, Rogers (1993) described the overlap between person-centered art therapy and person-centered talk therapy: both emphasize the three core conditions previously identified by Carl Rogers (empathy, genuineness, and unconditional positive regard) and acknowledge the importance of self-exploration and personal growth. In addition, the Creative Connection® approach emphasized the existence of creativity within all people and the ability of people to achieve self-awareness and emotional insight through their artistic expressions (Rogers, 1993).

Natalie Rogers' Creative Connection® method differs from a pure person-centered approach because some elements of psychodynamic theory are integrated. For example, Rogers incorporated the psychodynamic conceptualization of the unconscious, stating that "expressive arts lead us into the unconscious"

(1993, p. 8). While Rogers' Creative Connection® approach was not purely a person-centered approach, it was strongly influenced by the major components of Carl Rogers' approach to psychotherapy.

Liesl Silverstone. Another influential person-centered art therapist was Liesl Silverstone, a British art therapist who practiced, wrote, and taught about Rogerian theory (Rubin, 2009). Silverstone was originally trained as a social worker but later became a school counselor and then an art therapist. She wrote about her transformation from "authoritarian" (characterized by solving the client's problem for them and/or actively directing their process) to person-centered therapist who valued the relationship and emphasized a nonjudgmental approach (Silverstone, 1994). Silverstone found that her shift in method created therapeutic experiences that were more meaningful to clients, produced more significant personal growth, and increased clients' self-esteem. She authored two editions of a book titled *Art therapy—The Person-Centred Way* (1993, 1997). Although her texts embrace the core conditions and key elements of Carl Rogers' person-centered theory, Silverstone's approach, as written, is more directive and includes specific examples of art therapy exercises for use by trained therapists (1993, 1997, 2009).

Clinical example: Jeremy and the person-centered art therapist

Jeremy (a pseudonym used to protect client confidentiality) was a 14-year-old client who identified as male, White, heterosexual, and nonreligious. At the time of art therapy treatment, Jeremy was attending an alternative school for students with special needs and was in the eighth grade. Jeremy was referred for school-based art therapy due to difficulty with verbal communication. He had developed **selective mutism**, an anxiety-induced condition involving difficulty communicating in social situations, subsequent to being bullied by his peers regarding a moderate speech impediment. While Jeremy was silent and compliant at school, his mother reported angry outbursts at home, including verbal threats toward family members and destruction of property.

The art therapist approached Jeremy with a genuine interest in developing rapport, seeking to know this young man and understand his view of the world. Despite hearing that Jeremy could be physically violent at home, the art therapist maintained a positive view of the teenager and attempted to highlight his strengths. During the first several sessions, Jeremy did not communicate verbally with the art therapist. The art therapist took a nondirective approach, offering a variety of materials that he could choose from. Jeremy chose to engage in figure drawing or traced his hands on paper. A turning point came when the art therapist observed that Jeremy was drawing hands with long, pointed fingernails reminiscent of an old horror movie called *A Nightmare on Elm Street*. When the therapist asked, "Freddy Krueger?" Jeremy smiled and nodded. At the time of the next session, the art therapist presented Jeremy with plaster strips and asked if he would like to make a plaster casting of his hand.

FIG. 8.3 *A casting of the art therapist's hand created in art therapy session.*

They worked together on casting their hands, and as the hands dried Jeremy added long fingernails like Freddy Krueger (see Fig. 8.3, a casting of the art therapist's hand). At first, Jeremy communicated with the therapist by writing notes. As therapeutic rapport developed, Jeremy slowly began to speak, making verbal requests for supplies, such as when he asked the therapist for red paint. The therapist maintained a warm, empathic stance that helped Jeremy to find his voice. The therapist made observations aloud regarding the content or emotions depicted in Jeremy's artwork but did not analyze or evaluate his work. After several months, Jeremy began to speak in complete sentences during therapy. His progress gradually transitioned to other settings and he was able to communicate with his teacher and the speech language pathologist at his school (Fig. 8.3).

Summary: Person-centered art therapy

Person-centered art therapists, including Natalie Rogers and Liesl Silverstone, embrace Carl Rogers' emphasis on empathy, genuineness, and unconditional positive regard in the therapeutic relationship (Rubin, 2016). They value congruence on the part of both the therapist and the client, and believe that the client in therapy is more of an expert regarding their own life than the therapist.

While traditional person-centered therapy is definitively nondirective, person-centered art therapists do tend to offer suggestions and prompts to their clients (Silverstone, 1994, 1997, 2009). They may also integrate concepts from other theoretical frameworks, including the traditionally psychodynamic conceptualization of the unconscious (Rogers, 1993). However, the here-and-now processing that occurs in person-centered art therapy places value on the client's own perspectives and interpretations of the artistic experience (Hogan, 2015). The triadic relationship between client, artwork, and art therapist is central to person-centered art therapy.

A third humanistic approach to art therapy that shares similarities with both person-centered and existential art therapy is rooted in gestalt theory. In the segment that follows, gestalt therapy, the modern practice of gestalt therapy, and the emergence of gestalt art therapy will be explained.

Gestalt therapy

Frederick "Fritz" Perls was initially trained in psychoanalysis and subsequently developed gestalt therapy to integrate what he and his wife Laura Perls had learned from other schools of thought, including existential psychology (Perls, 1969). The German word gestalt does not translate directly into English. As Rhyne (1996) explained, "Form, figure, pattern, structure, and configuration are possible translations, but none is quite right" (p. 3). In the context of therapy, **gestalt** could be defined as the consideration of a whole person, including their way of being in the world and in relation to others.

Perhaps because both underlying theories were influenced by existentialism, gestalt therapy has traditionally shared characteristics with person-centered therapy (Herlihy, 1985). Similar to person-centered therapy, the therapist emphasizes staying in the present moment, as opposed to exploring the past, and values the development of a therapeutic relationship. Like Rogers, Perls believed in the importance of a holistic view of the client, to include their perceptions and emotions in response to their experiences (Yontef & Jacobs, 2010). Perls perceived that people could grow in their own psychological awareness without psychoanalysis by the therapist. However, the gestalt therapist takes a more directive and active role in therapy compared to the person-centered therapist (Herlihy, 1985).

Gestalt therapy focuses on each person's lived experience (Perls, 1969). Several ideas are central to the exploration of lived experience in gestalt therapy (Yontef & Jacobs, 2010). First, gestalt therapy relies on the assumption that people can grow and change throughout their lives, and this growth is inevitable unless obstacles arise that prevent the development of a person. For example, if a person does not learn from their experience and develops ways of being that are unhelpful, then they may benefit from the intervention of a gestalt therapist. Second, interactions between people inform our awareness of self within the world and influence both functional (or healthy) and dysfunctional (or unhealthy) behaviors within relationships. Third, the patterns that emerge during therapy emulate the patterns that emerge outside of the therapy session. The work of the gestalt therapist is informed by this theoretical assumption and the implication that change occurring in session may also elicit change outside of the session. As Yontef and Jacobs (2010) explained, the relationship between a client and the gestalt therapist is "a relationship in which the patient has another chance to learn, to unlearn, and to learn how to keep learning" (p. 13).

The method of change in gestalt therapy involves a series of exchanges between therapist and client that focus on the development of self-awareness (Perls, 1969). The goal is not simply for clients to relay a story that happened in the past, but for clients to actively reexperience a situation in the present. For example, rather than telling a story about something that happened between sessions, a client engaged in gestalt therapy may be encouraged to role play something that happened outside of the session. Unlike in psychodynamic psychotherapy where the therapist elicits free association and observes the verbalizations that come from the client, the gestalt therapist acts as an active participant during the therapy session. Perls used the term **contact** to describe the connections that occur between self and other, including connections between client and therapist (Perls, 1969). When engaging in contact with a client, the gestalt therapist is warm and caring, yet also may confront the client as needed. For example, in Fritz Perls now famous recording of a session with a client named Gloria, Perls' style was perceived by undergraduate and graduate students as being quite direct and confrontational regarding Gloria's behavior (Reilly & Jacobus, 2009). While confrontation may be an element of gestalt therapy, the approach used by modern gestalt therapists is likely to be more supportive and less abrupt.

Gestalt therapy in contemporary practice

What gestalt therapy looks like in contemporary practice is likely less confrontational and more accepting of the client than Perls' well-known interaction with Gloria (Yontef & Jacobs, 2010). However, the **enactments** or here-and-now exercises that were popularized by Perls are still utilized by many gestalt therapists (Brownell, 2016). For example, the **empty chair** (or **two-chair**) technique is still commonly used in gestalt therapy and involves the client engaging in dialogue with an empty chair that is thought to represent someone in their life with whom they have unfinished business. While this technique has some evidence of usefulness in therapy, contemporary gestalt therapists emphasize the need for creativity during sessions as clinicians experiment with directives that match the needs of their individual clients (Brownell, 2016; Yontef & Jacobs, 2010). Gestalt therapy's consistent emphasis on creativity and experimentation fits well with the contemporary practice of art therapy.

Gestalt art therapy

Several psychotherapists influenced gestalt therapy's crossover from talk therapy to art therapy (Rubin, 2009). After studying with several early practitioners of gestalt therapy, Psychologists Max Wertheimer and Wolfgang Köhler, Rudolph Arnheim developed a theory of visual perception and subsequently trained the gestalt Art Therapist Shaun McNiff (McNiff, 2007). Gestalt Psychologist Joseph Zinker (1991) wrote about the connections between visual arts and gestalt psychotherapy. However, the most frequently recognized contributor to the practice of gestalt art therapy in the United States was Art therapist Janie Rubin (2016).

Fritz Perls trained Art Therapist Janie Rhyne, author of *The Gestalt Art Experience* (Rhyne, 1973, 1996). Rhyne (1996) theorized that the desire to create art is inherent in people and is an emergence of an individual's experiences. According to Rhyne (1996), our visual perceptions directly relate to our thoughts and feelings, a relationship that is revealed when we use art materials to represent our perceptions. For example, a self-portrait of a person is not merely a self-portrait, but a reflection of someone's present thoughts and feelings about themselves as a person and their relationship with the surrounding world. Rhyne described the "Gestalt Art Experience" as

> *the complex personal you making art forms, being involved in the forms you are creating as events, observing what you do, and hopefully perceiving through your graphic productions not only yourself as you are now, but also alternate ways that are available to you for creating yourself as you would like to be (Rhyne, 1996, p. 9).*

Rhyne's definition of gestalt art therapy was clearly connected to the key elements of Perls' gestalt therapy. First, Rhyne emphasized the **uniqueness** of each individual and the contexts that surround them, a conceptualization that fits gestalt therapy. The implication for art therapy is that each piece of art is an individualized experience that is unique to the creator of the artwork, yet patterns or themes may emerge between and within pieces of art made by the same person. Second, Rhyne's use of the word "events" (1996, p. 9) connects to the emphasis on **experience** that is quintessential to gestalt therapy. As Rhyne explained, "Each time you and I draw, paint, or model we are actively living through an event: our own experiential event." Third, Rhyne's emphasis on **visual perception** draws from the work of Gestalt Psychologists Arnheim (1966, 1970) and Perls (1969). Rhyne extended their work by exploring how visual perceptions influence the making and processing of artwork in art therapy. Finally, Rhyne's emphasis on "yourself as you are now" and "as you would like to be" juxtaposes the here-and-now orientation of gestalt therapy with the eventual goal of awareness as art therapy progresses. While Rhyne's contributions were clearly rooted in Perls' gestalt therapy, she also made unique contributions by applying gestalt concepts to art therapy.

After presenting her theory, the remainder of Rhyne's (1973, 1996) writings included suggestions regarding experiential exercises alongside images and written clinical examples that may be helpful to students who are interested in learning more about her work.

Case example: Portraiture as a gestalt art experience

The second author of this chapter participated in a week-long art therapy training institute that was hosted by the University of Illinois at Chicago in Lake Geneva, Wisconsin, in 2002. The participants were asked to engage in a gestalt art experience by creating a portrait of someone with whom they had unfinished business. I utilized compressed charcoal to draw a picture of my beloved aunt and used the exercise to explore thoughts and feelings regarding my aunt's experience with mental illness. I spoke directly to the portrait, expressing empathy for my aunt, concern regarding her isolation, and sadness regarding my inability to improve her condition. This exercise, which resembles the traditional gestalt empty chair, helped me to engage in a here-and-now exploration of my thoughts and feelings regarding my relationship with my aunt.

Summary: Gestalt art therapy

Gestalt art therapists maintain a focus on here-and-now experiences that facilitate self-awareness and personal growth. Like other humanistic therapists, gestalt art therapists emphasize and value the perceptions of the client. The art therapist who practices from a gestalt perspective takes an active and creative role during the therapy session. The goal of the gestalt art experience is to experiment and examine new ways of knowing ourselves through art, exploring both who we are and who we want to be in relation to others.

Humanistic approaches to art therapy in cross-cultural contexts

Although humanistic psychology grew out of a desire to challenge the status quo in mainstream psychology, it is heavily influenced by Western culture and has been criticized for not adopting a multicultural perspective. The holistic nature of a humanistic approach emphasizes individualism, which can be seen as neglecting the influence of social and cultural contexts and ultimately perpetuating ethnocentrism (Hoffman et al., 2014). For example, while an emphasis on individual growth and change may be an acceptable treatment goal for a White client from the West, someone from a collectivist culture that emphasizes family and community may not want therapy to focus on them as an individual apart from their family unit.

For clients who are socioeconomically disadvantaged, the aspirational goal of self-actualization should not be the initial goal if the individual's basic needs are not met (e.g., if the client lacks food and shelter). For example, an art therapist asked her group of Black women at a domestic violence shelter if they felt excited or even empowered by Kamala Harris becoming the first woman of color to serve as vice president. To the art therapist's surprise, the group was ambivalent. Upon further reflection, she realized that the women in her group, who lacked secure housing and steady income, did not have the capacity to feel motivated or empowered by a change in the sociopolitical climate; their focus was on survival. Clients who are focused on survival may not view self-actualization as a realistic goal for themselves.

A person's environment, including experiences of bias, marginalization, and other struggles that they may contend with, gives context to their life experience (Hoffman et al., 2014). In order to be fully holistic, the humanistic art therapist must consider not just their client as an individual but also the sociopolitical world in which the client exists. Postmodern theories (e.g., feminist theory and relational-cultural theory) that were influenced by person-centered and other humanistic theories attend to interpersonal contexts. A few publications have emerged that apply these newer theories to art therapy; for example, British Art Therapist Susan Hogan (1997, 2012) has published two books on the subject of feminist art therapy.

While critiques regarding the cross-cultural applicability of humanistic art therapy are understandable and valid, many art therapists thoughtfully apply the theories described in this chapter to the practice of art therapy with diverse populations. Lucille Venture, a well-known art therapist of color whose contributions are described in Chapters 1 and 15, advocated for the use of humanistic art therapy within communities of color. Venture emphasized how the humanistic focus on the whole person was a better fit for clients of color than Freudian psychoanalysis. As Venture explained, "It is important to note that some black children have no wish to engage in the introspective self-analysis which may result after their drawing; their problems are frequently more tangible, requiring the exploration and application of alternative solutions" (Venture, 1977, p. 107, as cited by Potash, 2005). To successfully utilize existential, person-centered, and gestalt art therapy with diverse populations, art therapists must adapt techniques to fit the person engaged in therapy and also continually engage in critical self-reflection regarding their application of theory-based techniques.

Limitations

The critiques of humanistic theories in a cross-cultural context present some of the limitations of these approaches. As stated before, humanistic approaches can be excessively individualistic and minimize the influence of social factors. For example, a common critique of gestalt therapy is that clients may have cultural or social inhibitions related to confronting relatives/important people in their life, even in imagination.

Another potential limitation of the humanistic approaches is their unstructured nature. Some clients prefer a more directive, manualized approach and are uncomfortable with the open-endedness of humanism (Corey, 2016). Additionally, while humanistic approaches aim to investigate and illuminate the underlying causes of psychiatric symptoms, they do not strive to mitigate maladaptive symptoms that often need relief. The complex, searching nature of humanistic psychotherapy presents another limitation in that it requires an in-depth, philosophical consideration of the self as well as a willingness to challenge the status quo (van Deurzen, 2007).

Since the humanistic approaches are not manualized, meaning that the practitioner does not rely on a specific administration of intervention, they require a seasoned, confident practitioner who is capable of staying attuned to the client. Novice therapists may not be equipped with the adequate training, life experience, or inner wisdom to stay with their clients in an unstructured manner (van Deurzen, 2007). An inexperienced therapist may struggle to be supportive while also challenging their client, thus clinical supervision by a more experienced therapist would be important.

Conclusions

Humanistic approaches to psychotherapy have developed and expanded over the last 70 years to reach individuals in a holistic and comprehensive way. While the three approaches covered in this chapter differ in origin, they overlap in that each emphasizes the need for therapists to view their clients as more than psychiatric symptoms, and capable of achieving a meaningful and fulfilling life. Humanistic approaches to art therapy are not directive-based or manualized, but rather are defined by a way of being with clients that encourages empowerment and acknowledges their human experiences.

Art experiential and reflection questions

1. Create an expressive self-portrait that reflects the elements of this chapter. Consider incorporating concepts from the chapter including personal sense of meaning, self-actualization, and/or emotions in the here-and-now.
2. If you were seeking services from an art therapist, would you prefer a directive or a nondirective approach? Explain your response.
3. Give an example of how art-making supports your own sense of meaning or purpose.
4. Gestalt art therapists often address "unfinished business" in therapy. Describe one method of addressing unfinished business and explain why this might be helpful to a person in therapy.

Additional resources

APA Society for Humanistic Psychology: https://www.apa.org/about/division/div32
Association for Humanistic Psychology: https://ahpweb.org/
International Network on Personal Meaning: https://www.meaning.ca/
Journal of Humanistic Psychology: https://journals.sagepub.com/home/jhp
Viktor Frankl Institute of Logotherapy: https://www.viktorfranklinstitute.org/

Chapter terms

Being open to
Being with
Congruence
Contact
Empathy
Enactments
Existential neurosis
Existential vacuum
Experience
Genuineness
Gestalt
Holistic
Honoring pain
Logotherapy
Meaning making
Nondirective
Reductionistic
Self-disclosure
Unconditional positive regard
Uniqueness
Visual perception

References

Arnheim, R. (1966). *Toward a psychology of art: Collected essays* (Vol. 242). University of California Press.

Arnheim, R. (1970). Gestalt psychology. *Art Journal*, *30*(1), 85–85.

Brownell, P. (2016). Contemporary gestalt therapy. In D. J. Cain, K. Keenan, & S. Rubin (Eds.), *Humanistic psychotherapies: Handbook of research and practice* (pp. 219–250). American Psychological Association. https://doi.org/10.1037/14775-008.

Corey, G. (2016). *Theory and practice of counseling and psychotherapy*. Cengage Learning.

Elliott, R., Bohart, A. C., Watson, J. C., & Greenberg, L. S. (2011). Empathy. In J. C. Norcross (Ed.), *Psychotherapy relationships that work* (2nd ed.). Oxford University Press.

Farber, B. A., & Doolin, E. M. (2011). Positive regard. In J. C. Norcross (Ed.), *Psychotherapy relationships that work: Evidence-based responsiveness* (2nd ed.). Oxford University Press.

Farber, B. A., Suzuki, J. Y., & Lynch, D. A. (2018). Positive regard and psychotherapy outcome: A meta-analytic review. *Psychotherapy*, *55*(4), 411.

Frankl, V. E. (1959). *Man's search for meaning: An introduction to logotherapy*. Square Press, Inc.

Frankl, V. E. (1973). *The doctor and the soul: From psychotherapy to logotherapy*. R. Winston & C. Winston, Trans Vintage Books (Original work published 1946).

Frankl, V. E. (2006). *Man's search for meaning* (5th ed.). Beacon Press. I. Lasch, Trans. (Original work published 1959).

Freud, S., & Strachey, J. E. (1964). *The standard edition of the complete psychological works of Sigmund Freud*. Macmillan.

Herlihy, B. (1985). Person-centered gestalt therapy: A synthesis. *Journal of Humanistic Counseling Education and Development*, *24*(1), 16–24. https://doi.org/10.1002/j.2164-4683.1985.tb00274.x.

Hoffman, L. (2009). Introduction to existential psychology in a cross-cultural context: An east-west dialogue. In L. Hoffman, M. Yang, F. J. Kaklauskas, & A. Chan (Eds.), *Existential psychology east-west* (pp. 1–67). University of the Rockies Press.

Hoffman, L. (2019). Introduction to existential-humanistic psychology in a cross-cultural context. In L. Hoffman, M. Yang, F. J. Kaklauskas, A. Chan, & M. Mansilla (Eds.), *Existential psychology East-West: Revised and expanded edition* (pp. 1–72). University Professors Press.

Hoffman, L., Cleare-Hoffman, H., & Jackson, T. (2014). Humanistic psychology and multiculturalism. In *The handbook of humanistic psychology* (pp. 41–55).

Hogan, S. (1997). *Feminist approaches to art therapy*. Psychology Press.

Hogan, S. (2012). *Revisiting feminist approaches to art therapy*. Berghahn Books.

Hogan, S. (2015). *Art therapy theories: A critical introduction*. Routledge.

Joseph, S., & Linley, P. A. (2004). *Positive therapy: A positive psychological theory of therapeutic practice*. John Wiley & Sons, Inc.

Kolden, G. G., Klein, M. H., Wang, C., & Austin, S. B. (2011). Congruence/Genuineness. In J. C. Norcross (Ed.), *Psychotherapy relationships that work* (2nd ed.). Oxford University Press.

Levine, S. K., & Levine, E. G. (1999). *Foundations of expressive arts therapy: Theoretical and clinical perspectives*. J. Kingsley Publishers.

May, R., & Yalom, I. (2000). Existential psychotherapy. In R. J. Corsini, & D. Wedding (Eds.), *Current psychotherapies* (6th ed., pp. 279–302). Peacock.

May, R. (1975). *The courage to create*. Norton.

McNiff, S. (2007). *Art therapy and the soul. 3* (pp. 231–247). Whole Person Healthcare.

Moon, B. (2009). *Existential art therapy: The canvas mirror* (3rd ed.). Charles C Thomas.

Moss, D. (2014). The humanistic movement in psychology has emphasized the search for a philo. In *3. The handbook of humanistic psychology: Theory, research, and practice*. Sage Publications, Inc.

Neukrug, E., Bayne, H., Dean-Nganga, L., & Pusateri, C. (2013). Creative and novel approaches to empathy: A neo-Rogerian perspective. *Journal of Mental Health Counseling*, *35*(1), 29–42.

Perls, F. S. (1969). *Ego, hunger and aggression: The beginning of gestalt therapy*. Crown Publishing Group/Random House.

Potash, J. S. (2005). Rekindling the multicultural history of the American Art Therapy Association, Inc. *Art Therapy*, *22*(4), 184–188.

Reilly, J., & Jacobus, V. (2009). Gestalt therapy: Student perceptions of Fritz Perls in three approaches to psychotherapy. *Australian Journal of Guidance and Counselling*, *19*(1), 14.

Rhyne, J. (1973). *The Gestalt art experience*. Brooks.

Rhyne, J. (1996). *The gestalt art experience: Patterns that connect*. Magnolia Street Publishers.

Robbins, A. (1999). Chaos and form. *Art Therapy: Journal of the American Art Therapy Association*, *16*(3), 121–125. https://doi.org/10.1080/07421656.1999.10129652.

Rogers, C. R. (1961). *On becoming a person: A therapist's view of psychotherapy*. Houghton Mifflin.

Rogers, N. (1993). *The creative connection: Expressive arts as healing*. Science and Behavior Books.

Rogers, N. (2016). Person-centered expressive arts therapy: A path to wholeness. In *Approaches to art therapy* (pp. 230–248). Routledge.

Rogers, C. R., Gendlin, E. T., Kiesler, D. J., & Truax, C. B. (Eds.). (1967). *The therapeutic relationship and its impact: A study of psychotherapy with schizophrenics*, University of Wisconsin Press.

Rubin, J. A. (1987). *Approaches to art therapy: Theory and technique*. Brunner/Mazel.

Rubin, J. A. (2009). *Introduction to art therapy: Sources & resources*. Taylor & Francis.

Rubin, J. A. (Ed.). (2016). *Approaches to art therapy: Theory and technique*, Routledge.

Sartre, J. P. (1949). *Nausea (A. Alexander, & R. Baldick, Trans.)*. Editions Gallimard.

Schneider, K. J., & Krug, O. T. (2010). *Existential-humanistic therapy* (pp. x–164). American Psychological Association.

Schneider, K. (2015). The case for existential (spiritual) psychotherapy. *Journal of Contemporary Psychotherapy*, *45*(1), 21–24.

Schneider, K. J., & Krug, O. T. (2017). *Existential-humanistic therapy*. American Psychological Association.

Schulenberg, S. E., Hutzell, R. R., Nassif, C., & Rogina, J. M. (2008). Logotherapy for clinical practice. *Psychotherapy*, *45*(4), 447–463. https://doi.org/10.1037/a0014331.

Shostrom, E. L. (1965). producer *Three approaches to psychotherapy. (Part 1). [Film]*. Psychological Films.

Silverstone, L. (1994). Art therapy. *Self & Society*, *22*(2), 33–36.

Silverstone, L. (1997). *Art therapy: The person-centered way: Art and the development of the person*. Jessica Kingsley Publishers.

Silverstone, L. (2009). *Art therapy exercises: Inspirational and practical ideas to stimulate the imagination*. Jessica Kingsley Publishers.

van Deurzen, E. (2007). Existential therapy. In W. Dryden (Ed.), *Dryden's handbook of individual therapy* (5th ed., pp. 195–226). Sage.

van Deurzen, E., & Arnold-Baker, C. (2018). *Existential therapy: Distinctive features*. Routledge.

Venture, L. D. (1977). *The black beat in art therapy experiences* (Doctoral dissertation). Union for Experimenting Colleges and Universities.

Wong, P. T. (Ed.). (2017). *The human quest for meaning: Theories, research, and applications* (2nd ed.). Routledge.

Yalom, I. (1980). *Existential psychotherapy*. Basic Books.

Yalom, I. D. (2008). *Staring at the sun*. Jossey-Bass.

Yontef, G., & Jacobs, L. (2010). Gestalt therapy. In R. J. Corsini, & D. W. Wedding (Eds.), *Current psychotherapies* (pp. 328–367). Brooks/Cole.

Zinker, J. (1991). Creative process in Gestalt therapy: The therapist as artist. *Gestalt Journal*, *14*(2), 71–88.

Chapter 9

Using art to think and rethink: Cognitive-behavior therapy from behaviorism through the third wave

Marcia L. Rosal, PhD, ATR-BC, HLM
Florida State University, Tallahassee, FL, United States

Voices from the field

In my experience integrating art therapy with second- and third-wave behavioral therapies (CBT, DBT, and ACT), I have found that both the process and products of art-making contribute meaningfully to achieving therapeutic goals. For example, the process of creating an artwork about an avoided situation, emotion, or thought can serve as a behavioral exposure intervention. Then, the completed artwork product can be used to achieve further cognitive or emotional goals, such as re-framing cognitions in response to the artwork or using the artwork as a record of the client's ability to tolerate difficult emotions. Artwork can also be a visual aid to help clients understand and personalize complex concepts in behavioral therapies. For example, art therapy clients can create their own metaphorical representation of DBT's model of emotions as a house, road, or creature.

Frances Griffith, MS, ATR-BC

Learning outcomes

After reading this chapter, you will be able to

1. Discuss how CBT is an evolving theory and identify the three waves of CBT.
2. Name at least three art therapists who use CBAT techniques.
3. List at least three cognitive skills improved by art therapy.
4. Label at least three CBAT techniques.
5. Identify three outcomes of CBAT treatment.
6. Define CBAT.
7. Link therapeutic mindfulness practice with the third wave of the CBT evolution.

Foundations of Art Therapy. https://doi.org/10.1016/B978-0-12-824308-4.00015-6

Chapter overview

Historic and contemporary cognitive-behavioral art therapy (CBAT) practices are explored through the lens of three waves of behavioral theory and practice: behaviorism, cognitive-behavior therapy (CBT), and Buddhism/mindfulness philosophy and theory. From behavior theory, the groundwork of CBAT will be laid using the writings of Ellen Roth and other art therapists. Next a short exploration of how these beginnings morphed into CBAT will be discussed. The mindfulness evolution will be explored as an outgrowth of CBT theory and practice. The work of CBAT art therapists will follow and the CBAT techniques used in contemporary treatment will be illustrated through short case studies.

Introduction

Picture a young, White male called Tommy (a pseudonym). For his 12 years, he was taller than most other boys, gangly, and sullen. Other students in his class bullied him and once enraged by their jeers, he told the teacher that others picked on him. Often the teacher separated him from others so that he was not near other kids who taunted him. He was referred to an art therapy group because of his inability to deal with bullish behavior and because, at times, he became explosively angry, lashed out, and was found physically fighting with the boys on the playground or after school.

In an art therapy group with five other children, all about the same age, Tommy exhibited the same sullen and sulky behavior as in the classroom. Yet he was compliant with the art therapy interventions and stated that he liked to draw. When the group was asked to create two images based on two difficult to manage feeling states, he chose mad and sad. Once completed, members were asked to compare and contrast the two drawings/feeling states. The group members were confused about Tommy's two images, as was he. There was consensus that the figure he labeled "angry" looked sad and the "sad" picture looked angry. At first Tommy was confused by this feedback, but in the following session, he told us that when he gets mad, he quickly reverts to getting sad, which is why he cries or tells the teacher. It was revealed that he conflated the two emotions, and the consequence was that his behavior was inappropriate for his age and led to more problems with his peers, including physically lashing out at them.

Exploring his sadness came when the group created themselves as an animal. Tommy drew himself as a horse. Usually considered a strong animal, Tommy said his horse was stuck in the mud (see Fig. 9.1.

As illustrated before, **cognitive-behavior art therapy** (CBAT), like **cognitive-behavior therapy** (CBT), is equated with the identification and alteration of erroneous thinking, distorted cognitions and feelings, as well as problems with behavior. **Behavior therapy**, which focuses on changing or

FIG. 9.1 *Tommy's drawing of self as an animal stuck in the mud.*

elimination of dysfunctional behaviors, was developed in the 1950s to mitigate externally observable problem behaviors rather than delving into the interior world of the client. It is now known as the *first wave* of CBT. Behavior therapy was updated when the science of cognition (higher mental processes) was introduced into psychology in the 1970s. This is when attention shifted from modifying problematic behavior to altering distorted cognitions and uncovering how problematic reasoning led to feelings and behaviors that were difficult to manage. This change was called the *second wave* of CBT. During this time, CBT therapists attended to all aspects of higher mental processes: thinking, affect and feeling states, perceptions, imagery, language, and behavior (Hofmann & Asmundson, 2008). With this new psychological advancement, CBT theorists began to unravel the importance of emotions as part of the cognitive change process (Samoilov & Goldfried, 2000). It was during this second wave that art therapists began to embrace CBT and began work on how to use CBT in their work. Art therapists engaged all aspects of cognition, including emotions, in their work now called, CBAT.

CBAT first helps the client identify problem(s) which brought them to therapy. Once the problem is identified, the work of challenging, testing, and invalidating erroneous thought processes and emotions begins. When clients understand that their thoughts are flawed or emotional responses irrational, the final step is to alter or reconstruct cognitions to be more adaptive and effective (Hofmann & Asmundson, 2008).

Thus the main goal of CBT and CBAT is for clients to understand the origins of problematic or distorted cognitions (beliefs) and the maladaptive behaviors that are associated with erroneous thinking. The consequences of maladaptive behavior are various types of punishments or negative reactions (i.e., in Tommy's case, his tattling increased the taunts by peers). Once distorted thoughts or beliefs are identified, the development of **alternative actions** (adaptive behaviors) may ensue, which may be more productive and may lead to the client becoming more resilient. In Tommy's case, he allowed the behavior of others toward him (**antecedents** *or* **activating events**) hurt him in problematic ways because of his poor self-esteem (***beliefs***). Since 12-year-old boys are too old to tattle on their peers, this behavior led to more taunts by others. A cycle of sadness and explosive behavior ensued (***consequences***).[a] Once Tommy understood that when he got angry, sadness immediately followed. Only then he acknowledged these problem feelings and found alternative, age-appropriate ways to cope.

In this chapter, the theories behind how art therapy helped Tommy will be explored through the historical and contemporary cognitive-behavioral art therapy practices. This will be done through the lens of the *three waves* of cognitive-behavioral theory: behaviorism, cognitive-behavior theory, and Buddhism/mindfulness theory. Beginning with behavior theory, the groundwork of CBT will be laid using the writings of Ellen Roth and other art therapists. Next a short exploration of how these beginnings morphed into CBAT will be discussed. The mindfulness evolution will be explored next as an outgrowth of CBT. Finally, CBAT practices will be examined. The work of CBAT art therapists will follow and the CBAT techniques used in contemporary treatment will be illustrated with short case studies.

The first wave: Behaviorism

Behavioral Art Therapy (BAT) appeared in the art therapy literature during the late 1970s when art therapists began to theorize about the behavioral and cognitive aspects of art therapy: (1) Ellen Roth (1978) discussed using behavior therapy techniques and reality shaping as a means of conceptualizing art therapy for children with both developmental and psychiatric disorders and (2) Janice Carnes (1979) and Janie Rhyne (1979) explored **personal construct theory** (Kelly, 1955/1991) as a basis for helping individuals explore cognitive and emotional states. All three art therapists based their work on the assumption that drawn images and mental images can mediate or shape behavior (see Table 9.1).

Behavior therapy and art therapy

Roth (1987, 2001) used "behavioral modification techniques (operant conditioning and modeling procedures) to the practice of art therapy (with emotionally disturbed mentally retarded children)" (p. 1987, p. 216).[b] Roth based her

[a] The ABC (antecedent, belief, consequences) model of behavior therapy was developed by Ellis (1979).
[b] The terms, "emotionally disturbed" and "mentally retarded," are now out of favor. Today, we would use more sensitive terms such as "a child with emotional and behavior problems"; also, in place of "mentally retarded," we use, "someone with an intellectual disability."

TABLE 9.1 Behavior and CBT definition of terms.

CBT term	Definition
Operant conditioning	According to Roth (1987), "In operant conditioning, behaviors are controlled by events that follow…Positive reinforcement… increases the likelihood of a particular behavior reoccurring" (p. 214). Roth defines ***shaping*** as part of operant conditioning by bringing the client closer to the desired behavior by reinforcing small steps leading to the desired behavior
Classical conditioning	Term accredited to Pavlov (1927), is a learning process that occurs when a neutral stimulus is paired with a stimulus in the environment; the result is that the environmental stimulus elicits that same response as the neutral stimulus
Modeling	Treatment method where a client learns by imitation
Reinforcement	An action to either reward a behavior or extinguish a behavior. There are two types of reinforcement, positive and negative. **Positive** is when a reward is given after a desired behavior response is exhibited. **Negative** is when something is taken away when the desired behavior is achieved
Prompt	A suggestion to encourage an action or continued discussion from a client
Mental images/ imagery	Cognitive process where one has the capacity to picture things, experiences, or events even when the specific object is not present
Self-control	Is the ability to regulate one's emotions, thoughts, and behavior in the face of temptations and impulses
Self-efficacy	Bandura's concept for how well one can execute courses of action required to deal with prospective situations (1977)
In vivo	Term meaning in "real life." The therapist tries to recreate the real-life experience of an event in the therapy session
Systematic desensitization	An intervention to help overcome phobias by gradually exposing the person to the feared object alongside introduction of relaxation techniques
Implosion therapy	A form of behavior treatment which involves the client reviewing anxiety situations to develop coping strategies for similar situation in the future
Stress inoculation	A CBT method to arm clients with the tools to endure the effects of stress while avoiding the negative outcomes they experienced previously (Meichenbaum, 1985)
Flooding	Type of exposure treatment where the client is exposed to painful memories to bring repressed memories to current awareness (Stampfl & Levis, 1967)

Continuned

TABLE 9.1 Behavior and CBT definition of terms—cont'd

CBT term	Definition
Resilience	The capacity to recover from impediments and complications quickly
Locus of control (LOC)	The degree to which people believe they have control over the outcome of events (internal LOC) versus those who do not (external LOC) (Rotter, 1954)
Triggers	External events or circumstances that produce an emotional response
Mindfulness	A practice of bringing one's attention to the present moment. In mindfulness treatment, this type of practice is to be nonjudgmental regarding what is happening in the moment
Wise mind	The notion of the wise mind is from DBT (Linehan, 1993) and is between a rationale mind (driven by logic) and an emotional mind (driven by feelings) and uses both to inform behavior and decisions
Reality shaping	"Reality shaping begins by identifying a concept that is poorly conveyed in the child's productions during art therapy sessions. The concept is then developed into representational form through the construction—first by the art therapist and then by the child—of increasingly complex two- and three-dimensional models" (Roth, 1987, p. 218)
Prompts and prompting	A prompt is a verbal or nonverbal cue to initiate another's behavior. Prompts are usually positive interventions to encourage a person to begin an action or to continue to do the action
Personal construct psychology/ theory/personal constructs	This theory of psychology, developed by Kelly (1955/1991), explores how a person categorizes and uses information about the world around them. Kelly found that people develop hypotheses or personal constructs and by uncovering these constructs helps an individual examine and possibly modify them to better adjust to the reality of their world
Biofeedback	A technique to monitor a person's physiological states and sending this information to the individual in order to educate how the body is responding to various stimuli, as a means of helping the individual vary responses as needed

treatment on the **operant conditioning technique** of **shaping** (modeling) behavior or bringing a person closer to a "desired behavior by reinforcing small steps that gradually lead to the terminal behavior" (1987, p. 214). Additionally, **chaining**, another operant conditioning technique, helps a client to learn a sequence of positive behaviors. Both shaping and chaining are enhanced by reinforcements and prompts.

Roth called her combined approach of behavioral therapy and art therapy **reality shaping** (1978). This process involves identifying a concept or schema that eludes the understanding of the child. First, the art therapist helps the child bring representational form to the problematic concept (or **schema**) by creating an image of the schema. Second, the child constructs and reconstructs these schemas or images using art materials. Also, the child is encouraged to use increasingly more complex materials to explore the schema by using both two-dimensional (2D) and three-dimensional (3D) materials.

The goal of reality shaping is based on the principle that developing and constructing a schema (an idea based on a person's experience) through both mental and graphic means, particularly if it is psychologically sensitive, is one way to organize confused, dysfunctional thinking. Also, it can be useful in helping a client gain control of destructive urges. The result is the creation of a fully formed schema, created in the "here and now" of an art therapy session. Roth hypothesized that the well-formed schemas enhanced understanding of the object or idea and ultimately allowed the art therapist and the child to appraise both the value of the schema and the ramifications that might ensue if that creation were to be destroyed.

As an example, Roth used reality shaping with Larry, a White, male identified child with low intellectual abilities and destructive behavior, who set fire to the family home. Using craft sticks Roth formed a flat model of a house schema, which Larry used as a template to create and re-create houses. After several sessions of forming 2D houses, Larry was ready to build 3D houses. He treated the houses he drew and constructed with care, which coincided with a shift in seeing his family home as something that should be protected, not destroyed.

Roth (2001) and Sobol (1985) reminded art therapists that they use behavioral tenets in their work as a matter of course. For example, **reinforcement**, a common operant conditioning behavioral tenet that involves the shaping of behaviors through consequences, is an important component of working with children with behavior problems. Reinforcement also encourages those who have trouble engaging in the art process and helps other patients to continue to work on a problem even when it is difficult to do so. **Prompting** is a second behavioral technique widely used by art therapists (Melberg, 1998; Roth, 2001). An example of a simple prompt is *now it is time to work on your art project*. Offering a prompt helps a child learn that a specific behavior is expected of him or her.

A bridge to the second wave: Personal construct theory and art therapy

Janice Carnes and Janie Rhyne used the work of George Kelly (1955/1991) to conceptualize a cognitive approach to art therapy. Kelly's **personal constructs** (or perceptions or hypotheses about one's world view; or schemas) are easily translated from verbal to drawn constructs or what Rhyne called mind states.

Carnes

In the late 1970s Carnes (1978, 1979) was concerned that too little emphasis had been placed on understanding the cognitive aspects of art therapy. She proposed that through understanding cognition, art therapists could expand their understanding of the therapeutic value of art therapy. She noted that imagery, visual thinking, and creativity, all aspects of art therapy, are also features of cognition and suggested that art therapists might want to incorporate the importance of cognition into their work.

In particular, she posited that Kelly and his model, **personal constructs psychology** (PCP), could be a fitting basis on which to develop a cognitive approach to art therapy. She hypothesized that personal constructs could be nonverbal as well as verbal and that making art provides an opportunity to express nonverbal ideas, which may be situated within the core of an individual's construct system. Carnes also suggested that creating art may expand and enrich one's personal construct system. With a stronger personal construct system, the range of solutions to personal problems would be increased. She even postulated that engaging with the art created in treatment would be a quick and effective way to experiment with the creation of new constructions or alternative solutions to problems. An example of this approach would be to have an individual create a troubling situation in art. Viewing the drawing of this construct would then elicit reframing the drawing to be less troublesome or "provides the viewer...with a depiction of possible events" (p. 74). Additions or subtractions to the art could change the construct to be less toxic.

Rhyne

Rhyne[c] used Kelly's work as one of several theoretical bases for her 1979 doctoral research; like Carnes, she hypothesized that drawings and other works of art in treatment are expressions of personal constructs. She theorized that both cognitive and emotional components of experiences uncovered in treatment are interwoven and both need attention. She stressed the link between thoughts and feelings to her clients. By having participants in her dissertation research draw a set of personal construct "mind states" or feelings, she encouraged them to broaden understanding of themselves and their individual belief systems. Rhyne found that when participants understood the bipolar (or two-sided) nature of their drawn constructs, meaning was enriched and elaborated. Based on Kelly's ideas, she posited that each construct had two sides. For example, if one's construct is that many people are good, then it is implied that some people are bad. Using the personal construct model, she discovered that the cognitive and emotional components of experiences were inextricably connected, especially when the bipolar nature of a construct was uncovered.

Rhyne researched the use of **mind state drawings** to uncover common visual elements assigned to various emotions. She proposed 15 common feeling states might reveal a picture of how individuals deal with emotions and encouraged participants to create small black and white drawings of mind state

[c] Rhyne was first noted for the development of Gestalt Art Therapy. During her doctoral studies she began to explore cognitive approach to art therapy.

or personal construct emotions. Through the process of finding commonalities and differences among the drawn personal constructs, she hypothesized individuals: (1) uncovered how the emotionally charged situations in their life became out of control, (2) used the mind state drawings to understand which feeling states proceeded uncomfortable periods in their life, and (3) learned how to use mind states to regulate their emotional well-being.

The mind states were drawn in three thicknesses of black markers on white 5″ × 5″ squares. This uniformity lent itself to a process of comparing and contrasting the mind state drawings. The task of the participant was to compare and contrast the mind state drawings to ascertain common visual elements of emotions. One of the case study participants, a Chinese-American female named Li (a pseudonym), quickly grasped the task of comparing and contrasting her mind state drawings. Rhyne found that Li's decisions about the drawings were quickly and judiciously made as in contrast to her poor decision making in her real life.

Rhyne discussed one of what she called Li's similarity clusters (threatened and going crazy; see Fig. 9.2). In contrast, Li compared hoping and threatened (see Fig. 9.3).

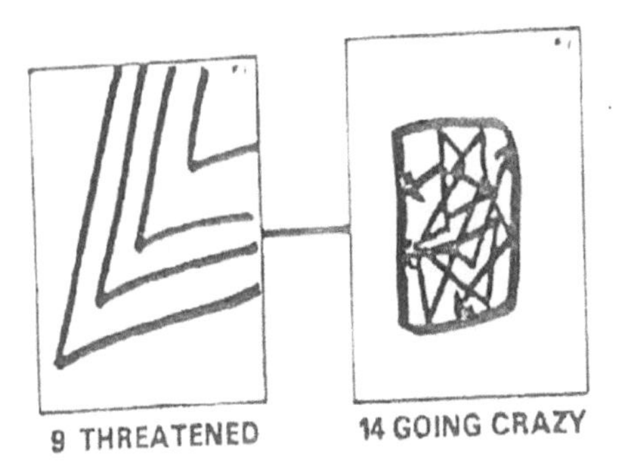

FIG. 9.2 *Li's similarity cluster threatened and going crazy have similar visual elements.*

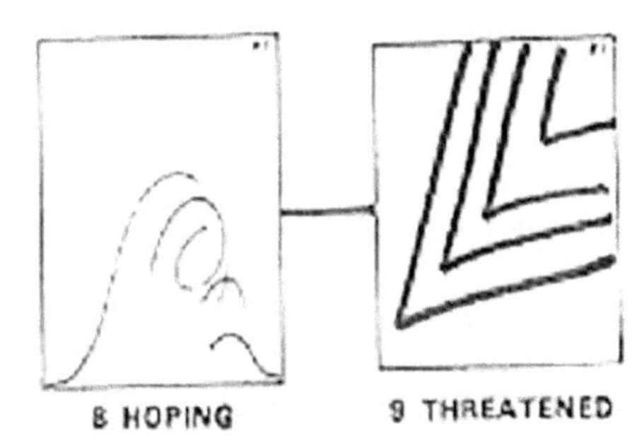

FIG 9.3 *Li's contrast cluster hoping and threatened have different visual elements; hoping has soft, curved lines and threatened has bold angular lines.*

During their discussions, Rhyne realized that Li was overwhelmed and threatened when "outside forces 'pressed in' on her" (p. 183). Li also admitted that she was afraid to hope. Rhyne found that using the mind state drawings or personal constructs assisted Li in understanding not only her visual language but also clarified her understanding of difficult emotions. Using the PCP model, the next step is for the art therapist to further explore these issues by formulating a plan for treatment.

Summary

Through the work of these art therapists, a behavioral and cognitive basis of art therapy was launched. They cautiously and courageously dipped their toes into the cognitive-behavioral realm. This was radical during the 1970s and 1980s. Roth (2001) admitted, "At first, the idea of a behavioral approach of art therapy may appear antithetical" to the process orientation of art therapy (p. 197). They found that by understanding thoughts and ideas, clients could better grasp how they interpreted the world around them. This understanding was fortified by drawing problems, issues, and feeling states. These beginnings helped many art therapists reframe the types of approaches and interventions used in their work.

The second wave: CBAT

In the late 1970s, psychotherapists were discovering that mental images were a powerful tool for clients to gain self-control and self-efficacy as conceptualized by social learning theorists. Bandura's (1977) approaches suggested that imagery contributes to **self-efficacy**. Singer and Pope (1978) proposed that imagery could be used constructively for adaptive escapism, self-awareness, self-regulation and **biofeedback** (a form of instant feedback of physiological responses to difficult situations), and for creativity and aesthetic experiences and stated:

Self-efficacy cognitions (or a person's beliefs that he/she can be effective in dealing with issues of daily life) are manifested in the form of imagery, fantasies, or self-communications and will determine whether successful behaviors will be initiated and, once a person is engaged in them, how long and how much effort will be expended to complete the behavior. The mental image that one can cope will help one stick it out in situations that are believed to be dangerous, embarrassing, or otherwise aversive (pp. 26–27).

Bandura (1977) hypothesized that private or mental images are self-reinforcing, which means that once in play, they bolster thinking and behavior even if the outcomes are problematic. "In art therapy, the reinforcement value of images may take three forms: (1) through the act of imaging in the mind's eye, (2) through reproducing the image in artistic form, and (3) through discussion of both the mental image and the artistic image" (Rosal, 2018, p. 81). Therefore, if images are linked with the acquisition of self-control, perhaps art therapy is a modality that can foster self-efficacy. Thus art therapists began understanding the power of mental images as part of their work based on the theories of cognitive psychology and Bandura's work and began to develop CBAT.

CBAT was developed using the theories and techniques from cognitive psychology, cognitive behavioral theory and therapy, as well as theories from the art therapy professionals. The ideas put forth by Roth, Carnes, and Rhyne made it possible to advance CBAT. Integrating all this information, it is possible to carefully craft CBAT programs for children, teens, or adults facing behavioral or emotional difficulties. CBAT therapies select the most efficacious treatment concepts from the information garnered from the CBT literature. The integration of art therapy with CBT is proven to be valuable for people of all ages with various emotional and behavior disorders (Rosal, 2016a).

The six-step CBAT process

CBAT therapists often use a six-step procedure for working with clients. This is illustrated in a study conducted by Morris (2014). The *first step* of CBT is to develop a strong therapeutic relationship. There are numerous art therapy techniques that open the door to rapport. Providing education about the treatment processes is one that is often used in CBAT and helps to build relationship (Hofmann & Asmundson, 2008). Morris utilized a brainstorming art therapy exercise to help clients with anxiety disorders explore the reasons for seeking treatment, to provide the therapist a picture of the needs of the client, to impart specific information on the client's problematic experiences, and to build relationship. Morris employed simple art materials such as magazine images, markers, and other dry colors to help her client think through and depict her panic cycle. The brainstorming drawing was used as a touchstone for discussing the panic cycle with a African-American, female identified, client named Shanice. Morris informed the client about "the different components of panic—physiological, cognitive, and behavioral—based on Jessica's insights from the brainstorm" (p. 347).

Having a problem focus is the *second step* in CBT work. Morris recognized that reducing the number of panic attacks needed to be the central theme of the art therapy with Shanice. Concentrating attention on this issue, Morris invited the client "to create a visual representation of her panic cycle" (p. 347). By having the client depict the panic cycle Morris was able to move Shanice into the *third step*, identifying irrational thinking. Worries about "floating in outer space" and "dying" were the two irrational thoughts that Shanice held during her panic states. Aurelia, an African-American, female identified client with generalized anxiety disorder, was also asked to draw her irrational thoughts. She felt that "all eyes were on her" when she found herself in an anxious situation.

Confronting irrational thoughts, the *fourth step* in the process may prove to be challenging for the art therapist. To provide a basis to explore irrational thoughts, Morris had the clients create two drawings: (1) *what they thought would happen when they find themselves in an anxious state* and (2) *what was more likely to occur while consumed by anxiety*. Drawing the two poles of an experience echoes Rhyne's (1979) work based on Kelly's (1955/1991) understanding that personal constructs are bipolar. For Morris, discussing the two drawings led to an examination of the validity of these irrational thoughts, the *fifth step* in the CBT process.

Morris' client, Aurelia, drew herself in the "lower right corner as proportionately small and powerless" (p. 349) with a large eye looming over her. When asked to depict a more realistic scenario, Aurelia painted herself in the middle of the paper thinking about what others are thinking about her which she labeled, "them." Her self-image was surrounded by smaller figures. She reported that all these people were, in reality, thinking about themselves and not her. The drawings helped to invalidate Aurelia's irrational thoughts (see Fig. 9.4).

Morris again employed the concept of bipolarity to work on *step six*: substituting irrational thoughts with rational ones (Hofmann & Asmundson, 2008, p. 4). In the first drawing (the desensitization drawing), the client is asked to depict an anxious situation. After discussion of the first drawing as an **in vivo** (or within the person) event, the client is instructed to create what Morris calls a "mastery image" (p. 350), one in which the client envisions a successful ending to an anxious event. To illustrate this process, Aurelia drew a situation where she wanted to approach a classmate to discuss course-related materials. In the first drawing, Aurelia was pictured as shaken and fragile; she portrayed people on one side as talking about her. In the mastery drawing, she depicted herself as having a successful interaction through finding common themes for a conversation.

FIG. 9.4 *Painting of others only thinking of themselves.*
(From Morris, F. (2014). Should art be integrated into cognitive behavioral therapy for anxiety disorders? The Arts in Psychotherapy, 41, *349. https://doi.org/10.1016/j.aip.2014.07.002.)*

Other CBAT interventions

Using mental imagery as a means for clients to become more internal thinkers is an important component of CBAT. In a CBAT program for behavior-disordered children, group members were taught how to use mental imagery (Rosal, 1993). For example, after very short relaxation exercises, children imagined what it was like to travel to school and to remember key aspects of this journey to draw or paint. Other short excursions were more imaginary and included hurdles to overcome such as preparing for a hike up a mountain or going into cave to slay a dragon and finding the treasure. One boy imagined himself in a tent the evening before a climb (see Fig. 9.5) and then overcoming a large boulder during the hike (see Fig. 9.6).

FIG. 9.5 *Mental imagery: night before mountain climb.*

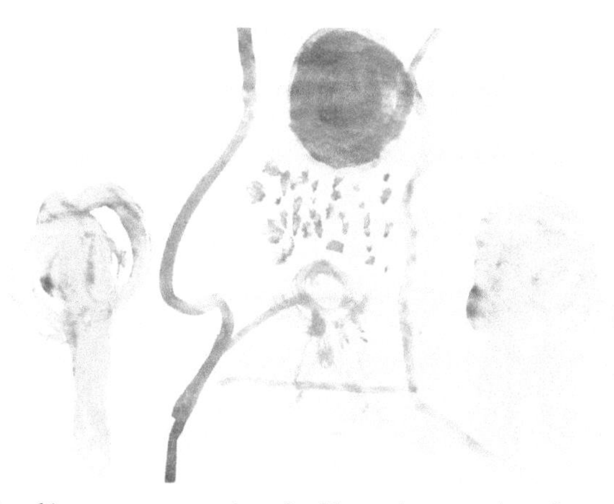

FIG. 9.6 *Mental imagery: encountering a boulder on the mountain path.*

Further aspects of the CBAT model include the emphasis on the human capacity to utilize higher mental processes such as categorization, problem-solving, thinking, as well as self-instruction and self-evaluation (Packard, 1977). In CBAT the therapist is active and directive. Verbal instructions aid the involvement in both uncovering mental and visual imagery-making. Education about art media is another important task of the art therapist. The art therapist also reinforces and rewards positive and prosocial behaviors.

Another CBAT technique based on PCP is having participants create drawings designed to help with reflection on the self and experiences. Tommy's art examining his feelings is one of these approaches. Other examples of this type of intervention might include thinking about life stages: me younger, me now, and me in a few years. Also, creating two drawings comparing aspects of school that are liked and aspects not appreciated is productive for children who have school-based problems to first identity specific issues and then allow the art therapist to use this information to assist the client in solving this problem. For reflecting on changes made during art therapy participants can be asked to complete two drawings: (1) *what were you like at the beginning of treatment* and (2) *what you are like today*. In Tommy's art therapy group, members were asked to create these two drawings during the final session. In Tommy's drawing of *what are you like today*, he drew himself smiling. He disclosed that he never knew what it felt like to have a friend and gave a nod to the friend he made in the art therapy group (see Fig. 9.7).

Like Roth's reality shaping, several art therapists had children create difficult personal and social situations to increase problem-solving. The depiction of complex events is then followed by the generation of alternative solutions, in graphic form, which increases choices. DeFrancisco (1983) and Gerber (1994) advocated four CBT techniques in art therapy: relaxation, systematic desensitization, implosion, and stress inoculation. Stress relief and lowered states of

FIG. 9.7 *Self-drawing before and after art therapy.*

anxiety are the goals of these techniques. The basic idea behind these techniques is the induction of relaxed states. Once relaxed, several other behavioral techniques can be introduced to mitigate difficult behavioral responses.

For example, both DeFrancisco (1983) and Gerber (1994) used images for slowly exposing children to challenging events, or systematic desensitization, to a feared object or situation. Implosion and stress inoculation were used to increase the coping abilities of children. Mental and drawn images were used to *flood* a person's affective experience (DeFrancisco, 1983), which led to stress resistance or served to *inoculate* the child as a means of mitigating the effects of stress and increase coping. Other uses of mental imagery include rearrangement of difficult memories and adding or eliminating aspects of the drawn image to make it less onerous or threatening. Creating images of tough events step by step can expose areas where the child can make changes to a cycle of aggression or offending behavior.

Two art therapists worked with people with eating disorders. Gentile (1997) wanted to increase both internal **locus of control** (LOC) and self-control with this population. She cited studies that indicated that anorexic patients have an external LOC orientation and found that art therapy produces "tangible, concrete and kinesthetic quality that words lack" (p. 196). Thus externalization of feelings was hypothesized to increase LOC. Likewise, Matto (1997) used a **systematic desensitization** technique by having women draw feeling states from least to most anxiety-provoking. Through this process, the client was able to gain control and accept each emotional state before moving onto the next. Reynolds (1999) also used a systematic desensitization protocol to help women experiencing unresolved grief. Through recreating photographs of the deceased person, bereaved clients recreated the photos into tapestries.

In working with sex offenders, Rosal et al. (1994) had patients draw triggers which led to offending behaviors. The art therapy program also included the creation of social milieus, like carnivals, which might lead to offenses and learning how to deal with their triggers in these situations. The aim of this CBAT treatment was to increase self-control. Improving a sense of control was also the goal of CBAT with an adult woman with an intellectual disability (Bowen & Rosal, 1989). Problem behavior plagued this person's performance at a sheltered workshop. Stress was one component of the client's troublesome behavioral issues and she was taught relaxation techniques to help with self-soothing and reducing stress. The result was to help her cope with the stressors of the workshop and to assist with her ability to stay on task.

Summary

Moving from theory to practice, art therapists began to experiment with using CBT techniques in their practice. For children experiencing critical behavioral and learning difficulties, CBAT was useful for creating an arena to change behavior and to understand uneasy feelings as well as mitigate the effects of those difficult feelings. CBAT with adults focuses on the use of systematic desensitization to externalize awkward feelings or challenging thoughts and triggers. The focus of CBAT for all age groups is to increase coping, self-control, and internal locus of control to mitigate the effects of stress and problematical situations, and adaptation. In summary, the CBAT approach uses delineated techniques, specifically applied imagery and media techniques, and a structured approach to aid in altering an external locus of control and maladaptive behaviors.

The effectiveness of CBT and CBAT practices is critical to this theoretical approach. If something does not work, it is not unusual for it to be eliminated. Each new practice is researched for its efficacy or ability to generate positive change. Once a practice has been thoroughly examined, it undergoes continual scrutiny to ensure that it can be considered an effective treatment. CBT has been widely researched and there is copious evidence that it is efficacious (that outcomes are positive); there is even ample evidence about the various populations who respond positively to CBT treatment.

The third wave: Mindfulness

Currently the evolution of CBT continues and there is new generation of CBT practices. Since the 1990s, CBT has been undergoing a transformation and a variety of *third wave* practices now exist. One commonality among these variants is that practitioners have borrowed contemplative and meditative traditions from Buddhist psychology and integrated them into CBT. These methods include mindfulness, acceptance, and compassion (Herbert & Forman, 2011). The third wave evolved from CBT that did not work for certain diagnostic groups including clients with relapsing depression. The original CBT strategies with this group of clients were effective for some time, but then clients relapsed. The search for treatments for individuals with relapsing depression led CBT researchers to the use of mindfulness and meditative practices.

Although it was not until the 1990s when third wave CBT variants began to take hold, Buddhism may have been at the core of CBT from its inception (Tirch et al., 2016). For example, Bankart (2003) cited Mikulas as one of the earliest psychologists to make connections between behavioral psychology and Buddhist tenets and in 1978 he identified several key areas where the two overlapped:

1. overriding emphasis on self-control
2. minimal use of theoretical constructs
3. focus on real problems in daily living
4. concern with objective study of observable behaviors
5. focus on the contents of conscious experience
6. symptom-specific application of relaxation and biofeedback
7. ahistorical, here-and-now focus
8. concern for the common people
9. discrimination between behavior and personality

10. increase awareness of subtle cues from the body
11. focus on behavior change, especially through guided practice
12. meditation as an adjunct for all forms of therapy
13. focus on helping the practitioner to be more fluid and empathic, less dogmatic
14. work to clarify the vantage point of the client
15. emphasis on peace of mind and happiness achieved through systematic self-observation (p. 58)

Mindfulness-based stress reduction

The most common Buddhist tenet in CBT work is mindfulness. The first individual to introduce mindfulness into therapeutic practice was Kabat-Zinn (1982). He established a meditative program in a class-based format, and he conducted outcome studies with positive results (Dryden & Still, 2006). He called his method ***mindfulness-based stress reduction*** (MBSR). Baer (2003) discovered that the mechanisms of change in MBSR include relaxation, self-management, exposure, cognitive change, and acceptance. Her research indicated that MBSR is an efficacious intervention for stress-related disorders and other diagnoses such as depression (Marchand, 2012) and chronic traumatic brain syndrome (Azulay et al., 2013). MBSR is also effective with healthy individuals dealing with life stressors or improving self-efficacy (Khoury et al., 2015; Sibinga et al., 2011). Although mindful practice was based on Buddhist psychology, Kabat-Zinn clarified that he used his practice as separate from Buddhism as a religion.

Integrating art therapy with MBSR

The integration of art into MBSR treatment as conceived by Kabat-Zinn (1982) caught the imagination of several art therapists. The short-term, class-based curriculum designed to relieve stress and improve self-regulation has applications for numerous client groups. The similarities between using art as a form of mindful practice with the therapeutic benefits of mindful meditation create a natural bridge between these two practices.

MBSR and art therapy for pain management

Fritsche (2014) hypothesized that "Art therapy can help to deepen observation of the pain experience and uncover its symbolic aspect" (p. 83). Through work with patients suffering with chronic pain, he found that engagement in making art mitigates the perception of pain. Using Kabat-Zinn's model, Fritsche outlined a Mind–Body Awareness Art Therapy Program. The program had seven stages, which included examination, expression, expansion, energetic release, redirection, recognition, and relief. Small groups met weekly for 10–12 weeks. Sessions began with a short discussion, a warm-up exercise using art and mindful attention, and an art directive. Themes for the directives included body scans; awareness of pain, surrounding space, and emotions; expressing anger; creating landscapes; painting in black and white; and themes of optimism and empowerment.

MBSR/MBAT for cancer patients

A study on the use of MBSR and art therapy (or MBAT) for cancer patients was conducted by Monti et al. (2006). Peterson (2014), the art therapist, and a lead author of the study described MBAT as the integration of art therapy with Kabat-Zinn's MBSR program for oncology patients (2014). Patients met weekly for eight sessions and the treatment followed Kabat-Zinn's curriculum, except for the seventh session when the clients met in a retreat-oriented setting meant to reinforce mindfulness practice and allow time to make art.

Peterson began with *mindful explorations of art materials* (MEAM), which were time-limited experiments with a wide array of art materials. Other practices included art exercises before and after mindful meditation, bringing attention to pain through using a body scan, pleasant and unpleasant event pictures, creating art about mindful practices, developing a feeling vocabulary of the body, creation of a healing place, and an exercise, she called, *walkabout* (Peterson, 2014, 2015). In the walkabout, patients were instructed to mindfully walk around outside the hospital or clinic and take photographs of what they saw. The photos become the basis for collage-making.

MBSR/Art therapy in community outreach

In 2000 an MBSR program was created for individuals with various stress-related medical, mental health, and emotional disorders in a community outreach program at a major hospital (Isis, 2014). Isis theorized that the sensory nature of the arts helped people stay in the present moment. Herring (2014) adapted an MBSR art therapy program for individuals with severe and persistent mental illness (SPMI) in outpatient treatment. Herring based his 16-week program on the tenets of Kabat-Zinn and the art therapy program conceived by Peterson. Isis created an eight-week combined MBSR and expressive arts program. The themes for each week are as follows:

1. There is more right with you than wrong with you
2. How you do or don't see things (present moment awareness)
3. Cultivating equanimity: pleasant, unpleasant, and neutral
4. Stress reactivity and stress hardiness
5. Everyday stress and life-changing events and their relationship to our health
6. To recognize stressful communication
7. Awareness of significant relationships and social support
8. Claiming the practice as your own

Two examples of Isis' MBSR art therapy interventions are body scans and mindful doodles. The **body scan** is a mindful exercise where the client reflects on all parts of the body and notes where he or she is holding emotions and stress. An outline of a body is then given to the client and he or she is asked to connect a color to various stress areas; the client then labels what the colors represent in the body. The **mindful doodle** hones mindfulness skills. Holding a mindfulness stance, the client is instructed to create a doodle without editing thoughts or judgments.

Art interventions included breath drawings, body scans awareness drawings, and response art to journey stories. Isis concluded that daily meditation is crucial to fully realize the power of the program. After participation, several clients noted changes in their ability to engage with others, had increased motivation, and felt more empowered—all crucial to improved daily functioning. The Herring program encompassed goals and art interventions similar to the Isis' program. Both Isis and Herring reported that participants continued the use of mindfulness and arts experiences after the conclusion of the program.

Dialectical behavior therapy (DBT)

DBT was developed by Marsha Linehan in the 1970s to treat individuals with a complex set of clinical issues, including treatment resistance and a client's propensity to commit acts of self-harm. She conceived DBT as a behavioral treatment to treat people with multiple suicide attempts. The components of DBT are rooted in evidence-based therapies, including behavior therapy and cognitive-behavior treatment (Brodsky & Standley, 2013). Linehan (1993) emphasized the underlying goal of DBT was to help suicidal individuals create a life worth living. The success of the program led DBT to become the treatment of choice for individuals with Borderline Personality Disorder (BPD)[d] and other intractable psychological conditions, including mood, eating, and substance use disorders.

According to Robins et al. (2004), focusing solely on behavior change that led to increased arousal rather than deescalation of emotional intensity because suicidal and BPD clients are sensitive to criticism. Emotional dysregulation is also an attribute of clients with these disorders and is triggered when problem behavior is the focus of treatment. Therefore Linehan imagined DBT as including both a skills practice program and an intervention that embraces the needs of the client with acceptance and compassion. Linehan underscored mindfulness skills are a core component of DBT and provide clients a means of learning to accept their own plight. Other skills taught and practiced in DBT include distress tolerance, emotional regulation, and interpersonal skills.

---

[d] Borderline personality disorder (BPD) is a mental health disorder which includes distorted self-image, difficulty developing stable relationships and managing emotions. They have intense fear of abandonment and have difficulty being alone.

DBAT in action

Art Therapists Lorenzo de la Peña and Jessica Masino Drass worked with patients using the DBAT paradigm. An art therapist at a major state psychiatric facility, Lorenzo de la Peña (personal communication, November 19, 2014) practiced DBAT in three formats: (1) in learning skill-based DBT groups, (2) in DBAT groups, and (3) in individual art therapy sessions. She infused art-based experiences with DBT as a means of having patients practice mindfulness, emotional regulation, stress tolerance, and a nonjudgmental acceptance. Drass (2015) provided art therapy group sessions in a DBT trauma treatment program for women.

Structure of the sessions

Both art therapists stressed the importance of structure and safety in their work. Lorenzo de la Peña planned each session with a clear vision of how to use an art medium. She then thought about how to convey the handling of a material to patients and taught, in tiny increments, how to interact with art materials. Since mixing colors can result in surprising, yet unwanted hues, she set out only a few colors for patient use. This reduced the risk of unwittingly inducing overwhelming emotional responses. Preparation for each session was planned from beginning to end including patient involvement in set-up, interacting with the media, and clean-up.

Drass wisely considered the "physical layout and organization of the art room" (p. 169). Carefully planned structure encouraged patients to internalize that structure. Art materials were arranged for easy access and patients knew where to find the supplies needed. Through the structure of the art room and the easy-to-access materials, patients could be autonomous and practice personal control.

Art experiences and art techniques employed by Lorenzo de la Peña included blowing bubbles with liquids infused with both colors and scents, experiencing materials with assorted textures and thicknesses, and basic media exploration. For emotional regulation, Lorenzo de la Peña encouraged patients to pay attention to their breath while they moved paint or other forms of color across large papers, to use the whole body to swirl a drop of liquid around a paper to form a circle on the page, and attend to each art process one step at a time until the patient experienced mastery before moving to the next step. For both emotional regulation and stress tolerance, Lorenzo de la Peña slowed down the art process, attended to the small steps in art-making, and had the patient use lines to create patterns rather than pictures or specific images. To practice nonjudgmental acceptance, she used layers of plastic sheeting with paint dribble and drops in between the layers. Patients shifted the paint around without mess and without the worry of being judged. If a patient noticed an interesting design in the paint, he or she used paper to make a mono-print of the enjoyable pattern.

Drass took DBT themes and developed eight art experiences that mirrored these topics. For *containment, control, and identity*, she had the patients create *wise mind books* and 3-D collages used to address such questions as, "'Who do I present to the world?' and 'What story do I have to tell?'" (p. 170). Another example of her DBAT interventions was *distress tolerance baskets*. Designed for skill-building and self-soothing, the baskets were crafted using a coiling technique to teach "self-soothing, relaxation, grounding and empowerment" (p. 171).

Suggestions for DBAT practice

Lorenzo de la Peña encouraged two essential aspects of practice: (1) using one's self as a model for mindful practice and (2) acquiring a deep understanding of media dimension variables (Kagin & Lusebrink, 1978). She proposed that understanding color theory, media properties, and other tools of art practice were necessities for DBAT. She posted thoughtful quotes about nonjudgmental attitudes around her art therapy space to as cues or reminders for her to pay attention, be present, and model mindful actions. At times, she practiced breathing exercises or her own art experiences before the session to prepare for mindful engagement with the patients.

For Drass, three therapeutic issues must be accentuated when working with people with BPD: (1) encouraging patient-generated art projects, (2) structuring both art-making and therapist-directed tasks, and (3) insuring choice-making and giving power to the client. She cautioned art therapists to stay on a metaphoric level when discussing artwork to protect individuals from disclosing too much personal information and to decrease the likelihood of a discussion arousing emotions or activating triggers.

Clark (2017) developed five models to practice DBT-informed art therapy. The first model integrated art therapy with teaching social skills. An example of this is a half-smile collage to assist clients with how facial expressions can help individuals accept reality and how facial expressions affect mood. The second model used art therapy to reinforce DBT skills. An illustration of this is the upside-down drawing to help the client integrate observational skills with a mindful and nonjudgmental mindset. Clients recreate a coloring sheet drawing upside down. Clark finds that clients are surprised by the accuracy of their work once it is turned right side up.

The third model, an art-based/parallel process, allows for an unstructured art therapy intervention that has a DBT theme but is not based on a particular set of skills. For example, a visual journaling group utilized DBT prompts. Other examples include an arts-based goals group designed to help patients structure time or a self-esteem workshop focusing on developing a life worth living. The fourth, an interdisciplinary model, incorporates art therapy and DBT skills training within a holistic residential treatment facility. The final model is what Clark labeled a free-standing program where the art therapy is the predominate focus, but the interventions are based on DBT principles.

Acceptance and commitment therapy

Acceptance and commitment therapy (ACT) was developed by Hayes and colleagues in the early 1990s. According to Hayes (2008), ACT "has always been a part of cognitive behavior therapy (CBT)" (p. 286) and was advanced through rigorous research. However, ACT rejected a key CBT construct: thoughts and feelings cause behavior. Rather, ACT theorists found that thoughts and feelings should be seen in "the context of a social/verbal community that linked private events to overt actions" (p. 287) and should be viewed through the lens of social interactions. It is valuable to include ACT as a third wave therapy because mindfulness is interwoven in the practice of ACT (Hayes, 2004).

Treatment constructs

There are six core therapeutic constructs in ACT. Hayes and colleagues identified these six constructs to be the mindfulness and behavior change processes that lead to the development and improvement of psychological flexibility (Flaxman et al., 2011). Three of the constructs are directly related to **mindfulness and acceptance processes** (acceptance, diffusion, and self-as-context) and the three others are related to **commitment and change processes** (contact with the present moment [mindfulness], values, and committed action). Levin and Hayes (2009) called the composite of these six constructs, the **hexaflex**.[e] As a treatment modality, ACT stands for accept, choose, and take action.

The ACT therapist has numerous roles, but the most critical is to "instigate, model, and support psychological flexibility" (Hayes & Lillis, 2012, p. 68). Hayes and Lillis find that using ACT exercises is the best way to activate therapeutic processes. In addition, the therapist must be emotionally honest with the client, which leads to positive modeling. The development of psychological flexibility is initiated through supporting the changes made by the client and reinforcing the progress made.

ACT and art therapy

Backos and Mazzeo (2017) chose ACT as the foundation for their work with veterans with posttraumatic stress disorder (PTSD). In their model, simple, structured art materials were deemed to be the most useful because they were easily controlled. An 8-week art therapy program, incorporating ACT principles framed by Waller and Westrup (as cited in Backos & Mazzeo), was created. According to the authors, "Each module included: a mindfulness art intervention, psycho-education, an ACT art therapy experiential, discussion, and art homework" (p. 169). Since the program was cognitive based and short term, they used controllable, familiar media (i.e., markers, pencils, and oil pastels).

---

[e] For more information on ACT, please read Levin and Hayes (2009).

One art exercise in the ACT model is the concept of contact with the present moment. Veterans created mandalas at the beginning of each session to ground and focus on the present moment. **Mandalas** originated from Asian and Indigenous people and is used for meditation (Robertson, 1992). Clients were asked to be present throughout all the art-making exercises. The concept of willingness to delve into painful memories was introduced through imaginal exposure. For dealing with the problem of control, group members were asked to compare freedom of what to create versus art-making when given instructions and specific media. The concept of cognitive diffusion was based on the *monster on the bus* metaphor of dysfunctional thoughts (Hayes et al., 1999; as cited in Backos & Mazzeo, 2017). Each vet created three monsters "that represent their commonly fused thoughts, as well as externalizing the details of these distorted thoughts via written descriptions including the age of the monster, what the monster says, other related monsters, and what situations bring out the monster" (p. 171). The close examination of internal demons led to externalization and understanding of difficult feelings and actions. Additionally, the use of opposites was introduced. For example, they asked the vets to compare free choice art experiences versus those that were more scripted.

Summary

The development of third wave CBT strategies encourages art therapists to embrace the power of cognition and mindful attention through connecting thoughts, physical sensations, emotions, and behavior into art processes. Art therapists have resonated with these third wave practices as they are closely aligned with the philosophy of the practice of art therapy: art as a means of getting in touch with the self. The idea behind third wave art therapy practices is to help clients focus attention and connect with the body through various types of mark making, which compels the client toward mindful intention. For example, Lorenzo de la Pena encourages clients to use their entire body to move paint around a large piece of paper. The client is asked to do this mindfully and to leave criticism or appraisal behind.

Conclusions

The goal of CBAT is for a client to gain self-control and self-efficacy, and achieve the ability to adapt (Bandura, 1977). For adults, CBAT alleviates the power of trauma, reexamines erroneous and problematic cognitions, decreases behavioral problems, increases awareness of triggers leading to self-harm or socially inappropriate behaviors, and improves locus of control. CBAT aids in achieving focus and mindfulness to alter the meaning of irrational thoughts. CBAT can improve coping strategies and led to adoption of rational solutions to improve life choices.

CBAT for children increases behavioral self-control, mitigates the impact of abuse, decreases the effects of bullying, and builds self-efficacy—all essential for positive development. Through CBAT, children learn to understand and manage their own behavior. For people of all ages, increased self-control can lead to more personal choice and freedom; and personal power, in turn, can lead to a richer and more meaningful life.

CBAT is not for all clients. From the literature reviewed herein, numerous client groups have benefitted for this theoretical perspective. Populations that may not be able to engage with CBAT could be very low functioning individuals or those with extremely serious mental illnesses (especially those whose grasp on reality is tenuous).

The importance of CBAT to our field can be discerned by reading art therapy literature through a CBAT lens and looking for key terms such as *stress reduction, problem-solving, regulating emotions, developing self-efficacy, modifying perceptions, coping strategies*, etc. (Rosal, 2016b). Acknowledging that CBT has a central place in the practice of art therapy is important and timely. CBAT is recognized as important to PTSD and anxiety treatment. A focus on societal problems such as childhood physical and sexual abuse and the effects of human trafficking points to a need for CBAT treatment. PTSD treatment includes numerous CBT approaches, including desensitization, coping, identification and reactivation of positive emotions, and enhancing self-efficacy (Collie et al., 2006). Other art therapists use CBAT techniques including cognitive restructuring, imagery rescripting, and mindful and meditative practices to lessen the impact of trauma and other disorders (Chapman et al., 2001; Pifalo, 2002, 2007; Rankin & Taucher, 2003). Because there is ample evidence that individuals experiencing trauma have responded well to CBAT, those dealing with the trauma of racial violence, managing adverse effects of Covid-19, or coping with gender identity issues may be helped by engaging in CBAT.

Sarid and Huss (2010) compared the tenets of CBT to art therapy principles. They found that both modalities provided a safe space to explore sensory experiences, modulate traumatic memories, construct new cognitions, and improve "the potential of creating new connections and pathways between the physical, emotional, and cognitive components of traumatic memory" (p. 10). The authors were surprised about how two seemingly different approaches (CBT and art therapy) include parallel components including "regulatory processes that decrease anxiety and negative emotional responses by inhibiting hypothalamic release of cortisol" (p. 11). These authors also hypothesize that CBT and art therapy have similar outcomes and use similar holistic methodologies to decrease stress and thereby aid in the "restructuring of more positive memories" (p. 11).

CBAT is also congruent with art therapy in the schools (particularly with behaviorally disordered students; Rozum, 2001) and in the prison system (Breiner et al., 2011). In these two arenas, increasing positive, prosocial behavior is valuable for both the clients and the settings. CBAT participants develop a sense of personal success and self-efficacy and these settings can become safer and more productive places to inhabit.

CBAT does not negate the importance of the sensory, emotive capacity of art therapy. CBAT embraces the significance of these concepts for envisioning new and adaptive patterns of thinking, behaving, problem-solving, and coping. Visualizing and reframing stressful, traumatic, disturbing thoughts, actions, and events is the domain of CBAT. I imagine art therapists embracing the CBAT concepts discussed not only in this chapter but in other CBAT literature. Comprehending, using, and reimagining CBAT constructs will benefit our clients for years to come.

Art experientials and reflection questions

1. *Mood states*: On each of four sheets of paper and using colored markers, draw the following emotional states: mad, sad, glad, and scared. After each feeling state is created, please write five other feelings that accompany that emotion on the back of the paper. Lay the four drawings in front of you and begin to reflect on times you felt each one. Ask yourself what two of the feeling states are similar by looking at the formal elements of the drawings: line, shape, color, etc. Once you find two that are similar, check to see how these two feeling states are related to you. Try to learn something about this pairing for yourself. Find one, if possible, that is different from the two that are similar. Ask yourself what the differences are and then check to see how this one is so different in your life. Now ask yourself what you learned from creating and thinking about these mood states.
2. *Safe place drawing*: Draw a place where you felt safe. On the back of the drawing, write about this place.
3. Create an image that represents each wave of cognitive behavioral art therapy as described above. Compare and contrast the images and approaches using the information in the chapter.

Additional resources

ACT Mindfully Free Resources: https://www.actmindfully.com.au/free-stuff/
Cognitive Behavioral Art Therapy: Behaviorism to the Third Wave by Rosal (2018)
Cognitive Behavioral Therapy Videos: https://www.psychotherapy.net/videos/approach/cognitive-behavioral-cbt
The Beck Institute: https://beckinstitute.org/
The Linehan Institute: https://linehaninstitute.org/

Chapter terms

Behavior theory and therapy
Cognitive-behavior art therapy (CBAT)
Distorted cognitions
In vivo
Mental imagery
Mindfulness

Mindfulness-based stress reduction
Personal constructs
Prompting
Reality shaping
Reinforcement
Resiliency
Self-efficacy cognitions

References

Azulay, J., Smart, C. M., Mott, T., & Cicerone, K. D. (2013). A pilot study examining the effect of mindfulness-based stress reduction on symptoms of chronic mild traumatic brain injury/postconcussive syndrome. *The Journal of Head Trauma Rehabilitation*, *28*(4), 323–331. https://doi.org/10.1097/HTR.0b013e318250ebda.

Backos, A., & Mazzeo, C. (2017). Group therapy and PTSD: Acceptance and commitment art therapy groups with Vietnam veterans with PTSD. In P. Howie (Ed.), *Art therapy with military populations: History, innovation, and applications* (pp. 165–176). Routledge.

Baer, R. (2003). Mindfulness training as a clinical intervention: A conceptual and empirical review. *Clinical Psychology: Science and Practice*, *10*, 125–143.

Bandura, A. (1977). Self-efficacy: Toward a unifying theory of behavioral change. *Psychological Review*, *84*, 191–215.

Bankart, C. R. (2003). Five manifestations of the Buddha in the west: A brief history. In K. H. Dockett, G. R. Dudley-Grant, & C. P. Bankart (Eds.), *Psychology and Buddhism: From individual to global community* (pp. 45–70). Kluwer Academic/Plenum Publishers.

Bowen, C. A., & Rosal, M. L. (1989). The use of art therapy to reduce the maladaptive behaviors of a mentally retarded adult. *The Arts in Psychotherapy*, *16*, 211–218.

Breiner, M. J., Tuomisto, L., Bouyea, E., Gussak, D. E., & Aufderheide, D. (2011). Creating an art therapy treatment anger management protocol for male inmates through a collaborative relationship. *International Journal of Offender Therapy and Comparative Criminology*, *XX*(X), 1–20. https://doi.org/10.1177/0306624X11417362.

Brodsky, B. B., & Standley, B. (2013). *The dialectical behavior primer: How DBT can inform clinical practice*. John Wiley & Sons.

Carnes, J. J. (1978). Toward a cognitive approach to art therapy. In L. Gantt, G. Forrest, D. Silverman, & R. Shoemaker (Eds.), *Proceedings of the ninth annual conference of the American Art Therapy Association* (pp. 91–92). American Art Therapy Association.

Carnes, J. J. (1979). Toward a cognitive theory of art therapy. *The Arts in Psychotherapy*, *6*(2), 69–76.

Chapman, L., Morabito, D., Ladakakos, C., Schreier, H., & Knudson, M. M. (2001). The effectiveness of art therapy interventions in reducing post traumatic stress disorder (PTSD) symptoms in pediatric trauma patients. *Art Therapy: Journal of the American Art Therapy Association*, *18*(2), 100–104.

Clark, S. M. (2017). *DBT-informed art therapy: Mindfulness, cognitive-behavior therapy, and the creative process*. Jessica Kingsley Press.

Collie, K., Backos, A., Malchiodi, C., & Spiegel, C. (2006). Art therapy for combat-related PTSD: Recommendations for research and practice. *Art Therapy: Journal of the American Art Therapy Association*, *23*(4), 157–164.

DeFrancisco, J. (1983). Implosive art therapy: A learning-theory based, psychodynamic approach. In L. Gantt, & S. Whitman (Eds.), *Proceedings of the eleventh annual conference of the American Art Therapy Association* (pp. 74–79). AATA.

Drass, J. M. (2015). Art therapy for individuals with borderline personality: Using a dialectic behavioral therapy framework. *Art Therapy*, *32*(4), 168–176. https://doi.org/10.1080/07421656.2015.1092716.

Dryden, W., & Still, A. (2006). Historical aspects of mindfulness and self-acceptance in psychotherapy. *Journal of Rational-Emotive and Cognitive-Behavior Therapy*, *24*(1), 3–28. https://doi.org/10.1007/s10492-006-0026-1.

Ellis, A. (1979). The theory of rational-emotive therapy. In A. Ellis, & J. M. Whitely (Eds.), *Theoretical and empirical foundations of rational-emotive therapy* (pp. 43–60). Brooks/Cole.

Flaxman, P. E., Blackledge, J. T., & Bond, F. W. (2011). *Acceptance and commitment therapy: Distinctive features*. Routledge.

Fritsche, J. (2014). Mind-body awareness in art therapy with chronic pain. In L. Rappaport (Ed.), *Mindfulness and the arts therapies: Theory and practice* (pp. 81–94). Jessica Kingsley.

Gentile, D. (1997). *Art therapy's influence on locus of control with eating disorder patients. [Abstract]* (p. 196). Proceedings of the American Art Therapy Association.

Gerber, J. (1994). The use of art therapy in juvenile sex offender specific treatment. *The Arts in Psychotherapy*, *21*, 367–374.

Hayes, S. C. (2004). Acceptance and commitment therapy, relational frame theory, and the third wave and behavioral and cognitive therapies. *Behavior Therapy*, *35*, 639–665.

Hayes, S. C. (2008). Climbing our hills: A beginning conversation on the comparison of acceptance and commitment therapy and traditional cognitive behavior therapy. *Clinical Psychology: Science and Practice*, *15*, 286–295.

Hayes, S. C., & Lillis, J. (2012). *Acceptance and commitment therapy*. American Psychological Association.

Hayes, S. C., Strosahl, K. D., & Wilson, K. G. (1999). *Acceptance and commitment therapy: An experiential approach to behavior change*. Guilford Press.

Herbert, J. D., & Forman, E. M. (Eds.). (2011). *Acceptance and mindfulness in cognitive behavior therapy: Understanding and applying the new therapies*. Wiley.

Herring, D. (2014). Mindfulness-based expressive therapy for people with severe and persistent mental illness. In L. Rappaport (Ed.), *Mindfulness and the arts therapies: Theory and practice* (pp. 24–36). Jessica Kingsley.

Hofmann, S. G., & Asmundson, G. J. G. (2008). Acceptance and mindfulness-based therapy: New wave or old hat. *Clinical Psychology Review*, *28*, 1–16. https://doi.org/10.1016/j.cpr.2007.09.003.

Isis, P. (2014). Mindfulness-based stress reduction and the expressive arts therapies in a hospital-based outreach program. In L. Rappaport (Ed.), *Mindfulness and the arts therapies: Theory and practice* (pp. 155–167). Jessica Kingsley.

Kabat-Zinn, J. (1982). An outpatient program in behavioral medicine for chronic pain patients based on the practice of mindfulness meditation: Theoretical considerations and preliminary results. *General Hospital Psychiatry*, *4*, 33–47.

Kagin, S. L., & Lusebrink, V. B. (1978). The expressive therapies continuum. *The Arts in Psychotherapy*, *5*(4), 171–179.

Kelly, G. A. (1955/1991). *The psychology of personal constructs*. Norton. Republished, 1991. Routledge.

Khoury, B., Sharma, M., Rush, S. E., & Fournier, C. (2015). Mindfulness-based stress reduction for healthy individuals: A meta-analysis. *Journal of Psychosomatic Research*, *78*(6), 519–528. https://doi.org/10.1016/j.jpsychores.2015.03.009.

Levin, M., & Hayes, S. C. (2009). ACT, RFT, and contextual behavioral science. In J. T. Blackledge, J. Ciarrochi, & F. P. Deane (Eds.), *Acceptance and commitment therapy: Contemporary theory, research, and practice* (pp. 1–40). Australian Academic Press.

Linehan, M. (1993). *Cognitive behavioral treatment of borderline personality disorder*. Guilford Press.

Marchand, W. R. (2012). Mindfulness-based stress reduction, mindfulness-based cognitive therapy, and Zen mediation for depression, anxiety, pain, and psychological distress. *Journal of Psychiatric Practice*, *18*(4), 233–252. https://doi.org/10.1097/01.pra.0000416014.53215.86.

Matto, H. C. (1997). An integrative approach to the treatment of women with eating disorders. *The Arts in Psychotherapy*, *24*, 347–352.

Meichenbaum, D. H. (1985). *Stress inoculation training*. Pergamon.

Melberg, C. (1998). *Increasing control: Watercolor painting and students with developmental disabilities [Abstract]* (p. 183). Proceedings of the American Art Therapy Association.

Monti, D., Peterson, C., Shakin Kunkel, E. J., Hauck, W. W., Pequignot, E., Rhodes, L., et al. (2006). A randomized, control trial of mindfulness-based art therapy (MBAT) for women with cancer. *Psycho-Oncology*, *15*, 363–373. https://doi.org/10.1002/pon.988.

Morris, F. (2014). Should art be integrated into cognitive behavioral therapy for anxiety disorders? *The Arts in Psychotherapy*, *41*, 343–352. https://doi.org/10.1016/j.aip.2014.07.002.

Packard, S. (1977). Learning disabilities: Identification and remediation through creative art activity. In R. H. Shoemaker, & S. E. Gonick-Barris (Eds.), *Proceedings of the seventh annual conference of the American Art Therapy Association* (pp. 57–61). AATA.

Pavlov, I. P. (1927). *Conditional reflexes*. Dover Publications.

Peterson, C. (2014). Mindfulness-based art therapy: Applications for healing. In L. Rappaport (Ed.), *Mindfulness and the arts therapies: Theory and practice* (pp. 64–80). Jessica Kingsley.

Peterson, C. (2015). "Walkabout: Looking in looking out": A mindfulness-based art therapy program. *Art Therapy*, *32*(2), 78–82. https://doi.org/10.1080/07421656.2015.1028008.

Pifalo, T. (2002). Pulling out the thorns: Art therapy with sexually abused children and adolescents. *Art Therapy: Journal of the American Art Therapy Association*, *19*(1), 12–22.

Pifalo, T. (2007). Jogging the cogs: Trauma-focused art therapy and cognitive behavioral therapy with sexually abused children. *Art Therapy*, *24*(4), 170–175. https://doi.org/10.1080/07421656.2007.10129471.

Rankin, A. B., & Taucher, L. C. (2003). A task-oriented approach to art therapy in trauma treatment. *Art Therapy: Journal of the American Art Therapy Association*, *20*(3), 138–147.

Reynolds, F. (1999). Cognitive behavioral counseling of unresolved grief through the therapeutic adjunct of tapestry-making. *The Arts in Psychotherapy*, *26*(3), 165–171.

Rhyne, J. (1979). *Drawings as personal constructs: A study in visual dynamics* (Unpublished doctoral dissertation). University of California Santa Cruz.

Robertson, R. (1992). *Beginner's guide to Jungian psychology*. Nicholas-Hays, Inc.

Robins, C. J., Schmidt, H., & Linehan, M. M. (2004). Dialectical behavior therapy: Synthesizing radical acceptance with skillful means. In S. C. Hayes, V. M. Follette, & M. M. Linehan (Eds.), *Mindfulness and acceptance: Expanding the cognitive-behavioral tradition* (pp. 30–44). Guildford Press.

Rosal, M. L. (1993). Comparative group art therapy research to evaluate changes in locus of control. *The Arts in Psychotherapy*, *20*, 231–241.

Rosal, M. L. (2016a). Cognitive-behavioral art therapy. In J. A. Rubin (Ed.), *Approaches to art therapy: Theory and technique* (3rd ed., pp. 333–352). Routledge.

Rosal, M. L. (2016b). Cognitive-behavioral art therapy revisited. In D. E. Gussak, & M. L. Rosal (Eds.), *The Wiley handbook of art therapy* (pp. 68–76). John Wiley & Sons.

Rosal, M. L. (2018). *Cognitive-behavior art therapy*. Routledge.

Rosal, M. L., Ackerman-Haswell, J. F., & Johnson, L. (1994). *Humanity behind the offense: Group art therapy with special needs sex offenders. [Abstract]* (p. 127). Proceeding of the American Art Therapy Association.

Roth, E. (1978). Art therapy with emotionally disturbed-mentally retarded children: A technique of reality shaping. In B. K. Mandel, et al. (Eds.), *The dynamics of creativity* (pp. 168–172). American Art Therapy Association.

Roth, E. (1987). Behavioral art therapy. In J. A. Rubin (Ed.), *Approaches to art therapy: Theory and technique* (pp. 195–209). Brunner/Mazel.

Roth, E. (2001). Behavioral art therapy. In J. A. Rubin (Ed.), *Approaches to art therapy: Theory and technique* (2nd ed., pp. 213–232). Brunner/Routledge.

Rotter, J. B. (1954). *Social learning and clinical psychology*. Prentice-Hall.

Rozum, A. (2001). Integrating the language of art into a creative cognitive-behavioral program with behavior- disordered children. In S. Riley (Ed.), *Group process made visible* (pp. 115–138). Brunner/Routledge.

Samoilov, A., & Goldfried, M. R. (2000). Role of emotion in cognitive-behavior therapy. *Clinical Psychological Science and Practice*, *7*, 373–385.

Sarid, O., & Huss, E. (2010). Trauma and acute stress disorder: A comparison between cognitive behavioral intervention and art therapy. *The Arts in Psychotherapy*, *37*, 8–12. https://doi.org/10.1016/j.aip.2009.11.004.

Sibinga, E. M. S., Kerrigan, D., Stewart, M., Johnson, K., Magyari, T., & Ellen, J. M. (2011). Mindfulness-based stress reduction for urban youth. *The Journal of Alternative and Complementary Medicine*, *17*(3), 213–218. https://doi.org/10.1089/acm.2009.0605.

Singer, J. L., & Pope, K. S. (1978). *The power of human imagination: New methods in psychotherapy*. Plenum Press.

Sobol, B. (1985). Art therapy, behavior modification, and conduct disorder. *American Journal of Art Therapy*, *24*, 35–43.

Stampfl, T. G., & Levis, D. J. (1967). Essentials of implosive therapy: A learning-theory based psychodynamic behavioral therapy. *Journal of Abnormal Psychology*, *72*(6), 496–503. https://doi.org/10.1037/h0025238.

Tirch, D., Silberstein, L. R., & Kolts, R. L. (2016). *Buddhist psychology and cognitive-behavioral therapy: A clinician's guide*. Guildford Press.

Part III

Art therapy with specific populations: Painting the picture

Chapter 10

Child development and artistic development in art therapy

Michelle Itczak, MA, ATR-BC, ATCS, LMHC
Department of Counseling, University of Indianapolis, Indianapolis, IN, United States

Voices from the field

Developmental art therapy *can be defined as a process for providing experiences in art to children and teens that encourages competencies for social and emotional development. Children's social emotional development emerges from experiences with others. (No one develops in a people-free vacuum.) So, an art therapist and art activity combine to become an "experience" for a child. Social emotional learning happens—seen and unseen—as the child interacts with materials and the art therapist in a uniquely personal and satisfying way. With such learning experiences children are able to express themselves, and experience satisfaction with themselves and others.*

Mary Wood (personal communication, May 14, 2020)

Learning outcomes

After reading this chapter, you will be able to

1. Delineate four domains of child development.
2. Name two developmental psychology theorists and briefly explain their theories.
3. Identify at least five people who have contributed to the study of child art development.
4. Describe developmental art therapy.
5. Identify characteristics of artistic stages in child artwork.
6. Give examples of developmentally appropriate art directives for children.
7. Explain ways to encourage art development in young children.
8. Verbalize the scope of practice for undergraduate pre-art therapy students.

Foundations of Art Therapy. https://doi.org/10.1016/B978-0-12-824308-4.00003-X

Chapter overview

This chapter will briefly introduce the reader to child development domains, developmental theorists, and their theories commonly used in the field of art therapy to help understand and determine approaches to working with children. Readers will learn about artistic development and four different perspectives of how children progress through creating art in both two-dimensional and three-dimensional media. Examples of child art are presented and discussed. Social emotional development is presented as a key component of understanding how to work with children from an art therapy perspective. Examples of art activities that can be used to help nurture social and emotional development with children from all age ranges are given. Additionally, a brief discussion about the scope of practice for undergraduate pre-art therapy students is presented.

Introduction

Early development of social emotional skills is foundational to healthy social functioning and well-being throughout one's life. In many therapeutic relationships an art therapist working with children is tasked with helping to nurture and develop the social emotional skills of a young client. In order for an art therapist to be most effective in this role, one must have a thorough understanding of child development, including, but not limited to cognitive, social, emotional, and artistic development. Oftentimes the work of an art therapist in this capacity is referred to as **developmental art therapy** (Williams & Wood, 2010). Some may assume that this term refers to working only with people who have been diagnosed with a developmental delay; however, a developmental art therapy approach is one that can be used with children and adults of all levels of functioning (Malchiodi et al., 2003). Thus an art therapist's knowledge of child development and artistic development is essential in this approach and helps create a well-equipped therapist to serve clients. An art therapist skilled in these areas can assess levels of functioning and integrate knowledge about all areas of child development to generate a nurturing environment and individualized art interventions to help each child express themselves. Many art therapists can speak to the power of their work with children and the importance of exposing a child to creative outlets in order to help one develop socially and emotionally. Two key voices in the niche of developmental art therapy agree that "at all stages of [development], the joy of art experiences should lead children to artwork as a means of self-expression" (Williams & Wood, 2010, p. 5).

Understanding child development

Understanding child development is fundamental to working with children, particularly in helping professions such as art therapy. A solid foundation of knowledge about how and when children develop helps inform art therapists about working with and treating young clients. **Child development** is a fascinating area of study that includes the physical, cognitive, social emotional, and language domains of development (American Psychological Association, 2020). The developmental process begins as an infant and continues rapidly in the first few years of life. These early years can have a significant impact on a child's overall health and well-being throughout life (World Health Organization, 2020). One's culture often plays an important role in their development as well. Each child develops at their own personal rate, so it is important to keep in mind that children of a similar age may differ in progress by weeks, months, or years. Some children may never crawl, but instead advance immediately to standing and walking. If there are no natural or biological causes that have created a developmental or atypical delay, then it is likely that a child provided with a stimulating and nurturing environment will progress at an appropriate pace for that child. While it may be tempting to compare children's developmental milestones, an art therapist would benefit most from examining each child as a unique human being. Furthermore, art therapists must be aware of how their own culture can influence their assessment in developmental domains (Slonim, 1991). The four domains of development are briefly discussed and Table 10.1 summarizes characteristics of each domain.

The information presented here is to help you understand theories that have been developed and that are commonly used to inform art therapists about general developmental markers. However, it is imperative to keep in mind that these theories are ideas that have value, but one must also recognize that at some point in time each of these theories has been challenged, criticized, and

TABLE 10.1 Developmental domains.

Physical development	Cognitive development	Social emotional development	Language development
Gross motor skills	Memory	Express feelings	Naming objects and materials
Fine motor skills	Decision-making	Understand others' feelings	Verbalizing thoughts, feelings, observations
Eye-hand coordination	Creativity	Manage emotions	Understanding spoken words
Balance, throwing, jumping	Problem-solving	Ability to share/cooperate	Fluency in speech
	Understanding cause and effect	Self-esteem	
	Naming shapes and objects	Explore social roles	
	Ability to compare and contrast	Establish relationships	

critiqued (Golomb, 2002). These are not one-size-fits-all theories and there is not one theory that could possibly encompass and include development for all people of all cultures. Art therapists must continually seek out information about development in many cultures in order to best understand and meet the needs of their unique clients.

Physical development

Physical development in children includes the changes that occur in the human body and its ability to move. Height, weight, gross, and fine motor skills, as well as coordination, are all a part of a child's physical development. The skeletal system plays a large part in one's physical development. Bones and cartilage make up the skeletal system, which grows rapidly in the first few years of life (Jenkins et al., 2016). This rapid growth creates challenges with balance and coordination, but opportunities to play and move give children practice in gaining control of their bodies. Physical development in the early years is often measured by a child's ability to sit, crawl, walk, and grasp and hold objects. A child's culture will influence physical development and their future attitudes about physical activity. Mary Ainsworth and many others have conducted a significant amount of research about cultures outside of North America to learn more about the impact of culture on physical development. For example, Western cultures frequently place infants in a crib or reclined position while some African cultures begin training in sitting as early as 3 months. Training may include digging a hole that would hold an infant upright for a specific amount of time each day. This emphasis on sitting is a result of the cultural naming ceremony that can only occur once a child achieves independent sitting (Cintas, 1989). Art therapists can begin working with young children once they are able to grasp objects and maintain some control over materials. Some children as young as 18 months are able to create scribbles if provided with the materials and opportunity.

Cognitive development

Cognitive development, or the growth of the brain, is heavily influenced by both nature and nurture. When referring to cognitive development, we often think about abilities such as memory, creativity, and decision-making. The brain tells our bodies what to do and how to operate. Amazingly, the brain doubles in size in the first year of life and is nearly full grown by the time a child is 6 years old (Brown & Jernigan, 2012). A baby is born with all of the brain cells it will have for its entire life. These cells require stimulation in order to grow and make connections. Early childhood experiences can have a significant impact on a child's developing brain by helping to strengthen the connections and increase the ability to achieve more complex tasks. When the brain does not have stimulating opportunities and experiences, there can be the potential for developmental delays (Berk, 2004). Cultural factors, such as poverty, can play a significant role in cognitive development. Children from families living in poverty typically have fewer books in the home and parents in these homes often read less to their children than parents from higher socioeconomic statuses (Maschinot, 2008). Researchers have noted that larger numbers of European American families read more frequently to their children than African American and Latino families (Maschinot, 2008). However, although there is a correlation between ethnicity and reading frequency, it is unclear whether these differences are due to ethnicity, socioeconomic status, or other factors. Art therapists can offer a variety of experiences to clients that may not be available in the home environment. Providing children with art materials and creative experiences at an early age is one way to positively impact their cognitive development. Allowing exploration of materials through sight, touch, and smell can stimulate the brain and help nurture its development.

Social emotional development

Development of healthy social and emotional skills is crucial to one's ability to relate to others in the world. Both biological and environmental factors can influence social emotional development. These skills begin developing in infancy and continue throughout childhood, adolescence, and even into adulthood. **Social emotional development** encompasses a wide range of skills and can significantly impact a child's overall health. A few examples include attachment, perception of others' facial expressions, the ability to identify and express emotions, the development of empathy, and the ability to follow rules (Berk, 2004). Art therapists who work with children frequently see clients in order to help with this aspect of development. Deficits in social emotional skills can be attributed to biological causes or lack of adequate environmental stimulation (Berk, 2004). However, an art therapist with knowledge of social emotional development can meet a client at their present social emotional level and work with them to encourage growth in this area. Art therapy interventions can address many social emotional issues such as identification and expression of emotions, while mastery of art materials can aid in mastery of managing emotions and self-control. Because all cultures have different ways of engaging with others and expressing emotions, art therapists must be vigilant in continually exploring awareness of how their own culture might influence the assessment and evaluation of a client's social emotional development.

Language development

Language development is sometimes discussed in connection to cognitive development; however, it may be considered a developmental domain of its own. Because language and communication can have a significant impact on the work an art therapist does, we will separate them into a different domain for the purposes of this chapter. **Language development** involves a child's ability to name objects, understand spoken language, verbalize their own thoughts and feelings, and speak their native language fluently. Researchers have discovered that, regardless of culture, there is a universal sequence in the development of language. Babies first distinguish between sounds, then they begin their first form of language, known as cooing. Babbling follows cooing, and finally children begin to use simple words to name objects or identify feelings. These skills continue to grow and develop into more complex language that begins to be affected by culture (Maschinot, 2008). As children develop, they build vocabularies and begin to understand grammar rules. Additionally, they acquire pragmatics or the social nuances of effectively communicating with others (Berk, 2004).

The development of conversational skills provides children with a new and oftentimes more effective way of expressing themselves. This ability has the potential to significantly impact relationships and how a child's needs are met. As with the other domains we have explored, environmental exposure to spoken language plays a huge role in a child's language development. Research data suggests that children raised in homes of a higher socioeconomic status are often exposed to more language, thus they tend to have larger vocabularies (Maschinot, 2008). Art therapists often tout the lack of necessity for language as a means of achieving therapeutic goals as a benefit of their work. And, when working with young children who have experienced trauma before they have the ability to verbalize their thoughts and feelings, the art is often the mode of communication and an avenue for healing. Thus there does not *need* to be language for art therapy to be beneficial; however, the combination of the art process and the verbal processing can have profound effects on a client.

While an art therapist's work may occasionally branch into and overlap with all of these domains, the primary goals and work of an art therapist will focus on the social emotional developmental aspects of a child or teen. The following theories frequently help art therapists to understand their clients' developmental level and where to meet the client when they begin and work through the art therapy process. In most professions, experts are always considering and synthesizing theories to help make sense of concepts in their chosen field or to explain a phenomenon that is yet to be understood. It seems only natural that as humans, we want to find a way to simplify information and help organize it in our minds; however, this can lead us to categorize people or characteristics in a way that ignores the uniqueness of all people and cultures.

Developmental psychology theories

Jean Piaget 1896–1980

In the early to mid-1900s, Swiss Psychologist Jean Piaget developed and refined his theory of cognitive development in children (Maier, 1969; Piaget, 1936; Piaget & Inhelder, 1969). Piaget understood cognitive development to be the way in which a child constructed an understanding of the world. His theory is composed of four developmental stages that describe a progressively sophisticated course of cognitive development. He focused on how children obtain knowledge and then how they employ that knowledge. Piaget indicated that all children experience these four stages in the same succession and that both biological and environmental factors influence a child's intellectual development (Maier, 1969; Piaget, 1936). The four phases Piaget identified and described are (1) the sensorimotor stage, (2) the preoperational stage, (3) the concrete operational stage, and (4) the formal operational stage.

Sensorimotor stage

The Sensorimotor Stage is the initial stage of development described by Piaget (Maier, 1969; Piaget, 1936; Piaget & Inhelder, 1969) and includes infants and toddlers from birth to approximately age 2. In this stage, children use their senses and motor skills to explore and learn about the world. They learn through seeing, hearing, sucking, and grasping during this phase of development (Berk, 2004). Much attention has been given to this stage because of the numerous developments that occur with the first 24 months of life. Piaget studied this stage extensively, so much in fact, that he further divided this stage into six substages that reflect a detailed examination of reflexes and reactions (Maier, 1969). The main achievement of this stage is **object permanence**. Piaget described object permanence as a child grasping the concept that "objects can endure in the passage of time" (Maier, 1969, p. 116). Or, in other words, this is when a child can understand that an object can exist, even when it is out of sight.

Preoperational stage

The second stage of cognitive development described by Piaget is the Preoperational Stage, which lasts from approximately 2 years of age until about 7 years of age (Berk, 2004; Maier, 1969; Piaget, 1936). Many exciting developmental milestones occur during this stage. Children begin talking and they develop symbolic play, which is often seen in the pretend or make-believe play of children at this stage. This is also a time when children are very **egocentric**, meaning they can only see situations from their own perspective. At this phase in life, children have not developed the mental capability of taking the perspective of another person. However, as children progress in this stage, they become more social, which Piaget indicates is necessary for decreasing egocentrism (Maier, 1969). The concept of **conservation**, or understanding that an object's appearance can change, while the physical quantity remains the same, is achieved at this stage, but rarely before the age of 5 (Berk, 2004; Piaget, 1936; Piaget & Inhelder, 1969).

Concrete operational stage

The Concrete Operational Stage spans the ages approximately 7–11 or middle childhood. Children in the beginning of this stage continue to think concretely as in the previous stage but gradually develop more logical and sophisticated thought processes (Maier, 1969; Piaget, 1936). Egocentrism decreases and children are able to understand others' perspectives. Children finally grasp the concept of conservation and they now understand constancy and reversibility, or the concept that an action can be reversed (Berk, 2004; Maier, 1969). Kids at this stage are now able to focus on multiple parts of a problem or situation, whereas previously, they could only focus on one part. Additionally, inductive reasoning takes hold during this stage and children can generalize a specific experience to a broader principle (Berk, 2004; Maier, 1969; Piaget, 1936). For example, a child's grandparent has gray hair and wears glasses; therefore, the child generalizes that anyone who looks like a grandparent with gray hair will wear glasses.

Formal operational stage

Piaget called the final stage of his theory the Formal Operational Stage, which begins around age 12 and develops into adulthood. This is a time of much more advanced thinking. Abstract thinking, theoretical concepts, and the ability to use logic to find creative solutions all develop during this stage. Children who have reached this stage can now form and test hypotheses. Rather than using trial-and-error to problem-solve, as in previous stages, youth in this stage can use logic to form a systematic or methodical way of solving problems. The important skill of long-term planning begins during the Formal Operational Stage and is evident when children and young teens begin to think about possible consequences and outcomes of various actions. Another key development of this stage is a person's ability to think about their own thoughts or the ideas and thoughts of others (Berk, 2004).

This is a simplified version of Piaget's theory that briefly highlights some of the key components of each stage. Piaget's theory has faced much criticism, but it has also been defended by some scholars (Lourenco & Machado, 1996). Criticisms have ranged from an ethical bias of studying his own children to misjudging the abilities of infants and adolescents. Additionally, he failed to include social and cultural implications on cognitive development (Babakr et al., 2019). While there may never be complete agreement about the accuracy of his theory, Maier (1969) pointed out,

> *Piaget's theory furnishes us with a frame of reference...variations may exist at any one point in an individual's approach to everyday problems. Basically, however, his theory pointedly demonstrates that there are regular patterns in cognitive development which are experienced by everyone. In turn, such understanding allows us to predict an individual's mode and range of comprehension all along on the course of development (p. 157).*

Piaget's theory provides art therapists with a basic starting point for understanding cognitive development when approaching our work with clients. This knowledge can inform the language we use with clients and help us to develop appropriate goals as we work alongside them. As an art therapist, it is vital to be knowledgeable of a variety of theories and allow those theories to serve as a frame of reference in helping us understand our clients; however, we must never forget to see our clients as unique individuals and to honor their diversity in our work with them.

Erik Erikson 1902–1994

Erik Erikson applied, expanded, and improved upon Freud's psychoanalytic theory when he created his psychosocial theory of development (Berk, 2004; Erikson, 1968; Maier, 1969). Unlike Freud, who focused on pathology, Erikson's work was more optimistic and centered around how individuals successfully resolve developmental crises based on what they learn and attain from their social relationships and interactions (Erikson, 1968; Maier, 1969). Erikson believed that humans are creative, adaptive, and continually revamping their personalities. He noted that as individuals acquire skills and attitudes at each stage of development, they become more active contributors to society (Berk, 2004; Erikson, 1968; Maier, 1969). Erikson's theory encompasses eight stages and covers the lifespan from birth to the older adult.

For the purposes of this chapter, only the first five stages will be discussed as they cover birth through adolescence. The last three stages of Erikson's theory address young adulthood, middle adulthood, and aging adults. Please bear in mind that Erikson's work was extensive and the information presented here is an extremely simplified version to serve as an introduction to the theory as an aid to understanding artistic development. The first five stages of Erikson's theory are (1) Trust vs. Mistrust, (2) Autonomy vs. Shame and Doubt, (3) Initiative vs. Guilt, (4) Industry vs. Inferiority, and (5) Identity vs. Role Confusion. Because the final three stages of Erikson's theory encompass adulthood, they are not included in this chapter. For your reference, these stages are (6) Intimacy vs. Isolation, (7) Generativity vs. Stagnation, and (8) Ego Integrity vs. Despair.

Trust vs. mistrust

In this stage, from birth to approximately 1 year, the infant gains a sense of trust when caregivers provide responsive and caring physical and emotional comfort when handling the child. Creating a sense of safety is vital to developing trust at this stage. When appropriate care is given, the infant develops confidence that the world is good and that trust can be extended to the environment and new experiences in the future. However, if the child experiences harsh physical or emotional responses, then fear, suspicion, and apprehension create a sense of mistrust (Berk, 2004; Erikson, 1968; Maier, 1969).

Autonomy vs. shame and doubt

From approximately 1 to 3 years of age, toddlers want to make decisions and choices for themselves. They are now mobile and eager to explore the world around them. Although it may be challenging, caregivers who provide gradual independence and structure while allowing the child age appropriate choices help to foster a sense of autonomy and success in mastering this stage. In contrast, a child who is forced and shamed when trying to exert their independence may develop a sense of shame and begin doubting themselves, their abilities, and their ability to become an independent person (Berk, 2004; Erikson, 1968; Maier, 1969).

Initiative vs. guilt

In this stage of Erikson's theory, the 3–6-year old should become more assertive through taking on some responsibility for their environment, such as dressing themselves and taking care of their toys. They learn how to assert themselves and take control of age-appropriate tasks such as planning activities and engaging in imaginative play where they may imitate various occupational roles to explore the person they can become. Children who are encouraged to play freely develop a sense of initiative and purpose as well as the belief that they can lead others. When adults are overly directive or controlling, the child can begin to fear trying new things and internalize a feeling of failure or guilt (Berk, 2004; Erikson, 1968; Maier, 1969).

Industry vs. inferiority

Social interactions and school become a significant part of children's lives from ages 6 to 12. When children successfully learn how to cooperate and work with peers, and feel competent at school through academic accomplishments, they develop a sense of industry and their self-confidence flourishes. If children have many negative experiences with peers, academics, or family, a sense of inferiority can arise and they may feel they are not "good enough." Parents and teachers are important during this stage and must maintain a healthy balance between encouraging a child's efforts and not excessively praising a child, which can encourage arrogance (Berk, 2004; Erikson, 1968; Maier, 1969).

Identity vs. role confusion

Adolescence, ages about 12–18, was intensely studied by Erik Erikson. The major achievement of the fifth stage of psychosocial development is the answer to the question, "Who am I?" The journey from childhood to young adulthood is ripe with experiences that impact one's personal identity such as parents, friends, school, society, and even popular culture. These influences as well as many others can help an adolescent develop a healthy sense of identity or role confusion. Adolescents should be encouraged to explore who they are and what they like so that they can determine their own path in life. Someone who successfully navigates this stage will achieve a sense of self, or personal identity, that remains strong throughout their life (Berk, 2004; Erikson, 1968; Maier, 1969). As previously noted, development continues into three more stages, according to Erikson. These stages represent adulthood and are thus not included in this chapter.

Now that we have examined some common developmental theories, let's take a look at theories about how children progress in artistic development. As noted in the previous section, one must consider that children exist within the context of their culture which includes relationships, environments, customs, beliefs, and many other aspects that can determine a child's exposure to the arts. Thus art therapists must learn about artistic development theories while continually remaining cognizant of the influence of their clients' cultures.

Artistic development in children

For nearly 200 years, many people have studied and explored the artwork and artistic development of children (Rubin, 2005). **Artistic development** is the process in which a child learns about, acquires experience in, and creates art from toddlerhood through adolescence, or an important part of "human development in the domain of art" (Darras & Kindler, 1997, p.17). Although there are differing opinions about the specifics of artistic growth phases and stages, there is great value in learning about and understanding what those who have come before us have learned about artistic development.

Interest in children's drawings began to flourish in the late 1800s with a surge in curiosity about child development and a desire to change art education. Intrigue about the human mind and children's growth started in England and then moved to the United States around 1883 (Richards, 1974). Many of the first observations of children focused on language and intelligence. These observations included an 1880 study by G. Stanley Hall, an American psychologist, that was implemented in a Boston school system. The study incorporated drawings by children who were between 4 and 8 years of age. Hall wrote an article about this study and included a discussion about the representation and growth of a human form in the artwork. In his writing, he referred to circular heads with lines for appendages (Richards, 1974), or what many art therapists now refer to as *cephalopods*, *globals,* or *tadpole* people. These figures are universal and appear across cultures (Golomb, 2011). Hall's notation of these types of figures may be the first reference to what many now describe as part of an artistic stage in Western culture.

Several individuals have examined children's art and attempted to find developmental patterns or consistencies within it. When looking at children's drawings, one must take into consideration many factors, including age, culture, individual life experiences, purpose of the artwork, and access to art materials (Boriss-Krimsky, 1999; Golomb, 2002; Lowenfeld & Brittain, 1987). Simone Alter-Muri (2002) emphasized, "Art therapists need to be aware of the developmental stages and their applicability cross-culturally" (p. 189). Please bear in mind that although you will sometimes see ages aligned with the stages discussed, these are not static, but rather an estimate of when some children *may* reach a stage. As previously noted, all children develop at vastly different rates and children's development can be dynamic and fluid, vacillating between stages depending on a variety of factors (Boriss-Krimsky, 1999; Rubin, 2005). Claire Golomb (1992) eloquently emphasized the importance of understanding a child's artistic development, "to bring the eye of the sophisticated adult to the work of young children without understanding the long route education and development take is likely to distort our vision" (p. 20).

Viktor Lowenfeld 1903–1960

Viktor Lowenfeld was an Austrian-born art educator with a diverse background who recognized the therapeutic value of art. He was a skilled artist and musician, earned a doctoral degree in education, and was colleagues with both Sigmund Freud and Erik Erikson. He has written many books, including texts that have been used across the United States for art education (Lowenfeld, 1954; Lowenfeld & Brittain, 1987). Lowenfeld lived in Austria until the late 1930s when his family moved in order to escape Hitler's regime. He moved to London briefly and then immigrated to the United States where he taught at universities like Harvard, Columbia, and then he eventually settled at Pennsylvania State University, establishing their first art department and serving as the department chair (Alter-Muri, 2002).

Lowenfeld is a well-known figure in the field of art therapy because of his studies of artistic development in children and the artistic stages he has proposed. Lowenfeld's stages are considered by some art therapists to be the "gold standard" (Shore, 2013, p. 10) in categorizing artistic development of children. Even so, these stages and his theory have been criticized by some for potential bias, a lack of statistical support, a lack of references and information about how he developed the stages, and whether or not the stages are applicable across cultures (Alter-Muri, 2002). Although Lowenfeld's methods in the development of the artistic stages have been questioned, he was acutely aware of how a person's background and family factors must be considered when looking at a child's artwork. He also noted that children develop at different rates and may occasionally regress in their artwork (Lowenfeld & Brittain, 1987). Some researchers have questioned the ability to apply Lowenfeld's stages cross-culturally; however, a study conducted by Alter-Muri with children in five European countries found that the first three stages Lowenfeld proposed were applicable across cultures in Europe (Alter-Muri, 2002). This was a small study and Alter-Muri emphasized that continued research in cross-cultural studies of Lowenfeld's stages is important. Because Lowenfeld's Stages are so predominantly used to inform art therapists' work with clients, a brief description of each follows.

Scribbling stage

The Scribbling Stage includes the time from when a child is first introduced to art materials and begins to make marks to the time when a child begins to name the scribbles or marks on the page. The scribbling stage can be further divided into disordered (or random) scribbles, controlled scribbles, and the naming phase (Lowenfeld & Brittain, 1987). This stage includes exploration of art materials and the child's realization that they have created something. In the beginning of this stage, mark-making is random and done with no intention. The child is often enjoying the movement involved and is intrigued by the materials and results. During the controlled scribble phase a child is gaining control over their physical movements and becoming more intentional with mark-making. Toward the latter part of this stage, as the child develops and adults speak to the child about the artwork, the child begins to provide words or names for the scribbles created. Color choice at this age is random and children often select the color that is closest in proximity to their hand. Scribbles on the page are sporadically placed and haphazard, often extending beyond the edge of the page (Boriss-Krimsky, 1999; Lowenfeld & Brittain, 1987). See Figs. 10.1 and 10.2 for examples of artwork from the Scribble Stage.

FIG. 10.1 *Disordered scribble. Marks are random, uncontrolled, and haphazardly placed. (Photograph courtesy of E. Itczak.)*

FIG. 10.2 *Controlled scribble. Repeated, controlled lines and dots. (Photograph courtesy of E. Itczak.)*

Preschematic stage

The Preschematic Stage is generally around the time a child enters preschool through kindergarten or first grade (Boriss-Krimsky, 1999). At this stage the child has developed some motor control and begins to be intentional with mark-making. One of the first recognizable figures at this stage is the cephalopod or tadpole person, which is a circular shape with lines extending from it as arms and/or legs (Lowenfeld & Brittain, 1987). The spontaneous drawings at this age are generally reflective of what is happening or what is important to the child at that moment in time (see Fig. 10.3). Because of a child's egocentrism at this age, objects in a picture will be placed in relation to how a child feels the objects connect to their life, as opposed to how an adult actually sees the objects. The child is just beginning to try to find a schema during this stage, so each time something is drawn, it will likely be different than the previous attempt (Boriss-Krimsky, 1999; Lowenfeld & Brittain, 1987). See Fig. 10.4 for an example of a drawing from the late Preschematic Stage.

Schematic stage

Children whose drawings fall into the Schematic Stage often reflect the child as a part of their environment instead of the center of it, as in the previous stage. The key development of this stage is a **schema** or a consistent concept that is applied over and over for people, houses, trees, etc. (Boriss-Krimsky, 1999; Lowenfeld & Brittain, 1987). The schema is a formula that the child uses whenever there is a need to express something, conversely the schema may be altered if a significant event impacts the child (Boriss-Krimsky, 1999). For example, a

FIG. 10.3 *Preschematic stage. An example of how an image reflects what is happening in a child's life. Water was leaking into the basement of the home and the child created this image stating, "Papaw and Daddy trying to figure out where the water is coming from. This (pointing to blue) is the water going into the basement."*
(Photograph courtesy of E. Itczak.)

FIG. 10.4 *Late preschematic. The floating objects revolve around the child and reflect the egocentrism of this stage. The ball and bump on the head are indicative of what was happening at the moment in time (created after recess when the child was injured). The person is more advanced than the beginning cephalopod but has not quite been solidified into a schema. This child is shifting into the schematic stage, evidenced by the groundline, skyline, and sun.*
(Photograph courtesy of E. Itczak.)

child may draw a house the same way each time, but if the family moves into a new home, the child may include more or different details. If the child previously drew a red square home with two windows and a door, but the new house is blue and has several windows, the child may still draw a square home but change or emphasize the details of the home. See Fig. 10.5 for a schema of a house.

Baselines are extremely common at this stage as children begin to realize spatial relationships. Children represent spatial relationships in a variety of ways, such as through x-ray drawings, folding over, and aerials views. An **x-ray drawing** shows the inside and outside of an object, such as a house, in the same image as seen in Fig. 10.6. **Folding over** is when an image appears to have an upside down area of the drawing that would be seen in water's reflection, or if the page of the paper were to be folded both images would be upright. Aerial views are drawn from a bird's eye view and may also be included when a child in this stage draws an image from multiple different views at the same time. Color becomes important in this stage and children want to use the "correct" colors as part of their schema. For many children, grass is green, skies are blue, suns are yellow and children do not like to stray from these consistencies at this stage (Boriss-Krimsky, 1999; Lowenfeld & Brittain, 1987).

Gang stage

As the name implies, the Gang Stage is when friends and group activities become very important to a child. Fear of judgment at this stage often prevents children from unrestrained creative expression. The child at this stage is becoming more

FIG. 10.5 *Schematic stage. The houses are grounded on the baseline and the schema of a house is repeated with only variation in the color of the home to signify different families' homes. (M. Itczak.)*

FIG. 10.6 *Schematic stage. X-ray drawing depicting outside and inside of house simultaneously. "Correct" colors are used for the grass, sky, and sun.*
(Photograph courtesy of E. Itczak.)

self-conscious and their drawings may be stiff and rigid. Typically, children at this stage include more details in their artwork. They may become interested in designs and more decorative features, such as clothing patterns and logos, jewelry and accessories, or even skin details such as freckles, blemishes, tattoos, or beauty marks. See Fig. 10.7 for an example of detailed artwork from a child in this stage. Children in the Gang Stage are beginning to want their work to look "right" and will attempt to copy artwork from images they see. There may be exaggerated gender characteristics based on assumptions of how a child thinks a specific gender should appear. Some children begin using a horizon line instead of the previous baseline and skyline. Additionally, children in this stage begin to understand variations in color. Some children stop making art around this age if they do not have an interest in developing their skills or if opportunities to continue being creative are not available or encouraged (Boriss-Krimsky, 1999; Lowenfeld & Brittain, 1987).

Pseudo-naturalistic stage

Young adolescents in the Pseudo-Naturalistic Stage are even more self-conscious than in the previous stage and this ego-centrism often leads some to be very strategic and thoughtful about planning their artwork. These youth want to be successful and tend to focus on creating a product that is acceptable in how it looks(Boriss-Krimsky, 1999; Lowenfeld & Brittain, 1987). At this point in development, youth who have had negative experiences with art-making, such as a peer or adult making inconsiderate comments, will most likely stop creating art. Topics of interest for drawing, to those who continue making art, can range from nature to fantasy. See Fig. 10.8 for an example of

FIG. 10.7 *Gang stage. Notice the details in the flowers and hands, the patterns in the planet, and the jewelry detail.*
(Photograph courtesy of E. Jansing.)

FIG. 10.8 *Pseudo-naturalistic. This perspective drawing includes details and is aesthetically pleasing in both form and shading.*
(Photograph courtesy of E. Jansing.)

a perspective drawing with attempts at more advanced drawing skills. Some young adolescents enjoy doodling as an easy way to continue being creative, but not necessarily judged since doodling may not be considered an attempt at creating a true artistic product. Most youth at this stage who have an interest in continuing with art have a desire to learn about perspective and often want to develop more advanced drawing skills (Boriss-Krimsky, 1999; Lowenfeld & Brittain, 1987).

Adolescent art

Adolescents begin to question everything in their lives, including parents and family values, society as a whole, people in positions of authority, and even their own art. At this stage, youth become more self-reflective and may begin exploring sexual identity through their artwork. Culture and society can have a significant impact on artwork created by teens as well. Depending on an adolescent's preference, some may desire to create realistic work, as in Fig. 10.9, while others strive for abstraction. Youth at this age begin to form very individualized ways to create art and their art can provide opportunities for self-expression that they may not find in other places. Graffiti may become appealing to some teens as another form of self-expression that can be a way to push limits in a creative and constructive way if done with respect and in acceptable settings (Boriss-Krimsky, 1999; Lowenfeld & Brittain, 1987).

For a quick summary of Lowenfeld's Stages of Artistic Development, see Table 10.2.

FIG. 10.9 *Adolescent art. Mixed media pen drawing with watercolor and acrylic paint. Increased skills in realistic drawing.*
(Photograph courtesy of M. Itczak.)

TABLE 10.2 Viktor Lowenfeld's artistic stages of development.

Artistic stage of development	Ages	Characteristics
Beginnings of self-expression Scribbling stage	2–4 years	1. Disordered scribbles (sometimes called Random or Uncontrolled) • Uncontrolled and unintentional marks may run off page • Minimal control over motor skills • Color use is haphazard and unintentional 2. Controlled scribbles • Discovery of connection between movement and marks • Repetition of marks, dots, etc. • Spend twice as long drawing • Can copy a circle around 3 years • Will try different colors 3. Named scribbles • Begin to name the forms created which signifies imaginative thinking • Marks distributed around page • More intent with mark-making
First representational attempts Preschematic stage	4–7 years	• Emergence of tadpole figure • Creation of various forms • Color is an exciting experience • Color is used for its own sake and may not align with reality • Objective spatial relationships have yet to develop
Achievement of a form concept Schematic stage	7–9 years	• Schemas for objects (peoples, trees, etc.) are developed, repeated, and highly individualized • Schemas are rigid, but an alteration of a schema suggests importance • Human figure includes more details/features, geometric forms • Beginning use of a baseline and skylines • "Folding-over" can be seen at this stage • Mixed plan and elevation (multiple views) • X-ray images • More intentional space relationships and use of color
Dawning realism Gang Age	9–12 years	• Expression of gender characteristics • Greater awareness and concern for detail, such as in clothing • Greater stiffness in figures • Exaggeration tends to disappear • Realization of properties of color, less rigid in color–object relationship • Begin using multiple planes/baselines • Overlapping is used

TABLE 10.2 Viktor Lowenfeld's artistic stages of development—cont'd

Artistic stage of development	Ages	Characteristics
Age of reasoning Pseudo naturalistic stage	12–14 years	• End of art as spontaneous activity and critical self-awareness of art skills • Art used as purposeful expression • Attempts at naturalistic expression, joints in human figure, sexual characteristics sometimes exaggerated • Keen awareness of color and design • Lettering and cartooning become popular • Attempts at incorporating depth • Increased use of overlapping
Period of decision Adolescent art stage	14–17 years	• Some teens developed highly individualized style of art • Abstraction and symbolism are used • Use art as a way to push limits • Interest in graffiti art • Color is very individualistic • Teen hone artistic skills of perspective and depth if they are motivated to continue

Developed from Lowenfeld & Brittain's Creative and Mental Growth 8th ed. and The Creativity Handbook: A Visual Arts Guide for Parents and Teachers.

Claire Golomb 1928–present

Claire Golomb taught psychology courses in child development for over 40 years at the University of Massachusetts (Jessica Kingsley Publishers, 2011). She was a well-respected, accomplished researcher and writer on the topic of artistic development (Golomb, 2002). Golomb posited that in order to best understand artistic development, one must look at a variety of mediums in both two-dimensional and three-dimensional artwork. She did not subscribe to stage theories that suggest artistic development is a natural progression toward visual realism, reminding us that the ability to draw in perspective is a skill that is taught, but it is not a natural acquisition for most people. She was of the opinion that "for children who are motivated to draw, paint, and model, there is a developmental progression toward greater competence that, however, need not be synonymous with optical realism" (Golomb, 2002, p. 132). Thus she believed that children's art development is a nonlinear trajectory with no specific endpoint, but rather several possible achievements in pictorial representation (Golomb, 1994). She endorsed a representational theory of drawing in which "the child who, in every generation, invents a basic vocabulary of universally similar and meaningful graphic shapes" (p. 18). She maintained that children progress in artistic development not based on their cognitive capabilities, but based on a continual search for better ways to represent what they are creating. Rather than describe children's progression of drawings by ages, Golomb looked more closely at the development of some key formal elements, including form, space, color, and composition.

Two-dimensional art

Golomb used the term **representational development** when discussing how a child progresses in art. The ability to create a representation or symbol of a three-dimensional object in a two-dimensional form is a sign of intelligence that is unique to humans (Golomb, 2011). She emphasized that when a child creates a tadpole figure the child is creating their own graphic system in which the simple form represents a solid, three-dimensional object or being. Simply stated, the child is beginning to understand that images can serve as symbols. She also pointed out the challenges inherent in creating a two-dimensional image from a three-dimensional object, noting that how a child represents a three-dimensional object with three-dimensional art materials aids in better understanding artistic development (Golomb, 1992).

Although Golomb respected Jean Piaget, she very much disagreed with his alignment of intelligence and artistic development. Rather, she maintained a perspective that "ages are merely convenient markers, and skill level, talent, motivation, practice, persistence, and the ability as well as the inclination to improve on one's creation affect the timing of certain pictorial achievements" (Golomb, 2002, p. 47). She reminded us that artwork created by many artistically untrained adults is evidence of the impact of culture, interest, and effort (Golomb, 1994). For a summary of Golomb's two-dimensional pictorial representation development, see Table 10.3. Readers are encouraged to continue their study of Golomb's (2002) work as this is a very simplified version of her extremely detailed description from *Child Art in Context: A Cultural and Comparative Perspective.*

Three-dimensional art

In addition to studying two-dimensional artwork, Golomb examined artistic development with three-dimensional media. She has noted the lack of studies of three-dimensional art and suspects that it may be due to some of the challenges of using these types of materials (Golomb, 2011). Clay or playdough can be messy, difficult to transport and store, and young children tend to struggle with constructing sturdy figures out of these materials. Although these challenges exist, Golomb believed it is important to look at children's work in these media so as not to inaccurately assume a lack of representational competence (Golomb, 2002). For example, a child may draw a person without a neck; however, the same child may sculpt a figure with a neck in the same session. Essentially, a child may be better able to recreate a three-dimensional object with three-dimensional materials. Asking someone to "translate" a three-dimensional

TABLE 10.3 Claire Golomb's development of two-dimensional representation.

Development of pictorial representation
Prerepresentational efforts include nonintentional scribbles and marks
Preliterate children across time and cultures use basic shapes, lines, dots, and scribbles to create stick figures, heads, and bodies
Form: • The major vehicle for creating a meaningful representation in the beginning. • Humans tend to be first subject; start with *globals*, or spheres with facial features and then move into tadpoles with arms and legs. • Early on, focus is on basic likeness of figure while size, proportion, or color is secondary. However once form is achieved, size may become important, especially in family drawings. • Emphasis on body parts of importance; inclusion of arms if throwing a ball or tummy if person is pregnant. • In early period and most of childhood, frontal views of humans and objects are preferred, figures are their own units and boundaries are clear. • Animal drawings commonly have mixed views (frontal view of head, but side view of body). • Progression to curved and bent lines, two-dimensional and three-dimensional lines occurs. Portrayal of movement and gestures occurs. • Experimentation of range of views (top, side, rear) while sizes and proportions gain importance
Space: • Young children represent nearness by creating forms that are close to one another on the paper. • Space becomes organized along horizontal and vertical axes on real or imagined lines (Horizontal axis = left to right direction and the Vertical axis = up and down/near and far directions). • Development of new ways to connect foreground, middle ground, and background into one composition. • Talented and motivated children may desire to create illusion and depth, thus they may overlap objects, use diminished sizes, use diagonals, foreshortening, and perspective
Color: • Serves many functions: expressive, aesthetic, etc. • Color at first may be due to personal preference. • After mastery of basic shapes, children may use a variety of colors to decorate and embellish their work, or for sheer pleasure. Realistic use of color is not important. • Gradually children become aware of and use realistic colors. Some children use color to create playful and imaginative patterns or designs. • In middle childhood color becomes a significant aspect of art and may unify or organize the composition. • Younger children do not use color to convey emotion, but as they develop, colorful media, such as paint, become appealing to them and color becomes a big factor in their preferences.

Continued

TABLE 10.3 Claire Golomb's development of two-dimensional representation—cont'd

Development of pictorial representation

Composition:

- In very early art, there is a brief period where objects are randomly placed around the paper and seem unconnected.
- Then, children cluster objects very closely to one another before moving onto the next phase.
- Two tendencies for composition in young and more experienced children:
  (1) figures aligned along horizontal or vertical axis; baselines are eventually introduced; objects usually placed on bottom of page; grouping of figures indicates special relationship
  (2) items organized around a pictorial center; creates stability for the figure; complexity of composition increases over time; strict bilateral symmetry declines as children progress in their skill, but a balanced composition may still be created

Developed from Child Art in Context: A Cultural and Comparative Perspective (Golomb, 2002). For even greater detail and further explanation, please take time to read Golomb's work.

object into a two-dimensional media is a challenge that has, in the past, been accounted for by assuming a lack of cognitive immaturity, which is not necessarily the case.

When discussing the progression of three-dimensional representation, Golomb used several terms which may not be familiar to many since there is a lack of information about development in this type of medium. Terminology used by Golomb included prerepresentational actions, romancing, imitative actions, reading off, and verbal designation (Golomb, 2002). **Prerepresentational actions** are how a child interacts with a three-dimensional media that have no representational intentions, such as pounding, poking, or squeezing. **Romancing** is when a child tells a story about something they have created, typically about a form that was not intentionally produced. Usually, the story that is created is not tied to what the form actually looks like, but rather it is a story that has no actual connection to the form. Children use **imitative actions** in place of or as a way to help support their representation, for instance flattening playdough to create pancakes, creating ring of dough and using it as a bracelet, or rolling a sphere of clay as a marble or ball. According to Golomb (2002), romancing and imitative action indicate a transition in development when a child is asked to create something they do not fully understand and are then unsure of how to move forward.

As children progress, the next step in three-dimensional representation development is known as reading off. **Reading off** is slightly more advanced than romancing because a child recognizes that what they have created resembles an actual object, and then the child attempts to provide meaning for their creation. Golomb considered **verbal designation** the most advanced development because the child identifies specific parts of a form that was intentionally created. The form may not be very detailed or even resemble a realistic object to the adult eye. However, the designation of parts is a result of the child recognizing that the parts are congruent with another object, for instance a head is located at the top and feet are at the bottom (Golomb, 2002). As in drawing, the child is beginning to develop an understanding of symbolism. For a brief summary of Golomb's examination of the development of three-dimensional representation, please see Table 10.4.

TABLE 10.4 Claire Golomb's development of three-dimensional representation.

Development of sculpture
• Young children between 2 years and 2 years, 8 months hold clay/playdough passively or hit it on a table. They may use it in conjunction with other toys by sticking it on cars or blocks
• Prerepresentational actions can be observed between 2 years, 8 months and 3 years, 2 months. • Examples include pounding, stretching, pulling apart and putting together, and hammering. Patting, folding, squeezing, poking/pinching, and flattening also occur. Eventually, rolling leads to the first shape: a snake
• At around age 3, children are more eager to explore media and learn quickly how to create simple forms. • Around age 4 children become representational in 3D media. • Human figures are a favorite subject of children in Western cultures. Blobs of dough become one of three models which lack significant detail: (1) Upright column (2) Ball or Slab with facial features (3) Separate parts laid out on a surface in an arrangement of a face or body. • Each of these models gradually increases in detail and differentiation of parts as the child progresses. As in drawing, globals become the beginning representation for humans. • Movement toward uprightness and details of facial features can be seen. • Models develop multiple components or body parts and the human figure becomes more differentiated. • Balance and symmetry develop in figures, which then leads to improvement in proportions. • Up to age 5, children predominantly create a frontal view with 3D materials. • Differentiation begins to level off around ages 8 or 9, similar to drawing

Developed from Child Art in Context: A Cultural and Comparative Perspective (Golomb, 2002). For even greater detail and further explanation, please take time to read Golomb's work.

Rhoda Kellogg 1898–1987

Rhoda Kellogg was a psychologist and nursery school teacher who devoted her life to studying art created by children. Over the span of more than 30 years, she collected, studied, and categorized several million drawings from preschool-aged children in the United States as well as 30 other countries. Rhoda had a significant impact on nursery school programs in New York and San Francisco from the late 1920s through her retirement in 1969. She believed that developmental stages and universal patterns could be identified within young children's artworks (Golden Gate Kindergarten Association, 2020; Kellogg, 1969; Kellogg & O'Dell, 1967; Primeaux, 2020). From her years of collecting and studying, she determined that children from across the globe create art that is identical until they start imitating art from their own cultures (Primeaux, 2020).

Kellogg (1969) often referred to art-making in the first 5 years as "self-taught art" (p. 39). She acknowledged that line formation exists in paintings and three-dimensional work; however, she primarily focused on line formations in two-dimensional art created with crayons and pencil. She excluded the use of color from her studies because she felt it could be limited by the materials provided to a child. In 1945 Kellogg realized that many of the 3-year-old children she observed were creating mandala (circular) shapes in their artwork. This observation was the catalyst into a search and classification system for other designs and structures that were repeatedly found in the artwork of children. The artwork examined included over a million pieces of art that were produced by children from all over the world and who were from various economic and social backgrounds (Kellogg, 1969). A table of her classifications (Table 10.5) and brief description of each follows.

Pattern stage

The Basic Scribbles are the first classification system Kellogg noted in her book *Analyzing Children's Art*. She identified 20 different scribbles made by 2-year-olds, which she concluded are the "building blocks of art" (Kellogg, 1969, p. 15). She further classified the scribbles into single or multiple scribbles and by the direction of line movement (vertical, horizontal, diagonal, circular). Because children often scribble over their work, it can be difficult to identify clear examples of scribbles. However, as children and their artwork develop, the different types of scribbles can be identified within the artwork of elementary aged children. Beyond line formation, Kellogg also examined and identified 17 different Placement Patterns in the artwork she collected from 2-year-olds (Kellogg & O'Dell, 1967). She determined that patterns created in a well-defined perimeter could be classified based upon where they were placed on a piece of paper. Furthermore, she pointed out that pattern placement required eye–hand coordination and the ability to see, while scribbles did not require eye control (Kellogg, 1969).

TABLE 10.5 Rhoda Kellogg's classification system.

Stage	Age range	Characteristics
Pattern stage	18 months–2 years	20 Basic scribbles
		17 Patterns
Shape stage	2–3 years	Emergent diagram shapes
		Diagrams
Design stage	3–4 years	Combines (2 units of diagrams)
		Aggregates (3 + units of diagrams)
		Humans (late)
Pictorial stage	4–5 years	Humans (early)
		Animals
		Buildings
		Vegetation
		Transportation

For detailed examples of each characteristic, please see Kellogg's Analyzing Children's Art (1969).

Shape stage

Kellogg (1969) noticed that children between ages 2 and 3 created formations which she called Emergent Diagram Shapes. This was a transitional period between the Pattern stage and the Shape stage. She distinguished 17 Emergent Diagram Shapes that included markings such as circular or crossing lines or parallel lines, which imply the beginnings of actual shapes. Children then move into making Diagrams or outlines of shapes that can easily be identified. Six Diagrams were identified and include an odd shape, which means any intentional line that creates an irregular but closed shape, as well as five typical geometric shapes: the rectangle/square, the oval/circle, the triangle, the Greek cross, and a diagonal cross. According to Kellogg, when a child begins making Diagrams, the child has begun to utilize memory and is gaining control over the use of lines. All of the aspects of drawings mentioned in the Pattern and Shape stages are common in artwork of children and adults. Kellogg (1969) reported that "these formations are, in fact, observable in the drawing and painting of all cultures" (p. 43).

Design stage

When a child places two Diagrams together Kellogg refers to this as a **Combine**, for example, an oval and a rectangle drawn together. An **Aggregate** is formed when three or more Diagrams are added to one another. Combines and Aggregates are classified as the Design Stage, which occurs roughly between ages of 3 and 4. The creation of Diagrams, Combines, and Aggregates indicates deliberate thought about the artwork. As children move into creating Aggregates, a sense of balance can be identified in the artwork (Kellogg, 1969; Kellogg & O'Dell, 1967). Observers begin to see what Kellogg calls Mandalas, Suns, and Radials. Kellogg described the various combinations of Designs and provided examples of the numerous different combinations. Kellogg's research into Combines and Aggregates is quite detailed and beyond the scope of this chapter. However, the work she has completed about Combines and Aggregates is quite fascinating and the reader is encouraged to review her work to fully understand the intricacies of the Design Stage (Kellogg, 1969).

Pictorial stage

The Pictorial Stage is situated between ages 4 and 5. Kellogg (1969) does not believe that children attempt to draw humans from what they are observing, but rather they are created as a natural progression in their artistic development when using Combines or Aggregates. The human-like figures begin to develop near the end of the Design Stage and are seen early in the Pictorial Stage. Often when children attempt to create animals the drawings appear to be humans on their sides with elongated torsos. In her book, Kellogg (1969) gives numerous examples of Combines and Aggregates that form together to create buildings. She also supplies countless examples of (vegetation) trees and flowers as well as (transportation) boats, automobiles, airplanes, trains, and rockets that are repeated in the Pictorial Stage. Moreover, the age of 5 can be a significant period in a child's artistic development. Spontaneous art may no longer be encouraged or as readily accepted because of the structure and demands of kindergarten. Upon entering the school years, children are frequently and unfortunately expected to replicate or copy the art of adults in their culture, thus impeding self-taught art. A child's art may be criticized, which may hinder a child from continuing to freely create (Kellogg, 1969).

Judith A. Rubin 1936–present

Judith Rubin, a licensed psychologist and art therapist, began her career in the 1950s as an art teacher in Massachusetts (Junge, 2010). She held various roles throughout her career and used art to influence children in several capacities. She worked with children diagnosed with schizophrenia at the University of Pittsburgh and she was the "art lady" on the PBS television show *Mr. Rogers' Neighborhood*. Rubin was fortunate to have learned from both Edith Kramer and Margaret Naumburg early in her career (Rubin, 2005). These experiences as well as many others throughout her career have provided her with over 50 years worth of studying the artwork of people of all ages.

In her work, Rubin (2005) found that she needed a way to describe artistic development that was not yet met by the present classification systems. In particular, she wanted to be able to include three-dimensional work as well as two-dimensional art, similar to Golomb. Rubin reminds us that these stages may overlap and that because of the variances in development, there could be up to a year's difference when a stage may begin or end for any given child. She categorized artistic development into seven stages: Manipulating, Forming, Naming, Representing, Consolidating, Naturalizing, and Personalizing. Table 10.6 summarizes Rubin's artistic stages.

Additional theories of artistic development

Clearly, there has been a significant amount of interest and research surrounding artistic development in children. In addition to the theorists mentioned here, one may also come across other notable scholars who have examined how children develop artistically. One would greatly benefit from looking into the work of Howard Gardner who studied graphic symbols in children's art. He is known for his proposed U-curve of artistic development, suggesting that adults and young children draw similarly based on their inclusion of expressive qualities while children in middle childhood include little expressive qualities in their artwork (Gardner, 1980, 1982).

More contemporary scholars of artistic development from the 1990s are Marianne Kerlavage, Bernard Darras, and Anna Kindler. Kerlavage (1998) has developed a theory based on her studies of the work of Lowenfeld, Kellogg, Golomb, and Gardner. Similar to Lowenfeld, she has identified six stages through which children progress as they develop artistically (Kerlavage, 1998). Kerlavage takes a more holistic view of art development and includes linguistic and aesthetic domains of development in addition to the traditional cognitive, physical, social, and emotional domains (Harris Lawton et al., 2019). Darras and Kindler (1997) disagree with a linear progression of artistic development. Rather, they have proposed a map-like model of artistic development in which they describe three stages and several ways one may develop in pictorial imagery. They heavily emphasize the interaction of culture and the social environment in the development of art (Darras & Kindler, 1997). Although these newer theories have yet to catch on in the field of art therapy, it seems they are worthy of further investigation and exploration as they include aspects that may have been previously omitted, such as the impact of aesthetic development, as well as social and cultural influences.

Conclusions and comparisons

This chapter could not possibly address all child development theories or theories of artistic development; however, what we have explored are theories frequently taught to students on the path to an art therapy career. While there will

TABLE 10.6 Judith Rubin's stages of artistic development.

Stages	Age range	Characteristics/behaviors
Manipulating	1–2 years	Kinesthetic and sensory exploration of natural materials through smearing, marking, molding, and building. Large body movements and recognition of one's ability to manipulate art materials in order to create a visual mark
Forming	2–3 years	Conscious, deliberate, and improved control with use of materials. Repetitive motions and new ways to manipulate materials (e.g., circular scribbling, pounding/squeezing of clay). Beginnings of nonrepresentational gestalts (shapes/objects). Development of the ability to make enclosed forms
Naming	3–4 years	This stage can overlap with Forming Stage. Giving names to objects or marks that do not actually resemble the identified name. These names of objects are often fluidly changed
Representing	4–6 years	Representations of true objects begin. Early human figures (cephalopods). Unique variations and symbols in sculptures, paintings, and drawings of what holds a child's interest at the time. Boundaries are created and lines are filled in. Exploration of different methods of doing and making
Consolidating	6–9 years	Children find their own preferences for creating and often repeat schemas in their artwork. Color is inconsistently realistic. Overall broadening of creativity during this time. Inclusion of people outside the family, vegetation, buildings, and transportation can now be seen
Naturalizing	9–12 years	Artwork looks more naturalistic. More realistic proportions are used, more accurate spatial relationships develop, sizes and colors of objects become closer to reality. Children at this stage are more concerned about making two-dimensional and three-dimensional artwork look real and may become discouraged or self-critical. Many kids stop making art at this stage
Personalizing	12–18 years	Some children continue developing their art abilities and become quite skilled in rendering realistic artwork. Others who do not develop the skills to create realistic work may turn to abstract work. Many begin to personalize their work and explore their identities and other ways to express themselves in media. Their artwork is more deliberate and egocentric than ever before

Developed from Rubin, J. A. (2005) Child art therapy (25th Anniv. Ed.) pp. 36–46.

always be holes to find in these theories and ways to challenge the ideas of these scholars, we can learn quite a lot from their efforts and apply the useful information they have gathered in our work with children. Whether one subscribes to the term "stage," "pictorial representation," "phase," or "developmental pattern," there does seem to be agreement that all young children under the age of 5 experience a similar progression when first beginning to make marks (Alter-Muri, 2002; Golomb, 2002; Kellogg, 1969), but rather quickly, the child's motivation, interest, talent, and culture begin to have an impact on artistic development (Berk, 2004; Golomb, 2002). Furthermore, there is a consistent message that a child's development is so uniquely individual that art therapist's must remember there will be fluctuations and fluidity in the developmental progression of their young clients. We cannot fit all children neatly into absolute artistic categories by ages, and therefore a broad knowledge base of child development, artistic development, and how to use this information as a guideline is essential for an art therapist.

In order to help organize your thoughts and understanding of the theories and stages just discussed, Table 10.7 contains key information from each (Golomb, 2002). Please take a few minutes to examine how the child development theories overlap and connect with the different artistic development theories. For example, a child who exhibits cognitive skills that align with Piaget's preoperational stage could create art that falls within Lowenfeld's scribbling stage or preschematic stage. Children use their imagination for pretend play in the preoperational stage and this is often reflected in their imaginative drawings. Additionally, Piaget's preoperational stage overlaps with Kellogg's shape, design, and pictorial stages which reflect the increasingly complex cognitive functions that children develop as they mature.

Developmental art therapy with children

The term developmental art therapy was first used by Geraldine Williams, an art educator and art therapist and Mary Wood, an expert in the fields of child development, special education, and psychology (Williams & Wood, 1977). Their work was primarily with children, but many art therapists use a developmental framework to inform their approach with a wide range of clients, including individuals with developmental delays, sensory impairments, and even adults who have experienced trauma (Malchiodi et al., 2003). Throughout this chapter, we have reviewed widely used developmental psychology theories and theories of artistic development. Once an art therapist has a solid foundation of knowledge in these areas, the next step is using these theories to inform one's practice of art therapy.

The following section includes examples of how an art therapist or art teacher might nurture social, emotional, and artistic development with a child. While some of these examples may seem simple enough that anyone could implement them, it is important to remember that art therapists have obtained

TABLE 10.7 Developmental theories and artistic development.

Piaget	Erikson	Lowenfeld	Golomb drawing	Golomb sculpting	Kellogg	Rubin
Sensory Motor Period Birth–2 Years	Trust vs. Mistrust Birth–18 months	Scribble Stage 2–4 Years Substages: • Disordered • Controlled • Naming	Early scribble patterns		Pattern Stage 1–2 Years	Manipulating 1–2 Years
Preoperational Period 2–7 Years	Autonomy vs. Shame/Doubt 18 months-3 Years		Pictorial Representation begins	Passive interactions with 3D media Approximately 2–3 Years	Shape Stage 2–3 Years	Forming 2–3 Years
	Initiative vs. Guilt 3–6 Years		Assigning ages is difficult because as children develop, form, space, color, and composition gradually evolve based on skill, talent, motivation, practice, and persistence.	Children learn quickly, make simple shapes, and eagerly explore media 3 Years	Design Stage 3–4 Years	Naming 3–4 Years
		Preschematic Stage 4–7 Years		Children become representational in 3D materials Age 4	Pictorial Stage 4–5 Years	Representing 4–6 Years
Concrete Operational Period 7–11 Years	Industry vs. Inferiority 6–12 Years	Schematic Stage 7–9 Years Gang Stage 9–11 Years		As child develops, 3D models gain greater detail and differentiation. Skills tend to level-off around 8–9 years of age unless there is motivation and practice, similar to drawing		Consolidating 6–9 Years Naturalizing 9–12 Years
Formal Operational Period 11–15 Years	Identity vs. Role Confusion 12–18 Years	Pseudo-Naturalistic Stage 11–13 Years Adolescent Art 14–17 Years				Personalizing 12–18 Years

hundreds of hours of clinical training, taken a considerable amount of psychology coursework, developed an in-depth knowledge of art materials, and a deep understanding of how art materials can affect a person. Art therapists are trained to understand how art materials can influence clients and how to respond appropriately if a client becomes upset or distraught. Art educators also receive extensive training about child development and have a plethora of knowledge about art materials. A brief section about how people who are not art therapists or art educators can nurture social, emotional, and artistic development is also included.

Goals of developmental art therapy

One of the beginning steps to working with any client in art therapy is to establish goals. Therapeutic goals are individualized for each client based on the needs and abilities of the specific person. When working with children, goals are typically generated with the help of the client and parent or guardian. Including a child in the establishment of goals gives them a voice in their treatment and empowers them to make decisions about the work upon which they are about to embark. Goals also provide a target and help a therapist know what to work toward when developing interventions for a specific client. When working from a developmental art therapy perspective, social emotional growth in behavior, communication, and socialization are some overarching goals (Williams & Wood, 2010). More specifically, an art therapist might have a goal of helping a client to identify and communicate their thoughts and feelings through the art process. Goals in these areas can be achieved through a multitude of methods including, but not limited to, adapting art materials as necessary, helping clients with acquiring more complex motor or social skills, or providing opportunities for sensory stimulation (Malchiodi et al., 2003).

An art therapist's approach

Williams and Wood (2010) noted five basic beliefs as foundational to a developmental art therapy approach. In order to best support a client from this framework one must:

focus on strengths and skills of the child/client
be knowledgeable of and follow developmental guidelines
create individually relevant art directives
help the child/client expand exploration of art materials
provide pleasurable and successful opportunities to create art.

Based on their experiences and research, Williams and Wood (2010) established five stages of working with children from a developmental approach. These stages align closely with Erikson's stages of development and each stage has its own comprehensive goal with objectives for social emotional growth in the areas of behavior, communication, and socialization. The ages associated with each stage are approximate guidelines and should not be rigidly held when working with clients. Additionally, clients who have experienced trauma, developmental delays, or sensory challenges may align with stages that are different than their chronological ages, thus emphasizing the importance of understanding developmental markers. Before working with a client, an art therapist must conduct an assessment in order to best understand the developmental level and to know where to begin working with an individual. A summary of key information about a developmental art approach is listed in Table 10.8. Please note the ages are approximate and should not be rigidly applied.

Art therapy examples

The following section provides an overview of information and examples of how an art therapist or an art educator might work with a client in each stage identified by Williams and Wood (2010). As previously noted, an art therapist would select interventions and materials based on their knowledge of a client's developmental level and the goals for that client. This type of work could take place in a school, hospital, outpatient clinic, or any another setting where an art therapist might work. For additional and more detailed information about working from a developmental approach, read *Developmental Art Therapy in the Classroom, 2nd Ed.*

Stage one

In Stage One of a developmental approach, the art therapist wants the client to have a pleasurable experience with the art environment. Children at this stage become engaged when their senses are stimulated and their interest can be maintained by frequently offering opportunities to explore new and varying materials that appeal to all of the senses. Utilizing commonplace materials or found objects such as egg cartons, cardboard, leaves, buttons, and scrap fabric can offer a variety of textures (Williams & Wood, 1977, 2010). Offering scented art materials, using shaving cream, or allowing children to smell a food before creating art are ways to incorporate the sense of smell. Letting children create art with food such as candy or fruit and allowing children to make or use lickable stickers are two ways to involve the sense of taste. The auditory sense can be addressed through incorporating music or rhythm during the art–making process. Williams and Wood (2010) provide the following suggestions for conducting a successful Stage One art activity (p. 15):

Find materials that are most arousing
Accept ALL first attempts to connect with the material
Begin with short, one-step experiences that have instant results
Keep activities to 3–5 min with brief instructions, using simple key words
Establish routine in a large work area that is easy to clean.

TABLE 10.8 **Developmental art therapy stages, goals, and objectives.**

Stage	Goal	Leading strategies	Art therapist task and role	Art environment
Stage One (birth to 2 years)	Responding to the art environment with pleasure	Offer stimulating materials, provide structure/routine, give comforting feedback and redirection, supportive physical proximity	**Task:** Assist children in responding to materials **Role:** Care and nurture, encourage responses, make positive things happen	Consistent routine, exploratory materials, enticing rather than demanding, attractive colors and textures
Stage Two	Responding to art materials with success	Abundant encouragement to participate, positive feedback, redirection, demonstrate desired actions	**Task:** Assist with art materials **Role:** Help them find abundant pleasure in artwork	Encourage imagination with and exploration of materials
Stage Three	Learning skills for successful participation in group art projects	Positive feedback about individual contribution, redirection, reflect positive words and actions, connect actions to feelings, establish positive rules	**Task:** Assist with successful participation with peers **Role:** Group leader, motivator, redirector	Focus on working as a group or team
Stage Four	Valuing individual artwork and contributions to group projects	Positive feedback from peers and adults, help students critique own artwork	**Task:** Encourage children to value contributing to the group project **Role:** Group facilitator, advocate, role model	Group projects with a focus on reality
Stage Five	Applying art skills independently in new situations	Positive feedback, encouragement (ideally from peers), reflection of values	**Task:** Teach children to use art skills independently **Role:** Mentor, advisor, supportive adult	Open studio settings to encourage independent work

Adapted from Developmental Art Therapy in the Classroom by Williams and Wood (2010).

Sample activity

Provide children a handful of clay, placing it directly in their hands. Encourage the children to squeeze the clay. Once they have explored this, and before they lose interest, demonstrate how to pound the clay. Then, encourage the children to explore this movement. Before they become distracted, demonstrate rolling the clay on the table. Finally, allow them the opportunity to manipulate the clay with an appropriate and safe clay tool. While this is taking place, playing a rhythmic song would engage another sense and perhaps respond with rhythmic motions while exploring the clay (Williams & Wood, 1977, 2010).

Stage two

According to Williams and Wood (2010) the primary goal of Stage Two is to help the client respond to art materials with success. In the previous stage, the art therapist frequently has to offer assistance both physically and verbally. However, in Stage Two, there is a focus on the client successfully partaking in art activities with minimal assistance from the facilitator. Clients in this stage may begin talking about or explaining their artwork without prompting and may ask to use specific materials. At this stage of development, one would want the client to, "respond to the art therapist as a significant, trusted adult and to the art activity with expectations of success" (Williams & Wood, 2010, p.28). An increased attention span improves the ability to follow directions at this age and children can create artwork on their own through coloring, drawing, and even cutting paper. Williams and Wood (2010) provide the following suggestions for conducting a successful Stage Two art activity (p. 30).

Use materials that each child can use successfully
Demonstrate the activity in a simple and brief manner before giving materials
Start by providing individual art supplies
Slowly move children from using their own supplies to sharing with a partner
Work toward a small group creating a collaborative piece by individually creating art and then displaying it together.

Sample activity

Demonstrate how to tear paper into mosaic pieces, use dramatic movements to keep children engaged. Provide children with colorful paper and encourage them to tear the papers into pieces. Role model how to attach torn pieces to a paper to make a collage. Ask the children questions to stimulate verbal exchanges, for example, ask them to talk about what they have created and how they created it. They can also be encouraged to observe others' artwork (Williams & Wood, 1977, 2010).

Stages three and four

Williams and Wood (2010) discussed Stages Three and Four together because the transition between the two can be very tenuous and challenging to discern.

Stage Three of a developmental art therapy approach aims to help clients learn the skills necessary for participating in group art projects with success. In Stage Four an art therapist wants to see clients value their own individual work while also contributing to projects with a group of peers. During this time, the artwork created is dramatically different from the previous stages. Children in these stages are able to create images that are more organized and they can express themselves through the representations they create. Trust in the art therapist and the art activity is vital during this stage. In order to help children trust themselves, creating an atmosphere where no one fails and each child's creative strives are respected is essential (Williams & Wood, 1977, 2010).

Some basic rules about behavior expectations within a group can be extremely helpful during Stages Three and Four. Williams and Wood (2010) offer a few that have been successful, including: (1) talk freely, but your hands should be creating while you talk; (2) put art supplies back where they belong when you are finished; (3) do not touch others' artwork; (4) do not throw away artwork that you think you have messed up, write your name on it and decide if you want to share it or not, then get a new piece of paper; (5) you can create as many pictures as you'd like; and (6) if you are being "mean" to others during group, you will be asked to step away from the group (p. 53).

Stage three sessions

When facilitating a session with clients in Stage Three it is best to focus on the involvement of the group members with one another through the art materials rather than the final art product. Planning sessions that entice and intrigue children of this age is key to a successful session. Basic art supplies are sufficient for this age group, but an occasional introduction of a nontraditional art material or varied materials can keep them engaged. Providing minimal instructions and efficiently giving the instructions are also important. As clients become comfortable, more complex, multistep activities can be given. As children begin to build their confidence they will start to use art materials with ease and will need little assistance or guidance from the adult, but instead, they will reach out to peers to ask for help (Williams & Wood, 1977, 2010).

Sample activities

Encourage a group of children to collectively create and perform a play. During art sessions, they can create props and a backdrop.

Ask children to use recycled materials to make musical instruments. They can create a band name, design a logo, and then perform a concert with their instruments.

Propose the idea of a group creating a collaborative book or game. After deciding on a topic and discussing the plan, each member can create a page for the book or they can all work together to design a game and the pieces needed to play the game.

Stage four sessions

Art sessions in this stage can be very exciting for participants because directives can include topics and ideas from real-world experiences and events. The structure of the art sessions can now be modified because while some routine is still important, children at this age can adapt to changes and art directives can be modified to varying artistic abilities. This is an age when children can attempt new and different art materials. They can be challenged with a variety of tasks and should be encouraged to attempt all art directives given. Once a child has attempted the provided activity, they can select free-choice art projects if the planned one does not interest them. Kids at this stage may be interested in learning new drawing techniques or ways that they can improve their work, thus opportunities for self-evaluation arise (Williams & Wood, 1977, 2010).

Sample activities

Take a group of children to the zoo and ask them to sketch several animals in a journal. Return to the art room and ask the children to work together to create a map or three-dimensional model of the zoo and the animals.

Magnify something that a child might not typically examine up close and have them draw the magnification. For example, drawing an enlarged insect or flower helps to increase awareness of the world around them.

Lead children on a nature walk or hike and ask them to look closely at leaves, rocks, sticks, etc., to find patterns that they can replicate in their artwork. Upon returning to the art room, have them create patterns on 5×5 square pieces of paper and then work together to arrange them into a nature pattern patchwork quilt.

Stage five

Learning how to apply art skills without assistance from adults in new settings and situations is the overarching goal for Stage Five of developmental art therapy. Williams and Wood (2010) do not specifically discuss this stage in as much detail as the previous four stages because a group is not required to achieve the goal. This fifth stage may begin for a teen as they are ready to leave a group and as they complete a journey through developmental art therapy groups. However, having support from adults in one's life beyond the therapeutic group is key to assisting these youth in continuing to reach developmental milestones in the teenage years. Teenagers in this stage do not need the specialized skills of a therapist, but they can continue to build problem-solving skills, self-esteem, and other skills through continued participation in art-making (Williams & Wood, 2010).

Exhibiting artwork from a developmental art therapy group

Art experiences within a developmental framework should achieve two criteria: inspire attainment of developmental markers and decrease emotional and behavioral issues. These criteria can be met through both the artistic process, which a child experiences during hands-on art-making, as well as through the actual finished products a child creates (Williams & Wood, 2010). These final products can then be exhibited in a manner that supports achievement of the two criteria. Whether or not an art therapist should exhibit client artwork is a regular topic in the field of art therapy, and can create ethical dilemmas with some populations for various reasons (Moon & Goldstein Nolan, 2019). While some settings may not be appropriate for displaying client artwork, there can be opportunities to support social, emotional, and other developmental progress through art exhibits. Careful consideration and planning should be undertaken when preparing for an exhibit of artwork from a developmental art therapy population. Structured and detailed recommendations for successfully facilitating an art exhibit with this population have been described in the literature (Williams & Wood, 2010).

Adapting art materials

Beyond these stages, art therapists must know how to adapt art materials for varying ages and abilities. This skill ensures that safety is a top priority when working with young clients or with clients who have different abilities. Adapting the environment or art materials is also a way to help clients be successful in the art-making process, thus achieving a common goal for this population of increasing self-esteem or confidence. Simple adaptations such as taping paper down to the table or adding foam or rubber grips to drawing materials can make a significant impact in a person's ability to use art materials. Retrofitting a paintbrush or ceramic tool can help clients more easily create and have control over materials. Utilizing adjustable tables or easels can make art surfaces more accessible. Adaptations such as these are limitless and invaluable when working with people who have developmental delays or differing abilities. These types of adaptations give clients an opportunity to work independently and achieve success in a world where their abilities are often dismissed or discounted.

These examples of developmental art therapy interventions barely touch the surface of the work that an art therapist can help facilitate through a developmental approach. A well-trained and experienced art therapist can create numerous art directives and utilize art materials in thousands of ways to help clients achieve developmental milestones in social, emotional, and artistic development. As previously noted, some of these activities may appear simple enough for anyone to facilitate, and there may be times when nonart therapists do lead these types of activities. The difference between an art therapist and a nonart therapist leading these activities is the goal, or intention, the knowledge of how children may react to art materials emotionally or behaviorally, and the therapeutic helping skills that an art therapist possesses. For a more extensive list of art activities and directives for children in Stages One through Four, please refer to *Developmental Art Therapy in the Classroom* (Williams & Wood, 2010).

Nurturing development through art

Art therapists have specialized training and skills that inform their work with children and adults of all ages. Art therapists are particularly equipped to know how to help people of all developmental levels and abilities because of their knowledge of child and artistic development. However, this does not mean that they are the only people who can nurture children as they grow. In fact, many people can support artistic development in a variety of ways. An open mind and an encouraging attitude about curiosity and exploration are key characteristics for nurturing artistic development(Boriss-Krimsky, 1999). A willingness to observe and accept art without judgment is imperative to creating positive art experiences for anyone courageous enough to create art and allow others to witness the process. Providing opportunities to safely explore art media without pressure or expectations allows children to discover and problem-solve. Constructing an inviting and appropriately stimulating environment for making art is crucial. Helping children notice the world around them helps to open their eyes and bring awareness to new and different experiences. Encouraging them to observe and examine their environment and culture, such as art, other people, and nature can enhance their developing curiosity and awareness. There will always be an opportunity to nurture a child when they are given the chance to explore art materials and express themselves. Here are a few things you can do the next time you have the opportunity to support a child's engagement with art:

- Help a child notice colors and textures in nature or while walking through a store.
- Make basic art supplies available at all times and encourage frequent exploration.
- Honor their artwork by hanging it for all to see.
- Encourage children to find creative ways to use household materials for art.
- Let a child see you creating art just for fun.
- Talk to children about artwork they see and artwork they create.
- Remind children there is no right or wrong way to create art.

Scope of practice

As an undergraduate student, where in the realm of art therapy is it acceptable for one to practice? At this point in your studies, you have only scratched the surface of learning about many topics. In order to practice art therapy, one must continue to delve more deeply into these topics, including theory and the art-making process, as well as developing professional helping skills. In the United States, one should only say they are an art therapist or that they are conducting art therapy after having completed a master's degree that meets the requirements of the Art Therapy Credentials Board. Even without being an art therapist, you can still be a person who nurtures artistic development in the children you come across in your life. Art therapists would agree that the more people who encourage children to engage with art materials throughout their childhood and adolescence, the better. If you have the opportunity to positively influence a child by creating art with them or introducing them to a new medium, take it! Find sites in the community where you can observe or help facilitate art-making opportunities for people of all ages. Take time to observe children in different settings while they play and make art. If possible, volunteer at a school, daycare, or summer camp as these could be valuable learning experiences. The more art-making you observe, the better you will understand child development and artistic development.

Art experientials and reflection questions

1. Find a drawing from your childhood or adolescence. In what artistic or developmental stage would you place the artwork? Can you remember what was happening in your family and life during this time? What stands out to you in the picture?
2. Reflect on your social emotional development. Who or what had a significant impact on your growth in this area? Create an image of what you see as the biggest influence on your social emotional growth.
3. Identify a family member or friend who would be willing to let you observe their child create artwork. Spend time observing how they work with drawing materials and clay or playdough. What materials do they handle well? Ask them to talk to you about what they create. Create art alongside them and see what happens.
4. What were your favorite art materials to use as a child? Who provided them? How often did you use them and why do you think you liked those particular materials? See if you can find similar materials and then create a piece of art in response to your feelings about creating art as a child.
5. Can you remember a positive or negative experience with creating art? Did someone influence your art experiences and your desire to continue or discontinue working with art materials? If so, how? Create an image about what you remember from the experience and how it has impacted you.
6. Pay attention to "child" artwork you see in movies and television shows. Can you align the artistic development of the artwork with one of the artistic stages discussed in this chapter? Do you think the artwork was actually created by a child and is the age implied by the movie or show realistic in relation to what characteristics are included in the artwork?
7. Discuss with your classmates: Do you agree with Piaget that a child's developmental domains parallel their artistic development, or does artistic development have an intrinsic process in its own right?
8. Which theory of artistic development is most appealing to you? Explain your thoughts about artistic development and how you will use the theories presented in this chapter to inform your studies and future work.

Additional resources

Netflix Docuseries "Babies" (2020)
Creative and Mental Growth, 8th edition (1987) by Viktor Lowenfeld and W. Lambert Brittain
Child Art in Context: A Cultural and Comparative Perspective (2002) by Claire Golomb
Yardsticks: Child and Adolescent Development Ages 4–14, 4th edition (2018) by Chip Wood
The Artful Parent: Simple Ways to Fill Your Family's Life with Art and Creativity (2019) by Jean Van't Hul

Chapter terms

Aggregate
Artistic development
Child development
Cognitive development
Combine
Conservation
Developmental art therapy
Egocentric
Folding over
Imitative actions
Language development
Object permanence
Physical development
Prerepresentational actions
Representational development
Romancing
Schema
Social emotional development
Verbal designation
X-ray drawing

References

Alter-Muri, S. (2002). Viktor Lowenfeld revisited: A review of Lowenfeld's preschematic, schematic, and gang age stages. *Art Therapy: Journal of the American Art Therapy Association, 40*(3), 170–192.

American Psychological Association. (2020). *APA dictionary of psychology*. https://dictionary.apa.org/child-development.

Babakr, Z., Mohamedamin, P., & Kakamad, K. (2019). Piaget's cognitive developmental theory: Critical review. *Education Quarterly Review, 2*(3), 517–524.

Berk, L. E. (2004). *Development through the lifespan* (3rd ed.). Pearson Education.

Boriss-Krimsky, C. (1999). *The creativity handbook: A visual arts guide for parents and teachers*. Charles C. Thomas.

Brown, T. T., & Jernigan, T. L. (2012). Brain development during the preschool years. *Neuropsychology Review, 22*(4), 313–333. https://doi.org/10.1007/s11065-012-9214-1.

Cintas, H. (1989). Cross-cultural variation in infant motor development. *Physical & Occupational Therapy in Pediatrics, 8*(4), 1–20.

Darras, B., & Kindler, A. M. (1997). Map of artistic development. In A. M. Kindler (Ed.), *Child development in art* (pp. 17–44). National Art Education Association.

Erikson, E. (1968). *Identity: Youth and crisis*. W.W. Norton & Company.

Gardner, H. (1980). *Artful scribbles: The significance of children's drawings*. Basic Books.

Gardner, H. (1982). *Art, mind, & brain: A cognitive approach to creativity*. Basic Books.

Golden Gate Kindergarten Association. (2020). *Welcome to the Rhoda Kellogg collection*. https://rhodakellogg.com/.

Golomb, C. (1992). Art and the young child: Another look at the developmental question. In *Making meaning through art conference, Urbana, IL*. https://files.eric.ed.gov/fulltext/ED352163.pdf.

Golomb, C. (1994). Drawing as representation: The child's acquisition of a meaningful graphic language. *Visual Arts Research*, *20*(2), 14–28. https://www.jstor.org/stable/20715828?seq=13#metadata_info_tab_contents.

Golomb, C. (2002). *Child art in context: A cultural and comparative perspective*. American Psychological Association.

Golomb, C. (2011). *The creation of imaginary worlds: The role of art, magic, and dreams in child development*. Jessica Kingsley Publishers.

Harris Lawton, P., Walker, M. A., & Green, M. (2019). *Community-based art education across the lifespan: Finding common ground*. National Art Education Association.

Jenkins, C., Fineran, K. R., & Lange, A. (2016). Birth and infancy: Physical and cognitive development. In D. Capuzzi, & M. D. Stauffer (Eds.), *Human growth and development across the lifespan: Applications for counselors* (1st ed., pp. 113–149). Wiley.

Jessica Kingsley Publishers. (2011). *An interview with author Claire Golomb on child development and "The Creation of Imaginary Worlds."*. http://www.jkp.com/jkpblog/2011/02/int-claire-golomb-the-creation-of-imaginary-worlds/#:~:text=Claire%20Golomb%20is%20a%20Professor,and%20graduate%20students%20of%20psychology.

Junge, M. (2010). *The modern history of art therapy in the United States*. Charles C. Thomas.

Kellogg, R. (1969). *Analyzing Children's art*. Mayfield Publishing Company.

Kellogg, R., & O'Dell, S. (1967). *The psychology of children's art*. Random House.

Kerlavage, M. (1998). Understanding the learner. In B. J. Potthoff (Ed.), *Creating meaning through art: Teacher as choice maker* (pp. 23–66). Prentice-Hall, Inc.

Lourenco, O., & Machado, A. (1996). In defense of Piaget's theory: A reply to 10 common criticisms. *Psychological Review*, *103*(1), 143–164. https://doi.org/10.1037/0033-295X.103.1.143.

Lowenfeld, V. (1954). *Your child and his art: A guide for parents* (1st ed.). Macmillan Publishing Company.

Lowenfeld, V., & Brittain, W. L. (1987). *Creative and mental growth* (8th ed.). Macmillan Publishing Company.

Maier, H. (1969). *Three theories of child development: The contributions of Erik H. Erikson, Jean Piaget, and Robert R. Sears, And their applications (revised)*. Harper & Row Publishers.

Malchiodi, C. A., Kim, D.-Y., & Choi, W. S. (2003). Developmental art therapy. In C. A. Malchiodi (Ed.), *Handbook of art therapy*. Guilford Press.

Maschinot, B. (2008). *The changing face of the United States: The influence of culture on early child development*. Zero to Three. https://kshomevisiting.org/wp-content/uploads/2015/09/Influence-of-Culture-on-devlopment-0-to-3.pdf.

Moon, B., & Goldstein Nolan, E. (2019). *Ethical issues in art therapy* (4th ed.). Charles C. Thomas.

Piaget, J. (1936). *Origins of intelligence in the child*. Routledge & Kegan Paul.

Piaget, J., & Inhelder, B. (1969). *The psychology of the child (H. weaver, trans.)*. Basic Books, Inc.

Primeaux, M. (2020). *Biographical database of militant women suffragists. Biography of Rhoda Kellogg, 1898–1987*. https://documents.alexanderstreet.com/d/1008297974.

Richards, A. E. (1974). History of developmental stages of child art: 1857 to 1921. *Faculty Lecture Series 1974–1975*. Ball State University. https://dmr.bsu.edu/digital/collection/FacLectures/id/1664.

Rubin, J. A. (2005). *Child art therapy (25th anniversary)*. Wiley.

Shore, A. (2013). *The practitioner's guide to child art therapy: Fostering creativity and relational growth* (1st ed.). Routledge.

Slonim, M. (1991). *Children, culture, and ethnicity: Evaluating and understanding the impact.* Garland Publishing, Inc.

Williams, G., & Wood, M. (1977). *Developmental art therapy*. University Park Press.

Williams, G., & Wood, M. M. (2010). *Developmental art therapy in the classroom* (2nd ed.). Xlibris.

World Health Organization. (2020). *Early child development*. World Health Organization. https://www.who.int/topics/early-child-development/en/.

Chapter 11

Art therapy for psychological disorders and mental health

Meera Rastogi, PhD, ATR-BC[a] and Janet K. Kempf, MA, ATR-BC, LPC, NCC[a,b]

[a]*Psychology and Pre-Art Therapy Programs, University of Cincinnati, Clermont College, Batavia, OH, United States,* [b]*Good Samaritan Hospital, Cincinnati, OH, United States*

Voices from the field

As you begin to express your imagery through art, you will discover your inner voice- the voice of your heart. With that voice to guide you, a voice that speaks in imagery not words, you will create healing art that will transform your body, mind, and spirit.

(Ganim, 1999, p. 19)

Learning outcomes

After reading this chapter, you will be able to

1. Define mental illness and discuss its prevalence in the United States.
2. Describe the development and current use of the Diagnostic and Statistical Manual of Mental Disorders.
3. Identify three ways stigma affects mental health treatment.
4. Articulate how mental health recovery and art therapy are related.
5. Explain the historical connection of the visual arts in attempts to understand mental illness and the role of art-making for healing in institutions.
6. Define the outsider art or the self-taught artist movement and name three self-taught artists.
7. Identify the specific ways art therapy support mental health and mental health recovery.
8. Discuss the results of qualitative and quantitative research on the effectiveness of art therapy with individuals diagnosed with specific mental health conditions.
9. Identify biological, psychological, and sociological influences on psychological disorders.
10. Explain the spectrum of treatment settings available to individuals seeking help for mental health issues.

Foundations of Art Therapy. https://doi.org/10.1016/B978-0-12-824308-4.00008-9

Chapter overview

This chapter begins by defining mental illness and provides criteria to understand when symptoms reach a significant level to be considered a mental health condition. Readers will learn about the history of diagnosing mental disorders and how therapists diagnose patients today. Historical connections are presented between art and mental illness and how these helped to shape the current field of art therapy. The chapter also describes ways art therapy supports mental health and mental health recovery. The chapter concludes with information about art therapy for specific disorders and in different settings.

Introduction

Imagine you are in a stadium filled with 50,000 fans. How many of those fans do you think have a **mental illness**? In the United States, one in five adults live with a mental illness (NIMH, 2021) which equates to 10,000 of the 50,000 fans. Who are these one in five adults?

Young adults between the ages of 18 and 25 have the highest rates of mental illness in the United States as compared to other age groups (NIMH, 2021). Most recently, COVID-19 pandemic surveys found the symptoms of mental illness remained high for college students (The Healthy Minds Network and American College Health Association, 2020) as students reported increases in fears related to financial stressors, changes in living situations, and difficulty accessing mental health care (The Healthy Minds Network and American College Health Association, 2020). Only 13.8% of adults age 50 or older report mental health symptoms. However, males over the age of 65 years have the highest rate of suicide as compared to younger individuals (NIMH, 2019, 2021). According to the National Institute of Mental Health (NIMH) (NIMH, 2021), the prevalence rate of any mental illness is higher among women (22.35%) than men (15.1%). This difference may be partially due to the socialization of men in the United States. Men are socialized to be strong and not seek help and thus are less likely to report symptoms of mental illness. Individuals who identify with two or more races report higher levels of mental illness symptoms (28.65%), followed by those who identify as White (20.4%), Native Hawaiian/Pacific Islander (19.4%), Indigenous people/Native American/Alaskan Native (18.9%), Black (16.2%), Hispanic (15.2%), and Asian/Asian American (14.5%) (NIMH, 2021). These rates may be due to cultural influences; for example, some people learn to internalize issues and tend not to share symptoms with others (U.S. Department of Health and Human Services, 2001).

The global economic impact of mental illness will cost the US $16.1 trillion between 2011 and 2030 "with dramatic impact on productivity and quality of life" (Bloom et al., 2011, p. 5). In 2012 the World Health Organization (WHO) adopted a resolution in response to the burden that mental illness places on global societies and developed the WHO Mental Health Action Plan,

2013–2020 (World Health Organization, 2013), which acknowledges that mental illness affects, and is affected by, other medical diseases.

How many of these people experiencing symptoms receive treatment? Less than half of the individuals who experience symptoms receive treatment in a given year (NIMH, 2021). Women (47.6%) and adults between 26 and 49 (43.3%) and over 50 years (44.2%) are more likely to seek treatment than men (34.8%) and young adults between 18 and 25 years (38.4%) (NIMH, 2021). **Stigma** was originally described as "an attribute that is deeply discrediting" (Goffman, 1963, p. 3). Therefore, being "labeled" with a mental illness may carry a stigma. This may be one reason that people do not seek treatment. Working to reduce stigma is an important challenge that prevents those living with a mental health diagnosis from obtaining treatment; stigma will be defined and discussed in depth later in the chapter.

Defining mental illness

In the United States, the NIMH differentiates any mental illness from serious mental illness. According to the NIMH, "**Any mental illness** is defined as a mental, behavioral, or emotional disorder" (2021, para. 3). **Serious mental illness** is the term frequently used when an individual experiences "serious functional impairment, which substantially interferes with or limits one or more major life activities" (NIMH, 2021, para. 4).

The American Psychiatric Association's (APA) **Diagnostic and Statistical Manual of Mental Disorders**, Fifth Edition, Text Revised (DSM-5-TR; American Psychiatric Association, 2022) defined a **mental disorder** as "a syndrome characterized by clinically significant disturbance in an individual's cognition, emotional regulation, or behavior that results in dysfunction in the psychological, biological, or developmental process underlying mental functioning" (American Psychiatric Association, 2022, Definition of a Mental Disorder section). But how do you know when a symptom crosses the line and becomes a mental illness or psychological disorder? Next, we will highlight some key criteria that can help differentiate when symptoms become a disorder.

Monte, a 10-year-old, African-American male, loves to draw with red pens only. When the art therapist asks him to use a different colored pen, Monte adamantly refuses. Does Monte's preference for red pens reveal symptoms of a mental health condition? Neema, a 10-year-old, Asian Indian female, scribbles all over the paper and onto the desk. She will also scribble on the wall, her clothes, and the floor. Neema's scribbling makes it difficult for her to develop friendships as other children do not want to be scribbled on. Is Neema's behavior a symptom of a mental illness? It can be difficult to differentiate a problematic behavior from a psychological disorder, even for therapists. When evaluating whether symptoms are part of a possible mental illness, the therapist will look for key features to help determine if the symptom has developed into a condition that needs treatment. These features used by clinicians are (1) clinical significance; (2) psychological, biological, or developmental dysfunction;

(3) distress to self or others; and (4) the behavior is not due to religion, politics, sexuality, or political views (Whitbourne, 2020).

Clinical significance is where the person is unable to accomplish daily goals due to the symptoms or behavior (Whitbourne, 2020). Can Monte go to school if he can only write with red pens? Can Neema go to work if she needs to scribble on things? Monte can probably attend school and perform daily activities even though he has a strong preference for red pens; however, Neema's scribbling prevents her from being able to attend events, make friends, and thus interferes with her ability to function.

In order to classify a behavior as part of a mental illness, the behavior must have a psychological, biological, or developmental dysfunction. Is Monte or Neema's preference for red pens and scribbling due to atypical psychological, biological, or developmental dysfunction?

Distress is when the symptoms cause the individual to feel upset or suffer. Does Monte suffer by only using red pens? Is Neema upset by the scribbling or by not having friends? In both cases, Monte and Neema do experience distress.

Does Monte's red pen preference reflect a political party practice? Does Neema's scribbling represent a religious practice? If the behavior can be attributed to a specific religion or political belief, the behavior would not be classified as symptoms of a mental illness.

By highlighting these criteria in the definition of a mental disorder, you can begin to differentiate behaviors as unique qualities of a particular person versus symptoms that need treatment. However, to make an official diagnosis, qualified clinicians receive training using the Diagnostic and Statistical Manual of Mental Disorders, Fifth Edition, Text Revised (DSM-5-TR; American Psychiatric Association, 2022). How did the DSM come into existence and what does the DSM contain? The next section describes how the DSM developed from its first edition (1952) to the version used today (5th ed., text revised; DSM-5-TR, American Psychiatric Association, 2022).

History and development of the Diagnostic and Statistical Manual of Mental Disorders

Emil Kraepelin, a German psychiatrist, developed the first known classification of mental diseases based on symptoms (Strous et al., 2016) in a textbook entitled *Clinical Psychiatry* (Kraepelin & Diefendorf, 1915). Kraepelin incorporated both psychological and medical explanations of mental illness but struggled with identifying clear distinctions among the disorders. In 1921, the American Medico-Psychological Association (later to become the American Psychiatric Association) worked with the New York Academy of Medicine to create the first American Medical Association Standard Classified Nomenclature of Disease (DSM History, n.d.). In 1952, the American Psychiatric Association developed the first Diagnostic and Statistical Manual of Mental Disorders (DSM) publication. A revised version, entitled the DSM-II, was expected to include clearer definitions of mental disorders but was similar to the original DSM (DSM

History, n.d.). The DSM-III was developed and subsequently published in 1980 and featured several key changes: a multiaxial diagnostic system, research-based diagnostic criteria, and avoided causal explanations for the disorders. The DSM-III-R (published in 1987) sought feedback from a workgroup to establish clearer criteria for disorders and resolve inconsistencies. After 6 years of work by more than 1000 professionals, the DSM-IV was published in 1994. Disorders were reorganized, some were added, and others were deleted. In 2000 workgroups were formed to create research-based arguments for the next version of the DSM, the DSM-5. After a 12-year process that involved hundreds of professionals and organizations (American Psychiatric Association, 2013), the DSM-5 is argued to have greater clinical utility than prior versions since it provides diagnostic criteria and science-based findings on each disorder. In 2019, the American Psychiatric Association created a Revision Subcommittee to review material in the DSM-5 that might be out of date, improve attention to the effects of racism and discrimination, and further clarify the criteria used for diagnosis (American Psychiatric Association, 2022, DSM-5 Text Revision Process section). A text revision of the DSM-5 (DSM-5-TR) was released by the American Psychiatric Association in March 2022. The DSM-5-TR clarifies several components used to make diagnoses, and includes one new diagnosis, prolonged grief disorder. The United States continues to use the DSM for psychopathology criteria and research, while 70% of the world prefers to use the **International Classification of Diseases** (ICD) (Neimeyer, 2020). The ICD is a free source that lists all health conditions. ICD codes are helpful for worldwide tracking of disease but differ from the DSM in that the ICD only lists the conditions. *The ICD-11 is available for free online* (https://www.who.int/standards/classifications/classification-of-diseases). Since the science and understanding of mental illness is constantly evolving, the DSM and ICD are revised every few years.

The DSM-5-TR is divided into three sections: (1) DSM-5 Basics, (2) Diagnostic Criteria and Codes, and (3) Emerging Measures and Modules. Section 2, Diagnostic Criteria and Codes, contains information and criteria for each of the mental health conditions or psychological disorders. The mental health conditions and psychological disorders are arranged by age of onset and are ordered by how related the disorders are to one another. The sections begin with neurodevelopmental disorders (such as intellectual disability, communication disorders, autism spectrum disorders, etc.). Please see Table 11.1 for a list of the 22 types of psychological disorders. This 1000 plus page book's goal is to aid in more reliable and consistent diagnoses by providing "the best available description of how mental disorders are expressed and can be recognized by trained clinicians" (American Psychiatric Association, 2013, p. xli).

Clinical diagnosis

Mental health professionals, such as art therapists, use a clinical diagnosis to help guide a client's treatment (American Psychiatric Association, 2013, 2022). The DSM-5 and DSM-5-TR assist in the diagnosis of mental health conditions

TABLE 11.1 Disorder types in the Diagnostic and Statistical Manual of Mental Disorders, fifth edition.

Disorder type	Description	Examples
Neurodevelopmental disorders	Disorders that have an early onset, often in childhood, that create a wider range of impairments.	Intellectual disability, communication disorders, autism spectrum disorder, attention-deficit/hyperactivity disorder, specific learning disorder, motor disorders
Schizophrenia spectrum and other psychotic disorders	Disorders that show one of these five features: delusions, hallucinations, disorganized thinking, disorganized or abnormal motor behavior, or inhibited emotional expression.	Delusional disorder, brief psychotic disorder, schizophreniform disorder, schizophrenia, schizoaffective disorder, substance-induced psychotic disorder, catatonia
Bipolar and related disorders	Disorder of mood that includes manic episodes.	Bipolar I disorder, bipolar II disorder, cyclothymic disorder, substance-induced bipolar and related disorder
Depressive disorders	Disorders that primarily feature a sad or irritable mood.	Disruptive mood dysregulation disorder, major depressive disorder, persistent depressive disorder, premenstrual dysphoric disorder, substance-induced depressive disorder
Anxiety disorders	Disorders where fear or anxiety is out of proportion to stimulus.	Separation anxiety disorder, selective mutism, specific phobia, social anxiety disorder, panic disorder, agoraphobia, generalized anxiety disorder, substance-induced anxiety disorder
Obsessive-compulsive and related disorders	Disorders where obsessions and compulsions are present.	Obsessive-compulsive disorder, body dysmorphic disorder, hoarding disorder, trichotillomania, excoriation, substance-induced obsessive-compulsive disorder
Trauma- and stressor-related disorders	Disorders that result from a traumatic event.	Disinhibited-social engagement disorder, posttraumatic stress disorder, acute stress disorder, adjustment disorders
Dissociative disorders	Disorders of an interruption in consciousness.	Dissociative identity disorder, dissociative amnesia, depersonalization/derealization disorder

Somatic symptoms and related disorders	Disorders that feature physical symptoms.	Somatic symptom disorder, illness anxiety disorder, conversion disorder, factitious disorder
Feeding and eating disorders	Dysfunction that is focused on eating.	Pica, rumination disorder, avoidant/restrictive food intake disorder, anorexia nervosa, bulimia nervosa, binge-eating disorder
Elimination disorders	Disorders of inappropriate elimination of urine or feces.	Encopresis
Sleep-wake disorders	Disorders that feature problems with sleep or wakefulness.	Insomnia disorder, hypersomnolence disorder, narcolepsy, breathing-related sleep disorders, circadian-rhythm sleep-wake disorders, parasomnias
Sexual dysfunctions	Disturbances in sexual functioning.	Delayed ejaculation, erectile disorder, female orgasmic disorder, female sexual interest/arousal disorder, genito-pelvic pain/penetration disorder, male hypoactive sexual desire disorder, premature ejaculation, substance-induced sexual dysfunction
Gender dysphoria	Inconsistency between one's internal sense of gender and the assigned gender.	Gender dysphoria
Disruptive, impulse control, and conduct disorders	Disorders involving problems with self-control.	Oppositional defiant disorder, intermittent explosive disorder, conduct disorder, pyromania, kleptomania
Substance-related and addictive disorders	Disorders that activate the brain reward system and behaviors to maintain the rewards.	Alcohol-related disorders, caffeine-related disorders, cannabis-related disorders, hallucinogen-related disorders, inhalant-related disorders, opioid-related disorders, sedative-, hypnotic-, or anxiolytic-related disorders, stimulant-related disorders, tobacco-related disorders, nonsubstance-related disorders
Neurocognitive disorders	Disorders that feature problems with cognition or thinking and not present in birth or early childhood.	Delirium, major and mild neurocognitive disorders

Continued

TABLE 11.1 Disorder types in the Diagnostic and Statistical Manual of Mental Disorders, fifth edition.—cont'd

Disorder type	Description	Examples
Personality disorders	Disorders of personality that are stable over time.	Paranoid personality disorder, schizoid personality disorder, schizotypal personality disorder, antisocial personality disorder, borderline personality disorder, histrionic personality disorder, narcissistic personality disorder, avoidant personality disorder, dependent personality disorder, obsessive-compulsive personality disorder
Paraphilic disorders	Disorders of sexual arousal due to behaviors that cause others to be uncomfortable or harmed.	Voyeuristic disorder, exhibitionistic disorder, frotteuristic disorder, sexual masochism disorder, sexual sadism disorder, pedophilic disorder, fetishistic disorder, transvestic disorder
Other mental disorders	Symptoms cause impairment but do not meet full criteria of a disorder	Other specified mental disorder due to another mental condition, unspecified mental disorders due to another medical condition, other specified mental disorder, unspecified mental disorder
Medication-induced movement disorders and other adverse effects of medication	These are not mental disorders but are possibly caused by medication or medical conditions	Neuroleptic-induced Parkinsonism, neuroleptic malignant syndrome, medication-induced acute dystonia, tardive dyskinesia
Other conditions that may be a focus of clinical attention	These are not psychological disorders but are noted for needing clinical attention	Relational problems, abuse and neglect, housing and economic problems, problems related to social environment, legal system, counseling and medical advice

Based on the American Psychiatric Association. (2013). Diagnostic and statistical manual of mental disorders (5th ed.). American Psychiatric Association; American Psychiatric Association. (2022). Diagnostic and statical manual of mental disorders (5th ed., Text revised). American Psychiatric Association. No permission required.

by trained professionals who determine a diagnosis only after careful assessment and consideration of multiple factors including the individual's level of distress and cultural background. The DSM-5 and the DSM-5-TR also provide a unified way for scientists and clinicians to communicate in an efficient and effective manner when describing the symptoms of mental illness.

Accredited graduate programs in art therapy are required to train students to recognize and diagnose mental illnesses (explore art therapy graduate education standards: Commission on Accreditation of Allied Health Education Programs, 2016). Art therapists are able to diagnose psychological disorders if the art therapist is licensed as a mental health professional or the state art therapy license includes the ability to diagnose. Mental health diagnoses are required by most insurance companies but in most states art therapists do not qualify for insurance reimbursement. The discrepancies among accreditation requirements, state laws, and insurance companies cause tension in the profession as many art therapists feel they have been trained to diagnose psychological disorders yet they are not allowed to do so due to state laws. On the other hand, some art therapists elect to receive direct payment from clients (often referred to as "private pay"), instead of from insurance companies, and therefore are not required to diagnose clients. Some art therapists may focus on psychoeducation that emphasizes teaching skills rather than treating a mental illness. Art therapists who prefer a strength-based approach may also feel a diagnosis labels people and may stigmatize clients.

Stigma

How can a diagnosis be harmful? As defined before, stigma was originally described as "an attribute that is deeply discrediting" (Goffman, 1963, p. 3) and therefore being "labeled" with a mental illness may carry a stigma. **Labeling Theory** (Goffman, 1963; Link et al., 1997) states that stigma demoralizes a person which can lead to income loss, unemployment, social isolation, as well as other negative consequences. Stigma and labeling are systemic as the label of mental illness can affect the person in a number of ways. **Public stigma** is when society believes the stereotypes about people with a mental illness and these beliefs can lead to systemic discriminatory practices. Examples of public stigma include the belief that people diagnosed with a mental illness are violent or unable to be contributing members of society. These societal beliefs can lead to self-stigma or internalized stigma.

Self-stigma is when a person with a mental illness *believes* the societal negative messages (Young et al., 2019). The combination of public and self-stigma can lead to individuals living with mental illness to face rejection, bullying, and discrimination. These consequences can lead to individuals not seeking help and suffering alone in silence. In fact, stigmas play such a role in the delay of treatment that, on average, individuals do not seek treatment for 8–10 years after they begin to experience symptoms of mental illness (NAMI, 2020b). Sadly, for some, mental illness can be terminal since people may feel so demoralized they may take their own life. Suicide is the second leading cause of death for individuals aged 15–24 years and the tenth leading cause of death for Americans (NAMI, 2020a, 2020b, 2020c). Perhaps, if the stigma related to mental illness were reduced or eliminated, lives would be saved, and those in pain due to mental illness might pursue relief from their symptoms sooner.

Becoming aware of one's ableism is an important step toward reducing stigma. **Ableism** is defined as having negative beliefs or actions toward people who are differently abled, such as those with a mental illness (Young et al., 2019). Awareness and reducing stigma have been emphasized by People First Language (People First Language, 2006). **People First Language** (PFL) "puts the person before the disability" and helps to identify the *person* as more than the disability. For example, instead of saying schizophrenic person, PFL replaces that statement with "the person with schizophrenia." The National Alliance on Mental Illness (NAMI) is an organization dedicated to individuals and families affected by mental illness. NAMI's Press and Media Division seeks to reduce stigma through their *CureStigma PSA*, *StigmaFree Pledge PSA*, and *Hope Starts with You* campaigns. These campaigns reduce stigma by openly discussing mental health, pledging to use stigma-free language, and sharing personal experiences to humanize mental illness.

Awareness of stigma has not always been present. As we will see next, early use of the visual arts was used to understand mental illness but did not consider the stigma that could result for the people with mental health condition; in fact, the visual arts, unfortunately, further "otherized" people in institutions.

Early understanding of mental illness through art

As early as the 1800s we can see professionals wanting to understand mental illness through the visual arts. There were two different ways art was used to explore mental health conditions: (1) artists who created images or portraits of people with a mental illness and (2) art created by those with a mental illness. Through these early portrayals of people with a mental illness, readers can see the beginnings of the field of art therapy, even if these early approaches are now considered inhumane and stigmatizing.

Medicine and art: Physiognomy

Two physician-artists are noted as using the visual arts to understand mental illness. These physician-artists drew and photographed patients to aid in understanding and documenting symptoms of mental illness. Although these artworks would be considered offensive today, they provide a window into how mental illness was viewed and understood at the time using the visual arts. These examples serve as early connections between the visual arts and mental health.

Sir Charles Bell (1774–1842) is well known for creating detailed neuroanatomical drawings of the facial expressions of people with a mental illness. Bell is also remembered for being one of the first artist-surgeons who documented brain anatomy through his detailed drawings. In his *Anatomy and Philosophy of Expression as Connected with Fine Arts* (Bell, 1877), Bell captured the physical changes that accompany mental illness. He created detailed drawings and descriptions of human anatomy and the physical features of emotional expression (Tubbs et al., 2012). Bell (1877) believed that "disease has characteristic symptoms, which we can accurately and scientifically reduce to description" (p. 147). Systematically documenting these physical characteristics of illness is called **physiognomy**. One of Bell's drawings depicts the emotional states of "madness" (Fig. 11.1). Bell drew a man with a "strong, rigid body" and "a vacant" gaze (p. 162). Bell's book also includes drawings of grief, sadness, fear, joy, and many other emotions. Not only is this an early artistic portrayal of the experience of mental illness, these visual explorations aided in the understanding of the nervous system, brain, and physical emotional expression (Tubbs et al., 2012) as connected to mental illness.

Hugh Welch Diamond (1809–86) grew up in his family home which housed people with mental illnesses. When he became old enough, Diamond attended medical school and eventually became a surgeon. While in school he also expressed an interest in ceramics, printmaking, and eventually photography. He

FIG. 11.1 *Emotional states of madness. One of Bell's drawings depicting the state of "madness." (No permission required.)*

began to study mental illness at Bethlem Hospital and later became the superintendent of another asylum. He began taking photographs of patients to capture their recovery process (Burrows & Schumacher, 1990). These photos are noted as the first psychiatric-photographic record of patients. Similar to Bell, Diamond was capturing the physical and emotional expressions of mental illness in order to diagnose and classify mental illnesses (Pearl, 2009).

Diamond hoped to prevent future relapses through the use of photographs which he believed aided patients in making a more accurate assessment of their mental state (Tucker, 2016). Diamond believed that the photographs could be used as a treatment by providing "accurate self-reflection required to force them to recognize their illness" (Pearl, 2009, p. 289). The goal for Diamond was to increase patient awareness of how they appeared on the outside as compared to their internal perception of their appearance (Pearl, 2009). His use of photography for psychological insight is an early connection of the visual arts and therapeutic interventions despite being an unacceptable practice by today's standards. Fig. 11.2 shows one of Diamond's photographs of a female patient. More

FIG. 11.2 *Patient, Surrey County Lunatic Asylum. Medium: Albumen silver print from glass; Date: 1850–58; Gilman Collection, Purchase, Ann Tenenbaum and Thomas H. Lee Gift, 2005; As part of The Met's Open Access program, the data is available for unrestricted commercial and noncommercial use without permission or fee.*
(No permission required.)

images of his work are available online at the National Gallery of Art, The J. Paul Getty Museum, and the National Portrait Gallery.

Although Bell and Diamond used art to depict the emotional expression and psychological states of patients in hopes of improving diagnosis and treatment, patient consent to be drawn or photographed probably did not occur (Pearl, 2009). Today, such use of art is unethical without the consent of the patients. Additionally, many of the patients probably came from poverty and lived in the asylums for many years which may have influenced the patient's hygiene, clothing, and hairstyles highlighted in the photographs. The patient's lack of resources and poor treatment were rarely considered in these portraits. Diamond's photographs have also been criticized for being "highly manipulated and staged" (p. 304) and for Diamond's lack of awareness of his influence on patients and possibly his beliefs about mental illness creating a self-fulfilling prophecy as the patients may have mimicked Diamond's expectations.

Psychiatrists, psychiatric institutions, and art

Moving from physician-artist portrayals of patients to observations of patient engagement in art-making, psychiatrists "began collecting and promoting exhibitions and appreciation of these works" (Cohen, 2017, p. 25). The burgeoning interest of patient art by several psychiatrists served as the catalyst in patient art that still exists today.

Hermann Rorschach (1884–1922) grew up spending most of his time painting and drawing. He struggled with choosing a career in art versus medicine. While attending medical school he spent Saturday afternoons at the local art museum and often asked his friends what they saw in the paintings (Searls, 2017). During this time in school, he also attended lectures by Jung and became familiar with the work of Jung, Freud, and Bleuler. After deciding to pursue a career in psychiatry, he began working at an asylum in Russia and then relocated to Switzerland. Rorschach kept visual patient files that included photographs and drawings by Rorschach. Rorschach also arranged for drama, art, and activities for patients. He even published an article where he analyzed a patient's drawing. Rorschach's colleague, **Walter Morgenthaler** (1882–1865), also encouraged his patients to draw and Morgenthaler began collecting patient drawings. Morgenthaler also noted that Rorschach "was vitally interested in patients' drawing. He had an amazing gift for getting patients to draw" (Searls, 2017, p. 100). Rorschach and Morgenthaler shared an interest in art, art-making, and mental illness. For Rorschach, his observations with Morgenthaler influenced his interest in patient art-making and the collection of patient art, and eventually led to the development of his famous Inkblot Test. Morgenthaler subsequently published *A Mental Patient as Artist* (1921), which focused on his patient with schizophrenia, Adolf Wolfli. In this text, Morgenthaler noted the healing qualities of art-making in helping Wolfli stabilize himself (Cohen, 2017). Wolfli's work is said to have subsequently influenced famous surrealist artists as well as Picasso (Searls, 2017).

Around the same time period, **Hans Prinzhorn** (1886–1933), a German psychiatrist and art historian, was similarly interested in the link between art, psychiatry, and emotional expression. Prinzhorn collected over 5000 pieces of art created by patients in an asylum. As described in Chapter 1, he published *Artistry of the Mentally Ill* in 1922 where he described the artwork of individuals who had been institutionalized (Vick, 2012). Prinzhorn discouraged using artwork to diagnose patients and instead emphasized the image-making process and the urge to create as a form of emotional expression (Cohen, 2017). These works created by patients later inspired the well-known artists: Franz Marc, Paul Klee, Max Ernst, and Jean Dubuffet (Cohen, 2017).

Self-taught artists

As stated before, the observations and collections by Rorschach, Morgenthaler, and Prinzhorn influenced numerous famous artists including Jean Dubuffet, a famous French artist (Hall, 2013). Dubuffet coined the term **Art Brut** which translates as "raw art" and describes artwork created without the influence of art culture and formal training (Raw Vision, n.d.). The term **outsider art**, also used in conjunction with art brut, was introduced by Roger Cardinal in 1972 and "refer[s] to any artist who is untrained or with disabilities or suffering social exclusion, whatever the nature of their work" (Raw Vision, n.d., para. 7). In response to the stigma associated with the words "outsider" and the implication of being uncultured, many prefer the terms **"self-taught artist"** or **visionary artist**. Due to space limitations, we describe the work of three self-taught artists who have been featured in the media, experienced a mental health condition, or used art to express their emotional suffering and social exclusion.

Henry Darger's (1892–1973) mother died during the birth of his sister. Darger lived with his father for a few years after the death of his mother but his father became too ill to take care of him, so Darger was sent to live in an orphanage. After "disciplinary problems, including making odd, repetitive motions with his hands and disruptive noises with his mouth, nose, and throat" (Trent, 2017, p. 45) he earned the nickname "crazy" and was sent to an asylum. At the asylum he was diagnosed with "masturbation," a behavior viewed at that time as unhealthy (Trent, 2017). At the age of 16, he began working as a custodian at a hospital in Chicago where he lived an isolated life in an apartment. In his apartment, he created a story about seven daughters who started a rebellion against child slavery which he illustrated with elaborate drawings and watercolor paintings with mixed media. The multivolume illustrated book is titled: *The Story of the Vivian Girls, in What is Known as Realms of the Unreal, of the Glandeco-Angelinian War Storm, Caused by the Child Slave Rebellion* was not discovered until after his death. The contents of his room have been relocated as a permanent exhibition at the *Intuit Art Museum: The Center for Intuitive and Outsider Art.*

Judith Scott (1943–2005) was born with Down Syndrome (Down Syndrome is classified as a neurodevelopmental disorder in the DSM-5-TR). As a toddler,

Judith had scarlet fever which caused her hearing loss. At 7, her parents, who were unaware of her hearing loss, placed her in an institution where she lived until the age of 44 (Trent, 2017). Her twin sister decided to move Scott to California where she began attending the Creative Growth Center for artists with disabilities. For 2 years, Scott showed no interest in art until a fiber artist came to the center as a guest speaker. Scott then began creating "enigmatic cocoon-like objects woven with colored yarn and scraps of cloth" (Wojcik, 2016) around "scavenged objects such as electric fans, magazines, foam packaging, coat hangers, and umbrellas" (p. 86). She is now considered an internationally known sculptor.

Martin Ramirez (1895–1963) was born in Los Altos de Jalisco, Mexico. He married and had three daughters. Ramirez migrated alone to the United States for work on the mines and railroad. He did not know English and ended up homeless. He was later diagnosed with catatonic schizophrenia and was hospitalized in 1931. However, this diagnosis should be read with caution since many immigrants at this time were viewed as mentally ill "because of their strange appearance, lack of language skills, and cultural habits" (Espinosa, 2015, p. 58). Ramirez remained hospitalized for the next 30 years. During his stay in the hospital, he created drawings and collages on any materials he could get his hands on (crayons, pencil, watercolor, and discarded paper that he pieced together to make large drawings). His work reflected Mexican folk traditions, tunnels and trains, and images that may represent his cultural heritage, journey to the United States, or the modernization at the time. His work shows a meticulous approach to creating art. Psychology Professor Tarmo Pasto, who specialized in approaches to teaching drawing, was introduced to Ramirez. Pasto spent several months studying the drawings and meeting with Ramirez and also introduced Ramirez to other artists. Ramirez' works have been shown in numerous galleries all over the country (Espinosa, 2015).

Art therapy's role in improving mental health

Over time, the treatment of individuals living with mental illness has developed and changed. Prior to the late 19th century, individuals living with mental illness were isolated from society and frequently physically confined in what was referred to as asylums (Jutras, 2017). Patients were dehumanized as can be seen by the works created by Bell and Diamond (see Medicine and art: Physiognomy section). However, in 1908, Clifford Beers wrote his autobiography, *A Mind that Found Itself*, which described his experiences living with mental illness. "I was continuously either under lock and key (in the padded cell or some other room) or under the eye of an attendant… While being subjected to this terrific abuse I was held in exile. I was cut off from all direct and all honest indirect communication with my legally appointed conservator—my own brother—and also with all other relatives and friends. I was even cut off from satisfactory communication with the superintendent" (Beers, 2010, p. 2054). In his book, he envisioned a society that focused on the prevention of mental illness or mental hygiene (Mandell, 1995). Before passing away in a mental health institution years later, Beers founded the Connecticut Society for Mental Hygiene, which evolved into Mental Health America (MHA), a community-based organization that assists individuals living with mental illness (MHA, 2020). Beers' introduction of mental hygiene subsequently created a national movement to introduce legislation, programs, and scientific research to explore the causes of mental illness (Mandell, 1995).

Art-making began gaining recognition as a treatment and positive coping mechanism around the 1940s. As described in Chapter 1, Adrian Hill engaged in art-making while recovering from tuberculosis and was the first to use the term "art therapy." In the United States, founding art therapists who were at the forefront of innovative mental health treatment were trained artists and art educators who partnered with psychiatrists. These founders taught art classes and demonstrated the therapeutic qualities of art-making. These early art therapists included Margaret Naumburg (New York State Psychiatric Hospital), Edith Kramer (focused on the healing power of the creative process), Harriet Wadeson (St. Elizabeth Hospital), and Myra Levick (Hahnemann Hospital in Philadelphia, Pennsylvania) (Junge, 2015). The Menninger Clinic established an expressive arts program in 1951 and trained several art therapists (Junge, 2015). Over the course of 20 years, these early art therapists published in journals and books about the benefits of working with individuals with mental illness using art therapy. What is the state of art therapy and mental health today? Can art therapy alleviate symptoms of mental illness and help people cope with the symptoms? When is art therapy harmful? The next section explores the current practice and research on art therapy and mental health. We begin by exploring some of the ways art therapy enhances mental health and mental health recovery.

How does art therapy help with mental health?

Symptoms of a mental illness can lower motivation, decrease cognitive abilities (e.g., concentration, memory, and focus), and increase one's avoidance of certain feelings or triggers. These negative consequences of mental illness can lower self-esteem and confidence and cause one to withdraw from much needed social support (King et al., 2016). King et al. (2016) and Uttley et al. (2015) state that art-making and art therapy increase **behavioral activation** as both call for engagement with the art materials and this requires physical movement. Through engagement with art-making, art therapy increases **self-efficacy** or a sense of mastery because the client tries something new. Art therapy also provides a nonthreatening way to explore emotions the client might be avoiding. Creating art can help the client see themselves as more than their illness and can also connect them to others, thus enhancing their identity and reducing their sense of isolation. Table 11.2 summarizes the factors King et al. (2016) and Uttley et al. (2015) identify how art-making supports mental health. These factors parallel the core principles of a more recent movement that shifts the focus from treating mental illness to mental health recovery.

TABLE 11.2 Connection between factors on how art-making improves mental health and mental health recovery principles.

Factors that improve mental health	Definition of factors	Mental health recovery principles
Behavioral activation	Art-making requires physical movement, outward expression of feelings, and empowers people with action.	Person-driven, self-direction, empowerment
Self-efficacy	Having successful art-making experiences increases one's confidence and builds a sense of mastery.	Hope, strength-based, responsibility
Emotion avoidance	Provides a nonthreatening outlet for addressing and expressing emotions.	Addressing trauma
Social connectedness	Engaging in community art-making or art therapy can build community and social support.	Peer support, relational
Identity	Art-making provides a chance to view one's self as more than just a person with a mental illness and can increase self-awareness.	Holistic, hope, self-direction

Modified from King, R., Baker, F., & Neilsen, P. (2016). Introduction. In P. Neilson, R. King, & F. Baker (Eds.), Creative arts in counseling and mental health (pp. 1–7). No permission required.

Mental health recovery is generally defined as "living a fulfilling and rewarding life in the context of mental health challenges" (Tondora et al., 2014). The principles of mental health recovery align with the ways art therapy aids in mental health as described before. Mental health recovery is a strength-based approach that guides the mission and vision of most mental health centers in the United States (Ellison et al., 2018). Instead of focusing on curing one's mental illness, the recovery model emphasizes living a meaningful life by pursuing one's full potential and focusing on one's strengths (Ellison et al., 2018). Mental health recovery also redefines the role of one's illness as only one aspect of the person's life. When treatment providers focus on mental health recovery, research shows that most people with a mental illness can lead a meaningful life and do not continue to deteriorate (Tondora et al., 2014).

Over the years, various organizations have worked to identify principles that guide recovery. The Substance Abuse and Mental Health Services

Administration (SAMHSA, 2012) has identified 10 mental health recovery principles: hope, person-driven, many pathways, holistic, peer support, relational, culture, addresses trauma, strengths/responsibility, and respect. Jacob (2015) reviewed the mental health recovery process and identified these key components: holistic view of patient, nonlinear, hope, support, identity, and purpose. Art therapy sessions typically implement these guiding principles. For example, in a community-based art therapy open studio, individuals gather to make and share art. In doing so, participants stimulate their minds, exercise their bodies, boost their spirit, and connect with others. Table 11.2 identifies ways the principles of mental recovery overlap with how art therapy can assist in promoting mental health.

Does research support the positive effects of art therapy for mental health? A systematic review of the effectiveness of art therapy for nonpsychotic mental health disorders was conducted by Uttley et al. (2015) and concluded that art therapy is effective for people with nonpsychotic mental health disorders. The researchers identified 15 separate, quantitative studies on art therapy and found 10 of the 15 studies reported significantly positive effects of art therapy on mental health disorders on at least some of the measured outcomes when compared to the control group. Four of the studies found no difference between the art therapy and the control group. More research is needed since only 15 different studies met the qualifications for the systematic review.

So, can art therapy help people cope even if they do not have a psychological disorder? Research generally supports the idea that engaging in art improves mental wellness. The World Health Organization's (WHO) synthesis report on the role of the arts for improving well-being found two main areas of how engaging in the arts benefits health: (1) prevention and promotion, and (2) management and treatment (Fancourt et al., 2019). Stuckey and Nobel (2010) found that engagement in the visual arts helps people gain insight, buffer strong feelings, distract from negative feelings, express strong emotions, improve medical outcomes (such as vital signs, earlier discharge), reduce stress, and improve one's sense of self-worth.

There are additional ways art-making helps to maintain mental health. Several researchers have found that engaging in art-making lowers the stress hormone **cortisol** (Beerse et al., 2019; Brown et al., 2017; Kaimal et al., 2016) while other researchers have found that drawing to distract improves participants' mood more than drawing to vent emotions (Drake et al., 2016). Some researchers argue that "art therapy and mindfulness practices have complementary effects on neurological and biological processes" (Beerse et al., 2019, p. 124) as research has shown engaging in art activated the medial prefrontal cortical region (a reward center) regardless of the type of art-making task (coloring a mandala, doodling, or free drawing; Kaimal et al., 2017). Research on how art therapy helps with specific symptoms and psychological disorders is discussed in the next section. To explore how art therapy is used in medical settings to help patients cope with chronic illness, please see Box 11.1.

Box 11.1 Medical art therapy

A setting where art therapists use art-making to enhance the psychological well-being of patients is in the medical setting. Medical art therapy is defined as using therapeutic art-making with people who are "physically ill, experiencing bodily trauma, or undergoing invasive or aggressive medical procedures" (Malchiodi, 1993, p. 66). Goodheart and Lansing (1997) note that when someone is diagnosed with a physical illness they experience multiple threats to their sense of well-being, comfort, privacy, independence, goals, relationships, and work. These multiple threats create a sense of internal disorganization that threatens the person's psychological health and well-being. Medical art therapy seeks to help the person reorganize and redefine their sense of self and possibly even to find meaning in the experience.

Art therapists who work with patients in a medical setting must consider a number of factors (Anand, 2015; Tedeschi & Calhoun, 2009). First, the therapist must focus on the unique patient's experience. The art therapist will want to learn about the patient's diagnosis and prognosis, assess the developmental stage of the patient, identify the patient's prior coping skills, level of treatment (family, individual, or group), social support, and identify any comorbid or co-occurring issues. Second, the art therapist will want to explore how the patient's identity has been impacted by the illness and how they are currently coping. Understanding the physical changes in disfigurement and ability is also important to assess. Finally, according to Anand (2015) the art therapist will want to consider options for media since the art therapist will need to follow any infection control or sterilization issues. Some materials have certain odors, sensations, and colors that may trigger negative, physical responses in clients. Additionally, art therapists need to be prepared to work at the bedside of patients, in public areas, and with family members (who may be present and benefit from art therapy).

Can art therapy be harmful? Scope et al. (2017) identified five factors that lead to poor outcomes when using art therapy for people with non-psychotic mental health disorders: (1) having an unskilled art therapist; (2) terminating the art therapy sessions too early, leaving the client with unresolved feelings; (3) engaging with art therapy that increased one's pain or anxiety; (4) if the client has a fear of engaging in art therapy; and (5) the participant was not interested in art therapy (Scope et al., 2017). The next section expands on the research discussed before by focusing on specific psychological disorders.

Art therapy for specific psychological disorders

Due to space limitations, this section focuses on more common mental health diagnoses and ones most frequently studied by art therapists. For each of the disorders, a brief overview of the DSM-5-TR criteria is provided along with research on the graphic indicators associated with drawings made by people with the diagnosis. Art therapy considerations with case examples from the authors' clinical work are included for each disorder. Lastly, research on the effectiveness of art therapy for the specific mental health conditions is provided.

Pattern matching and formal elements are artistic elements that are commonly found in artwork. Studies have identified certain patterns in the artwork of people with a specific disorder or symptom (e.g., people with major depressive disorder tend to use less color; Gantt & Tabone, 1998, 2012). Gantt and Tabone (1998, 2012) identified these patterns after collecting over 5000 drawings using a standardized assessment called the Person Picking an Apple from a Tree (PPAT; Gantt & Tabone, 1998, 2012). The results from the analysis of these drawings informed the development of the Formal Elements Art Therapy Scale (FEATS; Gantt and Tabone, 1998, 2012) which is used by art therapists and researchers when viewing client artwork. According to researchers (Gantt & Tabone, 1998, 2012; Pénzes et al., 2018) formal elements focus on *how* a client draws versus *what* they draw. Formal elements do not provide art therapists a way to "read" or "interpret" patient artwork since these patterns do not provide an explanation for what is happening to the person nor can one item in the drawing indicate a specific disease. Formal elements include the client's color usage, how much the color fits the objects the client is drawing, how much energy the client uses to create the image, the use of space, the cohesiveness of the picture, logic demonstrated in the image, the quality of line and form, repetitiveness of certain aspects in the image, and the visual balance of the image. Table 11.3 provides a summary of the Formal Elements Art Therapy Scale (Gantt & Tabone, 2012). Patterns noted for each disorder as follows should NEVER be used alone to make a diagnosis as patterns in drawings have not had consistent empirical support to predict psychological states or behaviors in research studies (Lilienfeld et al., 2000).

Art therapy considerations are noted throughout each section below. These considerations are ways therapists might work with clients based on the symptoms observed. The art therapy considerations described as follows are from clinical work by occupational therapists, art therapists, and the authors' clinical experiences.

Art therapy for depressive disorders

DSM-5-TR Criteria for Depressive Disorders: The DSM-5-TR includes the following types of depressive disorders: (1) disruptive mood dysregulation disorder, (2) major depressive disorder, (3) persistent depressive disorder, (4) premenstrual dysphoric disorder, (5) substance-induced/medication-induced depressive disorder, (6) depressive disorder due to other medical condition, (7) other specified depressive disorder, and (8) unspecified depressive disorder (American Psychiatric Association, 2022). Each one of these disorders has a list of specific diagnostic criteria and features, development and course, risk factors, and other diagnostic issues. However, all of the depressive disorders share feelings of sadness, emptiness, or irritability; affect one's body or thinking; and impair functioning. Symptoms must be present for at least 2 weeks and must show significant changes from prefunctioning.

TABLE 11.3 Formal Elements Art Therapy Scale.

Formal Elements Art Therapy Scale	Description	Example
1. Prominence of color	Amount of color used	Did the artist only outline the forms or color the forms in?
2. Color fit	Colors related to objects or task	Do the colors match the objects in the art image?
3. Implied Energy	Amount of energy used to create the art image "Vitality of the movement made" (Penzes et al., 2018, p. 5)	How much energy was used by the artist to create the image?
4. Space	Amount of space usage	Does the art image take up the entire paper or just a portion?
5. Integration	Cohesiveness of image, amount of organization, planning	Is the art image coherent, structured, or chaotic?
6. Logic	Image makes sense	Does the art image show logical thinking?
7. Realism	Drawing reflects actual objects	Does the art image resemble the identified subject?
8. Problem-solving	Solution derived to task	Is there a solution to the task?
9. Developmental level	Lowenfeld's Artistic Stage of Development	What stage of development is the drawing?
10. Details of object and environment	Amount of detail	Does the art image lack details, have too many details?
11. Line quality	Amount of control exhibited regarding in line quality	Is there steady pressure that results in an identifiable object?
12. Person	Resembles a human figure	Is the figure proportional?
13. Rotation	Amount of tilt	Is the image on a slant?
14. Perseveration	Repetition of response	Is there repetition of shapes, lines, objects?

Adapted from Gantt, L., & Tabone, C. (2012). The formal elements art therapy scale: The rating manual. Gargoyle Press. No permission required.

Depression can also accompany other mental health conditions (e.g., schizophrenia, anxiety), medical illnesses (e.g., multiple sclerosis, Parkinson's disorder), and major life events (e.g., divorce, loss) (Early, 2016). Clinical levels of depression affect one's ability to focus, problem-solve, and make decisions.

Genetic and physiological factors: People are at a 2–4 times higher risk of developing major depressive disorder if a first-degree family relative has major depressive disorder (5th ed., DSM-5, American Psychiatric Association, 2013), but this is not the case for persistent depressive disorder.

Demographics and cultural considerations: According to the DSM-5 (American Psychiatric Association, 2013), it is difficult to identify specific cultural features of depressive disorders because in many countries depression is undiagnosed. However, premenstrual dysphoric disorder is reported throughout several countries worldwide. Multiple adverse childhood experiences place someone at a higher risk for developing depression. **Adverse childhood experiences** are harmful experiences such as abuse, neglect, or loss that occur before age 18 (Felitti et al., 1998). If someone has experienced four or more adverse childhood events, then that person is at an increased risk for a number of risky behaviors (smoking, alcoholism, drug abuse, more than 50 sexual partners, physical inactivity) and health consequences (higher risk for depression, suicide attempts, sexually transmitted diseases, severe obesity, heart, lung, liver disease, or cancer) (Felitti et al., 1998).

Formal elements and depression: Both Wadeson (2010) and Gantt and Tabone (1998, 2012) noted that artwork done by those with clinical depression tended to score lower on color usage and implied energy, used less space on the page, and tended to use few details and less effort in the artwork. Wadeson (2010) also noted that several patients included immobile or restrained figures and depressive themes (such as death, suicide, or illness).

Art therapy considerations: "There is no single art therapy technique for people suffering from depression" (Wise, 2016, p. 359); however, the art therapist must show support for any small efforts to create when a client is depressed and should be keenly aware of any comments that can be perceived as critical (Wadeson, 2010; Wise, 2016). Therapists may choose to focus on a single or simple task, match the pace of the client, and reduce the amount of stimulation in the environment (Early, 2016; Wise, 2016). The therapist will want to ensure the client's success on the first art project and design the art directive appropriately such as making the art task highly structured, simple, and require minimal focus (Wise, 2016). As the client progresses in treatment, the art therapist may make note of the client's interactions with the art materials (e.g., physical movement, use of color, the addition of details) and adjust the art directive as appropriate to aid the client (e.g., provide fewer directions or allow for more open expression). When a client experiencing depression first enters treatment, they may add minimal detail to their images and avoid using colors. The depression lowers one's ability to engage, thus the art therapist may need to provide a lot of structure and a simple art project. As symptoms decrease, art images may have more detail and color, thus the therapist may provide more open art projects that allow the client to explore their creativity.

Case example

Ronald (pseudonym), an African-American 65-year-old male and long-time partner of Gladys (pseudonym), a 60-year-old, Asian American female, sought assistance from an art therapist to manage Gladys' depression. Ronald explained that Gladys retired 6 months ago after working as a patient care attendant in a hospital for over 40 years. Since her retirement Gladys has not been cleaning the house or cooking meals, two activities she used to enjoy. Instead, Gladys spends the majority of her day in bed watching courtroom reality shows on the television. When Gladys went to the art therapist's office, she made no eye contact, spoke softly, and responded to questions with one-word answers. The art therapist asked Gladys to choose which art material she would like to use and the art therapist asked her to draw a wave. Gladys slowly picked up a pencil and made one line on the paper and said she was done. The art therapist asked Gladys to indicate where she would be in the image and Gladys put a dot and said she is buried within the wave. The art therapist asked, "Gladys, do you feel like you're drowning?" Gladys looked up and made eye contact with the art therapist for the first time and said in a much louder tone, "Yes! I am completely underwater and no matter what I do I can't find a way to the shore." From there, the art therapist and Gladys explored what the depression felt like and how Gladys may be able to use techniques and supports to help her find her way to safety and alleviate the symptoms of depression.

Research on art therapy for depressive disorders: Eight common art therapy factors were found by Blomdahl et al. (2013) from their analysis of 16 journal articles on art therapy for depression. The common therapeutic factors in art therapy for depression were (1) using art directives that aid in self-exploration to increase awareness of self (e.g., examining goals), (2) encouraging self-expression through the use of color, shapes, and symbols to express one's inner experience (e.g., create symbols that represent your feelings), (3) creating a space for both nonverbal communication (the art piece) and verbal communication (client's explanation) that aids in (4) better understanding and explanation, (5) assisting with the integration, when the client is able to assimilate the new information with the self, using (6) symbolic thinking to aid in exploration and increase the personal connection, (7) stimulating the brain and problem-solving skills through creativity, and (8) stimulating the senses through work with the art media. When art therapists work with clients with depression they may seek to design art activities or discussions with clients based on these common therapeutic factors.

Case example

A common art therapy directive to assist in self-exploration and self-expression is to ask an individual to draw an image of themselves in a symbolic manner. For example, an art therapist working in a group with individuals on a behavioral health unit in a hospital asked the group members to "Draw an image of yourself as an animal exploring how the creature's thoughts, feelings, and behaviors are like yours. Be sure to include the environment where the animal is presently." After individuals had time to draw, they were asked to share. Elena (pseudonym), a 35-year-old, Latina, cisgender female, drew an image of a scarlet Macaw (a Central American bird) on the ground, under a tree with a branch holding a nest with three eggs in it. Elena shared with the group that she was the bird on the ground, and she had abandoned her children in the nest. With the assistance of the art therapist, Elena determined that the bird was taking a break and had no injuries that prevented the bird from returning to the nest to care for the eggs. Similar to the bird, Elena needed time away from her family to manage her depressive symptoms before she was able to return to care for her own family. Other group members shared that they too feared that their family would feel abandoned while they were hospitalized. The discussion evolved to the entire group exploring how the bird was eventually able to fly and symbolically represented how they were able to overcome the presently debilitating symptoms of their mental illness.

Art therapy for anxiety disorders

DSM-5-TR criteria for anxiety disorders: Anxiety is a natural response that we all experience. Low levels of anxiety are actually helpful because they can motivate us to complete assignments and warn us when we are in danger, but anxiety disorders feature high levels of fear that do not match the situation and may lead to avoidance of certain situations (American Psychiatric Association, 2013). The DSM-5-TR includes eleven types of anxiety disorders that are listed in developmental order: (1) separation anxiety, (2) selective mutism, (3) specific phobia, (4) social anxiety, (5) panic, (6) agoraphobia, (7) generalized anxiety, (8) substance-induced anxiety, (9) anxiety disorder due to another medial condition, (10) other specified anxiety disorder, and (11) unspecified anxiety disorder.

Anxiety is activated by the HPA axis (hypothalamus, pituitary gland, and adrenal glands). When the HPA axis is triggered, the adrenal glands release cortisol. "Cortisol is a glucocorticoid hormone and one of the most widely studied markers of stress" (Kaimal et al., 2016, p.74). Cortisol activates the sympathetic nervous system that prepares the body for a crisis (heart rate increases, lungs, and pupils dilate). When this system has trouble shutting down, symptoms of an anxiety disorder prevail.

Genetic and physiological factors in anxiety disorders: According to the DSM-5 and DSM 5-TR (American Psychiatric Association, 2013, 2022) anxiety disorders have a genetic component where people who have a relative with an anxiety disorder are at higher risk. Research has also shown that individuals who develop an anxiety disorder may also have a sensitivity to bodily sensations or respiratory issues.

Anxiety disorders and demographics and cultural considerations: According to the DSM-5 (American Psychiatric Association, 2013), anxiety disorders tend to emerge in childhood and most people need treatment to decrease symptoms. Approximately twice as many women as men are diagnosed with anxiety disorders. Environmental factors such as divorce, loss, and abuse can predict the development of an anxiety disorder.

The DSM-5 notes several important cultural considerations when diagnosing someone with anxiety. For example, culture can play a role in separation anxiety as some cultures may express more **somatic symptoms** (versus cognitive symptoms; somatic symptoms are defined as symptoms expressed through the body), and may have different expectations in regard to the amount of time children and adults have contact. Recent immigration may impact language fluency and may be mistaken for selective mutism. Finally, cultural beliefs may play a role in the expression of the disorder.

Formal elements and anxiety: Patterns have not been systematically studied in art therapy. Individual studies can provide some suggestions for graphic patterns of anxiety but additional research is needed. LaRoque and Obrzut (2006) examined **state anxiety** (which is anxiety in the present moment and due to external stressors) and **trait anxiety** (where anxiety is a characteristic of the person or anxiety caused internally) in 50, 6–11-year-old children and found that children with high and low levels of anxiety in the moment showed more **pencil pressure** while those with trait anxiety which is part of their temperament used less pressure. Although not a graphic indicator, pencil pressure is the force used "when pressing pencil to paper while drawing" (LaRoque & Obrzut, 2006, p. 382).

Art therapy considerations when working with clients with anxiety: Therapists should make the environment calming and seek art activities that will help to reduce the anxiety. Simple, repetitive tasks might be soothing to those with anxiety (Early, 2016; Hinz, 2019).

Case example

People with anxiety symptoms often struggle to calm themselves. Many of the art therapy directives for those experiencing anxiety focus on assisting clients to calm and stay in the moment. Cortez (pseudonym), a 19-year-old college freshman from Portugal who identifies as bisexual, sought assistance at the counseling center and reported increased anxiety since starting college 3 months ago. Cortez indicated that he initially noticed that he was struggling to focus and complete assignments and reach work on time. Eventually, he quit attending classes and going to work. He was failing all but one class and was fired from his job. He reported having debilitating panic when he left the dorm. Cortez created a goal with the art therapist to use art materials for 15 minutes prior to leaving his dorm room to assist with managing his anxiety. The art therapist encouraged Cortez to use fluid materials, such as watercolor paint or dry erase markers on a whiteboard so that the kinesthetic motion would be soothing. In the session, the art therapist played relaxing music and asked Cortez to paint to the music. During the 15 minutes that Cortez painted, the art therapist noted Cortez's posture becoming more relaxed and breathing less labored. When the art therapist and Cortez spoke about the artwork, Cortez said he got lost in the art-making and forgot about his anxiety. He titled the image *Peace of Mind* because he said the soft shades of blue and aqua looked like a tranquil sea.

Research on art therapy for anxiety and anxiety disorders: Several studies have found that engaging in art therapy significantly decreases anxiety but the type of interventions utilized by art therapists is not consistent. The studies are described below but the inconsistent findings underscore the need for additional research.

After a systematic review of the art therapy literature, researchers found only three randomized controlled studies (RCSs) measuring art therapy's effectiveness for treating symptoms of anxiety (Abbing et al., 2018). In these three studies, the art therapy intervention varied: coloring a mandala, working with clay, painting, collage, drawing, or the house-tree-person drawing. Two of the three RCSs yielded statistically significant differences in anxiety levels in the art-making group. The third RCS compared a trauma-related art-making group with a random art-making group. The researchers did not find significant differences in anxiety levels between the two groups (Henderson et al., 2007; Sandmire et al., 2016). The reviewers also argue that more evidence is needed to measure whether art therapy can effectively treat anxiety as the primary diagnosis when not related to another illness (Abbing et al., 2018).

One common art therapy intervention for anxiety symptoms is drawing or coloring a mandala. **Mandala** means circle in Sanskrit and originates from Asian and Indigenous people's religious artwork (Fincher, 2009; Robertson, 1992). In Asian cultures, the mandala "is usually a subject for meditation and contemplation, with the intent of leading the meditator progressively deeper into inner unity with the godhead" (Robertson, 1992, p. 178). Jung believed the containment of the circle provided space to express one's unconscious. Several studies have explored the therapeutic benefits of coloring a mandala for anxiety. When using mandalas and any other art practices, art therapists should be aware of cultural appropriation. **Cultural appropriation** is defined as "the action of taking something for one's own use, typically without the owner's permission" (http://Dictionary.com). To avoid appropriating art practices, Napoli (2019) argues that art therapists must acknowledge the source of practice and people.

Does coloring a mandala reduce anxiety? Research has examined the effects of coloring patterns, such as a mandala, on stress or anxiety reduction and has found mixed results. Curry and Kasser (2005) had participants write about their most fearful time to induce feelings of anxiety and then compared anxiety levels before and after coloring a pattern or freeform. The coloring pattern groups showed a significant reduction in anxiety as compared to the freeform group.

However, van der Vennet and Serice (2012) replicated this study but they found that the group that colored mandalas showed a significantly lower level of anxiety as compared to coloring a plaid design and free form groups.

Following these mixed results, Babouchkina and Robbins (2015) examined whether the shape of the intervention really matters. These researches compared participant mood after coloring in (1) a blank circle to express feelings, (2) a blank circle to draw freely, (3) a square to express feelings, or (4) a square to draw freely. The two circle groups reported more improvement in mood compared to the groups that colored in the squares. On the other hand, Campenni and Hartman (2020) examined which directives led to the least reported anxiety: (1) a structured mandala (patterned mandala), (2) a free expression circle drawing (outline of circle only), (3) free expression drawing (directions to complete the drawing in any way), or (4) directed instructions (complete the drawing based on how they feel). Anxiety significantly decreased and state body mindfulness increased in all conditions. The unstructured circle groups produced more emotion and insight word descriptions as compared to the structured mandala group.

The studies described above provide evidence that engaging in art-making can reduce anxiety; however, it was unclear whether the shape or amount of structure of the coloring activity makes a significant difference in anxiety levels. Støre and Jakobsson (2022) sought to resolve these inconsistent findings by conducting a meta-analysis on eight studies that all used mandalas, colored pencils, and measured state and trait anxiety. There results indicated that coloring, a mandala or free form, did reduce anxiety. However, coloring a mandala did not causes a greater reduction when compared to other forms of coloring. Majority of the studies were done with younger people with higher levels of education, took place in North America, Europe, and Australia and with people not diagnosed with anxiety, Støre and Jakobsson (2022) note the results "cannot be generalized to people with anxiety disorders" (p. 4).

Why does art-making reduce symptoms of anxiety? According to the polyvagal theory, the vagal nerve regulates the parasympathetic and sympathetic nervous systems. Art-making helps to calm and focus one's nervous system and increases control and activity of the vagal nerve (Sandmire et al., 2016). Others have argued that a focus on sensory art-making can aid in relaxation (Hinz, 2009) as evidenced by Campenni and Hartman (2020), or stimulate reward centers in the brain in similar ways as mindfulness practices (Beerse et al., 2019).

Art therapy for schizophrenia spectrum disorders

DSM-5-TR criteria for schizophrenia spectrum disorders: Schizophrenia is one of the schizophrenia spectrum and other psychotic disorders listed in the DSM-5-TR (American Psychiatric Association, 2022). The schizophrenia spectrum disorders share symptoms in five areas: (1) **Delusions** are strongly held beliefs not based on reality and resist changes even with evidence. These beliefs have a range of themes from persecution, referential, somatic, religious, or grandiose. (2) **Hallucinations** are perceptions of stimuli (sight, smell, sound, touch, taste) that are not present in reality. Auditory hallucinations or voices are the most common hallucination. (3) **Disorganized thinking** is defined as disconnected or unrelated thoughts expressed through speech. (4) **Disorganized/abnormal motor movement** is when someone has undirected bodily movements or lack of movement that impairs one's daily functioning. (5) **Negative symptoms** are a lack of emotional expression, motivation, pleasure, speech output, or social interaction.

Genetic and physiological factors in schizophrenia: Researchers have found a strong genetic link for schizophrenia. However, other risk factors include late winter or early spring birth, complications at birth, and the greater age of the father (American Psychiatric Association, 2022).

Schizophrenia and demographic and cultural considerations: Different cultures and religions positively value hallucinations [e.g., people from the Upper Amazon "brew ayahuasca as a spiritual guide" and "consider hallucinations that provide guidance" (Laroi et al., 2014), speech variations (e.g., "glossolalia is a poetic-rythmic utterance of pseudo-words …produced in a religious and spiritual context with particular reference to charismatic Christian and Pentacostal communities (Keri et al., 2020, p. 1), and cultural differences in family expressed emotion (López et al., 2004)]. In addition, the type of delusions, or strongly held beliefs not based in reality, can vary by culture (American Psychiatric Association, 2022). Rates of schizophrenia tend to be lower for females but females tend to report more mood-related and psychotic symptoms (Laroi et al., 2014).

Formal elements and schizophrenia: Gantt and Tabone (1998, 2012) found that people with schizophrenia or who were in a psychotic state tended to create artwork with mismatching color to object-fit, lower scores on integration, logic, and realism in the art piece. Ahmed and Miller (2003; as cited in Hinz, 2019, p. 10) found a "reverse developmental process [that] can be seen in art products created by the devolving brain."

Wadeson (2010) asked patients with schizophrenia to draw a picture of their psychiatric illness or whatever caused the patient to be admitted to the unit. She also asked patients to draw their hallucinations and delusions as a way "to gain further understanding of the psychotic experience" (p. 224). Many of the patients drew feelings of depression (pictures of tears, rain, and clouds). Religious, historical, and current event themes were present in many of the patients' drawings (Wadeson, 2010). Additional features in the drawings were symbols, distorted human figures and/or facial expressions, writing, fragments, lack of composition or organization.

Art therapy considerations when working with people with schizophrenia: Experiencing hallucinations can be very scary as the stimuli are often perceived as being real (Early, 2017; Whitbourne, 2020). Therapists should not argue with the patient about the hallucination or delusions but instead acknowledge and validate how the patient is feeling (Wadeson, 2010). Early (2017) recommends structured activities with others so that the patient focuses less on the hallucinations. Sometimes activities that provide sensory stimulation (music, scent, film) may distract the person from the hallucinations. Some art therapists suggest having patients engage in representational art-making (e.g., still life drawings) since this may help to refocus patients back to reality (McNiff, 2004; as cited in Hinz, 2019, p. 80). Shore and Rush (2019) use more controlled media (e.g., drawing, collage, geometric shapes) to help patients with psychosis have more control versus using media or art directives that might be less controllable (e.g., paint) and may lead to an increase of emotions.

Research on art therapy and schizophrenia: Ten journal articles that examined the effectiveness of art therapy for schizophrenia found that all the studies focused on group art therapy (Van Lith, 2016) but applied various theoretical approaches (role development theory, expressive arts therapy, group interactive, and psychoanalytic art therapy). Several studies showed improvement in interpersonal and task skills, role functioning, improved understanding of the disorder, increased coping skills, improved sense of self, decreased paranoia, and decreased dropout rates.

However, the Multicenter Study of Art Therapy in Schizophrenia Systematic Evaluation (MATISSE; Crawford et al., 2012) randomly assigned 417 participants with schizophrenia from four different centers to an art therapy group (free self-expression with art materials), an activity group (games, watching movies, café visits), or standard care. Results showed no significant difference between the art therapy group and the standard care group on overall functioning according to the Global Assessment of Functioning (GAF) scale and mental health symptoms but people in the activity group had a larger reduction in positive symptoms (i.e., hallucinations, delusions, etc.) of schizophrenia after 24 months. The study had several significant limitations: 40% of participants did not attend any session, many of the groups averaged 2–3 attendees per session, and short-term benefits were not measured. These researchers, therefore, argue that additional research must be done to determine whether art therapy is truly beneficial for those with schizophrenia.

Case example

The benefits and risks of introducing art materials to individuals who are in a current state of psychosis (or having experiences not based on reality) should be carefully evaluated before an art therapist proceeds. Symptoms of schizophrenia can lead individuals to lack a sense of security and live in fear and the art therapist will want to keep this in mind as they plan the art therapy session. An art therapy intervention that may help in this case is the safe place drawing. Solomon (pseudonym), a 23-year-old, white, cisgender male was just admitted to a long-term treatment facility where he was expected to spend the next several months as the treatment team worked with him to assist him in managing the symptoms of schizophrenia in hopes of eventually moving him to a less restrictive environment in the community. He was staying in his room, taking frequent showers, and reportedly held a conversation about God with a preacher, but no one else was in the room. The art therapist entered with a

FIG. 11.3 *Solomon's basketball drawing. This drawing was recreated by art therapist and chapter author, Janet Kempf.*
(No permission required.)

piece of paper and some markers and asked Solomon if he would like to draw. Solomon agreed by taking the materials and then returned to the conversation he was having before the art therapist entered. The art therapist waited and when there was a break in the conversation, the art therapist asked Solomon to draw his safe place. Solomon sat down and began to use the markers. A few minutes later he gave the drawing to the art therapist. The drawing contained two stick figures with an orange ball playing a game of basketball. Solomon did not say anything. The art therapist shared this with the treatment team and learned that before Solomon had his initial onset of symptoms he was a junior in college on a basketball scholarship. With this information, the team decided to advance Solomon's status on the unit so that he could go to the gym during recreation time. The next day, the art therapist saw Solomon on the court bouncing the basketball with a smile on his face. Fig. 11.3 is a therapist-recreation of Solomon's drawing.

Art therapy for manic episodes in bipolar disorder and related disorders

Bipolar and related disorders DSM-5-TR criteria: Bipolar and related disorders are considered to be related to both schizophrenia spectrum and other psychotic disorders and depressive disorders (American Psychiatric Association, 2022) and share common features of mood instability. A key feature that distinguishes bipolar disorders from depressive disorders is mania or hypomania. A **manic episode** is defined as an elevated or irritable mood (also called expansive), is not typical for the person, and lasts at least 1 week or longer. The elevated or irritable mood must have at least three of the following: inflated self-esteem, lack of sleep, increased speech, distractibility, increased goal-directed or at-risk behavior, and significant impairment or hospitalization. **Hypomania** has lower-level symptoms and impairment than mania and the change in mood needs to last only 4 days. These episodes fluctuate with depressive episodes. DSM-5-TR bipolar and related disorder diagnoses include bipolar I (manic and major depressive episodes), bipolar II (hypomanic and major depressive disorder episodes), cyclothymia (2 years of low-level symptoms of hypomania and depression that do not reach the level for full bipolar diagnosis), and substance use and medication-induced symptoms.

Bipolar and related disorder genetic and physiological factors: There is a strong genetic component to bipolar I disorder and people who have a relative with bipolar disorder have a "10-fold increased risk" (American Psychiatric Association, 2013, p. 130) and there is also an increased risk if a relative has schizophrenia. Bipolar II also tends to occur when relatives also have bipolar II. Cyclothymia is more common in relatives of people with major depressive disorder, bipolar I, or bipolar II disorder.

Demographic and cultural considerations with bipolar and related disorders: The DSM-5-TR (American Psychiatric Association, 2022) notes that experiencing adverse events in childhood places people at risk for early onset bipolar I disorder and can lead to a poorer outcomes and possibly more severe symptoms. Bipolar I is more common in high-income countries and people who are separated, divorced, or widowed have higher rates. Although rates for females and males are equal, females with bipolar I have more rapid cycles or mixed states, higher rates of eating disorders, and alcohol use disorders. The DSM-5-TR (American Psychiatric Association, 2022) notes that African Americans are more likely to be diagnosed with schizophrenia versus a mood disorder due to clinician bias (Hairston et al., 2019). Bipolar II tends to affect people at a younger age and has a higher likelihood of recovery with more education, fewer years of active illness, and being married. Females with Bipolar II also have more mixed and rapid cycling.

Formal elements and mania: Clients in a manic state tend to use a lot of color, space, numerous objects in the environment, and energy in the artwork (Gantt & Tabone, 2012). Wadeson (2010) also found that people in manic states used "wild, vivid, and hot colors" (p. 167), high space usage, and implied energy. Sexual symbols, euphoric themes, carelessness/impulsivity, and excitement were other patterns she found in the art of people in a manic state.

Art therapy considerations when working with someone in a manic state: Early (2017) cautions therapists to be prepared when working with people in a manic state as these patients may have difficulty focusing. She advises therapists to be consistent, set limits, and redirect problematic behavior. Reducing the stimulation or access to supplies may help limit distractions. Providing art directives that are portable and structured will allow someone in a manic state to move around and pick up easily when unfocused. Unfocused art activities or fluid art materials may be difficult for clients in this state; however, it is important for the art therapist to always review treatment goals to ensure they are meeting the needs of the clients at the moment. For example, the patient in a manic state may need a way to work off excess energy through more expressive art media.

Art therapy research and bipolar disorder: Art therapy research on bipolar disorder is rare. Henley (2007) wrote about several interventions he used with 16 children diagnosed with bipolar disorders (in the DSM-5 the bipolar disorder diagnosis in childhood has been removed). He called his intervention "Naming the Enemy." Each week children completed drawings on their "friend" and "enemy" aspects of their symptoms or behavior over the week. Henley argued this intervention helped the children to see themselves as separate from their symptoms. A second study with a 13-year-old participant found that art therapy helped to establish a strong alliance with a client who was resistant to therapy. The art therapy aided in identifying the onset of manic episodes. Lefebvre (2008) had the adolescent engage with art using a number of directives including drawing a superhero, building with tinfoil and masking tape, working with colored clay, mask making, and drawing emotions.

Case example

An art therapist conducted a group with six clients on an adult behavioral health unit. The art therapist directed the clients to fold a large piece of paper into fours and label each section with the words mad, sad, glad, and scared. Next, the clients were asked to create an image to show what each of these feelings looks like. When finished, the clients were asked to share their pictures. Connie (pseudonym), a 35-year-old, Asian-American client who identifies as a heterosexual female, shared her picture first. The image of the three more unpleasant feelings was very similar with simple small, black, blue, and red lines. However, the yellows and oranges used in the glad image were spilling into the other sections of the paper and almost seem to overtake the smaller images. Connie said, "This is what it feels like to be manic." The art therapist asked the other group members if they could relate. The group then had a conversation about the struggles of being in a manic episode and how it can be exciting and terrifying. At the end of the session, the clients were left with a better understanding of their emotions and the effects of manic episodes.

The cases described above take place at different treatment settings: private practice, behavioral units, and long-term care facilities. How do these treatment settings differ and what does art therapy work look like in these different settings? Next, we will explore a sample of settings where art therapists engage with individuals experiencing symptoms of mental health conditions.

Art therapy and mental health recovery treatment settings

This section describes a wide variety of treatment settings for people who experience mental health conditions. People may need different levels of treatment at different times as symptoms fluctuate and the needs of the individual changes. A **biopsychosocial** treatment approach must include an exploration of biological, psychological, and sociocultural influences that must be considered to treat the whole person. In order to restore the client's highest level of functioning, the client's history, treatment goals, and preferences must be considered. Settings follow a spectrum from highly restrictive to no restrictions. Highly **restrictive settings** (e.g., jails, prisons, forensic mental health units, or psychiatric units) are for clients who are perceived as being at risk of harm to one's self or others and thus are admitted to a locked unit to prevent and maintain the safety of clients, and others, until treatment is completed. Clients are typically admitted involuntarily to restrictive settings. In a nonrestrictive setting, clients meet with clinicians for a time limit but maintain their own independent life and schedule.

Art therapy in psychiatric (also called behavioral health) unit or hospital settings

Typically, when an individual experiences a life or death crisis related to mental health (e.g., suicidal thoughts, homicidal thoughts, or psychosis), they are directed to call 911 or go to the nearest emergency room. Some hospitals have specialized emergency rooms designated for psychiatric emergencies, while other hospitals admit patients to a locked psychiatric unit or a freestanding specialized psychiatric hospital. In these settings, clients receive medication and group therapy. Depending on the client's care needs and insurance coverage hospital stays are generally brief (3 days to a week). After clients stabilize, they may receive a referral, appointment for treatment outside of the hospital, or an evidence-based safety plan to assist them in maintaining and/or restoring their highest level of functioning in the community.

Shore and Rush (2019) note that the psychiatric hospital setting can feel "unpredictable and challenging" (p. 2) due to the rotation of clients and staff and heterogeneity in the group. Art therapy in psychiatric hospital settings primarily focuses on crisis stabilization (Spaniol, 2012). Group art therapy sessions focus on symptom reduction through structured art experiences that help to understimulate and not overwhelm the client (Shore & Rush, 2019). At this phase of treatment, it is important for the client to feel safe and the art therapist may choose interventions and materials that promote safety. Art therapy will also build on the client's strengths through creativity, increase a sense of control through the art directives, and may include art directives that orient someone to the present moment such as still life.

Art therapy in respite/residential care

Clients with severe symptoms may struggle to manage independently and may be placed in long-term or community-based treatment settings where they work with a treatment team to maintain their level of functioning. Community-based settings may include crisis respite centers and/or supported living apartments that provide 24-hour observation and support to residents (NAMI, 2020a). Assertive community treatment (ACT) is an example of a community-based approach where a multidisciplinary team provides around the clock support to people with mental health conditions (types of psychosocial treatments). Alternative treatment can include in-home support with family present or with providers meeting with the clients on a regular basis (NAMI, 2020a).

Individuals in this setting have the potential to isolate and feel detached from their communities whether due to the disruption that the symptoms of mental illness can cause or concerns about the previously mentioned stigma of mental illness. For these reasons, an art therapist may choose to focus on the person-driven principle of recovery and encourage "autonomy and independence to the greatest extent possible by" allowing the individual the opportunity to lead and choose how they would like to engage with the art materials (SAMHSA, 2012, p. 4). In doing so, the art therapist promotes resilience and empowers the individual.

Art therapy in partial hospitalization/day treatment programs

Partial hospitalizations/day treatment programs are options to assist clients to transition back to the community after hospitalization or when there is a decline in client functioning (NAMI, 2020c). In this treatment setting, clients typically have a treatment team composed of several providers and are offered medication, group, and individual treatment. At times, these programs also invite families to join their loved ones and offer family therapy.

External support networks (e.g., encouraging family and friends) and connections with peers who have similar shared experiences are guiding principles of recovery (SAMHSA, 2012). The art therapist in the partial hospitalization/day treatment program might work with clients to set goals related to building support systems. Interventions may include collaborative art projects and discussions about the importance of seeking support to gain a "sense of belonging, personhood, empowerment, autonomy, social inclusion, and community participation" (SAMHSA, 2012, p. 4).

Art therapy in dual diagnosis treatment centers

Clients experiencing symptoms of mental illness may also be using substances, such as alcohol, nonprescribed medications, or illicit drugs to cope with or dull symptoms. **Dual diagnosis** is where someone meets the criteria for a substance-use disorder and a psychological disorder. When this occurs, clients typically require treatment to manage symptoms of mental illness and substance use and are treated in settings where providers are trained to meet their unique needs. Art therapy treatment goals may focus on the recovery principle of hope, "that people can and do overcome the internal and external challenges, barriers, and obstacles that confront them" (SAMHSA, 2012, p. 4).

Art therapy in medical settings

When diagnosed with a medical illness, one's entire sense of self is shaken as one struggles to make sense of the diagnosis, adjust to changes in the body, desiring to return back to normal, and shifting roles in relationships. Although the patient's primary concern may be the medical illness, psychological issues as described in earlier sections may develop (Anand, 2015). An art therapist can help to address these issues in the medical setting. Art therapists in this setting must consider: (1) how the art materials might negatively affect the person physically (e.g., certain scents may cause nausea), (2) where the art-making will take place (e.g., at the bedside), and (3) the sterilization of art materials (Anand, 2015).

Art therapy in community mental health centers

When clients are in need of regular treatment to manage symptoms of their mental illness, at times unable to maintain employment, and lack insurance, community mental health centers may offer treatment (NAMI, 2020c). Treatment services may include medication management, individual and group therapies, peer support, and case management services. As mentioned earlier, open art studio sessions are common in these settings and the goal is to provide a safe and accessible place for clients to be expressive, make social connections, and focus on mental health recovery.

Art therapy in private practice settings and university counseling centers

Clients who are able to function in the community, yet need support to maintain stability or make improvements in their lives may seek treatment in private practice settings. These clients can receive art therapy as an individual, family, or group. Private practice offices are located in various locations in the community, including places of employment and medical office buildings. Most college campuses offer therapy services and a few offer art therapy to students in need of mental health treatment.

Art therapy and teletherapy

With the advent of technology, treatment settings are adjusting to meet the needs of their clients. When clients are unable to receive services in person, the art therapy provider may offer to meet with the client via secure telephone or internet. Teletherapy can be just as effective to assist clients with symptom management as in-person therapy (NAMI, 2020c). Since the COVID-19 pandemic, art therapists have found new ways to hold art therapy sessions via the internet, including online virtual support groups. For example, art therapists utilize two cameras, one to show the artwork and the other focusing on the client's face as the client makes art. While other art therapists have clients send images of their artwork via secure text or emails for the viewing and processing of art images in session. In all of these situations, clients must have access to art materials whether purchased independently, provided by the art therapist, or materials found in their environments.

Conclusions

This chapter began by traveling through history and exploring early connections of the use of art to understand mental illness, the effects of art-making on mental health, and the emergence of the art therapy profession in psychiatric institutions. We examined the criteria used to diagnose a small selection of psychological disorders and how therapists begin to formulate a clinical diagnosis. The chapter reviewed research on the benefits of art therapy, considerations for practicing art therapy when clients present certain symptoms, and case examples for the selected psychological disorders. Different treatment settings that use art therapy to help clients in different ways were presented. Since "art therapy has taught me that each individual is unique" (Wadeson, 2010, p. 168) we encourage readers to use the information, descriptions, and case examples provided before but remember that each client is unique and should be treated as such.

Art experientials and reflection questions

1. Define mental illness in your own words. What do you like or dislike about this term and definition? How has the definition changed since you read this chapter?
2. Fold a piece of paper in half and label one side as benefits and one side as risks of diagnosing clients. Create a collage that explores both the benefits and drawbacks of diagnosis.
3. Using a piece of paper and markers, create a poster to help reduce the stigma associated with mental illness that you can post on-campus or display on social media.
4. Do you think the artwork created by Bell and Diamond to understand mental illness was ethical? Why or why not? What might be other ways of using creative means to document symptoms of mental health conditions? Search online to learn about artists who are using creative means to express their emotions, experiences with social exclusion/prejudice, or highlighting social justice issues. How do these creative expressions counteract or contribute to the stigma of mental illness?
5. What resonates with you about ways art therapy helps to support mental health? How might you incorporate creative means to support your own mental health? Using your phone, take a photograph of a place you feel at peace and then make the image the main screen of your cell phone.
6. Share with a classmate a color, line, and/or texture that represents a mood or feeling. Ask them to guess the feeling based on what you shared. Compare your intention with their response. What does this exchange highlight about dangers of using of graphic indicators or patterns to diagnose people from their drawings? What are the potential drawbacks to this approach?
7. What are the current limitations of the research on art therapy and specific mental disorders? How might you improve studies on art therapy for the future?

Additional resources

Books

Burrows, A., & Schumacher, I. (1990). *Portraits of the Insane: The Case of Dr. Diamond.* Quartet Books.

Cohen, R. (2017). *Outsider art and art therapy: Shared histories current issues & future identities*. Philadelphia: Jessica Kingsley Publishers.

MacGregor, J. M. (1989). *The discovery of the art of the insane*. Princeton, N.J: Princeton University Press.

Prinzhorn, H. (1972). *Artistry of the mentally ill: A contribution to the psychology and psychopathology of configuration*. New York: Springer-Verlag. Originally published in 1922.

Videos

Kirsten Hatfield shares how her mood fluctuations that shape her artwork. Search YouTube for "This painter 'definitely wouldn't trade being bipolar.'" Documentary (4 minutes 22 seconds).

Between Insanity and Beauty: The Art Collection of Dr. Prinzhorn describes Prinzhorn's archives of patients with schizophrenia and their artwork. Documentary (1 hour 16 minutes).

As artist Louis Wain become more distant from reality, his art also paralleled his feeling of disconnection and paranoia. Documentary. Search YouTube for Louis Wain before and after schizophrenia (2 minutes and 55 seconds).

Search YouTube for Portraits of the Insane to view a short clip to see some of *Diamonds photographs* of people with a mental illness. Documentary (2 minutes 2 seconds).

Explore further

1. Explore the DSM-5-TR using a copy from your local or school library. What considerations or adaptations might be needed for people with different disorders?
2. Read, watch, or listen to any television, film, or podcast for 1–2 hours. Is person first language used? How might the language we use in society have an impact on people? How does our language affect how we see who is in our in-group or out-group?
3. Check out the National Alliance on Mental Illness campaigns such as CureStigma, StigmaFree, Hope Starts with You. Do you think the NAMI videos are helpful in reducing stigma? Design your own public service announcement.
4. Explore online information about the *Adverse Childhood Experiences* study.
5. There are many art centers that are focused on artists with disabilities, including those who have a mental health condition. Explore some of these sites (Check out Project Onward, Creative Growth Center, and the Art Therapy Studio). What do these centers have in common with information from this chapter? What do these centers offer that is different from what is discussed in this chapter?

Chapter terms

Ableism
Adverse childhood experiences
Any mental illness
Art Brut
Cortisol
Delusions
Diagnostic and Statistical Manual of Mental Disorders (DSM-5-TR)
Disorganized thinking
Disorganized/abnormal motor movement
Distress
Dual diagnosis
Formal elements
Graphic indicators
Hallucinations
Hypomania (hypomanic)
Impairment or dysfunction
International Classification of Diseases
Labeling Theory
Mandala
Mania
Manic episode
Mental disorder
Mental health condition
Mental health recovery
Mental illness
Negative symptoms
Outsider art
Pattern matching
Pencil pressure
People First Language
Physiognomy
Psychological disorders
Restrictive settings
Self-stigma or internalized stigma
Serious mental illness
Somatic symptoms
State anxiety
Stigma
Trait anxiety

References

Abbing, A., Ponstein, A., van Hooren, S., de Sonneville, L., Swaab, H., & Baars, E. (2018). The effectiveness of art therapy for anxiety in adults: A systematic review of randomised and non-randomised controlled trials. *PLoS One*, *13*(12). https://doi.org/10.1371/journal.pone.0208716, e0208716.

Ahmed, T., & Miller, B. L. (2003). Art and brain evolution. In A. Toomel (Ed.), *Cultural guidance in the development of the human mind* (pp. 87–93). Ablex Publishing.

American Psychiatric Association. (2013). *Diagnostic and statistical manual of mental disorders* (5th ed.). American Psychiatric Association.

American Psychiatric Association. (2022). *Diagnostic and statistical manual of mental disorders* (5th ed., Text revised). American Psychiatric Association.

Anand, S. A. (2015). Dimensions of art therapy in medical illness. In D. Gussak, & M. Rosal's (Eds.), *The Wiley handbook of art therapy* (pp. 409–420). John Wiley & Sons.

Babouchkina, A., & Robbins, S. J. (2015). Reducing negative mood through mandala creation: A randomized controlled trial. *Art Therapy: Journal of the American Art Therapy Association*, *32*(1), 34–39. https://doi.org/10.1080/07421656.2015.994428.

Beers, C. W. (2010). A mind that found itself: An autobiography. 1908. *American Journal of Public Health*, *100*(12), 2354–2356. https://doi.org/10.2105/AJPH.100.12.2354.

Beerse, M. E., Van Lith, T., & Stanwood, G. D. (2019). Is there a biofeedback response to art therapy? A technology-assisted approach for reducing anxiety and stress in college students. *SAGE Open*, *9*(2). https://doi.org/10.1177/2158244019854646. 215824401985464.

Bell, C. (1877). *Anatomy and philosophy of expression: As connected with the fine arts* (7th ed.). George Bell and Sons. Retrieved from https://www.google.com/books/edition/The_Anatomy_and_Philosophy_of_Expression/HCUtAAAAYAAJ?hl=en&gbpv=1&printsec=frontcover.

Blomdahl, C., Gunnarsson, A. B., Guregård, S., & Björklund, A. (2013). A realist review of art therapy for clients with depression. *The Arts in Psychotherapy*, *40*(3), 322–330. https://doi.org/10.1016/j.aip.2013.05.009.

Bloom, D. E., Cafiero, E. T., Jané-Llopis, E., Abrahams-Gessel, S., Bloom, L. R., Fathima, S., et al. (2011). *The global economic burden of noncommunicable diseases*. World Economic Forum.

Brown, E. D., Garnett, M. L., Anderson, K. E., & Laurenceau, J.-P. (2017). Can the arts get under the skin? Arts and cortisol for economically disadvantaged children. *Child Development*, *88*(4), 1368–1381. https://doi-org.proxy.libraries.uc.edu/10.1111/cdev.12652.

Burrows, A., & Schumacher, I. (1990). *Portraits of the insane: The case of Dr. Diamond*. Quartet Books.

Campenni, C. E., & Hartman, A. (2020). The effects of completing mandalas on mood, anxiety, and state mindfulness. *Art Therapy: Journal of the American Art Therapy Association*, *37*(1), 25. https://doi.org/10.1080/07421656.2019.1669980.

Cohen, R. (2017). *Outsider art and art therapy: Shared histories current issues & future identities*. Jessica Kingsley Publishers.

Commission on Accreditation of Allied Health Education Programs. (2016). *Standards and guidelines for the accreditation of educational programs in art therapy*. https://www.caahep.org/CAAHEP/media/CAAHEP-Documents/ArtTherapyStandards.pdf.

Crawford, M. J., Killaspy, H., Barnes, T. R. E., Barrett, B., Byford, S., Clayton, K., et al. (2012). Group art therapy as an adjunctive treatment for people with schizophrenia: Multicentre pragmatic randomised trial. *BMJ*, *344*(4), e846. https://doi.org/10.1136/bmj.e846.

Curry, N. A., & Kasser, T. (2005). Can colouring mandalas reduce anxiety? *Art Therapy: Journal of the American Art Therapy Association*, *22*(2), 81–85.

Drake, J. E., Hastedt, I., & James, C. (2016). Drawing to distract: Examining the psychological benefits of drawing over time. *Psychology of Aesthetics, Creativity, and the Arts*, *10*(3), 325–331. https://doi-org.proxy.libraries.uc.edu/10.1037/aca0000064.

DSM History. (n.d.). Retrieved from https://www.psychiatry.org/psychiatrists/practice/dsm/history-of-the-dsm. (Accessed 20 May 2020).

Early, M. B. (2016). *Mental health concepts and techniques for the occupational therapy assistant* (5th ed.). Wolters Kluwer.

Early, M. B. (2017). *Mental health concepts and techniques for the occupational therapy assistant* (5th ed.). Wolters Kluwer.

Ellison, M. L., Belanger, L. K., Niles, B. L., Evans, L. C., & Bauer, M. S. (2018). Explication and definition of mental health recovery: A systematic review. *Administration and Policy in Mental Health and Mental Health Services Research*, *45*, 91–102. https://doi.org/10.1007/s10488-016-0767-9.

Espinosa, V. M. (2015). *Martín Ramírez: Framing his life and art*. University of Texas Press.

Fancourt, D., Finn, S., Warran, K., & Wiseman, T. (2019). Group singing in bereavement: Effects on mental health, self-efficacy, self-esteem and well-being. *BMJ Supportive & Palliative Care*. https://doi.org/10.1136/bmjspcare-2018-001642.

Felitti, V. J., Anda, R. F., Nordenberg, D., Williamson, D. F., Spitz, A. M., Edwards, V., et al. (1998). Relationship of childhood abuse and household dysfunction to many of the leading causes of death in adults: The Adverse Childhood Experiences (ACE) study. *American Journal of Preventive Medicine*, *14*(4), 245–258. https://doi.org/10.1016/S0749-3797(98)00017-8.

Fincher, S. F. (2009). *The mandala workbook: A creative guide for self-exploration, balance, and well-being*. Shambhala.

Ganim, B. (1999). *Art & healing: Using expressive art to heal your body, mind, and spirit*. Echo Point Books & Media, LLC.

Gantt, L., & Tabone, C. (1998). *The formal elements art therapy scale: The rating manual*. Gargoyle Press.

Gantt, L., & Tabone, C. (2012). *The formal elements art therapy scale: The rating manual*. Gargoyle Press.

Goffman, E. (1963). *Stigma; notes on the management of spoiled identity*. Prentice-Hall.

Goodheart, C. D., & Lansing, M. H. (1997). *Treating people with chronic disease: A psychological guide*. American Psychological Association.

Hall, R. (2013). Art brut. *British Journal of Psychiatry*, *202*(4), 268. https://doi.org/10.1192/bjp.bp.112.122317.

Hairston, D. R., Gibbs, T. A., Wong, S. S., & Jordan, A. (2018). Clinician bias in diagnosis and treatment. In M. M. Medlock, D. Shtasel, N. T. Trinh, & D. R. Williams (Eds.), *Racism and psychiatry* (pp. 105–137). Springer International Publishing. https://doi.org/10.1007/978-3-319-90197-8_7.

Henderson, P., Rosen, D., & Mascaro, N. (2007). Empirical study on the healing nature of mandalas. *Psychology of Aesthetics, Creativity, and the Arts*, *1*(3), 148–154. https://doi.org/10.1037/1931-3896.1.3.148.

Henley, D. (2007). Aiming the enemy: An art therapy intervention for children with bipolar and comorbid disorders. *Art Therapy: Journal of the American Art Therapy Association*, *24*(3), 104–110.

Hinz, L. D. (2009). *Expressive therapies continuum: A framework for using art in therapy*. Routledge.

Hinz, L. D. (2019). *Expressive therapies continuum: A framework for using art in therapy* (2nd ed.). Routledge.

Jacob, K. S. (2015). Recovery model of mental illness: A complementary approach to psychiatric care. *Indian Journal of Psychological Medicine*, *37*(2), 117–119.

Junge, M. B. (2015). History of art therapy. In D. Gussak, & M. L. Rosal (Eds.), *The Wiley handbook of art therapy* (pp. 7–16). John Wiley & Sons.

Jutras, M. (2017). Historical perspectives on the theories, diagnosis, and treatment of mental illness. *British Columbia Medical Journal*, *59*(2), 86–88.

Kaimal, G., Ray, K., & Muniz, J. (2016). Reduction of cortisol levels and participants' responses following art making. *Art Therapy: Journal of the American Art Therapy Association*, *33*(2), 74–80. https://doi.org/10.1080/07421656.2016.1166832.

Kaimal, G., Ayaz, H., Herres, J., Dieterich-Hartwell, R., Makwana, B., Kaiser, D. H., et al. (2017). Functional near-infrared spectroscopy assessment of reward perception based on visual self-expression: Coloring, doodling, and free drawing. *The Arts in Psychotherapy*, *55*, 85–92. https://doi.org/10.1016/j.aip.2017.05.004.

Keri, S., Kallai, I., & Csigo, K. (2020). Attribution of mental states in glossolalia: A direct comparison with schizophrenia. *Frontiers in Psychology*, *11*. https://doi.org/10.3389/fpsyg.2020.00638. 638–638.

King, R., Baker, F., & Neilsen, P. (2016). Introduction. In P. Neilson, R. King, & F. Baker (Eds.), *Creative arts in counseling and mental health* (pp. 1–7). Sage.

Kraepelin, E., & Diefendorf, A. R. (1915). *Clinical psychiatry*. MacMillan.

Laroi, F., Luhrmann, T. M., Bell, V., Christian, W. A., Deshpande, S., Fernyhough, C., … Woods, A. (2014). Culture and hallucinations: Overview and future directions. *Schizophrenia Bulletin*, *40*(4), S213–S220. https://doi.org/10.1093/schbul/sbu012.

LaRoque, S. D., & Obrzut, J. E. (2006). Pencil pressure and anxiety in drawings: A techno-projective approach. *Journal of Psychoeducational Assessment*, *24*(4), 381–393. https://doi.org/10.1177/0734282906288520.

Lefebvre, A. D. (2008). *Art therapy interventions with an adolescent with bipolar disorder.* Unpublished master's thesis.
Lilienfeld, S. O., Wood, J. M., & Garb, H. N. (2000). The scientific status of projective techniques. *Psychological Science in the Public Interest, 1*, 27–66.
Link, B. G., Struening, E. L., Rahav, M., Phelan, J. C., & Nuttbrock, L. (1997). On stigma and its consequences: Evidence from a longitudinal study of men with dual diagnoses of mental illness and substance abuse. *Journal of Health and Social Behavior, 38*(2), 177–190. https://doi.org/10.2307/2955424.
López, S. R., Hipke, K. N., Polo, A. J., Jenkins, J. H., Karno, M., Vaughn, C., et al. (2004). Ethnicity, expressed emotion, attributions, and course of schizophrenia: Family warmth matters. *Journal of Abnormal Psychology, 113*(3), 428–439. https://doi.org/10.1037/0021-843X.113.3.428.
Malchiodi, C. A. (1993). Introduction to special issue: Art and medicine. *Art Therapy: Journal of the American Art Therapy Association, 10*(2), 184–186. https://doi.org/10.1080/07421656.1993.10758983.
Mandell, W. (1995). *Origins of mental health.* Retrieved from https://www.jhsph.edu/departments/mental-health/about-us/origins-of-mental-health.html.
McNiff, S. (2004). *Art heals: How creativity cures the soul.* Shambhala Publications, Inc.
Mental Health America. (2020). *Our history.* Retrieved from https://www.mhanational.org/our-history.
Napoli, M. (2019). Ethical contemporary art therapy: Honoring an American Indian perspective. *Art Therapy: Journal of the American Art Therapy Association, 36*(4), 175–182. https://doi.org/10.1080/07421656.2019.1648916.
National Alliance on Mental Illness. (2020a). *Getting treatment during a crisis.* Retrieved from https://nami.org/Learn-More/Treatment/Getting-Treatment-During-a-Crisis.
National Alliance on Mental Illness. (2020b). *Stigma free.* Retrieved from https://nami.org/Get-Involved/Pledge-to-Be-StigmaFree.
National Alliance on Mental Illness. (2020c). *Treatment settings.* Retrieved from https://nami.org/About-Mental-Illness/Treatments/Treatment-Settings.
National Institute of Mental Health. (2019, April). *Suicide.* https://www.nimh.nih.gov/health/statistics/suicide.shtml.
National Institute of Mental Health. (2021, January). *Mental illness.* Retrieved from https://www.nimh.nih.gov/health/statistics/mental-illness.shtml.
Neimeyer, G. (2020, March 13). *Contemporary diagnostic developments: The evolving relationship between the ICD and the DSM (webinar).* American Psychological Association. https://apa.content.online/catalog/product.xhtml?eid=17318.
Pearl, S. (2009). Through a mediated mirror: The photographic physiognomy of Dr Hugh Welch Diamond. *History of Photography, 33*(3), 288–305. https://doi.org/10.1080/03087290902752978.
Pénzes, I., van Hooren, S., Dokter, D., & Hutschemaekers, G. (2018). How art therapists observe mental health using formal elements in art products: Structure and variation as indicators for balance and adaptability. *Frontiers in Psychology, 9*. https://doi.org/10.3389/fpsyg.2018.01611. 1611–1611.
People First Language. (2006). Retrieved from https://odr.dc.gov/page/people-first-language (Accessed 2 June 2020).
Raw Vision. (n.d.). *What is outsider art?* https://rawvision.com/pages/what-is-outsider-art. Retrieved June 20, 2020.
Robertson, R. (1992). *Beginner's guide to Jungian psychology.* Nicolas-Hays, Inc.
Sandmire, D. A., Rankin, N. E., Gorham, S. R., Eggleston, D. T., French, C. A., Lodge, E. E., et al. (2016). Psychological and autonomic effects of art making in college-aged students. *Anxiety, Stress, & Coping, 29*(5), 561–569. https://doi.org/10.1080/10615806.2015.1076798.

Scope, A., Uttley, L., & Sutton, A. (2017). A qualitative systematic review of service user and service provider perspectives on the acceptability, relative benefits, and potential harms of art therapy for people with non-psychotic mental health disorders. *Psychology and Psychotherapy, 90*(1), 25–43. https://doi.org/10.1111/papt.12093.

Searls, D. (2017). *The inkblots: Hermann Rorschach, his iconic test, and the power of seeing* (1st ed.). Crown.

Shore, A., & Rush, S. (2019). Finding clarity in chaos: Art therapy lessons from a psychiatric hospital. *The Arts in Psychotherapy, 66*. https://doi.org/10.1016/j.aip.2019.101575, 101575.

Spaniol, S. (2012). Art therapy with adults with severe mental illness. In C. Malchiodi (Ed.), *Handbook of art therapy* (2nd ed., pp. 288–301). Guilford Press.

Støre, J. S., & Jakobsson, N. (2022). The effect of mandala coloring on state anxiety: A systematic review and meta-analysis. Art Therapy, 1–9. https://doi.org/10.1080/07421656.2021.2003144 (ahead-of-print).

Strous, R. D., Opler, A. A., & Opler, L. A. (2016). Emil Kraepelin: Icon and reality. *American Journal of Psychiatry, 173*(3), 300–301. https://doi.org/10.1176/appi.ajp.2015.15050665.

Stuckey, H. L., & Nobel, J. (2010). The connection between art, healing, and public health: A review of current literature. *American Journal of Public Health (1971), 100*(2), 254–263. https://doi.org/10.2105/AJPH.2008.156497.

Substance Abuse and Mental Health Services Administration. (2012). *SAMHSA's working definition of recovery: 10 guiding principles of recovery*. https://store.samhsa.gov/sites/default/files/d7/priv/pep12-recdef.pdf.

Tedeschi, R. G., & Calhoun, L. G. (2009). In C. L. Park, M. H. Antoni, S. C. Lechner, & A. L. Stanton (Eds.), *The clinician as expert companion* (pp. 215–235). American Psychological Association. https://doi.org/10.1037/11854-012.

The Healthy Minds Network, & American College Health Association. (2020). *The impact of COVID-19 on college student well-being*. https://www.acha.org/documents/ncha/Healthy_Minds_NCHA_COVID_Survey_Report_FINAL.pdf.

Tondora, J., Miller, R., Slade, M., & Davidson, L. (2014). *Partnering for recovery in mental health: A practical guide to person-centered planning*. John Wiley & Sons, Ltd.

Trent, M. S. (2017). Henry Darger and the unruly paper dollhouse scrapbook. In K. M. Brian, J. Trent, & W. James (Eds.), *Phallacies: Historical intersections of disability and masculinity*. Oxford University Press. https://doi.org/10.1093/oso/9780190458997.001.0001.

Tubbs, R. S., Reich, S., Verma, K., Mortazavi, M. M., Loukas, M., Benninger, B., et al. (2012). Sir Charles Bell (1774–1842) and his contributions to early neurosurgery. *Child's Nervous System, 28*, 331–335. https://doi.org/10.1007/s00381-011-1666-8.

Tucker, J. (2016). *Diamond, Hugh Welch*. Oxford Dictionary of National Biography. https://doi-org.proxy.libraries.uc.edu/10.1093/ref:odnb/7583.

U.S. Department of Health and Human Services. (2001). *Mental health: Culture, race, and ethnicity—A supplement to mental health: A report of the surgeon general*. https://www.ncbi.nlm.nih.gov/books/NBK44249.

Uttley, L., Scope, A., Stevenson, M., Rawdin, A., Taylor Buck, E., Sutton, A., et al. (2015). Systematic review and economic modelling of the clinical effectiveness and cost effectiveness of art therapy among people with non-psychotic mental health disorders. *Health Technology Assessment, 19*(18), 1–120. https://doi.org/10.3310/hta19180.

van der Vennet, R., & Serice, S. (2012). Can coloring mandalas reduce anxiety? A replication study. *Art Therapy: Journal of the American Art Therapy Association, 29*(2), 87–92. https://doi.org/10.1080/07421656.2012.680047.

Van Lith, T. (2016). Art therapy in mental health: A systematic review of approaches and practices. *The Arts in Psychotherapy*, *47*, 9–22. https://doi.org/10.1016/j.aip.2015.09.003.

Vick, R. M. (2012). A brief history of art therapy. In C. A. Malchiodi (Ed.), *Handbook of art therapy* (pp. 5–16). The Guilford Press.

Wadeson, H. (2010). *Art psychotherapy* (2nd ed.). John Wiley & Sons.

Whitbourne, S. K. (2020). *Abnormal psychology: Clinical perspectives on psychological disorders* (9th ed.). McGraw Hill.

Wise, S. (2016). On considering the role of art therapy in treating depression. In D. E. Gussak, & M. L. Rosal (Eds.), *The Wiley handbook of art therapy* (pp. 350–360). John Wiley & Sons.

Wojcik, D. (2016). *Outsider art: Visionary worlds and trauma*. University Press of Mississippi.

World Health Organization. (2013). *Mental health action plan, 2013–2020*. Retrieved from https://apps.who.int/iris/bitstream/handle/10665/89966/9789241506021_eng.pdf?sequence=1.

Young, R. E., Goldberg, J. O., Struthers, C. W., McCann, D., & Phills, C. E. (2019). The subtle side of stigma: Understanding and reducing mental illness stigma from a contemporary prejudice perspective. *Journal of Social Issues*, *75*(3), 943–971. https://doi.org/10.1111/josi.12343.

Chapter 12

Art therapy and older adults

Erin Elizabeth Partridge, PhD, ATR-BC
Art Therapy, Dominican University of California, San Rafael, CA, United States, Experiential Researcher-In-Residence, Elder Care Alliance, Alameda, CA, United States

Voices from the field
"This is new—we've never been this old before" Ruth, Advocate, Community and Nonprofit Worker. Because older adult voices are so often left out of the conversation, this chapter intentionally begins with the verbatim words of an older adult as opposed to a younger person providing care. In her nineties, Ruth serves her community through her work on several city task forces and a local nonprofit. She advocates for age justice. And she remarked aloud one day how, despite all her work, she sometimes felt unprepared for each new phase of aging.

Learning outcomes

After reading this chapter, you will be able to
1. Summarize the benefits of art-making for older adults.
2. State and define three diseases of later life that may present challenges and opportunities in art therapy.
3. Identify three ways to adapt art materials and processes to address the needs of older adult clients.
4. Identify at least three places art therapists may work with older adults and name at least one characteristic of each setting.
5. Summarize the benefits of engaging in art and creativity in therapeutic and community settings.
6. Identify at least three considerations when selecting materials and directives for working with people living with dementia.
7. Define and describe ageism.
8. State and describe at least three strengths older adults bring to the art-making process.

Chapter overview

This chapter will discuss the concerns, diseases, and important psychosocial milestones of later life. It will provide descriptions of diseases commonly encountered in older adult care settings and work with older adults, covering the particular implications for art therapy, including dementia, Parkinson's,

Foundations of Art Therapy. https://doi.org/10.1016/B978-0-12-824308-4.00012-0

aphasia, stroke, and sensory loss. Beyond specific diagnoses, it introduces the ideas of ageism and ableism, important issues for art therapists to address in clinical work as well as at a systemic level. The aging population has some specific needs with regard to topics that they often explore in therapy, including grief and loss and changes in identity. Art therapy provides a space to delve into these sensitive topics, providing creative enrichment and engagement in later life. Though the diseases of later life are covered, the overall lens takes a strength-based approach, acknowledging the lived reality of struggle while focusing on opportunities for creative growth and exploration.

Life transitions

Think of a time of transition in your life. What was exciting about it? What was scary or unknown? How did you move through that transition? What transitions are coming up for you in the next 5–10 years?

Now imagine you are working with someone at the transition into retirement, the transition into congregate living, memory care, skilled nursing, or at end of life? What do you imagine might be exciting about that transition and what might be scary or unknown? What concerns do you think an art therapist would address?

Jane Burns conducted her doctoral dissertation to investigate creative arts therapists' work with older adults (Burns, 2009). At the time of her dissertation study, Burns was one of three arts therapists working with people living with dementia in Scotland; her study involved creative arts therapists of all disciplines (art, music, dance/movement, and drama) across the United Kingdom. Burns interviewed practitioners about their work with older adults, asking questions about who they work with, where the work happens, what the work entails, and what patterns participants could identify in the practice of creative arts therapy with older adults. She described, in an interview in 2020, some of the barriers preventing more people from pursuing work with older adults: "It wasn't sexy enough, they weren't in tempo with the client group. The only people that went in [to work with older adults] were people who had previous experience." Burns reflected that while some of the practitioners had entered the field by way of being assigned to work in older adult settings, "none of them wanted to leave the field in the end." She found that the therapists made assumptions about the nature of the work—and that those often incorrect assumptions made the therapists in Burns' study hesitant about pursuing the work: "but that was a myth…they had misunderstood… that sense of it being too structured to allow people to flow. In fact, what they found, of course, is that the minute a memory is tapped, the person is away, into the art or into the music." Part of the role of the art therapist working in older adult care settings, according to Burns, is "creating a culture that is not so task-oriented…more relational culture. Where you're trying to be with the person in the moment, holding that, sustaining it."

When asked about the difficulties in working with older adults, Burns spoke about structural areas of friction art therapists may encounter: "A lot of it is to do with team-working. Working in multidisciplinary teams, divisions between public, private, and voluntary sectors. These are very different ways of working." She spoke about some of the difficulties in each sector and encouraged working collaboratively with the interdisciplinary team to support the work of art therapy: "Once the team is on board you have a chance to then locate yourself in the setting." She tells students who are just beginning to work in older adult settings to make friends with everyone in the environment and to "never sit aloof in your profession."

In the interview, Burns spoke about the importance of considering language to describe the work: "Think about what is appropriate language. How would you tell somebody with dementia about what you're doing? You must involve the client in what you're doing. You aren't treating them, you're working with them."

Burns described art therapy with older adults as incredibly impactful: "It's some of the most alive work I've ever done, I think. The people are just so alive towards the end of life. You never quite meet that energy elsewhere. I haven't anyway." She spoke about the need for the art therapist to "work with the here and now" in each session, rather than thinking about more long-term treatment trajectories. Burns said this is not a limitation but rather a gift of work with older people: "Each session is like a golden nugget by itself—held together by the image." She affirmed the transcendent quality of the images people make—to go beyond their diagnoses. She shared the experience she often had with clients living with dementia not remembering her, but immediately recognizing their images or the materials.

Reflecting on both the process and product of art therapy sessions, she stated that the art seemed to hold or bear evidence of the connection between therapist and client. Furthermore, Burns stated that using art materials helps to "keep the sensory world alive" for the person living with dementia. The process of creating work is the active making stage. The product is the finished art. Working with older adults provides access to a part of human life that can be incredibly rewarding for the therapist: "I suppose there is that sense of the not knowing…there's a slight fragmentation, but there's that sense of being witness to what may be the last time of telling a life story." She acknowledged that older adults often do a lot of sharing of their lives with many different providers in care settings, but that art therapists have the ability to sit with people and explore verbal and visual ways to express their memories, feelings, and life stories even as age-related illnesses limit other means of communication. When asked about her hopes for the future of art therapy for older adult clients, she noted the global prioritization of dementia as a positive shift. She also noted an increase in the number of students she has encountered in recent years who are interested in work with older adults. She summed up her hopes in the following quote: "More people, more interest, developing understanding of how to work in a way which they understand the need for supporting the person but also the need for that person to have some time of independence." She believes that to be successful and ethical in work with older adults, the art therapist must "know when to support somebody and not just take control but actually then offer some independence."

Purpose of the chapter

Art therapists need to have foundational expertise in working with older adults and the issues they may bring into therapy. Even if they do not work in an older adult-specific context, art therapists will undoubtedly encounter older adults and issues around aging with their clients in any setting. For example, when working in a locked forensic mental health hospital, an older adult in an open studio group was routinely caught stealing pens and other supplies. He did not hide his stealing; often the pens were resting on the top of his walker or sticking up out of his pockets. Understanding that his behavior was an expression of his advancing dementia and not evidence of ongoing criminal behavior was essential in providing ethical care for this individual. It was also important for the art therapists to recognize and document that he was exhibiting signs of dementia in order to keep him safe from predation from younger patients in the same hospital.

Work with older adults takes place in many different settings, though the stereotype is often the nursing home or other medical setting. Therapists can encounter older adults living independently in private practice, community settings, and museum spaces. Art therapy with older adults benefits from the rich stories and lived experiences that these clients bring into the session and into the art studio—their long lives, filled with joy, struggle, and triumph bring them into therapy in ways that are different than their younger counterparts. This reality is both a struggle and a strength: depression, experienced over many decades, may be more intractable, and yet, the older person experiencing depression is perhaps more resilient and has collected more coping skills across their lifetime. This chapter will cover the benefits of engaging in art-making, some of the concerns older adults face in later life, alongside the strengths they bring into their creative pursuits.

Who are older adults?

By 2030, 21% of the US population will be over the age of 65 (Vespa, 2018). Demographics worldwide are shifting in different ways, and unfortunately some of the narratives around aging are playing into ageist stereotypes (Applewhite, 2016). The United States is experiencing decreased fertility and increased longevity, along with many other countries worldwide. The aging of the Baby Boom generation is causing a steady increase in people over the age of 65 in the United States (Lakin & Burke, 2019). Called a "quiet demographic revolution" (Hayward & Zhang, 2001, p. 70) it entails a decrease in births paired with an increase in longevity.

Understanding these demographic shifts is important when considering working with, and around the field of aging as there is a worry that with the low fertility/low mortality rates, countries or regions will not have enough young people to provide care and support for an aging population. However, we need to be careful about how these conversations are framed, as they can contribute to negative feelings about older adults and ageist thoughts and behaviors (Levy, 2017; Sweetland & Volmert, 2017; van den Hoonaard, 2018). Changing health and lifespan trends impact how older adults are perceived in culture and how individuals experience their own aging. Negative perceptions at the individual and cultural levels can precipitate an older adult seeking therapy and are often relevant to other clinical concerns. Culture change movements suggest looking at how language impacts the perception of aging; the **Eden Alternative**, in reframing the way we think about care, suggests using the term "care partner" for everyone—acknowledging that it is possible to both give and receive care in this relationship (Eden Alternative, 2006; Thomas, 2006). A **care partner** can be the older adult, a family member, a medical provider, or a trained professional care provider.

As Burns (2009) discovered in her research and as described in the clinical literature (Houpt et al., 2016; Partridge, 2019b; Stephenson, 2010), art therapists can work in a wide range of settings with older adults. This range of settings suggests the need for training and ongoing education about approaches to the work. Settings where art therapists work with older adults, and the unique needs and approaches in these different settings will be covered later in this chapter.

Imagine you are an art therapist working with older adults. What would you do if your client(s)...

...walks into the room, carrying a box filled with memories and ephemera of life, ready to engage in a life-review project. He is self-directed and asks a few clarifying questions about material use, but generally likes to work on his own.

...come in one at a time from all different parts of the building. They have pockets filled with tangled necklaces, special trinkets they want to fix or repurpose, or empty hands ready to make something new. They have been waiting for this group all week.

...was referred to your service to supplement her physical and occupational therapy.

...was referred to you to cope with grief.

...was referred to you to lessen his loneliness.

...come into the room with the assistance of a private caregiver because "Art" is the next thing on the daily calendar. They don't want to be there. They are not interested.

...are all waiting for you at a table in a sunny corner of a skilled nursing center. They are curious about what you have brought with you this time.

...show up at least thirty minutes early for an open studio group, wanting to chat and have some individual time with you.
...tell you stories from their lives they have never spoken aloud before.
...discover they are artists in the last years of their lives.

Older adults show up for art therapy in many different ways. Likewise, art therapists support older adults by utilizing a wide range of therapeutic and artistic skills. Art therapists working with older adults need to not only have a working knowledge of art supplies, including adaptation of these supplies, but also need to maintain their knowledge about the diseases of later life as these frequently precipitate entry into therapy. Aging is a complex process—it is not solely the progression of human life toward an end. Like many aspects of human life, we must consider the intersectional concerns to gain a deeper understanding of each person's lived experience.

Consider the following scenarios; how might these scenarios influence a person's experience of aging?

Aging alongside a partner, in the home where you brought up your family, in a small town where you have lived for many decades.
Aging alone in a big city with no surviving family members.
Aging while experiencing homelessness.
Aging with increased medical care needs in a skilled nursing setting in an unfamiliar town because it is closer to family members.
Aging in a planned retirement community with a wide range of events and opportunities for connection with others.
Aging in an assisted living as an LGBT+ elder, unsure if you can safely be 'out' in the setting.
Aging with a comorbid mental health condition.
Aging in a multifamily household with responsibilities for providing care to grandchildren.
Aging while caring for an adult child with a disability.
Aging in a culture that reveres and celebrates older adults.
Aging in a culture that reveres and celebrates youth.

Models of aging

There are many different ways to conceptualize the aging process. These include the biological, chronological, and social. Interestingly, these factors are more intertwined—for example, Cruikshank (2013) described the connection between biological and social aging as "One mark of the social construction of aging is overemphasis on bodily decline. The entire meaning of old age then becomes deteriorating bodies" (p. 35).

Biological views of aging include consideration of the diseases and disorders of later life, which will be covered later in this chapter. It also encompasses some of the work to transcend or subvert aging—practices related to disease prevention and longevity. **Biological age** has to do with the changing status of cells and other bodily processes, generally described in terms of their decline (Hamczyk et al., 2020). Art therapists, and students working with older adults, need to know about biological aging issues such as those that relate to health status and physical changes that happen with age. Art therapists and students need to be aware that aging skin is thinner and more delicate and they are more sensitive to extreme temperatures, which may necessitate different adaptations of materials. For example, using a dye that stains skin may be less of a big deal when working with youth because the dye will easily scrub off their hands. But with an older adult, the dye may more deeply penetrate their hands or they may be more sensitive to scrubbing. When developing programming and services for older adults, understanding the age-related changes they experience is important (Cunha et al., 2016).

Chronological aging is the number of years (or other measurement of time) since someone's birth. Chronological age can give some hints to health status or possible concerns, but it is not a perfect system. Biological age recognizes that each individual person's body changes at a different rate, and considers how their functioning may be impacted as their bodily systems age and change. Biological age does a better job at predicting changes to a person's health and physiological well-being (Hamczyk et al., 2020).

Social aging takes into account the social and cultural aspects of aging, including how we perceive the aging process, older people, and the roles and tasks of later life. Some markers of social aging include life transitions like becoming a grandfather or retiring from a job. Social aging also includes visibly observable traits like gray hair, wrinkles, and use of certain assistive devices. Someone's perceived social age may be connected to their physical and chronological age or they might be divergent. Think of a time when you were perceived to be older or younger than your chronological age. What signs and markers was the other person using to place your social age? Depending on the culture, the understanding of later life can be positive or negative (Cruikshank, 2013).

One construction of social aging is the 'grandmother' stereotype; in a paper exploring the visual representation of the social identity of grandmother, Caldas-Coulthard and Moon (2016) identified many examples of ageism and sexism in how the role was depicted. Because women's worth is often tied to appearance and youth, older women are seen as low status (Clarke, 2017) or not seen at all. Think about representations of older adults you have seen in various media. Very often, the picture of older life painted in popular culture and the media is a stereotype, and it often conforms to one part of a binary at a time. The lived experience of aging is much more complicated.

Roca's (2016) graphic novel *Wrinkles*, which was adapted into an animated film, explores the rarely discussed, complex social lives in institutionalized settings. The main characters are roommates in a care-providing setting. In their interactions, the characters explore some of the difficulties rarely explored outside these settings—how to navigate friends and partners' decline, peer-to-peer bullying, boredom, and how to have 'fun' despite circumstances. Similarly, Cannon's (2018) novel *Three Things About Elsie* describes many common experiences in assisted living settings from the point of view of a woman struggling with social and cognitive change. The film *Ice Mother* (Sláma, 2017) depicts complex relationships in later life—both with self and others. These examples are unfortunately rare. Much more common are ageist stereotypes, where older adults are depicted as frail and often serve as the punch line to jokes.

Other important elements of social aging include those related to culture, race, and ethnicity.Additional factors also include religion, socioeconomic circumstances, lived experiences, and familial beliefs about aging. For example, five older adults brought LGBTQIA concerns into art therapy. One spoke often about his life as a gay man and the changes he saw across his lifespan. He was joyful, out to his peers in memory care, and kept everyone laughing. Another woman, described in Partridge (2019b), endured a great deal of discrimination, lost her partner, and used art therapy as a means to explore her trauma and grief. Two other individuals found community in different ways as they aged. One wondered aloud what his life would have been like if he had been able to explore life as a woman. His participation in a public art project put that question out to the world and enabled conversations with younger generations of transgender and nonbinary youth. The second individual attended an intergenerational picnic. He asked the art therapist, in a quiet voice as they approached the assisted living: "Do you think there is anyone else like me there?"

Beliefs and practices about aging impact care relationships as well. The Eden Alternative (2006) and other cultural change movements in aging care use the term **care partner** in order to recognize the reciprocal nature of the relationship. Activist Ai Jenn Poo's writing (Poo & Conrad, 2015) and work with the Domestic Worker's Alliance highlights the need for greater equity and dignity for those who work in care-providing and other care-related roles, both in and out of the home. Some families, cultures, and circumstances maintain older relative's presence in the home until the end of their lives. Others live collectively with multiple families and generations in the same home.

Ageism is discrimination against people because of their actual or perceived age. The World Health Organization identified it as a "widespread and an insidious practice which has harmful effects on the health of older adults" (World Health Organization, 2020). The COVID-19 pandemic brought ageism into stark focus; researchers across the world identified ways older adults were marginalized, ignored, and misrepresented (Fraser & Lagacé, 2020). They covered the different ways ageist beliefs and practices harmed us all as the world worked to respond to the crisis. As ageism was uncovered, intergenerational solidarity movements worked to counter the problematic biases. In a meta-analysis of how modernization impacts beliefs about ageism, North and Fiske (2015) highlighted the ways modern, industrialized societies' attitudes about age and aging have changed, comparing Eastern and Western cultures. The authors looked at collectivism, industrialization, and the population aging rate. One of the more interesting findings ran counter to stereotypes and suggested a difference between respecting elders in one's own family and a general positive regard for older adults. The authors concluded that the general East–West binary may not be nuanced enough to understand attitudes toward aging and the prevalence of ageism. Antiageism advocate Ashton Applewhite described why, as a society, we need to address ageism:

"Like racism and sexism, ageism is a socially constructed idea that has changed over time and that serves a social and economic purpose. Like all discrimination, it legitimizes and sustains inequalities between groups—in this case, between the young and the no-longer-young. Different kinds of discrimination—including racism, sexism, ageism, ableism, and homophobia—interact, creating layers of oppression in the lives of individuals and groups. The oppression is reflected in and reinforced by society through the economic, legal, medical, commercial, and other systems that each of us navigates in daily life. Unless we challenge stigma, we reproduce it. Like racism and sexism, ageism is not about how we look. It's about what people in power want our appearance to mean" (Applewhite, 2016, p. 9).

Older adults from any of these groups who are discriminated against face additional oppression through ageism and often ableism in their later life. **Ableism** is the discrimination against people living with a disability. As older adults experience these new forms of oppression as they age they may require assistance or help with coping. Wong (2020), in an edited volume of first-person stories about experiences of disability, identified storytelling and story-sharing as a way to ameliorate some of the detrimental impacts of ableism. Making images of their experiences is one way to tell and share stories. Art therapists can help share older adults' stories via visual documentation of memories to share with family, preservation of community and cultural memories, and exhibition of work. Facilitating opportunities to connect with sites of art and culture introduces perspectives that might otherwise go unheard.

Settings where art therapists work with older adults

Some settings where art therapists may work with older adults are outlined in the following paragraphs, from lowest to highest acuity—circumstances where older adults seek lowest to highest provision of care.

In private practice, art therapists may work individually or in groups with older adults. These clients may or may not come to therapy with issues specifically related to their aging. Regarding accessibility, the art therapist considers the access to the building and support for the person who may be living at home or with minimal care. Through years of adaptation and habits, older adults often function better in their own homes than they do in unfamiliar places; for example, someone with age-related vision loss who has lived in the same apartment for 30 years does not need to see where the light switch is—they just reach out and turn it on. But in an unfamiliar setting like an art studio or therapy office, they can become disoriented or struggle to move around on their own. For an older adult living alone, coming to therapy may be one of just a few social interactions per week. If the older-adult client is very lonely, they may linger after sessions or groups, hoping for more time in social connection. The client might also exhibit a strong reaction to a canceled or rescheduled session. If the therapist is the only other person the client sees each week, the therapist may see or suspect signs and symptoms of dementia, loneliness, or self-neglect and shift to a social work role. Connecting the client to resources and health and safety supports is an important intervention. Art therapists in private practice may also encounter older adults who are the primary caregivers for younger family members, or who live in the home and attend family therapy with parents and young people. Different family dynamics impact self-concept, identity, stress, and physical and mental health.

Some art therapists teach or lead groups in drop-in centers, adult education contexts, museum programs, or other places that bring older adults together. In these types of settings, depending on the employment arrangement and structure of the site, the art therapist may not have a full case history on each participant, the schedule can be variable, and the participants can vary from session to session. It can also be a very dynamic setting, reaching people who have just retired and are seeking out new ways to explore their creative ideas and develop new talents. Art therapists in these settings may be perceived at first to be art educators and will need to do some advocacy for the field by educating staff and older adults about the field and scope of practice of art therapists. Working in nonclinical settings offers an opportunity to advocate for the field and educating about the field and scope of practice of art therapists.

Another common place art therapists work is in care settings. **Care settings** for older adults have a range of levels of care and services offered; in these settings, art therapy is often but not always under the umbrella of "activities," "programming," or "life enrichment." **Independent living** settings are most similar to work with older adults in private practice or drop-in centers—these clients will often sign themselves up for groups or for individual work, and tend to be more self-directed. The greater independence in this level of care can make it more difficult to reach older adults who do not normally attend art groups. The art therapist can reach out through personal invitations, written notes, and phone calls in order to solicit participation.

In **assisted living**, older adults can receive support at a range of levels, which can include housing, meals, laundry, medication administration, some physical care. Assistance with **Activities of Daily Living (ADLs)** are the daily tasks done to maintain one's appearance and well-being, such as getting dressed or personal grooming, social and emotional programming, care coordination with outside providers, and transportation. Art therapists in this setting may offer groups and may also work with clients individually. Art therapists are familiar with a wide range of physical, cognitive, social, and mental impacts of aging in order to best support clients, as each group may include people with different diseases in later life requiring adaptation and support.

In **skilled nursing settings**, art therapists are most often part of an interdisciplinary team, and may do some case management or family coordination as needed, depending on the local and regional licensure regulations. These settings are often heavily influenced by the medical model, and an art therapist working in the setting will need to be aware of the medical needs of clients, adapting the art processes they provide, and coordinating with other providers in the setting. Clients in this setting may be there for long-term care, residing in skilled nursing for months to years at the end of their lives. Or clients may recently have transferred from more acute care for physical, occupational, or speech therapy or care that cannot be provided in home. The floor plans and daily schedule of this setting lend itself to art and art therapy groups as opposed to individual therapy. However, the art therapist may also do some one-to-one work with specific clients. Access to individual art therapy varies widely depending on the location and philosophy of the setting.

While the environment can often be sterile and medical, it does not preclude the use of interesting materials; Doric-Henry (1997) introduced wheel-thrown pottery in a skilled nursing setting. The research aimed to understand the impact of this medium. The study concluded that those participating in the program had increased self-esteem and decreased anxiety and depression. Another art therapist researcher has used clay manipulation in the treatment of people with Parkinson's disease (Elkis-Abuhoff & Gaydos, 2018). The study findings included both psychosocial and physical benefits, including decreased anxiety, fewer tremors, and improved affect. Art therapy in skilled nursing can help to bring clients together around a shared idea or shared project and it can disrupt and distract from the sometimes distressing setting.

The role of art museums

Art museums are sites of potential engagement in art and art therapy for older adults. The trip leader is aware of a range of access issues, including those specific to older adults, people with vision (Fogle-Hatch & Winiecki, 2020) and cognitive changes (Hollamby et al., 2020), and perception of who the museum is for (Partridge, 2016; Partridge & Harmon, 2019). Museums and galleries can provide both inspiration and psychosocial support for people as they age (Bennington et al., 2016; deBotton & Armstrong, 2013; Hollamby et al., 2020). Art therapists working with older adults can interact in fine art and exhibition settings to meet a range of treatment goals including social support, engagement, and to "facilitate an atmosphere of novelty and promote reflections about the past and present" (Salom, 2011, p. 82). It also enables older adults to remain part of the larger arts community in their communities (Box 12.1).

Finding ways to ensure older adults remain part of the arts in their communities is not always easy. The physical barriers to access include building size,

BOX 12.1 Part of the arts community

On a sunny Saturday, an art therapist pulled the big passenger van down a narrow, formerly industrial street in the arts district of Oakland, California. The van transported the art therapist, an undergraduate art student intern, six older adults, and one private caregiver escort. It also transported five walkers, who were intricately stacked in the back of the van. Once the vehicle was parked, the art student intern and art therapist got to work, untangling the walkers and assisting everyone out of the van. As the group slowly made their way over the uneven pavement toward the destination, there were grumbles about the distance, the terrain, and the cool fall air. The art therapist and intern exchanged glances and a smile, noting the familiar dialogue they had encountered so many times on these trips, trusting that once at the gallery, the complaints would fall away.

The art student intern ran ahead to hold the door wide open with her foot, and the art therapist came at the end, assisting one older adult who was moving much more slowly than everyone else: "I guess I need to be walking more places than back and forth to my room," he observed. The art therapist smiled and suggested he sign up for the monthly trips out to galleries and offered to remind him. "I want a reminder too," said the woman with the private caregiver, "please remind both of us!" She had dementia, but remained in her room in assisted living, supported by a daytime private caregiver to reduce the risk of her wandering away from the building.

Once inside the gallery, voices grew quiet. The lighting was dramatic, and it took a little time for their eyes to adjust from the bright light outside. The art therapist greeted the gallery sitter and then addressed the group: "We will take some time to just look—see what you see. I encourage you to notice things that you feel drawn to and the things that you don't especially like. Remember—there's not a right answer today. We are not looking for anything in particular. We are here to be part of the arts community and to see contemporary work." This statement set the tone for the trip—it would not be an educational lecture, though they were welcome to ask questions about materials, about the artists, and about the content.The art therapist and art student intern floated around the gallery from person to person, spending time looking at and discussing the work. The gallery attendant pulled out a few chairs for people to sit on, which was much appreciated. Each person voiced their impressions of the work—bringing their memories and previous experiences into the context of the contemporary gallery. They talked loudly—which seemed to both confuse and amuse the other visitors. They voiced their distaste for certain works and their delight in other pieces. One woman was mesmerized by a large-scale, detailed ink drawing; she talked about how much she liked the artwork but that it also made her sad because her hands had a tremor and it reminded her of what she could no longer do. Another older adult was fascinated by an installation piece and spent most of her time inside the work, hands clasped behind her back, just looking.

After thanking the gallery sitter, the group slowly exited the gallery, walked back down the street to the van, climbed aboard, and drove back to the assisted living. The conversation in the van was animated and full of life, in line with existing research on verbal fluency during museum visits (Eekelaar et al., 2012; D'Cunha et al., 2019). Later, the art therapist and art student intern compared notes about which artwork people responded to, noting both their positive and negative reactions to different works. They talked about how the art therapist might use some of what they learned from the trip in art therapy sessions and what the art student learned about future audiences for her own work.

FIG. 12.1 *Chalkboard response. The older adult group contribution to a community chalkboard wall at the museum. The community contributed the heart shape with the date and name of the community.*

proximity of galleries to communities where older adults live, and the stamina of elders while on the trip itself. Wherever possible, artists, art therapists, and older adults should make themselves visible in these spaces. Fig. 12.1 shows a chalkboard wall outside the Oakland Museum for visitors to write on. The older adults chose where to leave the message (next to the existing "send me [heart]) and asked the art therapist to add the chalk message. They also wanted their message as close as possible to the museum's name—they said they wanted to be sure to come back. Many museums have arts access programs and some are partnered with organizations designed to facilitate their use (Mittelman & Epstein, 2006; MoMA, 2021). Individual practitioners can also reach out to art spaces and request special time in galleries, museums, and studios—enabling a less chaotic and adapted time in the space.

Resistance to therapy

One thing art therapists are aware of is the stigma of the term therapy. Older adult clients in particular may bristle or pullback at the idea of engaging in therapy: "The art therapist needs to be aware of the potential discomfort art therapy introduces into the community. What long-held beliefs are challenged? What discomfort does invoking therapy stimulate?" (Partridge, 2019b, p. 118). The art therapist is particularly sensitive to this concern and needs to find ways to invite the older adults into the work and to meet them where they are. Language matters when addressing resistance. Usage of the word "art" or "art class" can scare away some older adults who have lifelong beliefs about themselves not having art skills, but inviting them to a creative discussion group may help them find a way into art therapy. Focusing on creativity and growth is one way to broaden reach (Partridge, 2019c). A playful, curious attitude can assist in overcoming an "I don't need therapy" mindset. Engaging older adults in community-facing group projects, such as in a "zine project at a skilled nursing" (Houpt et al., 2016), is another way to bring older adults into art therapy. Older adults created a hand-made, self-published magazine and sold it at a festival; they were the authors of the project, not patients. The zine contained their writing, drawing, and collage and the older adults were also coauthors on an academic article about the project (Houpt et al., 2016).

Aging and disease

The reality of working with aging populations is the need to understand and often directly address diseases of later life or experienced as part of the aging process. This section covers a review of some of the most common diseases and how they might manifest in art therapy spaces.

Dementia[a]

Dementia is not one illness, but rather an umbrella term for several different diseases and clusters of symptoms (The Alzheimer's Association, 2020). Although the term dementia is commonly used in clinical settings, the Diagnostic and Statistical Manual of Mental Disorders, Fifth Edition, Text Revised (DSM-5-TR; American Psychiatric Association, 2022, Neurocognitive Disorders section) uses the term neurocognitive disorders instead of dementia. The term neurocognitive disorders is a broader term and includes conditions affecting a wider age group (such as brain injury) and symptoms. The term **neurocognitive** refers to changes in cognitive abilities due to changes in the brain. **Cognitive abilities** "include powers of reasoning and understanding, the use of language, the ability to attach meaning to our perceived sensory information, the ability to pay attention…to form and recall memories, and…to place ourselves in another's position" (Whalley, 2015, p. 164). Neurocognitive disorders are listed in the DSM-5-TR as major, mild, and by cause (for example, due to Alzheimer's disease, Parkinson's disease, vascular, etc.). Alzheimer's is the most common cause of dementia or neurocognitive disorders (Alzheimer's Association, 2021).

---

a.This section was contributed by both Meera Rastogi, PhD, ATR-BC, Psychology and Art Therapy, Social Sciences Department, University of Cincinnati, Batavia, OH, United States and Erin "Elizabeth" Partridge, PhD, ATR-BC Dominican University of California, Art Therapy, San Rafael, CA, United States; Experiential Researcher-In-Residence, Elder Care Alliance, Alameda, CA, United States.

According to the DSM-5-TR, neurocognitive disorders can affect people in one, or up to six cognitive domains: (1) complex attention, (2) executive function, (3) learning and memory, (4) language, (5) perceptual-motor, and (6) social cognition. **Complex attention** includes the ability to sustain attention over a period of time, focus attention despite distractions, and attend to more than one task at a time. **Executive functions** include the ability to plan, make decisions, work with information in one's memory, respond to feedback, change behavior based on feedback, and shift between different tasks or concepts. **Learning and memory** include immediate and recent recollections as well as long-term memory. The **language domain** includes the ability to identify or list objects, grammar and syntax, and language comprehension. **Perceptual-motor** abilities include vision, hand–eye coordination, and implementing motor movements. **Social cognition** is the ability to identify different emotions and understand the emotional experience of others. When working with people living with dementia verbal means to establishing connection and interacting decline as the disease progresses. This decline does not, as Byers (2011) explored in a paper about aesthetics, preclude creative and artistic connection: "aesthetics can bring a point of resonance into the therapeutic relationship when connections may be hard to find" (p. 81). Though there is currently no cure for dementia, a recent meta-analysis pointed to clear, actionable steps people can take to prevent or slow the progression including reducing stress and engaging in learning (Yu et al., 2020). Art therapy provides both opportunities for slowing down via meditative art and learning through the art process.

Art therapists working with people living with dementia may work with clients individually, in group settings, or alongside their family members or care partners in all different types of settings. These different settings will require the art therapist to consider what materials they provide and the types of directives they introduce. For example, if facilitating a group project in a locked memory care program, where participants may be at different stages of dementia, the art therapist must take into account the possible size of the group, the amount of supervision they can provide, the amount of individual attention they can facilitate, and how that impacts the safety of the group. The art therapist makes appropriate choices about what materials they provide or make available. Generally speaking, it is best to use nontoxic, easy to hold and handle materials when working with people living with dementia. The art therapist should still select high-quality materials where possible, however, to avoid infantilizing the clients (Partridge, 2019b).

Parkinson's disease

Another disease art therapists are likely to encounter in older adult care settings is Parkinson's disease. **Parkinson's disease** involves a wide range of symptoms. Though the impacts on the motor system are often severe, people living with Parkinson's disease also experience a range of nonmotoric symptoms including depression and anxiety and mood changes that can include increased anger and irritability (Perepezko et al., 2018).

Art therapists working with people with Parkinson's disease will need to consider how their current level of symptom expression may impact their ability to feel successful with different materials. For example, one person with Parkinson's may need support in adapting their existing creative practice as the disease progresses. An art therapist who is working with someone as the disease progresses can support the person's continued creative expression. In recalling one session, the art therapist noted, "Valerie grew very excited as she explored the wide vocabulary of marks she could make with different brushes. She created vibrant patterns and mandala-like circular compositions" (Partridge, 2019a, p. 67). Older adults coping with Parkinson's disease may need to be supported in maintaining as much autonomy as possible; the range of choices offered in the art studio supports their feeling of autonomy (Partridge, 2019c).

In addition to the physical and physiological symptoms, the impact of Parkinson's has implications for the social and emotional well-being of the person with the diagnosis as well as their family and friends. Promising research about the use of clay in work with people living with Parkinson's found clay manipulation resulted in improved qualitative and quantitative measures of somatic and emotional distress (Elkis-Abuhoff & Gaydos, 2018). The researchers hypothesized the process of manipulating clay with both hands would decrease tremors and avoid the frustration of attempts at art engagement requiring fine motor movement. The study involved people living with Parkinson's disease as well as their care partners: both groups benefitted from the work with modeling clay. Additionally, the participants expressed interest in continued work with clay after the study was complete. This research suggests a need for the individual art therapist to incorporate clay into their work, both with people living with Parkinson's as well as for family or professional care providers.

Similar to the rationale behind using clay, the use of nontraditional materials in art-making is generally well received by people living with Parkinson's disease. Thinking outside the standard art materials helps to divorce the act of creative making from precise, traditional art processes which invite comparison to previous ability or lack of tremors. An art therapist facilitating a one-time art therapy experience for a support group for people with Parkinson's and their care partners brought large brush pens and graffiti art tools to facilitate bold mark-making on paper. The directive encouraged participants to engage in the kinesthetic experience and tell stories through their color choices and patterns. Several couples chose to work together on a single page, while others worked side by side. When complete, the group members shared both the content of their images as well as their experiences of using the new tools. One person said it had been several years since he had held a writing or mark-making tool of any kind, because he felt ashamed of his inability to write his own name: "If I can't do that—can't write my own name, what good am I?" He said he enjoyed the process of making bold dots of color with the acrylic marker and compared it to playing a drum. The other participants said they noticed his sounds and found themselves making marks along with his rhythm. One couple, who worked together on a single image, reported they felt playful as they created their image. At the conclusion of the group, the art therapist gave participants a list of suggested materials to encourage more art-making at home.

Stroke

Stroke impacts many people in the United States—both directly and indirectly; it is the fifth most common cause of death and the first most common cause of disability (American Stroke Association, 2020). A stroke occurs when the blood supply to the brain is limited through clot or rupture in the blood vessels. There are several types of strokes and they can have different impacts on the person's level of functioning in the short and long term after they occur. Some people are able to rehabilitate poststroke to a level of functioning near their previous state while others require lifelong care and assistance poststroke from family or professional care partners. The impact of a stroke can cause frustration, particularly as the person works to regain use of language or limbs. It may also cause depression or anxiety through the loss of independence or previous ability.

Creative arts therapies can address many of the concerns stroke survivors experience (Lo et al., 2018). There are many ways art therapists in particular can assist people coping with the short- and long-term impacts of a stroke. In some cases, it may be appropriate for the art therapist to collaborate with the speech, occupational, and physical therapy team. The art therapist can also assist in addressing the psychological impacts of stroke, as described in a case study of work with a woman whose stroke limited her access to her previous loves: nature and gardening (Partridge, 2019b). For some stroke survivors, exploring the use of art media on paper is less intimidating than relearning to write with a nondominant hand; the art therapist can work with the client in collaboration with the rehabilitation team to explore movement and mark-making where there is no right or wrong, develop the skills, and then help the person transition into writing with that hand. Another client in art therapy spent time mourning the loss of his previous art practice using glass and paint. The art therapist worked with him as an "expert guide" on trips to museums, sharing his art book library with others, and transitioning his art practice to collage. He was able to reconnect with his artist identity through adapting his approach and the community benefitted from his knowledge and humor. Toward the end of his life, he remade one of his glass pieces and hung it up in the skilled nursing hallway gallery.

Aphasia

Aphasia impacts people's ability to speak, read, write, and comprehend language (National Aphasia Association, n.d.). Aphasia is a common among those who experience a stroke. There are different forms of aphasia; it is important that people working with and supporting those who have aphasia find alternative means to communicate. Art therapy can provide a supportive, expressive, and adaptable way for people with aphasia to express themselves and get their needs met. In one example, an older adult with aphasia, secondary to a stroke, used animal drawings and gestures as a means to interact with his peers. He would draw and hold up his work to show his peers, who named aloud the animal he drew. His smiles and vigorous nodding signaled that they were correct in their interpretation of his work. These visual conversations kept him connected to his peers in assisted living and skilled nursing care settings.

Technology and art have the potential to support older adults in recovering from and/or coping with aphasia. In a study of audio-enhanced paper photos, researchers looked at both the functional and emotional potential (Piper et al., 2014). Using art materials, art therapists can support people with aphasia in expressing their needs as well as their emotions. For example, using human figure outlines or head outlines and encouraging use of line, shape, and color to express how the person is feeling can guide a conversation about the person's current lived experience, including pain, psychological distress, or social needs. One woman with mild aphasia was able to create an image depicting her experience of a peer's presence in the group—the jagged red lines coming from the direction where the peer was sitting and piercing the head outline. The worried, tired eyes she drew prompted and helped to guide a later discussion between care providers and the art therapist about where this woman would sit in subsequent groups. Changing the seating arrangement helped to reduce the distress she experienced from this peer. Her art stimulated the discussion and communicated her needs.

Multisensory loss

As humans age, so do their sensory organs, most profoundly impacting hearing, vision, taste, and smell. The senses are part of how people make sense of the world around them and a large part of how they interact and experience pleasure. Each of the senses can be impacted separately; research suggests that the impacts of the loss of multiple senses can be not just emotionally distressing, but also has cognitive and implications for quality of life and lifespan (Crews & Campbell, 2004; Khil et al., 2015).

Vision loss and hearing loss are the two senses most often associated with aging. Loss of these two forms of sensory input can arise from multiple medical and structural changes in the body associated with age. They are also common forms of ageist jokes seen in popular culture, like birthday cards, movies, and commercials (Box 12.2).

Because of the assumed ubiquity of these two forms of sensory loss, their impact has not been fully explored (Crews & Campbell, 2004); they are assumed to be part of aging. This assumption impacts the treatment of and research about new approaches in treatment and technology used to address sensory loss.

BOX 12.2 Sensory loss jokes

Think of a joke you have seen in popular culture (birthday cards, movies, TV shows, commercials) that makes fun of or relies on stereotypes about older adults' sensory losses.

How would you change the ageist message of the joke? Create a two-panel comic of you encountering and then responding to the joke.

Art therapists can work with vision loss in many different ways. They can introduce larger format work, kinesthetic work, tactile work, including weaving and fiber arts. In one instance, an older adult's desire to remain an artist was satisfied through the use of three-dimensional glue lines added to watercolor paper. She had the memory of the colors that she used to use when she could see them and a strong desire to remain an artist. The art therapist worked with her to reconnect with her artist identity and find a new way of painting (Partridge, 2019a, 2019b, 2019c).

Hearing loss can be very socially isolating, particularly for older adults who may have never struggled with hearing difficulties before and have fewer resources for adaptation. Reconnecting with community through focus on visual sharing in the art studio is one way for older adults to reconnect with their community. The art therapist can also introduce other visual communication techniques to enable greater sharing. Focusing on sharing the work as the voice itself as opposed to focusing on ending group with a discussion of the work is another way to be inclusive of people who experience hearing loss enabling them to have an equal experience as those who do not experience hearing loss.

The work of art therapy can adapt well around the loss of hearing and vision through the use of tactile materials, bright colors, larger format supplies, and adjustments to how the art therapist interacts in and prepares the space: adjustments to the qualities of the space and facilitator as described by Partridge (2019a, 2019b, 2019c). Art can be a means of understanding the impact of sensory loss, both for older adults and for art therapists and researchers (Partridge, 2020).

Dentures, dental health concerns, or loss of sense of taste may seem far removed from the work of art therapy. However, they very much impact the quality of life and may be part of a larger concern that brings an older adult into the therapy room. In a study of the connection between oral health and loneliness, researchers found "strong and robust association between oral impacts and loneliness both cross-sectionally and longitudinally" (Rouxel et al., 2017, p. 105). Though it might not be immediately evident, when one stops to think about all the social situations that might be impacted by poor oral health, the need to address it becomes clearer. Individuals may experience pain or discomfort from teeth, gums, or dental implants, which can impact both sharing meals in social situations as well as talking. They may have shame or another negative emotion about dentures or oral health concerns. If they are coping with an age or medication-related loss of taste, it can limit their ability to connect with others around shared sensory experiences.

Oral health also might be a topic the art therapist introduces into conversation with clients. In working with an individual who had Parkinson's disease and lost his sense of taste, the client often talked about how frustrated he was, how much he missed things like the taste of fresh peaches, and the difficulties he encountered in trying to explain his frustration to his doctors. His quality of life was severely impacted by the loss of taste—he often cried, describing how his eyes were so excited about a fresh peach, but then it would "taste like dust" when he bit into it. In art therapy, he explored drawing some of the foods he missed tasting, using color to depict the vibrancy and intensity he was no longer able to experience. He did not attend art therapy often, but when he did, he worked quietly on still-life drawings and would sometimes tear up when he described his work. The impact of the loss of taste was profoundly frustrating to him; he used art therapy to express his experiences.

Medical awareness with older adult clients

Working with older adults, whether individually or in congregate or medical care settings, requires knowledge of the diseases of later life as well as general physiological changes in aging. Art therapists use this physiological awareness to adapt and modify practices where necessary. Adaptations range from larger print text or larger materials (like thick markers or larger paper) to special materials and approaches for work in acute care and at end of life. When working bedside with older adults, art therapists need to adapt the materials, directives, and way of creating work. They need to be thinking about what materials they bring bedside, with particular attention to fumes, small parts, and concerns related to energy and range of motion. Other considerations include: whether the older adult is able to sit up in bed or adjust their bed at all, how much range of motion they have, and whether they are able to use both hands. Some common adaptations include using the hospital bed tray over the person's lap. These trays offer great support for art-making but are not very large for painting or offering a wide range of materials. They are also less effective if the person is not able to raise the bed to a more upright position for the upper body. Many ergonomic office tools are also well suited to adapting art supplies for older adults. Some art supplies for professional artists, like pencil extenders and painting bridges, support older adults with tremors, decreased stamina, decreased range of motion, and restricted movement due to medical devices. Some useful ways to adapt painting for bedside include the use of a water-brush instead of a cup of water for watercolors, colored brush pens, or tempera paint sticks. Using a sketchbook or clipboard can substitute for the bed tray, but the art therapist may need to hold or offer materials one at a time. Dual-tipped colored pencils and markers offer a wider range of choice with fewer individual items to carry or hold. Art therapists need to take care when working bedside to avoid interfering with any medical support. Making art bedside can often require navigating around things like heart monitors, IV poles, and other life-sustaining equipment.

The more creative the art therapist is about adapting materials for each individual, the more likely the older adults will experience creative and artistic success. Ideally, the art therapist has several sizes of clipboards, pads of paper, canvases, and other materials that they are able to use within the medical setting. These materials, loaded onto a rolling cart or tote, create a **mobile art studio** the art therapist can take from room to room or across the hospital to different areas. Doing so assists in meeting the needs of each of the older adult clients with materials on hand for each person. The medical setting in particular means that the art therapy work can be interrupted by necessary medical care, procedures, and diagnostic tests. For example, an art therapy session bedside may be interrupted by the need to get a blood pressure reading or administer medication. These interruptions are very common when working in skilled nursing or medical settings with older adults. Frequent interruptions are another reason to use materials that are easy to use and set aside and why the lap tray as an art studio is particularly effective. The art therapist and client can "pause" and "resume" the session to accommodate needed testing.

Use of natural materials introduces a therapeutic multisensory experience for bedside art therapy or art groups in high-care settings; items with bright colors and textures that are not generally found in a sterile medical environment, such as plants, rocks, and shells work particularly well. These items can be a stimulus for creative expression and reminiscence. Some examples of ways to use these materials include sorting stones, arranging leaves, and simply feeling the textures. In a small group of people who were nonverbal and with a limited range of motion and not able to participate in a discussion group for other residents, the art therapist used large shells to provide tactile stimulation. The participants moved their fingers across the surfaces of the shells, looked at the colors, and compared them to each other. The art therapist, communicating only in gesture, invited the participants to choose between two shells with touch or eye movement. Though very simple on the surface of things, this type of engagement provides visual and tactile stimulation as well as individual choice. The chosen shells, arranged on the nursing station countertop, served as a visual reminder of the ability of these residents to make personal choices: a subtle, yet powerful message to family, staff, and other professionals.

In a community with access to outdoor space, an art therapist and art student intern invited older adults to choose from an array of collected natural materials from the garden and surrounding land; they spent the afternoon creating a large circular arrangement on the ground. Later, they adapted the same approach for a table-top group in the skilled nursing unit. Starting from the center of the table, older adults took turns adding their items to the group arrangement. Once satisfied with the piece, each participant shared what they added and what they liked about the final work. The art therapist took a photograph of the piece and displayed it with a list of the reflection statements in the main gathering room in the skilled-nursing wing. In settings where infection control restrictions, allergies, or other logistics preclude bringing natural ephemera inside, prompts like "collage gardening" (Partridge, 2019a, 2019b, 2019c), collaged "flower arranging" (Buchalter, 2011), and art appreciation groups focusing on landscape and animals meet that need for engagement with the natural world.

Art therapists working in the medical setting with older adults need to be aware of not only the major medical diagnoses in later life but also common things that happen with aging, such as thinning skin, vision loss, and general loss of energy. These realities necessitate adaptation or use of alternative materials. For example, using materials that stain skin or is hard to wash away creates discomfort and may even be unsafe for older adult skin. Aging skin is thinner, easy to injure or irritate, slow to heal, and less hydrated than younger skin (Wiegand et al., 2017). In some cases, use of medical gloves or other barrier devices allows experimentation with materials that otherwise require solvents or scrubbing to remove. When a group of older adults wanted to tie dye clothing purple as a fundraiser for the community's Walk to End Alzheimer's (Alzheimer's Association, n.d.) team 1 year, the art therapist was nervous about using fabric dye with the group's thin skin and also worried about making a mess in the activity room in the skilled nursing center. In order to involve a large number of residents in the project, the art therapist worked with different older adults at different phases of the project. One group created fliers, inviting staff and family to purchase and donate white cotton clothing items for the cause. Once the items arrived, the art therapist worked with two different groups—one group of older adults in assisted living and the other in skilled nursing. Each group folded and twisted clothing items, working in a small circle to wrap and tie the items for the dying process. Each of these stages involved older adults at different levels of care; some were active participants while others were still able to contribute by folding, holding ends of items while others wrapped them with rubber bands, and making some of the creative decisions. When all the items were ready to dye, a small group came to the art room to help with mixing dye and putting the clothing in to soak. They all wore gloves and enjoyed the different shades of purple as they mused aloud about how different items would look when completed, which items they thought would "sell" best at the fundraiser, and which items they wanted for themselves. The art therapist planned to rinse and unwrap the items in the art room sink, but some warm weather and permission from the maintenance staff enabled doing this part of the process as a group as well. Residents from assisted living, memory care, and skilled nursing formed a semicircle around a grassy area in the courtyard. The art therapist placed all the items in a plastic wading pool and brought the hose over. One by one, she unwrapped and untied the items and rinsed them out with a hose. Each item hung to dry on a clothes line nearby, fluttering in the breeze like a bunch of purple flags. The older adults returned to their areas of the building with clean skin. The art therapist had purple hands for the next few days.

Grief

Working with the aging population necessitates working with grief in various different ways. Kumar (2005) identified two general types of loss: sudden loss and gradual loss. **Sudden loss** can take the form of an unexpected death or a change in living arrangements, as illustrated in the quote from the novel in the next section. **Gradual loss** happens with a deterioration of a relationship or the progression of a degenerative illness. Art therapists need to process loss in their own art and life as well—losses from their community and family as well as deaths of older adult clients.

The art therapist may be called upon to assist older adults in grieving losses from earlier in their life that are reactivated as new losses occur. They will also be called upon to assist in processing current losses, often of family and friends who have been together for lifetimes. Art therapists can support the grieving process of family after the older adult dies through workshops or individual treatment (Partridge, 2019b). Art therapists may also be part of determining if the person is experiencing grief or symptoms of major depression. The art therapist can help with the process of "untangling these subtle threads" (Kumar, 2005, p. 100) of grief, loss, and sadness.

When working with older adults in a medical setting like skilled nursing or acute care, the reality of grief and loss is ever present. Some settings have memorial rituals or services for staff or for the entire community each year. The art therapist can collaborate with other members of the community such as a chaplain or spiritual care director to incorporate an art-based component to this work. If there are no formalized means to process grief and loss, the art therapist might partner with a chaplain, spiritual care director, or other relevant staff to bring one into being. Some of the culture change practices in the field of aging suggest engaging with death in a different way than normal in the medical setting. These practices might include not taking the body of the deceased out the back door but rather covering the body with a special cloth and taking the stretcher out through the front door, sometimes covered in flowers, or making memorials to that person visible in the building. These types of settings are communities and homes, and it can be distressing for older adults when someone they have seen every day suddenly disappears. Rules and regulations of the Health Insurance Portability and Accountability Act or HIPAA prevent disclosing when someone transfers to a higher level of care or a medical diagnoses. Prominent memorials can help other older adults grieve the loss of a friend and engage in some of the thinking about their own end of life and death.

Retirement and other life transitions

Older adults face many transitions and changes as they age. These changes include job and career transitions, role changes, and changes in residence. So much of identity comes from a person's role or function in society. Cruikshank noted, "In America, where usefulness is defined as productivity, many who are old do not appear to themselves or others as useful because their paid work role has ended" (Cruikshank, 2013, p. 36). Older adults who are in the process of or immediately postretirement benefit from creative, generative time to explore their feelings about the change, opportunities to reinvent their identities, and work through the losses. Some later life transitions are celebrated and others are difficult and often not discussed. The protagonist in a novel set in an assisted living described what the transition to assisted living was like:

It didn't take them long to undo my life. I had spent 80 years building it, but within weeks, they made it small enough to fit in a manila envelope and take along to meetings. They kidnapped it. They hurried it away from me when I least expected, when I thought I could coat myself in old age and be left to it. A door doesn't sound the same when you close it for the last time, and a room doesn't look the same when you know you'll never see it again (Cannon, 2018, p. 196).

Often, the circumstances that precipitate a move into a care setting do not allow for sufficient time and space to process the change. Art therapists can work with older adults to explore the feelings they have about changes to the trajectory of their later lives, comparing what the older adults thought it would be to their current lived experiences. Art therapy creates opportunities for both verbal and visual comparisons in the interest of processing this change. Family also benefits from art-based processing of the care transition. Initially, this section of the book was to include examples from work in clinical and community settings, but life circumstances in the creative arts therapies, work with older adults, and our own lived experiences (Box 12.3) may require creative pivots or exploration (Partridge, 2021).

Hope, resilience, and opportunity in later life

Working with older adults can be incredibly fulfilling work—often filled with rich stories and laughter. While the decline and disease covered earlier in the chapter are realities art therapists will encounter, they are offset by the opportunities to work with people as they reflect on lives well lived (Bergman, 2017, Roher, 2021). Focusing on and celebrating the positive attributes of aging subverts problematic and ageist belief systems (Cruikshank, 2013; Partridge, 2019a; The Anti-Ageism Taskforce, 2006).

Older adults may experience increased access to and understanding of their emotions as they age. This increased access is called the "**paradox of aging**" (Samanez-Larkin et al., 2014), while older adults experience increased losses and decline, they also experience a stable or increased sense of well-being; the researchers posit they have higher ability of emotional control. Older adults also have a rich set of life experiences they can bring to conversations and once assumptions and stereotypes are addressed and set aside, they can bring so much wisdom and perspective to intergenerational conversations (Partridge, 2019b;

BOX 12.3 The art therapist's experience

In the process of writing this chapter, the author experienced a life-threatening health crisis followed by a few months of hospitalization with brain swelling. Close to the resolution of my own recovery from acute symptoms, my grandmother required care transition; my grandmother had moderately managed dementia with coexisting sensory losses. She loved to be outside and had a dog who was her guide and companion. At 99 years old with severe vision and hearing loss, her ability to navigate her home and property was remarkable, but often put her into precarious situations.

Art therapists are also humans experiencing their own aging process and that of others in their families and communities. Back when my grandfather required skilled nursing care, I started advocating for them to move into a continuing care retirement community. As I observed successful care transitions for couples, I advocated for my family to consider the move. After my grandfather's death, a change in setting was suggested again by a few additional family members. But for various reasons, grandma stayed at home. Prior to an increased escalation in sundowning behavior, my grandmother lived alone with care and family support. However, staying at home alone was no longer an option and she needed to move very quickly. **Sundowning** is a term referring to an increase in agitation and other negative symptoms observed in people living with dementia. The change has been connected to disruption to the circadian rhythm of people living with Alzheimer's disease (Volicer et al., 2001).

Due to the COVID-19 restrictions on travel and my still-recovering health status, I was not able to go to assist in person. As the family expert, I became the hub for communication, education, and client advocacy for grandma in the work to find an appropriate placement. I also assisted via phone, social media, email, and text messaging. Some of the assistance included logistics coordination and some was talking through guilt and sadness about Grandma not reaching that 100-year mark in her own home.

On the night before the transition, when all the paperwork was filed and a plan was in place to help her transition into care, I planned an art response for myself and my own mother. Initially, I intended to work through a structured process based on the Expressive Therapies Continuum (Hinz, 2009; Lusebrink, 2004, 2010). The Expressive Therapies Continuum suggests that different materials and media can be used to access different levels of emotion, sensory experience, and even brain function. Some art therapists use a very structured and systematic approach while other art therapists are informed by the continuum of what materials they use with clients or topics.

For the art process with myself and my mother, the initial plan was step by step over two days:

1. Watercolor wash on paper the night before.
2. Watercolor marks with large brush on dried paper the following morning.
3. Watercolor marks with smaller brush.
4. Larger mark-making tools.
5. Addition of collage.
6. Ink pens or colored pencil.
7. Discussing work with each other.

Continued

BOX 12.3 The art therapist's experience—cont'd

I planned to work on my own piece at the same time. One of the powerful benefits of letting go of some of the control and engaging in art process along with others is the way the art helps facilitate the exploration of shared experience. About three steps into this process, I realized, both in my own work and in what I witnessed in her mom's process, that the structured process was not in either person's best interests. When making my marks with the smaller watercolor, my mom stated "I didn't know what the meaning was but I already know this is Catherine the beautiful flower and we are all surrounding her with our love." At this point, I pulled out all the additional materials which had been tucked aside and we then worked freely for the duration of the time. Both of us began wondering aloud about creative choices we were making, saying that it was not the choice either of us had planned. Interestingly, neither of us glued down the collage material right away, which was a change in creative behavior for both of us.

When discussing the works, we noticed similarities in our pieces and reflected on shared materials and shared lived experience. We noted areas in the final art that connected to the family history. Each image appears with a quote from the sharing process of, a key point of change we noted (Figs. 12.2 and 12.3).

As the family continues to navigate this big transition, my role has shifted to debriefing, helping everyone better understand what is in the best interest of grandma as she approaches her one hundredth birthday. My own art illuminated some of these worries. In reflecting on the geometric components I said, "Maybe some of what I was worried about was that it was going to be an over-structured environment. It still has structure but not confinement." Helping people understand that orienting grandma to time and place and specific names can feel like quizzing

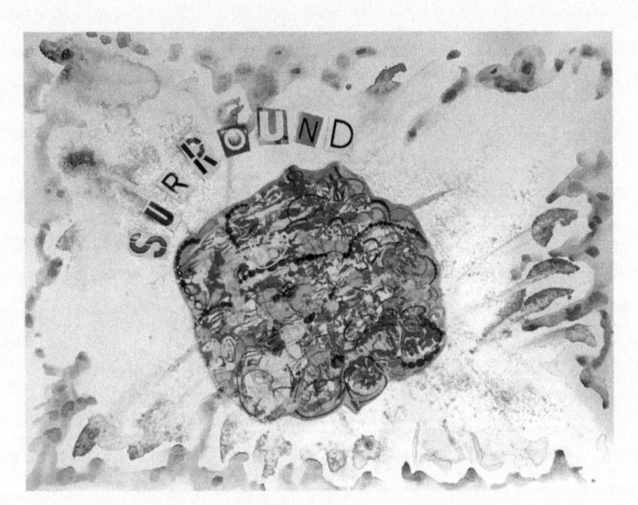

FIG. 12.2 *Surround. Mixed-media collage created by art therapist's mother. Includes paper collaged images and words from magazines and books and watercolor. "I started out not realizing I was using Grandma's colors. And then I used the pink and I thought, well that's like we're all surrounding her." "It has kind of a flower-like thing because that's what she and I talked about...we even talked about it yesterday."*

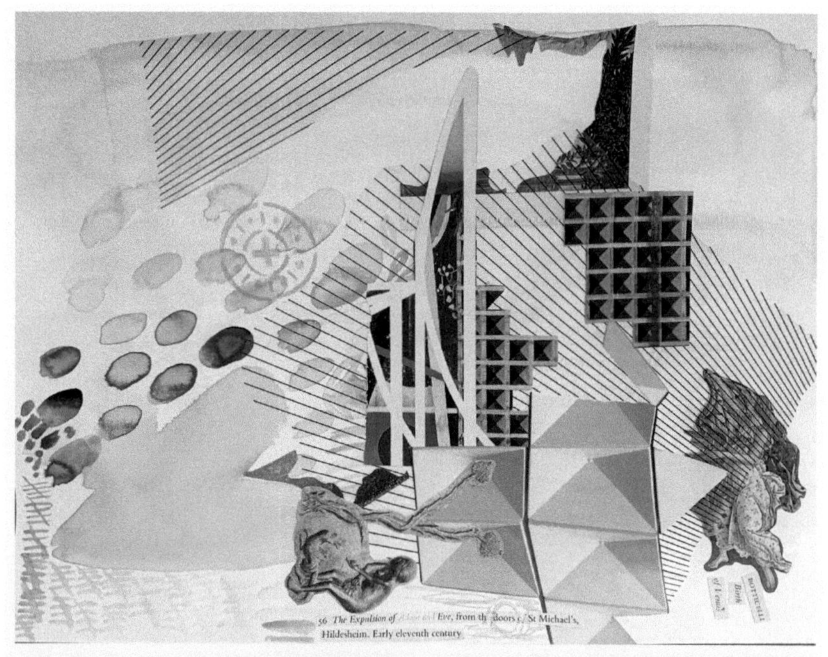

FIG. 12.3 *Doors. Mixed-media collage created by the art therapist. Includes paper collaged images and words from magazines and books, watercolor, colored pencil, ink, and vintage graphic design onlays. "When I added the larger brush strokes it was these strokes here and it was darker blue than I planned. I think because I was feeling worried that the transition wasn't going to happen. I had planned to do these light blue parts and I ended up working darker, I think because I was worried. When we came back to them today, the fan brush did something totally different than I had planned. I had planned to keep it all really muted. First I did stripes and then they got more and more blurry. And then I added the hatch marks, and you know what is so funny, I was trying to do her age, but you know how numbers are hard for me right now? I didn't do enough of them. When I planned this out, I thought we'd go from very, very fluid to the most structured...It's not at all how it went, which is better!"*

to people living with dementia. Emotions and shared present moment experiences provide opportunities to connect. Anecdotally, what I had observed what works best: shifting from specific names, places, and times, and instead having shared experience in the here and now. These shared experiences might include:

- Instead of "your grandkids George, Bob, and Frank" saying instead "the kids."
- Focus on stories that have a brief and positive outcome using simple words. These stories are best if they are about topics important to that person.
- If in person, reflect on and describe the things in the room where the visit is happening.
- Window gazing.
- Letters written to be read aloud by care providers.
- Shared favorite meals or foods.

Continued

BOX 12.3 The art therapist's experience—cont'd

One of the amazing things about the human brain and body is that the emotional connection and the things that are most important to people seem to be present right to the end—a final hug of an animal, smile, grasp of a paintbrush or hand-squeeze.

I suggested to my own family the earlier mentioned key points along with the encouragement to continue to connect around topics that are important in the family. I encouraged efforts to bring peace and positive emotions and sharing the stories of humor, tenacity, love, and resilience specific to the family with her current great grandchildren and the future generations.

On my side, being aware that each stage of my own healing from brain swelling made a certain kind of sense. As the swelling decreased, my ability to put reactions, movement, and later words and art to my experience in the world increased. Likewise, my grandma's behavior made sense, as her senses had fewer ways to provide input. The agitated behavior precipitating the move to memory care was a kind of grieving; her sadness about losing the ability to "age by the skin of her teeth" (Partridge, 2019a, 2019b, 2019c). I, too, had to grieve and feel shame as my brain became increasingly able to tolerate details about what I experienced, what I missed, and how things changed.

Rubin et al., 2015). In a multigenerational study initiated during the COVID-19 pandemic, researchers found that older adults experienced less emotional turmoil than younger generations (Edward Jones & Age Wave, 2020).

Art can play an important role in the well-being of older adults. It enables them, among other benefits, to hold the sometimes contradictory realities of aging—joys and difficulties at the same time. One elder described her increasing fatigue and acceptance of her aging body along with gratitude for the ways she is able to find growth and healing in art: "Creativity, that's taking care of ourselves! Art from the gut is what cures you!" (Partridge, 2019c, p. 205).

Aging in the future

What will the future of aging and of art therapy with older adults look like? Some recent advances suggest we will see an increased prevalence of the use of technology in older adult care settings—both to do tasks, but also to provide companionship or perhaps even inspiration and stimulate a sense of wonder. Recent experiments and innovations using virtual reality, social robots, and other technological tools have enabled older adults to revisit their birthplaces, connect with family at long distances, and form new kinds of relationships. Addressing ageism and directly examining the social construction of age will enable better ways to view aging—as a time of possibility and change rather than disease and decline. That said, advances in healthcare and longevity sciences with a focus on healthspan may enable more of us to live longer with better quality of life.

Art studios and art therapy spaces may look very different in future assisted living settings or older adult educational contexts. Paints may be stored near virtual reality headsets. A canvas could be clamped onto an easel or it could be the digital screen of a tablet. Art therapists can and should explore how technologies can support the expressive needs of older adults and they can also be part of ensuring older adult voices are at the table when technologies for other purposes are developed.

Art therapists can also be involved in redefining existing programs, finding ways to infuse greater amounts of creativity and self-expression in communities. For example, when piloting a project to introduce creativity into a friendly visiting program, an art therapist worked with participants in the program, an artist, and an educator to widen the definition of "creativity" and to design a project with more inclusive methods (Partridge, Harmon and Wade, 2020). The creative problem-solving skills and knowledge of adaptive techniques art therapists possess help them find ways to shift conversations of deficit, apathy, and disinterest toward connection and creativity.

Working with older adults is filled with the opportunity to engage in art-making, art appreciation, and the use of images in the service of growth. Art and visual imagery can tell older adult stories, providing opportunities to better understand the lived experience of aging from all perspectives: older adults, their family, their care providers, and society (Leonard, 2021; Chast, 2014; Baines, 2019, Leavitt, 2012). Aging is not an isolated issue. We all exist somewhere along the process toward older age. Art therapists have an important role to play in providing support, care, and creativity as we move through the years of our lives.

Art experientials and reflection questions

1. **"Old" exploration.** Think about the word "old." When you hear or read it, what comes to mind? Make a list of any words, images, or feelings you think of connected to the word "old." When you have completed your list, use two different colors, mark the things on your list that are positive in one color and negative in another color. Which list is longer?
2. **Collage of aging.** Make a collage about aging, using images of older adults you find in newspapers, magazines, and online. As you work, notice if it is easy or difficult to find images. Notice the tone and content of the images you are able to find. Notice where these images play into or run counter to stereotypes, not only stereotypes of certain age groups, but also of different decades.
3. **Fears and stigma about dementia.** Using the provided heading, create a visual representation of the impact of dementia. Once you have completed your image, reflect on it with some writing or conversation with a friend or classmate. In what ways does your image contain fear or stigma about dementia? In what ways is your identity tied to your memories? How much of your interpersonal world is connected through written or verbal language?

How else do you connect with your loved ones, community, and the world around you? What is your relationship to giving and receiving care? What would it be like for you to have someone assist you with intimate care tasks?

4. **Reframing aging—Create a positive image of aging.** Given everything you have read about and learned in this chapter and across your life, create a positive image of aging. This image might be a tribute to an important older adult in your life or community, an illustration around a word or phrase you find inspiring when you think toward your own aging process.

For more information

Graphic novels

Baines, N. (2019). *Afloat: A memoir about mum, dementia, and trying not to drown*. Flying Carp Books.

Chast, R. (2014). *Can't we talk about something more pleasant?* Bloomsbury.

Dunlap-Shohl, P. (2016). *My degeneration: A journey through Parkinson's*. The Pennsylvania State University Press.

Leavitt, S. (2012). *Tangles: A story about Alzheimer's, my mother, and me*. Skyhorse.

Moreu, M., & Batty, I. (2019). *Dolores y Lolo*. ASTIBERRI EDICIONES.

Roher, R. (2016). *Bird In A Cage*. Conundrum Press.

Steinaecker, T., Yelin, B., Reddick, J., & Steinaecker, T. (2020). *The summer of her life*. SelfMadeHero.

Walrath, D. (2016). *Aliceheimer's: Alzheimer's through the looking glass*. Pennsylvania State University Press.

Wright, A. (2015). *Things to do in a retirement home trailer park: When you're 29 and unemployed*. Penn State University Press.

Films

Wrinkles: https://www.imdb.com/title/tt1407052/
I See You: https://www.imdb.com/title/tt6079516/
Meet Me At MoMA: https://www.moma.org/visit/accessibility/meetme/
I Remember Better When I Paint: http://www.irememberbetterwhenipaint.com/

Chapter terms

Ableism
Activities of Daily Living (ADLs)
Ageism
Alzheimer's
Aphasia
Biological age
Care partner
Chronological age
Cognitive abilities
Complex attention
Dementia
Executive functions

Gradual loss
Language domain
Learning and memory
Multisensory impairment
Neurocognitive
Paradox of aging
Parkinson's disease
Perceptual-motor
Skilled nursing setting
Social age
Social cognition
Stroke
Sudden loss

References

Alzheimer's Association. (n.d.). *Walk to end Alzheimer's*. Retrieved December 2, 2021, from https://act.alz.org/site/SPageServer?pagename=walk_homepage.

Alzheimer's Association. (2021). 2021 Alzheimer's disease facts and figures. *Alzheimers Dement, 17*(3).

American Psychiatric Association. (2022). *Diagnostic and statistical manual of mental disorders: DSM-5-TR* (5th ed., Text revised). American Psychiatric Association.

American Stroke Association. (2020). *About stroke*. https://www.stroke.org/en/about-stroke.

Applewhite, A. (2016). *This chair rocks: A manifesto against ageism*. Thorndike Press.

Baines, N. (2019). *Afloat: A memoir about mum, dementia, and trying not to drown*. Flying Carp Books.

Bennington, R., Backos, A., Harrison, J., Etherington Reader, A., & Carolan, R. (2016). Art therapy in art museums: Promoting social connectedness and psychological well-being of older adults. *The Arts in Psychotherapy, 49*, 34–43. https://doi.org/10.1016/j.aip.2016.05.013.

Buchalter, S. (2011). *Art therapy and creative coping techniques for older adults*. Jessica Kingsley Publishers.

Burns, A. J. (2009). *An Interpretive description of the patterns of practise of arts therapists working with older people who have Dementia in the UK*. Queen Margaret University. http://etheses.qmu.ac.uk/117/%5CnRepository.

Byers, A. (2011). Visual aesthetics in dementia. *International Journal of Art Therapy, 16*(2), 81–89. https://doi.org/10.1080/17454832.2011.602980.

Caldas-Coulthard, C. R., & Moon, R. (2016). Grandmother, gran, gangsta granny: Semiotic representations of grandmotherhood. *Gender and Language, 10*(3), 309–339. https://doi.org/10.1558/genl.v10i3.32036.

Cannon, J. (2018). *Three things about Elsie*. Scribner.

Chast, R. (2014). *Can't we talk about something more pleasant?* Bloomsbury.

Clarke, L. H. (2017). Women, aging, and beauty culture: Navigating the social perils of looking old. *Generations, 41*(4), 104–108.

Crews, J. E., & Campbell, V. A. (2004). Vision impairment and hearing loss among community-dwelling older Americans: Implications for health and functioning. *American Journal of Public Health, 94*(5), 823–829. https://doi.org/10.2105/AJPH.94.5.823.

Cruikshank, M. (2013). *Learning to be old: Gender, culture, and aging* (3rd ed.). Rowman & Littlefield Publishers, Inc.

Cunha, A., Cunha, E., Peres, E., & Trigueiros, P. (2016). Helping older people: Is there an app for that? *Procedia Computer Science, 100*, 118–127. https://doi.org/10.1016/j.procs.2016.09.131.

D'Cunha, N. M., McKune, A. J., Isbel, S., Kellett, J., Georgousopoulou, E. N., & Naumovski, N. (2019). Psychophysiological responses in people living with dementia after an art gallery intervention: An exploratory study. *Journal of Alzheimer's Disease, 72*(2), 549–562. https://doi.org/10.3233/JAD-190784.

deBotton, A., & Armstrong, J. (2013). *Art as therapy*. Phaidon Press.

Doric-Henry, L. (1997). Pottery as art therapy with elderly nursing home residents. *Art Therapy: Journal of the American Art Therapy Association, 14*(3), 163–171. https://doi.org/10.1080/07421656.1987.10759277.

Eden Alternative. (2006). *Haleigh's almanac: Eden Alternative associate training manual*. Eden Alternative.

Edward Jones & Age Wave. (2020). *The four pillars of the new retirement*. The Harris Poll.

Eekelaar, C., Camic, P. M., & Springham, N. (2012). Art galleries, episodic memory and verbal fluency in dementia: An exploratory study. *Psychology of Aesthetics, Creativity, and the Arts, 6*(3), 262–272. https://doi.org/10.1037/a0027499.

Elkis-Abuhoff, D. L., & Gaydos, M. (2018). Medical art therapy research moves forward: A review of clay manipulation with Parkinson's disease. *Art Therapy: Journal of the American Art Therapy Association, 35*(2), 68–76. https://doi.org/10.1080/07421656.2018.1483162.

Fogle-Hatch, C., & Winiecki, D. (2020). *Assessing attitudes of blind adults about museums. MW20: MW2020*. Museums and the Web, LLC. https://mw20.museweb.net/paper/assessing-attitudes-of-blind-adults-about-museums/.

Fraser, S., Lagacé, M., et al. (2020). Ageism and COVID-19: What does our society's response say about us? *Age and Ageing, 49*(5), 692–695. https://doi.org/10.1093/ageing/afaa097.

Hamczyk, M. R., Nevado, R. M., Barettino, A., Fuster, V., & Andrés, V. (2020). Biological versus chronological aging: JACC focus seminar. *Journal of the American College of Cardiology, 75*(8), 919–930. https://doi.org/10.1016/j.jacc.2019.11.062.

Hayward, M. D., & Zhang, Z. C. N.-C. (2001). The demographic revolution in population aging: A century of change, 1950-2050. In R. H. Binstock, & L. K. George (Eds.), *Handbook on aging and the socal sciences* (5th ed., pp. 69–85). Academic Press.

Hinz, L. (2009). *Expressive therapies continuum: A framework for using art in therapy*. Routledge.

Hollamby, E., Homer, E., & Landes, J. (2020). Starting with art: Ben Uri artworks as a stimulus for art psychotherapy in dementia care. In A. Coles, & H. Jury (Eds.), *Art therapy in museums and galleries: Reframing practice* (pp. 108–132). Jessica Kingsley Publishers.

Houpt, K., Balkin, L. A., Broom, R. H., Roth, A. G., & Selma. (2016). Anti-memoir: Creating alternate nursing home narratives through zine making. *Art Therapy: Journal of the American Art Therapy Association, 33*(3), 128–137. https://doi.org/10.1080/07421656.2016.1199243.

Khil, L., Wellmann, J., & Berger, K. (2015). Impact of combined sensory impairments on health-related quality of life. *Quality of Life Research: An International Journal of Quality of Life Aspects of Treatment, Care and Rehabilitation*. https://doi.org/10.1007/s11136-015-0941-7.

Kumar, S. M. (2005). *Grieving mindfully: A compassionate and spiritual guide to coping with loss*. New Harbinger Publications, Inc.

Lakin, K. C., & Burke, M. M. (2019). Looking forward: Research to respond to a rapidly aging population. *Research and Practice for Persons with Severe Disabilities, 44*(4), 280–292. https://doi.org/10.1177/1540796919882356.

Leonard, B. K. (2021). *I see you*. Motion Picture.

Levy, B. R. (2017). Age-stereotype paradox: Opportunity for social change. *The Gerontologist, 57*(suppl_2), S118–S126. https://doi.org/10.1093/geront/gnx059.

Lo, T. L. T., Lee, J. L. C., & Ho, R. T. H. (2018). Creative arts-based therapies for stroke survivors: A qualitative systematic review. *Frontiers in Psychology, 9*(September), 1–12. https://doi.org/10.3389/fpsyg.2018.01646.

Lusebrink, V. B. (2004). Art therapy and the brain: An attempt to understand the underlying processes of art expression in therapy. *Art Therapy: Journal of the American Art Therapy Association, 21*(3), 125–135. https://doi.org/10.1080/07421656.2004.10129496.

Lusebrink, V. B. (2010). Assessment and therapeutic application of the expressive therapies continuum: Implications for brain structures and functions. *Art Therapy: Journal of the American Art Therapy Association*, *27*(4), 168–177. https://doi.org/10.1080/07421656.2010.10129380.

Mittelman, M., & Epstein, C. (2006). *Meet me at MoMA—MoMA Alzheimer's project*. MoMA.

MoMA. (2021). *MoMA | Meet Me*. Retrieved February 5, 2021, from https://www.moma.org/visit/accessibility/meetme/.

National Aphasia Association. (n.d.). *Aphasia definitions*. http://www.aphasia.org/aphasia-definitions/.

North, M. S., & Fiske, S. T. (2015). Modern attitudes toward older adults in the aging world: A cross-cultural meta-analysis. *Psychological Bulletin*, *141*(5), 993–1021. https://doi.org/10.1037/a0039469.

Partridge, E. (2021). *Getting on in the creative arts therapies: A hands-on guide to personal and professional development*. Jessica Kingsley Publishers.

Partridge, E. E. (2016). Access to art and materials: Considerations for art therapists (Accès à l'art et aux matériaux: facteurs à prendre en compte par les art-thérapeutes). *Canadian Art Therapy Association Journal*, *29*(2), 100–104. https://doi.org/10.1080/08322473.2016.1252996.

Partridge, E. E. (2019a). Ageism and ethics: Art therapy with older adults. In *International art therapy practice/research conference*.

Partridge, E. E. (2019b). *Art therapy with older adults: Connected and empowered*. Jessica Kingsley Publishers.

Partridge, E. E. (2019c). Dismantling the gender binary in elder care: Creativity instead of craft. In S. Hogan (Ed.), *Gender and difference in the arts therapies: Inscribed on the body* (pp. 196–206). Routledge.

Partridge, E. E. (2020). The pre-research sketchbook: A tool to guide future inquiry. *Art Therapy: Journal of the American Art Therapy Association*. https://doi.org/10.1080/07421656.2020.1729677.

Partridge, E. E., Harmon, S., & Wade, K. (2020, July 11-12). Creative friendly visiting: A collaboratively imagined program. *Art Together Now Art for Social Justice: Northern California Art Therapy Association Conference*. Rohnert Park.

Perepezko, K., Pontone, G., & Minton, L. (2018). *A mind guide to Parkinson's disease*. Parkinson's Foundation.

Piper, A. M., Weibel, N., & Hollan, J. D. (2014). Designing audio-enhanced paper photos for older adult emotional wellbeing in communication therapy. *International Journal of Human-Computer Studies*, *72*(8–9), 629–639. https://doi.org/10.1016/j.ijhcs.2014.01.002.

Poo, A.-J., & Conrad, A. (2015). *The age of dignity: Preparing for the elder boom in a changing America*. The New Press.

Roca, P. (2016). *Wrinkles*. Fantagraphics Books.

Rouxel, P., Heilmann, A., Demakakos, P., Aida, J., Tsakos, G., & Watt, R. G. (2017). Oral health-related quality of life and loneliness among older adults. *European Journal of Ageing*, *14*(2), 101–109. https://doi.org/10.1007/s10433-016-0392-1.

Rubin, S. E., Gendron, T. L., Wren, C. A., Ogbonna, K. C., Gonzales, E. G., & Peron, E. P. (2015). Challenging gerontophobia and ageism through a collaborative intergenerational art program. *Journal of Intergenerational Relationships*, *13*(3), 241–254. https://doi.org/10.1080/15350770.2015.1058213.

Salom, A. (2011). Reinventing the setting: Art therapy in museums. *The Arts in Psychotherapy*, *38*(2), 81–85. https://doi.org/10.1016/j.aip.2010.12.004.

Samanez-Larkin, G. R., Robertson, E. R., Mikels, J. A., Carstensen, L. L., & Gotlib, I. H. (2014). Selective attention to emotion in the aging brain. *Motivation Science*, *1*(S), 49–63. https://doi.org/10.1037/a0016952.

Sláma, B. (2017). *Ice Mother (Bába z ledu)*. FilmRise.

Stephenson, R. C. (2010). *The creative experience of women: Art making and old age*. New York University.

Sweetland, J., Volmert, A., & O'Neil, M. (2017, February). *Finding the frame: An empirical approach to reframing aging and ageism*. https://www.frameworksinstitute.org/wp-content/uploads/2020/05/aging_research_report_final_2017.pdf.

The Alzheimer's Association. (2020). *Types of dementia*. https://www.alz.org/alzheimers-dementia/what-is-dementia/types-of-dementia.

The Anti-Ageism Taskforce. (2006). *Ageism in America*. International Longevity Center.

Thomas, W. (2006). *In the arms of elders: A parable of wise leadership and community building*. VanderWyk & Burnham.

van den Hoonaard, D. K. (2018). Learning to be old. *International Journal of Qualitative Methods*, *17*, 1–8. https://doi.org/10.1177/1609406918810556.

Vespa, J. (2018). *The graying of America: More older adults than kids by 2035*. https://www.census.gov/library/stories/2018/03/graying-america.html.

Volicer, L., Harper, D. G., Manning, B. C., Goldstein, R., & Satlin, A. (2001). Sundowning and circadian rhythms in Alzheimer's disease. *American Journal of Psychiatry*, *158*(5), 704–711. https://doi.org/10.1176/appi.ajp.158.5.704. In this issue.

Whalley, L. J. (2015). *Understanding brain aging and dementia: A life course approach*. Columbia University Press.

Wiegand, C., Rascheke, C., & Elsner, P. (2017). Skin aging: A brief summary of characteristic changes. In M. Farage, K. Miller, & H. Maibach (Eds.), *Textbook of aging skin* (pp. 55–65). Springer.

Wong, A. (Ed.). (2020). *Disability visibility: First-person stories from the twenty-first century*. Vintage Books.

World Health Organization. (2020). *Ageism*. https://www.who.int/ageing/ageism/en/.

Yu, J.-T., Xu, W., Tan, C.-C., Andrieu, S., Suckling, J., Evangelou, E., et al. (2020). Evidence-based prevention of Alzheimer's disease: Systematic review and meta-analysis of 243 observational prospective studies and 153 randomised controlled trials. *Journal of Neurology, Neurosurgery & Psychiatry*. https://doi.org/10.1136/jnnp-2019-321913. jnnp-2019-321913.

Partridge, E.E., & Harmon, S. (2019, October 30–November 2). Remaking art spaces: Art therapists as architect-curators. In *American Art Therapy Association annual meeting*, Kansas City, Missouri, United States.

Chapter 13

Art therapy for trauma recovery and response

Joseph Scarce, PhD, ATR-BC[a] and Cynthia Wilson, PhD, ATR-BC[b,c]
[a]*University of Tampa, Tampa, FL, United States,* [b]*UniQue ImAging Art Therapy and Photo Therapy Techniques, Boise, ID, United States,* [c]*UniQue ImAging Art Therapy and Photo Therapy Techniques, Modesto, CA, United States*

Voices from the field

Since the dawn of humanity, art has been used worldwide as a redemptive force to cope with trauma. The Art Therapy for Trauma Recovery and Response chapter sheds new light on the current causes and consequences of trauma on the human condition and explores exciting treatments as a step toward unraveling the mystery of the healing power of art.

Wayne Ramirez (personal communication, May 9, 2021)

Chapter warning

This chapter discusses sensitive material. If the topic of trauma is potentially triggering for you, the authors recommend that you speak to your instructor and/or a mental health professional.

Learning outcomes

After reading this chapter, you will be able to

1. Define trauma.
2. Identify how trauma affects people in the United States.
3. Describe the long-term consequences of trauma.
4. Name and describe the Diagnostic and Statistical Manual of Mental Disorders, 5th Edition, trauma and stressor-related disorders.
5. Describe the four main clusters of symptoms for posttraumatic stress disorder.
6. Describe complex posttraumatic stress disorder.
7. Differentiate the theoretical approaches to trauma that can be used with art therapy.
8. Describe how art therapists work with children and adolescents recovering from trauma.
9. Describe how art therapists have responded to natural disasters, mass violence, and crisis.
10. Articulate the ways art-making can be useful for managing wellness and self-care.

Foundations of Art Therapy. https://doi.org/10.1016/B978-0-12-824308-4.00002-8

Chapter overview

This chapter explores how art therapy can help people recover from trauma. The chapter begins by defining trauma and examining why trauma is important to study. We learn about the different forms of trauma and how trauma is diagnosed. Four specific clusters of symptoms are discussed as well as how trauma affects the brain. Specific ways to prepare for trauma work are reviewed. Research evidence on art therapy interventions for trauma is provided and the chapter describes specific ways that art therapy is integrated into trauma treatment and work with children and adolescents. The second half of the chapter explores art therapy in response to disaster and tragedy. We explore art therapy interventions through Psychological First Aid, Art Therapy First Aid, and several real-life case examples. The chapter concludes with a discussion about the importance of self-care when working with clients who experience trauma.

Introduction

Jamie (pseudonym), a 19-year-old, White, gay, male college student was in a minor car accident. For Jamie, this was not a significant, traumatic event. He was able to manage his emotions; however, he noticed some fear related to riding in automobiles. Jamie adapted some cognitive flexibility by changing his thought process in response to what was happening in his situation. He pictured himself riding in a car, going safely from one place to the next, thus removing the threat of an accident in his mind. Jamie also had strong social support, as indicated by his willingness to verbalize his fear of riding in a car with his friends, who were supportive of him and did not minimize his fear. Jamie was fortunate to have used these skills to manage his trauma for some time and had become quite good at managing his fear of riding in a car in particular.

Unfortunately, Jamie was in another car accident in which he sustained injuries from shattered glass. When Jamie came home from the hospital, he became very anxious, and isolated himself in his room. He eventually realized he needed professional help to work through his fear. Jamie decided to see an art therapist since he liked to draw and had been able to use art-making to cope with other life events. Jamie worked with the art therapist to process his trauma and develop positive coping skills to assist with his isolation. Jamie saw the art therapist weekly, and during the first session he worked on a drawing of a bridge to help him visualize his current feelings. He discussed his ability to work toward getting over the "bridge" in order to reach his future goals. Jamie worked on a series of different art projects with his art therapist weekly, including creating mandalas and painting a canvas to further identify his emotions related to his fears and how to cope in the future.

We can see that things changed for Jamie from his initial accident when he was hospitalized and recovered as compared to the second accident when he was no longer functioning or managing his daily routine. It became important for him to seek out professional help. After his first accident, Jamie was able to recover on his own. Many people who have experienced traumatic events, like Jamie, often do not seek help. However, if the symptoms become debilitating and affect social interactions or other areas of life, treatment for trauma may be helpful.

Why is learning about trauma important?

The **Adverse Childhood Experiences** (ACEs) questionnaire is a survey that is used nationally to collect data on the traumatic experiences of people in the United States. The survey questions ask about childhood experiences with violence in the home or community, amount of emotional and physical stability in the environment, and family mental health and substance use problems. The ACEs study found that "About 61% of adults surveyed across 25 states reported that they had experienced at least one type of ACE, and nearly 1 in 6 reported they had experienced four or more types of ACEs" (Centers for Disease Control and Prevention, 2021, para. 2). Why is this important? The ACEs study results show that traumatic events in childhood are fairly common in the United States. Importantly, the study found that higher ACE scores are correlated to higher risk of disease, chronic health issues (cancer, diabetes, heart disease, suicide), and emotional and social problems (Anda et al., 2010). The study's findings note that "Toxic stress from ACEs can change brain development and affect such things as attention, decision-making, learning, and response to stress" (Centers for Disease Control and Prevention, 2021, p. 3). What is the cost of childhood trauma? The total cost of addressing the problems that result from childhood traumatic events costs "hundreds of billions of dollars each year" (Centers for Disease Control and Prevention, 2021, para. 2). This national study highlights the importance of learning more about the factors that cause trauma, and more importantly how art therapy might be able to ameliorate the long-term, negative effects of trauma.

What is trauma?

Trauma can result from an event that is "extremely upsetting and at least temporarily overwhelms the individual's internal resources" (Briere & Scott, 2006, p. 10). Experiencing trauma after a stressful event is a typical response; however, trauma can cause more serious consequences such as repression, dissociation, unpredictable or disconnected emotions, flashbacks, and even physical symptoms (Chapman, 2014; Dubi et al., 2017; Levine, 1997; Menakem, 2017; Ross & Halpern, 2009; van der Kolk, 2014). These consequences can lead to "lasting adverse effects on the individual's functioning and mental, physical, social, emotional, or spiritual well-being" (Substance Abuse and Mental Health

Services Administration [SAMHSA], 2019, para. 1) and possibly lead to a diagnosis of a trauma- or stressor-related disorder.

Trauma and diversity

Cultural context can play an important role in the expression of symptoms and the treatment of trauma. In fact, many communities of color are more likely to experience traumatic events yet these communities face multiple barriers to mental health services (Bryant-Davis, 2019). Factors that might affect symptoms and treatment include one's migration experiences, religion, family dynamics, ethnic identity, and other aspects of identity and "intersecting identities can result in multiple traumas or forms of oppression" (Bryant-Davis, 2019, p. 135) p. 135.

Exposure to incidents of racism can also negatively contribute to mental health and can be connected to negative health outcomes (low birth weight, higher risk of heart disease, higher rates of hypertension) (Carter, 2007). Race-based traumatic stress injury is a term that describes the effects that racism can have on a client's mental health. **Race-based traumatic stress injury** is defined as an emotional or physical injury due to racial harassment or discrimination that was viewed by the receiver as negative, memorable, sudden, and uncontrollable, and can result in reexperiencing the event or staying in a hyperarousal state (Carter, 2007). Thus cultural context is important to consider in trauma treatment.

How is trauma diagnosed?

The **Diagnostic and Statistical Manual of Mental Disorders**, 5th Edition, Text Revised (DSM-5-TR; American Psychiatric Association [APA], 2022) is the source for mental health professionals in the United States for diagnosing mental health conditions. The DSM-5-TR categorizes trauma disorders under the title of *Trauma- and Stressor-Related Disorders*. Although not all art therapists use the DSM-5-TR, understanding the different diagnoses and symptoms can aid our understanding of trauma disorders, increase our ability to be empathic, and help in identifying the best treatments for clients. **Trauma- and stressor-related disorders** included in the DSM-5-TR are (1) reactive attachment disorder, (2) disinhibited social engagement disorder, (3) posttraumatic stress disorder, (4) acute stress disorder, (5) adjustment disorders, and (6) prolonged grief disorder. Each of these disorders requires the criteria of "exposure to a traumatic or stressful event" (Trauma- and Stressor-Related Disorders section). Every disorder has specific criteria listed in the DSM-5-TR, with symptoms that may include anxiety, fear, sadness, anger, and even aggression. In the following section we provide a brief summary of each of the trauma- and stressor-related disorders.

The first two disorders, reactive attachment and disinhibited social engagement disorder, require a history of **social neglect**, which is defined as the "absence of adequate caregiving during childhood" (APA, 2013, p. 365).

Reactive attachment disorder

The first two years of a child's life are the most crucial for developing attachment to caregivers (Chapman, 2014). With an unattuned primary caregiver, a child may learn to not to cry when in need because no one will help meet their needs. This lack of emotional expression can lead to the child becoming very emotionally explosive at times, while at other times the child may show minimal responsiveness (APA, 2022). Disruption of the attachment phase during the child's development can lead to **reactive attachment disorder (RAD)**. RAD is related to the lack of attachment or connection between the child and their caregiver due to the caregiver's lack of attunement or attention to the child's basic needs (such as food, shelter, and love) as an infant or toddler.

When a child must rely on an adult to protect them and that bond of trust is broken by abuse, this can lead to **relational trauma**, which is when the child loses the sense of safety in their relationship with others or themselves. Relational trauma is complex because humans are relational or social creatures who function best together, supporting each other in family or community settings (Chapman, 2014; Danylchuck, 2015; Gottman & DeClair, 2001; Siegel & Bryson, 2011). "We survive in relationship and some of our most basic needs depend on the actions of others" (Danylchuck, 2015, p. 93).

Porges (2011) described how humans are constantly attuned to the nonverbal cues of others, such as through tone of voice, facial expressions, body postures, and eye movement or contact, to determine the level of threat in their environment and with others around them. People who have experienced relational trauma have a decreased ability to trust others, the environment, and/or themselves and tend to be hypervigilant or hyperaware of their surroundings. Therefore working with people who have experienced relational trauma can be challenging and establishing trust is not often easy. The way a therapist presents themselves in the room, the room décor or office location, clothes of the therapist, or their hairstyle are all important elements to consider before entering the room with your client who has a history of relational trauma (Chapman, 2014).

Disinhibited social engagement disorder

Similar to RAD, **disinhibited social engagement disorder** is caused by early social neglect and problems with early attachment to caregivers. Unlike RAD, the neglect leads to "culturally inappropriate, overly familiar behavior with relative strangers" (APA, 2013, p. 269) where the child is overly friendly and lacks appropriate boundaries with: "overly familiar verbal or physical behavior (that is not consistent with culturally sanctioned and with age-appropriate social boundaries)" (APA, 2022, Diagnostic criteria section). "Even after placement in normative caregiving environments, some children show persistent signs of the disorder, through adolescence … and into adulthood" (APA, 2022, Course modifiers section). One possible cause of the disorder is stress from the lack of consistent and higher than average number of caregivers (such as in multiple foster placements; APA, 2013).

Posttraumatic stress disorder

Posttraumatic stress disorder (PTSD) can be caused by experiencing or witnessing a traumatic event. Examples of **traumatic events** can include an implied, or actual threat of a natural disaster, serious accident, terrorist act/war/combat, rape, or assault (APA, 2022). Trauma can also result from events affecting loved ones or repeated exposure to details about traumatic events (APA, 2022). It is important to note that "The risk of onset and severity of PTSD may differ across cultural groups as a result of variation in the type of traumatic exposure (e.g., genocide), the impact on disorder severity can depend on the meaning attributed to the traumatic event (e.g., if one is unable to perform funerary rites after a mass killing), the ongoing sociocultural context (e.g., residing among unpunished perpetrators in postconflict settings), and other cultural factors (e.g., acculturative stress in immigrants)" (APA, 2013, p. 278).

There are four main clusters of symptoms (APA, 2022): (1) reexperiencing the event, (2) avoidance of things associated with the event, (3) negative thoughts and mood related to the event, and (4) increased arousal after the event. These symptom clusters are applied to people older than 6 years and the symptoms need to persist for more than 1 month (APA, 2022). A description of each of these clusters follows next. The DSM-5-TR does include criteria for children age 6 or younger but due to the brevity of this chapter those criteria are not included; please consult with the DSM-5-TR for more details on these criteria.

Cluster 1: Reexperiencing intrusive symptoms

Reexperiencing is when the person reports "Vivid images, sensations, and feelings are ever present, and the person has a sense of reliving the experiences, in the form of illusions, hallucinations, and flashbacks, as well as nightmares related to the event" (Schupp, 2004, p. 46). **Flashbacks** occur when a person remembers a traumatic event as though the event is currently happening. Differentiating between the trauma memory and the current time is extremely difficult. Sometimes the nightmares of the traumatic event(s) can be of a flashback nature where the event is replaying while the person is asleep. In children who are 6 years or younger, they may experience distressing dreams with unrecognizable or related content to the traumatic event (APA, 2022).

Cluster 2: Avoidance

Symptoms of **avoidance** include anything related to the evasion or avoidance of things associated with the event. The person may refrain from dealing with memories of the event or anything associated with the memory of the event (such as certain places or people). **Trauma triggers** are reminders of the trauma, for example, being exposed to the location of where the trauma originally happened, even a certain smell, color, sound, movement, or an image can elicit a memory that affects a trauma survivor.

Cluster 3: Negative thoughts and mood

Negative thoughts and mood include difficulty remembering details related to the event, persistent and negative beliefs about one's self or about the event, negative mood, feeling indifferent, or difficulty feeling positive after the event (APA, 2022).

Cluster 4: Hyperarousal

Hyperarousal includes symptoms of irritability, engaging in dangerous behavior, increased attention to one's surroundings, heightened startled response, difficulty concentrating, and sleep difficulties (APA, 2022) that disrupt daily life.

What is causing these symptom clusters? PTSD can be conceptualized as a rewiring of the system to recognize specific events or sensations as predictors of danger. In this case, there may be no distinction between past and present danger (van der Kolk, 2014). PTSD can affect the connections between the amygdala and brain regions associated with cognition, language, and the ability to modulate emotional responses (Sadeh et al., 2014). PTSD symptoms such as hypervigilance, intrusive memories, and impaired sleep can be associated with overactivation of the amygdala, while dissociative symptoms may be associated with insufficient activation of the amygdala and poor consolidation of the emotional memories (Diamond & Zoladz, 2016).[a]

It is important to monitor symptoms of PTSD and to see a mental health professional if you have experienced the trauma symptoms mentioned before. People who have been diagnosed with PTSD may be at an increased risk of suicidal ideation due to the distressing nature of their symptoms (APA, 2022), thus trauma-informed art therapists must be mindful of monitoring client safety and well-being.

Acute stress disorder

People who have symptoms that appear after 3 days but less than 1 month after exposure to trauma may be diagnosed with **acute stress disorder** (ASD; APA, 2022). In contrast, PTSD is diagnosed if symptoms last more than 1 month. To be diagnosed with ASD, individuals must report nine symptoms from the following areas after the traumatic event: involuntary and intrusive memories, negative mood, dissociation (altered sense or lack of memory), avoidance, and arousal (APA, 2022).

Adjustment disorder

Adjustment disorders occur when a person experiences distress within 3 months of an event that is out of proportion to a typical response, yet they do not meet the criteria of the disorders described before. According to the DSM-5-TR (APA, 2022) the stressors can be one or multiple events, due to developmental

---

a. This section was contributed by Christianne Strang Ph.D., ATR-BC, Behavioral Neuroscience Professor and Art Therapist.

changes (such as moving away for college, getting married, death of a loved one), and may affect one or more people. Individuals with an adjustment disorder are at an increased risk of suicide (APA, 2022).

Prolonged grief disorder

According to the DSM-5-TR, adults with prolonged grief disorder continue to experience impairments after 12 months since the death, while children continue to have debilitating symptoms after 6 months of the loss. Symptoms include: experience daily yearning or preoccupation with memories, have three of the symptoms (such as, identity disruption, disbelief, avoidance, intense emotional pain, difficulty socializing, emotional numbness, feeling a sense of meaningless, or loneliness). To be diagnosed with prolonged grief disorder, symptoms must affect the ability to function and are outside of cultural norms.

Complex posttraumatic stress disorder

Although not a diagnosis in the DSM-5-TR, **complex PTSD** (CPTSD) is defined as a form of PTSD with additional layers of complexity due to severe forms of trauma such as extreme physical or sexual abuse, repeated traumatic events, and/or various other types of trauma. The *International Classification of Diseases* (ICD) differentiates CPTSD as its own diagnosis. Judith Herman first defined CPTSD in her book *Trauma & Recovery* in 1992. She described CPTSD as "A history of subjection to totalitarian control over a prolonged period (months to years). Examples include hostages, prisoners of war, concentration-camp survivors, and survivors of some religious cults, domestic life, including survivors of domestic battering, childhood physical or sexual abuse, and organized sexual exploitation" (Herman, 1992, p. 121).

The effects of trauma on the brain[b]

It is important for art therapists to understand that there are emotional (van der Kolk, 2014), somatic (Ogden & Fisher, 2015), and cognitive components (Siegel & Bryson, 2011) to traumatic responses.

Emotional responses are mediated by the amygdala. As described in Chapter 4, the **amygdala** is a limbic system structure that is responsible for emotional learning and associated fear and danger with specific events or contextual fear associations (Kandel et al., 2013). The amygdala is involved with determining whether a sound, sight, or sensation represents a threat. If a sensation is perceived as a threat, connections with the autonomic nervous system (see Chapter 4) are activated to prepare us for the physical, somatic actions of fighting back or escaping (often described as fleeing, fainting, or dissociating) (King et al., 2019; van der Kolk, 2014). **Dissociation** is a survival skill used to escape

b. This section was contributed by Christianne Strang PhD, ATR-BC, Behavioral Neuroscience Professor and Art Therapist and Cynthia Wilson, Ph.D. MA, ATR-BC.

emotionally or psychologically from a situation that someone cannot physically leave, has no control over, or in which they have no voice (Miller, 2012).

Because the detection and avoidance of threat are involved in survival, emotional activation is faster and takes precedence over cognitive appraisal of the situation. This quick-acting emotional activation can affect how trauma is encoded in memory and impair the ability to communicate about the experience in words (van der Kolk, 2014). For example, intense and intrusive memories can result from overactivation of the amygdala during the creation of trauma memories (Diamond & Zoladz, 2016). The focus on immediate survival also results in fewer resources available for other learning, language, or other cognitive tasks. The effects on cognitive, emotional, and social development can be particularly severe if the trauma occurs during childhood (Miller, 2012; van der Kolk, 2014) due to the lack of resources directed to regular developmental processes.

When the traumatic events are objectively over, steps can be taken to restore the subjective sense of safety by decreasing the activation of the sympathetic nervous system. Ideally this shift will release resources for the other cognitive and emotional tasks associated with healing from trauma. Later in this chapter, we describe how art therapy treatments are specifically helpful at decreasing the activation of the sympathetic nervous system and thus addressing the ways trauma affects the body.

Preparing to provide services to clients with trauma

When a person is not an art therapist or other mental health professional and is entering a practicum, internship, or employment situation, it is important to understand how art-making is being used with survivors of trauma. When interviewing for these positions, be sure to ask questions about your role and responsibilities. For example, you might ask if you will be meeting with clients alone or with a qualified mental health professional, or who you should contact if clients need additional assistance that you are unqualified to provide. If you are asked to work in areas beyond your skill set or comfort zone, discuss these concerns with your supervisor and your instructor. A support network of professionals who are more experienced can aid with ethical, legal, and security issues (Wilson & Coleman, 2020).

An art therapy professional who is new to working with people who have experienced trauma should consult with an art therapist who is skilled in the areas of trauma treatment while they complete additional training on the subject. Even an art therapist who has been working with this population for years is ethically required to continue their education to stay up-to-date with current research. It is essential to maintain connections with other art therapists in the field for support and consultation. When working with this population it is important to be trauma-trained, survivor-centered, nonjudgmental, strengths-based, and culturally competent (Wilson & Coleman, 2020).

In my (second author, Cynthia Wilson) experience, one essential aspect of the art therapy process is making a safe space for the client to feel confident in sharing personal information. This includes building rapport and establishing a healthy, safe, trusting, supportive connection with the client. The client is not expected to (and likely will not) trust the art therapist at first—seeing the therapist as a stranger they just met—even though art therapy is a less threatening form of treatment. All clients, but especially clients who have experienced trauma, need to feel comfortable sharing their story with the art therapist at the pace they need and under their own control. Art therapy can be very powerful and if art therapy is not handled with caution the client can be further traumatized (Spring, 1993, 2001, 2004).

How can art therapy help with trauma?

Research on art therapy for trauma has shown promising results. Art therapists have worked with children and adults who have experienced various types of trauma caused by natural disasters (Roje, 1995; Chilcote, 2007; Linton, 2017; Scarce, 2021); terrorist attacks (Howie et al., 2002; Jones, 1997; Levy et al., 2002); sexual abuse (Becker, 2015; Hargrave-Nykaza, 1994; Kometiani, 2020; Piffalo, 2007; Spring, 1993, 2001); physical abuse (Culbertson & Revel, 1987); domestic violence (Mills & Kellington, 2012; Stronach-Buschel & Hurvitz Madsen, 2006); medical injury, illness, or procedures (Appleton, 2001; Malchiodi, 1999; Potash, 2018); community trauma (Gonzalez-Dolginko, 2002); neglect, deprivation, relational trauma (Chapman, 2014; Schore, 2009); and grief and loss (Johnson, 2007). Eaton et al. (2007) examined art therapy research from 12 peer-reviewed studies and found that art therapy was an effective treatment for children with trauma.

Art therapy provides a tangible, physical form of transferring a traumatic event from the mind to paper (Arrington, 2007; Chapman, 2014; Kubler-Ross & Kessler, 2007; Wilson, 2019). Art therapy can help clients find a renewed sense of self-worth as they find a voice for the traumas to be expressed and processed and this can lead to a healthier sense of self (Wilson, 2019; Wilson & Coleman, 2020). Orr (2007) conducted a **content analysis**, a technique that identifies content themes in articles, videos, and media that focused on art therapists who work with children who have survived disasters. Orr (2007) found that youth receiving art therapy were able to progress through grief and loss. She noted that "Art therapists had traumatized children create art to provide a temporary protected environment within the chaos, to help them to be optimistic and focus on the here and now, to provide assistance and resiliency practice to vulnerable highly stressed children, and to provide catharsis" (p. 356).

According to the American Art Therapy Association (AATA), art therapy has four primary contributions to the treatment of PTSD: (1) art therapy can reduce anxiety and other mood disorders; (2) art therapy can also improve emotional and cognitive functions; (3) art therapy can externalize, verbalize, and process trauma memories; and (4) art therapy can reactivate emotions of self-worth and self-esteem (AATA, 2017). If during the traumatic event there was a visual component, then it seems to reason that if the trauma processing work involves visual aspects as well

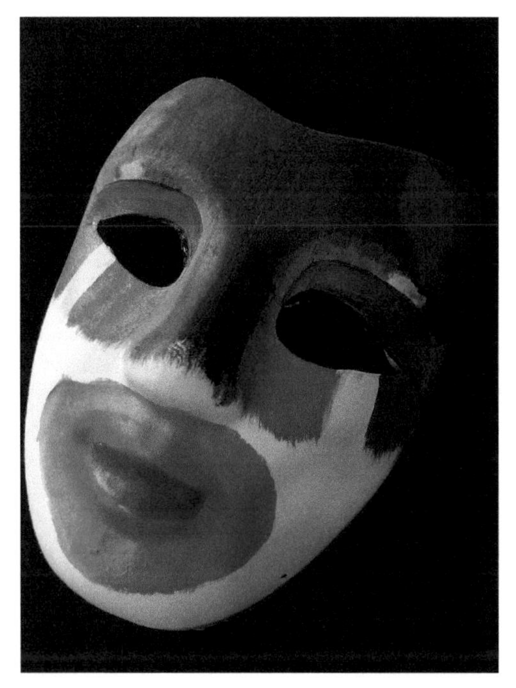

FIG. 13.1 *Mask.*
(Permission granted from Cynthia Wilson artist.)

(such as in art therapy), the memories may more easily become conscious and able to be processed effectively (Howie, 2016).

Veterans suffering from trauma and PTSD have reported benefitting from art therapy treatment (DeLucia, 2016). Active duty soldiers made and then used masks to tell their stories. The masks became a visual representation of their challenging, emotional experiences from active duty (Walker et al., 2017). Using masks for story telling has been used with many populations from military personnel to teenagers as a creative way to externalize the emotions and visually convey stories/narratives that can be worked with, talked to, and even tangibly held or handed off to another (Alexander, 2020; Chapman, 2014).

The mask above expresses the story of the second author Cynthia Wilson's experiences with the trauma of multiple car accidents (Fig. 13.1). This mask expresses my experience of surviving head trauma and severe bodily injury that caused routine migraines, chronic pain, and physical disabilities. The mask helped me express my grief and loss of who I once was, and who I imagined I would become. Creating and reflecting on this mask has helped me find myself again by voicing my emotional, physical, and spiritual pains. Being able to express these difficult emotions has created feelings of hope for the new me.

Art therapy, trauma treatment, and the brain[c]

In order to help an individual return to normal functioning, the first steps are to work toward objective and subjective safety. If the danger has not passed, if the individual is not objectively safe, then the amygdala is doing its job of ensuring survival by detecting cues associated with ongoing danger (Diamond & Zoladz, 2016; van der Kolk, 2014). If the danger has passed, the work may be to help the individual modulate the intense emotions and behaviors that are no longer needed to ensure safety.

The dependence of trauma processing on subcortical and autonomic circuitry means that verbal processing may be more difficult. However, integrating the cognitive and executive systems (see Chapter 4, Intersections of Neuroscience and Art Therapy) with emotional and sensorimotor processes is essential to processing trauma (Elbrecht & Antcliff, 2014; Gantt & Tinnin, 2007; Siegel & Bryson, 2011).

Art therapy is particularly well suited to meet the goals of integrating the systems. The brain regions responsible for processing visual imagery and connecting visual, emotional, and behavioral outputs are activated during the art-making process (Hinz, 2019; King et al., 2019) and can invoke body memories and visceral responses that can then be processed (Chapman, 2014; Hinz, 2019). Art therapy can improve attention, working memory, and executive function (Lee et al., 2019; Mahendran et al., 2018), while the properties of art material themselves can aid in somatosensory processing (Lusebrink & Hinz, 2020). Thus art therapy provides avenues to process trauma in ways that bypass the need for the verbal centers of the brain while balancing emotional or bodily needs. Balancing these other needs can aid in activating or reactivating the verbal centers again (Wilson, 2019).

Integrating art therapy with other therapeutic approaches to trauma

In addition to art therapy approaches, most art therapists are trained in general counseling and psychological approaches. Therefore art therapists are often well qualified to integrate other counseling theories with art therapy or in combination with other mental health therapy approaches (sometimes referred to as **adjunctive treatment**). Trauma treatment approaches can combine well with art therapy treatment because the creative arts can provide opportunities for rich insights, emotional expression, and integrating aspects of one's self (Kometiani, 2020; Scott & Ross, 2006).

Not all art-related interventions qualify as art therapy. However, providing art projects as a way to destress is common in many facilities that may not have an art therapist on staff. Without an art therapist, these facilities are probably using the therapeutic benefits of the arts to help their clients, but it is not the same as art

c. This section was contributed by Christianne Strang Ph.D., ATR-BC, Behavioral Neuroscience Professor and Art Therapist & Cynthia Wilson, Ph.D. MA, ATR-BC.

therapy. Similarly, the use of coloring book pages can be soothing just as taking photographs with friends can calm the nerves and leave a sense of connection to others. As therapeutic as these experiences may be, they are not art therapy without the art therapist who facilitates the relational art processing at deeper levels.

We will next explore specific types of art therapy trauma treatments including trauma narrative, forward-facing trauma therapy, cognitive behavioral therapy, trauma-focused cognitive behavioral therapy, cognitive processing therapy, eye movement desensitization and reprocessing, emotional freedom technique, and focused oriented art therapy. Due to space limitations, this chapter was unable to explore possible side effects of these treatments. Additional research is needed to explore the efficacy and possible drawbacks of the approaches shared below.

Trauma narrative

People affected by trauma can process traumatic events using a **trauma narrative**, that is, by telling their story in the form of written or artistic rendition. Bringing forth imagery through art therapy helps a person process the memory and then verbalize the event. Due to the brain's need to understand an event for survival's sake, we continue to replay an event over and over as our mind and body attempt to make sense of the event (Siegel & Bryson, 2011). Helping to desensitize and lessen the effect of the traumatic memory is a significant part of the healing process. Lanius et al. (2015) conducted a study with people diagnosed with PTSD and learned that stored memories were coming from various parts of the brain. The goal of a trauma narrative is for the brain to reconnect these scattered implicit memory pieces and make them explicit, which creates a linear and more cohesive story (Siegel & Bryson, 2011). Other benefits utlizing a trauma narative can include desensitization, gaining power over the narrative, and being able to share the narraive with others.

Art therapists often use the trauma narrative to assist the client in focusing on their story of the traumatic event through an art-making experience. This integration helps the client process the trauma and bring it forward to desensitize the traumatic event. Art-based interventions can facilitate connections to implicit, traumatic memory and create a bridge between unconscious states to the conscious explicit awareness (Talwar, 2007; Tripp, 2007). According to Hass-Cohen et al. (2014), "With balanced sensory and contextual processing, intrusive sensory memories gradually diminish, reducing the likelihood of unremitting stress responses" (p. 76).

Linda Chapman (2014), an art therapist in Northern California, has worked her entire career primarily with children with a trauma history. She developed a trauma narrative art therapy directive. This directive has the person first engage in a guided **bilateral scribble** (scribbling with both hands at the same time). Next, the person tells the trauma story through a series of drawings. Finally, a discussion with the therapist helps to integrate the scattered and fragmented pieces of the trauma story to make the story whole. The **Chapman Trauma Narrative** aids in connecting the trauma pieces in a linear way when the trauma experience otherwise makes no sense or cannot be described by words. "In the nonverbal mind, imprints of trauma memory lack narrative structure and therefore lack narrative closure" (Gantt & Tripp, 2016, p. 69).

A trauma narrative can be done in many ways, such as a teen creating a series of masks showing the inside and outside feelings associated with their experiences before, during, and after the traumatic event. In doing so, they also can be making a statement or establishing a sense of self through the art product. According to Gantt and Tripp (2016), an art therapy trauma narrative, called a **graphic narrative**, allows the client to retrieve traumatic memories in order to integrate them verbally. The art therapist is trained to use the art product and art materials to provide the client the necessary structure and linear sequence of the trauma story for integration and processing in a way that talk therapy cannot (Gantt & Tripp, 2016; Gantt & Vesprini, 2017).

Forward-facing trauma therapy

Eric Gentry is a highly regarded practitioner of trauma recovery who has trained thousands of professionals in trauma and disaster recovery. Gentry (2016) states **forward-facing trauma therapy** (FFTT) uses **self-regulation** (a way of managing responses to emotions) and self-scanning body techniques to identify stressors and create a relaxation response. Gentry bases his FFTT on the concept that one cannot have severe stress while in a relaxed body. The use of relaxation techniques is important not only for the client but also for the practitioner to provide treatment. Gentry (2016) cautions that this treatment should be only used with a professional, especially for people "dealing with severe depression, PTSD, an anxiety disorder, or a substance abuse disorder or if you are taking medications to treat these and other mental health conditions" (p. 36).

Art therapists are often accustomed to incorporating relaxation and meditative techniques into their art therapy practice, so Gentry's techniques are easily integrated into art therapy, especially when establishing and visualizing safety, a peaceful, relaxing place, or a brave space. Take note that the wording used with clients who have experienced trauma is just as important as the art materials and guided art projects. For example, some clients have difficulty with the idea of safe places since they have never felt safe before or have a difficult time believing a safe place can exist. Additionally, the idea of safety might be frightening since safety might imply letting one's guard down. The second author, Cynthia Wilson, uses the term brave space to complement what that particular client needs. So along with the choice of art materials or media and the guidance of the art creation activity, the art therapist must choose words that support the specific client's healing and coincide with the therapeutic orientation of the therapist and the technique being used.

Cognitive behavioral therapy

According to Dubi et al. (2017), cognitive behavioral therapy (CBT) is adaptable for shorter term treatment and focuses on changing client's thinking patterns to enable more adaptive responses (Rosal, 2015). **Cognitive behavioral art therapy (CBAT)** can be easily adapted with take-home art-making assignments that challenge thinking that is seen as distorted or to incorporate rational solutions to real-life problems. Marcia Rosal is an art therapist known for her work in CBAT (see Chapter 9, Using Art to Think and Rethink: Cognitive-Behavior Therapy from Behaviorism through the Third Wave). The cognitive behavioral art therapist incorporates art interventions to challenge the client in and out of the treatment setting with art-making that helps to process and question irrational thoughts, as well as provide guidance through visual timelines. There are two types of CBT that have specialized approaches in dealing with trauma: Trauma-Focused Cognitive Behavioral Therapy and Cognitive Processing Therapy. These two approaches are explored next.

Trauma-focused cognitive behavioral therapy

Trauma-focused cognitive behavioral therapy (TF-CBT) is an evidence-based practice that uses CBT techniques with the added emphasis and care that is needed when working with someone who has a history of trauma symptoms. Piffalo (2007) explains that CBT and trauma-focused art therapy work especially well together because both approaches help to recall the memory safely, while visually creating a narrative process that increases awareness of other aspects of the traumatic event that might be overlooked initially due to the power that the event had. TF-CBT use of the trauma narrative easily pairs well with art therapy trauma narrative techniques or protocols mentioned earlier in this chapter. Additionally, the "Art products externalize the individual's inner thoughts and feelings, rendering them in tangible, visual form, making them difficult to avoid or deny" (Tripp, 2016, p. 176). Being unable to deny a traumatic experience can be upsetting and care is needed to be sure the art being done is moving the client in a safe way and not causing severe unrest or further trauma. The reader should keep in mind that TF-CBT is an evidence-based practice that requires intensive training and is designed only for use with children.

Cognitive processing therapy

Cognitive processing therapy (CPT) is a type of cognitive behavioral therapy that challenges and helps to change treatment-hindering beliefs. CPT typically consists of 12 sessions where clients explore automatic thoughts, share details about the traumatic event, and examine their thinking patterns (Cognitive Processing Therapy (CPT), 2017). CPT has been shown to work well with art therapy to reduce depression and PTSD symptoms (Gantt & Tripp, 2016). According to Campbell et al. (2016), who conducted a study combining CPT and art therapy, "Improved trauma processing was one of the most significant contributions to art therapy intervention" (p. 175). Clients use art-making to express their internal experience with trauma. When the image is finished the trauma narrative is read back to them; it appears that the "auditory, verbal, and visual processing" (Campbell et al., 2016, p. 175) of hearing their stories read back to them is an important part of this treatment.

Eye movement desensitization and reprocessing

Eye movement desensitization and reprocessing (EMDR) is a theory that uses bilateral eye movement to process traumatic memories with a connection to both hemispheres of the brain (Parnell, 2008; Shapiro, 2001). Francis Shapiro (2018) believed that there are **little "t" traumas** such as being in a minor car accident, or being teased as a child and **big "T" traumas** such as sexual violence, physical abuse, going through a disaster such as war, catastrophic natural disaster, or mass violence. Francis Shapiro (2018) coined the term little "t" trauma and big "T" trauma and provided definitions to assist therapists in categorizing how trauma is affecting an individual. Tripp (2007), a well-known EMDR and trauma-trained art therapist and professor at George Washington University in Washington DC, described how art therapy and EMDR can be combined. Using tapping devices under each knee or in each hand while the participant is listening to calming music or sounds, the participant reconnects with imagery associated with a single traumatic event. The multimodal treatment allows for further exploration of the art response, and the artwork created can become a visual timeline to recovery. Old memories can be activated by bilateral tapping movements or through eye movements. Combining these movements with the awareness of the present is beneficial in helping to bring the trauma into better focus and helping to desensitize oneself to it (Parnell, 2008; Shapiro, 2001). This is also a way to increase awareness of time orientation for the client so their mind and body connect to the current time in recognition that the traumatic event is past, further allowing processing and emotional regulations to commence.

Other art therapists trained in EMDR have incorporated art-making into the steps of the EMDR process. One of the first steps involves the client creating a safe place in their mind, where they can go whenever they feel overwhelmed and need to be disengaged from the traumatic memory. Creating the safe space artistically provides a visual stimulus often used by clients, who may have flashbacks or intense disrupting triggers, while not in session. Creating a peaceful, relaxing place versus a safe place can be less triggering for a client who has a long history of relational trauma. Using art therapy during the EMDR process can be an added help to visualize the traumatic event and better process it with the EMDR-trained art therapist.

Many art therapy directives have aspects of EMDR. The **bilateral stimulation** of using both sides of your body at the same time to increase brain integration, relaxation, improved mood, and focused attention is easily done in art therapy (Chapman, 2014). Examples of bilateral stimulation include bilateral scribbling, drawing, painting, and writing, or doing art that naturally uses both hemispheres of the body and brain, such as knitting, crochet, sculpture, or woodworking. Mank (2021) describes how the building of a drum, adorning personal symbols or archetypal images on the drums, and using clients' personally created drums can be an expressive arts therapy intervention for bilateral movement both for processing and for healing. Art therapists can use these materials to come up with guided activities, or the materials can be used freehand by the clients; the artwork and body and brain response processing takes place during creation or afterward. Chapman (2014) applied developmental levels of bilateral scribbling stimulation for grounding and mastery of art. McNamee (2006) developed a nine-step protocol used to help alleviate harmful thoughts by replacing them with positive ones.

Emotional freedom technique

Emotional Freedom Technique (EFT) "combines elements of exposure and cognitive therapies with acupressure for the treatment of psychological distress" (Clond, 2016, p. 388). Ortner (2013, 2018) explains that EFT is the process of tapping on the body while addressing trauma-related anxiety and negative feelings or emotions while simultaneously pairing these feelings with a positive connection (such as love for self or safety in the current environment). EFT is used for acknowledging and releasing any blocks that may have formed during a traumatic event in a flexible and nonjudgmental manner framed in self-acceptance. EFT and art therapy both acknowledge the mind/body connection and acceptance without judgment (Wilson & Coleman, 2020). Art therapy can help highlight areas of the body where blocks may occur while EFT can reveal ideas for art directives to further work with the subconscious memories and connections of the traumatic event. EFT can help in discovering underlying shame or anger connected to a traumatic event. The underlying feelings can help guide the art therapist to suggest art materials or topics to be further processed in art therapy. The art therapist can also use the art before or after the tapping to visually gauge how things have shifted for the client. Sometimes, just seeing the shifts visually in one's own art helps to solidify and further the shift toward wellness and recovery.

Focus oriented art therapy

Focus Oriented Art Therapy (FOAT) is a protocol developed by Art Therapist Laury Rappaport and is a type of somatic treatment of trauma (Rappaport, 2009). **Somatic treatment of trauma** adds focus on the body sensations, responses and memories, and the interrupted body responses to the traumatic event (Levine, 1997; Ogden & Fisher, 2015). FOAT uses art therapy in combination with the felt sense within the body (Rappaport, 2009). Guided meditation with emphasis on the felt sense or sense of body and emotions combined with an art creation reveals a holistic healing approach of the mind and body that helps to create a homeostasis (or internal stability). The focus on the physical body seeks to relieve traumatic memories that may be stored in the muscles and actions involved in the traumatic event that were incomplete; for example, screaming, pushing, or running that occurred during the traumatic event (Wilson & Coleman, 2020).

Children and adolescents in trauma treatment

Children can be affected by trauma in similar ways as adults such as a result of loss of loved ones, being exposed to violence and disasters, or being abused by a loved one.

Art therapy, however, is also especially suited for children who have developmental delays, difficulty functioning because of behavioral disorders, or communication difficulties due to autism spectrum disorder or any form of disorder where it becomes difficult to tell their story (D'Amico & Lalonde, 2017; Emery, 2004; Martin, 2008). Eaton et al. (2007) examined both qualitative and quantitative research studies focusing on art therapy as an effective treatment for treating children experiencing trauma. Working with specific art materials in trauma focused settings allows for creative self-expression; many children are able to develop better control of their behavioral responses, be less reactive, and communicate visually and sometimes then even verbally when there were initially no words to express. Following is an example of how art-making assisted a teen in coming to terms with isolation during the pandemic.

Ethan, a 17-year-old adolescent, had difficulty expressing his emotions related to loneliness and isolation during the COVID-19 pandemic. After watching a report on the news about homeless shelters being closed, he also learned how other people were also struggling. Ethan painted this picture (Fig. 13.2) titled *Alone* to show his empathy and sadness for those struggling through the COVID-19 pandemic as well as feelings of being isolated himself.

One of the largest art therapy programs in the United States serving children in a school system is in Miami Dade County, Florida. Art therapists support children who need trauma processing and teach resiliency to help prepare children for when trauma occurs (Isis et al., 2010). When art therapy is offered in a school-based setting, the child or adolescent has an opportunity to make connections to the art process; this can often be integrated into other school subjects (Rosal et al., 1997). The art therapist can recognize behaviors that warrant follow-up with other professionals and work closely with school staff and caregivers to develop treatment goals that in turn address academic and behavioral challenges. Art therapists also assist caseworkers and mental health care workers who are having difficulty getting a child to express themselves verbally after experiencing or witnessing a traumatic event. In this case, the art therapist can sometimes be contracted by the school for support or the individual child can go to the therapist's office for treatment.

I (the second author) am careful to build rapport with the adolescent client since establishing trust is paramount. I have found that teenagers entering art therapy have many reasons to be guarded because they may have been hurt by societal wounds of systemic racism, cultural boundaries or expectations, and assumptions of what a child is capable of, as well as parental expectations and limits, and therefore are too acutely aware of their shortcomings. Furthermore, being exposed to a severe traumatic event can be debilitating, leading to increased depression, anxiety and suicidal ideations, thoughts, or attempts (Chapman, 2014; van der Kolk, 2014).

Case example: Art therapy intervention in school

In response to a suspect with a gun roaming the neighborhood around a school campus, the police entered the school grounds and locked it down just before

FIG. 13.2 *Alone.*
(Permission granted by Ethan Stephanis.)

lunch break. With the lockdown came many scared teachers and students, some of whom started rumors of what was going to happen and others who were just confused, wanting questions to be answered. Students from grades kindergarten to grade 12 huddled under their desks in darkened rooms with window blinds drawn shut and doors locked (some even barricaded). As the hours passed, the kids grew hungrier and more scared. Soon kids who had to use the bathrooms were escorted in small numbers down the hall, while others who were in classrooms outside the main building had to use a trash can in the corner of the room. Many teenagers used cell phones to make posts on social media with people outside the lockdown. Within 5 hours, the suspect was captured, the school and neighboring homes were taken off lockdown, and all the children went home safely. This was a successful preventative response to a possible tragic situation. There were many different experiences that the kids in each of these classrooms faced.

I (the second author) went in the very next morning to work with a classroom of third and fourth grade students. I used a simplified bilateral scribbling technique to help the children become grounded back into the present moment, making the classroom and the school campus feel safe again, without having to discuss the trauma verbally to avoid potential triggers. Within about 5 min the children completed the bilateral scribbling. I witnessed the once tense, muscles and postures relax. The children took deep breaths, blinked their eyes and looked around the room, connecting again to the environment and their fellow students. Several of the children began smiling and laughing, exhibiting pride in their artwork and joy in their bodies. One young girl on the autism spectrum stated, "That was the most fun art I've ever done!" Another boy was cheered on with support and relation to his comment as he stated, "I feel like my body has melted off my chair and I could just fall onto the floor". The teachers noted with gratitude how uplifting and relaxed the class now felt and how their giddy little kiddos were back.

Art therapy in response to disaster and tragedy

We are often affected by disasters and crises within our communities. Art can be a vehicle to send messages to uplift and unite people and communities. We have seen numerous community murals that have been created due to racial injustice. For example, artists used their "tool" of artwork to create the *George Floyd Mural* in Minneapolis as "a place to process" (Mizutani, 2021). Similarly, art therapists and students may feel called to volunteer with community response organizations to use art to instill hope such as after devastating hurricanes or creating art with a family who has lost their home to a house fire. Art therapy provides more than distraction from a painful event, the expressive arts therapies also seek to address healing.

Making art is rarely the first thing on someone's mind after experiencing a disaster. After first responders have attended to the tragedy and the individuals are in a stable place, art-making with a professional art therapist can help with processing the traumatic event. Art therapy can be a way to help those who have experienced trauma find healing in a time when many feel they have been forgotten (Scarce, 2021). The art therapy process can be extremely powerful to bring hope and inspiration for future recovery.

Art therapy can also provide members of a community a place to reconnect and create art together. This community art therapy work can create communal healing and helps individuals feel less alone. For example, creating tokens or art templates that are then sent out to other disaster sites lets everyone feel connected and acknowledged for the pain they are going through. Stars of Hope (SOH), a nonprofit organization in Florida, brings painted stars to other disaster sites to hand out to those who have gone through tragedy. Art therapists often work with SOH to engage the survivors in creating hope, through painting stars and processing trauma, grief, and loss.

Defining disaster

What defines a **disaster**? According to the International Federation of Red Cross and Red Crescent Societies (International Federation of Red Cross and Red Crescent Societies, 2021): "A disaster is a sudden, calamitous event that seriously disrupts the functioning of a community or society and causes human, material, and economic or environmental losses that exceed the community's or society's ability to cope using its own resources" (IFRC, 2021, para. 1). Disasters can have natural or human causes but they always have a negative impact on people (IFRC, 2021, para. 1). According to Webber and Mascari (2018), a person who survives a disaster can experience many of the symptoms described earlier in the trauma section in this chapter. How can art therapists and other mental health professionals assist in a disaster?

Psychological first aid

Psychological First Aid (PFA) is defined as an evidence-based approach to reduce the stress and increase the coping skills in people who have experienced a disaster (Brymer et al., 2006). PFA is a supportive intervention that helps provide immediate, nonintrusive connections with people who have been through a disaster. It is important to note that the provider of PFA is not providing counseling. Research has shown that counseling interventions or assessments (e.g., asking lots of questions) directly after a disaster can be harmful and can overwhelm a person (Brymer et al., 2006). The person providing PFA should be cognizant that their presence is part of a larger team approach and is part of a disaster survivor team in a place to provide help. Many organizations provide training in PFA and training is also provided online for free (https://www.coursera.org/learn/psychological-first-aid). There are eight core actions in PFA training that include how to initiate contact with survivors, provide safety and comfort, provide stability, gather information on people's needs, connect survivors with resources, provide education about coping, and linking people to additional services.

Brymer et al. (2006) identify specific things to avoid when offering PFA such as: assuming that you understand what the survivors are experiencing, assuming that everyone will be traumatized from the event, or that all survivors are interested in talking. They also recommend to focus on people's strengths, avoid asking details about the events, avoid diagnosing or labeling people, and when you do offer information, make sure to offer facts and not opinions.

Carla van Laar developed **Art Therapy First Aid** that parallels Psychological First Aid. Van Laar has trained over 500 art therapists in Australia on this approach and used it with her own clients (van Laar, 2021).

Example of art therapy approaches to disasters

Two examples are provided below of the ways that art therapy can help survivors of natural disasters.

Undergraduate art therapy learning experience with survivors of Hurricane Maria

In 2017 Hurricane Maria devastated Puerto Rico for many months. Survivors lacked basic needs such as running water and electricity and many people who became homeless resided in school gymnasiums as makeshift shelters. Art therapists from Florida and Puerto Rico joined together several months after the disaster to provide art therapy (Lugo-Axtmann, 2018). The art therapists worked with support organizations to not only provide help with basic needs but also art-making opportunities.

Haley Wilkins, self-identified as a cisgender, White, female, fourth year, undergraduate art therapy student at the University of Tampa. She was trained in Psychological First Aid, conversationally fluent in Spanish, and was interested in learning more about how art therapists work with people affected by disasters. Haley participated in the trip to Puerto Rico by assisting art therapists and engaging with children and families at several locations. One of the art activities was making pinch pots from clay and Haley assisted the children, helping them envision what the pot could hold for them in the future. Working with the clay provided the children with an art experience that included elements of safety and calmness. Thinking about the future helped open up the children's views of a potential future when their current life situations appeared so grim. Learning about how to work with clay and make pinch pots enhanced their self-efficacy. Haley learned from the art therapists about using clay as an outlet for stress and the frustration and anger from the loss of home and community. The group also promoted self-efficacy and connectedness among the participants. Haley felt empowered by her ability to communicate with children and families in their language and by learning to assist others in the resiliency building and hope inspiring art therapy experience. She also saw firsthand how art therapists practice self-care and manage trauma presented in group disaster settings. Haley later said that this experience changed her life; her new skills and conquering this challenge gave her the confidence to work towards a career as a professional art therapist. Subsequently, she applied for graduate school in art therapy.

Art therapy support and the 2018 California fires

In 2018 a registered and board-certified art therapist in the Central Valley of California teamed up with her local art therapy organization when the deadliest fire in US history wiped out the entire town of Paradise, California, and killed nearly 100 people. The Northern California Art Therapy Association took on the endeavor to provide a year of monthly art therapy support groups for the survivors and members of the surrounding communities. This devastating trauma affected the entire state of California and nearby states, as the toxic smoke billowed for weeks, and as the survivors fled to nearby towns and states to find housing and jobs. There was not only no home to go back to, but no town to go back to either. Nurses found that the hospital they worked at was burned to the ground, a security guard realized that there were no buildings to guard, and an optometry assistant had to change careers when the optometrist she had worked for left town to open practice elsewhere. The use of art therapy groups with this population helped provide a consistent, reliable, safe place to open up, explore, release, process, feel, ground, and balance in a new type of community. With the art therapist's support, guidance, and using the Psychological First Aid approach, they created a community of survivors that was mixed with direct, derivative, and vicarious trauma survivors. This new community bonded them and regrounded them in a current time while providing a sense of security and hope (BoBo et al., 2021).

Managing wellness while helping others

"Helping professionals are especially at risk, due to a focus on assisting others and a pervasive belief that focusing on self and one's own needs contradicts professional values of care for others" (Hinz, 2019, p. 1). The degree to which a helping professional is harmed by their caregiving increases drastically if they do not care for themselves along the way and can even leave them with chronic or severe illness or an early death.

In 2020–2021, therapists had the most traumatic collective experience of the 21st century: a global pandemic. COVID-19 forced therapists and clients alike to socially isolate and use face masks to reduce transmission. People worldwide lost their livelihoods and way of life as the world shut down and millions lost their lives. The majority of art therapists had to learn how to provide telehealth services, on the phone or online, to people who needed mental health treatment services.

Vicarious trauma

When a person shares their trauma story with another, that story can internally impact the listener in a way that alters their own experience of themselves and interactions in the world. This is called **vicarious trauma (VT)** or **empathetic distress** (Newell et al., 2016; Pearlman & Mac Ian, 1995; Singer & Klimecki, 2012). Vicarious trauma is common when working in this field since professionals have empathy for client's emotional and physical pains that have resulted from trauma. Being aware of vicarious trauma will help you to be more prepared and to practice good self-care (Busch-Armendariz et al., 2018). An art therapist who is hearing the trauma story or seeing it in the art created in art therapy can be easily overloaded by repeated or particularly traumatic descriptions and details from one client or many trauma stories from several clients. If the therapist is not taking the necessary precautions to maintain balance in their own life or seeking the support of a consultation group or doing their own therapy, they will increase the chances of having VT.

VT is common in new therapists who have yet to discover their own self-care needs and the available self-care tools that work best for them. VT can also happen when someone is not fully developed in their sense of self and might need to do their own therapeutic processing of life events or trauma(s) before being able to effectively hold the space for another person to share their trauma story. In this situation, the trauma story turns the therapist's intended compassion for the client into empathetic distress, leaving the therapist internally distressed by another's trauma story, because they internalized the empathy they had for the person's pain as their own pain (Singer & Klimecki, 2012; Singer & Lamm, 2009).

The symptoms of VT are virtually the same as those you would find in someone with PTSD (Jenkins & Baird, 2002). Because VT is a result of secondhand exposure to trauma stories, it is less likely to occur and more manageable when the therapist practices self-care. **Response art** is a form of art creation done after working with a client that can help to release the trauma that the client left with you to hold (Fish, 2012). Response art can even help process the session you had with the client to be clued in to some of the unspoken transmission of information the client presented via body language, emotion, and energy states.

I, Cynthia Wilson, the second chapter author, used response art to help me process feelings after a session with a client (Fig. 13.3). My free-drawn image was done with controlled media (colored pencil) in response to the intense and fast-paced first session with a highly aggressive and resistant young adult with trauma. After creating the image, I found the words to express what I thought the

FIG. 13.3 *Sorting out the unspoken. Art therapist response art to session with client. Texts reads in red colored pencil "Head trauma, Reaching for others, Anger, Confusion?, Fear, Envy, No voice (that is Xed out), Trouble walking, Trouble Speaking, Highly sexual" and in larger font yellow colored pencil the text reads "Awkward, Different, Lonely."*
(Permission granted by Cynthia Wilson artist.)

client's subconscious might be trying to show me through body language, gestures, facial expression, and energy presence during the session. The colors chosen and way the words are written showed me further into the hidden, vulnerable aspects of the work that was needed to be carefully addressed with this client.

Resiliency

Resilience is defined as the ability to adapt to difficult situations (Sun-Young et al., 2021) and **trait resilience** describes people who possess the personality characteristics to adapt to different situations (Genet & Siemer, 2011). Sun-Young et al. (2021) noted that resilience can be learned and the more resilience developed the better we will be able to manage crises. There are four areas of resilience that can help us to better cope with trauma; these include resilience of the mind, brain, body, and relationships (Sun-Young et al., 2021). Resilience of the mind is affected by our self-esteem and confidence. One trait that people with resilience tend to possess is cognitive flexibility. **Cognitive flexibility** is the ability to reframe and "shift" (Genet & Siemer, 2011, p. 381) one's thinking to better adapt to situations. Mental resilience is built by the continued ability to overcome obstacles and development of skills to deal with stress such as taking specific steps or reducing stressors (Swanson et al., 2018). Resilience in the brain is based on the idea of neuroplasticity (see Chapter 4, Intersections of Neuroscience and Art Therapy). As we learned in Chapter 4, the more the brain fires together it wires together; therefore, the more positive coping skills are used, the stronger the connections will be in our brain to more easily access these coping skills. Good sleep, balanced meals, and physical activity help to build bodily resilience (Sun-Young et al., 2021). Our early relationships can have a strong influence on our level of resilience as described earlier in the Adverse Childhood Experiences study. If you did not grow up with supportive relationships, you still have time to develop close, safe, secure relationships with others. These relationships can provide support and increase your ability to be resilient during tough times (Sun-Young et al., 2021).

Self-care

Reflective practices

Engaging in reflective practices is beneficial for clinicians to help stave off the onset of vicarious trauma (Hinz, 2019) and there are many ways to use the arts as a therapeutic tool for maintaining and gaining balance and grounding through all forms of trauma. Art therapists during the COVID-19 pandemic utilized many self-care techniques including creating their own studio art space in their home, making art solely for themselves, using photography, or journaling as a way to explore their creative self-expression, engaging in exercising, biking, running, roller skating, natural walks for fresh air and camping in the mountains (Scarce et al., 2021).

Establishing boundaries

Awareness of boundaries is another aspect of self-care. **Boundaries** are the emotional, physical, and psychological distance and space between two people (Anderson, 2012). Therapists need to be clear about boundaries while balancing flexibility in order to protect one's self and maintain a healthy therapeutic relationship (Wilson & Coleman, 2020). For example, keeping clear boundaries between the professional relationship and personal time off work is important for self-care. Some clients may require more or longer sessions, or frequent check-ins between sessions, but in maintaining boundaries for self-care, the therapist needs to regularly weigh what the client needs as well as what the therapist needs, and what other resources might be available for the client (such as group therapy or support, therapist on call, and creating a list of resources with the client).

Maintaining boundaries does not mean that you are to be robotic in nature and never disclose anything about yourself to your client, but rather be very specific as to what is disclosed, so that each item is clearly beneficial to the client's therapeutic process. The complexities of boundary setting are another example of how having your own therapist or a supervision group can be very helpful.

Eye on the Virus (Fig. 13.4) was created by the first author, Joseph Scarce, during the COVID-19 pandemic. My art helped me work through the tragedy

FIG. 13.4 *Eye on the virus. Art therapist response art work to Covid 19 Pandemic. (Permission granted by Joseph Scarce, Artist.)*

of COVID-19. To me, the artwork feels warm and welcoming but at the same time, it elicits a question about the nature of our existence within the area, as the foliage looks back at us and we deal with the virus between us. The sun-drenched bright purple, red, green, and angelic whites combined with earthy plant life merge with a human connection. The expressions between the adult and child question family communication and how this was strained during the pandemic. Through my art, I processed my emotions in a challenging time during the COVID-19 pandemic.

Examples of art therapy self-care techniques

To ensure one's own wellness, mental health therapists and art therapists commonly use a variety of self-care techniques to maintain balance and continue developing a solid sense of self throughout life. You might try some of these activities and see if they help you to relax and let go.

1. Draw a circle freehand or trace around a circular shape. Use a paintbrush to fill the circle with drops of paint, letting the colors mix as you first move along the perimeter and then to the middle of the circle. Enjoy the free, flowing movement of the paint and the way the circular shape provides continuous movement and freedom to express with a sense of containment and safety. When working in this field, being able to do art that is mindless can give needed mental relaxation and space.
2. Play several different styles of music that are reassuring and/or energizing for you; while listening to the music write down lyrics from different songs. Once you have created several verses, create an art response that you can use to visualize your new song. Use this to investigate ways to help support your growth. What is learned about yourself from the connection to your art work?
3. Visualization and meditation can be enhanced with the creative art responses. These integrated exercises can aid in grounding and help prevent vicarious trauma. Continuing to use creative self-expression—whether making art, writing, playing music, or simple movement exercises—you can help relax and reconnect with self, discover what makes us each valuable. Make an art response from your own guided visualization or meditation.

Future therapists and helping professionals need to be aware of one's own personal history of trauma(s) and be prepared if something arises during work with people who have experienced trauma. If you are working with people who have experienced trauma, we advise you to seek your own counseling in preparation for anything that arises and/or to clearly process your own past adverse childhood or adult experiences. We, the authors, believe that having personal traumas surface during this process is common. Some institutions are well aware of this phenomenon and even provide free or discounted therapy. Additionally, it is wise to experience mental health treatment as a client so that you can understand what it is like to be a client and the reasons mentioned before for self-care, self-discovery, and personal development.

Conclusions

This chapter explored the importance of understanding trauma and how art therapy approaches can help people who experience traumatic events. The chapter provided an overview of the different types of trauma and how the brain is affected by trauma. We specifically explored how art therapy is an excellent form of treatment due to the ways trauma affects the brain and body. Different art therapy approaches to trauma were described; these approaches included trauma narrative, forward facing trauma therapy, trauma-focused cognitive behavioral therapy, cognitive processing therapy, eye movement and desensitization and reprocessing, emotional freedom technique, and Focus Oriented Art Therapy. The second half of the chapter explored trauma as a result of disasters or tragedies and specific ways art therapists are working with these survivors. Finally, the chapter concluded with specific ways art therapists and students can build resilience and self-care.

Art experientials and reflection questions

1. Develop a chart of the treatments covered in this chapter. Create a unique symbol to represent the different approaches to treatment. Is there a treatment approach that you like more than others? Any that are less appealing?
2. Find a recent event where art was used to express feelings about a natural disaster or event. Describe how art was used to help the community cope with the event. What things did you read that paralleled things in this chapter? Create a piece of art about what you learned about the event.
3. Maintaining connections with others and not isolating is important when working with clients who have had trauma. Create an interactive scribble drawing with a friend, taking turns drawing a line and connecting to each other's line without crossing lines until a maze is formed. Make two of these drawings for each person to find an image in the maze. With markers, pencils, oil, or chalk pastels develop and/or color the found images. Interview each other, what kind of images did you find? How was the process working with each other to develop the images?

Additional resources

Films and articles

Art Can Heal PTSD's Invisible Wounds: https://www.ted.com/talks/melissa_walker_art_can_heal_ptsd_s_invisible_wounds/transcript?language=en
Art Therapy First Aid: https://carlavanlaar.com/art-therapy-first-aid/
The Wisdom of Trauma: https://thewisdomoftrauma.com/
How Shia LaBeouf's *Honey Boy* Delves Into his Arrest, Trauma, and Time on *Even Stevens:* https://www.esquire.com/entertainment/a29726423/honey-boy-shia-labeouf-true-story-dad-arrest-explained/

Books

Anderson, F. (2012). *Transcending Trauma healing Complex PTSD with Internal Family Systems*. Eau, Claire WI. PESI Publishing.

Hinz, L. D. (2019). *Beyond self-care for helping professionals*. New York: Routledge.

Junge, M. B. & Newall, K. (2015). *Becoming an art Therapist: Enabling growth, change, and action for emerging students in the field.* Charles C. Thomas, IL.

Perry, B. D. & Winfrey O. (2012). *What happened to You? Conversations on Trauma Resilience and Healing*. Flaitiron Books an Oprah Book.

Seigal, D. J. & Hartzell, M. (2003). *Parenting from the Inside Out: How a deeper self-understanding can help you raise children who thrive*. Tarcher/ Penguin, New York.

Chapter terms

Acute stress disorder (ASD)
Acute trauma
Adjunct treatment
Adjustment disorder
Adverse childhood experiences (ACES)
Amygdala
Art therapy first aid
Assessment of childhood experiences scale (ACES)
Avoidance
"Big T" traumas
Bilateral stimulation
Bio-psychosocial assessment
Brave space
Chapman trauma narrative
Chronic trauma
Cognitive behavioral art therapy (CBAT)
Cognitive flexibility
Cognitive processing therapy (CPT)
Cognitive-behavioral therapy (CBT)
Complex posttraumatic stress disorder (CPTSD)
Complex trauma
Content analysis
Diagnostic and statistical manual for mental disorders (DSM-5-TR)
Disaster
Disinhibited social engagement disorder (DSED)
Early childhood trauma
Emotional freedom technique (EFT)
Empathetic distress
Expressive therapies continuum (ETC)
Eye movement desensitization reprocessing (EMDR)
Flashbacks
Focus Oriented Art Therapy (FOAT)
Forward facing trauma therapy (FFTT)
Graphic narrative
Hyperarousal
Intensive trauma therapy
"Little t" traumas
Negative thoughts and mood
Posttraumatic stress disorder (PTSD)
Psychological first aid
Race-based traumatic stress injury
Reactive attachment disorder (RAD)
Relational trauma
Resilience
Resiliency
Response art
Self-care

Self-disclose
Self-regulation
Social neglect
Somatic treatment of trauma
Therapeutic art
Trait resilience
Trauma
Trauma- and stressor-related disorders
Trauma narrative
Trauma treatment involving neurobiological theory
Trauma triggers
Trauma-focused-cognitive behavioral therapy (TF-CBT)
Vicarious trauma/empathetic distress

References

Alexander, A. (2020). The Artopia program: An examination of art therapy's effect on veterans' mood. *Art Therapy: Journal of the American Art Therapy Association*, *37*(3), 155–161. https://doi.org/10.1080/07421656.2002.10129401.

American Art Therapy Association (AATA). (2017). *Who are art therapists?* (AATA website.) https://arttherapy.org/about-art-therapy/.

American Psychiatric Association (APA). (2013). *Diagnostic and statistical manual of mental disorders* (5th ed.). American Psychiatric Association. https://doi.org/10.1176/appi.books.9780890425596.

American Psychiatric Association (APA). (2022). *Diagnostic and statistical manual of mental disorders* (5th ed., Test revised). American Psychiatric Association.

Anda, R. F., Butchart, A., Felitti, V. J., & Brown, D. W. (2010). Building a framework for global surveillance of the public implications of adverse childhood experiences. *American Journal of Preventive Medicine*, *39*(1), 93–98. https://doi-org.esearch.ut.edu/10.1016/j.amepre.2010.03.015.

Anderson, F. (2012). *Transcending trauma healing complex PTSD with internal family systems*. PESI Publishing.

Appleton, V. (2001). Avenues of hope: Art therapy and the resolution of trauma. *Art Therapy: Journal of the American Art Therapy Association*, *18*(1), 6–13. https://doi.org/10.1080/07421656.2001.10129454.

Arrington, D. B. (2007). *Art, angst, and trauma: Right brain interventions with developmental issues*. Charles C. Thomas.

Becker, C. L. (2015). Integrating art into group dissociative for adults with post-traumatic stress disorder from childhood sexual abuse: A pilot study. *Art Therapy: Journal of the American Art Therapy Association*, *32*(4), 190–196. https://doi.org/10.1080/07421656.2015.1091643.

BoBo, K., Wilson, C., Valicenti, R., & Weinapple, D. (2021). The camp fire of 2018: California burning: Art therapist stories of response after the most destructive and deadly fire in California history. In J. Scarce (Ed.), *Art therapy in response to mass violence and crisis* (pp. 118–133). Jessica Kingsely. In press.

Briere, J., & Scott, C. (2006). *Principles of trauma therapy: A guide to symptoms, evaluation, and treatment*. Sage Publications, Inc.

Bryant-Davis, T. (2019). The cultural context of trauma recovery: Considering the posttraumatic stress disorder practice guideline and intersectionality. *Psychotherapy*, *56*(3), 400–408. https://doi.apa.org/doi/10.1037/pst0000241.

Brymer, M., Jacobs, A., Layne, C., Pynoos, R., Ruzek, J., Steinberg, A., et al. (2006). *Psychological first aid: Field operations guide* (2nd ed.). National Child Traumatic Stress Network (NCTSN). https://www.nctsn.org/sites/default/files/resources//pfa_field_operations_guide.pdf.

Busch-Armendariz, N., Nsonwu, M., & Heffron, L. C. (2018). *Human trafficking, apply research theory and case studies*. Sage.

Campbell, M., Decker, K. P., Kruk, K., & Deaver, S. P. (2016). Art therapy and cognitive processing therapy for combat-related PTSD: A randomized controlled trial. *Art Therapy: Journal of the American Art Therapy Association*, *33*(4), 169–177. https://doi.org/10.1080/07421656.2016.1226643.

Carter, R. T. (2007). Racism and psychological and emotional injury: Recognizing and assessing race-based traumatic stress. *The Counseling Psychologist*, *35*(1), 13–105. https://doi.org/10.1177/0011000006292033.

Centers for Disease Control and Prevention. (2021). *Adverse childhood experiences prevention strategy*. National Center for Injury Prevention and Control, Centers for Disease Control and Prevention.

Chapman, L. (2014). *Neurobiologically informed trauma therapy with children and adolescents: Understanding mechanisms of change*. W.W. Norton.

Chilcote, R. L. (2007). Art therapy with child tsunami survivors in Sri Lanka. *Art Therapy: Journal of the American Art Therapy Association*, *24*(4), 156–162. https://doi.org/10.1080/07421656.2007.10129475.

Clond, M. (2016). Emotional freedom techniques for anxiety. *The Journal of Nervous and Mental Disease*, *204*(5), 388–395. https://doi.org/10.1097/NMD.0000000000000483.

Cognitive Processing Therapy (CPT). (2017, July 31). American Psychological Association. https://www.apa.org/ptsd-guideline/treatments/cognitive-processing-therapy.

Culbertson, F. M., & Revel, A. C. (1987). Graphic characteristics on the draw-a-person test for identification of physical abuse. *Art Therapy: Journal of the American Art Therapy Association*, *4*(2), 78–83. https://doi.org/10.1080/07421656.1987.10758703.

Danylchuck, L. (2015). *Embodied healing: Using yoga to recover from trauma and extreme stress*. Difference Press.

DeLucia, J. M. (2016). Art therapy services to support veterans' transition to civilian life: The studio and the gallery. *Art Therapy: Journal of the American Art Therapy Association*, *33*(1), 4–12. https://doi.org/10.1080/07421656.2016.1127113.

Diamond, D. M., & Zoladz, P. R. (2016). Dysfunctional or hyperfunctional? The amygdala in posttraumatic stress disorder is the bull in the evolutionary China shop. *Journal of Neuroscience Research*, *94*(6), 437–444. https://doi.org/10.1002/jnr.23684.

D'Amico, M., & Lalonde, C. (2017). The effectiveness of art therapy for teaching social skills to children with autism spectrum disorder. *Art Therapy: Journal of the American Art Therapy Association*, *34*(4), 176–182. https://doi.org/10.1080/07421656.2017.1384678.

Dubi, M., Powell, P., & Gentry, E. J. (2017). *The 10 core competencies for evidenced-based treatment, trauma, PTSD, Greif & Loss*. Pesi Publishing & Media.

Eaton, L. G., Doherty, K. L., & Widrick, R. M. (2007). A review of research and methods used to establish art therapy as an effective treatment method for traumatized children. *The Arts in Psychotherapy*, *34*(3), 256–262. https://doi.org/10.1016/j.aip.2007.03.001.

Elbrecht, C., & Antcliff, L. R. (2014). Being touched through touch. Trauma treatment through haptic perception at the clay field: A sensorimotor art therapy. *International Journal of Art Therapy*, *19*(1), 19–30. https://doi.org/10.1080/17454832.2014.880932.

Emery, M. J. (2004). Art therapy as an intervention for autism. *Art Therapy: Journal of the American Art Therapy Association*, *21*(3), 143–147. https://doi.org/10.1080/07421656.2004.10129500.

Fish, B. J. (2012). Response art: The art of the art therapist. *Art Therapy: Journal of the American Art Therapy Association*, *29*(3), 138–143. https://doi.org/10.1080/07421656.2012.701594.

Gantt, L., & Tripp, T. (2016). The image comes first: Treating preverbal trauma with art therapy. In J. King (Ed.), *Art therapy trauma and neuroscience* (pp. 157–172). Routledge.

Gantt, L., & Tinnin, L. (2007). Intensive trauma therapy of PTSD and dissociation: An outcome study. *The Arts in Psychotherapy*, *34*(1), 69–80. https://doi.org/10.1016/j.aip.2006.09.007.

Gantt, L., & Vesprini, M. E. (2017). Using the instinctual trauma response model in a military setting. In P. Howie (Ed.), *Art therapy with military populations: History, innovation, and applications* (pp. 147–156). Routledge/Taylor & Francis Group. https://doi.org/10.4324/9781315669526-15.

Genet, J. J., & Siemer, M. (2011). Flexible control in processing affective and non-affective material predicts individual differences in trait resilience. *Cognition and Emotion*, *25*(2), 380–388. https://doi.org/10.1080/02699931.2010.491647.

Gentry, J. E. (2016). *Forward facing trauma therapy*. Healing the Moral Wounds, Compassion Unlimited.

Gonzalez-Dolginko, B. (2002). In the shadows of terror: A community neighboring the world trade center disaster uses art therapy to process trauma. *Art Therapy: Journal of the American Art Therapy Association*, *19*(3), 120–122. https://doi.org/10.1080/07421656.2002.10129408.

Gottman, J. M., & DeClair, J. (2001). *The relationship cure: A 5 step guide to strengthening your marriage family and relationships*. Three Rivers Press.

Hargrave-Nykaza, K. (1994). An application of art therapy to the trauma of rape. *Art Therapy: Journal of the American Art Therapy Association*, *11*(1), 53–57. https://doi.org/10.1080/07421656.1994.10759044.

Hass-Cohen, N., Findlay, J. C., Carr, R., & Vanderlan, J. (2014). "Check, change what you need to change and/or keep what you want": An art therapy neurobiological-based trauma protocol. *Art Therapy: Journal of the American Art Therapy Association*, *31*(2), 69–78. https://doi.org/10.1080/07421656.2014.903825.

Herman, J. (1992). *Trauma recovery: The aftermath of violence-from domestic abuse to political terror*. Basic Books.

Hinz, L. (2019). *Beyond self-care for helping professionals: The expressive therapies continuum and the life enrichment model*. Routledge.

Howie, P. (2016). Art therapy with trauma. In D. E. Gussak, & M. L. Rosal (Eds.), *The Wiley handbook of art therapy*. John Wiley & Sons.

Howie, P., Burch, B., Conrad, S., & Shambaugh, S. (2002). Releasing trapped images: Children grapple with the reality of the September 11 attacks. *Art Therapy: Journal of the American Art Therapy Association*, *19*(3), 100–105. https://doi.org/10.1080/07421656.2002.10129401.

International Federation of Red Cross and Red Crescent Societies. (2021). https://www.ifrc.org/en/what-we-do/disaster-management/about-disasters/.

Isis, P. D., Bush, J., Siegel, C. A., & Ventura, Y. (2010). Empowering students through creativity: Art therapy in Miami-Dade County public schools. *Art Therapy: Journal of the American Art Therapy Association*, *27*(2), 56–61. https://doi.org/10.1080/07421656.2010.10129712.

Jenkins, S. R., & Baird, S. (2002). Secondary traumatic stress and vicarious trauma: A validation study. *Journal of Traumatic Stress*, *15*(5), 423–432. https://doi.org/10.1023/A:1020193526843.

Johnson, C. (2007). Art therapy in the hospice setting. In D. B. Arrington (Ed.), *Art, angst and trauma: Right brain interventions with developmental issues* (pp. 208–229). Charles C. Thomas.

Jones, J. G. (1997). Art therapy with a community of survivors. *Art Therapy: Journal of the American Art Therapy Association*, *14*(2), 89–94. https://doi.org/10.1080/07421656.1987.10759262.

Kandel, E., Markram, H., & Matthews, P. (2013). Neuroscience thinks big (and collaboratively). *Nature Reviews. Neuroscience*, *14*, 659–664. https://doi.org/10.1038/nrn3578.

King, J. L., Kaimal, G., Konopka, L., Belkofer, C., & Strang, C. E. (2019). Practical applications of neuroscience-informed art therapy. *Art Therapy: Journal of the American Art Therapy Association*, *36*(3), 149–156. https://doi.org/10.1080/07421656.2019.1649549.

Kometiani, M. (2020). *Art therapy treatment with sex trafficking survivors: Facilitating empowerment, recovery and hope*. Routledge.

Kubler-Ross, E., & Kessler, D. (2007). *On grief and grieving: Finding the meaning of grief through the five stages of loss*. Scribner.

Lanius, R. A., Frewen, P. A., Tursich, M., Jetly, R., & McKinnon, M. C. (2015). Restoring large-scale brain networks in PTSD and related disorders: A proposal for neuroscientifically-informed treatment interventions. *European Journal of Psychotraumatology*, *6*, 27313. https://doi.org/10.3402/ejpt.v6.27313.

Lee, R., Wong, J., Lit Shoon, W., Gandhi, M., Lei, F., Eh, K., et al. (2019). Art therapy for the prevention of cognitive decline. *The Arts in Psychotherapy*, *64*, 20–25. https://doi.org/10.1016/j.aip.2018.12.003.

Levine, P. A. (1997). *Walking the tiger healing trauma the innate capacity to transform overwhelming experiences*. North Atlantic Books.

Levy, B., Berberian, M., Brigmon, L., Gonzalez, S., & Koepfer, S. (2002). Mobilizing community strength: New York art therapists respond. *Art Therapy: Journal of the American Art Therapy Association*, *19*(3), 106–114. https://doi.org/10.1080/07421656.2002.10129403.

Linton, L. (2017). A natural response to a natural disaster: The art of crisis in Nepal (Une réponse naturelle à une catastrophe naturelle: art de crise au Népal). *Canadian Art Therapy Association Journal*, *30*(1), 31–40. https://doi.org/10.1080/08322473.2017.1317201.

Lugo-Axtmann, A. (2018, April 26). *Puerto Rico and Florida AATA chapters offer group art therapy in wake of hurricane Maria*. American Art Therapy Association. https://arttherapy.org/chapters-art-therapy-maria/.

Lusebrink, V. B., & Hinz, L. D. (2020). Cognitive and symbolic aspects of art therapy and similarities with large scale brain networks. *Art Therapy: Journal of the American Art Therapy Association*, *37*(3), 113–122. https://doi.org/10.1080/07421656.2019.1691869.

Mahendran, R., Gandhi, M., Moorakonda, R. B., Wong, J., Kanchi, M. M., Fam, J., et al. (2018). Art therapy is associated with sustained improvement in cognitive function in the elderly with mild neurocognitive disorder: Findings from a pilot randomized controlled trial for art therapy and music reminiscence activity versus usual care. *Trials*, *19*(1), 615. https://doi.org/10.1186/s13063-018-2988-6.

Malchiodi, C. A. (1999). *Medical art therapy with children*. Jessica Kingsley Publishers.

Mank, J. (2021). *Self-expression through art and drumming: A facilitators guide to using art therapy to enhance drum circles*. Jessica Kingsley Publishers.

Martin, N. (2008). Assessing portrait drawings created by children and adolescents with autism spectrum disorder. *Art Therapy: Journal of the American Art Therapy Association*, *25*(1), 15–23. https://doi.org/10.1080/07421656.2008.10129348.

McNamee, C. (2006). Experiences with bilateral art: A retrospective study. *Art Therapy: Journal of the American Art Therapy Association*, *23*(1), 7–13. https://doi.org/10.1080/07421656.2006.10129526.

Menakem, R. (2017). *My grandmother's hands: Racialized trauma and the pathway to mending our hearts and bodies*. Central Recovery Press.

Miller, A. (2012). *Healing the unimaginable: Treating ritual abuse and mind control*. Routledge.

Mills, E., & Kellington, S. (2012). Using group art therapy to address the shame and silencing surrounding children's experiences of witnessing domestic violence. *International Journal of Art Therapy*, *17*(1), 3–12. https://doi.org/10.1080/17454832.2011.639788.

Mizutani, D. (2021, March 2). *Stunning Mural of George Floyd provides community a place to process*. Pioneer Press. Retrieved from https://www.twincities.com/2020/05/30/stunning-mural-of-george-floyd-provides-minneapolis-community-a-place-to-process/.

Newell, J. M., Nelson-Gardell, D., & MacNeil, G. (2016). Clinician responses to client traumas: A chronological review of constructs and terminology. *Trauma, Violence & Abuse*, *17*(3), 306–313.

Ogden, P., & Fisher, J. (2015). *Sensorimotor psychotherapy: Interventions for trauma and attachment*. W.W. Norton.

Orr, P. P. (2007). Art therapy with children after a disaster: A content analysis. *The Arts in Psychotherapy*, *34*(4), 350–361. https://doi.org/10.1016/j.aip.2007.07.002.

Ortner, N. (2013). *The tapping solution: A revolutionary system for stress-free living*. Hay House, Inc.

Ortner, N. (2018). *The tapping solution for parents, children and teenagers: How to let go of excessive stress, anxiety, and worry, and raise happy, healthy, resilient families*. Hay House, Inc.

Parnell, L. (2008). *Tapping in: A step by step guide to activating your healing resources through bilateral stimulation*. Sounds True Inc.

Pearlman, L. A., & Mac Ian, P. S. (1995). Vicarious traumatization: An empirical study of the effects of trauma work on trauma therapists. *Professional Psychology: Research and Practice*, *26*(6), 558–565. https://doi.org/10.1037/0735-7028.26.6.558.

Piffalo, T. (2007). Jogging the cogs: Trauma-focused art therapy and cognitive behavioral therapy with sexually abused children. *Art Therapy: Journal of the American Art Therapy Association*, *24*(4), 170–175. https://www.tandfonline.com/doi/pdf/10.1080/07421656.2007.

Porges, S. W. (2011). *The polyvagal theory: Neurophysiological foundations of emotions, attachment, communication and self-regulation*. W. W. Norton.

Potash, J. S. (2018). Special issue on medical art therapy. *Art Therapy: Journal of the American Art Therapy Association*, *35*(2), 58–59. https://doi.org/10.1080/07421656.2018.1490615.

Rappaport, L. (2009). *Focusing-oriented art therapy: Assessing the body's wisdom and creative intelligence*. Jessica Kingsley Publishers.

Roje, J. (1995). LA '94 earthquake in the eyes of children: Art therapy with elementary school children who were victims of disaster. *Art Therapy: Journal of the American Art Therapy Association*, *12*(4), 237–243. https://doi.org/10.1080/07421656.1995.10759171.

Rosal, M. L. (2015). *Cognitive-behavioral art therapy revisited* (pp. 68–76). John Wiley & Sons, Ltd. https://doi.org/10.1002/9781118306543.ch7.

Rosal, M. L., McCulloch-Vislisel, S., & Neece, S. (1997). Keeping students in school: An art therapy program to benefit ninth-grade students. *Art Therapy: Journal of the American Art Therapy Association*, *14*(1), 30–36. https://doi.org/10.1080/07421656.1997.10759251.

Ross, C. A., & Halpern, N. (2009). *Trauma model therapy: A treatment approach for trauma, dissociation and complex comorbidity*. Manitou Communications, Inc.

Sadeh, N., Spielberg, J. M., Warren, S. L., Miller, G. A., & Heller, W. (2014). Aberrant neural connectivity during emotional processing associated with posttraumatic stress. *Clinical Psychological Science*, *2*(6), 748–755. https://doi.org/10.1177/2167702614530113.

Scarce, J. (2021). *Art therapy in response to natural disasters mass violence & crisis*. Jessica Kingsley Publishers.

Scarce, J., Khalaf, E., Ballestas, A., Weinapple, D., Linton, J., & Wilson, C. (2021). Art therapists respond to COVID-19: Veiwing art therapy in the new virtual world, self-care in a pandemic. In J. H. Scarce (Ed.), *Art therapy and natural disasters, mass violence and crisis* (pp. 66–82). Jessica Kingsley.

Schore, A. N. (2009). Relational trauma and the developing right brain: An interface of psychoanalytic self-psychology and neuroscience. *Annals of the New York Academy of Sciences*, *1159*(1), 189–203. https://doi.org/10.1111/j.1749-6632.2009.04474.x.

Schupp, L. J. (2004). *Assessing and treatment trauma*. Pesi, Health Care LLC.

Scott, E. H., & Ross, C. J. (2006). Integrating the creative arts into trauma and addiction treatment: Eight essential processes. *Journal of Chemical Dependency Treatment*, *8*(2), 207–226.

Shapiro, F. (2001). *Eye movement desensitization and reprocessing: Basic principles, protocols and procedures* (2nd ed.). Guilford Press.

Shapiro, F. (2018). *Eye movement desensitization and reprocessing: Basic principles, protocols, and procedures* (3rd ed.). Guilford Press.

Siegel, D., & Bryson, T. P. (2011). *The whole brain child: 12 revolutionary strategies to nurture your child's developing mind*. Bantam Books.

Singer, T., & Klimecki, O. (2012). *Empathetic distress fatigue rather than compassion fatigue? Integrating findings from empathy research in psychology and social neuroscience*. Oakley.

Singer, T., & Lamm, C. (2009). The social neuroscience of empathy. *Annals of the New York Academy of Sciences, 1156*(1), 81–96. http://citeseerx.ist.psu.edu/viewdoc/download?doi=10.1.1.484.1623&rep=rep1&type=pdf.

Spring, D. (1993). *Shattered images: Phenomenological language of sexual trauma.* Magnolia Street Publishers.

Spring, D. (2001). *Image and mirage: Art therapy with dissociative clients.* Charles C. Thomas Publisher.

Spring, D. (2004). Thirty-year study links neuroscience, specific trauma, PTSD, image conversion, and language translation. *Art Therapy: Journal of the American Art Therapy Association, 21*(4), 200–209. https://doi.org/10.1080/07421656.2004.10129690.

Stronach-Buschel, B., & Hurvitz Madsen, L. (2006). Strengthening connections between mothers and children. *Journal of Aggression, Maltreatment & Trauma, 13*(1), 87–108. https://doi.org/10.1300/J146v13n01_05.

Substance Abuse and Mental Health Services Administration (SAMHSA). (2019, August 2). *Trauma and violence.* https://www.samhsa.gov/trauma-violence.

Sun-Young, K., Kim, S. I., & Weon-Jeong, L. (2021). Association between change in sleep duration and posttraumatic stress symptoms in natural disaster victims: The mediating role of resilience. *Sleep Medicine, 82*, 110–116. https://doi-org.esearch.ut.edu/10.1016/j.sleep.2021.03.042.

Swanson, A., Geller, J., DeMartini, K., Fernandez, A., & Fehon, D. (2018). Active coping and perceived social support mediate the relationship between physical health and resilience in liver transplant candidates. *Journal of Clinical Psychology in Medical Settings, 25*(4), 485–496. https://doi.org/10.1007/s10880-018-9559-6.

Talwar, S. (2007). Accessing traumatic memory through art making: An art therapy trauma protocol (ATTP). *The Arts in Psychotherapy, 34*(1), 22–35. https://psycnet.apa.org/doi/10.1016/j.aip.2006.09.001.

Tripp, T. (2007). A short term therapy approach to processing trauma: Art therapy and bilateral stimulation. *Art Therapy: Journal of the American Art Therapy Association, 24*(4), 176–183. https://doi.org/10.1080/07421656.2007.10129476.

Tripp, T. (2016). A body based art therapy protocol for reprocessing trauma. In J. King (Ed.), *Art therapy trauma and neuroscience* (pp. 173–194). Routledge.

van der Kolk, B. (2014). *The body keeps the score: Brain, mind, and the healing of trauma.* Penguin/Random House.

van Laar, C. (2021). Art therapy first aid: Growing capacity with arts therapists in communities affected by Australian bushfires. In Scarce (Ed.), *Art therapy in response to natural disaster, mass violence & crisis* (pp. 134–147). Jessica Kingsley. In press.

Walker, M. S., Kaimal, G., Gonzaga, A. M. L., Myers-Coffman, K. A., & DeGraba, T. J. (2017). Active-duty military service members' visual representations of PTSD and TBI in masks. *International Journal of Qualitative Studies on Health and Well-Being, 12*(1), 1267317. https://doi.org/10.1080/17482631.2016.1267317.

Webber, J. M., & Mascari, J. B. (Eds.). (2018). *Disaster mental health counseling: A guide to preparing and responding* (4th ed.). American Counseling Association Foundation. Wiley.

Wilson, C., & Coleman, S. (2020). Recommendations for working with individuals effected by sex trafficking. In M. Kometiani (Ed.), *Art therapy treatment with sex trafficking survivors: Facilitating empowerment recovery and hope* (pp. 55–94). Routledge.

Wilson, C. (2019). *Art based communication for individuals with dissociative spectrum disorders* (Dissertation). Proquest LLC. https://pqdtopen.proquest.com/doc/2307397271.html?FMT=AI.

Part IV

Profession of art therapy: Exhibiting the work

Chapter 14

Beginning concepts of group work

Heather J. Denning, MA, ATR-BC, ATCS, LSW
Art Department, Mercyhurst University, Erie, PA, United States

Voices from the field

The simple act of making art in the presence of other people who are engaged in creative work can be deeply satisfying and gratifying...Making art in the presence of others can evoke and intensify feelings while at the same time provide safe, concrete structures for their expression.

B.L. Moon (2016, p. 145)

Learning outcomes

After reading this chapter, you will be able to

1. Define the meaning of a group, group work, group art facilitation, and group art therapy.
2. Define the purposes of a group.
3. Understand stages of group development.
4. Understand the history of group work.
5. Identify therapeutic factors of group work.
6. Identify the benefits of group work.
7. Organize and plan a group art activity.
8. Distinguish between cultural competence and cultural humility.
9. Identify beginning level group facilitation skills.
10. Further understand group work concepts through a review of student narratives and clinical examples.

Chapter overview

Many undergraduate students studying art therapy will find themselves in group situations including in person or remote classrooms, student clubs, residence halls, social action groups, volunteer experiences, and required course placements in the community. These group configurations provide learning opportunities to understand what works in groups, when they function, and when they do not. Individuals in these groups may include other students in an art therapy class

Foundations of Art Therapy. https://doi.org/10.1016/B978-0-12-824308-4.00006-5

or group participants in a volunteer or fieldwork placement. The most common fieldwork placements for students identified within a survey of undergraduate art therapy educators were settings for older adults and community art programs (Schwartz et al., 2021). In these settings, participants are typically served in groups. Most students will encounter groups in some format; therefore, having foundational knowledge of the definition and purposes of a group will prepare students for community placement or fieldwork.

When studying art therapy, students may be making art alongside each other or collaboratively to deepen their knowledge about group art therapy. In these group situations, students will likely recognize how being with others is beneficial. Witnessing people coming together to create art and support one another demonstrates the deepest compassion creativity offers. Talking about art with others can improve our understanding of other people. Other lessons conveyed are the importance of feeling a sense of belonging and acceptance from others. These lessons speak to the human experience and the importance of being part of a group. Learning about group work and the associated skills to facilitate a group are fundamental concepts to the helping professions.

Within this chapter, information about group work will be initially approached from a broad perspective, then an examination of specific areas related to the study of art therapy at an undergraduate level will follow. Defining a group and exploring the purposes of the group will begin the chapter. Other topics presented will include defining group art facilitation and group art therapy, the history of group work, group art therapy approaches, therapeutic factors of group work, benefits of group work, and group work skills. Student narratives and examples from clinical experiences will be presented to further illustrate learning experiences about group work. Ideas for art experientials and reflection questions are offered for deeper exploration of group work. Additional resources about group work are provided to conclude the chapter.

Understanding and defining a group

The definition of a **group** can have many meanings. A basic definition of group involves people in face-to-face interactions with one another (Bales, 1950). Groups are "characterized as a collection of people bound to one another by some common experience or purpose…" (Brown, 2000 p. 4). Riley (2001) described group in the context of group therapy as "an extraordinary opportunity to look in the mirror of another's eyes and see one's own behaviors and prejudices reflected back with a clarity that is hard to receive" (p. 2).

Groups can be classified as formed or natural. People in **formed groups** are typically placed together by an outside influence such as an institution or agency. Examples of formed groups include students in an assigned course or coworkers on a job. **Natural groups** form more spontaneously. They include friendships and family groups (Toseland & Rivas, 2017).

Our first understanding about relationships in a group evolves from our interactions within a natural group, our family members. During infancy, we learn whether our environment is safe through relationships with our caregivers. When this environment is perceived as unreliable, we learn that others are not to be trusted (Springham & Huet, 2018). Conversely, when a secure attachment is established, we learn people can be trusted. Through the development of family relationships, we learn about boundaries, alliances, and hierarchies within the family (Reiter, 2017). Family relationships set the stage for us to belong to a group of people and then form our identities as we develop and join other social systems, such as school and groups of friends (Colapinto, 2017). These experiences inform individuals about what it means to be part of a group and shape our future relationships and feelings about being in a group. At times, we experience conflict then resolution as we navigate our relationships with family, friends, classmates, roommates, and coworkers.

As human beings, we cannot avoid being influenced by others in some manner as we are social beings (Siegel, 1999). We need support from others and seek human connection through acknowledgment, appreciation, validation, and acceptance (B.L. Moon, 2016). Baumeister and Leary (1995) pointed out:

> *At present, it seems fair to conclude that human beings are fundamentally and pervasively motivated by a need to belong, that is, by a strong desire to form and maintain enduring interpersonal attachments. People seek frequent, affectively positive interactions within the context of long-term, caring relationships. (p. 520)*

Being either rejected or accepted into a group can be sources of loneliness or contribute to well-being. Bruce Moon (2016) asserted "Few conditions are more distressing than loneliness" (p. 4).

Students routinely address the topic of what it means to be part of a group by confronting issues of social isolation or belonging on college campuses. Alghraibeh and Juieed (2018) reported for undergraduate students, feelings of isolation can lead to poor academic performance. Masika and Jones (2016) described a student's sense of belonging, feeling accepted and valued, contributes to engagement and retention in environments of higher education. Learning with peers in a communal setting, such as a classroom, can build confidence and shape identity (Masika & Jones, 2016). Fink (2014) supported college students finding a sense of community since social inclusion is a predictor of positive mental health. Thus, positive interaction with peers in the classroom can have both academic and interpersonal benefits as students feel part of a cohort. The following narrative reflects a student learning experience about groups and the anxieties associated with joining a new group. Pseudonyms are used throughout the chapter to describe student experiences for privacy. In addition, students provided consent for their presented and chosen descriptions.

Student experience

Katya, a student in her 20s of Russian decent and adopted, was enrolled in a group art therapy course I instructed. Katya expressed her feelings about joining

FIG. 14.1 *Katya's art reflection about joining the class.*

a class with students from a different cohort through her painting recorded in her art journal required for the course (Fig. 14.1). The experience enlightened her to what a new participant of a group might also encounter and deepened her empathy and consideration for others hoping to be included in a group. Katya had many reservations about participating with this slightly older group of students who had formed relationships in prior art therapy courses. In addition, she had experienced the death of a parent, an experience her peers had not faced. Her drawing expressed feelings of uncertainty as she began the course. Katya stated (personal communication, June 16, 2020):

> *As for the piece, I remember I really wanted to express the isolation I felt, and how I seriously considered dropping out of the class. I was afraid of how I really didn't know any of these students' past grief experiences and would have to open up and retell a lot of my deeply personal experiences revolving around my grief and experiences with it. That also coupled with the fact that most people my age did not have any experience with losing a parent, it really did make connecting at first hard and awkward.*

Katya did remain in the class and was able to connect with her peers and learn about group work. Classmates were supportive, and Katya was able to connect to her peers as the class became more cohesive. As students examine their own thoughts and feelings about groups, they can learn to understand the importance of group interactions and the purposes of a group.

Purposes of groups

Toseland and Rivas (2017) defined **group work** as goal-directed activity aimed at meeting socioemotional needs or to accomplish a specific task. Formed groups can have a wide range of purposes and goals, including socialization, social action, problem solving, conflict resolution, learning new interpersonal skills, developing healthier coping skills, resolution of symptoms of an illness, or efforts to maintain wellness or current functioning.

Groups can be task-oriented or treatment-focused. **Task-oriented** groups can meet individual, organizational, or community needs. Examples of task-oriented groups students may encounter in an academic environment include study groups for group assignments, a work team, academic clubs, team sports, or social action groups. When participating in task-oriented groups, individual members' needs may not be individually met as a larger task or goal is the purpose of the group (Toseland & Rivas, 2017). Examples demonstrating task-oriented groups with art would be students working together to paint a mural at a school, creating art in a community setting to raise awareness of a social issue, or teaching an art activity at a senior center. Students may find themselves in volunteer or fieldwork placements similar to those experiences described before while studying art therapy at an undergraduate level.

Working in a treatment-focused group is typically introduced while studying at the graduate level for art therapy. **Treatment-focused** groups are different from task groups as they address individual group member's needs (Toseland & Rivas, 2017). Examples of treatment-focused groups include support groups, self-help groups, and group art therapy. Table 14.1 outlines examples differentiating these groups. Treatment-focused groups may also offer education and opportunities to learn social skills. Some groups may serve both purposes to address individual needs and accomplish a task collaboratively and may not fit strictly in the definitions offered before. In both task-oriented and treatment-focused groups, group work occurs (Toseland & Rivas, 2017).

An example of a treatment-focused group in art therapy may include group members with substance use disorders creating art to reflect on a range of feelings surfacing during sobriety. Feelings of guilt, shame, and anger may be associated with addiction. Group members may experience **universality**, the concept that their experiences are similar, and they are not alone (Yalom & Leszcz, 2005, 2020). Often, this realization helps group members feel less isolated and better connected to their peers in treatment. Group members' art may reflect similar themes and elements that can be viewed and processed further in

TABLE 14.1 Examples of task-oriented and treatment-oriented groups.

	Task-oriented groups	Treatment-focused groups
Professional settings	Board meeting for a professional organization	
	Orientation meeting for new employees	
	Community walkathon benefiting a social cause	
Educational settings	Study groups for a group assignment	Student counseling center: Group therapy addressing student stress
	Academic Club	Student support group
	Social Action Group	Active Minds: Mental health awareness and education organization for young adults
Art-facilitated groups	Designing and creating a community mural	Art Hives: Building community through art
	Intergenerational group art activity at a residential facility for older adults	
Group art therapy	(The previous examples for art facilitated groups could also be conducted in an art therapy group)	Art therapy group addressing grief and loss
		Art therapy group at a veteran's hospital addressing trauma
		Art therapy group at an adolescent treatment center addressing self-esteem

group discussions. Art therapists can facilitate both task-oriented and treatment-focused groups.

Groups can be open or closed. Often, the purpose of the group dictates whether a group has open membership or is closed once the group commences. **Open groups** allow new members to join throughout the duration of the group. Examples include 12-step support groups, such as Alcoholics Anonymous (AA). Membership is open to individuals who wish to address their drinking problem (Alcoholics Anonymous, 2021). Student clubs are typically open where individuals may join in throughout the academic year. **Closed groups** are more typical in groups that are treatment-focused or follow a sequence of imparting knowledge or skills. Closed groups begin and progress with the same group members until the end. An example of a closed group may include a financial literacy class where basic budgeting skills are taught first, then more advanced financial skills are offered after (Toseland & Rivas, 2017).

Planning a group

Starting a group requires careful planning and consideration. Potential group members need to know practical information about the group such as the description, location and time, associated costs if any, and ways to access the group, which may include transportation and financial resources. A group must have a defined purpose so group members can learn about the potential benefits and general goals. "A statement of purpose should be broad enough to encompass different individual goals, yet specific enough to define the common nature of the group's purpose" (Toseland & Rivas, 2017, p. 162).

Frequently, treatment groups are formed when providers identify a group of individuals needing support with similar problems or needs. Groups may be promoted in numerous ways: word of mouth by a provider, family, or friend, printed flyers or announcements placed in the community, or agency websites and social media. Potential group members might express interest and self-refer by contacting an individual or agency listed in the promotion. Treatment providers might also refer individuals to a specific group to help their client build strengths, feel more empowered, or practice social skills.

Generally, group members are screened to align their needs with the group's purpose. There may be basic guidelines such as an age or residency requirement, legal status, or expressed interests. Other groups may require a full clinical assessment with specific diagnoses required, for example, a group at the Hospital of Veteran's Affairs that is addressing Post Traumatic Stress Disorder (PTSD). Ideally, group leaders can make direct contact with potential group members and provide an opportunity for an interview or dialogue to learn more about the individual, their needs, and goals, and determine if the group may be a good match.

Other considerations for planning are the size of the group and the space for the group to meet comfortably. Additionally, art therapists are mindful of the physical conditions of the group space, which include privacy, lighting, work surfaces, having a water source, proper ventilation, and room for working with and storing a variety of materials (Rubin, 2010). The size of the group can range depending on the needs of the group members and the type of group. There are advantages and disadvantages to small groups versus large groups. Smaller groups afford members more individualized focus and attention, while larger groups may offer more resources to more individuals (Toseland & Rivas, 2017). The group leader will need to carefully consider these advantages and disadvantages when planning a group.

Stages of group development

Groups develop in stages throughout their duration. Groups that are closed tend to develop in a more cohesive manner, while open groups may change and cycle through various stages of development. Group development does not always progress in a predictable linear fashion. However, literature reflects authors have identified stages of group from beginning, middle, and end with varying models and numbers of stages to categorize similar development (Bales, 1950; Henry, 1992; Trecker, 1972; Tuckman, 1965; Tuckman & Jensen, 1977; Wheelan, 1994). An early model, Tuckman's stages of group development, offered characteristics of each stage from forming in the beginning, to storming, norming, performing in the middle, and adjourning at the end (Tuckman, 1965; Tuckman & Jensen, 1977).

The beginning stage, forming, can cause uneasiness as group members wonder about the purpose and benefits of the group. Initial anxieties are common. Group members speculate about the other individuals and leaders in the group. They may question: Will the other group members like me? Can I add value to the group? What is my role? Group members learn about each other and typically look to the leader for direction and guidance during this initial stage (Tuckman, 1965).

The middle stages emerge with storming, norming, and performing as the group members develop relationships. After introductory pleasantries, storming may occur where group members become more competitive and tense as they struggle to find their place in the group. Disagreements are more common and group members still refer to the leader to intervene in discussion and disputes. This is also a period where cliques or subgroups form (Tuckman, 1965). **Subgroups** are separate alliances between smaller group members within the larger group based on mutual interests and emotional bonds (Toseland & Rivas, 2017). Subgroups are natural during the middle stages of group development. An example may be a support group for LGBTIQA+ adolescents where group members from the same school district and neighborhood form a subgroup as they relate by living in the same community. The group's relationships deepen with the stages of norming and performing. While norming, group rules are well established and agreed upon. **Group norms** "are shared expectations and beliefs about appropriate ways to act in a social situation, such as group" (Toseland & Rivas, 2017, p. 84). The group members function more independently from the leader and mutual trust and help are present. When the group is performing, the group members are actively solving problems and achieving goals. At this stage, progress is being made and the group is highly productive (Tuckman, 1965).

The group ends with the final stage of adjourning. Ending a group comes with a range of feelings from happiness to sadness as the group members celebrate successes and say goodbye. Evaluating the progress of the group may occur or individual reflection of goals accomplished. Group members depart and move in different directions as the group dissolves and ends (Tuckman & Jensen, 1977).

Group art facilitation and group art therapy

Foundational knowledge about group work can prepare the undergraduate student for group art facilitation. Students studying at an undergraduate level of art therapy will be focused on this level of group work, while group art therapy is conducted by a master's level prepared art therapist. **Group art facilitation** can be defined as assisting and helping a group of participants achieve an art activity. Group facilitation involves "motivating and coordinating people to perform their joint work" (Kolbe & Boos, 2009, p. 1).

A group facilitator can have many roles, including imparting knowledge and skills in a specific subject area and promoting respectful interaction and participation between group members. These roles encourage helping the group members complete and manage a task within a supportive environment. Additional roles of a group facilitator include managing a group agenda, which will be addressed later in the chapter under organization skills, and role modeling new skills and behaviors (McCain & Tobey, 2007). The role of the group art facilitator is to guide participants in the successful use of art materials in a group setting. Typically, the role of an art facilitator is task oriented and focused on wellness and support, while an art therapist expands this role to being treatment-focused and considers mental health concerns, developmental challenges, medical conditions, and other presenting concerns.

Collaborative art-making may demonstrate group work that is task-oriented and occurs in both group art facilitation and group art therapy. In addition, it can also occur in treatment-focused groups. **Collaborative art-making** "involves participatory art experiences in which the community cocreates..."(Bublitz et al., 2019, p. 323). Collaborative art-making can also be defined as a work of art where participants work together to create one piece of art. Artistry can be achieved by each person completing a portion of the art and combining or working on the art simultaneously. An example of collaborative art-making is drawing or painting together in the classroom to create a mural. Goals for mural making may include completing a decorative work of art for enjoyment or reflecting on student teamwork. Mural making historically has served many purposes, including decoration; empowerment; reflection of cultural, social, and political issues; and expression of individual and community concerns (Rossetto, 2012). This project is often given to students as a group task meant to demonstrate how creating art together can promote collaboration and highlight concepts of group art therapy. Problem-solving and interpersonal skills are needed to achieve completion of a mural. Students working together are simultaneously asserting themselves, compromising, and deciding the placement and arrangement of art media within the group's collective art piece. Typically, leaders and followers will emerge. At times, disagreements surface, and students will need to adjust and be flexible to achieve the group's goals. These interactions may highlight what is defined as group work that is facilitated within a classroom environment.

In this author's experience, group art therapy is challenging to define as the scope of settings, populations, and approaches are broad and continue to grow. Group art therapy can be offered in a variety of settings and with a wide range of participants. Settings for group art therapy include community art centers, art museums, outpatient counseling centers, telehealth and remote platforms, addiction treatment programs, schools, college counseling centers, group homes and residential centers, shelters, outpatient medical centers, hospitals, and correctional facilities. Participants served in these settings can range in age, cultural background, and intellectual needs. Intentions of a group range from addressing symptoms of an illness, or at the other end of a continuum, promoting wellness. Art therapists may adhere to a particular group art therapy approach due to their training or the setting they practice or blend approaches to meet the needs of the individuals they serve. Art therapists must remain flexible in their approaches to group art therapy and strive to find new ways of facilitating groups.

For a more specific understanding of group art therapy, emphasis should be placed within the context of enrichment and improvement through relationships to one's self, others (the group members and the art therapist), and art (the individual's and group members' art). It is through active art-making in relationship with others that treatment goals are addressed. Group art therapy can be viewed as a specific modality or specialty under the broader definition of art therapy or a format to deliver the services of the profession. Bruce Moon (2016, p. xv) offers this definition of "**art-based group therapy**":

> *...art-based group therapy can help group members achieve nearly any desired outcome, and/or address a wide range of therapeutic goals...Art-based groups offer therapists multiple opportunities for modeling appropriate artistic and interpersonal expression, as well as opportunities for helping clients learn new ways to cope with problems through artistic expression and by observing and interacting with others.*

I offer my own definition of **group art therapy** based on extensive experience working as an art therapist in group settings. Group art therapy is an art therapy service or intervention delivered with a group of people involving active art-making and the relationship between the individual, group members, art therapist, and their art. Group art therapy promotes intrapersonal and interpersonal communication (both nonverbally and verbally) through visual imagery and the groups' reflection on the artistic process to foster personal growth and connection to others. **Intrapersonal** communication occurs within one's self while **interpersonal** communication occurs between two or more people.

History of group work

Group work emerged as a practice from serving the needs of those who have been marginalized or oppressed and can be viewed through the lens of social justice, where the values of equity, access, and empowerment are central. People working together with a common goal can offer great social connection and empowerment. Early practitioners of group work recognized how groups can offer empowerment and healing through collaboration, advocacy, and self-determination. In the United States and Great Britain, group work developed in settlement houses meant to address assimilation of European immigrants in the late nineteenth century. Group work in settlement homes included self-advocacy, education, recreation, socialization, and community involvement. Groups, often in the form of clubs, offered residents a way to gain knowledge, support, and companionship (Toseland & Rivas, 2017). The first settlement house in the United States was the Neighborhood Guild founded by Stanton Coit in 1886 in New York. Groups of families living together were organized in clubs to meet for education and recreation and join together to promote social reform (Hansan, 2011). Jane Addams founded the Hull House in Chicago in 1889 to help immigrants address issues of assimilation. Groups were provided to assist residents in self-advocacy and developing life skills in a new country. Addams believed in treating all people with dignity and respect; tenants of all helping professions (Singh & Salazer, 2010).

Another early pioneer of group work was Dr. Joseph Pratt, who is often credited with the use of group as a treatment modality with patients suffering from tuberculosis in 1905. His method of monitoring patients with similar illnesses was originally referred to as the "class method," then was later known as "group therapy" (Ambrose, 2014). Pratt offered patients the opportunity to talk about their illnesses and gain support and methods of coping (Williams & Tripp, 2016). As patients talked and interacted in groups, Pratt observed they were less isolated and depressed and developed an improved morale (Singh & Salazer, 2010). Later, the human potential movement of the 1960s energized themes of social change and awareness of inequality related to race, gender, sexual orientation, and socioeconomic status (Horne, 1999). Group formats "were used to address issues of militarism, racism, sexism, and heterosexism" (Singh & Salazer, 2010, p. 100).

Early art therapists, Mary Huntoon, Edward Adamson, Edith Kramer, Georgette Powell, and Cliff Joseph, were artists who worked in group settings and within art studios placed within other institutions. Mary Huntoon in the United States during the 1930s and Edward Adamson in Great Britain during the 1940s worked in communal studios in psychiatric hospitals. Both Huntoon and Adamson considered "themselves to be facilitators whose role was to allow art to be the healing agent in the studio" and rejected directive approaches or interpreting patient artwork (Wix, 2000, p. 172).

Edith Kramer, also known for her "Art as Therapy" approach, entered the field of art therapy through her work in groups in educational settings; initially as an elementary school shop teacher in the late 1930s and then in the 1950s working in a therapeutic school for boys, where she was given the title art therapist. She preferred working in environments conducive to creating art and identified as an artist (Feen-Calligan, 2014).

Georgette Powell worked at D.C. General Hospital in the 1960s working on an acute psychiatry unit. Her work extended to community settings. She started the Art in the Park in 1966, an event where community members exhibited and created art and Tomorrow's World Art Center in 1970, offering art therapy and art education. Powell's career as an artist was notable. She was commissioned by the Works Progress Administration (WPA) to paint murals at the Harlem Hospital and Queens General Hospital in the late 1930s. Her mural *Recreation in Harlem*, completed in 1937 for the Harlem Hospital, represented people with racial diversity engaged in activities of daily life. Powell faced discrimination by hospital administrators who rejected imagery of people of color. Powell persevered with community support and the mural was completed (Gipson, 2019; Stepney, 2019).

Cliff Joseph, an art therapist, social activist, and the first African American member of the American Art Therapy Association, worked in group settings with a studio approach. These included psychiatric hospitals and forensic settings in New York. Joseph's work treating adult patients in inpatient psychiatric care at Albert Einstein College of Medicine led to him coauthoring the book *Murals of the Mind* in 1973, featuring his work with patients primarily with schizophrenia creating murals together during a period of a year (Harris & Joseph, 1973; Riley-Hiscox, 1997; Stepney, 2019). Joseph noted how this process promoted camaraderie and the development of family-like relationships among the patients. A democratic method of working together developed as the themes of the murals were developed by the patients. Additional themes of problem solving and finding solutions surfaced as a prominent topic for the patients while creating and discussing the murals, demonstrating at times an unconscious way of addressing difficulties (Riley-Hiscox, 1997).

In 1982 Kathleen Hanes compiled a bibliography of art therapy and group work literature in her book *Art Therapy and Group Work*. The book's format reflects the history of group art therapy through a literature review format examining publications from 1951 to 1980 and presents the theory, technique, and practice of group art therapy during this time period. Hanes (1982) noted "the first American article on art therapy in groups was published in 1951" by Dorothy Baruch and Hyman Miller titled, *The Use of Spontaneous Drawing in Group Therapy* in the American Journal of Psychotherapy (p. xi). The article explored how group members used their drawings to gain insight through associating personal meaning and peers' projections of drawings (Baruch & Miller, 1951). Group art therapy literature was minimal in the early development of the field through the 1960s, then began to increase in the mid-1970s (Hanes, 1982).

In 1986 Mariam Liebmann wrote *Art Therapy for Groups: A Handbook of Themes, Games and Exercises*. This book emerged after Liebmann became interested in structured art therapy groups while a student and interviewed 40 art therapists, group leaders, and teachers using art as a means for communication in group settings. Her book focused on these findings and themes used in groups by those interviewed (Liebmann, 1986). A second edition of the book was published in 2004 and was expanded in several areas: additional group themes with variations, a literature review of art therapy groups, safety factors, evidence-based factors in groups, and language more inclusive of diversity. This book was written for art therapists and other helping professions that wanted to expand their skills working with groups and art. The focus is on a themes-based approach where members share a common group art activity (Liebmann, 2004).

Shirley Riley published *Group Process Made Visible: Group Art Therapy* in 2001. Riley discussed the use of art as a tool for group communication. The book supports the idea of using art in group therapy as an additional language, aiding in group cohesion and building trust between group members. Art can be an "observable expression" of group members' thoughts and feelings which can be reflected upon in real time or referred back to when members are ready to process (Riley, 2001, p. 4). Art also captures the group's interactions in a visible way. These interactions may be less threatening than verbal exchanges. Members can also observe they are not alone in their struggles as common issues are represented visually. Quieter group members can share more personal expression through visual imagery while more talkative members can be prompted to listen as they view others' art. Art can allow individuals to function in areas of their personality they normally do not gravitate to (Riley, 2001).

In 2010, Bruce Moon published *Art-Based Group Therapy: Theory and Practice*. The book was designed as a textbook for graduate art therapy courses in group process. The art-based group therapy approach highlights how communion with others and art is therapeutic. In addition, the book distinguishes the differences between art-based group therapy theory and traditional group psychotherapy theory and emphasizes the advantages of art therapy. A second edition of the book was published in 2016 and is heavily referenced in this chapter. Additional goals of the book are to present essential therapeutic elements of art-based group work which are partially referenced in Table 14.2 and provide the reader case vignettes that support an art-based group therapy approach (B.L. Moon, 2010, 2016).

An additional group art therapy resource that was being written concurrently with this book chapter is Megan Robb's *Group Art Therapy: Practice and Research* (2022). The book presents common practice models and covers both history and contemporary practices in group art therapy.

Group art therapy approaches

In 2016 Williams and Tripp completed a review of group art therapy literature and found the format in which group art therapy services had been delivered could be categorized into three approaches: studio or community based, theme or task-focused, and process-oriented. While the following section does not address every approach to group art therapy, it provides an overview of broad categories. The first approach, studio or community based, is more applicable to the study of art therapy at an undergraduate level. Theme or task-focused group could apply to both the undergraduate or graduate level of training, depending on the themes focused on, and process-oriented approaches are more suitable to advanced training and education in art therapy. The reader should note the term task-oriented used earlier in the chapter is used more broadly by Toseland and Rivas (2017) while Williams and Tripp's (2016) category of theme or task-focused applies more specifically to group art therapy.

Studio or community-based approach

The studio or community-based approach to group art therapy focuses on art-making with others and is a communal experience (C.H. Moon, 2016). The setting is typically an art studio environment and may be open to the general public where wellness is focused on versus illness. An open studio approach may look like an art class or group of artists gathering to create art together in a studio space. Specific timelines for meetings may be less structured. Choices of materials and techniques are selected by the participants. This approach fosters community building and "healthy interactions within and among people" (C.H. Moon, 2002, p. 140). Communal art-making within this approach addresses social well-being where conversation and interactions through art occur more naturally. A sense of loneliness and isolation can decrease. Typically, the art therapist is also creating art and serving a flexible role, including being a teacher, mentor, cocreator, and collaborator (Allen, 1995; C.H. Moon, 2016).

Theme or task-focused approach

Group art therapy approaches that are theme or task-focused, meanwhile, provide a common directive given to all group members at the same time. In a community setting, a group of children in a camp setting might all be prompted with the same task, to create works of art from elements collected from nature. The theme might focus on appreciating nature and our environment. This group intervention may be suitable for a student trained at either an undergraduate or graduate level of art therapy education.

In a clinical setting, this structured approach is most often designed for a specific population of group members addressing similar issues. Examples may include adolescents in an anger management group, adults in substance use recovery meetings for peer support, or older adults addressing grief and loss. Added structure to the group process may reduce anxiety for group members participating. Structure is provided by a specific timeline and schedule, consistent leader and members, agreed upon group guidelines and expectations, and focus on a common group goal (Williams & Tripp, 2016). The group members may be given a specific theme to follow in the creation of their art; for example, "create an image of your anger," "depict in a drawing a road representing your recovery," or "put together a memory box to reflect on the loss of a loved one." These themes correspond to the examples of specific populations given before.

O'Neill and Moss (2015) wrote about their group work with adults with chronic pain and offer an example of a theme and task-focused group in 12 group art therapy sessions outlined in their article. The overarching goal was to offer support to those living with chronic pain. Each session offered a check-in and warm-up exercise and a main art directive based on a theme. Examples of shared themes offered for their main art therapy directive included "Draw/paint/create a landscape and place yourself in it," "Paint or draw your internal and external resources," and "Create a three-dimensional symbol... to symbolically represent the pain…" (O'Neill & Moss, 2015, p. 160). Each of these themes focused participants on supporting each other and expressing one's experiences of chronic pain.

Process-oriented approach

Process-oriented groups focus on thoughts and feelings evoked by art in the present moment. This approach was initially more dominant in England. An example of this approach might encompass the art therapist discussing with group members frustrations with the use of art materials and each other that occurred during the session. The art therapist might offer a wide range of methods to interact with the group: normalizing feelings of frustration, problem solving with materials, and considering different ways group members can communicate both visually and verbally. These interventions require more advanced education and clinical skills in art therapy (Williams & Tripp, 2016).

The history, pathfinders, and approaches provided focus primarily on developments in the United States and secondarily in Great Britain and are not presented in their entirety. Readers who are furthering their studies of group work are encouraged to research group work literature generated from other countries and cultures and investigate the study of collective art practices.

Therapeutic factors of group work

Group experiences described in this chapter can offer therapeutic factors that benefit individuals. In most groups, the element of social interaction occurs. Participating and being involved in a group can have distinct advantages encompassing social engagement, group cohesion, and secure attachments. Irvin Yalom empathized the therapeutic factors of a group: (a) installation of hope, (b) universality, (c) imparting of information, (d) altruism, (e) the corrective recapitulation of the family, (f) development of social techniques, (g) imitative behavior, (h) interpersonal learning, (i) group cohesiveness, (j) catharsis, and (k) existential factors (Yalom & Leszcz, 2005, 2020). Readers who are continuing their education in group therapy are encouraged to read Yalom and Leszcz's book *The Theory and Practice of Group Psychotherapy* and review each of these therapeutic factors in greater depth.

For the purposes of this foundational chapter about group work, the therapeutic factor of group cohesiveness will be highlighted with a student learning experience and narrative. **Group cohesion** is what pulls or attracts the group together and consists of a sense of unity and the ability to work as a team (Forsyth, 2014). When group members sense a high level of cohesion, perceived benefits include increased expression, willingness to listen, and increased self-confidence and self-esteem (Yalom & Leszcz, 2005, 2020). General satisfaction, attendance, and participation are higher when a group is cohesive (Prapavessis & Carron, 1997). Katya, an art therapy student also discussed earlier in this chapter, completed a colored pencil drawing to illustrate the concept of group cohesion she experienced with her classmates (Fig. 14.2). This occurred after her initial reservations about registering for the class as illustrated in Fig. 14.1. She described feelings of group cohesiveness within the classroom, the "make it or break it factor" and the

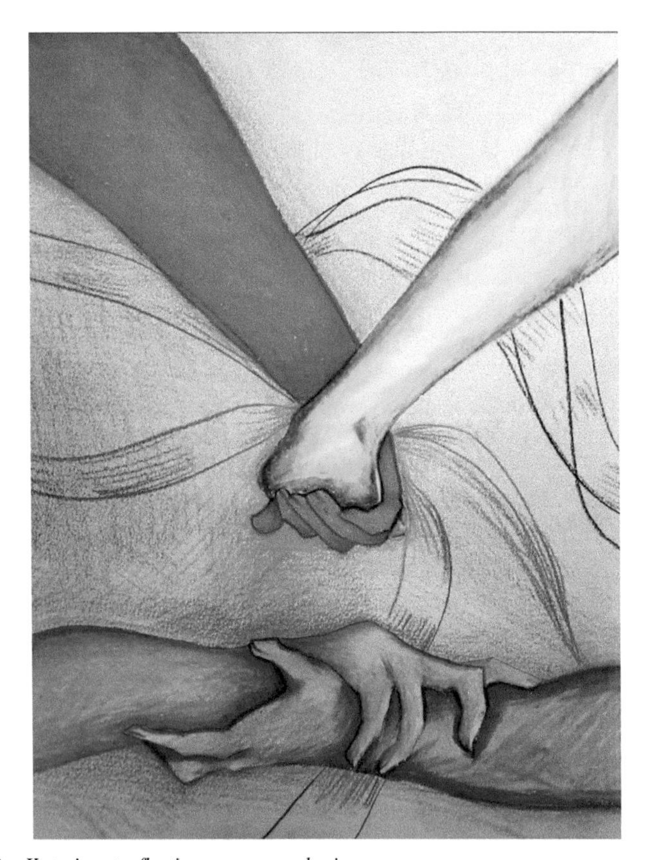

FIG. 14.2 *Katya's art reflection on group cohesion.*

"gateway of openness" allowing her to continue in the class. "I suppose I wanted to illustrate the bonds in the class and how it's an important factor to the life of the group..." (personal communication, July 29, 2020).

Student experiences while learning about Yalom's therapeutic factors of group in an undergraduate group art therapy course supported the benefits of being in a group. The added component of creating art alongside or collaboratively in the classroom emphasized these therapeutic factors. Utilizing art-based methods to teach beginning concepts of group art therapy appeared to enrich the learning environment and foster support among students as they navigated their college experience. Students reflected in an art journal with written and visual reflections, thoughts and feelings about learning about group work. Group cohesion was noted by students as the most prominent therapeutic group factor illustrated in the classroom. Another student, Cate, reflected on the topic of group cohesion. She reported that as the class progressed, she felt more comfortable and accepted. She felt the students came together although each was different (personal communication, July 8, 2020).

Gabel and Robb's (2017) thematic analysis examined therapeutic factors specific to group art therapy. Part of their analysis included Bruce Moon's book on art-based group therapy (2016). The authors found one of these therapeutic factors, relational aesthetics, strengthened group cohesion. **Relational aesthetics** is the process where co-occurring relationships, including the relationship to the art, promote verbal and nonverbal feedback and attachment in a group art therapy setting (Czamanski-Cohen & Weilhs, 2016). Schofield (2019) researched how group art therapy supports well-being and the functioning level for those impacted by Parkinson's disease. In her thematic analysis, she identified the theme of aesthetic group movement: "Aesthetic group movement describes the unique relational aspects of creating artwork together (individually in the same room or creating a group piece) and how this experience enhances group cohesion" (2019, p. 49).

In their research, Gabel and Robb (2017) identified other prominent themes or therapeutic factors specific to group art therapy: symbolic expression, embodiment, pleasure and play, and ritual. Symbolic expression is where an individual uses personal or universal symbols to communicate. Embodiment was defined as "the artistic action of personally confronting internal experiences" (Gabel & Robb, 2017, p. 129). Pleasure and play involve engagement in sensory experiences with art media (Hinz, 2020). Additionally, making art in a group can offer routine, ritual, and a sense of safety (B.L. Moon, 2016).

Table 14.2 provides a more detailed look at Yalom's therapeutic factors of group and Moon's 13 essentials and qualities of art-based group work. While Yalom's therapeutic factors and Moon's essentials are not provided in their entirety, similar themes described by the authors can be found supporting the benefits of group work and group art therapy (B.L. Moon, 2016; Yalom & Leszcz, 2005, 2020) (Table 14.2).

Theories of neuroscience offer added insights into how positive group experiences foster therapeutic factors in a group. These theories support how safe

TABLE 14.2 Comparison: Yalom's Therapeutic Factors of Group and Moon's Essentials and Qualities of Art-Based Group Therapy.

Yalom's Therapeutic Factors of Group (Yalom & Leszcz, 2005, 2020, p. 10):	Moon's (2016, pp. 8–9) Essentials and Qualities of Art-Based Group Therapy:
Installation of hope	Making art in the presence of others is an expression of hope
Universality	When members of a group make art they create shared experiences in the present
Altruism	Making art in a group setting promotes positive regard for the other members of the group
Development of socializing techniques	Making art with others is a gratifying and pleasurable experience
Interpersonal learning	Making art in a group setting provides ways to symbolize and express feelings regarding interpersonal relationships
	Making art in a group setting creates a sense of ritual that provides psychological safety and promotes interpersonal emotional risk-taking
Existential factors	Art-making in a group setting often leads to expression of the ultimate concerns of existence
	Making art in a group setting is an act of self-transcendence
Catharsis	Making art with others is a safe way to express pain, fear, and other difficult feelings
Group cohesiveness	Making art in the presence of others reduces isolation and creates a sense of community

environments promote social engagement. Increased attention and research are occurring within the field of neuroscience. **Neuroscience** encompasses studies of the brain and the nervous system. The concepts of polyvagal theory and neuroception offer another model to understand the benefits of social interaction and group work. Polyvagal theory proposes that within calm and secure environments, social engagement flourishes while in environments that are perceived as unsafe, defenses of fight or flight are activated (Flores & Porges, 2017). Group therapy can serve as a platform to exercise "neural pathways involved in social engagement behaviors" (Flores & Porges, 2017, p. 202). Response to stress, emotional regulation, and attachment styles are typically expressed in group therapy experiences and can help participants improve social functioning. Neuroception is the process of the nervous system evaluating risk without being consciously aware. When safety is perceived, desirable social behavior can unfold (Flores & Porges, 2017). Creating a safe environment emotionally for group members to interact in is critical for addressing and practicing social skills. Group members may feel safer when they trust the leader and the other group members.

Safety can also be fostered by providing group guidelines and acceptance as well as considering the actual environment where the group meets. The group environment should offer privacy and adequate space for the participants to comfortably create art and interact with one another. Additional considerations may include lighting, having a water source, and a secure area to store art supplies and keep artwork safe and confidential (Rubin, 2010).

Benefits of group work

The therapeutic factors of a group described previously lead to the benefits of group work. Group settings may be beneficial for practical reasons. A group format may be more advantageous economically as costs are typically higher for individual sessions in clinical settings. A group leader can serve more individuals at a time, which may be more critical when resources are limited. Group work is beneficial when group members are seeking peer and social support. A group format is especially helpful for those prone to isolating when symptoms of depression limit interactions with others. Many older adults in residential care or individuals with intellectual disabilities respond positively to group activities for the social benefits. Furthermore, a group format may also be advantageous to those with relationship difficulties, providing many opportunities to practice interpersonal skills (Toseland & Rivas, 2017).

The benefits of group work can enrich participants further with the added experience of art. Themes fostered through group art experiences or group art therapy include a sense of belonging, interpersonal communication, and attachment. Art therapy authors have presented more specific benefits of creating art in a group setting, including nonverbal ways for participants to build connections and practice interpersonal skills. Individuals participating in group art therapy services can present with a range of issues related to relationship difficulties and the need to develop interpersonal skills. A group setting can be the ideal format to address these skills.

Sense of belonging

Bruce Moon (2016) stated “Making art in the presence of others reduces isolation and creates a sense of connection” (p. 87). Liebmann (2012) outlined reasons for group work in art therapy including “people with similar needs can provide mutual support for each other and help with mutual problem solving” (p. 368). Seeing each other’s art in group art therapy adds a layer of therapeutic intimacy between participants (Riley, 2001). Art can serve as the channel to connect people in meaningful ways and promote multiple layers of well-being in a group setting.

Interpersonal communication

A study by the World Health Organization’s Regional Office in Europe examined the benefits of art for health and well-being. The definition of art was broadly defined, but results indicated involvement in the arts promotes health and well-being through social cohesion (Fancourt & Finn, 2019). The authors discussed how social engagement and inclusion contribute to social determinants of health (Fancourt & Finn, 2019). Rosal (2016) noted in her review of group art therapy authors, “it is clear that the premise behind using art in group work is the power of art to engender relationships through increased interpersonal interactions, viewing each other’s artwork, and uncovering connections with others through the artwork” (p. 232).

Attachment

Adding the experience of creating art with others can garner further benefits by developing attachments through relationships between participants, each other, and their art (Czamanski-Cohen & Weilhs, 2016). Building healthy attachments to others through creativity can help people learn to trust and form more secure bonds. Attachment and investment in one’s own artwork can promote self-empowerment.

Limitations of group work

While the benefits of group work are supported above, it is important to note a group format is not ideal for every individual. Some individuals may require more focus by the group leader to fully support their needs. An example may be an individual with limited dexterity who requires hand-over-hand assistance for completing particular tasks. Individuals may struggle with social anxiety, paranoid thoughts about others, or a lack of trust in peers; therefore, a group may seem overwhelming. In a clinical setting, confidentiality may be more limited then in a group setting due to multiple participants. In addition, group participants may not be ready for others to hear their difficult experiences (Corey et al., 2014). Those presenting with severe behavioral issues can disrupt groups and result in negative interactions for all (Toseland & Rivas, 2017). Finally, barriers may include lack of access and availability of services or having enough personnel with expertise to lead a group program. Therefore a group format must be carefully considered.

The definition, history, approaches, and benefits of art therapy provide further knowledge about how creating art with others can expand and deepen group work. The added component of art-making can offer widening or alternative pathways to help people express themselves and relate to others. When relating to others, students should seek to increase their knowledge about other cultures, their own culture and values, and nurture cultural humility.

Multicultural competence and cultural humility

Since a group is made up of interpersonal interactions, it is culturally bound. Group leaders can be more effective if they are aware of personal biases and work to expand skills and knowledge associated with multiculturalism and cultural humility. When working in a group setting, it is likely a leader will interact with people from varied cultures and experiences. The American Art Therapy Association's Ethical Principles for Art Therapists defined areas of multicultural and diversity competence (American Art Therapy Association, 2013). Several sections of the principles addressed groups, specifically ethical principles related to cultural groups:

> *7.2 Art therapists take reasonable steps to ensure that they are sensitive to differences that exist among cultures. They strive in their attempts to learn about the belief systems of people in any given cultural group in order to provide culturally relevant interventions and treatment. (p. 7)*
>
> *7.5 Art therapists acquire knowledge and information about the specific cultural group(s) with which they are working and the strengths inherent in those cultural groups. They are sensitive to individual differences that exist within cultural groups and understand that individuals may have varying responses to group norms. (p. 8)*

Cultural competence includes gaining knowledge and awareness of diverse cultures (Sue, 2001). In addition, **cultural humility** is a process of openness, self-awareness, self-critique, and mutually supportive relationships (Sue, 2001). It is a value informing one's behavior over a lifetime and cannot be achieved simply by attending a class or a training about a culture (Mosher et al., 2017). Cultural humility acknowledges power differences, including privilege and marginalization of cultural groups, and is a lifelong endeavor of learning for helping professionals (Foronda et al., 2016; Guth et al., 2019). Jackson (2020) contributed to our understanding and differentiates between cultural competency and cultural humility within the art therapy field and supports providers exploring cultural awareness on a deeper level through their own self-knowledge and art-making. Suggestions for deeper reflection with art materials include examining one's own cultural identity, relationships with others, and confronting thought patterns that lead to biases. Guth et al. (2019) provided another resource for cultivating cultural humility in their article *Ten Strategies to Intentionally Use Group Work to Transform Hate, Facilitate Courageous Conversations, and Enhance Community Building.* These strategies were developed to promote increased cultural awareness in self and others for group workers. These strategies are recommended for review in their entirety. Strategy Five states the rationale for cultivating cultural humility:

> *Group workers must continually strive to practice cultural humility by adopting an interpersonal approach that seeks to humbly understand how cultural identity shapes the worldview and experiences of others. This other-oriented concept is characterized by a lifelong commitment to self-evaluation, desire to bridge or eliminate imbalances of power, and commitment to systemically advocate for others (p. 13).*

The practice of cultural humility includes being open-minded and "welcoming of diversity of thought and expressions in groups" (Guth et al., 2019, p.13). Furthermore, allowing the group members to teach the group leader and acknowledging mistakes as teachable moments generate cultural humility (Guth et al., 2019).

Students developing leadership skills must not only be knowledgeable about the cultural groups they interface with but also examine their own cultural background and how this experience influences their worldview. Increasing multicultural competency and deepening cultural humility will aid in developing helpful relationships with members and prompt self-reflection and lifelong learning from others.

The relationship of the "group leader" and "group member" inherently holds a power imbalance with the leader often placed as an authority figure. College students who are typically young adults often underestimate this power differentiation. In addition, as we serve marginalized groups in our community, this divide of power may be even more emphasized if the leader is from a privileged position. By nature of being a student of higher education, privilege is afforded to students as they benefit from the resources and knowledge the institution provides (Jackson, 2020). Student leaders should be aware of this dynamic and work in partnership with others by being open to learn about another's worldview and experience. Cultural humility includes the stance that community members in a group are viewed as experts and can teach us about their own culture. Students will need to have the humility to recognize this expertise to build relationships with group members (Jackson, 2020).

The following narrative illustrates a student-led group art experience where both cultural competence and cultural humility were considered.

Students and I had the opportunity to travel to Kathmandu, Nepal, to volunteer at a school for "impoverished" students teaching art. In preparation for the experience, we read about the culture and customs of Nepal. A fellow student from Nepal presented to our group of traveling students as well as a professor with expertise in religious studies. We examined the beliefs of Hinduism and Buddhism in contrast to our spiritual beliefs, which were predominantly from a Christian viewpoint. This was part of our attempt to gain knowledge of the Nepali culture, thus improving cultural competency prior to traveling and teaching art in a group environment with the children. While this knowledge was helpful, our interactions were made deeper by having cultural humility.

As we reflected on our US centric concept of socioeconomic status which focuses on materialism, we opened up to another meaning of wealth. We left with an understanding the children were not necessarily "impoverished" as we understood this concept, but rich in generosity and kindness to us as visitors from a different country in their classroom. Although we were "volunteering," our group received as much as we attempted to give, and the experience felt more like a heartfelt exchange and connection. Reflecting on beliefs and values around socioeconomic status prompted greater understanding of different worldviews and increased cultural humility.

Group skills

The beginning skills needed to facilitate a group will prompt the student to consider areas of practice with group work. Learning skills associated with group facilitation may assist the student when encountering collaborative class assignments, leading art activities, volunteer or service learning experiences, and internship or fieldwork placements. Examples of group settings where undergraduate art therapy students may be placed include facilitating art lessons at art museums, art activities at a senior center, daycare, or afterschool program, supporting creativity at a studio setting, or promoting wellness through art at a community setting. Groups may meet in person, remotely, or mixed in a hybrid format with some group members in person and others remotely. Beginning in 2020, the use of online groups became popular due to infection control concerns relating to COVID-19. Therefore **group skills** encompass methods necessary to help the group meet goals, whether completing a task as a group or meeting individual members' needs in treatment (Toseland & Rivas, 2017).

Basic group work skills are delineated into three areas: organizational, listening, and leadership. Although these skills are fundamental, time and experience will allow students to develop and deepen these skills. Having trusted teachers and fieldwork supervisors will guide students in their first steps in facilitating a group. Developing and improving group skills is a continual endeavor for students and helping professionals further their skills to serve others.

Organizational skills

Developing and providing group structure requires organizational skills. Organizational skills will help the student be planful for a group art activity and provide a framework for participants. Tasks associated with organizing a group include ample preparation and consideration of available resources as well as presenting clear guidelines and directions to group participants. A common mistake made by students is not allowing enough time to properly plan an art activity. Thoughtful preparation will help students more successfully lead a group. A practical issue to consider is the resources available to effectively provide the art group.

Resources may be plentiful or restrictive and impact the planned art activity significantly. Being flexible, resourceful, and creative are all qualities to lean on when planning an art group. Students should always be familiar with any art materials they are presenting to others and complete the art activity themselves in advance. Art therapists' knowledge about art materials affords them the capability of assisting others with using materials in effective ways (Rubin, 2010).

Knowledge of safety considerations of art materials should be referred to when planning art activities. Safety considerations are addressed in more detail in Chapter 2 addressing art materials, but include mechanical and chemical hazards participants may encounter when using tools and materials for creating art. Potential risks include accidental injury, self-harm, or intoxication through cuts, burns, inhalation, and ingestion (Horovitz, 2018). Risks may increase in a group setting where one-on-one monitoring is not possible. Arrangements for access to art materials need to be considered for groups meeting remotely. Solutions may include art materials being mailed, delivered, or retrieved by group members or using materials available in group members' homes.

Being clear on the goals of the group and the theme of the art activity will also help focus and guide the planning for the group. Goals of group art activities may include practicing social skills and improving social supports, learning art techniques, improving frustration tolerance, increasing relaxation and enjoyment, building resiliency and promoting wellness, reducing stress, providing sensory stimulation and cognitive stimulation, decreasing isolation, and improving camaraderie. Goals addressing grief, trauma, and deeper feelings of emotional pain should be addressed after more advanced training as an art therapist. Examples of group themes include representing feelings of "being calm or at peace," representing "personal strengths," creating handmade cards for peers with inspirational quotes and images, building a group sculpture with peers, creating puppets for a group performance, designing a seasonal mural, or creating decorations for group members to enjoy in a shared space.

Leaders provide structure and direction to assist group members in remaining focused to the intended goals of the group. Having structure within a group provides group members a sense of control by having a sense of predictability and routine. When facilitating an art activity, many considerations must be addressed. The following template is provided to assist students with organizing, planning, and preparing a group. Students may find themselves practicing a group art activity with peers in the classroom or leading within a community setting. In preparation, state the directions for the art activity out loud to a peer who is not familiar with art. Do the directions make sense? Are they clear and concise? Avoid stating too many steps at once, and consider describing to participants step by step to avoid confusion. Consider the age group and development of the participants. Students studying art therapy may be more familiar with art materials than group members participating in an art group; therefore, participants may need more instruction how to use art materials and encouragement to engage (Table 14.3).

The following narrative provides an example of how an art therapy group session might be organized and structured. An 8-week art therapy group addressing grief and loss issues for adults is offered one evening a week for an hour and a half at a community outpatient health center. The group is a closed group and limited to eight participants due to the nature of the topic and to allow participants adequate time for creating art and sharing. The art therapist would set up the group space prior to each session, providing art materials and resources in a private area for confidentiality. The group would open each week with a check-in for 5–10 min, allowing participants to orient themselves and greet the

TABLE 14.3 Template: Group art facilitation planning guide.

Student Name:	**Date:**
Name of Group Art Activity/Theme:	**Timeframe:** (preparation, completing directive, clean up)
Goals: State 2–3 goals for your group art activity:	
Participants: Describe the group and/or population the group art activity is planned for	
Age Range (consider human development):	
Cultural Considerations: (consider cultural competence and cultural humility)	
Group Size: (consider how this will impact your timeframe and materials)	
Art Materials: Provide a list of art materials with amounts of materials needed. How will the materials be presented and prepared? (be specific)	
Safety Considerations:	**Costs:**
Variations:	
Directions: Provide a statement describing the directions for the group art activity. Include clearly stated steps.	
Other Information if Needed:	

other group members. The art therapy task would be introduced with clear directions and a choice of art supplies. The art therapist would develop the group art therapy tasks based on the theme of grief but consider the needs of the group members as the group evolves. "...The group informs the art interventions...the art informs the group" (Rosal, 2016, p. 238). Ideas are sparked directly from the group members and art created in previous group sessions. For example, the art therapist notices the group members expressing anger around their losses and considers an art therapy task to promote expression of anger. Art techniques might be demonstrated if needed. The art therapist would tell the group members how much time was allotted for creating art and group discussion. For example, "We have 40 minutes to create our art, then 30 minutes for a discussion after." It is helpful if the art therapist provides prompts around timelines throughout the session. The group might close by sharing an insight gained from the group that session. Additional time should be provided at the end for cleaning up the space and storing the artwork. An established routine offers consistency and predictability which may reduce anxiety for group members.

Listening skills and being present

While organizational skills are fundamental, a successful group experience will rely on more nuanced skills from the leader to flourish. These skills are interpersonal in nature and cannot always be learned through student reading assignments and classroom experiences. Some students may naturally possess these qualities, but all will expand these skills once venturing out of the classroom to community experiences with groups. Taking the stance of being a continual learner, whether a student or a helping professional throughout one's academic and professional career, will serve others and prompt ongoing self-reflection.

One skill that is often underestimated by students is simply listening to others—just listen. Students can be anxious about "what to say" to people when leading an art activity. At times, students may initiate discussion first without truly being present and listening to what the group members have to say or communicate through their art. The skill of active listening, also known as "empathic listening," has its roots in humanism and the work of Carl Rogers (Topornycky & Golparian, 2016). Rogers cited the positive acceptance of the person talking as a condition necessary for the "humanization of any interpersonal relations" (Topornycky & Golparian, 2016, p. 175).

Active listening has been defined as "the act of hearing a speaker, avoiding premature judgment" and "reflecting understanding" (Topornycky & Golparian, 2016, p. 175). A large component of active listening is paying attention. Paying attention involves focusing in the moment with others, showing genuine interest, displaying nonverbal affirmation, and comfortable eye contact (Hoppe, 2007). Active listening shows respect for others and builds relationships. Concepts of active listening can also be applied when witnessing and viewing another person's work of art and the act of active seeing (B.L. Moon, 2016). The group leader takes in images visually, sees another person's story, and pays attention to their expressions (B.L. Moon, 2016). "Art making provides group members opportunities to be seen, heard, and responded to" (B.L. Moon, 2016, p. 191). Listening in a genuine way can help others become more visible.

Being present with others is another key factor to successfully leading a group. Active listening is a part of being present but encompasses more skills and behaviors. Crane-Okada (2011) reviewed literature related to the concept of being present with others and found a range of meanings across disciplines of helping professions. Definitions of being present included a behavior that expresses being in the moment, focused awareness, nurturance, authenticity, care, compassion, and empathy (Covington, 2003; du Mont, 2002; Jonas & Crawford, 2004; Stanley, 2002). These are skills the leader also hopes to impart and nurture within the group members.

In the classroom, I role play and demonstrate behaviors that are the opposite of being present: looking at my cell phone and the clock, telling the class "I need to leave and check on something in my office," and looking out the window and commenting on individuals passing by. While I am exaggerating these behaviors as an example of not being present, students must be mindful that even subtle behaviors can give the message "I'm not interested."

For the leader, the meaning of healing presence was defined by Miller and Cutshall (2001, p. 12) as "the condition of being consciously and compassionately in the present moment with another or with others, believing in and affirming their potential for wholeness." Yalom and Leszcz (2005) described presence as "the hidden agent of help in all forms of therapy" (p. 106). Bruce Moon (2016) described art-based leadership skills which include "being with," "the leader's capacity to be open to what the group members' express" (p. 21). In addition, "leaders must pay attention to, respond to, and be with clients as they explore, create, and share" (B.L. Moon, 2016, p. 21). While remaining present and listening is essential, group members may also look to a leader for more direct support and guidance to accomplish their task or meet their needs.

Leadership skills

Leadership skills are fundamental to effective group work. Developing leadership skills will enable more successful facilitation of group experiences. **Leadership** has been defined as "the process of guiding the development of a group and its members" (Toseland & Rivas, 2017, p. 98) and helping them achieve their goals. Initial goals of leadership primarily focus on helping the group members feel supported. The organizational skills outlined previously may help develop structure and promote leadership. Leadership also requires flexibility within structure. The structure provided should not be overly rigid. In most group situations, the group unfolds in unpredictable ways, and a group leader must adequately prepare, but also adapt to unforeseen interactions within the group.

Students may find themselves in a range of positions requiring leadership skills: being an academic or social club officer, resident advisor, or student mentor to a group of incoming students. Students studying art therapy will most likely be charged with leading an art activity in the classroom, service learning experience, or fieldwork. Students may possess qualities and characteristics of leadership based on personal traits or prior experiences, and for some, these skills may not feel natural and intuitive and require significant development. At times, building leadership skills can be anxiety provoking and cause students self-doubt. Initially, being a leader can be uncomfortable. Even the most experienced group leaders confront challenges when leading a group. Fortunately, leadership skills can be learned about and practiced within a supportive classroom environment.

Cate, an art therapy student, reflected on practicing leading a group art activity with a peer in the classroom (personal communication, July 8, 2020):

> *Being a leader for this project, I was a little nervous, as I always am when having to get up in front of people. Even though I am very comfortable with the students in this class, I still get nervous having to get up in front of everyone. Once I got started, I relaxed a bit and got into the swing of things... Another thing that I was very nervous about was responding to the group's art pieces. That is my biggest worry about going into art therapy: wanting to know what to say in response to someone's art! However, I know that this takes time and practice, but for now it is scary...*

Cate accompanied her written reflection with a mixed media work of art contrasting black and white lines and warm colors (personal communication, July 8, 2020; Fig. 14.3):

FIG. 14.3 *Cate's reflection on leadership.*

I chose the colors red, orange, magenta, and gold because those are warm colors and I reflected those as being a leader. A good leader should be able to provide a warm and safe environment, hence the warm color choice. They should also provide hope for the clients, which I think is a valuable attribute in any setting. The leader should have a commanding presence, but should also know when to be respectful and kind. They should know how to refocus the group to the goal of the project and theme.

An effective leader offers support, encouragement, consideration, and help to work through conflicts that may arise in a group. Handling conflict in a group can be a source of anxiety for a new leader. It is normal for group members to experience conflict. In fact, if no conflicts surface, this may indicate the group is not ready or reluctant to explore deeper interpersonal skills within the group. A skilled group leader can address conflict and use these situations as opportunities for growth. A fairly common conflict that may arise in an art therapy group is experiencing frustration with the behavior of another group member. Examples may include a group member not sharing art supplies or intruding on a peer's work space while creating art. An art therapist might initially pause to allow the group members to work through the conflict, but if unresolved, encourage members to discuss ways of communicating and coming to a solution.

Group leaders may also encounter reluctance to participate in the group activity. Reluctance in group art therapy can occur for several reasons: coming to group therapy was not the participants' idea, feeling ambivalent and unsure if the group could be helpful, or knowing the difficulty or emotional pain that can arise in therapy (Schroder, 2005). Examples may be a participant referred to group therapy by the legal system or a participant reflecting on past traumatic events. In both cases, the art therapist should focus on building a relationship with the participant and acknowledge openly their reluctance. Initially, participants may only be comfortable observing the group until more trust is established.

Developing a rapport with group members is critical to effective leadership. Having a steady, calm, and genuine demeanor can help in building a rapport and trust with group members. Being genuine encompasses being interested in others, asking group members directly about their needs and understanding, and communicating a desire to be helpful. Group members often seek validation of their struggles and accomplishments and a caring leader acknowledges both.

Student group art collaborations

Group skills can be practiced in a classroom or community environment, and interacting with others creating art offers many benefits as previously discussed in this chapter. Students, throughout their education studying art therapy, will likely create art alongside their classmates to learn concepts about group work. These experiences differ when creating art alone and promote bonds within the classroom and learning outcomes related to group work. Collaborative art pieces where students work on the same piece of art may be introduced that elicit thoughts and feelings about ownership, cooperation, compromise, and boundaries. Working with others on the same piece of art may be satisfying as it offers another avenue to connect with classmates or it may be a source of discomfort and anxiety as students navigate peer relationships, dynamics within the classroom, and insecurities. Collaborative methods of art-making can range from working with a partner or smaller subgroup within the classroom to the entire group or class.

The art tasks shared were conducted with art therapy students enrolled in an undergraduate group art therapy course. As an instructor, I facilitated these experiences to illustrate learning about aspects of Yalom's therapeutic factors of group: the installation of hope and universality (Yalom & Leszcz, 2005, 2020). In addition, I modeled to the students, group skills needed for group art facilitation. Class guidelines were created by the students to promote increased sharing, safety, and learning. They included confidentiality, respecting each other, the right not to share in the classroom, and the expectation to be active with the art materials. This process modeled aspects of leadership. These ideas for collaborative art-making may be adaptable to student placements facilitating groups or integrated into future practice as an art therapist. As a group art therapist, I have found the most successful group interventions balance both the individual and collaborative art elements. These tasks contain elements of individual expression yet link participants together collectively.

Circle of hope painting

The circle of hope exercise illustrates a method for individuals to work with a partner. Hope is a critical component of group work and identified as a therapeutic factor of groups by Irvin Yalom (Yalom & Leszcz, 2005, 2020). The installation of hope can occur in a group setting when group members witness others improving, thus offering optimism (Yalom & Leszcz, 2005, 2020). In a group treatment setting, I have observed how clients at different stages of their recovery from a mental health or substance use diagnosis gain hope by hearing a peer with a similar experience. Group members both hear and see expressions of hope through group discussion and art. Recognizing oneself in others who are healing gives hope to group members in a more profound way than any encouraging platitude shared by the leader. Bruce Moon addressed the topic of hope by asserting the group leader must have hope for the group members and the creative process. In his 13 therapeutic essentials addressed earlier in this chapter, he stated "Making art in the presence of others is an expression of hope" (B.L. Moon, 2016, p. 8).

To examine the topic of hope, students were assigned to work with a partner in class on a painting representing hope. Organizational skills were considered by preparing in advance a square-sized canvas with a predrawn circle along with acrylic paints and various brushes. The predrawn circle was meant to provide a visual structure to prompt students to work together within the same space. Sharing space together while creating art elicits several choices: to integrate

FIG. 14.4 *Circle of hope.*

an image or separate. Some students had distinct areas or halves they worked within and others blended their imagery. This process in a group art therapy context might lead to discussion about personal space, boundaries, and the relationship with the partner.

Fig. 14.4 is an example of this directive and illustrates the concept of finding hope out of darkness or uncertainty and the idea that hope can grow. The left portion depicts the darkness of night, but light is present in the white spatter of paint representing the stars. The right portion presents the message of hope in writing and with the lotus-shaped flower image. Both the water lily and lotus have powerful symbolic meaning across many cultures. In Egyptian culture, the water lily rose out of the water in the morning then receded back into the water, representing the sun rising from the night and offering continual renewal (Kandeler & Ullrich, 2009). This theme echoed the message of the students' painting of hope. The students chose to work in separate areas and reinforced the meaning of the painting with a related quote by author, Amanda Hale (n.d.): "Trust the wait. Embrace uncertainty. Enjoy the beauty of becoming. When nothing is certain anything is possible." After class, the painting was left to dry off to the side of the classroom. A student in a different class observed the painting and message and approached me after class. She shared seeing the image and message of hope was something she needed to hear and see at that particular time in her life and asked I thank the artists who created the piece. In this example, art communicated a message carrying personal meaning beyond the artists' original purpose. This dynamic can also be observed in clinical settings, where observers project personal meaning onto imagery which may or may not align with the artists' original message.

Group class sculpture

Additional methods of group collaboration in art-making include artwork where each individual creates a portion, then all art pieces are combined into one work of art. An example of this method was a class sculpture depicting contrasting themes of being alone versus being part of a group (Fig. 14.5). The exercise promoted exploration of contrasting ways of being with self and others. Examining this theme may be considered developmental in nature as concepts of independence and dependence were explored. The students, who were adolescents and young adults, were transitioning to increased independence (Arrington, 2016). Within a group, members often strike a balance between expressions of individuality and conformity. Both expressions are important as we relate to others and develop our own identities and relationships.

Colored markers, utility knives, scissors, and a matboard with surfaces of black and white on each side were provided. The exercise started by having each student select a colored marker of their choice, then one at a time create a scribble on the white side of the matboard where the colored marker would be more visible. Students' scribbles and lines intersected but were identifiable to the student by color, thus offering a way to begin collaborating yet still have ownership over one's mark.

Students then outlined and cut out a shape of their choice to develop the theme further individually. The background lines of the group's scribble drawing could be used to develop the design further, thus, a symbol of how others may influence us. After each individual completed their piece, they

FIG. 14.5 *Collaborative group sculpture.*

were directed to cut slits in two areas of their pieces, then assemble the sculpture as a group. The exercise contained a problem-solving element, as the pieces being joined together had to be balanced in a way to support the sculpture remaining intact. Being engaged in relationships with others requires compromise, adjustment, and balance to remain healthy. In addition, the task required cooperation and patience to create stability, both qualities resonating in successful relationships. Other factors that can be observed are roles of leadership and followership that emerge in group art activities. Both roles are needed in a group environment and may reflect personal qualities outside the planned group art activity.

The class was able to successfully combine their pieces and reflect. Students were given the option to glue them permanently or leave them unglued to obtain their individual pieces at a later time. They chose to leave their pieces connected but not to glue them so they could retrieve their individual piece at the end of the class. This reflected a coming together and parting as the class progressed then ended. As an art therapist, I have utilized an adapted version of this directive in a clinical setting, and many therapeutic themes around relationships and group dynamics surface. Within the context of group art therapy, this process could be utilized to explore group relationships further, where relationships can be "solid" or "loose," "permanent" or "impermanent," and "come together" or "apart." While these themes were not all explored within a classroom environment, these suggestions may spark ideas for future group work.

Student themes did emerge in the classroom after the sculpture was assembled and discussed: stress and growth associated with being a student, life transitions, and self-care. These themes touched on Yalom's therapeutic factor of universality as students related to many demands of being a student (Yalom & Leszcz, 2005, 2020). Most students reflected on preferring to be part of a group, while others gained solace by having their own space and being alone. Some students found being with others energizing and empowering and most expressed positive feelings about being part of the group class and creating art together. Students practiced the skills of listening and being present with each other as they related to common experiences.

In retrospect, this exercise could also apply to examining White privilege as the class participants were all White young women. While the two-sided mat board happened to be the supply on hand in the classroom, it represented a missed opportunity to explore topics of race, privilege, and visibility in society, topics relevant to group work and art therapy. The white surface of the matboard and topic of visibility in society would have been a powerful metaphor to reflect on further and has informed me as a White educator to take more action in integrating these topics with art media. The duality of being felt visible or invisible to others is also a common theme I have observed in participants of group art therapy serving adults who confronted the stigma of mental illness.

Group work example in art therapy

The following vignette provides a description of group work of a professional art therapist. The narrative is a composite description of the group with identifying information changed to afford confidentiality of the group members. Key terms referenced in the chapter will be included to give examples of group concepts. Additionally, the topic of professional boundaries and how much the art therapist will personally share, or disclose, with group members will be addressed.

During the COVID-19 pandemic, I was approached by a community art center to develop a group focused on art and wellness. The art center staff recognized the communities' need for support during a period of time when many arts events and classes were canceled or restricted and sought out the services of an art therapist. The setting was not in a clinical environment, such as a mental health center; therefore, goals focused on promoting wellness and learning art techniques to reduce general stress during the pandemic. The group was a formed group since it was organized by the art center and closed, which did not allow new members to join once it started. The group was theme focused and structured with planned art techniques designed to promote wellness and coping. A written release was reviewed, obtained, and signed by the group members outlining the purposes and limitations of the group, and resources available if needing further mental health support.

Although the group was open to all adults in the community, four cisgender women joined the group, which ran weekly for five sessions for 1 ½ hour. One of the group members was a young adult in her 20s and three in their late 50s. One woman was Black and the other women White. Three of the four women were receiving Temporary Assistance for Needy Families and were able to utilize a grant to cover the costs of the group and art supplies. All women described themselves as creative individuals who in some way had been negatively impacted by the COVID-19 pandemic. Most notably, social isolation and lack of motivation to engage in creative outlets were identified as challenges faced. The group members hoped the group would provide them with camaraderie and new ideas to reinvigorate their creativity. A sense of universality, not being alone, was quickly established (Yalom & Leszcz, 2005, 2020).

The group members were given the option of meeting in person at the art center with safety protocols in place or remotely. The majority of the group felt more comfortable meeting remotely; therefore, the group began on camera, unmasked, and in our own spaces we had carved out in our homes for making art. Art supplies were ordered and prepared by the art therapist in individual boxes and picked up by the group members prior to the group starting.

As the group progressed, I myself could identify with many of the themes of the group: being limited from direct contact with others, missing live activities, and at times feeling boredom and a longing to return to the time before the COVID-19 pandemic. Then surfaced a decision art therapists encounter in group sessions—how much to personally reveal or not with the group members? When considering how much to share with a group member, in the middle of a spectrum between being "opaque" where "all aspects of the art therapist's life are withheld from the client" to being "transparent" where "the art therapy relationship is viewed as a mutual exchange of self revelations," there is being "translucent." In being translucent, the art therapist is careful about sharing and asks, "…how will my sharing be helpful to the client?" (Moon & Nolan, 2020, p. 157).

I considered this question during the second group. Group members were asked to collect natural and found items in their home, yard, or neighborhood to connect more deeply to sources of nature and comfort. A precut, neutral colored, circular piece of plastic shelf liner was provided to weave the materials. Group members were encouraged to fully be present in their environments and focus on their senses. A discussion ensued about some benefits of staying home: slowing down, having more time gardening or watching the bird feeder, walking outside more, and noticing the beauty in nature at hand. Materials gathered and shown on camera led to reflections about feeding the birds, sitting outside on a comfortable lawn chair, growing up playing outside and visiting grandparents, and enjoying simple pleasures.

I also participated in weaving and chose to share my example with the group. I shared that I turned to nature as a way of managing the stresses of the COVID-19 pandemic but stopped short of describing details of my personal life. My answers to the question "How will my sharing be helpful to the client?" encompassed several reasons: normalizing and validating stress associated with the COVID-19 pandemic, modeling the use of art techniques, and giving the message that we are all walking alongside each other in this experience as human beings during the COVID-19 pandemic (Fig. 14.6).

FIG. 14.6 *Art therapist's weaving.*

Conclusions

The topic of group work is central to students learning about art therapy and other helping professions. Group work offers many benefits to serving others. Being part of a group and relating to others is critical in our own personal development, education as a student, and work as future professionals. As we are social beings, belonging to a group promotes emotional well-being. Creating and making art with others in a group environment empowers individuals to be understood, express themselves, and tell their stories. Being in the presence of cocreators can offer a dimension to group interaction rich in authentic expression and interconnectedness. Learning about the skills associated with group work will develop as students gain knowledge and practice within their educational programs. The intersection of group work and art can offer students new ways of helping others and enriching their future study or practice.

Art experientials and reflection questions

The following art experientials prompt further exploration of group work:

1. Divide a paper into separate sections. In each section, represent a different group you are a part of (include both formed and natural groups). Variations: Dividing a large circle into pie-shaped sections or replicating the outline of puzzle pieces.
2. Draw a large circle with a smaller circle drawn inside. In the inner circle, represent your family. In the larger circle, represent your cultural group. Variations: 3D, use of clay with circular tiles or two bowl forms with the smaller bowl placed with a larger bowl.
3. Divide a paper in half. In one portion, represent "being alone" and the other "being with others."
4. Represent visually an "ideal leader."
5. Draw or paint a group environment which is calm and safe. Variations: 3D, use the format of a box and space within to represent the theme.

Further exploration on group work can be investigated with these reflection questions:

1. What groups are you a part of?
2. What did your family teach you about being a group member?
3. What has your cultural background taught you about being a group member?
4. What benefits have you experienced being part of a group?
5. How can you practice group work skills (organizational, active listening, leadership)?
6. What qualities are needed for an ideal leader?
7. How can making art with others promote a sense of belonging?
8. What group art activities promote communication and problem solving?
9. What group art activities promote group cohesion and a sense of community?

Additional resources

The following resources are provided for students volunteering or placed in fieldwork settings with older adults. These resources are provided due to the frequency of these placements for undergraduate art therapy students (Schwartz et al., 2019). Each book contains information about group activities that utilize art or multisensory modalities. In addition, resources for professional associations focused on group work are provided. These resources are not already listed in the reference section.

Chia, S.H., Heathcote, J., & Hibberd, J.M. (2011). *Group and individual work with older people: A practical guide to running successful activity-based programmes*. Jessica Kingsley Publishers.

Crockett, S. (2013). *Activities for older people in care homes: A handbook for successful activity planning*. Jessica Kingsley Publishers.

Dynes, R. (2017). *Positive communication: Activities to reduce isolation and improve the wellbeing of older adults*. Jessica Kingsley Publishers.

Jopling, S. & Mousley, S. (2018). *The multi-sensory reminiscence activity book: 52 weekly group session plans for working with older adults*. Jessica Kingsley Publishers.

International Association for Social Work with Groups, Inc: https://www.iaswg.org/resources

The Association for Specialist in Group Work: https://asgw.org/resources-2/

Chapter terms

Active listening
Art-based group therapy
Being present
Closed groups
Collaborative artmaking
Cultural humility
Formed groups
Group
Group art facilitation
Group art therapy
Group cohesion
Group norms
Group skills
Group work
Interpersonal
Intrapersonal
Leadership
Natural groups
Neuroscience
Open groups
Relational aesthetics
Subgroups
Task-oriented
Treatment-focused
Universality

References

Alcoholics Anonymous. (2021). *What is A.A.?* https://www.aa.org/pages/en_US/what-is-aa.

Alghraibeh, A. N., & Juieed, N. M. (2018). The relationship between affective and social isolation among undergraduate students. *International Education Studies*, *11*(1), 89–99. https://doi.org/10.5539/ies.vllnlp89.

Allen, P. B. (1995). Coyotte comes in from the cold. *Art Therapy: Journal of the American Art Therapy Association*, *12*(3), 161–166. https://doi.org/10.1080/07421656.1995.10759153.

Ambrose, C. T. (2014). Joseph Hersey Pratt (1872-1956): An early proponent of cognitive-behavioural therapy in America. *Journal of Medical Biography*, *22*(1), 35–46. https://doi.org/10.1177/0967772013479756.

American Art Therapy Association. (2013). *Ethical principles for art therapists*.

Arrington, D. (2016). The developmental journey. In D. E. Gussak, & M. L. Rosal (Eds.), *The Wiley handbook of art therapy* (pp. 201–209). John Wiley & Sons.

Bales, R. F. (1950). *Interaction process analysis: A method for the study of small groups*. University of Chicago Press.

Baruch, D. W., & Miller, H. (1951). The use of spontaneous drawings in group therapy. *American Journal of Psychotherapy*, *5*, 45–58.

Baumeister, R. F., & Leary, M. R. (1995). The need to belong: Desire for interpersonal attachments as a fundamental human motivation. *Psychological Bulletin*, *117*(3), 497–529.

Brown, R. (2000). *Group processes* (2nd ed.). Blackwell Publishing.

Bublitz, M. G., Rank-Christman, T., Cian, L., Cortada, X., Madzharov, A., Patrick, V. M., et al. (2019). Collaborative art: A transformational force within communities. *Journal for the Association for Consumer Research*, *4*(4). https://doi.org/10.1086/705023.

Colapinto, J. (2017). Belonging. *Journal of Systemic Therapies*, *36*(4), 91–94.

Corey, M., Corey, G., & Corey, C. (2014). *Groups: Process and practice* (9th ed.). Brookes/Cole.

Covington, H. (2003). Caring presence: Delineation of a concept for holistic nursing. *Journal of Holistic Nursing*, *21*(3), 301–317. https://doi.org/10.1177/0898010103254915.

Crane-Okada, R. (2011). The concept of presence in group psychotherapy: An operational definition. *Perspectives in Psychiatric Care*, *48*, 156–164.

Czamanski-Cohen, J., & Weilhs, K. L. (2016). The body mind model: A platform for studying the mechanisms of change induced by art therapy. *The Arts in Psychotherapy*, *51*, 63–73.

du Mont, P. M. (2002). The concept of therapeutic presence in nursing. In *International society for presence research, fifth annual international workshop on presence*. International Society. http://www.temple.edu/ispr/prev_conferences/proceedings/2002/Final%20papers/du%20Mont.pdf.

Fancourt, D., & Finn, S. (2019). What is the evidence on the role of the arts in improving health and well-being? In *Health evidence network synthesis report 67*. http://www.euro.who.int/en/publications/abstracts/what-is-the-evidence-on-the-role-of-the-arts-in-improving-health-and-well-being-a-scoping-review-2019.

Feen-Calligan, H. (2014). In memorium: Edith Kramer (1916-2014). *Art Therapy: Journal of the American Art Therapy Association*, *31*(4), 179–182.

Fink, J. E. (2014). Flourishing: Exploring predictors of mental health within the college environment. *Journal of American College Health*, *62*, 380–388. https://doi.org/10.1080/07448481.2014.917647.

Flores, P. J., & Porges, S. W. (2017). Group psychotherapy as a neural exercise: Bridging polyvagal theory and attachment theory. *International Journal of Group Psychotherapy*, *67*(2), 202–222. https://doi.org/10.1080/00207284.2016.1263544.

Foronda, C., Baptiste, D. L., Reinholdt, M. M., & Ousman, K. (2016). Cultural humility: A concept analysis. *Journal of Transcultural Nursing*, *27*, 210–217. https://doi.org/10.1177/1043659615592677.

Forsyth, D. R. (2014). *Group dynamics* (6th ed.). Wadsworth Cengage Learning.

Gabel, L., & Robb, M. (2017). (Re)considering psychological constructs: A thematic synthesis defining five therapeutic factors in group art therapy. *The Arts in Psychotherapy*, *55*, 126–135.

Gipson, L. (2019). Envisioning black women's consciousness in art therapy. In S. K. Talwar (Ed.), *Art therapy for social justice: Radical intersection* (pp. 96–120). Routledge.

Guth, L. J., Pollard, B. L., Nitza, A., Puig, A., Chan, C. D., Singh, A. A., et al. (2019). Ten strategies to intentionally use group work to transform hate, facilitate courageous conversations, and enhance community building. *Journal for Specialists in Group Work*, *44*(1), 3–24. https://doi.org/10.1080/01933922.2018.1561778.

Hale, A. (n.d.). https://www.goodreads.com/quotes/7844747-trust-the-wait-embrace-the-uncertainty-enjoy-the-beauty-of (Accessed 3 December 2021).

Hanes, K. M. (1982). *Art therapy and group work: An annotated bibliography*. Greenwood Press.

Hansan, J. E. (2011). Settlement houses: An introduction. In *Social Welfare History Project*. http://socialwelfare.library.vcu.edu/settlement-houses/settlement-houses/.

Harris, J., & Joseph, C. (1973). *Murals of the mind: Image of a psychiatric community* (p. 274). International University Press.

Henry, S. (1992). *Group skills in social work practice: A four-dimensional approach* (2nd ed.). Brooks/Cole.

Hinz, L. D. (2020). *Expressive therapies continuum: A framework for using art in therapy* (2nd ed.). Taylor & Francis.

Hoppe, M. H. (2007). Lending an ear: Why leaders must learn to listen actively. *Leadership in Action*, *27*(4), 11–14.

Horne, S. (1999). From coping to creating change: The evolution of women's groups. *Journal for Specialists in Group Work*, *24*(3), 231–245. https://doi.org/10.1080/01933929908411433.

Horovitz. (2018). *A guide to art therapy materials, methods, and applications: A practical step-by-step approach*. Routledge.

Jackson, L. C. (2020). *Cultural humility in art therapy: Applications for practice, research, social justice, self-care, and pedagogy*. Jessica Kingsley Publishers.

Jonas, W. B., & Crawford, C. C. (2004). The healing presence: Can it be reliably measured? *Journal of Alternative and Complementary Medicine*, *10*(5), 751–756. https://doi.org/10.1089/acm.2004.10.751.

Kandeler, R., & Ullrich, W. R. (2009). Symbolism of plants: Examples from European-Mediterranean culture presented with biology and history of art. *Journal of Experimental Botany*, *60*(9), 2461–2464. https://doi.org/10.1093/jxb/erp166.

Kolbe, M., & Boos, M. (2009). Facilitating group decision-making: Facilitator's subjective theories on group coordination. *FQS: Forum: Qualitative Social Research*, *10*(1).

Liebmann, M. (1986). *Art therapy for groups: A handbook of themes, games and exercises*. Brookline Books.

Liebmann, M. (2004). *Art therapy for groups: A handbook of themes and exercises* (2nd ed.). Brunner-Routledge.

Liebmann, M. (2012). Developing themes for art therapy groups. In C. Malchiodi (Ed.), *Handbook of art therapy* (pp. 368–382). The Guilford Press.

Masika, R., & Jones, J. (2016). Building student belonging and engagement: Insights into higher education students' experiences of participating and learning together. *Teaching in Higher Education*, *21*(2), 138–150. https://doi.org/10.1080/13562517.2015.1122585.

McCain, D. V., & Tobey, D. D. (2007). *Facilitation skills training*. American Society for Training and Development.

Miller, J. E., & Cutshall, S. C. (2001). *The art of being a healing presence: A guide for those in caring relationships*. Willowgreen Publishing.

Moon, B. L., & Nolan, E. G. (2020). *Ethical issues in art therapy* (4th ed.). Charles C Thomas Ltd.

Moon, C. H. (2002). *Studio art therapy: Cultivating the artist identity in the art therapist*. Jessica Kingsley Publishers.

Moon, B. L. (2010). *Art-based group therapy: Theory and practice*. Charles C Thomas Ltd.

Moon, B. L. (2016). *Art-based group therapy: Theory and practice* (2nd ed.). Charles C Thomas, Ltd.

Moon, C. H. (2016). Open studio approach to art therapy. In D. Gussak, & M. Rosal (Eds.), *The Wiley handbook of art therapy* (pp. 112–121). John Wiley & Sons.

Mosher, D. K., Hook, J. N., Farrell, J. E., Watkins, C. E., & Davis, D. E. (2017). Cultural humility. In E. L. Worthington, D. E. Davis, & J. N. Hook (Eds.), *Handbook of humility: Theory, research, and applications* (pp. 91–104). Routledge.

O'Neill, A., & Moss, H. (2015). A community art therapy group for adults with chronic pain. *Art Therapy: Journal of the American Art Therapy Association, 32*(4), 158–167.

Prapavessis, H., & Carron, A. V. (1997). Cohesion and work output. *Small Group Research, 28*(2), 294–301. https://doi.org/10.1177/1046496497282006.

Reiter, M. D. (2017). Salvador Minuchin, MD: Innovator and challenger. *Journal of Systemic Therapies*, 16–22. https://doi.org/10.1521/jsyt.2017.36.4.16.

Riley, S. (2001). *Group process made visible: Group art therapy.* Routledge.

Riley-Hiscox, A. (1997). Interview—Cliff Joseph: Art therapist, pioneer, artist. *Art Therapy: Journal of the American Art Therapy Association*, 273–278. https://doi.org/10.1080/07421656.1987.10759297.

Robb, M.A. (2022). *Group art therapy: Practice and research.* Routledge.

Rosal, M. (2016). Rethinking and reframing group art therapy: An amalgamation of British and US models. In D. Gussak, & M. Rosal (Eds.), *The Wiley handbook of art therapy* (pp. 231–241). John Wiley & Sons.

Rossetto, E. (2012). A hermeneutic phenomenological study of community mural making and social action art therapy. *Art Therapy: Journal of the American Art Therapy Association, 29*(1), 19–26. https://doi.org/10.1080/07421656.2012.648105.

Rubin, J. A. (2010). *An introduction to art therapy: Sources & resources* (2nd ed.). Routledge.

Schofield, S. (2019). Group art therapy, aesthetic experiences of difference and belonging. *Language and Psychoanalysis, 8*(1), 30–68. https://doi.org/10.7565/landp.v8i1.1591.

Schroder, D. (2005). *Little windows into art therapy.* Jessica Kingsley Publisher.

Schwartz, J. B., Rastogi, M., Pate, M. C., & Scarce, J. H. (2021). Undergraduate art therapy programs in the United States survey report. *Art Therapy: Journal of the American Art Therapy Association*, 33–41. https://doi.org/10.1080/07421656.2019.1698226.

Siegel, D. J. (1999). *The developing mind: How relationships and the brain interact to shape who we are.* Guilford Press.

Singh, C., & Salazer, C. (2010). The roots of social justice in group work. *The Journal for Specialists in Group Work, 35*(2), 97–104. https://doi.org/10.1080/01933921003706048.

Springham, N., & Huet, V. (2018). Art as relational encounter: An ostensive communication theory of art therapy. *Art Therapy: Journal of the American Art Therapy Association, 35*(1), 4–10. https://doi.org/10.1080/07421656.2018.1460103.

Stanley, K. J. (2002). The healing power of presence: Respite from the fear of abandonment. *Oncology Nursing Forum, 29*(6), 935–940. https://doi.org/10.1188/02.ONF.935-940.

Stepney, S. A. (2019). Visionary architects of color in art therapy: Georgette Powell, Cliff Joseph, Lucille Venture, and Charles Anderson. *Art Therapy: Journal of the American Art Therapy Association, 36*(3), 115–121. https://doi.org/10.1080/07421656.2019.1649545.

Sue, D. W. (2001). Multidimensional facets of cultural competence. *The Counseling Psychologist, 29*(6), 790–821. https://doi.org/10.1177/0011000001296002.

Topornycky, J., & Golparian, S. (2016). Balancing openness and interpretation in active listening. In *Collected essays on learning and teaching* (pp. 175–184). https://doi.org/10.22329/celt.v9i0.4430.

Toseland, R. W., & Rivas, R. F. (2017). *An introduction to group work practice* (8th ed.). Pearson.

Trecker, H. (1972). *Social work group: Principles and practices.* Association Press.

Tuckman, B. W., & Jensen, M. C. (1977). *Stages of small group development revisited.* Group & Organization Studies.

Tuckman, B. W. (1965). Developmental sequence in small groups. *Psycological Bulliten, 63*(6), 384–399. https://doi.org/10.1037/h0022100.

Wheelan, S. (1994). *Group processes: A developmental perspective.* Allyn & Bacon.

Williams, K., & Tripp, T. (2016). Group art therapy. In J. A. Rubin (Ed.), *Approaches to art therapy: Theory and technique* (3rd ed., pp. 417–432). Routledge.

Wix, L. (2000). Looking for what's lost: The artistic roots of art therapy: Mary Huntoon. *Art Therapy: Journal of the American Art Therapy Association, 17*(3), 168–176. https://doi.org/10.1080/07421656.2000.1012.

Yalom, I. D., & Leszcz, M. (2005). *The theory and practice of group psychotherapy* (5th ed.). Basic Books.

Yalom, I. D., & Leszcz, M. (2020). *The theory and practice of group psychotherapy* (6th ed.). Basic Books.

Chapter 15

Community-based art therapy and community arts

Michelle Pate, DAT, LCMHC, ATR-BC[a], Meera Rastogi, PhD, ATR-BC[b], and Vittoria Daiello, PhD[c]

[a]*Psychology and Applied Therapies, Lesley University, Cambridge, MA, United States,* [b]*Department of Social Sciences, University of Cincinnati, Clermont College, Batavia, OH, United States,* [c]*Art Education, College of Design, Architecture, Art, and Planning, University of Cincinnati, Cincinnati, OH, United States*

Voices from the field

(C)ommunity art therapy acknowledges that the fabric of culture provides the necessary healing context for individual healing, therapeutic art making, and transformative community dialogue.

Timm-Bottos (2011, p. 63)

Learning outcomes

After reading this chapter, you will be able to

1. Describe the origins and key elements of community-based art therapy.
2. Compare and contrast community-based art therapy and community arts.
3. Describe how art can contribute to rebuilding and strengthening communities.
4. Articulate how art therapists are uniquely trained to work in community-based settings.
5. Distinguish the similarities and differences between community-based art therapy and community arts settings.
6. Identify and explain the roles and responsibilities for facilitators of community-based arts programs.
7. Provide examples of community-based art therapy and social practice art.
8. Explain two main criticisms of community-based arts programs.

Chapter overview

In this chapter we explore the connections between community-based art therapy and community arts while also articulating differences between art therapy and arts programs. We begin the chapter by defining community-based art therapy, community, and community arts. We try to identify ways these programs

Foundations of Art Therapy. https://doi.org/10.1016/B978-0-12-824308-4.00016-8

overlap, how they differ, and we provide the basic roles and responsibilities for those interested in this work. Several key reasons are identified as to why arts programs are important to communities which include increasing accessibility and affordability of support services, providing services that have less stigma, and rebuilding and strengthening communities. Historical conflicts in the field of art therapy that have led to the development of community-based art therapy work and the theoretical foundations of the community-based approach are explored next. The second half of the chapter describes types of community-based art therapy programs and also provides examples of social practice art. The chapter concludes with criticisms about community-based arts programs.

What is community-based art therapy?

Community-based art therapy has been defined as therapeutic, collaborative art-making experiences that enhance the connections among community members and focus on themes determined jointly by the art therapist and the community (Ottemiller & Awais, 2016). Community-based art therapy provides a place where interactions among people, in arts contexts, can create social change and individual empowerment (Reyhani Dejkameh & Shipps, 2018). Art plays an important role in communities, serving a variety of different needs and interests. However, artists' and art therapists' community work is often motivated by a deep commitment to social justice. **Social justice** values human rights, accessibility to resources, fairness, and equality for all people and understands people's experiences through a systemic lens (Talwar, 2018). Given their overlapping interests in social justice and the variety of ways in which artists and art therapists work with communities, it may be difficult to distinguish between community-based art therapy and other forms of community arts. In this chapter we explore community-based art therapy as a continuum of practices that involve experiential, interactive processes, interest in social change, and the use of art to create transformations for communities and individuals, empowering them to shape the future they desire (Kapitan et al., 2011).

Thinking together: An invitation to a conversation

Does it matter if arts practices within a community are called "community-based art therapy" or referred to as "community arts" initiatives that help people? The authors have debated this question, and many others, during the writing of this chapter. After reviewing the research in the field, reflecting on our work as artists, art therapists, a psychologist, and an art educator we found that the distinctions are not always clear. We believe that there is still much to learn about community arts interventions and their specific effects on an individual's quality of life as well as their long-term effects on community health and well-being. Therefore, in the spirit of community, we envision this chapter as a conversation about an art therapy topic that is currently being defined, articulated, and understood. We invite you into this conversation and encourage you to bring curiosity, critical perspectives, and questions to your encounter with the ideas. In sum, we invite you to think together with us. As a form of engagement that opens up a dialogue with the world (Bennett & Zournazi, 2019; Serres, 2020), thinking together is both an individual and communal project, a generative and creative process of sense making, not unlike the critical, dialogical work that art therapists do with individuals and communities.

The scope of community-based art therapy

It is difficult to know how many art therapists facilitate community-based art therapy. The most recent membership survey assessed the work settings of art therapists, several of which we consider community-based (American Art Therapy Association, March, 2021). For example, 15.6% of respondents identified their work setting as an art center/studio, 1.5% at a homeless shelter, and 1.1% at a domestic violence shelter (American Art Therapy Association, March, 2021). If we combine these three community-based settings, community art therapy may encompass the third largest work setting for art therapists (following independent practice and outpatient mental health settings). Despite possibly being the third largest work setting for art therapists, community-based art therapy has received minimal attention. Yet, healthcare inequities worldwide have increased the need for community wellness and prevention resources; these demands have outpaced the rate of research on community-based art therapy (Ottemiller & Awais, 2016). To address these gaps, Feen-Calligan et al. (2018) encourage art therapists and art therapy students to engage in service work and community-based research to respond to community needs.

Determining the number of art therapists who are working in community-based art therapy can be difficult due to the elasticity of the definition of "community." For instance, a group of people who live within a bounded geographic location could be called a community. Community could also refer to people who come together around a shared identity such as LGBTQ+, yet reside in different geographic places while interacting online. We therefore begin our exploration of community-based art therapy by defining the concept of community.

What is a community?

When you hear the word community, what comes to mind? Maybe you think of the town you live in, the individuals who attend your school, or those who belong to a religious organization. While these are communities, there is a much broader view of what encompasses a community. For the purposes of this chapter we are defining **community** as the coming together of people in provisional groups as a result of specific circumstances such as shared concerns about neighborhood policing, or individuals engaged in short-term, collective action such as an artist-initiated public dialogue that serves as the artwork in a community (Khan, 2015; Meban, 2009).

The phrase "community-based" used in relation to art therapy and community arts practices draws our attention to the broad systems of society and the diverse relationships and interactions in which individuals make meaning for themselves and in relation to others. Within a community-based context, art therapy and arts practices can be thought of as forms of collective, creative action. These practices can even become opportunities for individual and group **self-reflexivity**, using art to develop critically conscious perspectives on the sociocultural systems that shape the distinctive nature of each community (Karcher, 2017). Developing a **critically conscious** perspective begins with asking questions that seek out assumptions and self-reflexivity grows from questioning one's own assumptions. As you think about all the different communities in which you participate, ask yourself, what are the defining characteristics of each? What do the members of these communities have in common? Who is not part of these communities and why? Finally, how might art help facilitate personal growth and collective flourishing within these social systems?

Community arts

Community-based art therapy has a close affinity with community arts not only because of their community-centric context but also because their roots are entwined with developments in the Western art world that validated the many forms of arts practices occurring beyond museums, in communities.

In this chapter we use the phrase **community arts** to refer to those artistic activities within a community setting that are characterized by interactions among people who may not otherwise engage in the arts and that involve professional artists or others who may collaborate with community members (Tate Britain, 2021). Community arts can encompass a range of socially engaged and social practice art initiatives that include art created by people with shared interests and goals that are attended to by people living in a common area (Adejumo, 2000), art that is produced to express concerns and issues affecting that community (Carter, 2012), and efforts to organize and maintain networks of people whose support of arts and culture will facilitate inclusivity, creativity, and change based upon a community's needs (Kirk et al., 2012).

Community arts take many different forms such as public viewing of music and dance performances, attending museum exhibitions and poetry readings, learning about art in a community's schools, and making art for personal or professional reasons. Art, in some form, touches the lives of everyone in a community. In fact, art has been called one of the "most complex and diverse of human achievements" created through "free human will and conscious execution" (Dutton, 2009, p. 1). Art, art-making, and receptiveness to art have even been described by some as an evolutionary trait, an adaptive human characteristic that reinforces communality and solidarity of a group while passing on emotional dispositions that contribute to community cohesiveness (Dissanayake, 2013; Mithen, 1996).

Community arts and community-based art therapy have emerged within a contemporary aesthetic perspective which embraces a broad and diverse view of art. Within this expanded aesthetic field, a vast range of phenomena in the world can be considered art, from fine art to popular visual culture, to objects and experiences that exist outside museums, to performances and ephemeral happenings (Irvin, 2008; Shusterman, 2000). Some of these art forms are described as relational aesthetic and social practice projects (Bourriaud, 2002; Kester, 2004; Thompson, 2012).

French Art Critic Nicolas Bourriaud (2002) coined the term **relational aesthetics** to describe art practices that feature interactions among people as the primary means of artistic production. Artist Rirkrit Tiravanija's *pad thai*, featured at the Paula Allen Gallery in New York in 1990, is often cited as an early example of relational aesthetics. Rejecting the creation of art objects in a traditional sense, Tiravanija instead focused on the act of cooking and serving food and the interactions of people around the cooking itself, bringing attention to art as a potential social space (Yao, 2019). While the concept of relational aesthetics was initially employed in explaining artists' work that defied fine arts traditions and resisted elite museum culture, this phrase sometimes appears in descriptions of the more overtly activist socially engaged or social practice art that developed later (Kester, 2004).

The phrase **social practice art** emerged to describe "deeply participatory" experiences that seek to create social change, blurring lines among "object making, performance, political activism, community organizing, environmentalism and investigative journalism" (Kennedy, 2013, para. 4). Artist Rick Lowe's *Project Row Houses* in Houston's Third Ward community is an example of social practice art that changed the landscape and social trajectory of a neighborhood through the transformation of a block and a half of dilapidated shotgun houses into a site of sustainable opportunities for artists, young mothers, small businesses, and Third Ward residents (Project Row Houses, 2021).

We began this chapter by inviting you to think with us as we develop a definition of community-based art therapy and explore its meaning for individuals and communities. To this end, we defined the concepts of "community" and "community arts" in an effort to build an understanding of the context within which community-based art therapy is operating. In the process, we learned how community arts initiatives may be referred to as relational aesthetics or socially engaged arts practices within the art world. We further learned that socially engaged, community arts practices often emphasize human relationships, interactive art processes, participation in dialogues, and activist motivations. We are now ready to ask, how are community arts endeavors similar to or different from community-based art therapy? The answer, it seems, is very complicated.

Community-based art therapy and community arts

The complexity of defining community-based art therapy and community arts arises from the nature of their overlapping qualities and the reality that community-based art therapy will function not as a single method or technique, but as a continuum of experiences that respond to the situation in which an art therapist is working (Potash et al., 2016). In essence, the art therapist who engages in community-based art therapy and artists who work in community arts projects must be highly sensitive to the needs of a community while using the specific tools and training of their own discipline.

Similarities

As described in the previous paragraphs, community-based art therapy and community arts share these common elements:

1. Work is based *within the community*. Both community-based art therapy and community arts have the professional (therapist or artist) working within the community itself. The community setting for the work separates it from the standard practice of the therapist or artist who have clients visit their offices or studio space.
2. Both types of work *focus on collaboration* between the professional and the community. According to Ottemiller and Awais (2016), **collaboration** means that both parties work together, utilize their strengths and skills, and make decisions together. The professional listens to the needs of the community and identifies goals that meet the community's needs.
3. *Prioritizes interactions among people*. These interactions may be the primary purpose of the work or may even be considered the "artwork" itself, as in the 2005 UK project *Lounging on Red Couches: A public dialogue on safety in Hyde Park* which consisted of an outdoor public lounge where residents engaged in dialogues about safety concerns in their community (Blundell Jones & Fiala, 2005).
4. Addresses a *social issue*. Both community-based art therapy and community arts utilize art to address social issues of concern. Examples of social issues that have been addressed through art by both artists and art therapists include individual and collective trauma resulting from natural disasters such as hurricanes, and community threats such as gun violence, sexual assault, and terrorist attacks (Shipley et al., 2021). Artist Mel Chin's 2006 *Fundred Dollar Bill Project* is an example of a long-term arts endeavor that generated financial relief for New Orleans in the aftermath of Hurricane Katrina. In *Revival Field* (1991), Chin used art pragmatically and metaphorically in the environment with a conceptual sculpture artwork consisting of living plants that draw toxic metals from the soil (Bhatt, 2021).

Differences

Although there is overlap between community-based art therapy and community arts practices there are some differences. Interdisciplinary theorist and writer Allen Weiss (1992) made a clear distinction between art therapy and artists' workshops observing that "art therapy has therapy as its primary goal, and not the creation of art," while "art workshops have the creation of 'art'—even if at a rudimentary, didactic level—as its primary aim" (p. 67). We find a space for productive dialogue in the overlap of the two practices and we offer the following comparisons and contrasts, not as a final word on the boundaries of community-based art therapy and community arts but as observations to point the way toward continuing explorations.

1. *Boundaries and discipline*. An important distinction between community arts and community-based art therapy is found in the training and qualifications of those who work in community arts endeavors. Artists, activists, and art educators may work in community settings in which art therapists are practicing (Hacking et al., 2008; Junge et al., 2009; Lawton, 2019; Lawton et al., 2019); however, there are differences in this work. Kalmanowitz and Potash (2010) call for a "**sensitive**" or "**ethical use of art-making**" in which arts professionals who are not trained in art therapy must observe their own disciplinary boundaries (p. 22). For instance, an art educator who engages in community arts work is not practicing art therapy, but is instead using their art-making skill set "within their own professional boundaries and scope of practice" as a teacher of art (p. 22). These boundaries are important, because although community arts endeavors may bring positive outcomes for individuals and communities, only art therapists have specific training for using art-making to guide social actions into therapeutic outcomes, observing their responsibility toward the client and the integrity of the art therapy profession (Kalmanowitz & Potash, 2010).
2. *Focus of facilitation*. Although nonart therapists and art therapists are facilitators of community-based arts projects, each has a discipline specific focus in their facilitation. For art therapists, the facilitation focuses on what Potash et al. (2016) refer to as the **spectrum of art therapy practice**. This spectrum refers to behavioral health practice, but we can apply the spectrum concept to describe the variety of work community-based art therapists are trained to do: prevention (adaptive coping), lifestyle management (promoting healthy choices), wellness (self-care, stress management), therapy (insight, change), rehabilitation (returning to health), and social action (social issues or community empowerment) (Potash et al., 2016, pp. 121–123). In contrast, nonart therapists who are involved in community arts projects may vary their focus more on the art process, the people involved in the project, or the art itself; however, only the art therapist has the specialized training to use art in implementing the spectrum of art therapy outcomes. While therapeutic benefits may be derived from

having an expressive artwork in a community, these benefits are often not the main point of the community art project.

3. *Facilitator's role in the art-making process.* An art therapist has been trained to encourage the community member to make all decisions about their artwork. This member-led art-making process encourages independence which builds self-confidence and leads to multiple art therapy outcomes. To this end, the art therapist rarely touches the art piece and instead acts as a coach or mentor by supporting the member through a problem-solving process. Art Therapist Edith Kramer described this process as the "Third Hand." Kramer defined the **third hand** as "a hand that helps the creative process along without being intrusive, without distorting meaning or imposing pictorial ideas or preferences alien to the client ... [art therapists] must cultivate an area of artistic competence ... employed solely for empathic service to others" (Kramer, 2000, p. 48). In contrast, artist-led community projects will engage community members for input, but the artist designs the community art product. In some projects, residents may work with the artist to complete the art piece; in others, the artist and their team might perform all of the work.

Unique fit: Art therapist in the community setting

Ottemiller and Awais (2016) argue that art therapists have a unique set of skills that are particularly useful in the community setting. Art therapists have completed academic coursework in several different types of fine arts media which provides them with knowledge of art media and aesthetic understandings. Art therapists are also trained in group facilitation, conflict resolution, how to handle participants' emotional responses to their work (Lawthom et al., 2007; Ottemiller & Awais, 2016), and working with art materials and artwork in therapeutic ways (Hinz, 2019). In addition, an art therapist's counseling skills are helpful when working with groups and processing emotions (Finkelpearl, 2013). The combination of the fine arts skills with the counseling skills makes art therapists uniquely suited to community-based art therapy. Table 15.1 identifies the specific skills of the artist, art educator, counselor, and art therapist.

In spite of the differences between community arts and community-based art therapy noted before, these practices may be conflated due to their overlapping interests, motivations, values, histories, and locations within the community. One overlap, in particular, stands out: ethical issues. Both art therapists and artists who engage in community artwork must be aware of the ethical responsibilities that come with activities involving dialogic interactions, social and political activism, and the application of art to address concerns of personal and communal consequence (Meban, 2009). Indeed, social practice art is a topic of robust debate among art historians and theorists, some of whom celebrate the positive effects of these collectivist actions in communities (Kester, 2004), and others who question the ethical implications of art interventions

TABLE 15.1 Art therapist's unique skill set.

Characteristics	Artist	Art educator	Counselor	Art therapist
Knowledge of material	X	X		X
Understanding of aesthetics	X	X		X
Conflict resolution			X	X
Group dynamics		X	X	X
Trauma training			X	X

This chart outlines the unique skills of an art therapist compared to those of an artist, art educator, and counselor.
Adapted from Ottemiller, D. D., Awais, Y. J. (2016). A model for art therapists in community based practice. Art Therapy: Journal of the American Art Therapy Association, 33, 144–150. https://doi.org/10.1080/07421656.2016.1199245.

that rely on the uncompensated labor of community members (Bishop, 2012a). Adding another provocation to the debate, Thompson (2009) asserts that community arts practices addressing power, privilege, and oppression are themselves a form of therapy. This raises the question, can community-based art therapy also be considered a form of social practice art?

In focusing on the different ways in which community artists and community-based art therapists approach the issues of healing and facilitation, we find some important distinctions between community arts and community-based art therapy. However, we recognize that the experience of healing, in particular, can be challenging to pinpoint in these settings because of the subjective nature of human experience. That is, healing and therapeutic experience can be inextricably intertwined. Catherine Moon (2016b) acknowledged the complexity of art therapy's relational qualities, an observation that is especially apt in community-based art therapy contexts. She noted that a traditional view of the "relationship between the therapist and client, contained within the private space of the office or studio" is perhaps unrealistic; the experience of art therapy in our contemporary context is in actuality a "much wider and and more complicated" situation (p. 60). Assessing the relational context of community-based art therapy through artist Mel Chin's observation about his practice, we find a succinct summary about community arts work that we believe also rings true for community-based art therapists: "This is not about me making an art project; it's about people's lives" (Gordon, 2019, para. 6). After reading the similarities and differences between community-based art therapy and community arts noted earlier, do you think some of these distinctions are more or less important than others?

Why are community-based art therapy and community arts important?

Now that we have defined community-based art therapy and community arts along with outlining their similarities and differences, we will address why this work is important to communities. Community-based art therapy increases the accessibility of art therapy services to underserved and often marginalized populations (Ottemiller & Awais, 2016). **Marginalized communities** are "those excluded from mainstream social, economic, educational, and/or cultural life" (Sevelius et al., 2020, p. 1). Additionally, persons of color and other marginalized groups have been mistreated by the medical community which has created a lack of trust in traditional healthcare (Kumagai & Lypson, 2009; Talwar, 2016; Vick & Sexton-Radek, 2008). These community members may be drawn to community-based art therapy as a shift away from traditional settings that may not recognize their needs (Kapitan, 2008). When used to identify and address social problems in communities, art can have an enduring impact in people's lives. While public discussions and community forums may fade from memory, art can remain, building a collective sense of self-esteem (Che, 2007).

As introduced in Chapter 1, Art Therapist Georgette Powell (1916–2011) is an example of an art therapist who offered art therapy in communities. Powell saw a need in Washington D.C. for community members to come together and support each other, so she began organizing art-making and exhibitions for community members using grocery store parking lots that were closed on Sundays (Gipson, 2018; Hurtibise, 2008). Powell also opened the Powell Art Studio (Gipson, 2018; Hayden & Stearns, 2006) where she offered space for community members to create in addition to Tomorrow's World Art Center and Art in the Park (Boston & Short, 2006; Gipson, 2018; Hurtibise, 2008).

In addition to serving marginalized communities, community-based art therapy offers services associated with less stigma. According to the National Institute of Mental Health (NIMH, 2021), only 44.8% of adults 18 years and older diagnosed with any mental illness sought out treatment in 2019 and stigma may be preventing people from seeking treatment. As discussed in Chapter 11, **stigma** are the stereotypes, beliefs, or preconceived ideas toward members of a certain group, including those diagnosed with a mental illness or those seeking mental health treatment (Rössler, 2016). The stigma of mental illness can occur on three levels: public, structural, and self-stigma (Corrigan & Bink, 2005; Ong et al., 2020; Rüsch et al., 2005). **Public stigma** is "defined as the endorsement of stereotypes, prejudices, and acts of discrimination toward people from a stigmatized group" (Ong et al., 2020, p. 2), **structural stigma** is associated with policies whether intentional or not that create inequities (Corrigan & Bink, 2005; Ong et al., 2020; Rüsch et al., 2005) and finally, **self-stigma** is when an individual believes the public and structural stigmas that have been placed and begins to identify themselves with the stigma (Corrigan & Watson, 2002; Ong et al., 2020; also mentioned in Chapter 11).

The stigma of mental illness can be found across different cultures, genders, races, and socioeconomic statuses (Angermeyer & Dietrich, 2006; Ong et al., 2020; Thornicroft et al., 2009). Specifically, in Western cultures, the stigma toward mental health services often prevents individuals from seeking services (Hackler et al., 2010; Topkaya et al., 2017; Vogel et al., 2009), which can result in exacerbated symptoms and increased isolation, depression, and lower self-esteem (Chronister et al., 2013; Ottemiller & Awais, 2016; Perlick et al., 2001). Community-based art therapy participants can begin to deepen their artistic sensibility by embodying the "sense of self as an artist through the integration of artistic and aesthetic attributes of self and others" (Thompson, 2009, p. 159). By building this sensibility, people can identify themselves positively, rather than as damaged, marginalized, or stigmatized.

In addition to the benefits offered by community-based art therapy, community arts can also help in rebuilding and further strengthening communities. Investment in the arts can inspire community regeneration through the establishment of positive behavior patterns and commitment to shared goals (Supple & Plunkett, 2011). These changes help community members to take pride in their community and feel supported which in turn can decrease crime (Blackman, 2011). Art facilitates change through participation and regeneration (Jones & Wyse, 2005; Kay, 2000) and can serve as a voice for community empowerment (Hocoy, 2005) that can rebuild damaged communities by bringing people together to discuss even the most difficult issues using a shared art medium (Goldbard, 2009). Art has also been an element in a city's process of economic revitalization that has "linked creative industries and peoples with economic development" (Che, 2007, p. 34) as community members are often able to earn income from their art, consequently strengthening the economy of their families and neighborhoods (Ritok & Bodoczky, 2012).

There are many communities in the United States that are thriving, in part, because of a strong community arts presence. For example, St. Paul, Minnesota has collaborated with artists as partners with the city government. "Here, artists don't merely make sculptures and murals to adorn the urban landscape; they have a meaningful role in city government and participate in the conception, development, and implementation of all manner of city projects" (Schoweiler, 2013, p. 57). St. Paul is a model of a city that is thriving from the activities of its arts community. St. Paul offers several artists-in-residence programs in which artists work with the Public Works Department to develop creative options for building the city. Such programs are intended to encourage "long-lived connections among neighborhood artists, residents, and business owners" (Schoweiler, 2013, p. 60). For example, a local artist and student proposed to make vacant storefronts available to local artists and small organizations with short-term leases, a win for all parties: low-cost rent, encouraging community engagement through art, and giving property owners income.

Having explored some of the ways in which community-based art therapy and community arts play an important role in a community's quality of life, we now look to the history and theory of these practices and ask the question: How did community-based art therapy develop?

Historical approaches and theoretical approaches

Defining the practice of art therapy has been an ongoing discussion since art therapy began. The dominant conflict surrounding the definition of art therapy has focused on viewing art therapy as psychotherapy versus viewing the art as the therapy (Talwar, 2016). What are the differences between these two approaches? How did this division contribute to the development of community-based art therapy?

Historical art therapy foundations

Clinical approach: Art therapy as psychotherapy

As briefly described in Chapter 1, the dichotomy between the two approaches (art psychotherapy versus art as therapy) began with Margaret Naumburg who was a "dynamically oriented" therapist and wrote about her work through this lens (Junge, 2016, p. 7). Naumburg viewed art therapy as a form of psychotherapy, underwent analysis herself, and worked at the New York State Psychiatric Institute (Junge, 2016). This psychotherapy orientation was further supported by the emphasis on psychoanalysis at the same time, the emergence of numerous artists working at mental health institutions, and the development of several art therapy programs in psychiatric units in hospitals in the Midwest (Menninger, Winter General Hospital, Marlboro State Hospital, Menninger Clinic, and the Columbus State Hospital; Junge, 2016, p. 11).

At the first formal meeting of art therapists in 1968, the definition of art therapy as ***art psychotherapy*** was the subject of debate and this perspective continues to be challenged today. Allen (1992), who believed that art therapists are uniquely skilled in facilitating and observing the client's work with art materials, claimed that the concept of art psychotherapy "clinified" the field of art therapy. Allen (1992) defined the **clinification** of art therapy as the therapist placing emphasis on the following: clinical skills at the expense of art skills, discussion of the art image is predominant, and the image is interpreted in relation to the person's diagnosis. Spooner (2016) further criticized the art therapy profession for continuing to align itself with mental health counseling which can be seen today in the Standards and Guidelines of Educational Programs in Art Therapy (2016) and in the American Art Therapy Association's definition of art therapy (see Chapter 1). How does this clinical approach compare to the studio or art as the therapy approach?

Studio approach: Art as the therapy

Art as the therapy, known as **art as therapy,** emphasizes the process of creating the art product. This approach was originally described by Art Therapist Edith Kramer. As mentioned in Chapter 1, Kramer did not view herself as a therapist, as she did very little talking during her sessions (Gray, 2012; Junge, 2016). In fact, Kramer believed the "art making process provides the means to dwell deeply and fully in those memories and feelings" (Junge, 2016, p. 23) and that the art-making provides a space to help clients regulate and contain emotions, so they are not overwhelmed. According to Block et al. (2005), a **studio approach** to art therapy is characterized by "intention, art-making, witness-writing, and sharing, as well as no commenting and no forced participation," while also being "versatile enough to nurture people within their respective circumstances" (p. 33). Therefore, studio work prioritizes the process of art-making over verbal descriptions and underlying meaning. The studio approach uses the art-making process to increase self-awareness through self-direction (McGraw, 1995). More often, the studio approach to art therapy may also offer artists the opportunity to exhibit their work in galleries, storefronts, or community gatherings. Read more about the studio approach in the "Community-based art therapy settings" section.

Challenging the dichotomy: The emergence of community-based art therapy

Although there have been many differing views of what art therapy is (Agell & McNiff, 1982; Ault, 1976; Kramer et al., 1994; Moon, 2002; Shoemaker et al., 1976; Timm-Bottos, 1995), the dichotomous views of art psychotherapy versus art as therapy remain (Talwar, 2016). Potash et al. (2016) asserted that this "binary thinking" (p. 120) does not reflect the actual practice of art therapy. Sajnani et al. (2017) critically analyzed the traditional practice of art therapy and suggested art therapists and other expressive art therapists can practice a more flexible approach to expressive therapies that focused on people's strengths and acknowledges the influence of social and political environment. Similarly, Talwar (2016) stated that art therapy should reflect more than our psychological state and should also include the social and political influences that surround and influence our daily lives.

These differing views and debates have a long history in art therapy. For example, Potash and Ramirez (2013) recalled the early meetings of the art therapy founders and their attempts to narrow the definition of art therapy. Yet, in 1970, Art Therapists Wayne Ramirez, Lucille Venture, and Edith Kramer spoke against the narrowing of the definition of art therapy that emphasizes the psychiatric setting while excluding other settings, such as community-based or studio art therapy (Potash, 2005; Potash & Ramirez, 2013). Despite these early attempts, and many attempts since, to address the inequities of a narrowed art therapy definition the profession has continued to move into the direction of viewing art therapy as a clinical practice. One way for art therapists to engage in social justice work is to view art therapy on a spectrum instead of the hybrid perspective (Potash et al., 2016; Sajnani et al., 2017). Thus community-based art therapy expands the dichotomous definition of art therapy. The next section explores theoretical foundations that have contributed to the community-based art therapy practices we see today that further challenge a dichotomous approach to art therapy.

Social action art therapy

Social action art therapy combines concepts from community-based art therapy with critical and liberation psychology. **Social action art therapy** uses art activities outside of the traditional mental health therapy setting to address social problems, help individuals cope with environmental and social issues, and "create a stronger sense of community … through … shared activity" (Kaplan, 2016, p. 790). Several art therapists practice social action art therapy and their work is described next.

Leah Gipson, a Chicago-based art therapist, artist, educator, and community activist, focuses on black feminism and social change. Gipson has been a board member of A Long Walk Home, a Chicago-based organization, for over 12 years. "A Long Walk Home empowers young artists and activists to end violence against all girls and women. We advocate for racial and gender equity in schools, communities, and our country-at-large" (A Long Walk Home, 2021). The organization was founded in 2013 by sisters Salamishah Tillet, who is a writer, activist, and rape survivor and Scheherazade Tillet, who is a photographer, youth organizer, and art therapist. As a board member and art therapist, Gipson created a series of art therapy projects to empower young girls and women and respond to violence against women (Gipson, 2021). In 2016 Gipson received the Propeller Fund Award for her work with the Austin Neighborhood Studio Co-op on the construction of The Rectory, a partnership with an Episocopal church to develop a collaborative artist studio partnership (Propeller Fund, 2021).

Cliff Joseph (1922–2020), a graduate of Pratt University's Illustration Program, started his career as a commercial artist but was inspired to join the field of art therapy by the civil rights movement and his desire to have a greater impact (Gipson, 2018; Riley-Hiscox, 1997). Joseph went on to obtain a job at Abraham Jacobi Hospital in the Bronx in the activities department. Joseph was familiar with the writings of Art Therapists Edith Kramer and Margaret Naumburg but did not pursue the education of an art therapist until he met Edith Kramer, who also worked at the Hospital (Riley-Hiscox, 1997).

Along with Joseph's work in hospitals, he cofounded The Black Emergency Cultural Coalition (BECC) with fellow artist Benny Andrews in response to exclusion of Black artists in the 1969 exhibition *Harlem on My Mind, Cultural Capital of Black America, 1900–1968* at the Metropolitan Museum of Art (Stepney, 2019). BECC continued on to develop "an arts exchange program in correctional facilities" and support arts programs in mental health facilities and juvenile detention centers (Schomburg Center for Research in Black Culture, The New York Public Library, n.d.). Joseph continued to be an activist, worked with oppressed communities, and called attention to inequities through art (Moon, 2016; Stepney, 2019).

Nonart therapy theoretical foundations and concepts

Although the roots of community-based art therapy have not been explicitly explored in the art therapy literature, community-based art therapy shares theoretical ideas with community psychology, liberation psychology, critical psychology, disability studies, harm reduction, socially engaged art, and art education. Some of these theoretical underpinnings were noted by Moon and Shuman's (2013) chapter on the community art studio. These foundations of community-based art therapy are explored next.

Community psychology

Community psychology, officially founded in 1965 (Fryer & Duckett, 2014), has been defined as an approach to psychology that shifts the focus from the individual to the interactions between individuals and their environment in hopes of making changes through social action (Kloos et al., 2020). Community psychology addresses problems by examining structural changes instead of only treating the individual. Community psychology looks at the multiple systems that affect individuals such as those that have a direct influence on the individual (called **microsystems**) to larger societal and cultural influences (called **macrosystems**) (Kloos et al., 2020), and levels in between these two. The type of interventions in community psychology include prevention, consultation, organizing or bringing members together, and community-based research. Kloos et al. (2020) identified eight core values in community psychology. They define **values** as "deeply held ideals about what is moral, right, or good" (p. 23) and these values help to inform "research and action" (p. 24). The eight core values of community psychology include social justice, respect for diversity, importance of community, collective wellness, empowerment and participation, collaboration, empirical grounding, and multilevel, strengths perspective (p. 25).

Similar to community psychology, we believe that community-based art therapy shares the focus on the interactions among the individual person and context or environment. Community-based art therapists and community psychologists share the values of social justice, human diversity, importance of community, collective wellness, empowerment, and collaboration. In our review of the literature for this chapter, community-based art therapy research has not placed emphasis on empirical grounding or the use of the multilevel strength-based perspectives. The lack of attention to these two areas highlights the differences between these two approaches. How might empirical grounding and/or the multilevel strength-based perspective enhance or hinder the development of community-based art therapy?

Liberation psychology

Liberation psychology has roots in community psychology and movements in Latin America. This approach seeks to understand and address oppression and its systemic effects on the individual (Rivera & Comas-Díaz, 2020). Therapists who practice liberation psychology use collaborative approaches, understand the systemic consequences of oppression, and highlight people's strengths. We believe all of these qualities are reflected in the community-based art therapy approach.

Critical psychology

Critical psychology examines the abuses of "power" in psychology. For example, critical psychology challenges the use of psychological categories to describe and diagnose people and believes traditional psychology often does not take into account "power, history, and context" (Teo, 2015, p. 246). Similarly, community-based art therapy shifts the focus of art therapy practice from individual diagnosis and treatment to exploring and validating the perspectives of community members through art (Moon & Shuman, 2013).

Critical disability studies

Critical disability studies views disability as important as other identity markers (such as ethnic identity, gender, etc.) and is deserving of attention when addressing social justice issues (Wexler & Derby, 2020). Critical disability studies assert that people with disabilities are often ignored, overlooked, and viewed through a deficit lens (Moon & Shuman, 2013; Wexler & Derby, 2020). Disability studies seek to disrupt "the white, abled dominance of the art world" (Wexler & Derby, 2020, p. 5) by challenging "exclusionary practices" (p. 6). Similar to disability studies, approaches in community-based art therapy seek to address issues related to diversity, equity, and inclusion through collaboratively run art programs that seek to empower members of the community.

Harm reduction and radical acceptance

Harm reduction is the approach described by Moon and Shuman (2013) which they defined as "radical acceptance of all people" (p. 298). **Harm reduction** or **radical acceptance** is an approach that is used to reduce the surrounding community's discomfort with particular groups. Radical acceptance provides a safe environment for all community members to share their discomfort and possibly change their perceptions of others. In community-based art therapy, the projects may address stigma or seek to empower community members (Ottemiller & Awais, 2016) and therefore the project may directly or indirectly seek to address the perceptions of the surrounding community; however, the focus of community-based art therapy is not addressing the perceptions of the surrounding community (Ottemiller & Awais, 2016).

Similar to the harm reduction approach, community art and **socially engaged art** have the goals of using art to facilitate social change, increasing empathy, and community participation that take place in a public setting (Maguire & McCallum, 2019; Wexler & Sabbaghi, 2019). Through collaboration with the community, these arts projects focus on engaging viewers in a debate, exchange, or expand the perceptions of both the viewers and the artists (Maguire & McCallum, 2019; Rutten et al., 2018).

Art education

The final theoretical foundation of community-based art therapy is art education. Defined in the broadest terms, **art education** is the teaching and learning of art in its various distinctive disciplinary forms through a sequential, focused approach or a curriculum that integrates the art into other subject areas (Arts Education Partnership Working Group, 1993). Art education occurs in many different formal and informal settings such as public and private schools, institutions of higher education, and community centers.

As a distinctive kind of community, schools are microcosms of the societies in which they are situated. As such, societal issues such as abuse, neglect, poverty, and other household challenges that impact students' well-being also have a profound effect on classroom culture. With a growing number of students identifying as having adverse childhood experiences (ACEs) consisting of potentially traumatic events occurring before the age of 18 (Meeker et al., 2021), teachers and school counselors are increasingly faced with social, behavioral, and emotional issues that these students carry into the classroom (Kay & Wolf, 2017). Within classroom contexts shaped by traumatic stress, and in teaching expressive art-making forms, art educators may find that their work resembles the practice of an art therapist. There are key differences, however. Lisa Kay, art educator and art therapist, and Denise Wolf, art therapist (2017), make the following succinct observation: "art teachers teach; art therapists treat" (p. 27). They note that while "some teaching occurs in art therapy, and some healing may occur in teaching, the main purpose of art therapy is self-awareness and therapeutic change" (p. 27).

The historical and theoretical foundations of community-based art therapy provide multiple lenses for community-based work, but what do people need to know before they engage in this work? The next section describes the nuts and bolts of community-based art programs.

Community-based arts programs: Shared roles and responsibilities

What do art therapists, artists, and volunteers do in community-based art programs? Despite the unique skill set of art therapists as described before, there are a number of overlapping roles and responsibilities. In the following sections, we discuss these in detail while noting the specific contributions of an art therapist in a community setting.

Specialized preparation and training

Kazmierczak (2017), a visual artist, graphic designer, and academic who created the Art for Empowerment (A4E) program for survivors of domestic violence, suggests learning about the group you plan to work with through books, experts, and individuals from the community. It is important to examine one's own privilege, values, biases, and power differentials, especially when working with communities from different cultural or ethnic identities (George et al., 2005; Ottemiller & Awais, 2016).

Kazmierczak (2017) also attended a 40-hour training in crisis intervention before creating a program for survivors of domestic violence. She states that the goal of this training was to decrease the chances of causing harm while increasing one's knowledge and correcting misperceptions. Art therapists tend to receive training to handle emotional crises and trauma but still may want to receive additional training prior to starting community work. We suggest seeking training suggestions from the community organization where your arts program will take place. As your collaborators, the community organization will be able to highlight issues and concerns, and possible trainings, to prepare you for your work.

Facilitator

Although we described earlier the different ways an art therapist focuses the facilitation of community-based programs, community-based art therapists, artists, and volunteers often view community work as cocreation (Wadeson, 2000). A **facilitator** emphasizes people's strengths and personal power and seeks to create a safe and accepting environment that "is conducive to creativity, reflection, and open communication" (Kazmierczak, 2017, p. 351). To this end, community-based arts program facilitators seek to encourage community members to ascribe their own meaning to their artwork while facilitators should refrain from interpretations of community artwork (Kazmierczak, 2017). General comments may be shared about the aesthetic aspects or objective observations about the artwork (line quality, space and color usage, etc.) "but otherwise facilitators create a nonjudgmental environment by listening empathetically, showing understanding, acceptance, and concern" (Kazmierczak, 2017, p. 350). In the **open studio** approach, described in more detail in the "Community-based art therapy settings" section, the art therapists did not encourage comments on one another's work and this may be due to the young age of participants or desire to create an atmosphere free of judgment. As mentioned before, art therapy facilitators may have members reflect on and work with the artwork to enhance healing, well-being, personal, and/or relational growth. Empowerment is enhanced by the facilitator as they emphasize self-expression, assist members in connecting with their strengths, encourage members to make their own artistic and stylistic choices, and determine their own pace (Kazmierczak, 2017).

We suggest that nonart therapists consider the "sensitive use of art-making" as defined by Kalmanowitz and Lloyd (1997, as cited by the American Art Therapy Association, 2010, para. 3). An art therapy training model for the education of nonart therapists, "the sensitive use of art-making" is an approach that emphasizes "how to make use of the arts within one's own scope of professional practice" (American Art Therapy Association, 2010, para. 3). Gaining training about the intentional use of art materials, how and when to structure art experiences, focus on sharing instead of interpretation, and considering different contexts are the main components of the art therapy training model for nonart therapists (Kalmanowitz & Potash, 2010).

We recommend that artists and volunteers collaborate with an art therapist when they want to deepen the reflections on the artwork to focus on healing, well-being, personal growth, and interpersonal relationships, especially when related to trauma, conflict resolution, and complex group dynamics.

Witness

Sharing our experiences in a validating and accepting community environment can be healing. **Bearing witness** or **witness consciousness** is defined as witnessing without judgment (McNiff, 2013) and attending to others' artwork without commenting (Allen, 2013). Witnessing provides validation, support, sharing in the burden of one's pain, and can result in an emotional release and healing (McNiff, 2013). Witnessing requires one to be present in the moment, giving "quality attention," "silently observ[ing]" (McNiff, 2013, p. 43), and is an active process. As McNiff (2013) explained, even a "completely silent and still" witness can convey "interpersonal energy" and support through "an intentional process of infusing the immediate environment with a sense of significance" (p. 44).

A witness will focus on the present moment, let go of thoughts and feelings outside of the present moment, and be attuned to people making art (McNiff, 2013). The facilitator models witnessing for other group members while also encouraging the community to be good witnesses to one another.

Art as a witness

Can sharing our artwork digitally allow others to bear witness? Although not documented in academic research, we, the authors of this chapter, have observed how the sharing of art images through social media provides community, and thus may help people feel support and validation. Posting pictures helps to create a community of support, decrease isolation (Goldsmith, 2019), and share in the grief process (Gan, 2019). Writing and sharing narratives online is also a form of bearing witness to one another's suffering and can be a step toward healing. Following we share two examples of how people used social media to share their painful experiences and create a sense of community and support. However, we also caution you to weigh the pros and cons of sharing personal images and disclosing personal experiences online since we have little control over who and how people respond, which may make you feel worse (Gan, 2019).

Angelo Merendino shared a series of images documenting his wife, Jennifer's, struggle with breast cancer (Murray, 2013). The images begin with the Merendinos drinking beer together on the stairs of their upper West Side apartment. Each following image reveals Jennifer's step-by-step fight with cancer. These images include a picture of her hair falling out after chemotherapy, Jennifer with her brain radiation mask, Jennifer at the beach, and finally, Jennifer's head stone. The Merendinos shared the images to inform people about the reality of dying from cancer and Angelo believes the images "help people understand better how they could be there for a family member or friend" (Murray, 2013, para. 23). Please search online to see The Battle We Didn't Choose to see Angelo's photographs and read more about the Merendinos.

As we write this chapter, a story of witnessing is unfolding in social media in the form of visual and written narratives created by people experiencing "Long Covid" or Covid-19 "long-hauler" symptoms. Created by citizens in the United Kingdom as an appeal to their Prime Minister for public healthcare assistance, the initiative LongCovidSOS is an example of social media witnessing that not only became a social support network but also influenced medical research and patient care. Callard and Perego (2021) referred to Long Covid as a patient-made illness, crediting individuals' persistence in finding one another online as the reason why Long Covid is thought to be the first illness collectively discovered and named by patients "through Twitter and other social media" (p. 5). In this way, a community formed through collective witnessing of a shared experience was able to influence how the pandemic is understood and potentially how people suffering from Long Covid can manage their illness (Callard & Perego, 2021). The phenomenon of witnessing in art therapy has similar potential to shape community discourse and health outcomes, whether the community exists in an online forum or is engaging in a community-based art therapy experience in a local neighborhood.

Consents and records

In a traditional clinical setting, art therapists and clients are required to document consent for treatment, payment structure, treatment plans, and session notes. Artists, art therapists, and volunteers should consider both the needs of the community and any ethical and legal guidelines they are required to follow. The facilitator may need to create documents for the community-based arts program. We suggest creating written consents for participating in the program and for photographing and/or exhibiting artwork. We also suggest keeping a record of each session that includes the art prompt or project, number of participants, and observations. Art therapists and other mental health professionals should follow state and national guidelines for record keeping.

Privacy

Facilitators should discuss with participants the aspects of privacy or confidentiality, boundary setting, and safety protocols (Ottemiller & Awais, 2016). Since community art therapy takes place in the community, typical guidelines for privacy and confidentiality are difficult since members are from the same community and share various roles: neighbors, friends, or peer artists.

Boundaries

In any therapeutic setting, boundaries need to be considered. Even more so, in a community or open studio setting, the role of the therapist, artist, or volunteer is blurred as the facilitators may be cocreating and collaborating in a community space (Nolan, 2019). Since formal boundaries may be blurred, art therapists will need to consistently reflect upon their multiple roles in the community (Kapitan, 2017; Moon & Shuman, 2013) by engaging in self-reflection as well as outside supervision. Artists and volunteers may also want to reflect on the boundaries and discuss challenges that may need to be addressed.

Group norms

Many art therapists, artists, or volunteers will want to establish group or studio rules or norms. **Norms** are "rules and expectations that govern the life of a group" (Meyer Kiser, 2016, p. 181). Examples of group norms might include being respectful to fellow participants, materials, and the studio space. Norms can be posted in the community setting for all participants to review. Additional information about group work can be found in Chapter 14.

Goals

Treatment plans or care plans are typically used in outpatient therapy and include the short- and long-term goals that the consumer and therapist have identified to work on (Meyer Kiser, 2016; please see Chapter 6 for more details on treatment planning), whereas in a community setting, detailed histories and individual treatment plans are rare. Instead, art therapists, artists, and volunteers will work with the community to develop broader community goals and may reflect a different focus depending on the facilitator.

Supplies

Artists, art therapists, and volunteers will need to think about how to fund and budget for art materials and supplies. If the program is just starting out, we suggest creating a list of basic art supplies that can be used with a variety of different projects while also taking into consideration the population as well as the setting. Basic supplies might include paper (include drawing paper and watercolor paper), pencils, pencil sharpeners, erasers, paint brushes, acrylic or watercolor paint, glue, and canvases. Materials that are available at local thrift stores or around the house include old magazines, containers for water, and paper towels or rags. As the program develops and more funding is available, supplies could be ordered based on specific projects. Additionally, if the program is well supported, having a range of materials from low cost to professional artist quality materials is recommended.

Kazmierczak (2017), who created the Art for Empowerment (A4E) program for survivors of domestic abuse, suggests using donations of supplies to help the program start with no or minimal funding (her specific ideas are provided later). Once the program is successful, additional donations or a line in the budget for the program can be added to sustain the program in future years.

Storage of the supplies depends on the location of the community program. Some programs will have a locked space for the art supplies to prevent the supplies being used for nonarts programing. Other centers might want the materials to be accessible to everyone who enters the community space. The second author found the use of an art cart essential to her community-based art therapy program to transport the art materials from a locked room to the group art-therapy space.

Payment

Typically, discussing the payment structure, insurance, and fees for services would be addressed with a consumer's consent for treatment and outlined in the initial paperwork. In community-based arts settings, there is no typical payment structure. Many studios charge nominal fees with no contracts, while others operate by donations, grants, and public funding.

Funding

Unlike traditional art therapy that takes place in a hospital or mental health treatment facility, community-based arts models do not necessarily receive reimbursement from insurance. Funding for community-based arts models can come from a variety of places and is usually made up of multiple funding sources that can include community fundraising and grant funding.

Donations and fundraising

Using social media to raise funds can be done relatively easily. There are several websites dedicated to setting up an account where community members can contribute to the creation of an arts program. Community members can share the links with their contacts while increasing the community's awareness of the arts program. Kazmierczak's (2017) A4E program sought supply donations from art retailers, art teachers, and art departments. Seeking donations of art materials from community members is another avenue to support a community-based arts program by posting on social media or requesting donations from businesses. There are also a variety of internet sites (free cycle, list serves, front porch forum, etc.) where you could post requests for specific materials or find someone giving away materials. The second author recommends finding local art supply thrift stores, many of which offer art supplies based on what you can afford or very low prices (e.g., Indigo Hippo, Scrap It Up, and Scrap Creative Re-Use). Finally when all else fails, be creative in finding materials even if they are not typical art media. Found objects can offer a great creative outlet and also helps to save the environment by recycling objects that otherwise would go to the trash.

Funding through grants

Grant funding can be found locally and nationally. Small grants are available through state-wide art councils. For example, the Acadia Family Center in Southwest Harbor, Maine provided funds to create a mobile art therapy studio to reach community members who were unable to afford services and attend the center (Acadia Family Center Receives Grant for Mobile Art Therapy Studio, 2021). The National Endowment for the Arts has supported over 585 placemaking grants for the past 10 years (Carter, 2019). **Placemaking** is a term that refers to developing public spaces to attract people by bringing them together to build and create a better community. Placemaking has opened a partnership between artists and public policy professionals to rebuild communities (Spayde, 2012).

Exhibition of artwork

The exhibition of artwork helps to increase awareness of issues facing a community, informs the public about the arts program, showcases the power of artwork in healing, increases the self-esteem of artists, and can be empowering to community members (Kazmierczak, 2017; Potash, 2012; Spaniol, 1990; Vick, 2011). For art therapists, the exhibition of artwork poses several ethical issues that artists are not bound to consider. Potash (2012) and Vick (2011) recommend that art therapists and clients should thoughtfully discuss the therapeutic value in exhibiting artwork while balancing out the feelings of empowerment, enhanced artist identity, creating a shared experience, memorializing or bearing witness to an experience, or encouraging social change that can be gained from exhibiting work. Overall, art therapists and client/community members should consider whether exhibiting the work helps or hinders the focus of the art therapy. Vick (2011) suggests that conversations also include weighing the pros and cons of exhibiting the artwork and examining how might the artist respond to negative comments or criticisms about their work.

Spaniol (1990) noted several "safeguards" she employed when exhibiting client artwork. She considered the language used in describing the exhibit. For example, she discouraged the use of the term "outsider art" since this term often refers to people who are on the fringes of society. On the other hand, should the term mental illness be used in the description (Spaniol, 1990)? When selecting artwork, Spaniol suggested that members submit their work directly instead of artwork chosen by caregivers or art therapists. The direct submissions and collaboration with the members on the exhibition increased the sense of empowerment and ownership for the members.

Finally, the *Ethical Principles for Art Therapists* (American Art Therapy Association, 2013) requires written consent to exhibit artwork. The consent must include (1) the art piece to be exhibited; (2) how, if at all, the client's identifying information should be written; (3) permission to sell the work and who receives the money; and (4) where the exhibition is held (Potash, 2012).

Thus far we have explored the similarities and differences among community-based art therapy and community arts, the historical and theoretical underpinnings, and social action art therapy. We have also described the roles and responsibilities for those doing community-based arts work. Now we explore the range of settings where community-based art therapy and community arts take place.

Community-based art therapy settings

Community-based art therapy can be provided in many different settings. This section explores these different settings for art therapy. This section covers the open studio, public and community art, disability studios, art hives, and museums. Are there other community-based art therapy settings you would want to add to this list?

Open studio

Open studios are a form of art therapy practice that provides art supplies, space, and time to create art (Moon, 2016). In the United States, Art Therapist Mary Huntoon started the first art therapy open studio in the late 1930s. Edward Adamson, a British art therapist, opened an art therapy studio shortly after (Moon, 2016). Both open studio programs were located in psychiatric hospitals and focused on the freedom of choice in the creative process. Art Therapist Pat Allen introduced the term open studio from her own exploration of her artist identity (Allen, 1983; Allen, 1995; Finkel & Bat Or, 2020). Similar to Huntoon and Adamson, Allen offered open studios in a short-term psychiatric unit where patients could determine their own art direction while Allen created art next to the patients (Finkel & Bat Or, 2020). Allen continued her open studio work over the years and cofounded the Open Studio Project in 1995 (described in detail below). The open studio concept shifted from psychiatric units to community centers, correctional facilities, and parks. Today, open studios emphasize opportunities for personal expression, artistic growth, and a place to exhibit one's work. These settings emphasize the connection among people as everyone makes art together, and even the art therapist may create alongside the artists (Block et al., 2005; Malchiodi, 1995).

Huntoon, Adamson, and Allen approached the open studio not as experts or directors but rather as facilitators (Adamson, 1984; Hogan, 2001; Moon, 2016; Waller, 1991; Wix, 2000). Typically, the role of the facilitator is to encourage expression with little to no intervention, as compared to clinical art therapy. Sajnani et al. (2017) described how a nondirective approach provides space for the client to express, discover, and experiment without the therapist's influence.

Moon (2002) noted that an open studio art therapist's roles are that of a witness, role model, and peer. There may be an emphasis on witnessing each other's art-making, that is, listening without interjection while others explain their creative process, as opposed to a more active critique or verbally processing the meaning of the art (Allen, 2008) and the art therapist takes on the role of someone who can hold the space for others (Gadiel, 1992). The role of the witness can be taken on by both the art therapist and other artists in the studio. Open studios might allow reflection to happen more organically than in clinical settings (Moon, 2002). On the other hand, Allen (2008) views the role of the art therapist in an open studio as an "artist-in-residence." An artist-in-residence is someone who is there to create alongside other artists in the studio, share supplies and ideas while coaching others in fine art techniques.

Allen's Open Studio Project (OSP; Block et al., 2005) combined the open studio concept with social action where clients and art therapists created artwork for personal transformation. The OSP was not considered art therapy since diagnoses of the participants were unknown and treatment plans were not utilized (Allen, 2008). Instead the OSP emphasizes the artistic process as an emotional outlet and for self-expression. To this end, the OSP process includes the following components: intention, art-making, witness, and sharing. During the sessions, the art therapist also creates their own artwork to model "artistic energy" (p. 34) and problem solving. The one rule is that no one is to comment on others' artwork or writing. The components are noted in Table 15.2.

TABLE 15.2 Open studio project process components.

OSP process components	Description
Intention	At the start of each session, each participant writes their intention to promote personal responsibility. An example of an intention might be "I relax and have fun" (p. 33).
Art-making	The art therapist introduces a simple art technique and supplies are freely available to participants.
Witness	Each person participates in "witness-writing" where they pay attention to their artwork without judgment. The writing describes and/or dialogues with the artwork or is a catalyst for a story or poem.
Sharing	At the end of the session, members share what they wrote to increase empathy among participants.
Art therapists create work alongside the participants.	
No one is allowed to comment on writing or artwork.	

Adapted from Block, D., Harris, T., & Laing, S. (2005). Open studio process as a model of social action: A program for at-risk youth. Art Therapy: Journal of the American Art Therapy Association, 22(1), 32–38. https://doi.org/10.1080/07421656.2005.10129459.

The OSP exhibits work as a form of community sharing and empowerment. The attention, praise from community members, emphasis on strengths, and sense of accomplishment have resulted in an increase in the self-esteem of participants.

Should facilitators participate in art-making alongside community members?

Many art therapists such as Bruce Moon (2008) and Catherine Moon create artwork alongside clients, consumers, and community members (Teoli, 2020). Benefits of creating work next to members include: (1) the therapist can focus on one's art instead of staring at the client and this may enhance safety and trust (Havesteen-Franklin, 2014; Marshall-Tierney, 2021; Moon, 2002), (2) creating a balance in power as both the art therapist and member are creating beside each other (Allen, 1995; Moon, 2016; Teoli, 2020), (3) demonstrating or assisting to show a specific technique, (4) modeling how to engage in artwork, or (5) when there is a joint art project (Mehlomakulu, 2017; Wadeson, 2010).

Other art therapists identify several drawbacks to making art during sessions (Mehlomakulu, 2017; Wadeson, 2010). Many art therapists find it difficult to be able to be fully present to witness the art-making process if they make art, the art therapists artwork can make others feel inferior, the artwork may influence the artwork of others, shifting the attention of the art therapist from the group, and the art therapist may become too absorbed in the artwork and lose track of attending to the group (Mehlomakulu, 2017; Wadeson, 2010).

While there is no clear answer as to whether art therapists should engage in their own artwork during sessions, we encourage the readers to ask the following questions:

1. When might engaging in artwork enhance the work with the client or participants? When might it hinder the session?
2. What type of artwork can the art therapist (or you) engage in that will allow the art therapist (or you) to stay focused on the group?
3. How might the art therapists' artwork affect the group (Teoli, 2020)?

Community-based art programs for people with disabilities

There are numerous studios for people with disabilities where they can make art (Vick, 2016). These studios or centers are grounded in the work of Psychologist Elias Katz and Educator Florence Ludins-Katz (Finley, 2013; Vick, 2016). Ludins-Katz and Katz (1990) created a model for art centers for people with disabilities and they identified 17 goals that include supporting and helping people reach their artistic development, promoting personal and emotional expression, increasing self-esteem, encouraging independence and individual choice, increasing communication and social skills, improving motor coordination, marketing artwork, helping people to remain in the community, involving caretakers, volunteers, children and youth, and educating the general public (pp. 15–17). Most of these studios do not employ art therapists but emphasize the therapeutic qualities of art-making and therefore share similar goals as art therapy (Vick, 2016). These centers differentiate the work they are doing from art therapy by stating they are not "treating" or doing "therapy" with the people attending the programs (Ludins-Katz & Katz, 1990; Vick, 2016).

Art Therapist Vick (2016) identified two types of studios, those that serve artists with disabilities and others that employ artists with disabilities. Vick (2016) described his role as a consultant for Project Onward, a Chicago-based studio for persons with disabilities. In his role, he did not offer art therapy services. Instead, he believes that art therapists can work in disability studios by setting aside notions of being the expert, removing the client/therapist lens, and shifting from the process to the art product (since the artists will be exhibiting and selling their work). Disability studios such as Gateway Arts in Brookline, Massachusetts are places of employment for artists with disabilities. These environments help foster independence and self-worth (Becker et al., 2007; Sandys, 1999) while highlighting individuals as artists instead of emphasizing their disability (Peterson & Etter, 2021). Artists' work is showcased in studio galleries and storefronts where a portion of the revenue from the sales of their art is given back to the artist.

Should we use the word "disability"?

A **disability** is defined as "any condition of the body or mind (impairment) that makes it more difficult for the person with the condition to do certain activities (activity limitation) and interact with the world around them (participation restrictions)" (CDC, 2020, para. 1). People who have disabilities can be affected by physical (vision, movement, hearing), cognitive (thinking, memory, learning), social (relationships, communication), and mental health impairments and thus represent a diverse group of people (CDC, 2020). Twenty-six percent of people (1 in 4) in the United States have a disability (CDC, 2020, infographic).

Using the word disability can be a problematic title since it implies "incapacity rather than capacity" (Vick, 2016, p. 837). "Disability" divides people into two opposite categories, the abled or those without impairments and the disabled or those with impairments. This dichotomous perspective may contribute to exclusion and discrimination (Harpur, 2012). The term "dis"-abled implies "not" abled and reflects the medical-model perspective by viewing a person who is disabled as needing fixed or helped by others (Yi, 2019). These views of disability validate a narrow view of ability versus challenging society to widen its perception of ability and being differently abled (Harpur, 2012).

On the other hand, Disability Culture grew out of the 1960s–1970s International Disabled People's Movement and acknowledges a shared history, set of values, and experiences with oppression (Yi, 2019). This shared experience has created connections and closeness among people and has led to the empowerment of people who have this shared experience. Disability Arts seeks to explore the meaning of disability (Yi, 2019), "promote disability identity and culture" (Wexler & Derby, 2020, p. 5), and create accessible spaces for people who are often excluded (Yi, 2019) in the arts.

What are your thoughts about how the term disability might be empowering or disempowering?

Creators of Art Hives

Art Hives offer people a place to connect, interact, exchange ideas, and make art (Timm-Bottos & Reilly, 2015). At an art hive, the meeting space is based on a concept called the third space theory (Bhabha, 1994). **Third space theory** is a physical place where everyone is equal and is located "in-between" work and home in hopes of offering a safe and stimulating environment (Timm-Bottos & Reilly, 2015, p. 161). Initially the first art hive began as pop-up spaces to create art within communities. A few years later, the first art hive became more established as the La Ruche d'Art: Community Studio and Science Shop in Montreal, Canada (Timm-Bottos, 2017). Since establishment of La Ruche d'Art, over 114 hives have developed across North America, Canada, and Europe and many of the hives employ art therapists.

Janis Timm-Bottos, art therapist and founder of OFFCenter Community Arts in Albuquerque, NM, provides space for any community member to create and share in the artistic process. This free hive space offers drop-in visual art sessions, scheduled expressive art workshops, writing workshops, and art classes (Hives, n.d.). Timm-Bottos identified the hive studio model as "mingling of the best in art education (lifelong learning), the best of art therapy, and the view that we are each teachers and students of each other" (Gamble, 1997, p. 32). Gamble (1997) observed that Timm-Bottos's studio offered an encouraging environment that involved people from diverse backgrounds joining in a safe place with the intention of exploring and becoming creative.

Portable studio

Portable studios are movable art studios that operate outside mainstream services providing direct and accessible therapeutic support to those in need (E. Bryant, personal communications, October 1, 2021). These mobile studios, containing art materials and tools, can go directly to where the need is greatest. By plugging gaps left by other services, portable studios provide a sense of security for participants whose environments and safety have recently changed (Kalmanowitz, 2018; Potash & Ramirez, 2013). Although portable studios can be run by nonart therapists, in this chapter we feature an art therapy portable studio.

Bryant and Burr (n.d.) defined their The Portable Wellbeing Studio as a fully equipped, mobile art therapy space that seeks to improve the well-being of people in different communities. Burr and Bryant's vision is to provide services to underserved communities, to increase accessibility while reducing the stigma toward mental health services, and to promote creativity as a part of one's overall health practices. They evaluated their work using a well-being scale and found that "the average child's wellbeing improves by 18%, and they get 40% closer to reaching the personal goals" (Bryant & Burr, n.d., para. 4). Figs. 15.1 and 15.2 show the Portable Wellbeing Studio.

Art Therapists Kalmanowitz and Lloyd identified the need for portable studios through their work in the former Yugoslavia (Kalmanowitz, 2018; Kalmanowitz & Lloyd, 1997, 1999, 2005, 2016) and in a temporary refugee

FIG. 15.1 *The Portable Wellbeing Studio from the outside.*
(Image credit: Alex Burr. Printed with permission.)

FIG. 15.2 *The Portable Wellbeing Studio from the inside.*
(Image credit: Ella Bryant. Printed with permission.)

camp in Greece (Kalmanowitz, 2018). When a disaster or a crisis emerges, direct and immediate response is usually limited to workers, but portable studios can help provide structure and safety for those affected and provide a safe space physically, emotionally, and mentally (Kalmanowitz, 2018; Kalmanowitz & Lloyd, 2005).

Similarly, Art Therapist Wayne Ramirez created a portable studio in response to the local school needs following Hurricane Hugo (Potash & Ramirez, 2013). Hurricane Hugo was a category five storm that hit the US Virgin Islands in September 1989. The shortage of resources and emotional trauma motivated Ramirez to renovate a discarded 1974 Ford, 24-passenger school bus that became known as the "Arts Mobile." The bus was carpeted and brightly painted with colorful tropical murals inside and out. A multidisciplinary group of artists, teachers, counselors, and an art therapist used the Arts Mobile to visit 13 schools throughout the islands providing services to 300 students each week (Potash & Ramirez, 2013, p. 173).

Museum-based art therapy

Historically museums were known as places for the affluent to view private art collections (Reyhani Dejkameh & Shipps, 2018). But, during the Great Depression many museums were turned into public institutions to serve the community (Brown Treadon, 2016). Museums now offer unique spaces that enable conversation, self-reflection, and art-making, and even art therapy. Although museum-based art therapy is not new, it has only recently gained attention and research.

So, what is museum-based art therapy? **Museum-based art therapy** primarily focuses on helping people personally connect to art (Reyhani Dejkameh & Shipps, 2018) by using the museum's exhibitions for inspiration, exploration of thoughts, feelings, and self-reflection (Hartman & Irwin, 2021). Museums can also offer spaces for open studios, community gatherings, and arts education (Reyhani Dejkameh & Shipps, 2018).

Museum-based art therapy yields a wide range of benefits for diverse populations depending on the type of program. A California museum-based art therapy program found improved well-being among older adults when the adults journaled after viewing art and analyzed their responses using De Botton and Armstrong's seven functions of art: remembering, hope, sorrow, rebalancing, self-understanding, growth, and appreciation (De Botton & Armstrong, 2013, cited in Bennington, Backos et al., 2016). In addition, patients with chronic health issues, developmental deficits, and mental health struggles reported increases in self-awareness and self-esteem when viewing artwork in museums as a way to connect with images while processing and reflecting on their week (Alter Muri, 1996; Brown Treadon, 2016; Winn, 2001). The museum-based art therapy program, *ArtAccess* at the Queens Museum in New York, offers several programs to the community (Reyhani Dejkameh & Shipps, 2018) with the goals of meeting visitors' special needs, providing opportunities for people to express their creativity, and creating personal connections with art (What is ArtAccess?, 2010, para. 2–3). *ArtAccess* programs have included open studios, art shows for people in or recently out of adult behavioral or psychiatric units, programs for people associated with medical settings, using costumes with children in a hospital school, programs for children on the autism spectrum, and even the creation of saleable art.

Although not museum-based art therapy, several museum educators have discussed the importance of Trauma-Aware Art Museum Education (T-AAME) for museum educators who engage with visitors. The type of conversations that are led by a museum educator focus on strengths and resilience, while an art therapist in the museum setting will focus on therapeutic goals by working with the visitor's pain, therefore differentiating T-AAME from therapy (Murawski, 2020a, May). The following box provides more details about T-AAME.

What is Trauma-Aware Art Museum Education?

Museum educators have observed how museum visitors are attracted to artworks that reflect their internal emotions, thus developing personal connections to specific pieces of art. "Museums, by their nature, are environments where people's collective and individual narratives are elicited and we cannot ignore, in good conscience, that this includes stories that are traumatic" (Legari as cited by Murawski, 2020a, May, para. 8). Andrew Palamara, Associate Director of Docent Learning at the Cincinnati Museum of Art, asserted that museum educators therefore need to create safe spaces for sharing these personal connections at museums. By creating safer spaces in museums, museums become more relevant and inclusive to the community (Murawski, 2020c, August).

Trauma-Aware Art Museum Education enhances personal and interpersonal connections at museums and is based on principles that are informed by those doing trauma work. This education guides the work of museum educators or docents. Trauma-Aware Museum Education differs from other museum education methods such as **visual thinking strategies** (VTS) which uses a structured set of questions to facilitate visual awareness, critical inquiry skills, and visual literacy with museum visitors (Housen & Yenawine, 2000–2001; Yenawine, 2013). While trauma-aware museum educators might use visual thinking strategies as they provide tours and engage with visitors, the T-AAME work is specifically mindful of and responsive to implicit or explicit trauma (Murawski, 2020b, June).

Trauma-Aware Art Museum Education principles include:

1. Importance of collaboration with art therapists since trauma-aware conversations can easily cross the line from conversations to therapy.
2. Setting clear intentions for the group about the purpose and limitations of the group discussions and holding conversations in an atmosphere of "warmth, openness, curiosity and can include playfulness and humour" (Murawski, 2020b, June, para. 5).

3. Facilitators' awareness of their own trauma, triggers, and ability to use grounding/self-soothing techniques for self-care.
4. Creation of ground rules for discussions.
5. Prepared warnings for images that might cause strong emotional reactions. Warnings should be empowering and encourage visitors to use their own self-regulation skills to address the situation (e.g., if something feels uncomfortable, express your feelings, reach out, or decide how much you want to see).
6. Discussion leaders use the skill of paraphrasing and reflective visitor comments while also encouraging visitors to speak to one another, thus building a sense of connection and community.
7. Providing time for deep-level processing through quiet and anonymous written reflections that can be shared in the group without commentary, sensory experiences (such as touching cloth or smelling aromatherapy scents), or incorporating movement to indicate responses (stand closer to the painting if you like it).

Social media and virtual community-based art therapy and arts programs

Social media and virtual platforms have started hosting community-based art therapy and therapeutic arts programs, thus increasing the reach of the power of arts to more people. In the following we describe three different platforms that bring art therapy into people's homes through TikTok, Facebook, and Zoom. These platforms offer new opportunities for providing community-based programs that are accessible to a wider audience.

Megan Mitts, an art therapist, created Art from Anxiety on TikTok. Mitts' goals are to share her own experiences with anxiety and depression and how she uses art as a positive coping mechanism. Her videos feature her use of art materials to manage her anxiety, creating art for comic relief, and modeling self-care. Art from Anxiety has over 11,000 followers.

Amy Maricle of Mindful Art Studio offers free mindful art sessions on Facebook and her website. Her goal is to teach people how to create in a slow, mindful way, tuning in through the senses. She begins by leading people through a brief mindfulness meditation and then she slowly draws while emphasizing the importance of being present and enjoying the process. Students relax into this process-oriented approach, and as a result, progress in their art skills. She teaches a new nature-based pattern every week, and encourages students to listen to their artistic impulses and take them in new directions. Her teaching emphasizes grounding through connection with self, other, nature, and art. What is amazing is that through her online platforms, she is able to reach over one thousand people each week.

Find Your Groove and the Dempsey Family Education and Resource Center offer virtual arts-based programs and art therapy via Zoom and are both run by art therapists. Find Your Groove is an Indiana-based, therapeutic arts program that offers free, weekly sessions for people with Parkinson's Disease. The programs include a community mural, choir, dance, and art. The Dempsey Center is based in Columbus, Ohio and offers free art therapy sessions every other week.

While the section above featured community-based work predominantly done by art therapists, the following section provides social practice art initiatives that address issues of injustice.

Examples of social practice art

Social practice art emerged in the 1970s when Mierle Laderman Ukeles created a performance art series to raise awareness of the amount of "maintenance" that caretakers shoulder (such as the amount of cleaning and caring for others that is often done by mothers, public service workers, and others) (Lawton, 2019, p. 207; Steinhauer, 2017). Originally from the graffiti-art scene, Jean-Michel Basquiat (1960–1988) explored police brutality through his art (Gural, 2018) and Keith Haring (1958–1990) used his art to raise awareness of the AIDS epidemic (Warnes, 2019). As stated earlier in the chapter, artists engaging in social practice art seek to advocate, raise awareness, and create social change (Kennedy, 2013) by using the arts to highlight issues of injustice and inequality in communities (Lawton, 2019). There are so many examples of this type of art, and due to space limitations, we have chosen to highlight the following social justice art projects: AIDS Memorial Quilt, the Heidelberg Project, 5.4 million and counting. We encourage you to seek additional examples in your community.

AIDS memorial quilt

As a response to the growing number of San Francisco residents who died from acquired immunodeficiency syndrome (AIDS), Activist Cleve Jones organized a march in November 1985. He asked fellow marchers to place names of friends and family that had died from AIDS on placards to carry with them in the march. After the march, Jones and other organizers gathered the placards and tapped them together on the side of the San Francisco Federal Building, giving the appearance of a quilt. This event led to a meeting 1 year later to discuss how the AIDS Memorial Quilt could come to life. The first quilt square was created by Jones in 1987, in remembrance of his dear friend Martin Feldman. The response to the Quilt was overwhelming as people from all over the United States began to send their own quilt squares.

The Quilt was first displayed on October 11, 1987 "during the National March on Washington for Lesbian and Gay rights" (National AIDS Memorial, 2021, para. 5). During the display all 1920 names from the panels were read aloud, this tradition continued as the Quilt moved to various cities over the next 4 months. During this time of display the Quilt raised over $500,000 for AIDS organizations and over 4000 panels were added. The AIDS Memorial Quilt continues to grow and evolve to address the changing climate including Black lives lost to HIV/AIDS and Native lives lost to HIV/AIDS. As of the time of this writing, the AIDS Quilt is "nearly 50,000 panels dedicated to more than 105,000 individuals" and is "considered the largest community arts project in history" (National AIDS Memorial, 2021, para. 29).

Heidelberg Project

The Heidelberg Project, created by Tyree Guyton, has been a staple of the Detroit arts community since 1986. Fig. 15.3 features the welcome sign to The Heidelberg Project. Guyton's program transformed abandoned homes and recycled discarded items into art in order to help rebuild the community by bringing people together to raise awareness about the city's struggles (Scott-Dorsey, 2014). Guyton used found objects as metaphors to acknowledge the community's struggles. For example, faces on car hoods identified as the *Faces in the Hood* or shoes suspended from a tree that represent slaves who were hanged and the continued struggle with racism. The project raises awareness and conversations surrounding some tough controversial issues. For nearly 30 years, The Heidelberg Project has drawn attention to the plight of the city while developing youth art programs and volunteer opportunities. Its mission is to inspire and educate others not to give up, and to see the beauty in the midst of change (The Heidelberg Project, 2013).

FIG. 15.3 *Heidelberg Project welcome sign.*
(Image credit: Michelle Pate. Printed with permission.)

The Heidelberg Project has also influenced community members from surrounding areas to join together to clean up the land and create beautiful works of art. The Project has encouraged people to take pride in their community. However, in 2014 the Heidelberg Project experienced 12 alleged arson incidents that destroyed many installations and homes. Community members suspect that the arson may be due to people who did not like raising awareness of the city's lack of resources to assist blighted communities. In response, Guyton and the affected community have banded together to create an even bigger and better project, raising funds to purchase seven solar-powered street lights and security cameras placed at strategic areas of the houses. They increased community activities by inviting more dialogue, presentations, volunteer opportunities, and increased clean up to show their resilience despite the negative incidents (Aguilar, 2015).

5.4 Million and counting

In 2016 the case of Whole Woman's Health vs. Hellerstedt headed to the supreme court. The case would affect 5.4 million women in Texas from accessing reproductive healthcare and would dramatically restrict, and possibly lead to the closing of Texas clinics that offer abortions. Artist Chi Nguyen partnered with Textile Arts Center and The Center for Reproductive Health to create "stitch-ins." These stitch-ins used craft as activism which culminated into a visual representation of the 5.4 million women possibly affected by this case. The first image (Fig. 15.4) is from the Somerville, Massachusetts "Stitch-in" (May 2016). Participants from 36 states and nine countries used 10"×10" fabric panels and embroidered tallies to represent each woman who may have lost their

FIG. 15.4 *Quilt Squares from Somerville, Massachusetts "stitch-in" May 2016. (Image credit: Lauren Leone. Printed with permission.)*

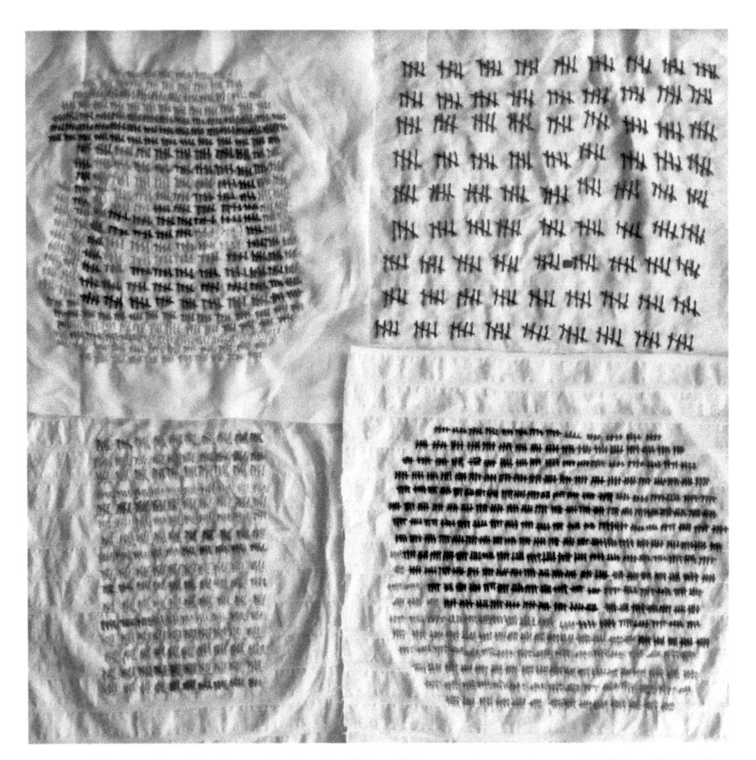

FIG. 15.5 *Additional quilted panels for the 5.4 million and counting quilt, March 2015. (Image credit: Lauren Leone. Printed with permission.)*

right to a safe and legal abortion. These embroidered panels were combined into a larger quilt that was presented in front of the US Supreme Court during the oral argument for this case (Nguyen, 2021). This is the largest quilt that addresses the protection of access to abortions. See Fig. 15.5, a panel quilted by Art Therapist Lauren Leone.

We hope the examples of social practice arts have you excited about this type of work. In the final section of this chapter, we explore several criticisms of community-based arts work.

Criticisms

As we noted earlier, this chapter is envisioned as a conversation in which readers are welcomed to think with us as we explore the parameters, different uses, and varied outcomes of community-based art therapy. We have shared examples of community-based art therapy and community art and discussed how these projects variously contribute to health, healing, and quality of life for many people. We would be remiss, however, if we did not invite you to explore with us some of the assumptions associated with community-based art therapy that could unintentionally undermine its effectiveness. We turn now to the important work of developing a critically conscious perspective on community-based art therapy and socially engaged community art. In challenging ourselves to articulate and examine assumptions that shape our work, we affirm the importance of self-reflexivity and its relationship to professional accountability.

As discussed earlier, community-based art experiences can cover a range of activities, from community-based art therapy as practiced by art therapists, community arts projects led by artists, classes provided by art educators, and other experiences, such as sharing images and stories online, that do not fit neatly into the categories of community-based art therapy or community arts. Most people would agree that community-based arts and art therapy can provide unique benefits for individuals and groups, filling a need in society for therapeutic experiences that promote well-being and strengthen community ties. There can be a tendency, however, to focus only on the positive attributes of community arts and community-based art therapy practices and miss issues that, when addressed, could lead to more positive outcomes for communities. We highlight two issues here that bear consideration when assessing both community-based art therapy and artists' projects that are intended to address a social issue of concern and benefit a community.

Need for nuanced criteria in assessing community-based arts projects. Writing about social practice art, Art Historian Bishop (2006, 2012b) points out that art critics' reluctance to assess work in which a community and its participants are heavily involved has led to a lack of criticality about these projects, especially the possible negative outcomes of such projects. One problem is a lack of consensus on how best to judge the quality of a community-based art project (Kester, 2011). Traditional aesthetic judgments focusing on the beauty or craftsmanship of art (Kant & Bernard, 1951) may be a poor fit for participatory social practice arts projects that emphasize human relationships and social change rather than the production of objects (Klein et al., 2015). In these cases, the judgment of a project's success may default to a general set of ethical principles that evaluate a project's beneficial outcomes for society. However, broad judgments about societal benefits may mask the subtle power structures at work in a project. For example, Bishop (2012b) notes how a heroic narrative of public participation in a community project can hide the less positive narrative of commodifying participants through the unpaid labor they provide in an artist's project. One potential solution is to develop specific criteria for the community-based project with the participants and community stakeholders themselves. This idea is taken up in the following section, as we explore how an art therapist could engage a critical perspective on their own role in community-based art therapy.

Need for self-reflexivity. Art Therapist Karcher (2017) advises that it is an art therapist's responsibility to be consistently self-reflective about their own participation in societal structures that ignore collusion with oppressive systems that disenfranchise others. To this end, Karcher recommends Goodman's (2015) deconstructive approach, noting how it can be "used directly with clients by examining dominant narratives and creating counternarratives" (p. 4) that may lead to awareness of the social, political, and emotional forces that shape clients' realities. Karcher also offers a framework for self-questioning. This framework addresses how a therapist can be shaped by their own experiences of trauma and oppression; how therapists access resiliency themselves; and how therapists understand their clients' "barriers to health" as well as how clients find "safety, resiliency, and strength" (p. 4). Karcher's self-reflection recommendations can also help guide development of criteria for assessing the goals, potential impacts, and intended outcomes of a community-based art therapy endeavor or community arts project by looking at the intersection of the personal and the political and asking: "(a) What impact do my identities, social positioning, actions, words, and approaches have on my clients? (b) How does the current sociopolitical state of identity politics in the United States affect my clients?" (p. 5).

As you reflect on the projects described in the previous pages, challenge yourself to identify what assumptions might have shaped these projects, the art and therapy processes, and the resulting outcomes. What questions come to mind in regard to a project's participants and their role(s) in the project? What underlying assumptions can you identify about the communities, participants, and focus of a project? Whose voices are silenced or missing? Whose needs are prioritized in the project? Whose interests are served? And, what are the potential long-term implications of this project's effects in this community?

Conclusions

As you can see, community-based art therapy and arts programs can provide great benefits for individuals and communities. Community-based arts can fill gaps in healthcare while also serving as a catalyst for change and advocacy. While we are still working on differentiating art therapy from arts programs, we are able to identify numerous similarities and some key differences between these two approaches.

Art experientials

1. Research a current social issue and advocate for this social issue by creating artwork in the form of a press release, flyer, blog post, etc.
2. Attend a community arts program. After attending, create a piece of reflective art to culminate and record your experience.
3. Locate an open studio (virtually or in person). Reflect on how the open studio was similar or different to an art class, therapy session, or art therapy class. Create an image to identify the similarities and differences between these different approaches to using the art-making process and art product.

Additional information

1. Explore several Facebook groups that relate to this chapter topic (search Facebook for Art Therapist for Human Rights, Art Therapist for Social Responsibility, Art Therapy Students for Social Justice).
2. Explore the Critical Pedagogies in Art Therapy website. This website explores how the expressive arts therapies can address oppression. Critical Pedagogies also offers an annual conference and a journal. https://www.criticalpedagogyartstherapies.com.
3. Search Vimeo for "Wheels of Diversity: Pioneers of Color" or click on this link: https://vimeo.com/261157000 (21 min). This video highlights the work of several art therapists of color.
4. Search Ted Talks for "Powerful Art Activism" or click on the link here: https://www.ted.com/playlists/476/powerful_art_activism. The videos featured on the Ted Talks page feature different forms of art that are making social statements.
5. Art Hives Network provides the common features of art hives, latest news, kits, videos, and connects community art studios.
6. Search Vimeo for "Art Therapy and Behavioral Health: Exploring the Continuum of Practice" to watch the 2016 American Art Therapy Association Annual Conference presentation by Jordan Potash https://vimeo.com/178606133. This video demonstrates how the spectrum of art therapy practice is highly compatible with the spectrum of behavioral health practice.

Chapter terms

Art as therapy
Art education
Art hives
Art psychotherapy
Bearing Witness
Clinification
Collaboration
Community
Community art
Community psychology
Community-based art therapy
Critical disabilities studies
Critical psychology
Critically conscious
Disability
Ethical use of art making
Facilitate
Harm reduction
Liberation psychology
Macrosystems
Marginalized communities
Microsystems
Museum-based art therapy
Norms
Open studios
Placemaking
Portable studios
Public stigma
Radical acceptance
Relational aesthetics
Self-reflexivity
Self-stigma
Sensitive use of art-making
Social action art therapy
Social justice
Social practice

Social practice art
Socially engaged art
Stigma
Structural stigma
Third hand
Third space theory
Trauma-Aware Art Museum Education
Treatment plans
Values
Visual thinking strategies
Witness consciousness

References

A Long Walk Home. (2021). *About us. Our mission*. https://www.alongwalkhome.org/about-us/.

Adamson, E. (1984). Art as healing. *Coventure*.

Adejumo, C. O. (2000). Community-based art. *School Art*, *99*(6), 12–13. Retrieved from http://www.davisart.com/portal/schoolarts/sadefault.aspx.

Agell, G., & McNiff, S. (1982). Great debate: The place of art in art therapy. *American Journal of Art Therapy*, *21*, 121–123.

Aguilar, L. (2015, February 20). Arsons at Detroit art project unsolved, despite reward, publicity, security video. *Detroit News*. Retrieved from http://www.detroitnews.com/story/news/special-reports/2015/02/20/heidelberg-arsons-detroit-hard-solve/23769375/.

Allen, P. B. (1983). Group art therapy in short-term hospital settings. *Art Therapy: Journal of the American Art Therapy Association*, *22*, 93–97.

Allen, P. B. (1992). Artist-in-residence: An alternative to "clinification" for art therapists. *Art Therapy: Journal of the American Art Therapy Association*, *9*(1), 22–29. https://doi.org/10.1080/07421656.1992.10758933.

Allen, P. B. (1995). Coyote comes in from the cold: The evolution of the open studio concept. *Art Therapy: Journal of the American Art Therapy Association*, *12*(3), 161–166. https://doi.org/10.1080/07421656.1995.10759153.

Allen, P. B. (2008). Commentary on community-based art studios: Underlying principles. *Art Therapy: Journal of the American Art Therapy Association*, *25*(1), 11–12. https://doi.org/10.1080/07421656.2008.10129350.

Allen, P. B. (2013). Intention and witness: Tools for mindfulness in art and writing. In L. Rapport (Ed.), *Mindfulness and the art therapies: Theory and practice* (pp. 51–61). Jessica Kingsley Publishers.

Alter Muri, S. (1996). Dali to Beuys: Incorporating art history into art therapy treatment plans. *Art Therapy: Journal of the American Art Therapy Association*, *13*(2), 102–107. https://doi.org/10.1080/07421656.1996.10759203.

American Art Therapy Association (2010). *Art therapists training non-art therapists*. https://www.arttherapy.org/upload/ECTrainingNonATs.pdf.

American Art Therapy Association. (2013). Ethical principles for art therapists. https://arttherapy.org/wp-content/uploads/2017/06/Ethical-Principles-for-Art-Therapists.pdf.

American Art Therapy Association. (2021, March). *Member demographics report*. https://arttherapy.org/upload/MemberDemographics_2021.pdf.

Angermeyer, M. C., & Dietrich, S. (2006). Public beliefs about and attitudes towards people with mental illness: A review of population studies. *Acta Psychiatrica Scandinavica*, *113*(3), 163–179. https://doi.org/10.1111/j.1600-0447.2005.00699.x.

Arts Education Partnership Working Group. (1993). *The power of the arts to transform education*. John F. Kennedy Center for the Arts.

Ault, B. (1976). Are you an artist or a therapist—A professional dilemma of art therapists. In R. H. Shoemaker, & S. Gonick-Barris (Eds.), *Creativity and the art therapist's identity: Proceedings of the 7th annual American Art Therapy Association conference* (pp. 53–56). American Art Therapy Association.

Becker, D., Whitley, R., Bailey, E., & Drake, R. (2007). Long-term employment trajectories among participants with severe mental illness in supported employment. *Psychiatric Services*, *58*(7), 922–927. https://doi.org/10.1176/ps.2007.58.7.922.

Bennett, J., & Zournazi, M. (2019). Introduction: Thinking in the world. In Bennett, & M. Zournazi (Eds.), *Thinking in the world: A reader* (pp. 1–12). Bloomsbury Academic.

Bennington, R., Backos, A., Harrison, J., Reader, A. E., & Carolan, R. (2016). Art therapy in art museums: Promoting social connectedness and psychological well-being of older adults. *The Arts in Psychotherapy*, *49*, 34–43. https://doi.org/10.1016/j.aip.2016.05.013.

Bhabha, H. (1994). *The location of culture*. Routledge.

Bhatt, C. (2021). Mel Chin's revival field. *Arts help*. https://www.artshelp.net/mel-chins-revival-field/.

Bishop, C. (2006). The social turn: Collaboration and its discontents. *Artforum*, 178–183.

Bishop, C. (2012a). *Artificial hells: Participatory art and the politics of spectatorship*. Verso.

Bishop, C. (2012b). Participation and spectacle: Where are we now? In N. Thompson (Ed.), *Living as form: Socially engaged art from 1991–2011. Creative time* (pp. 34–45). MIT Press.

Blackman, M. (2011). Public art discourse: A case study of Gateshead, England. *The International Journal of Arts in Society*, *6*(3), 137–151.

Block, D., Harris, T., & Laing, S. (2005). Open studio process as a model of social action: A program for at-risk youth. *Art Therapy: Journal of the American Art Therapy Association*, *22*(1), 32–38. https://doi.org/10.1080/07421656.2005.10129459.

Blundell Jones, C., & Fiala, J. (2005). Lounging on red couches: A public dialogue on safety in Hyde Park lbrochure. In *Burley & Hyde Park Community Safety Project, in conjunction with situation Leeds, a festival on public art*.

Boston, C., & Short, G. (2006). Notes: Georgette seabrooke powell. *Art Therapy: Journal of the American Art Therapy Association*, *23*(2), 89–90. https://doi.org/10.1080/07421656.2006.10129649.

Bourriaud, N. (2002). *Relational aesthetics*. Les Presses du Reel.

Brown Treadon, C. (2016). Bringing art therapy into museums. In D. E. Gussak, & M. L. Rosal (Eds.), *The Wiley handbook of art therapy* (pp. 487–497). John Wiley & Sons. https://doi.org/10.1002/9781118306543.ch11.

Bryant, E., & Burr, A. (n.d.). *The Portable wellbeing studio*. https://www.theportablewellbeingstudio.com/.

Callard, F., & Perego, E. (2021). How and why patients made long Covid. *Social Science & Medicine*, *268*(113426), 1–5.

Carter, D. (2012). Art in the community: A "neighbourhood watch" scheme in Germany. *Contemporary Review*, *294*(1706), 335–342.

Carter, M. (2019). Creative placemaking in government: Past and future. *Community development Innovation Review*, *13*. https://www.frbsf.org/community-development/publications/community-development-investment-review/2019/november/creative-placemaking-in-government-past-and-future/.

CDC. (2020, September 15). *Disability and health overview | CDC*. Centers for Disease Control and Prevention. https://www.cdc.gov/ncbddd/disabilityandhealth/disability.html.

Che, D. (2007). Connecting the dots to urban revitalization with the Heidelberg project. *Material Culture*, *39*(1), 33–49.

Chronister, J., Chou, C., & Liao, H. (2013). The role of stigma coping and social support in mediating the effect of societal stigma on internalized stigma, mental health recovery, and quality of life among people with serious mental illness. *Journal of Community Psychology*, *41*(5), 582–600. https://doi.org/10.1002/jcop.21558.

Corrigan, P. W., & Bink, A. B. (2005). *On the stigma of mental illness* (pp. 11–44). American Psychological Association. https://doi.org/10.1037/10887-001.

Corrigan, P. W., & Watson, A. C. (2002). The paradox of self-stigma and mental illness. *Clinical Psychology: Science and Practice*, *9*(1), 35–53. https://doi.org/10.1093/clipsy.9.1.35.

De Botton, A., & Armstrong, J. (2013). *Art as therapy*. Phaidon Press Limited.

Dissanayake, E. (2013). Art as a human universal: An adaptationist view. In A. W. Geertz (Ed.), *Origins of religion, cognition and culture* (pp. 121–139). Acumen.

Dutton, D. (2009). *The art instinct: Beauty, pleasure, and human evolution*. Bloomsbury.

Feen-Calligan, H., Moreno, J., & Buzzard, E. (2018). Art therapy, community building, activism, and outcomes. *Frontiers in Psychology*, *9*, 1–17. https://doi.org/10.3389/fpsyg.2018.01548.

Finkel, D., & Bat Or, M. (2020). The open studio approach to art therapy: A systematic scoping review. *Frontiers in Psychology*, *11*, 1–16. https://doi.org/10.3389/fpsyg.2020.568042.

Finkelpearl, T. (2013). *What we made: Conversations on art and social cooperation*. Duke University Press.

Finley, C. (2013). *Access to the arts: History and programming for people with disabilities*. Vanderbilt Kennedy Center for Excellent in Developmental Disabilities. https://vkc.vumc.org/assets/files/resources/ArtsManual-P1-adj.pdf.

Fryer, D., & Duckett, P. (2014). Community psychology. In T. Teo (Ed.), *Encyclopedia of critical psychology*. New York, NY: Springer. https://doi.org/10.1007/978-1-4614-5583-7_53.

Gadiel, D. (1992). *Working as an artist-in-residence as a method of practicing art therapy* (Unpublished master's thesis). School of the Art Institute of Chicago.

Gamble, H. (1997). ArtStreet: Joining community through art. *Arts & Activities*, *121*(1), 29–31.

Gan, E. (2019, February 16). Sharing on social media can help grieving hearts heal, say experts. *Today*. https://www.todayonline.com/singapore/sharing-social-media-can-help-grieving-hearts-heal-say-experts.

George, J., Greene, B. D., & Blackwell, M. (2005). Three voices on multiculturalism in the art therapy classroom. *Art Therapy: Journal of the American Art Therapy Association*, *22*(3), 132–138. https://doi.org/10.1080/07421656.2005.10129492.

Gipson, L. (2018). Envisioning black women's consciousness in art therapy. In S. Talwar (Ed.), *Art therapy for social justice: Radical intersections* (pp. 96–120). Routledge.

Gipson, L. (2021). Art & Discursive Practice. *Archiv*. http://www.leahgipson.com/locations.

Goldbard, A. (2009). Arguments for cultural democracy and community cultural development. *Grantmakers in the Arts Reader*, *20*(1). Retrieved from http://www.giarts.org/article/arguments-cultural-democracy-and-community-cultural-development.

Goldsmith, B. (2019, January 22). Can social media help you heal? No one has to be isolated anymore; help and support are a mouse click away. *Psychology Today*. https://www.psychologytoday.com/us/blog/emotional-fitness/201901/can-social-media-help-you-heal.

Goodman, R. (2015). A liberatory approach to trauma counseling: Decolonizing our trauma-informed practices. In R. Goodman, & P. Gorski (Eds.), *Decolonizing "multicultural" counseling through social justice* (pp. 55–72). Springer.

Gordon, M. S. (2019). Interview: Mel Chin's Fundred Project takes the next step. *Art21*. https://art21.org/read/mel-chins-fundred-project/.

Gray, B. (2012). The babushka project: Mediating between the margins and wider community through public art creation. *Art Therapy: Journal of the American Art Therapy Association*, *29*(3), 113–119. https://doi.org/10.1080/07421656.2012.

Gural, N. (2018, December 13). Rarely viewed Basquiat exposes timely exploration of racial identity, activism, and police brutality. *Forbes*. https://www.forbes.com/sites/natashagural/2018/12/13/basquiat-under-new-lens-timely-exploration-of-race-identity-activism-in-little-seen-defacement/?sh=6d5e4b74d0f9.

Hacking, S., Secker, J., Spandler, H., Kent, L., & Shenton, J. (2008). Evaluating the impact of participatory art projects for people with mental health needs. *Health and Social Care in the Community*, *16*, 638–648. https://doi.org/10.1111/j.1365-2524.2008.00789.x.

Hackler, A. H., Vogel, D. L., & Wade, N. G. (2010). Attitudes toward seeking professional help for an eating disorder: The role of stigma and anticipated outcomes. *Journal of Counseling & Development*, *88*, 424–431. https://doi.org/10.1002/j.1556-6678.2010.tb00042.x.

Harpur, P. (2012). From disability to ability: Changing the phrasing of the debate. *Disability & Society*, *27*(3), 325–337. https://doi.org/10.1080/09687599.2012.654985.

Hartman, A., & Irwin, C. (2021). Exploring cultural identity: Connections between art history and museum-based art therapy practices. *International Journal of the Inclusive Museum*, *14*(1). https://doi.org/10.18848/1835-2014/CGP/v14i01/119-133.

Havesteen-Franklin, D. (2014). Consensus for using an arts-based response in art therapy. *International Journal of Art Therapy*, *19*(1), 3.

Hayden, C., & Stearns, S. (2006). (Interviewer). (Videographer). *Georgette Seabrooke Powell remembers the Harlem arts workshop [video file]*. The History Makers Digital Archive.

Hives. (n.d.). OFF center community arts project. https://www.offcenterarts.org/.

Hinz, L. D. (2019). *Expressive therapies continuum: A framework for using art in therapy*. Routledge. https://doi.org/10.4324/9780429299339.

Hocoy, D. (2005). Art therapy and social action: A transpersonal framework. *Art Therapy: Journal of the American Art Therapy Association*, *22*(1), 7–16. https://doi.org/10.1080/07421656.2005.10129466.

Hogan, S. (2001). *Healing arts: The history of art therapy*. Jessica Kingsley.

Housen, A., & Yenawine, P. (2000–2001). *VTS curriculum*. Visual Understanding in Education.

Hurtibise, R. (2008). *Daytona beach news*. Retrieved from www.youtube.com/watch?v=4sgaaZ-I6eU.

Irvin, S. (2008). The pervasiveness of the aesthetic in everyday experience. *British Journal of Aesthetics*, *48*, 486–500.

Jones, R., & Wyse, D. (2005). *Creativity in the primary curriculum*. David Fulton.

Junge, M. B. (2016). History of art therapy. In D. E. Gussak, & M. L. Rosal (Eds.), *The Wiley handbook of art therapy* (pp. 7–16). John Wiley & Sons. https://doi.org/10.1002/9781118306543.ch1.

Junge, M. B., Alvarez, J. F., Kellogg, A., Volker, C., & Kapitan, L. (2009). The art therapist as social activist: Reflections and visions. *Art Therapy: Journal of the American Art Therapy Association*, *26*(3), 107–113. https://doi.org/10.1080/07421656.2009.10129378.

Kalmanowitz, D. (2018). Displacement, art and shelter: Art therapy in a temporary refugee camp. *Journal of Applied Arts & Health.*, *9*(2), 291–305. https://doi.org/10.1386/jaah.9.2.291_1.

Kalmanowitz, D., & Lloyd, B. (1997). *The portable studio: Art therapy and political conflict*. Health Education Authority.

Kalmanowitz, D., & Lloyd, B. (1999). Fragments of art at work: Art therapy in the former Yugoslavia. In *vol. 26 (1). The arts in psychotherapy special issue: 'Healing troubled communities through the arts'* (pp. 15–25).

Kalmanowitz, D., & Lloyd, B. (2005). *Art therapy and political violence: With art without illusion*. Routledge.

Kalmanowitz, D., & Lloyd, B. (2016). Art therapy at the border: Holding the line of the kite. *Journal of Applied Arts & Health*, *7*(2), 143–158. https://doi.org/10.1386/jaah.7.2.143_1.

Kalmanowitz, D., & Potash, J. S. (2010). Ethical considerations in the global teaching and promotion of art therapy to non-art therapists. *The Arts in Psychotherapy*, *37*(1), 20–26. https://doi.org/10.1016/j.aip.2009.11.002.

Kant, I., & Bernard, J. H. (1951). *Critique of judgment*. Hafner Pub. Co.

Kapitan, L. (2008). "not art therapy": Revisiting the therapeutic studio in the narrative of the profession. *Art Therapy: Journal of the American Art Therapy Association*, *25*(1), 2–3. https://doi.org/10.1080/07421656.2008.10129349.

Kapitan, L. (2017). *Introduction to art therapy research* (2nd ed.). Routledge.

Kapitan, L., Litell, M., & Torres, A. (2011). Creative art therapy in a community's participatory action and social transformation. *Art Therapy: Journal of the American Art Therapy Association, 28*(2), 64–73. https://doi.org/10.1080/07421656.2011.578238.

Kaplan, F. F. (2016). Social action art therapy. In D. E. Gussak, & M. L. Rosal (Eds.), *The Wiley handbook of art therapy* (pp. 787–793). John Wiley & Sons. https://doi.org/10.1002/9781118306543.ch77.

Karcher, O. P. (2017). Sociopolitical oppression, trauma, and healing: Moving toward a social justice art therapy framework. *Art Therapy: Journal of the American Art Therapy Association, 34*(3), 123–128. https://doi.org/10.1080/07421656.2017.1358024.

Kay, A. (2000). Art and community development: The role the arts have in regenerating communities. *Community Development Journal, 35*(4), 414–424. https://doi.org/10.1093/cdj/35.4.414.

Kay, L., & Wolf, D. (2017). Artful coalitions: Challenging adverse adolescent experiences. *Art Education, 70*(5), 26–33.

Kazmierczak, E. T. (2017). Engaging communities through an art program at a domestic violence shelter. In L. Hersey, & B. Bobick (Eds.), *Handbook of research on the facilitation of civic engagement through community art* (pp. 339–366). IGI Global. https://doi.org/10.4018/978-1-5225-1727-6.ch016.

Kennedy, R. (2013, March 13). *Outside the citadel, social practice art is intended to nurture*. New York Times. https://www.nytimes.com/2013/03/24/arts/design/outside-the-citadel-social-practice-art-is-intended-to-nurture.html.

Kester, G. H. (2004). *Conversation pieces: Community and communication in modern art.* University of California Press.

Kester, G. H. (2011). *The one and the many: Contemporary collaborative art in a global context.* Duke University Press.

Khan, R. (2015). *Art in community: The provisional citizen*. Palgrave MacMillan.

Kirk, R., Bennett, K., & Lembke, A. (2012). What is community art?: Three women's professional journeys through Lesley University's master's program. *The International Journal of Arts in Society, 6*(6), 23–29. https://doi.org/10.18848/1833-1866/CGP/v06i06/36108.

Klein, J., Bishop, C., Thompson, N., & Phelan, P. (2015). Social practice then and now [review of artificial hells: Participatory art and the politics of spectatorship; living as form: Socially engaged art from 1991–2011; live art in LA: Performance in Southern California, 1970–1983]. *PAJ: A Journal of Performance and Art, 37*(2), 103–110. https://www.jstor.org/stable/26386770.

Kloos, B., Hill, J., Thomas, E., Case, A. D., Scott, V. C., & Wandersman, A. (2020). *Community psychology: Linking individuals and communities* (4th ed.). American Psychological Association.

Kramer, E. (2000). *Art as therapy: Collected papers*. Jessica Kingsley Publishers.

Kramer, E., Drachnik, C., Anderson, F., Landgarten, H., Levick, M., & Riley, S. (1994). How will art therapy change in the next 25 years? Responses by past award winners. *Art Therapy: Journal of the American Art Therapy Association, 11*(2), 91–101. https://doi.org/10.1080/07421656.1994.10759057.

Kumagai, A. K., & Lypson, M. L. (2009). Beyond cultural competence: Critical consciousness, social justice and multicultural education. *Academic Medicine, 84*(6), 782–787.

Lawthom, R., Sixsmith, J., & Kagan, C. (2007). Interrogating power: The case of arts and mental health in community projects. *Journal of Community & Applied Social Psychology, 17*(4), 268–279. https://doi.org/10.1002/casp.932.

Lawton, P. H. (2019). At the crossroads of intersecting ideologies: Community-based art education, community engagement, and social practice art. *Studies in Art Education, 60*(3), 203–218. https://doi.org/10.1080/00393541.2019.1639486.

Lawton, P. H., Walker, M. A., & Green, M. (2019). *Community-based art education across the lifespan: Finding common ground*. Teachers College Press.

Ludins-Katz, F., & Katz, E. (1990). *Art and disabilities: Establishing the creative art Center for people with disabilities*. Brookline Books.

Maguire, C., & McCallum, R. (2019). ArtsAction group: Fostering capabilities through socially engaged art. In A. Wexler, & V. Sibbaghi (Eds.), *Bridging communities through socially engaged art* (pp. 38–47). Taylor and Francis Group/Routledge.

Malchiodi, C. (1995). Studio approaches to art therapy. *Art Therapy: Journal of the American Art Therapy Association, 12*(3), 154–156. https://doi.org/10.1080/07421656.1995.10759151.

Marshall-Tierney, A. (2021). Therapist art making as a means of helping service users with anxiety problems. *International Journal of Art Therapy, 26*(1–2), 47–54. https://doi.org/10.1080/17454832.2021.1918193.

McGraw, M. (1995). The art studio: A studio-based art therapy program. *Art Therapy: Journal of the American Art Therapy Association, 12*(3), 167–174. https://doi.org/10.1080/07421656.1995.10759154.

McNiff, S. (2013). The role of witnessing and immersion in the moment. In L. Rapport (Ed.), *Mindfulness and the art therapies: Theory and practice* (pp. 38–50). Jessica Kingsley Publishers.

Meban, M. (2009). The aesthetic process of dialogical interaction: A case of collective art praxis. *Art Education, 62*(6), 33–37.

Meeker, E. C., O'Connor, B. C., Kelly, L. M., Hodgeman, D. D., Scheel-Jones, A. H., & Berbary, C. (2021). The impact of adverse childhood experiences on adolescent health risk indicators in a community sample. *Psychological Trauma: Theory, Research, Practice, and Policy, 13*(3), 302–312. https://doi.org/10.1037/tra0001004.

Mehlomakulu, C. (2017, June 11). *Should therapists make art in session: 10 things you must consider*. https://creativityintherapy.com/2017/06/should-therapists-make-art-in-session-10-things-you-must-consider/.

Meyer Kiser, P. (2016). *The human services internship: Getting the most from your experience* (4th ed.). Cengage Learning.

Mithen, S. (1996). *The prehistory of the mind: The cognitive origins of art, religion, and science*. Thames and Hudson.

Moon, B. (2008). *Introduction to art therapy: Faith in the product* (2nd ed.). Charles C. Thomas.

Moon, B. (2016). *Art-based group therapy: Theory and practice* (2nd. ed.). Charles C. Thomas.

Moon, C. H. (2002). *Studio art therapy: Cultivating the artist identity in the art therapist*. Jessica Kingsley.

Moon, C. H. (2016b). Relational aesthetics and art therapy. In J. A. Rubin (Ed.), *Approaches to art therapy* (3rd ed., pp. 50–68). Routledge.

Murawski, M. (2020, May). *Trauma-aware art museum education: Principles & practices*. Newstex. https://artmuseumteaching.com/2020/06/.

Murawski, M. (2020, June). *Trauma-aware art museum education: A conversation*. Newstex. https://artmuseumteaching.com/2020/05/04/trauma-aware-art-museum-education/.

Moon, C. H., & Shuman, V. (2013). The community art studio: Creating a space of solidarity and inclusion. In P. Howie, S. Prasad, & J. Kristel (Eds.), *Using art therapy with diverse populations: Crossing cultures and abilities* (pp. 297–307). Jessica Kingsley.

Murawski, M. (2020, August). *Museums must become more trauma informed*. Newstex. https://artmuseumteaching.com/2020/08/03/museums-must-become-more-trauma-informed/.

Murray, R. (2013, April 15). *Husband documents wife's battle with breast cancer through photo series*. New York Daily News. https://www.nydailynews.com/life-style/health/husband-photos-wife-breast-cancer-battle-article-1.1315041.

National AIDS Memorial. (2021). *The history of the quilt: Activist beginnings*. https://www.aidsmemorial.org/quilt-history.

Nguyen, C. (2021). *5.4 million and counting*. http://whatchidid.com/.

NIMH. (2021). Mental health information: Mental illness. National Institute of Mental Health. https://www.nimh.nih.gov/health/statistics/mental-illness.

Nolan, E. (2019). Opening art therapy thresholds: Mechanisms that influence change in the community art therapy studio. *Art Therapy: Journal of the American Art Therapy Association*, *36*(2), 77–85. https://doi.org/10.1080/07421656.2019.1618177.

Ong, W. J., Shahwan, S., Janrius Goh, C. H., Hng Tan, G. T., Chong, S. A., & Subramaniam, M. (2020). Daily encounters of mental illness stigma and individual strategies to reduce stigma-perspectives of people with mental illness. *Frontiers in Psychology*, *11*. https://doi.org/10.3389/fpsyg.2020.590844.

Ottemiller, D. D., & Awais, Y. J. (2016). A model for art therapists in community based practice. *Art Therapy: Journal of the American Art Therapy Association*, *33*, 144–150. https://doi.org/10.1080/07421656.2016.1199245.

Perlick, D. A., Rosenheck, R. A., Clarkin, J. F., Sirey, J. A., Salahi, J., Struening, E. L., et al. (2001). Stigma as a barrier to recovery: Adverse effects of perceived stigma on social adaptation for people diagnosed with bipolar affective disorder. *Psychiatric Services*, *52*(12), 1627–1632. https://doi.org/10.1176/appi.ps.52.12.1627.

Potash, J. S. (2005). Rekindling the multicultural history of the American art therapy association. *Art Therapy: Journal of the American Art Therapy Association*, *22*(4), 184–188. https://doi.org/10.1080/07421656.2005.10129522.

Peterson, J., & Etter, A. (2021). Empowerment through mentorship peer-lead craft workshops in a forensic psychiatric hospital. In L. Leone (Ed.), *Craft in art therapy diverse approaches to the transformative power of craft materials and methods* (pp. 204–217). Rutledge.

Potash, J. (2012, July). *Art therapy ethics of exhibiting and displaying client artwork (conference panel presentation)*. American Art Therapy Association. https://vimeo.com/78718537.

Potash, J. S., Mann, S. M., Martinez, J. C., Roach, A. B., & Wallace, N. M. (2016). Spectrum of art therapy practice: Systematic literature review of art therapy, 1983–2014. *Art Therapy: Journal of the American Art Therapy Association*, *33*(3), 119–127. https://doi.org/10.1080/07421656.2016.1199242.

Potash, J. S., & Ramirez, W. (2013). Broadening history, expanding possibilities: Contributions of Wayne Ramirez to art therapy. *Art Therapy: Journal of the American Art Therapy Association*, *30*(4), 169–176. https://doi.org/10.1080/07421656.2014.847084.

Project Row Houses. (2021). *About us*. https://projectrowhouses.org/about/about-prh.

Propeller Fund. (2021). *Austin neighborhood studio co-op*. http://propellerfund.org/projects/austin-neighborhood-studio-co-op/.

Reyhani Dejkameh, M., & Shipps, R. (2018). From please touch to ArtAccess: The expansion of a museum-based art therapy program. *Art Therapy: Journal of the American Art Therapy Association*, *35*(4), 211–217. https://doi.org/10.1080/07421656.2018.1540821.

Riley-Hiscox, A. (1997). Interview—Cliff Joseph: Art therapist, pioneer, artist. *Art Therapy: Journal of the American Art Therapy*, *14*(4), 273–278. https://doi.org/10.1080/07421656.1987.10759297.

Ritok, N., & Bodoczky, I. (2012). The positive influence of art activities on poor communities. *International Journal of Education through Art*, *8*(3), 329–336. https://doi.org/10.1386/eta.8.3.329_7.

Rivera, E. T., & Comas-Díaz, L. (2020). Introduction. In L. Comas-Díaz, & E. T. Rivera (Eds.) (p. 3). American Psychological Association. https://doi.org/10.2307/j.ctv1chs1sn.7.

Rössler, W. (2016). The stigma of mental disorders a millenia-long history of social exclusion and prejudices. *Science & Society*, *17*(9), 1250–1253. https://doi.org/10.15252/embr.201643041.

Rüsch, N., Angermeyer, M. C., & Corrigan, P. W. (2005). Mental illness stigma: Concepts, consequences, and initiatives to reduce stigma. *European Psychiatry*, *20*, 529–539. https://doi.org/10.1016/j.eurpsy.2005.04.004.

Rutten, K., Van Beveren, L., & Roets, G. (2018). The new forest: The relationship between social work and socially engaged art practice revisited. *The British Journal of Social Work*, *48*(6), 1700–1717. https://doi.org/10.1093/bjsw/bcx118.

Sajnani, N., Marxen, E., & Zarate, R. (2017). Critical perspectives in the arts therapies: Response/ability across a continuum of practice. *The Arts in Psychotherapy*, *54*, 28–37. https://doi.org/10.1016/j.aip.2017.01.007.

Schomburg Center for Research in Black Culture, The New York Public Library. (n.d.). *Black emergency cultural coalition records.* https://snaccooperative.org/ark:/99166/w6vh9k8s#biography.

Sandys, J. (1999). "It does my heart good": How employers perceive supported employees. In R. J. Flynn, & R. A. Lemay (Eds.), *A quarter-century of normalization and social role valorization: Evolution and impact* (pp. 305–316). University of Ottawa Press.

Schoweiler, S. (2013). Public art/public works: St. Paul brings public artists into city hall as partners in creating the city. *Public Art Review*, *48*, 57–60.

Scott-Dorsey, M. (2014). Creative reinvention. *American Craft*, *74*(2), 100–105.

Serres, M. (2020). *Branches.* (Translated by R. Burks. Bloomsbury).

Sevelius, J. M., Gutierrez-Mock, L., Zamudio-Haas, S., McCree, B., Ngo, A., Jackson, A., et al. (2020). Research with marginalized communities: Challenges to continuity during the COVID-19 pandemic. *AIDS and Behavior*, *24*(7), 2009–2012. https://doi.org/10.1007/s10461-020-02920-3.

Shipley, M. J., Coggins, K., Shipley, K. C., & Ellison, D. (2021). Community-based art therapy program to honor 9/11. *Journal of Creativity in Mental Health*, *16*(2), 140–152. https://doi.org/10.1080/15401383.2020.1757003.

Shoemaker, R., Ulman, E., Anderson, F., Wallace, E., Lachman-Chapin, M., Wolf, R., et al. (1976). Art therapy: An exploration of definitions. In R. H. Shoemaker, & S. Gonick-Barris (Eds.), *Creativity and the art therapist's identity: Proceedings of the 7th annual American art therapy association conference* (pp. 89–96). American Art Therapy Association.

Shusterman, R. (2000). *Pragmatist aesthetics: Living beauty, rethinking art* (2nd ed.). Rowman & Littlefield.

Spaniol, S. E. (1990). Exhibiting art by people with mental illness: Issues, process and principles. *Art Therapy: Journal of the American Art Therapy Association*, *7*(2), 70–78. https://doi.org/10.1080/07421656.1990.10758896.

Spayde, J. (2012). Public art and placemaking. *Public Art Review*, *24*(1), 23–25.

Spooner, H. (2016). Embracing a full spectrum definition of art therapy. *Art Therapy: Journal of American Art Therapy Association*, *33*(3), 163–166. https://doi.org/10.1080/07421656.2016.1199249.

Steinhauer, J. (2017, February 10). *How Mierle Laderman Ukeles turned maintenance work into art hyperallergic.* https://hyperallergic.com/355255/how-mierle-laderman-ukeles-turned-maintenance-work-into-art/.

Stepney, S. (2019). Visionary architects of color in art therapy: Georgette Powell, cliff Joseph, Lucille venture, and Charles Anderson. *Art Therapy: Journal of American Art Therapy Association*, *36*(3), 115–121. https://doi.org/10.1080/07421656.2019.1649545.

Supple, A. J., & Plunkett, S. W. (2011). Dimensionality and validity of the Rosenberg self-esteem scale for use with Latino adolescents. *Hispanic Journal of Behavioral Sciences*, *33*(1), 39–53. https://doi.org/10.1177/0739986310387275.

Talwar, S. (2016). Is there a need to redefine art therapy? *Art Therapy: Journal of the American Art Therapy Association*, *33*(3), 116–118. https://doi.org/10.1080/07421656.2016.1202001.

Talwar, S. (2018). Beyond multiculturalism and cultural competence: A social justice vision in art therapy. In S. Talwar (Ed.), *Art therapy for social justice: Radical intersections* (pp. 96–120). Routledge.

Tate Britain. (2021). *Art term: Community art*. https://www.tate.org.uk/art/art-terms/c/community-art.

Teo, T. (2015). Critical psychology: A geography of intellectual engagement and resistance. *The American Psychologist*, *70*(3), 243–254. https://doi.org/10.1037/a0038727.

Teoli, L. A. (2020). Art therapists' perceptions of what happens when they create art alongside their clients in the practice of group therapy. *Arts in Psychotherapy*, *68*, N.PAG. https://doi.org/10.1016/j.aip.2020.101645.

The Heidelberg Project. (2013). *What we do*. Retrieved from www.heidelberg.org.

Thompson, G. (2009). Artistic sensibility in the studio and gallery model: Revisiting process and product. *Art Therapy: Journal of American Art Therapy Association*, *26*(4), 159–166. https://doi.org/10.1080/07421656.2009.10129609.

Thompson, N. (Ed.). (2012). *Living as form: Socially engaged art from 1991–2011* Creative Time.

Thornicroft, G., Brohan, E., Rose, D., Sartorius, N., Leese, M., & Indigo Study Group. (2009). Global pattern of experienced and anticipated discriminationagainst people with schizophrenia: A cross-sectional survey. *Lancet*, *373*, 408–415. https://doi.org/10.1016/S0140-6736(08)61817-6.

Timm-Bottos, J. (1995). Artstreet: Joining community through art. *Art Therapy: Journal of the American Art Therapy Association*, *12*(3), 184–187.

Timm-Bottos, J. (2017). Public practice art therapy: Enabling spaces across North America. *Canadian Art Therapy Association Journal*, *30*(2), 94–99. https://doi.org/10.1080/08322473.2017.1385215.

Timm-Bottos, J., & Reilly, R. (2015). Learning in third spaces: Community art studio as storefront university classroom. *American Journal Community Psychology*, *55*, 102–114. https://doi.org/10.1007/s10464-014-9688-5.

Topkaya, N., Vogel, D. L., & Brenner, R. E. (2017). Examination of the stigmas toward help seeking among Turkish college students. *Journal of Counseling & Development*, *95*(2), 213–225. https://doi.org/10.1002/jcad.12133.

Vick, R. M. (2011). Ethics on exhibit. *Art Therapy: Journal of the American Art Therapy Association*, *28*(4), 152–158. https://doi.org/10.1080/07421656.2011.622698.

Vick, R. M. (2016). Community-based disability studios. In D. E. Gussak, & M. L. Rosal (Eds.), *The Wiley handbook of art therapy* (pp. 829–839). John Wiley & Sons. https://doi.org/10.1002/9781118306543.ch82.

Vick, R., & Sexton-Radek, K. (2008). Community-based art studios in Europe and the United States: A comparative study. *Art Therapy: Journal of the American Art Therapy Association*, *25*(1), 4–10. https://doi.org/10.1080/07421656.2008.10129353.

Vogel, D. L., Wade, N. G., & Ascheman, P. L. (2009). Measuring perceptions of stigmatization by others for seeking psychological help: Reliability and validity of a new stigma scale with college students. *Journal of Counseling Psychology*, *56*, 301–308. https://doi.org/10.1037/a0014903.

WAB15. (2021, June, 4). *Acadia Family center receives grant for mobile art therapy studio*. https://www.wabi.tv/2021/06/05/acadia-family-center-receives-grant-mobile-art-therapy-studio/.

Wadeson, H. (2000). *Art therapy practice: Innovative approaches with diverse populations*. John Wiley & Sons.

Wadeson, H. (2010). *Art psychotherapy* (2nd ed.). John Wiley & Sons.

Waller, D. (1991). *Becoming a profession: The history of art therapy in Britain 1940–1982*. Tavistock/Routledge.

Warnes, K. (2019). *Street art*. Salem Press Encyclopedia.

Weiss, A. S. (1992). *Shattered forms: Art brut, phantasms, modernism*. State University of New York.

Wexler, A., & Derby, J. K. (2020). Contemporary art and disability studies. *Routledge*. https://doi.org/10.4324/9780429260902.

Wexler, A., & Sabbaghi, V. (2019). *Bridging communities through socially engaged art*. Taylor and Francis Group/Routledge.

What is ArtAccess? (2010). https://queensmuseum.org/2010/06/what-is-artaccess.

Winn, P. (2001). The National Gallery of Australia. *Art Therapy and Health Country Communities. 6th National rural health conference, Canberra, Australian Capital Territory, 4–7 March 2001*.

Wix, L. (2000). Looking for what's lost: The artistic roots of art therapy: Mary Huntoon. *Art Therapy: Journal of the American Art Therapy Association*, *17*(3), 168–176. https://doi.org/10.1080/07421656.2000.10129699.

Yao, P. J. (2019, June 23). *The lives of objects: Rirkrit Tiravanija in conversation*. M+ Magazine. https://www.mplus.org.hk/en/magazine/the-lives-of-objects-rirkrit-tiravanija-in-conversation/.

Yenawine, P. (2013). *Visual thinking strategies: Using art to deepen learning across school disciplines*. Harvard Education Press.

Yi, C. (2019). Res(CRIP)ting art therapy: Disability culture as a social justice intervention. In S. K. Talwar's (Ed.), *Art therapy for social justice: Radical intersections* (pp. 161–177). Routledge.

Chapter 16

Pathways to developing a career in art therapy

Dana Elmendorf, MA, ATR-BC, LPC
Art Therapy Program, Seton Hill University, Greensburg, PA, United States; Accreditation Council for Art Therapy Education, Alexandria, VA, United States

Voices from the field
Tell everyone about art therapy, sing its praises, and be willing to explain what it is many, many times over. Find your passion either within or on the fringes of the field. And then make things happen. Don't expect your dream job to fall into your lap, but be willing to advocate and fight and create and educate and search and work and fail and try again to make your professional dreams come true.

C.H. Moon (2015)

Learning outcomes

After reading this chapter, you will be able to
1. Recognize characteristics of a successful art therapist, according to national standards
2. Identify curricular and extracurricular activities at the undergraduate level which support application to a graduate program.
3. Describe aspects to consider when searching for a graduate program.
4. Define art therapy scope of practice and professional credentialing options.
5. Discuss professional challenges and growth opportunities fostered by art therapy studies.
6. Compare career options in fields closely related to art therapy.

Chapter overview

When art therapists talk about the most memorable aspects of their career, in my observation they often mention four common elements: professional relationships that foster lifelong friendships, seeing resilience and progress, learning to work through experiences of disappointment or failure, and staying creative throughout life. Art therapists have differing interests, personalities, and

Foundations of Art Therapy. https://doi.org/10.1016/B978-0-12-824308-4.00011-9

backgrounds, but generally enjoy hands-on work and art-making and share an appreciation for genuinely relating to individuals, groups, and families. While it is common for art therapists to express a hope to be helpful to others, they also value people's inborn ability to creatively overcome challenges. Professional education also teaches the importance of growing as a person in order to demonstrate the ability to handle one's own personal problems before trying to help others. In addition, art therapists often work in settings that require creative problem-solving and flexibility in approaching situations.

Students interested in art therapy are introduced to a profession that invites creative thinking and lifelong learning. The art therapist must be committed to a lifetime of education, continuously developing competency, and being invested in growing with the field. Choosing a career that combines a love of art and psychology requires information about educational options that are available in order to learn, to take risks, to own one's success, and to prepare for future professional contributions to the world. As is often the case with creative approaches to work and learning, however, there is not just a single entry-level pathway option. Each pathway entails certain steps that must be taken, both in preparation during schooling and once working after graduation, in order to succeed in advanced training and to go on to become a strong employee and practitioner.

This chapter discusses the process of becoming an art therapist, from entering college to becoming credentialed. The confidence and ability to provide art therapy services is built over many years and a long-term pathway of development even as at times it involves specific steps that are focused on such as **credentialing**, which refers to documented evidence one has undergone a certain level of training. Topics in this chapter include undergraduate courses and experiences that can prepare one to apply to a graduate program, the art portfolio for applications, and aspects to consider when searching for a program. Basic career information on characteristics/dispositions of a successful art therapist, common types of work settings, job titles along the continuum of care, and projected job growth of the profession are included. In addition, professional challenges and growth during initial entry-level years will be discussed, including postgraduate credentialing possibilities such as becoming a registered and board-certified art therapist along with state licensure. The chapter concludes with career options for students who may not have the opportunity to complete graduate studies or who wish to explore pathway options in closely related fields.

Introduction

Art therapists gravitate to visual thinking, and one of the more powerful ways to engage visual thinking is with metaphors. A **metaphor** communicates by using a phrase, idea, image, or object to suggest a likeness to something else. Metaphorical thinking is used in art therapy to help solve problems because the visual metaphors and symbols people create and refer to can generate new ideas for solutions (B.L. Moon, 2007).

A metaphor that offers a useful framework for our exploration of pathways to developing a career in art therapy is that of standing on the beach at the edge of the ocean, where the water meets the sand. Can you feel the cold water lapping at your toes and the wet packed sand under your feet, creating a firm foundation to stand or walk on? Imagine, as the next wave comes in, the water gently washing over your feet. Is it cold or is it warm? How does the rest of your body react to the temperature? Can your eyes scan and see out to the distant horizon along with any people or fish who might be closer in the water? Imagine the wave then slowly receding back out to sea and as it does so, the sand which is now being pulled by the water under your feet shifts, at times rapidly and at other times ever so slowly. The shifting sand as the water recedes requires you to adapt your stance in slight ways, to adjust to the new sand foundation under your feet. With each wave that washes in and recedes, you slightly adjust your footing, even as you continue to be able to stand and scan the horizon or notice what is happening in the water. Against the background of this experience are the rhythmic sounds of the waves breaking on the beach, like a heartbeat that has existed for a long time and to which you feel in sync.

Much like the firm foundation with a shifting stance which is held by this metaphor, individuals interested in a career in art therapy must be prepared to understand the foundation of national education standards with related competencies which exist in the United States, and ways these standards and competencies function as a firm grounding of quality art therapy practice, even as the profession continues to develop. **Competencies** are the stated areas of knowledge, skills, and attitudes which are formally defined in published education standards. Another way to understand competencies is to think of them as what entry-level art therapists know, can do, and value and the related education standards as the published definition of these. Formal education standards and the competencies detailed within them are continually being refined and improved, and most recently the education standards for Art Therapy were updated in 2016 and are under continuous quality improvement (Accreditation Council for Art Therapy Education, 2016). It is also important to begin to understand the longer-term aims of credentialing requirements and state regulations of mental health care that exist in the United States, along with the knowledge that there are several pathway options available in order to achieve credentialing.

As we return to our metaphor of standing at the edge of the water and feeling the waves wash over our feet, can you imagine and feel the water shifting the sand under your feet? Adapting your stance as you gaze out to the far horizon, then looking more closely around, will you continue that walk along the shore, enter the water to swim, walk out up to your knees, or maybe return to your beach towel to relax? Choices to respond exist but as you stand scanning the horizon and adapting to the waves lapping at your feet, our metaphor speaks to the ways requirements and clear educational standards exist as a foundation on which to stand and which seek to define what quality art therapy work is, even as these elements are continually being improved and required health care regulations shift. At the same time, there is not just one single pathway choice for becoming a professional who is authorized to provide safe, ethical, and competent mental health care as an art therapy practitioner. Instead, career decision-making for students interested in art therapy is much like standing on the beach at the water's edge, and entails consideration of options along with a core question.

How do I begin as I consider a career pathway in art therapy and how do I know if the field is right for me?

Brief history

The art therapy profession in the United States has been developing its pathway options for education standards and credentialing for over 60 years and in the very early days, as the profession was being established, specific coursework was not required to practice as an art therapist. Early art therapists were trained by reading, doing, writing, consulting with, and collaborating with others (Rubin, 2009). Art therapists are still learning in this way, but changes to require specific coursework and eventually to require a master's degree as the entry level for art therapy practice were brought about in order to enhance the status of the profession, to increase accessibility to art therapists under mental health care regulations, and to further define the skills needed to be an effective and ethical art therapist.

The **American Art Therapy Association (AATA)**, formed in 1969, was key in the development of formal training. AATA is a membership organization composed of professionals, educators, students, and others interested in Art Therapy (https://arttherapy.org/). Lively give-and-take has often been a part of discussions as the profession has evolved. Debates in the early years of the 1970s focused on defining a competent practitioner, and then articulating guidelines for training. Judith Rubin, past president of the American Art Therapy Association, shares further details about this early growth period of art therapy training as she writes: "After intense debate within AATA about the adequacy of undergraduate preparation, the master's degree was ultimately recognized as the entry-level for the practice of the profession...training by observing, assisting, and being supervised by an art therapist remains a central part of art therapy education. Undergraduate programs in existence are viewed as preparation for graduate work" (Rubin, 2009, p. 245).

While the master's degree has been established as the entry level for the profession, undergraduate coursework in art therapy and undergraduate majors exist as preprofessional training opportunities. In spite of their popularity at a number of colleges and universities across the United States, Schwartz et al. have noted that undergraduate art therapy education has received little attention in terms of clarification of undergraduate training objectives and scope of practice (Schwartz et al., 2019). **Scope of practice** is a term that helps to identify procedures, actions, and processes an individual is permitted to perform. An individual's scope of practice is also based on specific education, experiences, and demonstrated competence. The authors review the history of art therapy training programs, including reference to doctoral programs that have been established, but more importantly detail the results of a survey of undergraduate art therapy programs in order to determine best practices and needs of this preprofessional level of training. The survey results reveal that undergraduate art therapy is growing and expanding, and its value in mentoring future art therapy leaders and providing for the unmet art enrichment needs of communities is highlighted (Schwartz et al., 2019).

While Rubin described the early years of art therapy as a period of incubation then rapid growth, and Schwartz et al. share the history of attempts to develop various training levels in the field, recognition of the work by other health care professionals along with the need to remain competitive in the health care marketplace has more recently emerged as an essential focus. Indeed, in a pilot study of Creative Arts Therapy students found a statistically higher rate of responses indicating student's desire to locate more information about employment opportunities and finding a job in their chosen career as compared with lower rates of responses for obtaining educational training information (Orkibi, 2010). In other words, career identity and training interests appear to be closely linked with pressures regarding potential employment. In addition, increased national- and state-level requirements in the United States to be a mental health care provider have entailed a related need within the art therapy profession to establish credentials. A credential, otherwise known as becoming **credentialed**, serves to assure a baseline level of competency and is often thought of as the alphabet soup after professionals' names (American Heritage® Dictionary of the English Language, 2011). Credentialing mechanisms in human service professions exist primarily to protect the public from incompetent practitioners and as the practice of art therapy has grown in popularity, Greenstone (2016) provided support to the idea that training requirements and credentialing offer protection to the consumer about who is qualified to deliver art therapy services.

Only those individuals who have applied and been approved for credentialing are legally entitled to use the credential designations as evidence of their professional status. The very first credential for art therapy, **Registration as an Art Therapist (ATR)**, was first instituted in 1970 by the American Art Therapy Association. The ATR credential was then shifted to be managed and conferred by the Art Therapy Credentials Board in 1993 and all credentials for art therapists are now overseen and administered by this organization (https://www.atcb.org/). The ATR is available to individuals who have a master's degree and also a minimum of 1000 hours postgraduate of direct provision of art therapy services under clinical supervision with an approved clinical supervisor. The option to become a **Board-Certified, Registered Art Therapist (ATR-BC)** was then instituted in 1994. ATR-BCs pass an empirically produced, statistically vetted examination, thereby demonstrating knowledge of the theories and clinical skills used in art therapy. The option to become a **Certified Art Therapy Supervisor (ATCS)** became available in 2010 to experienced art therapists who provide clinical supervision and have met specific training requirements. The newest credential to now be offered, first conferred in 2017, is the **Registered Art Therapist-Provisional (ATR-P)** for recent master's level graduates and new professionals, allowing a credential in the first few years of entry-level employment as one continues to work toward the more advanced ATR and ATR-BC levels (Art Therapy Credentials Board Credentials at a Glance, 2017).

Table 16.1 provides an overview of levels of credentialing. In order to maintain board certification, each individual is required to accumulate 100 Continuing Education Credits (CECs) every 5 years (Art Therapy Credentials Board, 2020).

State Licensure as a mental health provider is a second level that is achieved in addition to becoming board certified. Depending on the state you are living and working in, or the kind of work you want to do, it may be important to eventually become both board certified and licensed. In addition, Rubin added that

TABLE 16.1 Types of professional art therapy credentials.

Credential	Explanation
ATR-P—Registered Art Therapist-Provisional	Achieved with a master's degree and confirmed supervisory oversight from a qualified supervisor while beginning entry-level work years
ATR—Registered Art Therapist	Achieved after completing a required number of postgraduate art therapy experience work hours under supervision
ATR-BC—Board-Certified Art Therapist	Achieved after becoming Registered and also taking and passing the national Board Certification exam, demonstrating comprehensive knowledge of the theories and clinical skills used in art therapy.
ATCS—Art Therapy Certified Supervisor	Achieved after becoming board certified and undergoing additional training to offer clinical supervision
State Licensed Mental Health Provider—Depending on the state, might include LPAT, LCAT, LPC, LGPC, LMHC, LAT, LAC, MFT, LICSW, PhD/PsyD to name a few credential options.	The type of license needed is specific to the state where one is working and where a client is living. A growing number of states have passed an Art Therapy license. For states that have not yet achieved this regulation, practitioners might earn a Counseling or Marriage and Family Therapy license.

Various levels of credentials exist and can be progressively worked toward over several years following graduation.

being compensated for the work by insurance companies is difficult unless one becomes licensed in a field they recognize (Rubin, 2015). Because occupations are regulated on a state-by-state basis and also due to recent shifts in the insurance industry, obtaining a state **mental health license** may lead to insurance reimbursement for the services of a therapist as it is considered the highest form of regulation within a state which determines if a provider is qualified.

State licensure is applicable to the state a therapist works in along with, in the case of teletherapy, the state a client lives in. Some states have a license specifically for art therapy, and some states license art therapists under a related license at this time (as opposed to an art therapy license) even as national efforts are underway to develop an art therapy license in all states, a multiyear initiative being led by the American Art Therapy Association (2021a). At the time of this writing, an art therapy specific license is available in 11 states (with more in development) even while art therapists have historically qualified for licenses in related mental health professions such as Counseling or Marriage and Family Therapy in many, if not most other states. However, movements by these related professions to solidify their own professional identity have made it more and more difficult for art therapists to qualify for these related licenses (Keane, 2019). To continue to advance the profession, solidify art therapists' own professional identity and to also ensure access to licensure for art therapists, a priority of the American Art Therapy Association and art therapists in states across the country has recently been to seek distinct licensure for art therapists in all 50 states. Until that is achieved an art therapist may, at time of this writing, seek to obtain a license specific to Art Therapy, Creative Arts Therapy, Counseling, Marriage and Family Therapy, or even Social Work, depending on the state and courses taken in graduate school. Many art therapists are dual credentialed as both board-certified art therapists along with being state licensed and may even hold two state licenses. License initials after art therapists' names may thus include LPAT, LCAT, LPC, LGPC, LMHC, LAT, LAC, MFT, LICSW, PhD/PsyD to name a few credential letters. Because opportunities for gaining a license vary from state to state and are governed by different boards and regulatory philosophies, Greenstone (2016) has rightly referred to state licensure as a "complex web" (p. 79).

In addition to needing to tend to varying state regulations around licensure, there may also be a concern about the financial costs of maintaining multiple credentials given there are annual fees one must pay to do so. A lot of people do say this all seems expensive and like such a long process! It is important to acknowledge there are benefits and drawbacks to the long-term professional development and the credentialing steps an art therapist must typically go through. The drawbacks may be around finances and the annual costs to maintain various credentials and membership in more than one professional association along with a potential lack of confidence in one's professional identity. The benefits are a wide range of resources and relationships with other professionals that inspire innovation and quality work. This has potential to be an exciting part of the work, as it keeps a person growing, and there is always something new to learn. Think of it as a vocation, a calling, not just a job.

Meanwhile, the very definition of what makes art therapy unique, as compared to closely related fields, including mental health and community health professions, has been in development and continuous discussion among art therapists. Art therapy is an interdisciplinary field and practitioners have much in common with other helping professions even as the work entails art-based approaches and theories which are unique to the field. In the United States and Great Britain, the art therapy profession has struggled to assert a clear and bounded identity while simultaneously having to participate in an increasingly regulated health care system (Kapitan, 2010). While art therapy is unique in its focus on art, art-making, art materials, and nonverbal information processing, art therapy also shares important foundations and training with other mental health professions.

Art therapy moving forward

New questions are also currently arising within the profession about how to best define the focus of the work and the actions associated with art therapy. Perhaps because of the relatively small size of the field, or because creative people are a part of it, individual art therapists have opportunities to regularly contribute to the collective identity of the profession. In fact, numerous art therapists volunteer their time to writing, committee work, building state chapters, and offering presentations. Four recent examples highlight the range of volunteer efforts occurring which seek to further develop the profession:

1. An Undergraduate Education Subcommittee of the volunteer AATA Education Committee was formally established in 2018 and seeks to establish guidelines for undergraduate art therapy education (Schwartz et al., 2019). The article asserts that such guidelines would better position undergraduate art therapy programs to increase the number of trained, nonclinical art facilitators who understand the scope and limit of their skills, which in turn would also increase access to art-making experiences by underserved populations (p. 7).
2. Since 2016 the Accreditation Council for Art Therapy Education, an all-volunteer council, has begun to manage newly developed accreditation processes for art therapy graduate programs that are transitioning to accreditation (https://www.caahep.org/ACATE).
3. Since 2018, the Critical Pedagogies in the Arts Therapies group has hosted conferences and offered writings that address social justice questions such as, "How do we contribute to equity and social justice through how we teach, supervise, mentor, write and research in and through the arts therapies and across educational contexts? When do we risk reinforcing oppression and, conversely, how can our work increase access and inclusion?" (Lepere, 2019).

4. During the Spring of 2020, the Covid-19 pandemic required a fast-moving learning curve as art therapists shifted to providing services through Telehealth. **Telehealth** is the use of digital information and communication technologies, such as computers and mobile devices, to access health care services remotely and manage physical and mental health care. Online forums became active with art therapists sharing ideas for virtual art therapy, digital art media, and safe protocol for materials. Blogs, webinars, and social media allowed art therapists and even graduate students to connect and volunteer their ideas, challenges, and tips for responding to the new mental health care landscape (American Art Therapy Association, 2020).

Collaborations, partnerships, and even participation in the political process for state licensure support the clients art therapists serve. As rigorous standards of art therapy education have been established, strict systems and steps have been developed for credentialing, and as the profession becomes more clearly defined, the goal is to expand the numbers and reach of qualified art therapy practitioners. A career in art therapy includes collective striving with other art therapists and as Kapitan (2010) writes, "Even the longest-standing, most familiar construction of what we mean when we say 'art therapist' needs to be reimagined frequently" (p. 107). Moon (2016) goes on to invite further reflection in the form of a question. "Maybe the efforts to delineate the boundaries of our profession will never, and should never, end. Perhaps we will always need to wrestle with the parameters of our field that so clearly combines ideas from multiple perspectives, but isn't that just like art?" (p. 232).

Characteristics of a successful art therapist

Art therapy is practiced worldwide, though more highly regulated and with clearer education standards in the United States and Great Britain. People interested in becoming art therapists come from all walks of life, though there remains an ongoing need for more diversity within the field. While not all art therapists in the United States are members of the American Art Therapy Association, and membership actually includes individuals from over 50 countries worldwide, a membership survey conducted by AATA in 2021 of its 4357 members offers some interesting demographic highlights and shifts. AATA membership is getting younger, as noted by the 2021 survey results in which close to a half of members (44%) said that they were under 40 years old. By comparison, only a third (36%) of members in 2011 were under 40. The portion of professionals that are just entering the field is growing. When asked about years of experience working in the field, more than a third (37.8%) said they had worked four or fewer years. In prior surveys, this portion ranged from 18% to 31%. While small increases in diversity by race and ethnicity were found, membership continues to be majority White, based on current data set. Since 2016, there were slight increases in the number of people who identified in all other racial and ethnic categories except for "Multiracial," which decreased slightly. (Members who identified as Asian increased from 2.9% in 2016 to 4.3% in 2021, Black or African American from 1.2% to 3.5%, and Hispanic or Latino from 2.9% to 5.9%. The percentage of members who identified as Indigenous American or Alaska Native remained the same at 0.6%.) Finally, AATA members continue to be majority female. In 2021, 88.3% of members identified as female, compared with 93.0% in 2016. However, since 2020, AATA has been offering additional "Gender Identity" options for members in their profiles which will help to better capture the gender diversity of members in the future (American Art Therapy Association Member Demographics Survey, 2021).

Because art therapists do not always work under the job title of an art therapist, as discussed later in this chapter, it can be difficult to determine how many exist, but the Art Therapy Credentials Board offers useful information in its Annual Reports in terms of numbers of credentialed art therapists it oversees in a given year. The ATCB Annual Report for 2018 indicates a total of 6540 actively credentialed art therapists. This number is reflective of art therapists working in the United States primarily, as ATCB credentialing is part of the US system. This number is not reflective of all new art therapists who are working toward credentialing and thus who are obtaining the required number of supervised work hours, nor does it include those art therapists who choose not to become credentialed (Art Therapy Credentials Board, 2018).

A common concern students have about becoming an art therapist is in regard to their own life history. Some people enter the field as "wounded healers" and want to give back a part of what they felt they needed while they were experiencing life difficulties. Others are just naturally drawn to helping. Both pathways are valued as each carries their own wisdom (Roots & Roses, 2020). Art therapy students are commonly asked to reflect on how they might relate to this continuum and how this might impact the personal growth required for studies to be a therapist. In addition, students and art therapy practitioners continually reflect on areas of potential growth along with ways to avoid letting one's own life history dictate the direction of therapy. Without sufficient self-awareness and reflection, art therapists run the risk of overly meeting their own needs through clients. This is known as **critical self-reflection** and Hogan (2014) has written extensively about the role of experiential learning in art therapy programs, and how this supports the self-reflection needed to manage the personal emotional reactions an art therapist may experience in their work. Hogan and Coulter (2014) write "In teaching art therapy, it is important for students to realize the uniqueness of their own perception and the advantages and disadvantages of this" (p. 26). The authors go on to detail avenues for laying the foundations of reflective practice through experiential learning such as art-making, workshops, discussion, and journaling activities which are a common part of art therapy training, in addition to didactic teaching such as content lectures and presentations.

Practicing as an art therapist is more than knowing your educational content, systematic planning, enjoying hands-on art-making, and interacting with clients. Art therapists must also demonstrate the professional attitudes and conduct that facilitate emotional exploration and personal growth in others and which convey a positive image of the profession. These attitudes and modes of conduct are known as **professional dispositions** which describe the values, actions, attitudes, and beliefs of art therapists as they interact with clients/patients, families, community members, and professional colleagues. In conversations by this author with program directors of master's art therapy programs, the professional dispositions they most frequently mention that seem to make a quality art therapist or art therapy student and thus ones generally sought out by graduate art therapy programs include:

1. A strong work ethic and self-direction;
2. The ability to be empathic and emotionally present with others;
3. The ability to tolerate situations that are ambiguous, without definite answers all the time, while remaining curious;
4. A passion for art-making that supports emotional growth rather than focusing on perfection of technique, but which also combines creativity and knowledge of art-making processes;
5. A commitment to learning about the multicultural experience, marginalized communities, and one's own biases, privilege, and automatic reactions;
6. An investment in personal growth and interest in obtaining feedback in order to understand how the people we work with might experience us;
7. The ability to reflect on and articulate personal attitudes and thoughts, especially in classroom groups or treatment team meetings;
8. The ability to write, read, research, and present at the graduate level.

Employment prospects

The demands of today's mental health care require thinking about continuous quality improvement as new research and worldwide health crises prompt changes to the types of mental health services being provided. College students will enter a world that demands the creative application of skills in new ways, new approaches to learning, and new requirements to practice. While new jobs and new job settings will emerge, common questions will continue to be asked about employment prospects in the field which tend to include, "Where do art therapists work?" and "Do they actually find work?"

Art therapists work along a **Continuum of Care**, which is a term used to convey a broad array of services. It is a fairly common stereotype that art therapists just work with children, but art therapy is actually provided to people across the lifespan, including adults and elders. Additionally, while many art therapists work in what can be described as **clinical** roles, a term used to mean the formal addressing of mental health treatment needs, some art therapists work in community-based settings that offer alternatives to mental health care and which emphasize community empowerment. Ottemiller and Awais (2016) expand on this as they write, "This shift of definition allows for more diverse and inclusive ways of practicing, which means that art therapists can offer their services to a wider range of people through community-based practices that embrace wellness and prevention, thereby also reducing the stigma associated with traditional mental health treatment" (p. 144). A review of graduate program websites, member survey reports from the American Art Therapy Association, and AATA State Chapter job surveys reveal that art therapists carry the skill set to work in a range of settings such as, to name a few: Bereavement and Hospice Care, Family Therapy Wrap-Around Services, Victim Trauma Services Centers, Child Therapy Outpatient Clinics, Drug and Alcohol Treatment Centers, Private Practice, Hospitals, Outpatient Mental Health Clinics, Nursing Homes, Prisons and Juvenile Detention Centers, Homeless Shelters, Art Studio, and Wellness Centers. While education standards for art therapy training do emphasize a core of knowledge, skills, and values along with specializations that may be fostered, students are also taught, and practitioners are called upon, to generalize skills from one setting to another.

When an online search of "art therapy jobs" is conducted, it may appear as if not many employment opportunities exist in some parts of the country. Family members and loved ones may express concern to students that they "have never met an art therapist and do people really get a job?" It is important to note that while individuals with art therapy training work along a continuum of settings and with people across the lifespan, it remains less common to have a job title of "art therapist." While obtaining an "art therapist" job title is on the rise, especially with the advent of art therapy licensure in increasing numbers of states, individuals with art therapy training often do employment searches using related job title keyword searches. While the job title of art therapist may offer clarity on the skill set one is bringing, other job titles and jobs also foster the integration of the art therapy skill set such as a primary therapist, clinician, mental health therapist, counselor, school-based therapist, addictions therapist, community advocate, activity therapist, artist in residence, etc. Indeed, the author of this chapter, while entering her 36th year as an art therapist, has never had the job title of "art therapist"!

Art therapists might also be referenced as a **Creative Arts Therapist** or work as part of an **Expressive Arts Therapy** department, both umbrella terms which refer to human service professionals who use arts modalities and which, under that umbrella, may include art, music, drama, dance/movement, and poetry therapies (National Endowment for the Arts, 2021). Whereas traditional single modality arts-based approaches (such as dance/movement therapy, music therapy, drama therapy, art therapy, and poetry therapy) emphasize the particular modality and may be referred to as Creative Arts Therapy, Expressive Arts Therapy integrates and embraces all the modalities, sometimes layering several art modalities in one session. Some art therapy programs even include training in related Creative Arts Therapy modalities/Expressive Arts Therapy integrations as part of the curriculum.

Given that job prospects for art therapists require the ability to generalize and weave skills across a range of settings, and to realize a job may not necessarily entail the job title of an art therapist, it is important to understand the work of art therapy and most mental health care involves participating in **Interdisciplinary Treatment Teams.** An interdisciplinary approach, which is the most common approach in mental health care, involves integrating the knowledge, skills, and experience of multiple disciplines who discuss and work together to enhance and improve the care of the people they serve. Art therapists do not work in isolation, but rather are members of teams committed to what could be considered a multilevel model of care. Art therapists certainly have a unique strength to bring to the team as they foster ways of knowing that encourage emotional exploration without relying solely on words, even as the skills also overlap with other mental health disciplines and support the skills others on the team have to bring. Because of this, art therapists spend a significant amount of time explaining to others what their work entails (sometimes jokingly saying it is one-third of the career), even as they learn to work alongside and in collaboration with a team and value other approaches. Rubin (2015) offers a pathway for success as she conveys, "You will need to become not only a good practitioner but also *a good salesperson.* In order to convince others of the value of your work, you will need to be able to explain it clearly in language they can comprehend. You will therefore need to learn different languages for different audiences" (p. 149).

Salaries for art therapists vary depending on the part of the country one is living and working in. Tools for understanding typical salaries of art therapists, including a range of work settings, job titles, and annual salaries are available through the American Art Therapy Association membership survey which is conducted every 2 years, with results found via the biannual Member Demographics Report posted on the AATA website (https://arttherapy.org/upload/MemberDemographics_2021.pdf). While not all art therapists nationally are members of AATA, it is interesting to note that according to the 2021 Member Demographics Report, the most common median annual salary range reported was $50,000–$79,000. These figures do not reflect only entry-level salaries, however, given that while more than a third of the members who participated in the survey in 2021 had 0–4 years of experience, the next highest range of survey participation was members with 5–9 years experience and additional years of work were reported in ranges up to 30+ years. State chapters of the American Art Therapy Association also conduct an annual jobs survey of state chapter members on a regular basis and these results may offer information on salary ranges in particular regions of the country.

Additional salary research tools are provided by two departments within the federal government. The US Bureau of Labor Statistics (BLS) does not specifically collect data on art therapists at the time of this writing (though a multiyear effort by the American Art Therapy Association is advocating for specific data on art therapists) (Torpey, 2015). Instead, the annual mean wage of "Substance

Abuse, Behavioral Disorder and Mental Health Counselor," which by implication includes art therapists as part of mental health professions, may be found on the BLS Website and their *Occupational Outlook Handbook* (https://www.bls.gov/ooh/). An online search of basic entry-level job salaries for a mental health worker, rather than searching specifically for art therapy salaries, has the potential to yield information. In the beginning few years right after graduating with a master's degree, full-time jobs on the lower-paying end of the salary scale are the norm for most entry-level mental health professional work. While not always the case, starting in what is commonly known as "entry-level" roles, then advancing into higher levels of responsibility and thus salary increases, are standard avenues for advancement in mental health professions. Some art therapists begin with several part-time jobs to make ends meet, or engage in what is known as contract services, where they provide specific art therapy services to one or more agencies for a few hours a week but are not officially part-time. Self-care and advocacy for inclusion in professional opportunities for advancement become essential and a pathway to further success and promotions.

An additional tool for career exploration and job analysis may be located at O*NET OnLine, which is part of the US Department of Labor, Employment and Training Administration (https://www.onetonline.org/). The Summary Report for art therapists covers skills, work activities, work contexts, and wages and employment. The provided links for wage data are instrumental and allow for state-specific searches along with typical entry-level to median wages for this type of human service profession even within a zip code area. Anyone who wants to become an art therapist will be glad to know that Art Therapy is listed as a "Bright Outlook" occupation on the O*NET OnLine website (National Center for O*NET Development, 2021).

Educational preparation of the art therapist

With so many terms, titles, and changes, it is common for college students interested in becoming an art therapist to have questions about the kind of education required, where to locate degree programs, and how to become certified and licensed. Even more common questions often relate to the types of courses or major college students should choose as preparation for graduate studies, what sort of person makes a good art therapist, what types of jobs art therapists do, and what work options exist with a bachelor's degree if one is not able or chooses not to go directly on to graduate school. The pathways to a career in art therapy can at times be experienced as confusing, while also inspiring, as the career offers the opportunity to make lifelong professional contributions to the world.

A common question people often begin with is, "Where do I find a list of graduate Art Therapy programs?" The website for the American Art Therapy Association (AATA) has an *Education and Practice* link that will answer many of your questions and can be a resource for you (American Art Therapy

Association, 2021b). There you will also find links to explore Art Therapy master's programs that have undergone a formal quality review process which ensures their resources, curriculum, faculty, and policies are prepared to meet your learning needs. Important information to be aware of is the current (at time of this writing) 7-year transition of many graduate art therapy programs from being reviewed for quality and thus "approved" by the Educational Programs Approval Board (EPAB), which is a part of the American Art Therapy Association, to being "accredited" by the **Commission on Accreditation of Allied Health Education Programs** (CAAHEP). CAAHEP accreditation is a quality review process being managed, for the art therapy profession, by the **Accreditation Council For Art Therapy Education** (ACATE), https://www.caahep.org/ACATE. Information provided from the AATA webpage will explain the transition occurring from program approval to program accreditation processes and take you to graduate art therapy program websites after you follow a series of steps detailed (https://arttherapy.org/). It is important to note that both approved and accredited programs will fully prepare you to become a Registered Art Therapist (ATR) and programs that are still approved, but not yet accredited at time of the writing of this chapter, have simply not yet been given the green light to apply for accreditation as the shift is happening over a longer term transition period of several years in order to allow the volunteers overseeing the shift to complete their work. Be sure to check back to both the AATA website and the ACATE website for ongoing updates and current lists of graduate art therapy programs nationally (and in future years, some even internationally perhaps).

It is also important to know that in addition to master's program links provided from the American Art Therapy Association website, there are additional programs at other universities, which can also offer the needed training to become an art therapist. The reason they may not appear on the AATA website is that they are fairly new and have not yet had the required number of years in existence to be able to apply for program accreditation (at least one graduating class is needed). While a newer program has the potential to be very strong and may be an exciting program in an area that has not previously had an art therapy program offered, they are still too new to be listed while they are establishing their foundation. You are encouraged to look into them on your own, however, as institutions from many states across the country are in the process of rolling out art therapy programs. It is an exciting time in the growth of the profession! These newer programs are *also* likely to be structured to prepare graduates to become credentialed art therapists.

Because it is common to have questions about where to find art therapy graduate programs and how to become an art therapist, an FAQ sheet was developed by this chapter's author to provide information related to the most common questions received (https://www.caahep.org/ACATE). Following are the *top questions* received, in the words of individuals seeking to understand the various pathways which exist and their options for study in the field, with responses included as if speaking directly to the person inquiring. These words of guidance provided by the author may speak to readers of this chapter as well (Elmendorf & Accreditation Council for Art Therapy Education, 2019).

Do I have to have an undergraduate art therapy major to apply to grad school? It is important to know that a master's degree is the required entry level into art therapy work. The undergraduate art therapy majors which exist are preprofessional and prepare students in terms of lowering anxiety and providing foundational information but are *not* required to apply to graduate school. You may find further information about art therapy education on the AATA website (American Art Therapy Association, 2021a). While a graduate degree is required for art therapy work, there are many options for undergraduate preparation studies. You could choose an undergraduate preprofessional art therapy major, a double major in art and psychology, a major in art with a minor in psychology, a major in psych with a minor in art, a relevant major with elective coursework in studio art and psychology, or other majors or minors that would be highly applicable and still allow you to earn the needed prerequisites to apply to the graduate programs. While the bachelor's in art therapy preprofessional majors may specifically provide a well-rounded exposure to fieldwork through a practicum or internship experience, keep in mind it is important to gain some volunteer experience working with people during whatever option you choose for an undergraduate major or minor.

What prerequisites do I need to apply to a graduate program? Each graduate program institution establishes its own acceptance criteria but in general, a 2017 survey of graduate programs and their prerequisite course requirements indicated some commonalities (Rastogi, 2017). These include 18 credits of studio art with a class in drawing, painting, claywork (prefer some hand building, not just wheel). The additional nine credits of studio work would then be in other media or advanced studies in the earlier mentioned media, as a variety of art materials experience is needed when working with clients. It is important to be able to fully understand what it feels like to make art and to express oneself in a wide variety of materials. This need for 18 credits of studio art coursework is also a prerequisite requirement of the Art Therapy Credentials Board and supports future application for becoming board certified (ATR-BC). Graduate programs will likely require, as part of their application, a portfolio of artwork completed as part of prerequisite studio art coursework. Many people wonder how many pieces and what kind of work they should include. While each program will have instructions on their website, the general range tends to be around 13 pieces, in drawing, painting, clay work, and a self-chosen variety of additional media you have explored. An artist statement that reflects the ways art-making has fostered personal growth is also often requested.

In addition to studio art, 6–12 credits of study in Psychology (which may include coursework in closely related disciplines) are likely to be needed. This involves a course in Abnormal Psychology, a course in some sort of Developmental Psychology (which might be titled Child Psychology, Adult

Psychology, Lifespan, or some such title addressing people across the lifespan). Typically, to take these sorts of classes at an undergraduate level, an Introduction to Psychology class is needed first. Some graduate programs require an additional three credits, which can be in many other related areas such as a Psychology Research class, Statistics, Personality Theory, or many other sorts of classes that might prepare students with important foundational skills for graduate studies. Many types of courses, for example, those in Sociology, not just those offered by Psychology departments, can be a helpful supplement if they teach you about people, working with people, and studying their needs.

Should I go to an Art Therapy program that also offers Counseling, a Counseling program that also offers Art Therapy, a Family Therapy program that offers Art Therapy, or something else? How do I know if it's an actual Art Therapy program? Generally, the title of any degree a program offers is not something to really worry about; however, it is best to check with the state you plan to practice to find out if the title of the degree matters. Typically, the title of the art therapy programs are in accordance with that state's requirements. That's something the program directors and faculty have to think about. What is really more important for you is what *classes* the program offers. You want to look at their list of classes, not the title of the degree because the classes are what prepare you to go on to become board certified and licensed. Art therapy graduate programs offer a number of differing degree titles and some may identify as offering a master's focused on art therapy, while others may seem to emphasize counseling or marriage and family therapy in addition to art therapy.

Art therapy programs, whatever the title of the degree, offer classes that teach about art-based approaches, and classes that teach about what is more often thought of as traditional mental health content even as they all focus on combining two sides of learning in both clinical and creative skills to train as a competent and effective art therapist. To be an art therapist, one needs to know how to engage in the relational therapeutic process and use art materials within that. In the past, we used to call some of those skills "related mental health" and some "art therapy" but now it all falls under a set of skills any art therapist needs. So whatever the title of the degree, whether the first word is Art Therapy, or Counseling, or Marriage and Family Therapy, the classes taken together will teach you to work with people and use art-making to do it. Look at the list of classes they offer and use that as part of your decision.

What types of courses are typically in a graduate degree in art therapy? Art therapy has historically been referred to as an integrative profession with coursework from what is known as related mental health professions being combined with coursework taught by board-certified art therapists and which focuses on art therapy theories and methods. This distinction is a somewhat false dichotomy as art therapy work is not "separate" or distinct from the skills needed by other mental health practitioners, although that is a common perception. As I often say, I am not a counselor when I am talking, and an art therapist only when I am using my hands, and if you ever met me you would know I often do both at the same time! Art Therapy programs are typically designed to address national education standards, which provide an outline of content for courses that are considered best practices and which confirm that art therapy education is equivalent to education in related mental health professions. Additionally, graduate programs typically pay attention to curriculum content requirements delineated by the Art Therapy Credentials Board and also by any from the state licensing boards. While each art therapy program has its own unique coursework that highlights the expertise of its faculty or needs of the region it is located in, the following content areas reflect the types of coursework typically in a graduate degree in art therapy. Note these are *content areas, not course titles,* so when reviewing a program you might see, in its class list, a different course title for what essentially covers the following content areas:

1. Psychopathology
2. Human Growth and Development
3. Psychological Assessment
4. Counseling/Psychological Theories
5. Helping Relationships
6. Research
7. Professional Orientation
8. Ethical and Legal Issues
9. Multicultural and Social Issues
10. History and Theory of Art Therapy
11. Materials and Techniques of Practice in Art Therapy
12. Creativity Studies
13. Studio Art
14. Application of Art Therapy with People in Different Treatment Settings
15. Art Therapy Assessment
16. Group Art Therapy
17. Culminating Thesis or Project
18. Practicum and Internship

Programs may also have coursework that highlights Family Therapy studies, Trauma studies, Studies in Addiction, Studies in related Creative Arts Therapies such as Drama Therapy, Music Therapy or Dance-Movement Therapy, Vocational and Career Development, additional Studio electives, Medical Art Therapy, etc., depending on the requirements of their state for state licensure, the expertise of their faculty, or needs of the region they are located in.

Does it matter where I attend school, as far as which state? In terms of what state to study in, that is a more important question for graduate studies. An undergraduate student can really study anywhere in the country. For a master's program though, at this time the best place to attend graduate studies depends in large part on where a person might want to live and settle once working. The reason for that is that each state has its own regulations for what classes need to be taken in order to go on and become a licensed mental health provider in that state, even as various states may also share very similar requirements with other states. As mentioned earlier, some states have an Art Therapy license (and lots of people are working hard to have more states that offer that). Some states at this time just offer an option for a Counseling License or, more rarely, a license in Marriage and Family Therapy. Each program develops its classes to meet the requirements of whatever state it is in, though most programs *also* include the classes needed by many other states as well. It is important to also consider that graduate school can be a time to make professional connections and to develop networking connections through internships and class activities that may lead to jobs and references.

Reach out to programs and ask them if they will prepare you for licensure in the state you want to live in. If you are not sure where you want to live (which keeps life interesting), choose a school you are drawn to. Some things in life you just cannot plan for sure. Work in art therapy requires one to be very flexible and to not always know exactly how things will turn out with clients, and that is often the best attitude to take when figuring out where to study as well. Choose a program that will help you grow.

I want an online program because I am unable to relocate. If your life does not allow you to immerse yourself in a new setting by moving to a school program, it is important to know that there are some options to consider. *Fully online... Hybrid...Low-Residency...*these are the names of the sorts of program designs that may offer you a livable option. Online education can occur with all classes online or with the classes mostly online but only 1–3 weeks back on campus a year. These are called Hybrid or Low-Residency options. When looking for an art therapy program without moving, it can be helpful to not just look for an online option, but rather to review *all* program websites to see what ones offer an online, hybrid, or low-residency component. What is known as face-to-face programs may also offer a few online classes but this is different from what is considered a fully online or hybrid program.

I want to become a certified art therapist. There are a couple of terms that are important to define. Here are the terms and then they will be explained. (a) *Board-Certified Art Therapist*, (b) *Licensed*, and (c) *Accredited*. While the master's degree is the required entry level of art therapy, after graduating people can spend a few more years of work and go on to become a ***Board-Certified Art Therapist***. That is why you see ATR-BC after many art therapists' names. Most graduate programs will want their students to have the courses needed, so you could ask a program you are applying to if the courses they offer will prepare you to go on to apply to become board certified. Most, if not all, will. Being able to put ATR then ATR-BC after your name signifies that you are highly trained and competent.

The next term is about becoming ***licensed***, which is different from becoming board certified. See the explanation of state mental health licenses earlier in this chapter. State Licensure as a mental health provider is a second level that is achieved in addition to becoming board certified. Depending on the state you are living and working in, or the kind of work you want to do, it may be important to eventually become both board certified and licensed. A lot of people tell us this all seems like such a long process! That's an exciting part of our work though.

Finally, let's talk about the term ***accredited***. We get a lot of questions from people saying they want to be an accredited art therapist. That is a slight confusion of terms. What they really are asking about is how they can become a board-certified art therapist and licensed mental health provider. The term "accredited" applies to the graduate education programs. An education program can be accredited, not a person.

What else do I need to understand about accreditation of graduate programs? The importance of accreditation as a way that students, employers, the public, and government officials can know that a quality education is being provided is something you will continue to hear a lot about in Art Therapy, and also in the mental health fields that are closely related to Art Therapy including Psychology, Counseling, and Marriage and Family Therapy. More on what accreditation is, how it works, and why it is starting to matter can be learned through materials available on the Council for Higher Education Accreditation (CHEA) website (Council for Higher Education Accreditation, 2021). While the several years long transition of art therapy programs to being accredited was explained earlier in this chapter, there are some additional items to keep in mind. Readers who are exploring the possibility of pursuing a master's degree are encouraged to learn more about the connections between program accreditation and licensure in some states. While not yet a requirement for the art therapy license, program accreditation is written into the counseling licensure law in some states, and applicants for a counseling license may need to graduate from a program accredited by the Council for the Accreditation of Counseling and Related Educational Programs (CACREP, 2021). In the meantime, as noted previously, Art Therapy programs are transitioning to accreditation through CAAHEP, which is a different organization from the counseling group of CACREP, but the importance of accreditation quality standards and reviews for graduate programs, including art therapy programs, is becoming increasingly valued for state licensure, by employers, by federal and state governments, and by students. This area is a fast-changing landscape but specifics of art therapy program accreditation and its relationship to the increased credibility of art therapy as a regulated mental health profession can be found through information provided by the American Art Therapy Association (2021a). Graduate programs are also now required, by federal law, to provide information to applicants on how their program curriculum prepares for state licensure in the profession and you may contact an institution's admissions office to ask for this information or look on the institution/program website. To also assist, it may be helpful to know that in addition to the accreditation organizations mentioned before, Psychology and also Marriage and Family Therapy have accreditation organizations overseeing their discipline-specific programs.

In addition to foundational coursework, what else can I do to prepare for graduate school? A favorite story the author of this chapter likes to tell her students is that the undergraduate class that in many ways most prepared her to become an art therapist was Astronomy. The class taught her how to look up and around with wonder and curiosity and to hear stories in the stars all around, and this open attitude fosters responsive therapeutic relationships as well. Consider all the ways life and learning can teach you to notice beauty and growth and awe, even as you consider the following activities as well:

1. Engage in art-making for your own means of self-exploration and expression.
2. Show you have a desire to work with people by volunteering or working with a human service, medical, educational, or similar agency offering support to community members. Some college programs offer therapeutic art-making practicum classes or internships/fieldwork at the undergraduate level, which provide an opportunity for a student to work with participants and get a better understanding of what it entails. These are very basic assisting-type jobs. This is important in some programs since masters-level programs often do want to know if the student has volunteer experience working with people. This provides the student with a "first job" and may also provide some basic knowledge of working with children or adults to see if it is something they want to pursue. Fieldwork experiences, participating in service learning, volunteer or work experience allows students to gain experience and determine if this is the career for them.
3. Participate in your own personal therapy (not necessarily art therapy if unavailable) to develop self-awareness while getting a sense of what a therapeutic relationship is like.
4. Consider connecting with the state art therapy chapter in your state, to meet art therapists and participate in trainings they might be offering.

In their own words

A quantitative study in the form of a 10-question survey was sent in 2017 to graduate art therapy students in programs across the United States and 84 participants responded with results reported in *Who Are the Next Generation of Art Therapists: A Survey of Graduate Students* (Shortell, 2018). While not representative of a cross-section of graduate students across time, the results provide an interesting snapshot of a moment in time that serves to address the question, "Who is entering into the art therapy profession and what are their future aspirations?"

Question three of the Graduate Art Therapy Student Education, Goals, and Demographic Survey, summarized in the thesis, asked participants to identify their top reasons for choosing their current graduate program, and more than one answer was allowed (Fig. 16.1). A total of 154 responses were recorded, with the top answer being that the program met specific state licensure requirements (29.76%). The second most common response with one less respondent (28.57%) was the program's proximity to the participant's home. A program's

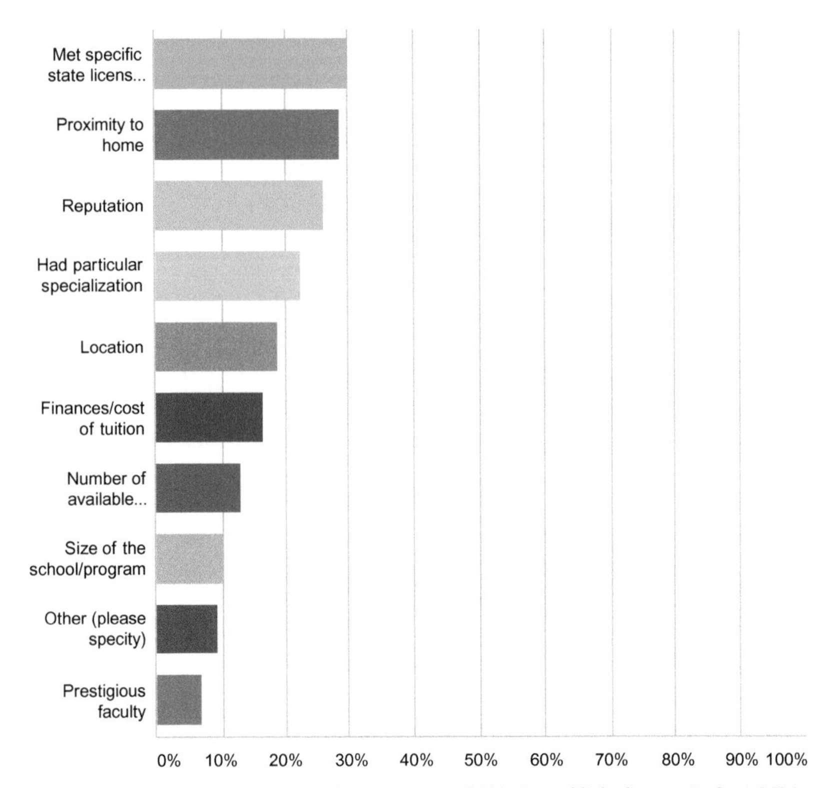

FIG. 16.1 *Reason for Choosing Graduate Program (2018) [unpublished master's thesis] Kristen Shortell, Identify top reasons for choosing your graduate program.*

reputation was the third most common reason for attendance, with 22 responses (26.19%). A total of 19 participants (22.62%) stated that they chose their program because it had a specialization of interest. A program's location was the fifth most common answer (19.05%). A total of 14 participants (16.67%) stated that the cost of tuition and other financial reasons led them to choose their current program (Shortell, 2018, p. 33) (Fig. 16.1).

Question six of the Graduate Art Therapy Student Education, Goals, and Demographic Survey asked participants to identify their top two ideal work settings. Fig. 16.2 provides the ideal work settings noted by the 157 answers recorded. Those who answered other, "reported being interested in work at museums, shelters, community centers, correctional facilities, VA hospitals, nonprofits, and refugee camps" (Shortell, 2018, p. 41).

Hidden costs of being an art therapist

While the benefits of a career that foster lifelong growth and job satisfaction through creativity are hopefully evident, by now you may be wondering why people might leave the field. What are the hidden costs of being an art therapist?

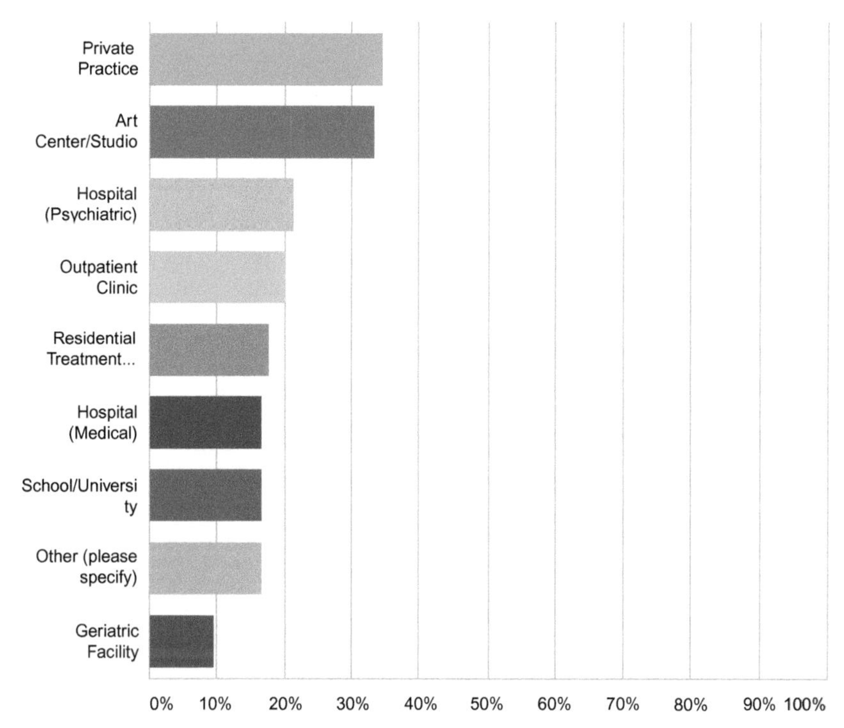

FIG. 16.2 *Ideal Work Settings (2018) [unpublished master's thesis] Kristen Shortell, Identify your top two ideal work settings.*

Some challenges of being an art therapist have been discussed previously in this chapter, such as a lack of familiarity with art therapy, and the lengthy process to be trained and credentialed. There are pros and cons to any career, but art therapy has several specific challenges which are most commonly reported by art therapists. At the same time, the work of art therapy allows avenues for resilience that are unique to the field.

The act of caring for others can come at an unspoken cost. Professionals in the fields of health care, mental health, community, and social services are at a higher risk for compassion fatigue and vicarious trauma. While **compassion fatigue** (Figley, 1995) refers to the profound emotional and physical erosion that takes place when helpers are unable to refuel and regenerate, the term **vicarious trauma** describes the significant shift in worldview that occurs in helping professionals when they work with clients who have experienced trauma (Pearlman & MacIan, 1995). For example, a therapist may begin to see the world as an unsafe place after repeatedly being exposed to continuous stories about trauma that clients share. Art therapy work carries a unique risk of being impacted by vicarious trauma. Rather than listening to recollections of traumatic events as in traditional talk therapy, traumatic experiences are visually expressed in client artwork and the visual images clients create in therapy, inclusive of sensory art media that may be experienced by the therapist on an embodied level (with empathic felt bodily senses), may increase the susceptibility of the art therapist to experiencing vicarious trauma or compassion fatigue. Some work settings may also include a risk of physical trauma when working with potentially violent clients.

Managing one's personal life challenges is taxing, as are critical incidents (e.g., death of a loved one, divorce, illness) that impact both personal and professional roles. The importance of adaptation to professional demands while also accommodating their personal lives is an ongoing challenge for mental health professionals. Sometimes a personal crisis may be so challenging that a practitioner leaves a profession altogether, but avenues for self-care do exist, including the importance of personal art-making. Peers often have the best sense of what is helpful, as conveyed by a Blog post from art therapy student Trica Zeyher at the height of the Covid-19 pandemic: "Our professional and educational training is about helping others, but we must also look at ourselves first to see if we are ready, willing, and able to help them. When we provide ourselves with love, non-judgment, and support, we can model this to our clients, our community, and our families. Please meet your health needs, get rest, eat healthy, exercise, take breaks, practice a ritual, make a schedule with boundaries you set, obtain telehealth art therapy for yourselves and reach out for help when you need it. I recommend scheduling time to make art just for yourself" (Zeyher, 2020).

Moss (2017) has researched the anxiety and insecurity many new graduates experience during the years between graduating with their master's and becoming a board-certified art therapist, ATR-BC. This process can take from around 2–3 years or longer, and it is a time described as an important period of transition often filled with "challenge, difficulty, frustration, marginalization, feeling misunderstood and under-appreciated, and feeling like there are more walls than roadways to provide the services art therapists are trained to do" (p. 2). A feeling of loneliness is sometimes reported by art therapists due to the fact that there are usually no other art therapists at the agency where one works. Feelings of inadequacy with respect to their skills, confusion about their roles, a felt lack of validation, and an overall sense of ambiguity may result (Moss, 2017).

Attention is then drawn in Moss's research, to the importance of supervision specifically as a key in developing as an art therapist. The unique role that supervisors can play in the development of the art therapist as they normalize and work with newcomer's disillusionment and frustration is highlighted (Moss, 2017, p. 10). External support, which can be offered by a supervisory mentor, is not only helpful but is also a required part of the work of art therapy as one completes hours toward board certification and licensure and also meets with the supervisor during a required number of weekly hours. While supervisory mentors are essential for reassurance, reinforcement, and modeling, because an art therapy-specific supervisor may not be available at the agency one is working at, some supervision may occur by people in related professions who may not understand the theories of art therapy, potentially creating a felt lack of opportunity to observe a mentor practicing the specific skill set one had trained so long for. Supervision by a non-art therapist can expand the art therapist's skill set and knowledge, though it might also challenge the art therapist's professional identity. Meanwhile, if it becomes necessary to pay for a credentialed art therapy supervisor outside of the work setting, a financial burden is created which adds to the already existing burden of student loans. External supervision also dips into what might be very little personal time for a new professional while they are striving for a work-life balance and practicing self-care. Fortunately, supervision by an art therapist is a required part of graduate art therapy education during an internship, either by a faculty supervisor, a site supervisor, or both. Learning and being encouraged by an art therapy mentor during graduate training provides a foundation for seeking additional sources of learning after graduating.

It may be interesting to note that some of the hidden costs of art therapy training may also be encountered by undergraduate students who are studying art therapy at a preprofessional level. These may include trauma impacts and role confusion. For example, part of undergraduate learning may involve a fieldwork experience either shadowing an art therapist or providing art facilitation within the community to various groups of individuals. Given that the master's degree is the entry level for art therapy, undergraduate students are not to be thought of as "doing art therapy" even as they may be providing high-quality art facilitation that meets community needs (Schwartz et al., 2019). Role confusion can result, and sites may at times expect an undergraduate student to provide services beyond the level of their training, and to even claim they are conducting art therapy, leading to anxiety and insecurity for the student or unethical practice. As with graduate art therapy students and new practitioners, the role of a supervisor, including a faculty supervisor who is a trained and credentialed art therapist, can be essential to offering support to a student as they negotiate these concerns.

A sentiment often discussed in art therapy circles is that the art therapy profession is not easy, which can lead to resentment. Moss (2017) affirms that "the process of becoming a practitioner of any helping profession can be expected to include considerable effort, and art therapy is no exception" (p. 17). Through her research and writing, Moss invites students, practitioners, and supervisors to consider whether acknowledging and normalizing the professional difficulties likely to be encountered can function "as knowledge that can combat resentment or unrealistic ideals" (p. 107). This idea is affirmed by an instructive metaphoric story that emerged from the art-based research Moss conducted with a group of art therapists who were newly credentialed with their ATR-BC. Responsive artwork was collected from the participants and upon review, it was noted that a story with a theme emerged across the series of works collected. In the story, a bee (a pollinator) launches from a hive and confronts a tangle of yarn which represents the natural disillusionment and challenges of becoming established in the art therapy profession (Fig. 16.3). The bee must overcome tasks that allow it to move through and wind up the red yarn in order to reach the goal through patience, focus, trust, and tenacity.

A core question is posed of whether "the tangle is in the way, or on the way?" and the reader is invited to consider whether the tangle represents a barrier to success or is instead a necessary part of becoming successful (Fig. 16.4). In other words, as Moss, writes: "The journey can't be skipped, patience and compassion are essential. Credentialing is a wonderful professional goal, but so

FIG. 16.3 *Encounter (2017) [unpublished doctoral dissertation] Danielle Moss, Confronting the tangle.*

FIG. 16.4 *Flying Across the Mountains (2017) [unpublished doctoral dissertation] Danielle Moss, Was it in the way, or on the way?*

is learning to believe in one's self and permitting their inevitable transformation. Their hard work and sometimes painful experiences may lead them to a rewarding life as art therapists if they stay the course and always remember what they love about this work" (Moss, 2017, p. 100).

Career options in fields closely related to art therapy—Options to pursue a related master's degree or to begin to work with a bachelor's

Whether you are reading this book because you are taking a class about art therapy, are enrolled in a preprofessional art therapy major, or simply exploring ways to connect to your work passion, a master's in Art Therapy is not the only option for a student to combine their love of art and psychology into a career. Although a master's degree is the entry-level requirement for the Art Therapy profession, undergraduate studies still have the potential for students who plan to continue into graduate studies or who plan to enter a variety of related types of work and get further on-the-job training. Your undergraduate courses allow you to develop a broad understanding of the world, leadership skills, and an enhanced ability to think creatively and critically. While graduate school may be an ideal option for you, not all students will desire or are an ideal fit for a master's degree. *Regardless of what you decide to go on to do after graduation, during your time as an undergraduate student, you have the opportunity to practice generalizable job skills, and to gain a sense of what you are truly good at and the kind of impact you wish to make in the work world.*

Career options exist. There is ample opportunity to take advanced and more specialized courses in the field of Art Therapy or instead in related fields after admission to graduate school. Options to explore undergraduate coursework, then to pursue a master's degree exist not only in Art Therapy but also in Community Arts, Counseling, Psychology, Marriage and Family Therapy, Clinical-Community Psychology, School Psychology, Creative Arts Therapy, Teaching Artistry, Arts Administration, Arts in Medicine, Occupational Therapy, Child Life Specialty, and other related fields. Several of these fields have introductory, mid-level, and more advanced levels of training through undergraduate coursework and graduate degrees. For example, Arts in Health (also sometimes referred to as *arts in medicine* or *arts in health care*) now has both undergraduate and graduate coursework available that supports earning a certificate and courses are offered for those who want to pursue training in this area. More information on this may be found through the National Organization for Arts in Health (2021).

Readers of this text are also encouraged to review the list of resources provided at the end of this chapter and to familiarize themselves with the following closely related fields, in order to obtain a sense of work and career options with a bachelor's degree which have potential to offer on-the-job training or further educational training. These fields incorporate an artist's identity and value creativity as a transformational process in the world. It can be exciting to explore both worldwide programs and also those across the United States that are exploring curiosity, the power of stories, using art to spark collaboration, and amplifying human potential. This information, including the list of resources, is by no means exhaustive.

1. **Art Facilitation**—Should a student desire to just complete an undergraduate degree alone, and not go on to graduate school, opportunities for *art facilitation* work that do not involve the job title nor specialized responsibilities of an art therapist exist in a variety of art, recreation, education, human service, health care, and community organizations. For example, you will be prepared to utilize art facilitation skills in settings such as children's art camps, retirement homes, community arts agencies, or to begin a career in an entry-level psychology setting. If your interests best match an alternate area of specialization, it is expected that in addition to any introductory undergraduate coursework you might take about art therapy, you will prepare yourself for further education or on-the-job training and will not refer to your art facilitation as art therapy.
2. **Arts in Health**—Arts in health is a field dedicated to using the power of the arts to enhance health and well-being in diverse institutional and community contexts (Rollins et al., 2009). Comprised of many subfields and affiliated fields, arts in health support health as defined by the World Health Organization (WHO), as "a state of complete physical, mental, and social well-being and not merely the absence of disease or infirmity"(National Organization for Arts in Health, 2017).
3. **Teaching Artist**—Someone who works as a Teaching Artist is different from an art educator although they learn and combine teaching theory while working with individuals who may not otherwise have access to art experiences. Social transformation grounded in creativity is also a focus. Growth of the field and knowledge of what being a Teaching Artist involves is supported by the Association of Teaching Artists (https://www.teachingartists.com/). This field is also supported by an international consortium titled Creative Generation (https://creative-generation.org/).
4. **Community-Based Arts**—Also known as *community art,* it refers to the practice of art generated in a community setting and through collaboration with community members. This work is focused on interaction with or a dialogue with the community through art-based ways of collaborating and often has a social justice focus in particular where creativity is utilized for transformation within individuals, communities, and societies. Undergraduate areas of focus along with master's degrees are available in Community Arts (https://en.wikipedia.org/wiki/Community_arts).

The core question introduced at the beginning of this chapter was, *How do I begin as I consider a career pathway in art therapy and how do I know if the field is right for me?* Beginning, taking the first steps, and exploring options have been our focus throughout this chapter. Google career coach-turned-author

Jenny Blake (2016) counsels those searching for a new career to think smaller so that they can get started on testing whether their ideas hold up in the real world. She suggests you ask yourself, "What are small experiments I can run right now that will not drastically shift my day-to-day life, but involve skills, or test a new hypothesis of something I'm interested in?". Blake goes on to explain how launching little experiments, like making a quick turn or pivot while playing a basketball game, can help people transition into work they love. Blake adds that it is common to worry, "What if I make the wrong move? What if I make the wrong decision?" She goes on to convey, however, that each move (or pivot) teaches people very valuable information for their next move after that (Blake, 2016).

If the pivot method of trying smaller experiments seems as if it might help to begin to explore an art therapy career, the following sampling of *Human Services & Arts Agencies* job titles may provide valuable information for your next move:

- Activities Specialist/Activities Therapist.
- Arts Facilitator.
- Artist in Residence.
- Autism Specialist.
- Child-Welfare Specialist.
- Case-Worker.
- Care Manager.
- Counselors (undergraduate level jobs).
- Child-Life Specialist.
- Therapeutic Recreation Specialist/Recreation Worker.
- Special Education Aide.
- Teacher's Aide/Personal Aide.
- Charter School Teacher (may not require a teaching certification, just a BA).
- Teaching Artist.
- Therapeutic Support Staff (TSS)/Behavior Health Technician (BHT)—(part of wraparound service).
- Senior Center staff.
- Group Home worker/residential counselors/resident advisors.
- Milieu Therapist.
- School-Based Therapist.
- Staff at Community Club Houses or Drop-In Centers.
- Staff at Partial Programs/Day Treatment Centers.
- Life Skills Counselors (a term often used in Drug and Alcohol Treatment Centers).
- Child Mental Health Worker.
- In-Home Family Counselor.
- Outreach/Education Coordinator (at a museum).
- Art Teacher—but may require art teacher certification, unless working as a substitute.

Summary

Think about the core question posed as you read through this chapter, *How do I begin as I consider a career pathway in art therapy and how do I know if the field is right for me?* Return also to considering the opening metaphor of this chapter. Imagine you are standing at the ocean, gazing outward, on slightly shifting ground as the waves wash over your feet. What do you feel drawn to do? There may be treasures to be found if you wade deeper into the water, figuring out how to body surf. Or you might have a good time digging around in the sand and turning over seashells in your hand. Or does gazing at the distant horizon bring it closer? What draws your attention or what do you feel a pull to respond to? What might you find or discover? How, then, might the images that surface for you as you consider this metaphor relate to your career decision-making and standing with a sense of firm footing while also adjusting to shifts, new directions, and pivots? Many exciting pathways exist, which will allow you to integrate creativity into whatever you go on to do. A person pursuing a career in art therapy must be ready to seek solutions to challenges, embrace long-term professional goals, and enjoy flexibly working with diverse clients and settings. With that mindset, a career in art therapy has the potential to be very rewarding.

Art experientials and reflection questions

1. **Current to future self**: Imagine that it is 5 years from today. The "future you" is working toward their ideal career and is thanking the "current you" for a gift that helped them enormously. What gift did the current you give the future you? Consider creating a collage, or use art media of your choice, including digital media possibly, to create an art response to this prompt. **Reflection**: On a separate sheet of paper, consider writing a brief letter from your future self, thanking your current self in a conversation. What is important for your current self to know and understand about what your future self has to say? How did the gift allow the future self to be touched or inspired? How does the artwork bring insight into your sense of your professional development needs? Ask yourself how you might integrate personal growth into your professional goals.
2. **Responding to life's callings**: As you think about the ways you feel called to integrate creativity into your career, consider who or what can help you succeed. Now imagine yourself as a tree. What would a tree look like if you were a tree? What might the roots and branches of your inspiration look like or consist of? What would the environment around this tree consist of? What else would be important to include? **Reflection**: Notice where you see the need for support or space for growth. Why do you think you drew this particular tree and environment? What was it trying to convey? What does the

tree that you drew illustrate about the kinds of support and mentoring that can help you succeed?

3. **Making unique contributions to a professional field and the world**: In a world of infinite possibilities and as a person with numerous professional choices, you have something unique to contribute to the world. Using art media of your choice, express what unique contribution(s) to professional work and the world you dream of making. What does the world need more of that you want to offer through a career you choose? **Reflection**: What do you notice about what the image reveals about how you value yourself? What strengths, resources, and goals can be identified in the image? What changes to the image might better allow a good fit of a positive sense of self with the work environment? After discussion, notice how you feel now about what gifts you have to bring to your work. Journal your reactions to this creative experience.
4. **Interview an art therapist and respond**: Interview an art therapist, then create a visual response piece. What sorts of colors, shapes, lines, or even symbols express what was sparked for you during the interview? While you are creating, pick up the art piece and rotate it in different directions in order to spark new curiosity. **Reflection**: Describe the space, form, and balance of this symbolic representation. What do the lines and colors in your artwork convey? What stands out to you in this image? What feelings are expressed?

Additional resources

American Art Therapy Association (AATA): https://arttherapy.org/
Americans for the Arts: Animating Democracy: https://www.americansforthearts.org/by-topic/social-change
Accreditation Council for Art Therapy Education: https://www.caahep.org/ACATE
Art Therapy Credentials Board (ATCB): https://www.atcb.org/
ArtCorps (arts program based on Peace Corp model): https://artscorps.org/
Association for Creativity in Counseling: https://www.creativecounselor.org
Creative Generation: https://creative-generation.org/
Expressive Therapies Summit: http://www.summit.expressivemedia.org/
International Arts + Mind Lab: https://www.artsandmindlab.org/
International Expressive Arts Therapy Association (IEATA): https://www.ieata.org/who-we-are
National Coalition of Creative Arts Therapies Association: https://www.nccata.org
National Guild for Community Arts Education: https://www.nationalguild.org/
National Organization for Arts in Health: https://thenoah.net/
Teaching Artists Guild: https://teachingartistsguild.org/
Thirsty for Art Podcast: https://www.thirstyforart.com/podcast

Chapter terms

Accreditation Council for Art Therapy Education (ACATE)
Accreditation/Accredited Program
American Art Therapy Association (AATA)
Approved program
Art facilitation
Art Therapy Certified Supervisor—ATCS
Art Therapy Credentials Board (ATCB)
Arts in healthcare
Board Certified Art Therapist—ATR-BC
Commission on Accreditation of Allied Health Education Programs (CAAHEP)
Community-Based Arts
Compassion fatigue and vicarious trauma
Competencies—knowledge, skills, values/attitudes
Continuum of care
Creative Arts Therapy/Expressive Arts Therapy
Credential/Credentialing
Critical self-reflection
Dispositions
Education standards
Interdisciplinary Treatment Teams
Mental Health License
Metaphor
Prerequisites
Provisionally Registered—ATR-P
Registered Art Therapist—ATR
Scope of practice
State Licensure
Teaching Artist
Telehealth

References

Accreditation Council for Art Therapy Education. (2016). *CAAHEP standards and guidelines for the accreditation of educational programs in art therapy*. https://www.caahep.org/ACATE.

American Art Therapy Association. (2020). *COVID-19 resources for art therapists*. https://arttherapy.org/covid-19-resources/.

American Art Therapy Association. (2021a). *Becoming an art therapist*. https://arttherapy.org/becoming-art-therapist/.

American Art Therapy Association. (2021b). *2021-2023 Strategic plan*. https://arttherapy.org/strategic-plan/.

American Art Therapy Association Member Demographics Survey. (2021). https://arttherapy.org/upload/MemberDemographics_2021.pdf.

American Heritage® Dictionary of the English Language. (2011). *Credentialed*. https://www.thefreedictionary.com/credentialed.

Art Therapy Credentials Board. (2018). *Annual report* (p. 2018). https://www.atcb.org/Home/AnnualReports.

Art Therapy Credentials Board. (2020). *ATR application handbook*. https://www.atcb.org/resource/pdf/ATR_ApplicationHandbook.pdf.

Art Therapy Credentials Board Credentials at a Glance. (2017). https://www.atcb.org/wp-content/uploads/2020/07/ATCB-Credentials_at_a_Glance.pdf.

Blake, J. (2016). *Pivot: The only move that matters is your next one*. Penguin Random House.

CACREP. (2021). *Understanding accreditation*. Retrieved from: https://www.cacrep.org/accreditation/ (Accessed 5 August 2021).

Council for Higher Education Accreditation. (2021). *Accreditation and recognition*. Retrieved from: https://www.chea.org/about-accreditation (Accessed 5 August 2021).

Elmendorf, D., & Accreditation Council for Art Therapy Education. (2019). *So you want to be an art therapist?—FAQ sheet*. https://www.caahep.org/ACATE.

Figley, C. R. (1995). Compassion fatigue: Coping with secondary traumatic stress disorder in those who treat the traumatized. In C. R. Figley (Ed.), *Brunner/Mazel psychological stress series, no. 23*. Brunner/Mazel.

Greenstone, L. (2016). Issues in credentialing and licensing for art therapy in the United States: Who ate my pie? In D. Gussak, & M. Rosal (Eds.), *The Wiley handbook of art therapy* (pp. 802–813). John Wiley & Sons.

Hogan, S., & Coulter, A. M. (2014). *The introductory guide to art therapy: Experiential teaching and learning for students and practitioners*. Routledge.

Kapitan, L. (2010). Art therapists within borders: Grappling with the collective "we" of identity. *Art Therapy: Journal of the American Art Therapy Association*, *27*(3), 106–107. https://doi.org/10.1080/07421656.2010.10129662.

Keane, C. (2019). *5 Building blocks to achieving art therapy licensure in all 50 states*. https://arttherapy.org/blog-5-building-blocks-to-art-therapy-licensure-strategy/.

Lepere, R. (2019). Critical pedagogies in arts therapies 2019: Curating dignity and other points of view. *Drama Therapy Review*, *5*(2), 293. http://link.gale.com/apps/doc/A604896681/AONE?u=anon~27bef77b&sid=bookmark-AONE&xid=eacf96c1.

Moon, C. H. (2015). Letters to a young art therapist. In M. B. Junge, & K. Newall (Eds.), *Becoming an art therapist: Enabling growth, change and action for emerging students in the field* (p. 143). Charles C. Thomas Publishers.

Moon, B. L. (2007). In *The role of metaphor in art therapy: Theory, method, and experience*. Charles C. Thomas Publisher.

Moon, B. L. (2016). *Introduction to art therapy: Faith in the product*. Charles C. Thomas Publishers.

Moss, D. (2017). *The art therapist's professional developmental crisis: The journey from graduation to credentialing* (Unpublished doctoral dissertation). Mount Mary University.

National Center for O*NET Development. (2021). *29–1129.01—Art therapists*. https://www.onetonline.org/link/summary/29-1129.01.

National Endowment for the Arts. (2021). *Creative forces national resource center*. https://www.creativeforcesnrc.arts.gov/.

National Organization for Arts in Health. (2017). *Arts, health, and well-being in America*. https://thenoah.net/wp-content/uploads/2019/01/NOAH-2017-White-Paper-Online-Edition.pdf.

National Organization for Arts in Health. (2021). Retrieved from: https://thenoah.net/ (Accessed 5 August 2021).

Orkibi, H. (2010). Creative art therapies students' professional identity and career commitment: A brief pilot study report. *The Arts in Psychotherapy*, *37*, 228–232. https://doi.org/10.1016/j.aip.2010.04.008.

Ottemiller, D. D., & Awais, Y. J. (2016). A model for art therapists in community based practice. *Art Therapy: Journal of the American Art Therapy Association*, *33*, 144–150. https://doi.org/10.1080/07421656.2016.1199245.

Pearlman, L. A., & MacIan, P. S. (1995). Vicarious traumatization: An empirical study of the effects of trauma work on trauma therapists. *Professional Psychology: Research and Practice*, *26*, 558–565.

Rastogi, M. (2017). *Creating a successful career in art therapy: Advising guide for psychology faculty and students*. Office of Teaching Resources in Psychology. http://teachpsych.org/resources/Documents/otrp/resources/Advising%20Guide%20for%20Art%20Therapy-edited4.docx.

Rollins, J., Sonke, J., Cohen, R., Boles, A., & Jiahan, L. (2009). *Arts in healthcare: 2009 State of the field report*. Arts and Health Alliance. https://www.americansforthearts.org/by-program/reports-and-data/legislation-policy/naappd/arts-in-healthcare-2009-state-of-the-field-report.

Roots, R., & Roses, R. (2020). Wounded healer experiences in art therapy. *Art Therapy: Journal of the American Art Therapy Association, 37*(2), 76–82. https://doi.org/10.1080/07421656.2020.1764794.

Rubin, J. A. (2009). *Introduction to art therapy: Sources and resources* (2nd ed.). Taylor and Francis.

Rubin, J. A. (2015). Letters to a young art therapist. In M. B. Junge, & K. Newall (Eds.), *Becoming an art therapist: Enabling growth, change and action for emerging students in the field* (p. 149). Charles C. Thomas Publishers.

Schwartz, J. B., Rastogi, M., Pate, M. C., & Scarce, J. H. (2019). Undergraduate art therapy programs in the United States survey report. *Art Therapy: Journal of the American Art Therapy Association*. https://doi.org/10.1080/07421656.2019.1698226.

Shortell, K. (2018). *Who are the next generation of art therapists: A survey of graduate students* (Unpublished Master's thesis). College of New Rochelle.

Torpey, E. (2015). *You're a what? Art therapist career outlook. U.S. Bureau of Labor Statistics*. https://www.bls.gov/careeroutlook/2015/youre-a-what/art-therapist.htm.

Zeyher, T. (2020). *From an online art therapy grad student, here are 5 tips for making the transition to virtual*. https://arttherapy.org/blog-5-tips-for-virtual-art-therapy-grad-students/.

Index

Note: Page numbers followed by *f* indicate figures, *t* indicate tables, and *b* indicate boxes.

B

C

D

F

G

N

S

T

U

V

W

Y

X